Breaking Point

World War II: The Global, Human, and Ethical Dimension

G. Kurt Piehler, *series editor*

Breaking Point

The Ironic Evolution of Psychiatry in World War II

Rebecca Schwartz Greene

Fordham University Press | New York 2023

Copyright © 2023 Fordham University Press

All rights reserved. No part of this publication may be reproduced, stored in a retrieval system, or transmitted in any form or by any means—electronic, mechanical, photocopy, recording, or any other—except for brief quotations in printed reviews, without the prior permission of the publisher.

Fordham University Press has no responsibility for the persistence or accuracy of URLs for external or third-party Internet websites referred to in this publication and does not guarantee that any content on such websites is, or will remain, accurate or appropriate.

Fordham University Press also publishes its books in a variety of electronic formats. Some content that appears in print may not be available in electronic books.

Visit us online at www.fordhampress.com.

Library of Congress Cataloging-in-Publication Data available online at https://catalog.loc.gov.

Printed in the United States of America

25 24 23   5 4 3 2 1

First edition

In memory of my son Ethan Frederick Greene

Contents

List of Illustrations   ix
Foreword by Noah Tsika   xi
Preface   xv

Introduction   1

Part I   Before the War

1. **Mobilizing for War**   13
2. **Military Necessity Overrides Psychiatric Skepticism**   34
3. **Debating Screening's Viability**   46

Part II   During the War

4. **Psychiatric Policy Making in the Throes of War**   77
5. **The Public Reaction**   101
6. **The Response of Psychiatrists**   120
7. **The Horrors of War and Beginnings of Change**   138
8. **From Prediction to Prevention**   153
9. **Limits to Prevention and Treatment**   177

Part III   After the War

10. Return to Normalcy — 209

11. From "War Man" to "Peace Man" — 232

Conclusion — 247

List of Acronyms and Abbreviations — 253
Principal Physicians and Social Scientists — 255
Appendix A: Medical Circular No. 1 — 275
Appendix B: Circular Letter No. 19 — 277
Appendix C: Key Investigations of Military Psychiatry — 279
Acknowledgments — 281
Notes — 287
Select Works — 405
Index — 441

Illustrations

1	Inductees Waiting to Be Examined, Mar. 1942 (Med. Dept. of U.S. Army, *Physical Standards in World War II*, ed. Robert S. Anderson, MC, 1967)	41
2	Proposed Examination Process (Created by author)	41
3	The Screening Program in 1941 (Created by author)	50
4	U.S. Marines Marching Through the Mud to Front Lines, Bougainville, Nov. 4, 1943 (Library of Congress Pictures)	81
5	Psychiatric Casualties, 26th Infantry, Sicilian Camp. July 1943 (Annual Report, Neuropsychiatric Consultants Div., FY 1945)	160
6	"Hit th' dirt, boys!" (Bill Mauldin, *Up Front* [NY: Norton, 2000])	165
7	"Joe, yestiddy ya saved my life. . . . Here's my last pair of dry socks" (*Up Front*)	165
8	"Maybe Joe needs a rest. He's talkin' in his sleep" (*Up Front*)	166
9	"I guess it's ok. The replacement center says he comes from a long line of infantrymen" (*Up Front*)	166
10	"I'm depending on you old men to be a steadying influence for the replacements" (*Up Front*)	166
11	"I feel like a fugitive from th' law of averages" (*Up Front*)	166
12	"Mack and Mike" (Pamphlet, Robert Cohen, M.D., from Committee on Neuropsychiatry, Overholser Papers, St. Elizabeth's Hospital, R.G. 418, NA)	187
13	"Marines Crouching Behind a Rock as They Blow Up a Cave on Iwo Jima, 1945 (Getty Images)	193
14	"The 2000 Yard Stare" (from Tom Lea Institute)	194
15	American Psychiatric Association Membership, 1910–1950 (from Carolyn Gifford, Table, American Psychiatric Association, Washington, D.C.)	213

Foreword

Noah Tsika

Speaking at the New York Academy of Medicine in 1944, Colonel Walter S. Jensen, Deputy Air Surgeon of the United States Army Air Forces, acknowledged the negative psychological effects of war while bemoaning their apparently perverse appeal to the general public. Defining war trauma as the source of multiple psychological symptoms, Jensen underscored the military's commitment to educating both soldiers and civilians on the subject. In so doing, he also warned that popular media were particularly pernicious in promulgating misinformation about various psychic disorders. Mainstream commercial representations had, in Jensen's view, so accustomed Americans to "thinking in terms of weaknesses rather than strength" that such individuals were likely unaware, by 1944, of major, "strength-restoring" developments in military psychiatry. Suggesting that "the lay public ... may tend to view with alarm the incidence of neuropsychiatric casualties in this war," Jensen prescribed efforts to "place the subject in its proper perspective."[1]

Among the most admired of such efforts is a 1977 dissertation entitled "The Role of the Psychiatrist in World War II," which Rebecca Schwartz Greene submitted as part of a PhD in American history at Columbia University. A comprehensive account of the relationship of war and medicine in the 1940s, Greene's groundbreaking research offered a foundation for several key interdisciplinary works, from Allan Bérubé's *Coming Out under Fire* in 1990 to Ellen Herman's *The Romance of American Psychology* in 1995. As Eric Jaffe rightly put it in his 2014 book *A Curious Madness*, "The best place to begin a study of psychiatry in World War II is a doctoral dissertation by Rebecca Schwartz Greene, 'The Role of the Psychiatrist in World War II.'"[2] While writing the dissertation, Greene was a Josiah Macy Historical Research Fellow at Cornell Medical Center, New York Hospital. She attended grand rounds and diagnostic sessions with psychiatric residents and gave papers before psychiatrists and historians at Cornell's Section on Psychiatric History. That Greene's pioneering dissertation is now available in book form is cause for celebration. An updated version of "The Role of the Psychiatrist in World War II," *Breaking Point* retains and expands the earlier work's emphasis on the complex and at times contradictory influence of individual medical professionals on institutional and public perceptions of behavioral health. Beginning in the mid-1970s, Greene interviewed a number of those professionals—psychiatrists whose military service during World War II helped transform their field: Dr. John W. Appel, who worked in an "exhaustion center" near the battlefields of Cassino and Anzio and who would proclaim the inevitability of "neuropsychiatric casualties" among combat personnel, arguing that no one could sustain more than 240 consecutive days of fighting; Dr. M. Ralph Kaufman, who developed hypnosis techniques for the treatment of those traumatized in the Battle of Okinawa, in which he also served; Dr. Herbert Spiegel, who promoted therapeutic hypnosis while serving as a battalion surgeon in North Africa; and Dr. Abram Kardiner, a psychoanalyst who joined Spiegel in asserting that "the normal state for the soldier in battle is fatigue and fear."[3] A rigorous yet accessible account of psychiatry's entwinement with World War II, Greene's book is also, via these interviews, an invaluable record of the field's self-image as it took shape during a later, perhaps equally pivotal period, when the war in Vietnam raised new—and reanimated old—questions regarding the individual mind and the national soul.

During World War II, the prevalence and severity of post-traumatic conditions far exceeded the military's capacity to treat them, and efforts to rehabilitate the victims of war trauma were consistently compromised by the relative scarcity of psychiatrists, both stateside and at or near the front. Various crash courses were meant to spread psychoanalytic lessons beyond a small coterie of skilled practitioners, but even these proved difficult to administer. Qualified instructors were hardly abundant, even as the military continued to call for the "transmission" of psychiatric knowledge from doctors to "everyone else." Setting up a series of so-called mental hygiene lectures for officers and enlisted men, the Neuropsychiatry Consultants Division would later conclude that these formal talks "undoubtedly contributed to the mental health of the Army by removing some of the mystery connected with psychiatry and by properly explaining many of the misconceptions commonly connected with this specialty." But consultants, like psychiatrists in uniform, were forced to confront the fact that they alone could not meet the educational needs of all officers and enlisted men. The busy schedules of psychiatrists rarely allowed for much lecture time, and many inexperienced orators worried that they were unable to convey crucial information "in an impressive and instructive manner." Compounding these problems was the fact that lectures on psychiatry were occasionally given during soldiers' off-duty hours, leading to "much dissatisfaction" among enlisted men.[4]

With one out of every four white draft registrants rejected on the basis of a newly diagnosed "nervous condition," and with General George C. Marshall attributing the spread of psychoneurosis to failures in the field of education, urgent questions regarding the country's pedagogic and therapeutic obligations began to be asked. The epidemic proportions of psychoneurosis demanded immediate action, but severe manpower shortages meant that such action could not be limited to the use of psychiatrists alone. To begin with, those tasked with interviewing draft registrants and determining their "psychological conditions" were, in fact, only rarely psychiatrists; often, they were drafted physicians forced to make up for the dearth of psychiatric professionals in the military by providing services for which they were scarcely qualified.

In *Breaking Point*, Rebecca Schwartz Greene tackles all of this and more, offering indispensable insights into the lasting relevance of her subject. Psychosomatic illnesses—also known as "organ neuroses" or, more appropriately, "somatization reactions"—were much discussed in the immediate post-1945 period, their explication by military psychiatrists widely appreciated amid an explosion of pop-psychological self-help literature, widespread health reform, and sheer therapeutic optimism. During World War II, recalled William C. Menninger, pernicious somatization reactions "ran the gamut of illnesses in which the organs of the body act as mirrors for the emotional maladjustments of the individual."[5] Menninger and others also anticipated a different mirroring process, however, one in which diverse civilians would increasingly reflect this symptomatology, their complex psychological experiences rendered reasonably intelligible by the wartime labors that *Breaking Point* lays bare.

Preface

While this book is about the contributions of a diverse group of psychiatrists to the war effort, drawn from neurologists, private practitioners, mental hospital superintendents, psychoanalysts, military psychiatrists, and psychiatrists in veterans' hospitals and clinics, it in no way is able to cover everyone. Hence, we begin by thanking everyone who rendered some service for doing their part in the war.

The attitudes expressed by some in the military, medicine (psychiatry), and even the White House toward women and minorities were very different from those of today. While today we might term that language "prejudice" or "politically incorrect," back then it was common parlance and not often objected to. In order to achieve a complete historical narrative, this book has not minced words. However, the attitudes expressed by some in World War II decidedly do not reflect this author's views.

Breaking Point

Introduction

The fear of death has broken many a soldier in battle. Troops have been emotionally torn by the sight of comrades maimed and killed. Panic has stricken the most stalwart, spreading like a disease among the ranks. Soldiers have suffered concussions from blasts of shells; been worn down by relentless campaigns under harsh conditions; succumbed to hysterical amnesia, paralysis, deafness, and blindness, or self-medicated on drugs and alcohol. Returning home, they have suffered flashbacks and nightmares for decades, sometimes inflicting violence on themselves or others.

This book explores the ambitious and unique effort of American psychiatry in World War II to eliminate the psychological scourge of war. It begins with an in-depth review of the origins and implementation by Selective Service, the army, and the navy of universal psychiatric examinations ultimately administered to more than 18 million men and women before service in World War II. Of these, Selective Service and the military rejected at least 1.8 million. Additionally, by the end of the war, approximately 700,000 more were discharged on neuropsychiatric grounds from military service.[1]

This book traces the slow evolution from psychiatric screening to preventive psychiatry and treatment at the front. Despite many wartime missteps and policy battles and failures, the story of psychiatry in World War II ironically culminates in a tremendous growth in popular demand, transforming a profession primarily engaged in caring for the chronically ill in isolated mental asylums to one caring for the everyday problems of the common man and woman.

Traditionally, the history of medicine has focused on the contributions of doctors to the development of concepts and practices. While this book provides a medical and intellectual history, it also provides a social, political, and military one. The entire psychiatric program in World War II could not have occurred without ongoing debate and compromise among the psychiatric profession, the military, and the president. Psychiatry in 1940 was in no way monolithic. Mental hospital superintendents, neurologists, career military psychiatrists, psychoanalysts, and private practitioners differed among themselves on whether to screen military recruits altogether: If so, how to do it, and if not, what role psychiatry would take instead. The military was not in unison either. Line officers in the field were more likely to be tolerant of soldiers' psychiatric breakdowns than commanding generals. Beyond documenting the roles of policy makers, this book describes the impact of wartime psychiatry on the common soldier and sailor, his or her family, and American society at large both during and after the war.[2]

Chapter 1 begins with the psychiatrist Harry Stack Sullivan and his William Alanson White Psychiatric Foundation (WAWPF), Washington, DC, starting to design a psychiatric examination for military service in 1938. Approved by President Franklin Roosevelt in September 1940, the examination became part of the general medical examination authorized by the Selective Service and Training Act of 1940, known as Medical Circular No. 1, published that November. (For the full text of the psychiatric examination, see Appendix A.) Concerned that America's youth were worn out psychologically by the Depression and imbued with rampant pacifism, Sullivan and his associates believed they had the ability to weed from service and thus protect from breakdown those unable to adjust to the rigors of the military or to later readjust to civilian life.[3] Proponents such as Winfred Overholser, superintendent of Washington's St. Elizabeth's Hospital, the first federal institution for the insane, established in 1855, promoted the examination to save the government from long-term, prohibitive costs hospitalizing veterans as had occurred after World War I.

Broadening the concept of mental unfitness, Sullivan's examination sought to identify and reject not only those with traditional psychoses or neurological disorders but also those with the slightest propensities, possibilities, or tendencies for maladjustment. As America's entry into the war drew nigh in 1941, the army and navy added their own routine pre- and postinduction psychiatric examinations. (For a full text of the army's preinduction examination Circular Letter No. 19, see Appendix B.) By war's end, America had rejected before service or discharged during service more than two and a half million men and women on neuropsychiatric grounds. More than 10 percent of those examined were rejected on neuropsychiatric grounds. Neuropsychiatric rejections accounted for at least 35 percent of all medical rejections. Neuropsychiatric discharges accounted for more than 49 percent of all medical discharges.[4]

No other Allied or Axis nation conducted such a program in World War II. To the contrary, the bloodbath of World War I on European soil confirmed to Britain and Germany the need for immediate total mobilization without a moment or a man to lose to some vague possibility of maladjustment. Consequently, they little tolerated the disqualification of recruits who might potentially prove disloyal, cowardly, or weak.[5] Less concerned than Americans about "undemocratic" mind control, they engaged in widespread propaganda to instill unity. Unable to afford the loss of recruits, instead of screening they turned to tougher discipline, mandatory national service, and psychiatric treatment, hoping to restore the mentally injured to military fitness.[6]

Across the Atlantic, America, isolated from the imminent threat of war on its own soil, approved a broad Selective Service psychiatric examination (Medical Circular No. 1; see Appendix A) to meticulously screen all draftees. Throughout the war, Selective Service and military examiners sought to reject a sweeping array of recruits, including those with reservations about training for national defense or who were employed by the WPA, had a history of unemployment, wet their beds, or stuttered. Native Americans might be eliminated for "wanderlust," Blacks for indicating opposition to segregation. The author Jack Kerouac was discharged from the navy for "grandiosity" for expressing concern about not being able to complete his book.[7] A recent obituary of the underworld boss John Franzese quotes him saying that the army discharged him for being "psychoneurotic with pronounced homicidal tendencies" after he pressed them for a transfer from kitchen duties to combat so he could kill the enemy.[8] As demonstrated in this book, many were rejected on an examiner's gut reaction or suspicion of maladjustment, out of racial or regional bias, by a mere facial expression, or because of perceived tendencies toward alcoholism or addiction, homosexual "proclivities," or, in the case of women, not meeting contemporary notions of respectability.

Psychiatrists asked a few questions at best. "Did you wet your bed?" "Did you have a happy childhood?" "Do you have any worries?" "How do you feel about the war?" But mostly, registrants recalled years later being asked only one question: "Do you like boys?," which became a popular cliché.[9] This focus, as discussed by Allan Bérubé in *Coming Out under Fire*, reflected a change from a prewar military practice of court-martial and conviction of homosexual sodomists to the elimination of a larger group suspected of "homosexual proclivities" through psychiatric rejections, psychiatric discharges, or administrative discharges, often without benefits.

These changes, however, were in no way unique to military policy toward homosexuals. As this book will make clear, they were part and parcel of the psychiatry program's overall goal, covering all groups within the two and a half million, of rejecting or discharging from military service anyone suspected of, likely to, having a tendency to, or possibly being unable to adjust to military life. This goal significantly expanded the definition of mental illness. It contrasted significantly with the earlier practice of psychiatry of focusing on those committing an actual offense or having blatant neurological defects.

Soon after implementing this ambitious screening program, problems in its execution emerged, as described in Chapters 2 and 3. Psychiatrists confronted frequent contradictions and inconsistencies in diagnoses and practices, due largely to the lack of any standard diagnostic nomenclature at the time. A registrant might be passed by a local board examiner only to be rejected by an army induction board, because of separate army and local board examinations with different criteria. Examiners were supposed to spend about fifteen to twenty minutes inspecting each candidate. In reality, they often spent no more than a few minutes at most. Some psychiatrists recalled examining one hundred, two hundred, even five hundred candidates in a single day.[10]

Overseas, in North Africa, army psychiatrists including Roy Grinker and Frederick Hanson, as described in Chapter 4, began working with their British and Canadian associates in developing new treatment modalities. But separated by thousands of miles from the front, American civilian psychiatrists who sought to take the reins of military psychiatric strategy after Sullivan resigned in November 1941 were relatively cut off from war's bloody realities. With few career military psychiatrists with any clout, these civilian leaders, led by Overholser, filled the vacuum and replaced the career military psychiatrist Patrick Madigan as director of army psychiatry with their own civilian mental hospital superintendent, Roy Halloran. In the months following, from mid-1942 to mid-1943, mental hospital superintendents, neurologists, psychoanalysts, and private practitioners debated strategy at National Academy of Sciences and American Psychiatric Association meetings. They considered abandoning their focus on psychiatric screening for a combined psychiatric and psychological vocational classification system similar to that of the British and Canadians. But ultimately, as shown in this book, any thought of this was rejected in favor of ever-tighter psychiatric screening, as demanded by military leadership and fostered by a lack of sufficient interest in collaboration between psychologists and psychiatrists.[11]

With screening ever more dominant, the numbers rejected swelled to over a million, discharges climbing precipitously as well. Not surprisingly, the public and the military raised Cain. General George Patton famously slapped two psychoneurotic patients in military hospitals in Sicily, calling them yellow-bellied cowards and ordering them immediately to the front. Not as well known were similar sentiments against "malingerers" expressed in more constrained, less public language by such top brass as Army Chief of Staff George C. Marshall and Supreme Allied Commander Dwight D. Eisenhower. Even Roosevelt, while not endorsing Patton's attitude, refused to fire him, harking back to Lincoln's defense of another successful general, Ulysses S. Grant, that he liked his "brand of liquor."

In a particular spike of criticism, young fathers and their families facing the newly enacted "Father's Draft" plaintively asked in 1943 and 1944 why they had to serve when seemingly "normal" 4-Fs did not. As discussed in Chapter 5, Blacks, Native Americans, and other minorities repeatedly complained of bias in their screening, often with some merit. Reflecting their concern about inequities in selection, the president and members of Congress in February 1944 introduced a National Service bill to assign all service-age men to work either in the military or in agriculture or industry on the home front. Great Britain and Germany had adopted such programs in World Wars I and II. But in the United States, organizations that promoted free labor and free enterprise, such as the American Labor Movement and the Chamber of Commerce, campaigned against it. Had this bill become law, the role of psychiatry in World War II might have been different, with far fewer men rejected or discharged on psychiatric grounds. Once more, an opportunity was passed by.

What, then, was the reaction of psychiatrists to all this criticism? Did they change their policies? If not, why not? For a long time, leading psychiatrists persisted in focusing on screening, supported by presidential, Army Surgeon General, and Inspector General investigations that failed to call for any change, even as mental breakdowns in military service severely mounted, belying the notion of predisposition and the ability to forecast behavior.

To improve the screening process with its acknowledged inconsistencies and biases, as shown in Chapter 6, psychiatrists worked on designing supplemental written personality tests. But being based on civilian data, the tests failed to measure how someone would react in the military. Consequently, the tests continued a pattern of false positives (i.e., rejecting men who could have successfully served). Why continue to develop these tests when faced with poor results? Most probably because once the machinery was put in motion there was an urge to finish the job—and because certain psychiatrists and psychologists clung to an exaggerated belief in their own acumen.

Ultimately, as the sociologist Paul Starr has noted in *The Social Transformation of American Medicine*, for a profession like psychiatry to achieve moral authority, it needed competent, "scientific" expertise, nurtured by a standardization of training and licensing and enhanced diagnostic technology.¹² These elements were largely lacking during World War II and only subject to refinement thereafter, such as in the *Diagnostic and Statistical Manual of Mental Disorders (DSM-I)* in 1952.

Late in the war, military psychiatrists finally endorsed a policy of psychiatric prevention and treatment at the front. This followed Marshall's criticism of excessive evacuation of psychiatric casualties as well as Roosevelt's avid promotion of psychiatric treatment and the growing realization that combat experience, not predisposition, precipitated most breakdowns. Originally, it had been assumed that examiners could simply screen out the predisposed. But as the war progressed, it became increasingly apparent that an examiner could not forecast behavior. As discussed in Chapters 8 and 9, the concept that "everyone has a breaking point" given the proper stress became ever more accepted in medical and popular thought. Hence, if a doctor could modify the environment by preventing certain stressors (e.g., by limiting the length of tour) or reduce stress by providing a worn-out soldier with rest, good food, sleep, and medications, it was believed he could restore the soldier's health and return him to combat. While this regimen was most associated with combat exhaustion, psychiatrists also treated soldiers facing extremes of climate and topography, crippling isolation, or endless boredom.

Some historians see the shift in emphasis from psychiatric screening to treatment and prevention as beginning as early as February 1943 in North Africa, but this book will point to mid-1944 as the official change.¹³ While army psychiatrists in North Africa developed methods of treatment early on, the change did not occur everywhere. Particularly during the crucial grueling battles in the South Pacific, without benefit of doctors trained in psychiatry and with severe shortages of medical supplies and staggering combat losses, the military routinely evacuated psychiatric casualties to the rear without treating at the front.¹⁴ The lack of division psychiatrists, who had been eliminated from the army's Table of Organization in 1940, severely hampered change. The Neuropsychiatric Branch's Annual Report for 1943 reported that 95 percent of army psychiatrists were posted in general and station hospitals, often hundreds of miles from the front, where doctors saw soldiers only after symptoms had calcified. Not until November 1943 were psychiatrists ordered back to the divisions, nor did they actually arrive in the field until a month later. Only thereafter could they discover for themselves the battlefield precipitants of mental breakdown.

Further hampering change was the limited number of psychiatrists for most of the war, aggravated by a failure to assign psychiatrists to jobs in their own specialty. Herbert Spiegel, for example, an early advocate of hypnosis who trained at St. Elizabeth's, was assigned not as a psychiatrist but as a battalion surgeon in North Africa. Sullivan had conducted two-day Selective Service seminars throughout the country to train nonpsychiatrist examiners in the rudiments of diagnosis.[15] The army did establish its own training program in military psychiatry at a hospital in Georgia, and Columbia University and New York University arranged programs as well, but still battalion surgeons, and even some clergy, sometimes had to fill in on the job.

Once in the field, psychiatrists confronted new problems. As the psychiatrist John Appel, director of the army's Mental Hygiene branch under William Menninger, recalled: "Psychiatrists soon learnt ... they had to change their oath of allegiance from ... Hippocrates ... to General Marshall. ... [They] were working for the army not ... the individual soldier."[16] Military doctors were caught between promoting health and life and adhering to military orders. While psychiatric leadership attempted to defend its core value of patient care, out in the field military priorities held sway. The leading Pacific Theater psychiatrist Moe Kaufman acknowledged that in Okinawa he was forced to send men back to combat before they were psychologically ready because of the dire military need for manpower.[17]

Motivating men to kill in combat tended to collide with considerations about their health. Menninger shared Marshall's and his generals' concern that American youth was soft and selfish, uneducated in the importance of sacrificing for the cause, and spoiled by government largesse, an opinion widely reiterated during and after the war.[18] Worried that American soldiers would fail in combat, Marshall and Frederick Osborn, chief of the army's Information and Education Division (I&E) and a close friend of Roosevelt, arranged for the social psychologist Samuel Stouffer, working with the psychiatrist Appel, to survey the attitudes of thousands of soldiers to determine the best arguments to motivate them to fight.[19] Menninger and Appel particularly promoted political orientation, because unlike the Russians, they said, American servicemen did not have the added impetus of fighting for survival on their own soil. But while psychiatrists sought one way or another to stimulate soldiers to kill the enemy in battle, others, such as Frederick Hanson, cautioned that programs inspiring hatred for the enemy could well have long-term destructive psychological effects. Herbert Spiegel maintained that love, not hate, inspired men on the battlefield: love of comrades, commander, country.[20]

The conflict between individual health and group cohesion was also apparent. Experts in psychology agreed that inspiring men to cover for their buddies instilled the will to fight. But as the war progressed, it became apparent that devotion to friends only made it harder to go on after seeing one buddy after another killed in combat.

Military considerations may also have inhibited psychiatrists' potential role as advocates for racial integration. While the war was on, Menninger gave a lecture arguing that segregating Black troops was actually beneficial to their mental health, but after the war, in *Psychiatry in a Troubled World*, he changed his tune, clearly espousing integration.[21] On the other hand, the psychoanalysts Lawrence Kubie and Moe Kaufman, who had been active in the 1930s in helping European analysts emigrate to the United States, promoted racial integration in the military to enhance mental health. Which view was correct? Was it, in Menninger's case, deference to the opinions of his superiors, including War Department Secretary Henry Stimson?

By war's end, as shown in Chapter 10, not only had over 2.5 million men been rejected or discharged on neuropsychiatric grounds, but more than a million came home with physical wounds and amputations, many with accompanying mental disorders. Though the number of women who served was relatively minimal, the largest group consisting of 150,000 in the Women's Army Corps, by late 1944, women had much higher rates of psychiatric discharges than men, reflecting—in part—a growing societal intolerance for women in the military as the war came to a close.[22]

Families had a hard time caring for these returning casualties. Even in the absence of mental or physical wounds, many families had difficulty readjusting after fifteen years of the Depression and war. The media and movies popularized psychiatry, including psychoanalysis, as never before. Increasingly, people who'd had no contact with psychiatrists before the war attended burgeoning clinics and private practices. For some, the challenges of readjusting from war to peace were onerous. Responding to growing demand, President Harry Truman signed the National Mental Health Act in 1946. At the same time, some mental health specialists who had worked together in the war studying the human character and its predilection toward war now shifted their inquiry to how to achieve global peace by ensuring international mental health.[23]

What were the lessons of the war for American psychiatry? Menninger wrote in *Psychiatry in a Troubled World* that one of the greatest benefits of the war experience was the recognition by psychiatrists of the impact of environment on mental health.[24] Hanson in particular claimed high rates of success in treating soldiers at the front and returning them quickly to battle.[25] Looking back, however, psychiatrists found that in hundreds of cases, there was a higher percentage returned successfully to noncombat than combat assignments.[26] Nevertheless, historians such as Gerald Grob credited the experience in World War II of treating men close to the front and recognizing the importance of environment as precursors to the community mental health movement.[27] However, the historian and sociologist Andrew Scull has noted that the community health movement did not fulfill its expectations due in part to underfunding and neglect.[28] Appel and other military psychiatrists made valuable contributions by emphasizing the need for limited tours of duty and fewer days of continuous combat, plus rest and recuperation. But these reforms occurred late in the war and were barely applied at the time. Sadly, the military in recent times has seemed to forget the lesson of limited tours of duty by sending men back again and again to combat in Iraq and Afghanistan. By 2009, with suicide rates in the military climbing significantly above the civilian rate, the Army Vice Chief of Staff after extensive study connected "involuntary enlistment extensions" and "extended deployment rotations," in addition to drug and alcohol addiction, to the alarming rise.[29] Is this not déjà vu?

As to the vaunted psychiatric screening program, it was never repeated on any such scale, with the Korean War and later conflicts relying more on aptitude tests. As the historian Edgar Jones has noted, a considerable percentage of those rejected in World War II constituted false positives who could have contributed much more to the war effort.[30] Instead, they suffered with stigmatic mental labels, often finding it difficult to obtain work in a full-employment economy. At a time of postwar "normalcy," with the husbands as breadwinners and wives as stay-at-home moms, those rejected were burdened with shame.

On a more positive note, the war led to the medicalization of certain disorders that previously had been considered crimes and subject to punishment or even execution. Before World War II, military men accused of an overt homosexual act, abusing drugs or alcohol, or deserting were almost always criminally prosecuted or court-martialed. On the other hand, under the influence of psychiatric medical thinking in the war, "proclivities" or "tendencies" could lead to a medical diagnosis, treatment, or discharge, often a coerced Section VIII (Blue) discharge, usually without veteran's benefits. Hence, criminal punishment for behavioral traits occurred less in World War II, but its medical or administrative replacement also had its drawbacks.

Ironically, the huge numbers of rejections and discharges on psychiatric grounds of men with physical and mental disabilities, and the close contact of soldiers with a branch of physicians previously derided as "nut-pickers" isolated in institutions, led to a familiarization with and acceptance of the profession. Returning home, veterans and their families, with few qualms, clamored for care from psychiatrists in clinics, private practices, and hospitals, not only for severe conditions but for everyday problems of adjustment. Psychiatrists became doctors for everyone.

Yet still there were the forgotten. Some came back unable to convert in their minds from "war man" to "peace man," suffering from, according to then-prevalent medical theory, transient combat-related disturbances of mind. Some suffered for years, ignored by doctors and their own families who could not understand why they just could not recover. Not until 1980 did the APA officially recognize Post-Traumatic Stress Disorder (PTSD) as a disorder. This severe delay in medical recognition of PTSD may possibly have been the largest failure in the psychiatric response to World War II, already marred by an overreliance on screening and an underemphasis on psychiatric prevention and treatment.

Part I
Before the War

1   Mobilizing for War

> And it shall be, when you draw nigh unto the battle, that the priest shall approach and speak unto the people, and shall say unto them: "Hear, O Israel, ye draw nigh this day unto battle against your enemies, let not your heart faint; fear not, nor be alarmed, neither be ye affrighted at them . . ."
> And the officers shall speak further unto the people, and they shall say: "What man is there that is fearful and faint-hearted? Let him go and return unto his house, lest his brethren's heart melt as his heart."
> —Deuteronomy 20:2–8, from J. H. Hertz,
> *The Pentateuch and Haftorahs* (1960)

Every nation involved in World War II faced the challenge of unifying its armed forces and citizens to defeat the enemy. But the "solution" the United States initially adopted differed widely from anything engaged in by the other combatants and anything done before or since in America. For the first time in American history, Selective Service, the army, and the navy routinely administered psychiatric examinations to each enlistee and draftee as well as examinations to those already in service. In all, the military rejected at least 1.8 million men in World War II before service and discharged another 700,000 already in service on psychiatric grounds.[1] A total of 2.5 million.

Put another way, at least 10 percent of the 18 million men between the ages of eighteen and thirty-seven examined for military service in World War II were rejected for neuropsychiatric conditions. Psychiatric rejections accounted for more than 35 percent of all rejections for medical conditions.[2] And unlike the practices in other countries, these psychiatric rejectees were not assigned to any alternative form of national service.

Why did America embark on such a lonely path? Clearly, influential psychiatrists such as Harry Stack Sullivan, the designer of the Selective Service examination and director of the William Alanson White Psychiatric

Foundation (WAWPF), and Winfred Overholser, superintendent of St. Elizabeth's Hospital, the first federal hospital for the insane in America, influenced the president's approval of the screening program. Yet, fundamentally, psychiatric screening was adopted and survived because it satisfied America's unique political, socioeconomic, military, and medical needs at that time. In contrast, America's allies and enemies did not employ screening in World War II because it did not satisfy their own very different needs.

When Sullivan and his psychiatrist/social science associates at the WAWPF began drafting a psychiatric examination for military service in 1938, America was economically and psychologically crippled by the Depression and isolationism. Over the next four years, Americans showed little appetite for risking their lives over the arcane affairs across the ocean in Europe. Even after the partition of Czechoslovakia in 1938, the invasion of Poland in 1939, and Germany's conquest of France in June 1940, isolationism remained the attitude of large segments of the American populace. Congress stalled funding for military mobilization, and Roosevelt had to tap other federal agencies' surplus funds to finance the military equipment and buildup he felt were urgently needed. With fiscal conservatism paramount, the president and his director of Veterans Affairs were particularly influenced by Overholser's touting screening to reduce the numbers of neuropsychiatric veterans who would be hospitalized should the United States enter the war.

At a time when peacetime conscription had been legislated but barely tolerated, Selective Service welcomed screening to persuade the public it was employing the most scientific, fair, and objective methods of selection. Believing that America's participation in war, if it came, would be like World War I—quickly over—policy makers favored a highly selective screening program, since they assumed that more young men would be available than needed for military service. Reflecting this attitude, Sullivan's Selective Service examination expanded the definition of mental illness beyond gross neurological and psychotic defects to include even potential problems of interpersonal relations. Concerned about the ability of men emotionally scarred by the Depression to cope with military service, Selective Service instructed examiners to watch for those with reservations about training for national defense, with histories of problems getting employed, or even with histories of WPA work.

After World War I, some American psychiatrists expressed misgivings about failing to follow the lead of their French and British counterparts in treating soldiers at the front and returning them soon to combat. But between the wars, the American military and psychiatrists largely forgot this lesson. Instead, they recalled the army general John J. Pershing's cablegram in 1918 charging psychiatrists with failing to screen enough men out of service before they embarked for overseas, leading to excessive psychiatric casualties among replacement troops at the front in Europe.[3]

Smarting from this criticism, Sullivan and Overholser, among other psychiatrists, sought to vindicate their predictive expertise through a more thorough psychiatric examination. Sullivan and members of the WAWPF also advanced screening to enable psychiatry to play a key patriotic role in America's massive mobilization. They also looked to put to the test their broad theories of mental health and interpersonal relations, both in war, should it come, and in peace thereafter.

Sullivan envisioned and implemented a detailed Selective Service screening of America's youth to locate the slightest scintilla of interpersonal maladjustment. But the army's own examination, published in May 1941, focused on a narrower goal of quickly culling a Depression-raised generation of questionable motivation, ability, and loyalty to ensure an army imbued with the all-important element of discipline. By mid-1941, a draftee would be required to pass both the Selective Service and the army examination, the standards of which often proved contradictory.

Certain unique conditions in America converged to promote screening while discouraging adopting alternative roles. Because the United States had not engaged in war for over twenty years and had fought relatively briefly in World War I, the military had little experience with psychiatric treatment at the front or even in hospitals behind the lines. A severe shortage of military doctors had led in interwar years to a policy of spending as little time as possible on treatment in hospitals for the small number of servicemen. Instead, the doctors concentrated on diagnosing ailments and quickly discharging from service.[4]

Because of America's democratic heritage, political leaders were reluctant to use political propaganda ("thought control") to promote morale instead of screening malcontents. Indeed, freedom of speech and expression was one of Roosevelt's cherished Four Freedoms.

In contrast to America, other combatant nations showed little interest in screening. This striking difference can be attributed to not only long-standing differences in military and political traditions and objectives but also, more importantly, to the exigencies of war. Unlike the Americans, who recalled World War I as a brief heroic interlude, for the Europeans, World War I had been a brutal and deadly struggle fought on a massive scale by countries deadlocked for years. By the late 1930s, less than twenty years later, they were again fighting a war on their own home soil for their very survival, a war in which every available citizen had to be utilized. They could not afford to siphon off amorphous potential psychiatric cases. Instead, they relied on vocational placement to find suitable jobs where men would not break down, propaganda to motivate men to kill, and treatment to preserve every drop of manpower. As the war intensified in 1940 and 1941, the British and Canadians also learned from their new experiences in combat and in bomb shelters during the Blitz that even the seemingly least stalwart could in fact withstand stress. Therefore, they saw little reason to needlessly siphon off men in advance. Although they tried to convey the value of psychiatric treatment and prevention to American psychiatrists, their interests were not appreciated until late in the war. Had they influenced Americans earlier, the story of American psychiatry in World War II might well have been very different.

Antecedents to Psychiatric Screening in World War II

In 1907, the federal government passed a law prohibiting entry of immigrants who were insane, feebleminded, epileptic, or criminal. About this time, they also assigned five alienists, as psychiatrists were then called, including the well-known Thomas Salmon, to inspect about half the immigrants arriving daily at Ellis Island, deporting an average of only two hundred a year on grounds of "insanity."[5] Hence, the program had little impact.

In World War I, doctors medically examined a total of 3.5 million men for service, referring only a limited number to psychiatrists for examination. Of the 3.5 million, a little more than 2 percent, or around 70,000, were disqualified on neuropsychiatric grounds from entering service and another 35,093 discharged thereafter.[6] Unlike World War II, where the detection of subtle or potential maladjustment or behavioral "proclivities" was encouraged, examiners in World War I were told when in doubt to accept and to focus on gross psychotic or neurological disorders.

Independent of psychiatrists, American psychologists in World War I administered a routine intelligence quotient (IQ) test to at least 1,750,000 recruits. The test was developed by the psychologist Robert Yerkes, president of the American Psychological Association, who, like Sullivan in World War II, aggressively sought to enhance his up-and-coming profession's contribution to the war effort. After the war and through the 1920s, IQ results were used to validate such questionable practices as restricting immigration of Southeastern Europeans, justifying racial discrimination, and sterilizing the "feebleminded." By the 1930s, leading psychologists attacked the IQ test for its skewed, biased, and confusing questions. Hence, the IQ did not play a central role in determining acceptance for military service in World War II, though psychologists did use such tests as the Army General Classification Test (AGCT) for vocational placement to determine intelligence, occupational experience, and ability to learn.[7]

Another important predecessor to screening in the 1920s and 1930s was the National Committee for Mental Hygiene's (NCMH) program to examine juveniles for psychiatric disorders at child guidance clinics. But while the clinics were also supposed to improve juvenile development and avert delinquency through teacher training, instructions to parents on nurturing, educational courses on child development, and psychiatric and social work intervention, the NCMH Division on the Prevention of Delinquency concluded they did little more than test.[8]

Originally, the NCMH had a different focus. Founded in 1909 by Clifford Beers, who had written about the awful conditions he had experienced as an asylum inmate two years earlier in *A Mind That Found Itself*,[9] the NCMH initially sought to improve conditions in mental institutions. But after Beers, the committee adopted a broader agenda. Thomas Salmon, a director of the NCMH who had been an alienist at Ellis Island and played a leading psychiatric role in World War I, called for the eradication of syphilis and alcoholism. Later, Adolf Meyer, director of the Phipps Clinic at Johns Hopkins University, and William Alanson White, Overholser's predecessor at St. Elizabeth's, acknowledged the social and biological causes of mental illness, with White taking an activist stance, calling for birth control, decent food, clothing, sanitation, and child labor laws.[10]

But in the 1920s and 1930s, the NCMH concentrated mostly on screening children. It also contributed to psychiatry in World War II by providing some of its leading psychiatric policy makers, including Meyer; Raymond Waggoner, director of the University of Michigan Psychiatric Clinic; John Appel, director of the Lancaster, Pennsylvania, juvenile guidance clinic; and George Stevenson, NCMH's director.[11]

Predisposition

Behind the concept of screening was a long-standing belief in "predisposition," shared by many psychiatrists: that personality traits were stable either from birth, attributable to heredity, or from early childhood, attributable to socialization, thereby enabling psychiatrists to examine a young person and forecast their future personality.

In World War I, the psychiatrist F. W. Mott at first attributed mental breakdowns in combat to "shell shock," literally the impact of a nearby exploding shell, or to extreme physical fatigue.[12] Gradually, however, he and C. S. Myers, a British Expeditionary Force psychiatric consultant, concluded that shell shock arose from an inherited predisposition or early defective socialization. The predisposed soldier, they argued, could not resolve the contradiction between the herd instinct and the instinct of self-preservation. The instinct of "self-preservation" encouraged him to flee the battleground, but the "herd instinct" compelled him to remain with his comrades. The "normal" soldier resolved the conflict by repressing his drive to save his life. The predisposed, unable to resolve the conflict, unconsciously escaped from combat through hysterical symptoms. Even in training camps, though not yet confronting the conflict between life and death, the weaker-constituted individual experienced a similar unresolved conflict between regimentation and individualism, which led him to escape through breakdown.[13] These opinions were widely shared by Salmon and Pearce Bailey, the heads of army psychiatry in World War I overseas and in the United States, respectively, and by Edward Strecker, a psychiatrist in World War I and later both the army's and navy's psychiatric consultant in World War II.[14]

After World War I, Bailey and Salmon concluded that both in war and peace, neuropathologic individuals unconsciously escaped from unbearable situations through hysterical reactions.[15] Sigmund Freud's protégé Ernest Jones recalled that "those persons more easily fall ill [in battle] who in spite of real cowardice, are compelled from ambition to perform courageous deeds." Another protégé, Karl Abraham, stated: "War neurotics ... before the trauma were labile people ... especially as regards sexuality. Many... unable to carry out their tasks in practical life, others ... capable ... showed little initiative."[16] Some German psychiatrists linked men breaking down, demanding pensions, or becoming revolutionaries to "a pathological lack of male behavior." British psychiatrists similarly tied physical breakdown, cowardice, and pension opportunism to resistance to male norms or military authority.[17]

Several variants of predisposition were advanced in the profession. In the 1920s, American psychiatrists attributed personal psychopathology to defective early childhood socialization, warranting juvenile examinations. While Freudian theory connected oral, anal, and genital stages of childhood to later personality formation, "habit theory" tied predisposition with childhood habits.[18] As explained by White, family social conditioning influenced later problematic traits of character. Meyer held similar views, employing his well-known system of using individual case histories to trace problems adjusting to life experiences to biological or social factors.[19]

While Sullivan was influenced by White's opinions and corresponded with Meyer about the social and biological causes of mental illness,[20] he and the WAWPF developed their own brand of predisposition. Their theory concentrated on problems of communication between two individuals or within a group, caused by either a lack of self-confidence or excessive hostility in an earlier stage of life that could reemerge later on, culminating in adult schizophrenia or psychopathy.[21] Sullivan's major concepts were set forth in *Personal Psychopathology*, based on a 1932 manuscript; *Conceptions of Modern Psychiatry*, which first appeared in *Psychiatry* (1940); and in his articles from 1924 to 1935 collected in *Schizophrenia as a Human Process*.[22]

Eugenics

Eugenics was a pernicious form of predisposition, asserting that defective physical or mental traits passed from one generation to the next could consequently be predicted and eliminated by controlled breeding or by barring certain immigrant stocks from the country. Army medical statistics from World War I, plus IQ results, reinforced the popular notion that Southeastern Europeans were inherently genetically inferior, encouraging passage of the 1921 and the even stricter 1924 laws severely limiting immigration. Salmon favored immigration restriction and the prohibition of feebleminded marriages. Ultimately, in the United States, thirty states sterilized at least 60,000 "genetically inferior" or "feebleminded" individuals before World War II.[23]

Henry Fairfield Osborn, president of the American Museum of Natural History and a world-renowned paleontologist, was an avid eugenicist, as was his nephew Frederick Osborn. With the sociologist Frank Lorimer, in 1934 Frederick Osborn authored *Dynamics of Population*. In 1940, Frederick Osborn promoted the use of the IQ test, sterilization, and the prohibition of the marriage of the feebleminded in his *Preface to Eugenics*. As we shall see, Roosevelt appointed Osborn head of the Selective Service Psychiatric Advisory Committee, a position of great policy influence. There, his interest in eugenics informed his work, with Sullivan refining the screening exam.[24] Roosevelt's personal polio specialist, Dr. George Draper (a fellow Groton and Harvard man), also adhered to a form of eugenics, called constitutionalism, and headed the Constitutionalism Clinic at Columbia University for thirty years. The doctrine of constitutionalism found a positive relationship between physical body types and personality characteristics and afflictions. After doing a study of some of his young polio patients, Draper concluded that the afflicted children and their parents shared certain physical features not shared by others.[25] Roosevelt's association with Draper and Osborn may well have facilitated his own interest in psychiatric screening.

The Roots of World War II Screening

The Military

After World War I, the military and its psychiatrists supported a routine preinduction examination to reduce psychiatric casualties. Recalling Pershing's cablegram, Salmon called on the military to toughen its psychiatric screening to avoid soaring costs in military training and hospitalization during and after the war, writing in the army's *The Medical Department of the US Army in the World War*, volume 10, on neuropsychiatry in World War I.[26] About the same time, the army's *Handbook for the Medical Soldier* predicted that "future psychiatric casualties would be weeded out during the induction process."[27]

In 1933, Captain Lewis Hershey, then a student at the Army Command and General Staff School, Fort Leavenworth, Kansas, later to serve as Selective Service director from 1941 through the war in Vietnam, wrote a paper on "Fear as a Factor in Leadership Problems." That paper espoused screening out soldiers unable to tolerate combat who might spread panic among troops.[28] In 1936, the Army-Navy War Readiness Committee, with Hershey as its executive secretary, began drafting a Selective Service bill, which included a provision for a universal medical examination.[29] Four years later, in August 1940, Roosevelt established a Joint Army Navy Selective Service Committee (JANSSC) to coordinate plans for conscription, with Hershey as secretary and Osborn in charge.[30]

Isolationism and Pacifism

In the 1920s and 1930s, America largely withdrew from world events. Despite Woodrow Wilson's vision for world peace, the United States failed to join the League of Nations. In 1936, the American Student Union organized half a million students in a peace strike, including the signing of the "Oxford Oath" not to serve in future wars. America's leaders eschewed negotiations with Japan over its invasion of Manchuria in the early 1930s or confrontation with Germany over its annexation of Austria in March 1938 or partition of Czechoslovakia in Munich the following September. In the months before passage of the Selective Service Act, congressional leaders, major newspapers, and labor leaders opposed it. On the other hand, Archibald MacLeish, the ninth librarian of Congress and three-time Pulitzer Prize winner for drama and poetry, later to head the War Department Office of Facts and Figures, bemoaned American youth's lack of moral and spiritual preparation for war and absence of interest in defending democracy against fascism. He attributed it to a pacifism inculcated by such novels as John Dos Passos's *Three Soldiers*, Ernest Hemingway's *A Farewell to Arms*, and Richard Aldington's *Death of a Hero*. The terrifying description of warfare in *All Quiet on the Western Front* had tremendous popular impact. Dalton Trumbo's *Johnny Got His Gun* was also effective. Popular magazines such as the *Atlantic Monthly* and *Outing* described shell shock in graphic terms.[31]

In July 1940, the president of the graduating class of George Washington University explained to a Senate committee considering a peacetime draft why American youth was opposed:

> We youngsters have not suffered through ten years of contemporary depression ... and these days of foreign and domestic difficulty ... to be forced into military conscription of war. No youth group in the entire history of America has had so little opportunity, has had to bear so much difficulty, pain, and sorrow. We beg you oppose [this bill]. For what kind of soldiers will conscripted American youth who have grown up in an atmosphere of disillusionment and frustration make?[32]

Sensitive to public opinion, Roosevelt, a month after signing the Selective Service Act, felt the political need to disingenuously promise Americans in an October 30, 1940, election-eve speech that "your boys are not going to be sent into any foreign wars."[33]

Selective Service's Need for a Perception of Scientific Fairness in the Draft

Aware of the tenor of the times, Hershey also attempted about the same time to offset popular and congressional reservations by praising the democratic nature of the draft: Its local boards would be composed of a registrant's own neighbors making the decisions regarding "whose 'boy' would go and whose stay behind," the neighbors being the ones most familiar with the registrant's personal problems. The local boards, Hershey maintained, would be "little schools," teaching the populace how democracy worked in times of emergency. Instead of a large standing army, which America had historically abhorred, the draft would be an army of "citizen soldiers" patriotically engaged in military service during war, returning home to civilian lives thereafter.[34]

Praising Selective Service on similar grounds, Charles Spruit, medical advisor to the JANSSC and a Selective Service medical officer, stressed that well-designed psychiatric screening would "promote confidence in the fairness of the system" by adding scientific credibility. Screening would fairly, accurately, and objectively determine the ability of men to perform in service as well as weed out those malingering to avoid service.[35]

Sullivan's Thoughts and Plans

But the real force behind the success of psychiatric screening was Sullivan. As early as 1938, he and the WAWPF started designing a routine Selective Service psychiatric examination. That a civilian psychiatrist would be the one to lead the development of a military examination can partially be explained by the dearth of military doctors between the wars and by Sullivan's association with Chief Army Psychiatrist Patrick Madigan and Navy Psychiatrist Dallas Sutton, both WAWPF members. Sullivan had been a medical officer in Pershing's 1916 expedition to Mexico, director of veterans' rehabilitation for the Federal Board for Vocational Education in World War I, and liaison between the Veterans Bureau and St. Elizabeth's Hospital in the 1920s and 1930s.[36] From his experiences with psychiatric veterans, he felt confident that a thorough psychiatric examination could and would prevent wartime casualties and vindicate the expertise of psychiatrists against prior military criticism.

After Czechoslovakia's partition in 1938, writing in Sullivan's journal *Psychiatry*, Sutton called for a routine psychiatric examination to promote the morale necessary to win a prospective war against fascism. In June 1940, with the fall of France, the WAWPF published its "Memorandum on the Utilization of Psychiatry in the Promotion of National Security." Soon thereafter, Clarence Dykstra, Hershey's predecessor at Selective Service, on leave as chancellor of the University of Wisconsin, appointed Sullivan as Selective Service psychiatric consultant.

In the civilian world as well, Sullivan had much influence. According to an oral history with Osborn, Sullivan was one of the five highest-paid psychiatrists in New York City. He also had a private practice in Washington, DC.[37] Members of the WAWPF, which he founded in 1933, included the political scientist Harold Lasswell (co-editor of *Psychiatry*); the anthropologist Ruth Benedict; and the émigré psychoanalysts Erich Fromm, known for *Escape from Freedom* (1941), about the sociopsychological effects of Nazism, and Karen Horney. Both brought him direct accounts of Europe's duress.[38]

Perhaps because of conversations with these associates, Sullivan held a uniquely broad vision of the role of the psychiatrist. To him, psychiatrists were specialists in interpersonal relations, capable of reforming social maladies through detecting and healing those who might incite war, revolution, economic depression, fascism, communism, or antisemitism.[39] Hence, he would see no ethical conflict between political participation and being a medical doctor.

Echoing Roosevelt's interest in unity, Sullivan believed the United States could win a war against fascism only through the mobilization of every American. Yet Sullivan feared that such unity was far from real in 1940. Americans, he said, appeared selfish, cynical, "discouraged, embittered, and hostile." After years of the Depression, they seemed to him scarcely ready to "conform to ... unaccustomed ... restrictions ... [such] as [a] declining ... standard of living and curtailment of liberty." It was up to psychiatrists, he wrote, to ensure that "every member of the democratic states ... function usefully in times of crisis" or, if not, to "at least ... inhibit [certain persons] from malfunction costly to the common weal."[40]

In May 1940, a month before France surrendered to Germany, Sullivan wondered how a "disillusioned youth would become an effective fighting force." Reflecting the general concern about fifth columnists, who some believed had undermined French unity with pro-German sentiment, he wrote: "Not for nothing have many agencies worked diligently through the years of economic hardship to inculcate a vivid realization of the horrors of war, a conviction of exploitation by the privileged, and a cynical distrust of all public information."[41] The same kind of German propaganda that had plagued France, he feared, might incite American racism and antisemitism, as well as opposition to enter the war. This opinion was shared by the president. In a fireside chat that same month, Roosevelt scolded those who had "closed their eyes to events abroad." He worried that the Nazi propaganda minister Goebbels's methods of spreading disunity in Europe might soon plague the United States, leading to "confusion of counsel, public indecision, political paralysis, and eventually a state of panic."[42]

Sullivan's aforementioned remarks about propaganda appeared to link pacifism with communism, referring to "conviction of exploitation by the privileged" immediately after the phrase "vivid realization of the horrors of war." This may have referenced the Soviet-Nazi nonaggression pact in effect from August 1939 through June 1941, which was respected by the American Communist Party.[43] Sullivan's coeditor Harold Lasswell was similarly anxious about the divisiveness of communism, reflected in his 1939 article in *Public Opinion Quarterly* on "The Volume of Communist Propaganda in Chicago."[44]

As WAWPF director, Sullivan well knew the literature on the stress of unemployment. As early as 1933, the leading psychologist J. E. Wallace Wallin had proposed to the outgoing Hoover and incoming Roosevelt administrations that a morale department be established to combat cases of maladjustment from the Depression.⁴⁵ Five years later, the sociologists Philip Eisenberg and Paul F. Lazarsfeld pointed to American and European studies, including their own of Marienthal, Austria, to confirm the psychological impact of unemployment. According to these authors, the unemployed lost self-esteem, withdrew from social activity out of a fear of ostracism, and became dependent, submissive, and pessimistic about their chances of getting work. Their children also felt inferior, ostracized, increasingly lacked respect for their parents, and lost ambition.⁴⁶

Sullivan feared that people unemployed for years had undergone changes in their belief in democracy and capitalism. "How are we to overcome the effects on personality of the last ten years?" he asked.⁴⁷ Sullivan's attitude reflected popular opinion at the time. As the economy improved and more jobs became available in the private sector, Americans came to believe that any hard-working, decent person could find a job in industry and that only the indolent or impaired would remain unemployed or in lower-paying, less demanding WPA work.⁴⁸ This, as we will see, led to an interest in screening from military service those on the WPA.

In 1940, while Roosevelt and Secretary of Labor Frances Perkins worried about a lag in industry converting to military production, Sullivan proposed that in addition to the military, the government authorize psychiatric screening of civilian workers to prevent absenteeism, accidents, sickness, poor moral attitudes, and "mindless submission to union leadership" and instruct psychiatrists to alert authorities about subversives. He even proposed that psychiatrists treat executives whose industries lagged in production.⁴⁹

None of these plans came to fruition, possibly because personality tests had not proven effective forecasters of individual productivity in the 1920s, or because Sullivan himself feared that eliminating too many workers from industry might cripple wartime production, or because Sullivan recognized that psychiatrists reporting cases of sedition or propounding propaganda could infringe on America's traditional civil liberties. On the other hand, Sullivan's Medical Circular No. 1 did claim to be designed to determine the propensity for mental maladjustment in the year of acceptance into service and in the ten years of reserve duty after service—in other words, predicting both military and civilian adjustment over many years.

By November 1940, Sullivan sought to bring psychiatry squarely into national prominence. Writing in almost messianic terms to his close friend Dorothy Blitsten, author of *Social Theories of Harry Stack Sullivan* and wife of the Chicago psychoanalyst Lloyd Blitzsten, Sullivan not only envisioned training seven thousand physicians in psychiatry to become examiners and over seven hundred psychiatrists for advisory boards, but also educating many psychiatrists and physicians in psychiatry for industrial mobilization and, later, for promoting civil and military morale.[50]

Other leading psychiatrists were more reluctant than Sullivan to play a political role. In 1938, the *American Journal of Psychiatry* mentioned the deteriorating European situation only once in its 1,400 pages, in that case referring to Freud's safe escape from Germany. In 1939, the APA's president, after Kristallnacht, condemned Hitler's behavior but still advised its members not to get involved in world affairs until America did more to prevent crime in its own cities. Even less interested was *Mental Hygiene*, the organ of the National Committee for Mental Hygiene, not commenting once on events in Europe from 1938 to 1940.[51]

On the other hand, American psychiatrists did facilitate the migration of their European peers to America, quite a few of whom were Jewish, especially after Germany's acquisition of Austria in March 1938. In 1939, Clifford Beers, director of the NCMH, intervened with the State Department to bring over the Berlin forensic psychiatrist Karl Birnbaum. Starting in March 1938, the American Psychoanalytic Association (APsaA) formed its own Emergency Committee on Relief and Immigration. Led by Lawrence Kubie, secretary of the APsaA and president of the New York Psychoanalytic Institute (NYPI), it also included, among others, the NYPI member psychiatrist Bettina Warburg, a member of the Warburg banking family, and M. Ralph Kaufman and John Murray, members of the Boston Psychoanalytic Society (BPS). Kubie, Kaufman, and Murray would later play major psychiatric roles in World War II. Working with Freud's disciple Ernest Jones in England, Kubie arranged for funds to be transferred to Europe to support émigré analysts immigrating to England and émigrés struggling to leave Austria and Germany for the United States. This included funds for living expenses in Europe while waiting for visas and for transportation to the States. Aided by Warburg, the committee also provided thousands of dollars to émigrés to support them in the United States or arranged for psychiatric positions in hospitals and professorships in order to persuade the State Department that the doctors would not be public charges. The committee also negotiated with the State Department about visas. Concerned that the field of psychoanalysis was overcrowded in New York, the committee encouraged new immigrants to settle elsewhere in the United States. In what would become a long internecine conflict, Kubie corresponded with the International Psychoanalytical Association (IPA) about APsaA's concern that European lay analysts would subvert the reputation of the field and decided that the APsaA would require émigré analysts to have medical licenses before they could be accepted as members of the APsaA. Among the émigrés Kubie personally assisted was Heinz Hartmann, the last person Sigmund Freud trained. Thanks to Kubie's correspondence with Eleanor Roosevelt, the State Department eventually agreed to allow Hartmann to emigrate.[52]

Yet, while other psychiatrists focused mainly on protecting their brethren and ensuring the viability and reputation of their field, Sullivan took a unique stance in mobilizing psychiatry for war.

Winfred Overholser's Role

While Sullivan designed Medical Circular No. 1, Winfred Overholser, superintendent of St. Elizabeth's, lobbied the president for its approval. Most likely, Sullivan began professional contact with Overholser through his work at St. Elizabeth's with Overholser's predecessor, William Alanson White.

As an army psychiatrist in World War I, Overholser had personally treated victims of shell shock. In the 1920s, while director of the Massachusetts Division for Examining Prisoners, he engineered passage of the first law in the United States requiring a routine psychiatric examination for every defendant prior to criminal trial. As commissioner on mental diseases for the Massachusetts Hospital Service and superintendent of St. Elizabeth's starting in 1937, he was well aware of the deplorable conditions in mental hospitals. Upset by the army's criticism of insufficient screening in World War I, he and Harry Steckel, APA military mobilization director, as well as others, were eager to vindicate their profession's expertise in a new war through a sufficiently thorough psychiatric screening examination.[53]

The Roosevelts' Part

Psychiatrists promoted screening, and the Roosevelts' receptivity to the method led to its adoption. At a time when few Americans had much if any contact with psychiatrists, when the public associated psychiatry with grossly aberrant patients treated by strange doctors in isolated mental hospitals, the Roosevelts and their family and friends were much less apprehensive about the field, associating with psychiatrists as their physicians and friends. Frankwood Williams, a leading World War I psychiatrist and one of the authors of volume 10 of *Neuropsychiatry in the United States*, had analyzed Harry Hopkins. Frances Perkins's husband was institutionalized.[54] Eleanor Roosevelt consulted Strecker and Kubie to care for family members.[55] Responding to speculation during Roosevelt's presidential campaign in 1931 that Roosevelt would not be able to withstand the pressures of the office, three doctors, including the neurologist Foster Kennedy, examined him and found him healthy.[56]

In the ensuing years, Kennedy gave Roosevelt periodic checkups, advised the Roosevelt clan on personal matters, and, with his wife, dined with the Roosevelts the night before the attack on Pearl Harbor.[57] Psychiatric illness was profoundly personal for Eleanor Roosevelt. As a child, she had experienced her mother's rejection and her alcoholic father's undependability. He entered a Paris mental asylum for several months and an alcohol rehabilitation center for over a year.[58] Orphaned by age ten, both parents and a brother having died, Eleanor sought throughout her life to help others with problems like her father or, later, like her remaining brother, also alcoholic, who died of cirrhosis of the liver.[59]

Not surprisingly, the Roosevelts urged the US surgeon general in 1939 to create a neuropsychiatric institute to research alcoholism, addiction, and schizophrenia. During the war, both Roosevelts contributed to decisions on military psychiatric policy. Immediately after the war, Eleanor Roosevelt returned to the campaign for a National Mental Health Act.[60]

In the months before enactment of the Selective Service psychiatric examination, Eleanor and Overholser corresponded frequently on the deplorable conditions in mental hospitals, many still housing World War I veterans. In 1940, she condemned such conditions in her "My Day" syndicated newspaper column. From May to July that year, Veterans Affairs Director Frank Hines corresponded with Eleanor about the high cost of hospitalizing World War I psychiatric veterans. Having visited St. Elizabeth's Hospital during World War I, Eleanor Roosevelt was well aware of the plight of neuropsychiatric soldiers and veterans there. (During World War II, she would continue to visit the hospital, frequently invited by Overholser.)[61]

Since she and New York City's mayor Fiorello La Guardia were codirectors of the Office of Civilian Defense, in charge of improving civilian morale, she no doubt knew of his position on screening. To La Guardia, in screening, science joined hands with humanitarianism. Reflecting the popular fear of shell shock in past decades, he told Congress at Selective Service Act hearings in July 1940:

> The one we have to look out for is the boy that just cannot face it. That is the type. It is pathetic, but some types just cannot face fire. They go to pieces. Now medical science can easily discover those types, which we could not during the last war, as we did not know much about those things during the World War. But with the progress in medical science today you can discover those things. We can save those boys from horror. . . . And we can pick those boys out with medical observation, and that is why I would eliminate them, and it will take care of itself.[62]

Franklin's personal experiences and the advice he received from associates also contributed to his receptivity to psychiatry. Born privileged and isolated, polio transformed him into "a traitor to his class," a person identifying with the plight of the downtrodden.[63] Distressed by the abject poverty around Warm Springs, Georgia, he developed an institution there to treat polio.[64] As a victim of polio, he knew well the need for critical psychological support to combat a disability. As he perceived it, he was not a patient but "Doc," who cared for patients and inspired Americans through hard times. Seeing himself that way, he associated socially with his doctors. Age thirty-nine when he contracted polio, he was crippled for the rest of his life, wearing fourteen pounds of steel braces on each leg to locomote, often using two crutches and pivoting his head and torso forward, though he preferred to use a cane and lean heavily on someone's arm.[65]

At first, doctors misdiagnosed Roosevelt's ailment as a cold and then a blood clot on the spinal cord. After a couple of weeks, through the intercession of his uncle, the nationally known polio specialist Dr. Robert W. Lovett confirmed that it was polio.[66] Later on, Dr. Draper treated Roosevelt for polio. Though not a psychiatrist, Draper, analyzed by the Swiss analytic psychologist Carl Jung, had a holistic approach to medicine, instructing his students to look broadly at physiological, anatomical, psychic, and immunological factors.[67] Draper continually encouraged Roosevelt to have faith that he would get better, never telling him that he would remain a cripple, urging him that politics was the best therapy for his constitution.[68] As a cripple, Roosevelt sought through preinduction examinations to prevent militarily unsuited inductees from incurring the unnecessary physical or mental disorders he'd had to endure. As assistant secretary of the navy from 1914 to 1921, he knew particularly the emotional plight of the American sailor. In World War II, he appointed his personal physician Ross T. McIntire as navy surgeon general. So close was McIntire to Roosevelt that during the war, Overholser and others frequently asked him to convey psychiatric policy issues to the president.[69]

Putting Medical Circular No. 1 into Effect

Lobbying the Roosevelts for psychiatric screening began in earnest around the time of the fall of France in June 1940, when the possibility of America's entering a war became more real. In addition to La Guardia's missive to Congress, the Michigan juvenile court justice and syndicated columnist Malcolm Hatfield wrote the president. Recalling victims of shell-shock from World War I who had appeared before him between the wars, he believed that screening would spare "mentally untrained boys" from the horrors of war.⁷⁰

At the same time, Director of Veterans Affairs Frank Hines corresponded with both Roosevelts about the hospital costs and care of World War I psychiatric veterans, a concern he also conveyed in a speech to the American Legion on August 16, where he rued the excessive number of World War I veterans and families receiving pensions and hospitalization or death benefits for service- and non-service-related disabilities.⁷¹ On August 19, Overholser sent a memorandum to the Federal Board of Hospitalization, of which Hines, McIntire, and Overholser were members, estimating that the cost for neuropsychiatric veterans from a second world war would be even higher; that is, at least 400 men per 100,000 on duty would require long-term veterans' hospitalization for nervous and mental diseases should America enter the war, at a cost of over $30,000 per patient per year. Citing World War I figures, he warned that the numbers would be higher in a second world war because of the increasing mechanization of German aerial and naval warfare. (While Overholser's memorandum did not specify a number, he estimated to Selective Service several months later that the cost would exceed one billion dollars, since the cost for World War I had come to $641 million for service-related claims and $282 million for additional hospital maintenance.)⁷² To avoid these costs, Overholser called for preinduction psychiatric screening.

Most likely aware of Overholser's memorandum, on September 8, Sullivan cabled him to attend a meeting at the WAWPF "to outline the recommendations concerning psychiatric examination of conscripts." On September 11, the WAWPF published its psychiatric examination in a "Bulletin from the William Alanson White Psychiatric Foundation to the Chairman and the Physician-Member of Each Local Selection Board." This document essentially became Selective Service Medical Circular No. 1.⁷³

On September 16, Roosevelt signed the Selective Training and Service Act, authorizing the president to "select and induct" each registrant, provided "his physical and mental fitness . . . have been satisfactorily determined" and he was "morally sound" (thus legislatively justifying the psychiatric screening program).⁷⁴

On September 26, the Bureau of the Budget forwarded to Roosevelt Overholser's August 19 cost estimate memorandum, which the director had received from Hines. Since McIntire had seen the memorandum a month earlier, he may well have conveyed its importance to the president. McIntire himself addressed the College of Physicians and Surgeons on the same subject a few weeks later.⁷⁵

The next day, September 27, the president sent Overholser's memo to Frederick Osborn, head of the JANSSC, as well as to the war and navy secretaries.[76] Osborn was well aware of the plight of neuropsychiatric soldiers from his experience as head of the American Red Cross in World War I. In January 1941, Army Chief of Staff George C. Marshall would appoint Osborn chair of the Committee on Welfare and Recreation, to improve housing and recreational facilities for servicemen, and, in August 1941, director of the Army Morale Branch (later converted to the Information and Education Division).[77] But for now, Roosevelt chose Osborn to head the Selective Service Psychiatric Advisory Committee, with the objective of working with Sullivan to adapt the WAWPF examination to military specifications.

Besides Osborn, Sullivan, and Overholser, the committee included Selective Service doctors and psychiatrists from the Army Surgeon General, Walter Reed Hospital, Veterans Affairs, the American Psychiatric Association, the APA Military Mobilization Committee, and other mental hospital superintendents and neurologists.[78] In the years to come, some of the same individuals and organizations would continue to advocate for tougher screening.

On November 7, 1940, Medical Circular No. 1 was published, and Selective Service ordered all 6,403 local boards and 108 induction stations to employ the circular to routinely examine draftees throughout the nation.[79] From January 1941 through July 1941, Sullivan conducted two-day seminars for draft board members and examiners on psychiatric diagnoses at nine induction centers around the country, including Washington, DC, and Boston in January; Atlanta in February; New York in April; Chicago in May; Dallas, Los Angeles, and San Francisco in June; and Buffalo in July. Sullivan trained examinees on the first days of the seminars. Other specialists conducted sessions on the second day on subgroups of diagnoses. Sullivan used the seminars not only to educate nonpsychiatrists in basic diagnostics, including interpersonal relations and morale, but to express his views as a psychiatrist/social scientist on such topics beyond traditional psychiatry as agriculture, commerce, communications, civilian and industrial morale, counterespionage, propaganda, and violence.[80]

Medical Circular No. 1

Sullivan's Medical Circular No. 1 was the first-ever routine psychiatric examination for draftees, and it greatly expanded categories of illness. As originally published on November 7, 1940, it contained five categories: I—mental defect or deficiency; II—psychopathic personality; III—major abnormalities of mood; IV—psychoneurotic disorders; and V—pre- and postpsychotic personalities and schizophrenia.[81] The last category included paranoid personalities and catatonic and prepsychotic states. Medical Circular No.1 instructed examiners not only to detect those who had such disorders but also to look for men with possible problems in interpersonal relations who might not be able to adjust to others or to the stress of military or civilian life thereafter. Before 1940, an individual with such concerns might have consulted a minister or his family, not a doctor. Though technically a psychiatric rejection was simply a judgment of unsuitability for the military and not a diagnosis of mental illness, this distinction was too subtle for popular opinion, and thus a new, broader concept of mental illness became an important byproduct of screening, which would have a major impact after the war.

Medical Circular No. 1 emphasized that the psychiatric examiner was to be trained not only to look for current ailments but for any hint of possible future maladjustment. While World War I examiners had been instructed to accept anyone unless he had a "definite corroborated history of a mental disease that required hospital treatment or observation," Medical Circular No. 1 probed for the least hint of maladjustment. The examiner was to interview his subject in an isolated area and to ask questions in a "straightforward," respectful manner. In this way, the doctor was to gain full confidential disclosure. If the registrant said anything deemed unusual, the doctor was to explore further.

According to the circular, the examination was to be done in the nude to disarm the candidate of pretense. (This later created a controversy in the examination of prospective WACs.) Sullivan told medical interviewers at diagnostic seminars in New York City and Washington, DC:

> If a person, for example, has marked shyness about disrobing in front of a doctor, one cannot help but wonder why, and what . . . this tendency will be when he is flung into [the] anything but private world of the training camp. Also, when a person is unable to carry out . . . instructions of disrobing, if you ask him questions while he is doing it, that immediately excites your interest as to first, the intellectual grasp; that is, how much this man can carry in his mind; and second, tendencies to obsessional preoccupation.[82]

The circular instructed examiners that the men chosen for induction were anticipated to remain mentally fit for both the year of training and service and the ten years thereafter in the reserve.[83] Selective Service Director Clarence Dykstra went further, telling examiners in January 1941 in Washington, DC, to screen out the one who could not adjust to military life and the one unable to readjust to civilian existence.[84] Reflecting this dual interest, the circular instructed examiners to probe for a history of problems relating to others at work, at home, or socially with men and women, plus possible former criminality or subversion. The circular gave this example:

> The registrant being a machinist whose left index finger is badly scarred, the examiner asks how the injury occurred. There may follow a question as to just what job he has been doing; how many others are similarly employed in the shop; is it a pretty good crowd; does he like the work; is the employer fair? Have they treated him right. . . . What does he do with his spare time? . . . Sociable, or prefers his own company? . . . Is he self-reliant . . . shy? With men, with women? If anything . . . unusual comes to light, pursue the topic. . . . Does he like the idea of being trained for the national defense?[85]

The circular stressed the ability to get along in a group. "Military life," the circular stated prominently on its first page, "requires that the soldier shall be able to live comfortably in continued close contact with a variegated group of other men. He cannot depend on any self-evolved protective mechanism that sets him apart from his fellows."[86]

Medical Circular No. 1 reflected Sullivan's apprehensions about political skeptics. While psychiatric screening did not specifically call for the elimination of men with doubts about military service, it did suggest that examiners look out for such individuals. Circular No. 1 instructed examiners to ask the registrant if he "liked the idea of being trained for the National Defense."[87]

Examiners were trained to look for those who had been emotionally afflicted during the Depression, whether attributable to nature or nurture. A Selective Service medical officer told examiners in September 1940: "A man who is constantly out of work, as a general rule, is so because of certain personal qualities in the man." He called for a "careful examination to cull these people out."[88] One of Sullivan's closest associates, Dr. Dexter Bullard, recalled in an interview years later:

> Sullivan's general proposition was, if you're warped in one area of development it is much more difficult to adjust in later areas of development, so if you find a guy who has a long history of being discharged from work many times because he couldn't get along with the boss, the chances are he's going to have a hell of a time with the military boss, where orders are orders and you carry them out or else.[89]

The clinical chief of psychotherapy services at the Menninger Clinic instructed Chicago Selective Service examiners in early 1941 to reject not only those on relief but those employed by the WPA, because they were emotionally immature, clung in a dependent fashion to strong figures, and expected to be taken care of by a strong agency or individual. Social workers, he said, were very aware of this and called it the "WPA attitude."[90]

At the Washington training seminar in January, examiners were instructed to weed out those unable to resolve the conflict between the peacetime belief in killing as against the Commandments, illegal, and criminal and the wartime doctrine that killing was necessary, commendable, even praiseworthy. This objective sought to cull from service those who had unspecified religious or moral objections to serving but who had not gone through the formal process of filing for conscientious objector (CO). It is not known how many of these were rejected on psychiatric grounds or were admitted to service only to be discharged later. We do know, however, that about one out of seven of the 7,000 COs assigned to Civilian Public Service (CPS) camps were later discharged for psychiatric reasons. Another 5,000 assigned to CPS worked outside the camps, largely as aides in mental hospitals and as guinea pigs for medical experiments.[91]

From 1938 through 1940, Sullivan and the WAWPF drafted a routine, universal psychiatric examination for military service, known as Medical Circular No. 1. The objective: to eliminate anyone who might possibly have emotional problems in military service and to substantially reduce the cost of any future hospitalization. Approved by Franklin Delano Roosevelt as part of the medical examination authorized by the Selective Service Act of September 1940, Medical Circular No. 1 soon encountered skepticism from prominent American and European psychiatrists. Their skepticism and the response of the American military is the subject of the next chapter.

2
Military Necessity Overrides Psychiatric Skepticism

Months before the United States' publication of Medical Circular No. 1 in November 1940, British and Canadian psychiatrists had raised serious questions about the efficacy of the screening program. Prompting these questions was graphic evidence from the Battle of Dunkirk in June 1940, the evacuation thereafter, and the early North African campaign.

In July 1940, only a few weeks after the evacuation of Dunkirk, the psychiatrists William Sargant and Eliot Slater, clinical director and deputy director, respectively, of Belmont Hospital, England, reported that patients returning home from France were broken not because of individual predisposition but because of the stress of continual physical exertion, insufficient sleep, irregular meals, recurrent bombing, comrades killed, and the shame of retreat. Soon after, British forces in North Africa disclosed that a majority of their casualties were normal men unpredictably broken by the stress of combat.[1]

Instead of screening, the British endorsed preventive psychiatry. Instead of simply rejecting them, they placed mentally deficient or maladjusted men into "pioneer corps," a form of labor battalions to work in agriculture and factories. For those inducted into the military, they developed educational courses, recreation, counseling, and vocational placement to boost morale, plus emphasizing rest, chats with psychiatrists, satisfactory nutrition, and housing.

As to treatment, they evacuated men from Dunkirk to hospitals in England. But in North Africa, they treated increasingly at the front, using drugs such as sodium amytal to encourage the soldier's recall of battle experiences to resolve conflicts (narcosis). They also used drugs to induce rest and sleep. They enticed the shell-shocked to gain weight with supplemental nourishment. And they employed coma and electroconvulsive therapy (ECT).[2]

American psychiatrists on the National Academy of Sciences, National Research Council (NRC) Committee on Neuropsychiatry, which reported to the Office of Scientific Research and Development (OSRD), the chief military policy-making body during the war, were well aware of their European and Canadian colleagues' doubts. Indeed, the American Psychiatric Association (APA) included Canadian members.

But they did not heed the evidence and warnings. In October 1940, John Cathcart, chief psychiatrist for the Canadian Department of Pensions, cautioned Harry Steckel, head of the APA Military Mobilization Committee, that "unwise [selection] can ruin otherwise useful material." Both Cathcart and Aubrey Lewis, director of the Mill Hill Emergency Hospital in London, emphasized that a liberal neuropsychiatric discharge policy would encourage men to feign illness so they could remain at home in "relative freedom" with better civilian pay.[3] In another letter in December 1940, Lewis urged his American colleagues to adopt British methods of preventive psychiatry and treatment instead of screening.[4]

In April 1941, Canadian psychiatrists advised their American peers on an NRC Committee on Neuropsychiatry tour of Canada that seemingly fit recruits had proved "abject cowards" on the battlefields of North Africa, while "little squirts" with rejectable defects could be heroes.[5] (A refrain to be echoed among Americans later on.)

As early as 1939, Emilio Mira y Lopez, a professor of psychiatry at the University of Barcelona, had praised the Loyalist Army in the Spanish Civil War for accepting homosexuals, bedwetters, and alcoholics in noncombat positions, where they performed well and rarely needed to be discharged. (All three categories would later be subject to rejection in Medical Circular No. 1.) Mira reiterated these views at the New York Academy of Medicine in 1942, advising Americans that there was no need to eliminate these men from an effective army.[6]

Several leading American psychiatrists expressed the same skepticism. Impressed by a Scottish study reported at the NRC/APA Conference on the Neurotic Soldier in December 1940, which revealed that fifty out of one hundred previously known "neurotics" in one Scottish town had exhibited no change in emotional status after German aerial bombings, twenty-five showed improved morale, and twenty-five became worse, the psychiatrist Frank Fremont-Smith, who was also medical director of the Josiah Macy Foundation, questioned the predictive power of screening.[7]

Charles Mac Fie Campbell, director of the Boston Psychopathic Hospital and professor of psychiatry at Harvard Medical School, raised in Scotland, had examined inductees in World War I and industrial workers in the 1920s. From this experience, he told Selective Service examiners in January 1941 that regardless of the time spent on examination and investigation, psychiatrists, if they were honest, had to admit they were only guessing about diagnoses.[8]

The well-known criminal psychiatrist Bernard Glueck, who had examined immigrants at Ellis Island, prisoners at Sing Sing, and soldiers in World War I and worked at St. Elizabeth's Hospital, affirmed in February 1942 that the classic military conflict between the "avoidance of annihilation" and loyalty might even be "unmanageable in the best of men."[9] In January 1941, the Public Health Service psychiatrist Lawrence Kolb told Selective Service and Army Induction Board psychiatrists that he doubted Sullivan's claim that psychiatrists could predict a registrant's adjustment to the military and postmilitary civilian life based on early or latent mental problems.[10]

Reviewing his experience treating one thousand Bronx VA veterans from 1920 to 1924, Abram Kardiner maintained in March 1941 that psychiatrists could not determine a person's psychological fitness for war. Though analyzed by Sigmund Freud himself, he disputed the master's contention that war and civilian neuroses were similar. Rather, he contended that "war is a unique life death situation" where one minute a man might live, the next, die. Even the strongest-willed individual might break down. Recalling his personal experience, Kardiner noted that some "severely neurotic personalities" unable to adjust in their premilitary life actually "accommodated themselves excellently to the military routine and . . . lost all their neuroses." Denying that psychiatrists could use the peacetime experiences of examinees to predict war neuroses, he opposed screening out almost all categories, including those with a history of convulsions, tiqueurs, stammering, or demonstrated disturbances of the autonomic nervous system. All these men, he said, could be given noncombat assignments.[11] Advocating early treatment at the front, he recalled that the conditions of most of his World War I VA patients had become calcified because no one had treated them until four years after service.[12]

What, then, was American psychiatry to do? Sullivan insisted on the value of prediction. "When the mind has once gone bad," he is quoted as stating, "there is every likelihood that it will go bad again. . . . Even the best of psychiatrists cannot always tell that a man has had a breakdown but the strains of the service will find the weakness and the man will go down again."[13] Despite studies that questioned predisposition, Sullivan pointed to earlier British reports and a study by St. Elizabeth's Hospital to promote psychiatric predictive expertise. The Veterans Affairs psychiatrist Martin Cooley likewise referred to the Army Medical Department's volume 10 on *Neuropsychiatry in the World War*, which found that most men who broke down soon after reaching camp had shown symptoms before entering service.[14]

More Screening in Preparation for War

Despite the objections of some British, Canadian, and American psychiatrists, screening in the United States continued as the predominant function of military psychiatry from 1941 onward. What was it that explained this persistent devotion? For one, the alternatives to screening did not particularly appeal to Americans at this time. But more importantly, the military feared that without screening, they would be dragged into war with an undisciplined, uncooperative, unruly, and unmotivated group of young men unable to withstand the fascist military machines of Hitler and Tojo.

While some American psychiatrists preferred preventive psychiatry (including moral persuasion) and treatment over screening, civilian and military policy makers were opposed. Roosevelt maintained publicly that using propaganda to inspire national unity would be against America's freedom of belief and expression. As the president put it, in a war fought against totalitarianism, the unity of "free men and women who recognize the truth and face reality with intelligence and courage" would overcome "the false unity of people browbeaten by threats, misled by propaganda."[15] In no way would the United States emulate the propaganda of the World War I American Creel Committee, which had been accused of suppressed dissent, or the widespread, invasive lies of the Nazis. When Roosevelt established a propaganda agency, he acted cautiously, seeking to present "facts" only, calling it the Office of Facts and Figures, the precursor to the Office of War Information. Likewise, Osborn's Army Morale Branch, renamed the Special Services Division, became the Information and Education Division (I&E). Learning the truth, it was argued, would enable soldiers to appreciate the justice of the war and the need to sacrifice.[16] The agency issued seven propaganda films directed by Frank Capra, the Why We Fight series, but only two were shown in public theaters because of congressional opposition. They were *Prelude to War*, which won an Academy Award in 1942, and *Battle of Russia*, nominated for an Academy Award in 1944.[17]

Nor did the army show much interest in labor battalions or "universal service" to assign everyone, regardless of mental, psychiatric, or physical disabilities, to some vocation in the military or civilian work. This, despite endorsement from European psychiatrists at NRC meetings where colleagues from both America and Europe conversed. To the extent the military supported such battalions in late 1940 and 1941, they were for physical, not mental, limitations, for example, a Selective Service regulation authorizing limited service for those "who cannot do heavy work."[18]

In a similar vein, American psychiatrists in the military espoused little preventive psychiatry until late 1944, when they began promoting rest and recuperation (R&R), limited tours of duty, and reduced the number of continuous days in combat. Nor did American psychiatrists treat much until late in the war, given their enduring faith in screening and a belief by the military that they were "not a welfare agency."[19]

Nor could the military rely on more rigorous training to ensure discipline, motivation, and coordination. By early 1941, time and resources were short, and America needed to catch up with the fascist enemy, already victorious throughout continental Europe. In the two decades before the war, the army had trained only 100,000 reserve officers, a cadre grossly insufficient for troop strengths of 800,000 by September 1940 and 1,500,000 by August 1941. And not only leaders but essentials like rifles were in short supply, with some rifles as much as thirty years old. As war became ever more likely, the president lobbied Congress for billions of dollars for ammunition, guns, and planes, but when funds lagged, he had to turn to other federal agencies to supplement the defense budget.[20]

Facing the nightmare of American soldiers failing under fire, Chief Army Psychiatrist Patrick Madigan saw psychiatric screening as essential to ensuring a military where the "team worked together and stayed together [even when] authority vanishes . . . members of the team . . . drop out . . . and . . . the only driving force . . . remains a strong and incomparable spirit of attainment."[21]

The Army and Navy's Examinations

So it was that the idea of screening did not die but was in fact reinforced by army and navy examinations. In May 1941, the army published its preinduction examination, Army Circular Letter No. 19, and the following October its postinduction examination, Army Medical Bulletin No. 58.[22] In April 1941, the navy adopted its own psychiatric examination. Supervised by the navy psychiatrist Dallas Sutton and the Public Health Service psychiatrist Lawrence Kolb, the navy exam was more basic, focusing on current neurological and gross behavioral defects. For example, examiners were told to look for abnormalities of gait, deviations of psychomotor activity, significant physical defects, severe migraine headaches, enuresis (bedwetting), psychopathy, and manic depression.[23]

Karl and William Menninger, sons of Charles Menninger, the founder of the Menninger Clinic, also developed their own Selective Service examination for the state of Kansas. Karl Menninger was one of the first Americans to be trained as a psychoanalyst. His brother William trained as a psychiatrist at St. Elizabeth's Hospital in 1927, where he became personally aware of the plight of hospitalized neuropsychiatric veterans from World

War I.²⁴ The two brothers published their examination, more traditional than Medical Circular No. 1, in the army journal *War Medicine* (November 1941). The Kansas examination devoted half of its ten psychiatric criteria to social history or intelligence and had a substantial neurological section on gait, reflexes, and speech but little about mere possibilities of disruptive behavior, as described in the Selective Service and army examinations.²⁵

Army Circular Letter No. 19

By mid-1941, the predominant military psychiatric examination became Army Circular Letter No. 19. Selective Service Medical Circular No. 1, developed in peacetime by civilians, broadly focused on forecasting military and postservice civilian adjustment. But Circular Letter No. 19 emphasized a narrower goal of ensuring inducted soldiers were well motivated, well disciplined, and physically and mentally capable. It sought to quickly detect behavior problems at a time of massive troop buildup, to locate those who would bully or be bullied, who would not get along because of being strange, introverted, not team oriented, addicted, alcoholic, syphilitic, or neurologically impaired.²⁶ The army intended that both Selective Service and the army's examination be given to every draftee before admission to service.

Patrick Madigan, the designer of Circular Letter No. 19, unlike Sullivan had a long-standing military medical career, beginning in World War I, when he served in France with the 7th Division, 64th Infantry. Afterward, he became the chief army psychiatrist in the Philippines, then chief psychiatrist at Walter Reed, and then the psychiatrist in the Army Surgeon General's Office. Two of his brothers and a son were also military doctors. From his military experiences, he grew acutely conscious of the characteristics needed to be a good soldier.²⁷

Circular Letter No. 19 instructed examiners to detect those who found it hard to conform with regimentation or derived pleasure from inciting insubordination in others.²⁸ Similar instructions appeared in the army's postinduction Medical Bulletin No. 58 (October 1941)²⁹ but little in Sullivan's Medical Circular No. 1.

Circular Letter No. 19 instructed examiners to look for such "personality deviations" as "seclusiveness," "lonesomeness," "discontent," "suspicion," "overboisterousness," "lack of initiative and ambition," "resentfulness to discipline," "suicidal tendencies," and lastly, "homosexual proclivities."³⁰ In a separate journal article, Madigan made clear that "proclivities" or "possibilities" also referred to other deviations of character beyond the explicitly stated categories of homosexuality and addiction.³¹

Circular Letter No. 19 called for detecting such "psychopaths" as "many homosexuals," "grotesque and pathological liars," "vagabonds . . . swindlers, kleptomaniacs, pyromaniacs, alcoholics . . . guardhouse lawyers." It also included addicts and syphilitics. While the revised Selective Service exam added addiction, alcoholism, and syphilis to synchronize the two examinations, it did not go into the letter's detail, such as describing "suffused eyes, prominent superficial blood vessels of nose and check, flabby, bloated face" as evidence of alcoholism, or, for addiction, white scars on thighs, trunk, and arms, "pallor and dryness of the skin," "an attitude of flippancy" or, if withdrawn, "cowardly and cringing." Army examiners were to elicit responses to questions about heroin addiction with such words as "deck," "quill," "package," or "an eighth." For syphilis, they were to look for facial symptoms or speech distortions.

For the first time, Circular No. 19 medicalized many traits previously handled under the Code of Military Justice. Thus, while the circular aimed to screen out a wide range of potential disciplinary problems, it did ostensibly spare soldiers and their officers the agony of a military tribunal and potential harsh punishment in the stockade or brig. This was an enlargement of function for the psychiatric profession and an arguably more humane way of treating personality variations as medical rather than criminal matters. However, as will be seen, those found "guilty" of mental illness or certain personality characteristics could be and often were discharged without due process, without benefits, without honor, and with a stain on their record for life. Nor did court-martials and imprisonment related to these status characteristics totally disappear.

The Screening Process in Operation

By mid-1941, male inductees had to navigate a complex labyrinth of examinations. First, at least in theory, local board medical examiners were to question each registrant for twenty minutes, either rejecting or accepting. If undecided, they were to refer to a Selective Service Medical Advisory Board (MAB) psychiatrist. The MAB psychiatrist was to reject or pass the registrant and send him back to the Army Induction Board. The Induction Board psychiatrist would then reject or accept. If accepted, the registrant could still be examined by army reception center doctors and at a training camp as well. Only if he passed every examination would he continue in service. Later in the war, a soldier might also be examined by a psychiatrist at an army embarkation camp before going overseas, then again before going into combat, then after initial combat and before being discharged.[32]

Military Necessity Overrides Psychiatric Skepticism | 41

Figure 1. Inductees waiting to be examined.

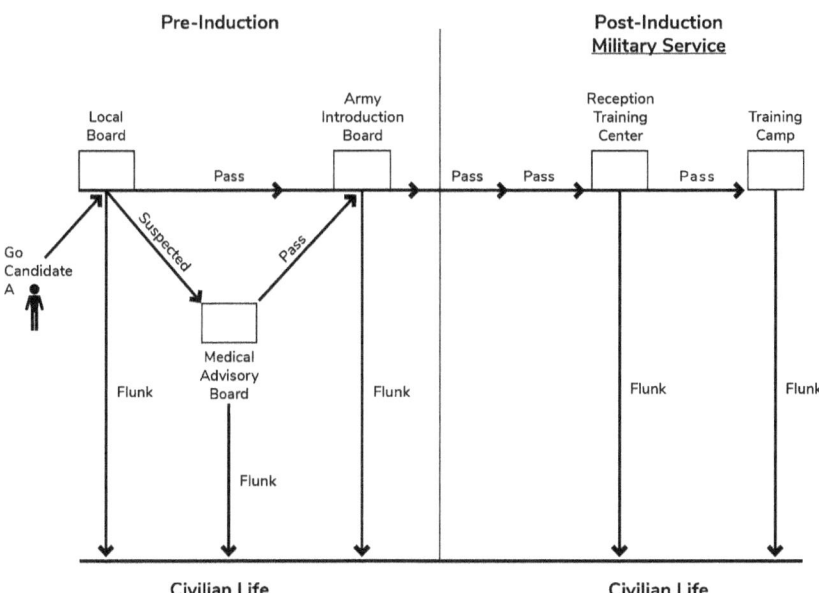

Figure 2. Proposed examination process.

The navy also had a series of examinations, which continued even after the armed forces instituted a joint induction program in February 1943. Before then, the navy accepted a man at a recruiting station, then sent him to a training station. After he filled out several forms regarding schooling, health, and jobs, he saw a psychiatrist and a psychologist. If the psychiatrist suspected a disability, he referred him to another psychiatrist for a more thorough examination. If the second psychiatrist had questions, he referred him to a two-week observation platoon or a neuropsychiatric ward. If the navy still had reservations, they could send him to their aptitude board, which included a psychiatrist and sometimes a psychologist, for further inspection. Then they could approve him for service, discharge him, or send him to St. Elizabeth's or another hospital.[33]

Psychiatry in the Allied and Axis Nations

Britain

The lonely path the United States chose to pursue—screening and little else—was particularly significant because other Allies and the Axis did not share it.

To the extent British screening existed, personnel specialists administered aptitude and intelligence tests, particularly because they were anxious about sophisticated German weaponry and equipment. They referred a recruit with low scores to psychiatrists to determine if a man had an "inadequate personality." But even those men were not rejected from service, instead being placed in noncombat assignments.[34]

Psychiatrists from both Britain and Germany discouraged soldiers from thinking they were mentally ill, in part to avoid the loss of useful soldiers and to stem the demand for disability pensions. Indeed, not until 1944 did Britain permit pensions for psychiatric disabilities. Some British psychiatrists believed that receiving a pension would be a disincentive to getting better.[35] The British tended to view psychiatric diagnoses as a cover for cowardice.

Germany

The Germans did even less screening than the British, as most of their political opponents or those who were "different" were disposed of by other means. Beginning with dismissals from jobs or political positions, the Nazis continued throughout the 1930s and 1940s with mass imprisonment, torture, humiliation, and degradation. In 1933, they enacted the "Law for the Prevention of Hereditarily Ill Offspring," which eventually led to the sterilization of 400,000 alcoholics, epileptics, and mentally "retarded." Another 200,000 "congenitally inferior" individuals were killed through starvation, medication, overdoses, or gassed in concentration camps. This included one-third of those in asylums for the mentally ill. All this apart from the "final solution" for Jews and the extermination of other nonfavored groups, which eliminated millions. Instead of psychiatry, within the military the Germans stressed training and harsh discipline. Over 15,000 German soldiers were shot for cowardice, and many more were court-martialed or imprisoned. Large numbers committed suicide. For those Germans not subject to execution or imprisonment, unity of thought and action was achieved through propaganda and indoctrination of youth and by keeping men from the same province or town in the same unit. The only place the Germans favored screening was in aptitude tests to select officers, because officer candidates lacked geographic or economic cohesion and because technological aptitude and leadership skills in the military were critical.[36]

As with the British, the Germans believed that everyone should play a role, and their experience with a plethora of cases of shell-shock victims applying for pensions during and after World War I led them to consider those claiming mental illness before being inducted as examples of "pension opportunism" and exhibiting a "pathological lack of male behavior."

The Soviet Union

With the German invasion of Russia on June 22, 1941, the Russians were faced with the need to immediately mobilize. Every male or female was called up unless he or she had a blatant physiological incapacity. The only way one could receive a "psychiatric" exemption was to have an obvious physiologic disorder confirmed by a neurologist or be an imbecile or psychotic. Not surprisingly, according to one historian, the Soviet Union rejected only 50,000 to 75,000 from military service for neurological disorders out of a total of 22 million conscripted, compared to America's 1.8 million neuropsychiatric rejectees out of 18 million. The Russian focus on physiological causes also pervaded their efforts at psychiatric treatment and preventive psychiatry on the battlefield. The Russians had no tolerance for anyone who exhibited fear or anxiety. These were considered normal reactions to war that a person should be able to get over. If he or she did not, they were referred to a "political officer" or to their immediate commander for reorientation. If this did not work, they might be sent to penal battalions or executed. Barely anyone was evacuated. Even if someone was schizophrenic, which was considered to be an organic disruption of the brain, he could only receive treatment or be evacuated if he also exhibited physical symptoms such as paralysis. Not surprisingly, the Russians had rates of return of "psychiatric" cases to combat four to six times greater than the Americans. To the extent the Russians treated or prevented mental illness, they focused on rest, nutrition, and political orientation. They also used herbal and chemical medicines to induce long-term sleep or to revive and stimulate. Because the Germans waged horrific battles on Russian soil, the Russians were easily motivated to hate their enemy and to fight with intensity to survive.[37]

Japan

Unlike other combatant countries, some Japanese military psychiatrists did believe in "predisposition" and did develop a system of classification during the Sino-Japanese War in the 1930s, which designated men from A (the best) to D (the worst) in terms of physical and psychological condition. But a severe shortage of manpower in World War II and psychiatrists' lack of faith in their ability to predict neuroses led them to not employ screening in World War II.[38]

On the eve of the war, with only 22,000 out of 70 million Japanese in mental hospitals, with an average stay of 40 days, the country had little incentive to weed men out from service to reduce state hospital bills.[39] The army had a severe shortage of psychiatrists, hampering all types of psychiatry; mostly nonspecialists took care of those with hysteria. Reports of low rates of British psychiatric casualties in 1941 also motivated Japanese psychiatrists not to engage in psychiatric screening. Indeed, instead of rejecting the "insane" from service, the Japanese placed them under long-term confinement and surveillance. In other cases, they used the threat of institutionalization to persuade soldiers to ignore their psychological ailments.[40]

In actuality, the Japanese military leadership had little interest in supporting any form of military psychiatry, let alone screening. The military refused to authorize psychiatric treatment at the front throughout the entire war. Only one Japanese army hospital specialized in treating psychiatric casualties, admitting 10,454 soldiers during the war; the Japanese navy was even more opposed to psychiatry, having no hospitals and only a limited number of psychiatric wards after 1942. In contrast, 1.2 million Americans were admitted to army psychiatric hospitals during the war. Fundamentally, the ethos of the Japanese army and that of the nation extolled self-sacrifice. Unlike American culture, the Japanese found individualism anathema; an activity such as psychiatric treatment, which might inspire negative attitudes or encourage cowardice, was considered unpatriotic defeatism. In the interest of the state, psychiatrists discharged a limited number of "mentally disordered" from one military hospital when they found them "contradict[ing] government propaganda." But they did not recognize them as having a medical condition or to be suffering; nor did they give them disability pensions.[41] They were, as we will see, like American servicemen who later received Section VIII discharges, without honor and without benefits. As for suicides, from the end of the 1930s through World War II, Japanese military psychiatrists distinguished between those who committed suicide in obedience to the state and those who self-inflicted death; the latter were cases of mental illness, the former approved behavior.[42]

Thus, we see that by mid-1941, America had embarked on a unique path of psychiatric screening unlike any other medical venture in any other Allied or Axis nation. The interest of America's military in fostering well-motivated, disciplined, regimented troops by eliminating potential troublemakers, plus the pride of Sullivan and his associates in their psychiatric expertise, overrode skepticism of others in the profession about the program's efficacy. With the publication of Selective Service Medical Circular No. 1 and Army Circular Letter No. 19, Selective Service and the army joined hands in coordinating the screening of America's youth from the hazards of war. But as it went into operation, basic problems with screening emerged.

3   Debating Screening's Viability

As soon as the examinations launched, practical problems emerged. Far fewer psychiatrists agreed to work with Selective Service than Harry Stack Sullivan had anticipated. A September 1940 American Psychiatric Association (APA) questionnaire found only 1,500 psychiatrists willing to volunteer for national defense.[1] Though not all 6,403 local boards were expected to have a psychiatrist, as of November 1940 only 584 psychiatrists had signed up. Though Sullivan hoped that all 660 regional Medical Advisory Boards (MAB) would have a psychiatrist, not all did. Doctors sometimes lacked adequate credentials.[2] With transportation scarce, some psychiatrists, who lived as far as fifty to two hundred miles from local boards, rarely appeared. As late as August 1942, only 561 doctors were working as psychiatrists in the army, a mere fifty-one of those certified by the American Board of Psychiatry and Neurology.[3]

The army and Selective Service's failure to pay psychiatrists to examine candidates made matters worse. There was also a tendency to assign psychiatrists to nonpsychiatric positions, giving little incentive to leave profitable practices, especially before Pearl Harbor.[4] To stem the shortage, Sullivan trained nonpsychiatric doctors, social workers, psychologists, and military officers in psychiatric diagnosis at nine two-day seminars in 1941. But other psychiatrists, such as the University of Michigan's Raymond Waggoner, did not appreciate these seminars, criticizing Sullivan for minimizing the expertise of the profession.

Sullivan had envisioned a twenty-minute examination. But given the shortage of examiners and high induction quotas, psychiatrists frequently examined as many as one hundred to 150 a day. In such short exams, psychiatrists could not implement Medical Circular No. l's thorough probe. According to the circular, every verbal hint of maladjustment, strange body movement, or curious dart of the eye was to invite intense cross-examination.

Years later, one examiner recalled that one day he actually examined 512 men. On a good day, he might ask in rapid fire: "How do you feel?" "Have you ever been sick?" "Are you nervous?" "How do you think you will get along in the Army?"⁵ Most examinees recalled only one or two questions: "Do you wet your bed?" and "Do you like girls?" For many, the only one they remembered was about sexual preference.⁶

Initially, the military and Selective Service had anticipated four routine psychiatric examinations: at the Selective Service local board, the army induction center, the army reception center, and the army training camp. Only those who passed all four were to be accepted. But only two of the four examinations were in effect in 1941, the local board and the induction station, leading an army psychiatric investigating committee to complain of inadequate screening at army training camps.⁷ (The navy, on the other hand, had extensive screening in the training camps.)

A divergence in philosophy between Selective Service and the army further exacerbated problems. While the army prioritized the enlistment of disciplined, motivated troops, Sullivan emphasized ensuring a man's long-term military and civilian durability. First, a Selective Service local board examiner assessed each candidate's emotional fitness, either rejecting or passing the individual. Then, the army induction board reexamined the emotional status of each individual. Though efforts were made to synchronize the two exams, in operation, they differed widely. Selective Service might accept a man only to have the army reject him.

Registrants and their families complained of inconsistencies. Sometimes, a recruit received a clean bill of health from a psychiatric examiner at his local draft board, left his job assuming he was off to war, only to have a psychiatric examiner at an army induction center reject him as mentally unfit. Americans wondered how much psychiatrists could really know if a person one examiner called "normal" was later deemed "abnormal" by another; when men with identical physical and mental characteristics were treated unequally—one accepted, the other rejected; or when men considered healthy for years were suddenly found mentally ill.⁸

The initiators of psychiatric screening assumed the army and Selective Service could synchronize their two examinations. Yet between May 1941 and December 1941, the contents and execution of the examinations differed widely. The army preinduction examination targeted men with obvious disciplinary, psychotic, and neurological defects. Its list of mental disorders included schizophrenia, syphilis, and hysterical paralysis. Addicts, alcoholics, psychopaths, and sex perverts were also included for rejection, as well as those with misbehavior tendencies. As criticized by Sullivan, designers of the army examination were not so much interested in "building up a trained army" as in "throwing together [one] to meet an acute emergency," whereas

Sullivan's group was more "keenly concerned with durability . . . than numbers," focusing on tendencies toward personal maladjustments rather than eliminating troublemakers.[9]

Psychiatric standards could be arbitrary. John Aita, a psychiatrist at the Fort Snelling, Minnesota, induction board, noted in his study of 9,652 men: "From day-to-day standards of rejection . . . vary. . . . In a group of meager prospects the proportion of disqualifications was frequently no greater than in other groups," while "in a group composed of essentially urban student material, less impressive specimens were more likely to suffer rejection."[10]

Some of Sullivan's own policy decisions seemed arbitrary. While he could point to only 10 percent of 183 veterans in St. Elizabeth's who'd had prior mental hospitalizations, he favored rejecting all former inmates of asylums. Though no more than 20 percent of the same sample had repeated arrests for drunkenness, he advocated rejecting anyone arrested for drunkenness more than once. On the other hand, while Sullivan found that 34 percent of the same sample had psychotic relatives, he nonetheless concluded that heredity did not provide sufficient evidence to reject an individual.[11] Clearly, something beyond logic and scientific reasoning was at work. Moreover, to be valid a study would have required comparison of neuropsychiatric ex-servicemen with a similar number of normal veterans.

Screening's goals also confused examiners. Some psychiatrists thought they were checking fitness for military service; others thought that rejection or acceptance would place men in the most suitable work—either in service or in domestic industry. In September 1941, the Menninger Clinic psychiatrist Douglass Orr wondered why psychiatrists could not substitute a "vocational classification" for the neuropsychiatric rejection to avoid misunderstanding.[12] Years later, psychiatrists recalling their experience in World War II expressed similar confusion: "We were led to believe that the fighting soldier was only one member of the team and that if a person was rejected from military service, he was not lost to the cause but played his part in production."[13] This was not to be the case.

Ironically, the supposed use of psychiatric screening to reject persons better suited for civilian work led to employment problems in civilian life. Burdened with a neuropsychiatric label, the rejectee often returned to an employer likely to refuse to retain him and a community likely to refuse to accept him. In August 1941, *Psychiatry* reported just such complaints from registrants returning home to the big cities.[14] Years later, Hershey wrote: "Because mental illness was not well understood by the public . . . no mental[ly] rejected [person] could gain from [it] and . . . in many cases he would fail to get employment he could have gained had he not had this record."[15] Exacerbating this problem was that under the law at that time, enlistment records were open to the 4F and his community. Aware of this, the army cautioned examiners to be conservative in rejections, rejecting only those who could not perform soldiers' duties. Reflecting similar concerns, Sullivan suggested giving rejectees a card, which stated that they could still contribute to the national defense through civilian employment even though they had been rejected from military service. But this did not occur.[16]

To make screening more objective, in January 1941 Lewellyn Barker, professor emeritus at the Johns Hopkins Medical School, advocated observing recruits for several weeks in an army encampment before rejecting them. The next month, the National Academy of Sciences, National Research Council (NRC) Neuropsychiatry Committee endorsed observations of up to five days at induction centers of individuals suspected of nervous weakness. Instead, the Army Surgeon General's office proposed sending ambiguous cases to special training battalions, which did not occur either.[17]

Some feared screening would incite draft evasion. Members of the NRC Subcommittee on War Neuroses were concerned that the neuropsychiatric label would encourage normal men to assume they were sick and act accordingly. Waggoner warned Selective Service that the public would criticize psychiatrists for enabling and encouraging registrants not to do their share in a national emergency.[18] In April 1941, Army Major William S. Iliff complained to Selective Service that the seminars were teaching registrants to evade service. He cited a New England induction center doctor suspected of receiving pay for psychiatric examinations from men who wanted to stay out of the army.[19]

Nor were all psychiatrists and military leaders sure that America's participation in a war would be short or that sufficient manpower would remain after widespread psychiatric rejections.[20] Screening, they worried, would "skim off for combat ... [the] 'cream' of American youth to the serious detriment of the stock." Others could not understand why psychopaths should be rejected since the army could make them into good soldiers or, if not, "break" them so they could not cause trouble in civilian life.[21] Writing to the head of Selective Service's Medical Division, Waggoner warned that "Medical Circular No. 1 might well exclude ... many men who would be adequate or even exceptional soldiers."[22] Several years later, Hershey, remembering this letter, appointed Waggoner as Sullivan's successor at Selective Service.[23]

THE SCREENING PROGRAM IN 1941

	What They Planned	What They Did
Number of Examinations	Four.	Two.
Coordination of Examination Program	The Army and Selective Service to have the same program. Uniform standards throughout the United States.	The Army and Selective Service widely differ in examinations. Standards vary from region to region, psychiatrist to psychiatrist.
Time Per Examination	15-20 minutes.	1-2 minutes.
Type of Examination	Detailed analysis of current and future ailments.	Cursory inspection.
Number of Psychiatrists Available	1,500.	Many fewer.
Method of Examination	Objective.	Sometimes racially biased or influenced by political or military consideration.

Figure 3. The screening program in 1941.

Controversies over Specific Diagnoses and Lack of Uniform Classification

Confusion about criteria for rejection was rampant. As one psychiatrist later recalled: "I think the concept of what constitutes potential neuropsychiatric casualties varied according to the number of psychiatrists involved, in the ratio of about one different concept per psychiatrist."[24]

Definitions of terms used in Medical Circular No. 1 (November 1940) had not yet crystallized when the army introduced its own pre- and postinduction psychiatric examinations. Though examinations were supposed to be synchronized, they differed greatly. Nor did civilian psychiatrists or civilian neurologists have any widely accepted uniform psychiatric classification or manual. The American Medical Association had published a *Standard Nomenclature of Disease* in 1937. But it had little practical impact on the work of neuropsychiatrists, possibly because most psychiatrists dealt with obvious, severely impaired residents of mental institutions.[25] The first *Diagnostic and Statistical Manual of Mental Disorders* (*DSM*) for psychiatry was not published until 1952.[26]

Hence, military and civilian psychiatrists on the eve of World War II disagreed over the categories to be disqualified and the definitions of those categories. They debated the acceptance or elimination of, among others, malingerers, persons with doubts about entering service, former inmates of mental institutions, stutterers, homosexuals, and registrants with psychotic relatives. Categories such as "psychoneurotic," "psychopath," and "schizoid personality" tended to be defined broadly, covering almost anyone who might not cooperate or might encourage insubordination. The army's Circular Letter No. 19 referred to "psychopathic personality" as being an "ill-defined, more or less heterogeneous group." Categories were so broad that one person might be classified psychoneurotic while someone else with almost identical characteristics might be labeled psychopathic. Differences existed between military line officers and psychiatrists over whether to discharge or court-martial, since for the first time, categories such as addiction, alcoholism, and homosexuality, which used to be considered subject to punishment, were now frequently considered medical, subject to treatment or medical or administrative discharge. Also, the screeners' focus was not just on present status but on future potentialities, not only regarding homosexuality but other categories as well. This expansive intent to eliminate aided the military by reducing the time officers had to spend away from troops participating in military courts, quieting tensions between enlisted men and officers over officers' court-martialing comrades, and avoiding criticism from superiors of an inability to control troops.[27] But it victimized many recruits and enlistees who could have fulfilled successfully military careers but were unnecessarily rejected or discharged for merely potential or hypothetical disruptive behavior.

Psychopaths

Both civilian and military psychiatrists questioned their ability to diagnose psychopaths. Army Circular Letter No. 19 recognized that psychopaths comprised a broad, ill-defined, heterogeneous group, all of whom had in common their inability to learn from experience. Such individuals broadly included those who could not respond in an adult way to demands for honesty, decency, or consideration of others; who acted impulsively with poor judgment; got in trouble with the law; or had problems with military regimentation and discipline. Such examinees, it was recognized, could appear quite presentable. Despite or because of the many different characteristics falling under this label, designers and implementers of the examination were attracted to it as an all-purpose diagnosis that could cover almost anyone.

Although Sullivan's Medical Circular No. 1 was supposed to be revised to conform with the army's examination, Sullivan himself had misgivings about the practicality of the psychopathic diagnosis. He did not believe psychiatrists could often detect a psychopathic personality through a superficial examination. In a brief interview, a psychopath could appear intelligent, healthy, pleasant, and intent on joining the military. Hence, Sullivan favored reviewing an individual's social history records as well and actually initiated the early beginnings of a social history program in 1941. But social services and juvenile courts were at that time reluctant to provide information because Section 8a of the Selective Service and Training Act (also called the Selective Service Act) permitted registrants to see their files.[28]

Additionally, Karl Bowman, a member of the Selective Service Psychiatric Advisory Committee and director of psychiatry at Bellevue from 1936 to 1941, was concerned that even normal people might evince some degree of duplicity and irresponsibility. He wondered where to draw the line when it came to diagnosing psychopathy. Since various psychiatric clinics drew the line differently, he said, it was impossible for the military to develop a uniform, nationwide definition of psychopathy. Bowman complained that one clinic would call someone with a mild deviation a psychopath while another would only classify if the deviation were pronounced. At the same seminar, according to the minutes of the recording secretary, several psychiatrists wondered: "Who is there who has not his own special little psychopathic trend which needs only sufficient provocation to blossom out unmistakably?"[29] In this way, they stressed how all-encompassing the diagnosis of psychopathy could be.

Even so, the army and Selective Service insisted on screening psychopaths. Medical Circular No. 1 stated that by definition psychopaths were "inadaptable to employment or to enduring group life and [were] wholly disqualified for any form of military service."[30] Army Circular Letter No. 19 and Army Medical Bulletin No. 58, the postinduction examination, told doctors to look out for those who did not accept authority and would "cultivate insubordination in others."[31] Given the broad definition, which included alcoholics, addicts, those with sexual pathology, and those with tendencies to such conditions, psychopathy comprised the second-largest category of neuropsychiatric rejections during the war, after only "psychoneurosis."[32] From the beginning, psychopaths were often given administrative, Section VIII discharges. These discharges could be either white or blue: white (being honorable) with benefits, blue being without honor and without some or all veteran's benefits. Out of a total of 168,000 soldiers discharged under the diagnosis of psychopath during the war, 42,000 (25 percent) received blue discharges, without benefits.[33]

At a meeting of the Congress of the American Prison Association in 1942, the psychiatrist M. Ralph Kaufman, later to play a key role in military psychiatry in the South Pacific, emphasized the need to discharge psychopaths from service. Referring to the army's definition of psychopathy as involving dishonesty and irresponsibility, he reported that 13 percent (96) of his hospital's patients had been diagnosed as psychopaths for such wide-ranging defects as homosexual proclivities, pedophilia, alcoholism, and theft. These cases reflected the growing medicalization of groups formerly court-martialed or imprisoned even early in the war, categories still criminally prosecuted by other countries at the time.[34]

Alcoholism and Addiction

At the same meeting, Kaufman told of two patients who had been diagnosed as psychopaths and were heavy drinkers, both receiving administrative Section VIIIs instead of Certificates of Disability for Discharge. In one case, the alcoholic had gone AWOL, been court-martialed twice, was imprisoned for five months, and engaged in sexual activity with little girls and petty theft. Hence, his psychopath diagnosis was also attributable to pedophilia and theft and supplemented earlier incarceration.

While the army's pre- and postinduction examinations included alcoholism as a separate medical category, and although the army admitted 42,044 alcoholics to its neuropsychiatric hospitals between 1942 and 1945 with "character and behavior disorders," according to William Menninger, severe alcoholics could at times receive Section VIII blue discharges. This practice reflected the army's belief that alcoholism was a volitional offense requiring punishment because it otherwise would threaten the morale of troops. Still, the number of times the army gave blue discharges to self-destructive, alcoholic soldiers was rare.[35] It is not known whether they were given blue discharges as early as 1942 when Kaufman made his determinations.

Stutterers

Another variant of military intolerance was stutterers, who were also classified under psychopathy. In World War I, the Freudian psychoanalyst Ernst Simmel had found mutism, stammering, and stuttering indicative of an obedient soldier's repressing his objections to his officer's placing him in mortal peril. His repression of an urge to curse, shout, or hit his officer resulted in distorted speech or no speech at all.[36]

Perhaps aware of this analysis, Roosevelt's neurologist, Foster Kennedy, opposed sending speech defectives to a school for rehabilitation, favoring instead rejection or discharge. On the other hand, the director of the speech clinic at Oklahoma Agriculture and Mechanics College advocated rehabilitation. Yet both the army and navy refused to treat stutterers though they acknowledged that they could be rehabilitated. McIntire explained to the director of Oklahoma Agriculture's speech clinic that the reason for the military's refusal was that they were not a "welfare agency." Further, he qualified his belief that stutterers could be treated by noting that the few cases he had observed in service had generally been "incapable of full recovery to the point of renewing military duty." In fact, he said, the "underlying psychopathic state" of these patients required that they be separated from service.[37] (Again, the term "psychopath" was broadly used to cover almost anyone who might possibly disturb a fellow serviceman.)

"Schizoid Personality"
Though psychiatrists differed in their concept of "schizoid personality," many used it as a catch-all to encompass virtually anything. At a Selective Service training seminar in Boston in early 1941, the child psychiatrist Douglass Thom found "no dependent common denominator for men with schizoid personalities. They are not all 'shut in,' queer, peculiar, dreamy . . . friendless. . . . Some show not only a desire for friends but an ability to make them; . . . some display an aggressiveness . . . at times [bringing] them into conflict with society . . . some . . . mild mannered . . . considerate." Because the concept was so broad and contradictory, he instructed examiners to inquire into the person's social history, records that were difficult to obtain at the time.[38]

Dexter Means Bullard, a member of Sullivan's Selective Service Psychiatric Advisory Committee, likewise conceived of schizoid personality in broad, amorphous terms, albeit somewhat differently. He instructed examiners at Selective Service training seminars in Washington, DC, and Atlanta to detect those whose behavior was indicative of prepsychotic behavior or potential schizophrenia, reflected in "observable signs of disassociated phenomena during the examination." In this way, he anticipated finding those who might break down either in the army or afterward, in the ten years of reserve.[39]

Malingering
Some psychiatrists believed anyone who faked illness should be disqualified. Others distinguished between the emotionally stable, conscious malingerer and the one with psychoneurosis.

Mobilization Regulations (MR) 1-9, August 31, 1940, distinguished three groups of malingerers: real malingerers, "who injure themselves" or "simulate disease with full consciousness and responsibility" to evade service; psychoneurotics, who "try to get out of every disagreeable thing in life; perhaps only partially conscious ... of the seriousness of what they do," many of whom could become "good soldiers"; and, third, "confirmed psychoneurotics" who have a "long history of nervous break-downs" who "persistently" evade military service and "from whom not much can be expected in the way of reconstruction."[40]

Despite these distinctions, most psychiatrists favored eliminating all malingerers with little concern for a person's intent. S. Spafford Ackerly, who received a leg wound that never healed from fighting against the Germans in France in World War I and who was later on the medical faculty at the University of Louisville, Kentucky, instructed examiners in January 1941 that regardless of symptoms, a person is sick if he malingers.[41] William Menninger reasoned that since a malingerer may be seriously maladjusted, he should not be admitted to service. More adamant was William Porter of Walter Reed Hospital, finding malingering "always a psychiatric problem for disposal." On the other hand, the forensic psychiatrist and psychoanalyst Edward Strecker believed psychiatrists should only be rejecting malingerers with an underlying psychoneurotic or psychopathic personality.[42] Hence, again, these individuals were placed in the catch-all diagnosis of psychopath or psychoneurotic.[43]

Depending on diagnosis, psychiatrists differed on disposition. The relatively stable they hoped to place in hypothetical labor battalions; the unstable they wanted to reject or discharge. As it turned out, almost every identified malingerer was rejected or discharged; the army IG charged late in the war that officers used discharges for "malingering" to hide discipline or morale problems in their units. However, the army court-martialed at most forty-seven soldiers for malingering during the war.[44]

Political Activists and Those Opposed to Entering Military Service

Psychiatrists also differed over whether persons reluctant to serve should be accepted. The forensic psychiatrist Nolan D. C. Lewis believed they should. Referring to the "socially maladjusted, the religious, political, the general Bolshevik, and the bellyacher," he told other NRC psychiatrists that "many of these people ... become splendid soldiers, and are the type of men who win medals of honor."[45]

On the other hand, Sullivan wavered on this subject. While designing the local board examination, he expressed concern about the ability of men imbued with isolationism to be effective soldiers. The original Medical Circular No. 1 instructed examiners in November 1940 to ask the registrant if he "liked the idea of being trained for national defense."[46] By August 1941, however, Sullivan told examiners at the seminars that there was no reason such men should not make fine soldiers, since, as he put it, the men were simply the product of "a culture ... indifferent to ... civic responsibility" and "could easily learn a new pattern of behavior once in the forces."[47]

But the eugenicist/psychiatrist Joseph S. de Jarnette, superintendent of Western State Hospital, Staunton, Virginia, was adamant that men who were reluctant to serve should be rejected. Likewise, the criminal psychiatrist Paul de River, who had examined pilots for navy service in World War I and headed the Los Angeles Sex Offense Bureau in the 1930s, opposed accepting "intellectuals and homosexuals" into service. As he explained in a letter to Roosevelt's secretary Stephen P. Early, there was "an apparent lack of loyalty and enthusiasm [for] military service ... of our younger generation ... largely [due] to an inroad of a homosexual pervert and his weaklings among the so-called intellectuals."[48]

Despite differences in psychiatric opinions, in practice Selective Service appears to have paid special attention to weeding out those who opposed the draft for political reasons, referring their records to the FBI. This policy began when a neurologist at Temple University Medical School in January 1941 wrote to Pennsylvania's Selective Service, complaining that a Russian-born registrant had threatened to "jump overboard" if he were inducted. The writer suggested that Selective Service give such cases a careful psychiatric evaluation and investigation. Shortly thereafter, Hershey notified Sullivan, who contacted the FBI. The FBI requested that Selective Service let them know about such cases in the future.[49] (It should be noted that the Soviet Union and Nazi Germany had a nonaggression pact at this time.)

History of Prior Treatment and Heredity

Psychiatric opinion varied on the emotional stability of men who had previously consulted psychiatrists, had relatives in mental institutions, or had been in institutions themselves and whether heredity determined psychiatric disability. Anyone who had visited a psychiatrist more than two or three times, Sullivan believed, should be rejected—an opinion that would not appear today, when many see psychiatrists regularly. Yet Waggoner wrote the director of the Selective Service Medical Division that such men "would make far better than average soldiers."[50]

While Sullivan and Roscoe Hall, another member of the Selective Service Psychiatric Advisory Committee, opposed rejecting men just because of relatives in an asylum, de Jarnette, an advocate of sterilizing the unfit, favored it. Noting that four generations in one family at his Virginia mental hospital had been manic-depressives, he assumed manic-depressive parents could transmit their disability to their children. But he was not sure that a brother or sister of a manic-depressive could transmit the illness to the brother's or sister's children.

Sullivan and Hall, on the other hand, did not believe heredity dictated a person's ability to serve. Speaking to examiners at a Selective Service seminar in January 1941, Sullivan contended that "no bad heredity would ever convince me that a person is not a good risk. I would have to have ... some findings on the person himself." At the same meeting, Hall stressed that psychiatrists "did not know enough to reject individuals on the basis of heredity alone."[51] Psychiatrists similarly disagreed about whether psychopathic conditions were inherited. William Dunn, later an instructor in psychiatry in World War II at the army's Lawson General Hospital, Atlanta, and its Mason General Hospital, Long Island, contended in *Psychiatry* (May 1941) that a man did not become a psychopath because of heredity.[52] But a navy psychiatrist at the Great Lakes Naval Training Station, Chicago, argued that the "psychopathological constitution ... is definitely a hereditable defect" and urged the navy to reject men with a family history of psychopathology.[53]

Proof of Institutionalization

Sullivan instructed Selective Service and army induction board psychiatrists in January 1941 to reject anyone who had been in a mental institution. Yet Canadian psychiatrists told Hall on an NRC observation trip the following April that they had accepted former inmates because they would be useful in the military.[54]

Homosexuality

Though years later many men and women examined for military service recalled only one question in their preinduction psychiatric examination—"Do you like boys?" or "Do you like girls?"—the actual number of individuals rejected or discharged for homosexuality from military service in World War II was minimal if not indeterminate. More importantly, therefore, is the evolution of a dramatic change in military policy toward homosexuality in World War II, which began in the period under study, 1940 through 1942, and has had major ramifications to this very day.

Little occurred in the period between the world wars to account for the major change in military policy on homosexuals away from court-martials and toward medical and administrative rejections and discharges. Though Circular No. 22, the army's World War I *Examinations in Nervous and Mental Disease*, included "homosexuals" as a category under its list of "psychopaths," the numbers eliminated under this ground in that war constituted a mere handful in a few army camps.[55] In virtually all cases, the army did only one thing: court-martial sodomists, try, and imprison them.

According to the Articles of War, "sodomy" consisted of the "unnatural carnal copulation with another person of the same or opposite sex."[56] With two persons of opposite sex, "sodomy" referred to nonconsensual sex, rape, or juvenile sexual assault. With two persons of the same sex, it applied to both nonconsensual and consensual sex. In practice, sodomy in the military referred to both oral and anal sex. A soldier convicted of sodomy could be imprisoned at hard labor for up to five years, his wages and benefits forfeited, and given a dishonorable discharge. A sailor found guilty of sodomy could be imprisoned for as many as ten years with the same punishments, a naval officer for twelve years.[57]

While military leaders were familiar with psychoanalytic theory between the wars conceiving of homosexuality as a stage of psychological development rather than a criminal offense,[58] most continued to consider sodomy a crime requiring punishment, in line with the law in all forty-eight states on the eve of World War II. They also believed that without the threat of court-martial and imprisonment, men would feign homosexuality to evade service.[59] Hence, the navy did not employ psychiatrists in court-martials at all during this time and the army only rarely.

Not until November 1940 did the United States institute a preinduction examination requiring an individual psychiatric examination for each registrant as part of the physical. Not until May 1941 did the army introduce the term "homosexual proclivities" as grounds for rejecting men from military service in Circular Letter No. 19. This represented a major change—a medicalization of what was previously considered a criminal offense—an emphasis on tendency or suspicion rather than on an actual action. Once in the military, most soldiers and sailors alleged to be homosexuals were not tried for sodomy. Instead, for the first time, the military discharged them from service. Some received a medical discharge, a Certificate of Disability for Discharge (CDD). But mainly, they received Section VIII, administrative, blue discharges, without honor, benefits, or hospitalization and without due process.[60] This applied to women in the service as well.[61]

Principally involved in this change was Harry Stack Sullivan, who developed his theories about homosexuality in the 1920s at Enoch Pratt Hospital in Baltimore. There he conducted experiments on homosexual schizophrenic patients, modifying their interpersonal relations to improve their health. He studied how adolescent patients adjusted their sexuality to comport with self-esteem. He advised his aides to encourage the patients to relate better to one another. He trained his aides to discuss their patients' previous homosexual urges, which contributed to their illnesses, and to soothe their patients' anxieties by assuring them that they too had had similar experiences as a natural stage in normal adult development. As a result, Sullivan reported a high rate of recovery from mental illness among a population generally considered incurable.[62] Published in 1932, Sullivan's *Personal Psychopathology* maintained that a homosexual episode in preadolescence, only a few years younger than some draftees, was normal. It referred particularly to a study of gang members that had found that the members who had gone through a homosexual episode as teens were more successful as heterosexuals later on than those who had not had such experience.[63] Significantly, the age of the patients was not that different from many in the military in World War II, as eighteen- and nineteen-year-olds were being drafted.

Possibly reflecting these beliefs, Sullivan's original Medical Circular No. 1 (November 1940) did not include the category "homosexuals," and members of Sullivan's Advisory Committee expressed reservations at examiner training seminars about disqualifying homosexuals. Ackerly, for example, who had had much personal experience as a soldier on the front in World War I, instructed examiners in Washington, DC, in January 1941 to reject suspected homosexuals only if they showed other personality problems. Recalling excellent soldiers who were homosexual, such as the great World War I warrior T. E. Lawrence of Arabia, he stated: "Colonel Lawrence's natural courage, partly the result of careful home nurture, was undoubtedly reinforced by the terrible energy bound up in his psychosexual frustrations." On the other hand, he added, psychiatrists must reject a homosexual if he "manifested socially useless symptoms." Ackerly's views presaged those of the American Psychiatric Association in the *DSM-III* (1980), which unlike the *DSM-I* and *DSM-II*, did not classify homosexuality as a disorder at all, per se.[64]

At the same training seminar for examiners, Sullivan cautioned: "The mere fact that there is something of a homosexual tendency ... seems ... to indicate that he is one of an extremely large section of humanity, and it is the individual that should be dealt with rather than a somewhat poorly delineated field."[65] Hence, homosexual proclivity was not to be considered disqualifying. Yet, in the same statement, he also cautioned that in conformity with contemporary army regulations, homosexuals who manifested "moral turpitude in the sexual field" must be rejected.

Sullivan's reluctance to reject homosexuals may have reflected his long-held medical views and his own homosexuality.⁶⁶ Yet, while he was personally sensitive to the stigma and social pressure of this status, he balanced his private and medical persona against his obligations as a government official and modified Medical Circular No. 1 in accordance with the army's regulations and examinations. By the end of March 1941, while the army was in the last stages of drafting Circular Letter No. 19, Sullivan added "homosexual proclivities" along with other personality deviations to his draft of a revised Medical Circular No. 1. A few months later, after the revised circular was published, he told examiners at the San Francisco Selective Service training seminar that American social mores required a man to have "a strong interest in a member of the other sex."⁶⁷

Yet, at the same time, at the NRC War Neuroses Subcommittee, he opposed court-martialing "sex perverts" as "archaic." Instead, he endorsed rejecting from service homosexuals who could not withstand the rigors of military life. For example, he interceded with Selective Service to make sure that a private patient of the psychoanalyst Clara Thompson was rejected from military service. But because he was afraid of the stigma of homosexuality, he made sure that the term was not used in the diagnosis.⁶⁸

This was about as far as he and his associates would go. While the army's Circular Letter No. 19 placed its list of "deviations" prominently on its first of three pages, beginning with "instability" and ending with "homosexual proclivities," Medical Circular No. 1 REVISED inserted the list at the tail end of its final page with "homosexual proclivities," the final words in the entire examination, almost hiding the concept altogether. Similarly, the phrase "many homosexual persons" headed Circular Letter No. 19's list of "those exhibiting irresponsiveness to social demands" in Group II on its first page under "Psychopathic Personality Disorders." But in Medical Circular No. 1 REVISED, the phrase failed to appear.⁶⁹

Those in Sullivan's camp, such as Dexter Bullard and Leo Bartemeier, if they had to reject, chose to use amorphous, all-embracing categories, such as "schizoid," "psychopath," or "psychoneurotic," with the hope of avoiding the stigma of the "homosexual" label.⁷⁰ But psychiatric rejections, whatever the specific label, engendered public condemnation and problems getting employed throughout the war and immediately after.

Psychiatrists working with the army, on the other hand, took a more aggressive stance. In April 1941, Tracy Putnam, chair of the NRC War Neuroses Subcommittee of the Committee on Neuropsychiatry and chair of the Columbia University Neurology Department, drafted revisions to the War Department's Mobilization Regulations (MR) No. 1-9, Section XIX,

Mental and Nervous Disorders. The draft provided for the elimination of those who engaged "occasionally" or "habitually" in homosexuality or "other perverse sexual practices." Reflecting the army's interest in spotting "proclivities" or tendencies, he instructed psychiatrists to look for men with "feminine bodily characteristics, effeminacy in dress or manner," language not included in the revised Medical Circular No. 1 or its original.[71]

M. Ralph Kaufman, a key psychiatric player in the South Pacific campaign later, discharged a Walter Reed Hospital patient administratively from service in 1942 for homosexual proclivities under Section VIII after finding out that the patient's family had dressed him in feminine attire early on. Though the patient had gotten married and had sexual relations with his wife, he could not "shake the habit." Kaufman concluded that the man needed to be discharged to shield him from being the butt of jokes from other soldiers or from disrupting morale.[72] (This is an early example of the use of an administrative discharge. According to historians, it was most likely blue.)

Years later, the Rutgers alumnus Lionel Greer told an oral historian about an army psychiatrist at Jefferson Barracks, Missouri, who had rejected a man from the Army Air Force because he was a ballet dancer and might cause "crew problems." When Greer sought to assure him that he had known the guy for almost five months and had seen him "pick up broads with the best of them," the psychiatrist admitted it was a hunch. As for Greer, he assured him his four years of college made it certain that he would not have emotional problems.[73] Hence, it was suspicion rather than offense that counted.

Echoing Madigan's concerns in Circular Letter No. 19, in early 1942 an army colonel advised the Commonwealth Club in San Francisco not to accept homosexuals into the army, because "the homosexual may make one of the neuropsychiatric weaklings a victim of sexual assault or may himself be used, abused, threatened with disclosure, and in many cases undermine the morale of his unit."[74]

For some, the military's actions were not stringent enough. In November 1941, Dr. J. Paul de River, a specialist with the Los Angeles Police Department Sex Crimes Unit, wrote to Stephen Early, Roosevelt's secretary, that too many "sex perverts" were still being admitted into the army. Responding, Madigan, then a psychiatrist in the Surgeon General's office, agreed that known homosexuals had no place in army camps given the proximity of living quarters. He assured de River that the War Department was encouraging civilian authorities to send names of recognized homosexuals to local boards and army induction centers to have them surveyed and rejected. Others shared this opinion.[75] This was a forerunner of the witch hunts that were to occur on a much larger scale in the 1950s.

From 1940 to 1942, psychiatrists debated among themselves and with the military over whether homosexuals should be discharged administratively or medically, court-martialed and imprisoned, or subjected to conversion therapy. NRC neurologists at a meeting in March 1941 criticized glandular treatment for increasing rather than reducing homosexual proclivities. More research, they said, was needed. In the meantime, discharge appeared the best option.[76]

As early as July 1941, the AG refused to honor the judge advocate general's recommendation to permit the army to administratively discharge soldiers who had consensual homosexual sex with another adult. The representative from JAG based his request on a tour of army bases in the United States, where he found a substantial number of generals informally discharging alleged homosexuals for bad character instead of instituting court-martials. Despite this recommendation, however, the AG, with the approval of Secretary of War Henry Stimson, officially opposed administrative discharges in lieu of trial as contrary to War Department policy and congressional intent.[77]

Psychiatrists, however, took a different position. They continued, like Kaufman, to discharge soldiers administratively. Asked for his opinion by Navy Surgeon General Ross T. McIntire in January 1942 about a sailor who was imprisoned for sodomy, Overholser maintained that most cases of latent homosexuality involving only "incidental or casual activity" did not deserve court-martial.[78] The following November, when McIntire asked for the committee's approval of a navy officer's being given a discharge instead of a court-martial, Overholser similarly replied that "legal punishment" against homosexuals in the military was "meaningless and unjust." Like the judge advocate, Overholser excepted from this policy sexual offenders who used physical or mental coercion during sex or who sexually abused a child. If, on the other hand, the act was consensual, he believed that given the "compact" conditions of military life, the individuals should be given a "dishonorable discharge" or a discharge "for inaptitude" (that is, administrative).[79] It is interesting to note that at this early stage, he spoke about giving dishonorable discharges, not just discharges without honor, the latter of which became more the policy later on. Despite McIntire's approval of Overholser's position and despite the fact that a month later Overholser condemned as "sadistic" the imprisonment of two soldiers at Fort George Meade, Maryland, for ten years in a federal prison (when ten years was for the navy, not the army) based on "gossip," the official army policy did not really change much until over a year later. In January 1944, the War Department issued Circular No.

3, allowing for the hospitalizing of those who were "reclaimable" and a "blue" discharge, dishonorable, without benefits for those who were not.[80]

Yet, in reality, as historians have noted, military psychiatrists from America's entry into the war on, with the approval of lower-level officers, discharged many alleged homosexuals with administrative blue discharges. As a result, as the historian Allan Bérubé has stated, the switch to administrative discharges from court-martial had a widespread personal impact. No more than a few hundred were convicted of sodomy in the military from 1900 through World War II, compared to at least 4,000 sailors and 5,000 soldiers discharged for homosexuality in World War II alone.[81] This meant that some homosexual veterans, regardless of their contributions to military service including combat, ended up receiving Section VIII blue discharges, discharges without honor, benefits, or hospitalization, based on an administrative procedure, without due process, no attorney, no trial. Since the military and psychiatrists focused on "tendencies" and suspicions rather than individual actions, the accusations were often baseless. In some cases, as homosexual and lesbian veterans recalled years later, they were based on the giving of names and pressure to do so or be court-martialed.[82]

Yet, on the positive side, many soldiers accepted their homosexual comrades during the war in a way not expressed later on, indicating that tolerance and acceptance could work. Gay comrades in World War II were sometimes not discharged or reported even when their fellow soldiers and sailors knew they were homosexuals, because there was a war going on and everyone was needed to do their share, a feeling especially prevalent in combat settings.[83]

Group solidarity and teamwork discouraged "troublemakers" from spreading rumors about fellow soldiers that might lead to imprisonment and reflect badly on morale. Ted Allenby, a columnist for *Gay Life* in Chicago, told Studs Terkel that while Allenby was "in the closet" in the marines, there was "no witch-hunting." He "would even hear reports of guys found secretively having sex and nobody turned them in. Officialdom made no big thing about it. There was a war on." Only later when he became a navy chaplain in peacetime in the 1950s was he arrested, charged with sodomy, and discharged under conditions other than honorable.[84] Dr. Ted Winn, educated with the help of the GI Bill at Harvard Medical School after the war, told another oral historian that he did not experience any problems in the navy with his sexuality in World War II. But when Winn embarked on a naval ship for Korea in 1951, "each ship would lose in a period of six months overseas as many as 20 or 30 men . . . just because someone said they were gay."[85]

Social scientists and military leaders recognized during and after World War II that homosexual soldiers and sailors had made major contributions to military service and the winning of the war, auguring well for future employment in the military. Herbert Spiegel, the first battalion surgeon/psychiatrist to experience combat, well known for treating soldiers with hypnotism, recalled in an interview after the war that gay men proved excellent soldiers. The Yale psychiatrist Clements Fry likewise reported in 1945 that only five out of 132 homosexual patients at Harvard and Yale were discharged, those remaining performing competently as officers. In several other studies published in the *American Journal of Psychiatry* in 1945, the authors found that the men discharged under Section VIII for sexual psychopathy (mainly homosexuals) were above average in intelligence, did not have histories of neurosis, were cooperative, had lower rates of alcohol use, and had been decorated for bravery.[86] Also generated from the war was a sense of identity and community among gays from being together for long stretches of time, an identity that presaged the gay movement in decades to come.[87]

And yet, no matter how one estimates the numbers of gay men and women rejected or discharged from service in World War II based on suspicion of sexual status, it scarcely in any way compares with the gargantuan sum of at least 1.8 million rejected and 700,000 or more discharged on neuropsychiatric grounds. Hence, almost all the men and women in World War II rejected or discharged on neuropsychiatric grounds were not homosexual, even though many prospective inductees recall having been asked only one question, that about their sexual orientation. According to Bérubé, the army in actuality discharged 5,000 soldiers from service for homosexuality, and another 4,000 were discharged from the navy as well.[88] The army based its estimate of 5,000 on the numbers admitted to hospitals for "psychopathy, mainly homosexual," most unreclaimable and therefore discharged. In addition, an unknown number of homosexuals were discharged from the army for homosexuality with a medical diagnosis of schizoid or psychoneurotic or with an administrative Section VIII without mentioning the specific diagnosis and often without benefits.[89] Even if one were to take into account Menninger's opinion that for "every homosexual ... referred to or [who] came to the Medical Department, there were 5 or 10 who never were detected,"[90] the fact is that a tenfold increase beyond 5,000 would still be very small in number compared to the total number of over 700,000 discharged from the military. Similar figures of 4,000 or 5,000 have been given for rejections from the army and navy.[91] Again, even if those numbers were multiplied, it would be a very, very small number compared to the total rejected of over 1.8 million. As to the specific number of women discharged from the military for homosexuality, even if it were known, which it is not, it would not add that much more to the number for homosexuals, since no more than 350,000 women served in the military in World War II, 150,000 in the Women's Army Corps (WAC). While by 1944, the rates for WACs of medical rejections and medical discharges on psychiatric grounds rose to more than 20 percent and 60 percent respectively, rates higher than those for men, and although suspected lesbians, after arduous investigations, were given discharges for "drunkenness" or "inaptitude," often without honor or benefits, the actual numbers were still quite small.[92]

More significant was the policy debate on homosexuality among psychiatrists and the military from 1940 through 1942, which influenced the development of military policy on gay servicemen and women during the rest of the war and since then. The general fluidity of discussion on psychiatric terminology and policy during these years also pervaded the policy on homosexuals. A man labeled homosexual, a drug addict, alcoholic, stutterer, bedwetter, even one who had gone AWOL, might one day be classified psychoneurotic, another day psychopathic, for the same characteristics, in some cases given a Section VIII, in others, still court-martialed.

Regional Bias
Initially, Selective Service was attracted to screening as a way of achieving an objective, fair, scientific method of selection. But relatively quickly, critics complained of socioeconomic, regional, and racial bias in examinations. To promote objectivity, Medical Circular No. 1 stipulated that only psychiatrists from the local area should examine registrants. Yet Colonel Richard Eanes, assistant executive director of Selective Service, complained to Hershey that few psychiatrists came from the "particular environment" of their registrants.[93] One psychiatrist noted that because most examiners came from urban areas, they could not understand Southern farm boys: "The boys from the Southern hills in the service looked withdrawn, autistic and were often diagnosed schizophrenic, with no reference to their taciturn cultural pattern."[94] World War II's registrants and their examiners had "problems of communication," Hershey later recalled. Registrants had "different character traits not always understood by a psychiatrist with a far different background."[95]

Native Americans
The case of Malcolm Jay Harrison ("Malcolm H") particularly revealed racial bias. In March 1941, Oklahoma City's induction board rejected Malcolm H,

a Native American, for "psychopathic personality and first-degree pes-planus [flat feet] with symptoms." The examiner concluded that H "is unstable, has wanderlust, hitchhiking and freight riding, never stays on a job for any appreciable length of time . . . drinks excessively. . . . In every case of this type . . . [the writer who brought it to the attention of the board] has been impressed that the psychopathic personality of the rejectee is an indication that the selectee rejected is crazy." Upon learning his diagnosis, Malcolm H was so ashamed that "rather than have to tell the folks . . . he was turned down because of 'being crazy,' he told them about his flat feet."[96]

He simultaneously appealed the decision on grounds of psychiatric bias to the Oklahoma City induction board and the Oklahoma State Selective Service headquarters and eventually to Hershey and Stimson. In his appeal, Malcolm contended that the Oklahoma examiner's charges were groundless, based on prejudice, and reflected ignorance of Native American culture and Oklahoma's socioeconomic mores. To prove the charges groundless, he noted that another psychiatrist at the same induction board and his local board psychiatrist had both accepted him for the draft a month earlier. Contesting the charge that he drank excessively, he stated, according to the records from the appeal, that "in his whole life, he hasn't drunk as much as one gallon of liquor and in the last few years has not taken a drink." He found many of the examiner's questions insulting and unfair, such as "the difference between a penny, a nail, and a piece of wire," "the difference between a bird, snake, and a fish," and "the difference between a mistake and a lie." He believed the examiner would not have accused him of "wanderlust" if he knew anything about oilfield work, which required moving from one community to another and not staying anywhere long.

Malcolm's appeal proved relatively successful. Though the acting assistant AG at Fort Sam Houston recognized that the preinduction examiners had been practicing in Oklahoma for many years, which should make them entirely familiar with the "characteristics of the natives, including the Indians," he nevertheless wrote Oklahoma's Selective Service that if they desired, Malcolm H could be reexamined.[97] Available records do not indicate whether H was ultimately inducted.

Malcolm H's case was not only important but also representative of discrimination against Native Americans in preinduction psychiatric examinations for military service. At the same time an examiner was rejecting Malcolm, local board and induction board doctors throughout Oklahoma were rejecting over 40 percent of the Native American registrants on psychiatric grounds; this, when nationally, local board and army induction board examiners were probably rejecting no more than 6 percent of draftees for mental disease.[98] Nor was this just an Oklahoma problem. Since over 20 percent of all Native Americans lived in Oklahoma in 1940, possible psychiatric discrimination against them had national ramifications.[99] Thus, while reviewing Malcolm's appeal, Stimson ordered a national investigation.

Between March 1941 and January 1942, psychiatrists and Selective Service and army officials debated whether Oklahoma's examining psychiatrists had discriminated against Native Americans. Harry Deutsch, Malcolm's consulting psychiatrist, was the first to accuse Oklahoma's army induction and local boards of psychiatric bias. While defending Malcolm, he noted that the rate of Native Americans rejected for psychiatric reasons in Oklahoma was much higher than for whites, while he claimed that Native Americans' mental health was actually superior: "The vast majority are much more stoical than the average white person and less inclined to develop symptoms of psychoneuroses or psychopathic personalities. The percentage [with] schizophrenia, involutional melancholia, manic depressive psychoses [is] comparatively low." Then why were they rejected? The answer, according to Deutsch, was the medical officers at army induction centers in Oklahoma did not understand the personality characteristics of Native Americans, such as their shyness, reticence, and stoicism and instead assumed these traits indicated mental deficiency. This especially occurred, he said, when Native Americans were transferred for induction to a quite different environment in a large city, with brusque examiners and overwhelming medical procedures.[100]

Top-ranking army and Selective Service officials expressed suspicions. Colonel Carlton Dargusch, JAG, and Hershey both believed the 40 percent psychiatric rejection rate for Oklahoma Indians was "abnormally" high.[101] On the other hand, army and Selective Service officials in Oklahoma denied that the high rate of psychiatric rejection of Native Americans reflected examiners' bias. Rather, they attributed the rejection rate to the state of health of Oklahoma's Native Americans and the examiners' exceptional vigilance and superior training. Moreover, they stressed, the doctors were well acquainted with the ways of the Native American. Noting the exceptional qualifications of Oklahoma's examiners, Oklahoma's Selective Service medical director emphasized that "Oklahoma was one of the first states [to] recognize the importance of psychoanalysis in conjunction with the physical examination of draftees." The district recruiting officer wrote army investigators that the examiners were licensed by the American Board of Psychiatry and approved by Selective Service Medical Adviser Richard Eanes. Oklahoma's medical director concluded by extolling examiners for their experience in dealing with all races, including Native Americans, and for making special effort to make Native American and Black selectees feel comfortable during the examination. Finally, he insisted they received the same exam as white inductees.[102]

Sullivan defended the expertise of Oklahoma's examining psychiatrists. Responding to Deutsch's letter, he admitted the 40 percent rejection rate for Oklahoma's Native Americans was higher than the rejection rate in other sections of the country, yet he attributed it to the "application of more rigid standards than those being taught by Army and Selective Service through our seminars." He predicted that "the psychiatric classification over the country will tend to rise toward the figure at present experienced in Oklahoma." Though he "sympathized" with Deutsch's contentions that examiners were ignorant of Indian ways, Sullivan wrote: "I sympathize too with any psychiatrist who has to give an opinion about an Indian, if he has not had long acquaintance with them." "Perhaps," he asserted, "this is a suitable time [for a] good piece of public relations."[103]

Yet the army's investigation concluded otherwise, finding much higher mental rejection rates in the southeastern and eastern counties of Oklahoma, the rate alone for Malcolm H's Adair County being 33.8 percent.[104] In January 1942, the US Public Health Service likewise reported that rejections were surprisingly high, even though Indian Service officials had always believed that mental disease was not very common among Indians. The Health Service concluded that the high rate was attributable to the very thorough examination of Native Americans by doctors in service as well as the insufficient knowledge and understanding of Native American ways by examiners not in service.[105]

Throughout the war, issues of racial and ethnic bias in psychiatric selection would continue to occur against Native Americans, Blacks, and other minorities, but for the time being, the most blatant was that of Malcolm Jay Harrison. Even so, 25,000 Native American men from reservations served in the war, 21,767 in the army, 1,910 in the navy, and 874 in the marines, plus hundreds of Native American women and thousands of men and women from off the reservations as well. This amounted to around 10 percent of the total population of 332,397 Native Americans in 1940.[106]

Attempts to Reduce Rejections

As America's entry into the war became increasingly imminent, requiring more and more servicemen, Hershey and Roosevelt investigated ways to reduce the numbers being rejected on psychiatric and physical grounds. This occurred while in June 1941 Germany invaded Russia; German U-boats also sank an American merchant steamer that month and torpedoed an American destroyer the following October. Japan and the United States increasingly clashed over Japan's stationing troops in Indochina.[107] By that October, those rejected from military service approached half the number inducted, or one million men. To increase the numbers available for service, Roosevelt and Hershey proposed combining the army and Selective Service preinduction exams and paying private doctors to rehabilitate 4Fs for military service. Hershey also supported labor battalions not only for those rejected on physical grounds but for the 13 percent excluded for venereal and mental diseases as well.[108] Hershey's interest in rehabilitation may well have reflected the fact that he himself had had a severe eye injury since 1927 when he got hurt during a polo match. If he could serve his country while disabled, why not everyone else?[109]

Responding to these efforts, Sullivan, Overholser, and Osborn accused Roosevelt and Hershey of sabotaging their screening efforts and argued that the elimination of the examination, labor battalions, and rehabilitation would encourage the admission of persons with disciplinary problems. Stimson and Army Chief of Staff George C. Marshall would also express similar concerns.

On October 6, 1941, Hershey proposed to the American College of Physicians in Philadelphia a Selective Service program to pay private doctors to treat 4Fs. Four days later, Roosevelt proposed the same plan at a White House meeting with Hershey, Marshall, and Stimson and the next day at a press conference, with the objective of restoring 200,000 men for military service.[110]

However, Sullivan's *Psychiatry* objected that while treating a tooth might produce reliable results, there was no way of knowing whether neuropsychiatric disorders could be cured, even if such dramatic methods as electroshock or lobotomy were utilized.[111] Marshall opposed psychiatric rehabilitation as too costly, projecting it would come to $1 billion. Echoing Circular Letter No. 19, Stimson called rehabilitation more a welfare than a military program. Instead, he urged Hershey to focus on treating "teeth and a few other minor defects," adding that "Mrs. Roosevelt has apparently butted into this herself." (Clearly, Stimson did not see eye to eye with the First Lady; she was, as Osborn recalled years later, more interested in ensuring social justice and welfare while her husband focused more on winning the war.)[112]

Osborn too wrote Overholser, opposing rehabilitation. Reflecting the army's primary interest in ensuring morale, he argued that men restored to service might have been previously imprisoned or committed to mental hospitals or taken addictive drugs. The president's rehabilitation proposal "holds great dangers from the point of view of psychiatry," he wrote. He "wondered how far this is realized by the President, the Surgeon General, or the staff sections of the Army."[113] By December 1, this message had apparently gotten across, and the rehabilitation proposal was abandoned.[114]

About the same time, Roosevelt and Hershey also considered combining the army and Selective Service preinduction exams into one to avoid inconsistent medical standards and doctors' reluctance to serve on local boards without pay. Again, Sullivan and Overholser objected. In October, when Selective Service proposed cancelling its own exam, Overholser contacted Osborn, protesting that with only the army's policy remaining, many "defective" persons might slip in. Without local board examinations, he argued, it would be harder to obtain data on prior criminal convictions, commitments to mental hospitals, or drug use, since such information came from local communities. And cancelling the local exams would cost time and money, since examiners would be compelled to travel from base to base.[115] Editorials in *Psychiatry* were also opposed, as was Sullivan, who stated in the *American Journal of Sociology* that with the absence of a local exam, more men would slip into the military, become disciplinary problems, or go off on their own in battle, washing out the entire maneuver. Ultimately, President Roosevelt announced at a press conference on October 9, 1941, that Selective Service "would continue to perform at least a minute examination."[116]

Hershey also proposed to Stimson placing rejectees with minor physical or mental defects, including mental deficiency and morale problems, into developmental battalions. But after much opposition from Osborn, Sullivan, and the army psychiatrists Madigan and Porter, Stimson only approved battalions for those with less than a fourth-grade level of reading or writing.[117]

Extension of Service Raises Fears of Insubordination

A key factor influencing Roosevelt not to totally abandon the local board examination and not to rehabilitate psychiatric 4Fs was the concern that troublemakers might slip into the military. Apprehensions grew in August 1941 during peacetime after Roosevelt signed a controversial bill, passed in Congress by one vote, extending military service for a year and a half beyond the original term.[118] Predictably, trainees complained bitterly and even rioted in camps about the unexpected extension.

Soldiers protested to Congress that the act constituted an unfair breach of contract. According to *Time*, they chalked "Ohio," or "Over the Hill in October," on latrines and artillery and threatened to desert.[119] The Roosevelts were aware of these circumstances, as was Stimson. Marshall told the House Committee on Military Affairs that "these disturbing activities" constituted "sabotage." Believing that the problem of morale would be "the most difficult task in the development of the Army during the coming months,"[120] on August 18 he appointed Osborn, a man of many hats, to become chief of the Army Morale Branch.[121]

Reports in *Life, Readers Digest,* and *Time* heightened apprehensions. Most distressing was an ultimately squelched report by Hilton Howell Railey, a veteran journalist of twenty-five years and a War Department field representative in World War I. After traveling eight thousand miles, visiting nine training camps on the East and West Coasts, and interviewing "thousands" of officers and enlistees for the *New York Times,* Railey concluded in October 1941: "From coast-to-coast conviction as to the gravity of the international crisis is lacking. The men of all branches preponderantly do not believe that the United States is imperiled, even should Hitler defeat the British and bring about the collapse of the British empire!"[122] Railey even quoted a War Department special investigation, which had revealed "a veritable nest of Anti-Semitism at Fort Benning, Georgia, many of the men expressing open admiration for the German Army."[123]

More frightening for Marshall was Railey's finding of widespread fraternization, against army dictum. As explained by a leading historian, the goal of military training was for officers to remove American individualism by breaking down and rebuilding a man through shock, exhaustion, and intimidation. The process was supposed to ensure that even if forsaken by officers and comrades, the soldier would stay perfectly drilled and under control in battle.[124] If officers and enlistees became pals, however, the men would lose respect for officers, not follow orders, and not be willing to risk their lives.

But fraternization seemed endemic when Railey toured a training camp for thousands of guardsmen in Alexandria on a random Saturday. Railey found none of the officers or enlistees on the street in uniform, none with hats, shirts unbuttoned to the waist, some wearing red patent-leather high-heeled boots. Officers and enlistees were sprawled together in gutters vomiting or in drunken brawls. Others were visiting prostitutes and taking drugs. As comrades in sin, superiors lacked the will to discipline their friends, and enlistees refused to take orders. Indeed, when officers tried to discipline men, guardsmen fought with officers or even shot at them. So widespread was all this that an anonymous high-ranking officer in Alexandria told Railey: "We are scared to death of them, and most of us feel that the sooner we get out of this mess the better we'll like it." (This, only a few months before Pearl Harbor.)

Elsewhere, insubordination did not reach the peaks—or sink to the depths—of Alexandria, but Railey reported: "Faith in their junior officers, lieutenants and captains and respect for their qualifications is extremely uncertain, if not generally lacking in all branches."[125] The intellectual inferiority of many officers to their men—a substantial number of whom were college graduates—accounted for much of this lack of respect. Enlistees found it hard to follow the orders of officers who, according to Railey, held reviews in temperatures above 120°, were afraid to inspect the men's loaded rifles because they did not know how to load their own, got lost in the woods despite "using" a compass, and mistakenly took battalions on training maneuvers into dangerous areas.

This was not the troop morale necessary to win a war against totalitarianism. On October 14, after reading Railey's report, General Lesley McNair (in charge of training) warned Marshall: "These revelations are astounding. I have known from the training viewpoint that leadership was bad, but I had no idea discipline was in such a shocking state."[126] So upset was Marshall that he instructed the army chief of information to prohibit publication of Railey's report, which was done. This occurred because the *New York Times* had granted the chief of information the unusual right of prior approval before publication in order to access information for the report.[127]

The NRC's War Neuroses Subcommittee also expressed concern about press and magazine coverage of training camp unrest. The Columbia University neurologist Tracy Putnam stated that "many soldiers have no idea why they were drafted and see no danger to the country and want to go home."[128] Based on a survey of press and radio coverage over several weeks, the well-known psychoanalyst/neurologist Lawrence Kubie concluded that "long debunking of ideals has had the effect of dividing public opinion." He called for a "nonpartisan voluntary propaganda agency to repeat over and over" the importance of "unification of purpose." It was not clear exactly what this agency was supposed to do, but the NRC turned it down as "against Freedom of the Press."[129] At the same time, Marshall's suggestion to Roosevelt that the army should produce films politically motivating soldiers to fight led Osborn, as head of the Army Morale Branch, to order its head of research, the sociologist Samuel Stouffer, to survey the political attitudes of thousands of servicemen. But while this was a beginning, in the months before Pearl Harbor the focus remained not on propaganda but on psychiatric screening.[130]

By November 1941, with over 1 million rejected by Selective Service on medical grounds, relations between Hershey and Sullivan worsened to the point that Sullivan resigned. Alarmed by the large number of rejectees, Hershey proclaimed that too many were being rejected who were not "queer" enough to "justify deferment."[131] Sullivan, on the other hand, could not tolerate the one- to two-minute local board examination, writing to Stimson on

November 4 that examiners needed at least fifteen minutes to detect psychopaths, hysterics, and mood disorders. He was upset that his training of nonpsychiatrists in detecting psychiatric disorders had not worked out as planned, since the men were not sufficiently trained to detect psychiatric disorders and scarcely referred anyone to psychiatrists. He warned that the failure to reject "unsuitable people" would "imperil their precarious adjustments in the community." He called for more public relations about the importance of screening, since the less the public "suspects that mistakes are being made and injustices done, the less harm we shall be doing to the registrants and to civilian morale and solidarity."[132] Not receiving a favorable response from Stimson, five days later, on November 9, he sent Hershey a letter resigning from Selective Service because, he said, there was little further need for him, given that "the principal medical examinations in the future will be made by Army boards employing their own psychiatrists."[133]

In an interview years later, Osborn pointed to long-standing differences between Hershey and Sullivan. Hershey, an astute politician, he said, recognized that Selective Service had to be run by local committees instead of national headquarters. Sullivan, on the other hand, wished to impose national standards. While Osborn persuaded Hershey to retain a local board psychiatric examination, Hershey had a much simpler idea of what it should contain than did Sullivan. "You cannot imagine Hershey sitting down with a psychiatrist and discussing studies," Osborn stated. "His idea would be a doctor would look at a man and say this fellow was no good and we won't take him, but it's much more complicated than that."[134]

For his part, Sullivan was upset about Selective Service's and the army's lack of appreciation for psychiatry. "There are selective-service local boards," he wrote, "that regard psychiatrists as feebleminded, persons who indiscriminately reject everyone sent to them, and army-board chairmen who ignore psychiatric opinion entirely."[135] Resigning before Pearl Harbor, he spent the war teaching psychiatry at Chestnut Lodge, a psychoanalytically oriented mental hospital in suburban Maryland, outside Washington, DC. He died in 1949 after attending the International Conference on Mental Health. He was a month shy of fifty-seven. Per his instructions, he had a military funeral.[136]

As more and more men were inducted and America's entry into World War II became a growing reality, psychiatric policies changed. Originally, Sullivan had introduced an examination that emphasized adjustment to military and civilian life. This satisfied a time when entry into the war was distant, when being in stateside training camps in peacetime was not that different from staying at home, and when the expected duration in military service was no more than one year. But with the time in service extended another year and a half in August 1941 and the probability rising of servicemen being sent overseas to fight a long, grisly war against fascism, the psychiatric quest for adjustment to civilian life became less relevant. The army preinduction examination, with its emphasis on ensuring the American soldier's full cooperation, regimentation, and mental and physical acumen, became the panacea instead. Not surprisingly, as the focus changed, the army sought to eliminate the local board examination altogether, only retaining a minute examination after presidential intervention. Sullivan left, disgusted that his goal to put psychiatry on the map had not been met. But the unique ambitiousness of his examination program cannot be ignored. The idea of being able to determine both military and civilian adjustment proved of major importance after the war when soldiers returned home, fully trained to succeed in war but not trained to readjust to peace, with little concern from the public about their prospects. That dilemma had been ignored in 1941 by the all-consuming need to take a nation worn out by the Depression into the boiling cauldron against fascism.

Part II
During the War

4

Psychiatric Policy Making in the Throes of War

Despite extensive efforts at designing and fine-tuning pre- and postinduction psychiatric examinations, when the Japanese struck Pearl Harbor, the American military was not prepared. In 1942, the nation's armed forces suffered shockingly high psychiatric casualties. From late 1942 to mid-1943, neuropsychiatric cases rose from 20 to 34 percent of medical casualties in North Africa and by May 1943, to more than 40 percent on Guadalcanal.[1] Some American psychiatrists treated psychiatric patients in North Africa. But few in the Pacific did anything more than evacuate psychiatric patients far from the front. Taking up the cudgel of policy where Harry Stack Sullivan had left it, America's leading civilian psychiatrists at home, isolated from events overseas, evaluated various psychiatric options. Ultimately, however, by mid-1943, most joined with military leaders and the executive branch in supporting tougher psychiatric screening and little else.

The Pacific War

On the eve of America's entry into World War II, as dramatized in books like *From Here to Eternity*, Pearl Harbor exuded a country club atmosphere. The night before the attack, the ranking general in Honolulu ignored Washington's warnings. He allowed men their usual Saturday night off. Only 195 of 780 navy antiaircraft guns and four of thirty army antiaircraft batteries were manned. Most lacked ammunition, which was in storage.[2] Some 2,330 Americans perished in the attack. Eight hours later, Japanese bombers and fighters attacked the Philippines, where eighty-six out of 160 American aircraft on Luzon were destroyed. By mid-December, 430 American marines and sailors had surrendered on Guam to 5,400 Japanese.[3] After sixteen days of fierce fighting, on December 23, the Japanese vanquished the Americans on Wake Island.

Americans and Filipinos were not ready for the Japanese in the Philippines. The Filipino army was untrained, the American military little better, recalled the veteran Thomas Calderone years later. Though Calderone was assigned to a mortar platoon, he had not fired a rifle for a year. Nor had he been given any training in throwing a live hand grenade. A week before Pearl Harbor, he was finally given ammo. Awaiting the landing of Japanese paratroopers, Calderone's unit moved from Manila to Clark Field. For ten days, they stood in defense lines, each with an M-1 rifle, ten feet apart. But they "didn't have enough guys to cover the defense lines," so the Japanese were able to get through. Nor did they have phones to connect with the next company.

American troops then experienced their first combat. Screaming like "banshees," Japanese "made their *Banzai* charge." The enemies' screams "scared the hell" out of them. They waited for ammo and water during lulls in fighting but got no water. "Nobody's got food. . . . Go to the mess hall . . . they won't feed you. . . . Supposed to get the priority . . . didn't." Some at the frontlines desperately stole food. Many contracted dysentery or malaria. There was no penicillin. Others developed night blindness because of the lack of vitamin A in their vegetables. Some lost so much weight they "couldn't even carry their rifle. . . . The sergeants used to carry it for them." The Japanese bombed, strafed, and "swooped down" on American planes, destroying them. "Their fighter pilots wasn't scared of nothing. They come right down, come right over your head." The Americans had no air cover, because their airplanes had been destroyed.

Retreating to the fortified island of Corregidor, where they sheltered in tunnels, Calderone and his buddies faced thirty days of Japanese bombing. Many, like Calderone, were unable to take it and broke down.[4] Everett D. Reamer, a corporal at Corregidor, recalled years later: "We also had Sergeants who were hardcore army guys who had been in service for a period of time and in charge; they cracked under the bombardment. One guy . . . a gung-ho Sergeant in peacetime left his post, became a zombie, and had to be taken to the hospital in Malinta Tunnel. I never saw him again." A "quiet young fellow from Somerset, Kentucky," started to take cover when an air raid began. He ran off into a 12-inch Coastal Battery pit. It killed him when he hit the lower elevation of the gun pit." A third, in a communications center eight feet below ground, alone too many days, "lost it." "When one of our officers went to check on him at the command center, he told the officer that he had had it . . . left his post . . . held for court martial; they would have killed him . . . for deserting his post, but . . . the invasion came about 10 days later. . . . He was sent to the front and that was the end of his being tried for deserting."[5]

General MacArthur and his family left Manila for Corregidor on December 24. On February 21, Roosevelt ordered him to leave the Philippines altogether. On March 11, he and his family boarded a PT boat to Mindanao Island. On March 17, they flew to Australia.[6]

MacArthur left thousands of troops behind to fight, suffer, or die. In April, 76,000 (12,000 Americans and 64,000 Filipinos) surrendered to the Japanese on Bataan. Sick, tired, and starving, they were marched sixty-six miles to a railhead for transport to POW camps elsewhere on the island or on mainland Japan. During this "March of Death," they were clubbed, beaten, and bayoneted; six hundred Americans and at least five thousand Filipinos perished.[7] Survivors, like the diarist Ben Steele, by the end of the war had experienced forty-one horrendous months in Japanese camps and after liberation were treated in military hospitals for what would later be termed post-traumatic stress disorder. In the hospital, even under the influence of phenobarbital, Steele thrashed every night, his mind reliving slaps, punches, and kicks from the enemy.[8] Similarly, as recounted in the bestselling book and motion picture *Unbroken*, the army air force bombardier Louis Zamperini suffered for years after surviving brutal Japanese POW camps.[9]

Even after the pivotal naval battle of Midway in June 1942, it took a harsh six months, August 1942 to February 1943, to defeat the Japanese at Guadalcanal. American troops became emaciated; three out of seven contracted malaria, jungle rot, or dengue fever. Sleep-deprived, they endured repeated hand-to-hand combat, struggling to rout an enemy often hidden in caves. They faced frequent Japanese bombardment. One Japanese naval attack in August 1942 cut off marines from communication with the outside world for over a month. "They suffered the unpleasant and harrowing experience of seeing numerous friends and buddies . . . blown to bits," the navy psychiatrist Robert S. Schwab later wrote.[10] The sight and stench of mounds of dead Japanese bodies was sickening, Richard Tregaskis recalled in his bestselling *Guadalcanal Diary*: "Bodies torn apart from . . . artillery fire . . . remains fried by . . . blast of shells."[11] Martin Berezin, the only psychiatrist as well as acting division surgeon and medical inspector in the Army's Americal Division on Guadalcanal, saw a man at the front "who remained half conscious, sometimes talking gibberish, who practically had convulsive seizures whenever a bomb dropped."[12] One marine evacuated from Guadalcanal told the psychiatrist Albert Rosner he had been exposed to repeated bombing and had continued to fight on the front line despite malarial chills. The soldier confided: "I'd like to be a guard, sir. . . . I better take that back . . . I don't know about the gun part of it. I am afraid something might happen. I might hurt or kill someone." Trembling, he went on: "You can never tell about fellows that went through Guadalcanal. Everything I hear makes me think of that place. I could not handle another rifle. The slightest noise makes me jump ... a good soldier, but not anymore."[13] At the American Psychiatric Association's (APA) annual meeting in May 1943, Navy Lt. Commander E. Rogers Smith told psychiatrists about the horrors of battle experienced by "500 neurotic marines," not weaklings but steady men. Soon, *Time*, followed by *Newsweek*, publicized it.[14] Altogether, over 40 percent of the men shipped from Guadalcanal to the United States for hospitalization were neuropsychiatric, compared to only 5 percent from Pearl Harbor and 15–20 percent throughout most of the war.[15] The army medical staff estimated that neuropsychiatric cases accounted for an even higher 50 percent of all evacuees to the United States from the Southwest Pacific (including Australia, the Philippines, and New Guinea).[16]

Americans feared Japanese ruthlessness, "cunning," and refusal to surrender. Unlike the Germans, whom Americans generally found to honor the international convention of surrender, the Japanese had their own 1908 Army Criminal Code, which declared: "A commander who allows his unit to surrender to the enemy without fighting to the last man or who concedes a strategic area to the enemy shall be punishable by death."

Kiyoshi Kinoshita, a Japanese veteran of the battle of Quinaun Point on the Bataan Peninsula in Luzon, Philippines, in January and February 1942, recalled his experience later on. Ashamed of becoming a prisoner in an American army hospital bed, he "wanted to die, but he was ... too weak to kill himself. ... He had betrayed his comrades ... his colonel ... the stink of that failure ... would always be on him ... his survival ... an act of treachery."[17] Japanese military psychiatry sought to harden soldiers against fear of combat, believing that the ethic of the samurai, to commit suicide rather than surrender, underpinned their national identity and was in no way pathological.[18]

Returning from Malaya, the *Life* reporter Cecil Brown wrote that the Japanese had "one mental vitamin ... contempt for the white man." Lieutenant General Lesley McNair, in charge of training, cautioned soldiers that the "Jap" was "a hard, relentless fighter," a killer with "no fear of death" who fought with every weapon available, was fully abreast of modern technology, and could equally adjust to warfare in the country, jungle, or mountains. He urged his soldiers to "hate with every fiber of our being. ... Our object ... must be to kill. ... There need be no pangs of conscience. ... We must hurry to catch up ... if we are to survive."[19]

A severe shortage of medical doctors, nurses, dieticians, dentists, physical therapists, qualified surgeons, and, even more, psychiatrists pervaded the entire Pacific. The army did not send a medical consultant to the South Pacific until July 1943. Then, those sent were unprepared for the conditions of jungle warfare. In Guadalcanal, one out of ten mosquito bites resulted in malaria.[20] Though the army officially blacked out statistics on malaria throughout the war, an estimated 60,000 out of 152,000 soldiers and marines in the South Pacific had contracted the disease by 1943.[21] With so many unable to fight, the military had no choice but to pressure Berezin in Guadalcanal to return his cases to the front as many as three times before allowing him to send them to hospitals. Since Guadalcanal was an island, it was also difficult to evacuate. Having insufficient drugs, Berezin developed an innovative form of therapy, ordering psychiatric casualties to dig dugouts and wells for the hospital areas.[22] Elsewhere in the Pacific, with no psychiatrists at all at the front and scarcely any doctors of any sort, with insufficient medical supplies and equipment and no psychiatric training programs until late 1944, the military ordered massive psychiatric evacuations and little else.[23]

Doubtless, some of those evacuated could have benefited from returning to their units. A South Pacific hospital report at the end of 1943 stated: "Many cases of acute neuroses, with stable backgrounds suffered from prolonged fatigue and lack of sleep. Earlier sedation and rest would have been beneficial for these soldiers more than evacuating to the rear."[24]

Figure 4. U.S. Marines marching through the mud to front lines, November 4, 1943.

Psychiatric cases were last in line in the process of evacuation; the army first evacuated the physically wounded, starting with the most severe. Consequently, combat-exhausted soldiers could wait six months before being evacuated. In the meantime, they were frequently held in "corrals," a phrase usually referring to horses. The army padlocked "psychotics" in wire enclosures. As the number of psychiatric cases arriving at station or evacuation hospitals rose, the milder ones were commingled with the more disturbed in stockades. Sometimes, officers labeled them "discipline problems" and imprisoned them in hastily constructed jails with violent criminals free to assault them. It often took a month for psychiatric patients to sail from the Pacific to California. Aboard ship, officers locked the more serious patients in cages. Psychoneurotics were placed in stifling bunks near the psychotic. Psychiatrists rarely staffed these ships.[25]

North Africa

As the army mushroomed from 1,686,000 in 1941 to 5,397,000 in 1942, Army Chief of Staff George C. Marshall feared that the paucity of effective leadership and adequate equipment would depress morale. The British medical officers' reaction to a tour of an American training camp in the United States further alarmed him. The British concluded that Americans needed to learn far more before they could effectively engage the Germans in North Africa. It would be murder, they wrote, to put the young Americans they had seen against trained continental troops.[26]

Spirits sagged in late 1942 and early 1943 while soldiers waited to ship out of the Hampton Roads Port of Embarkation in Virginia. Almost half of the camp's dispensary calls were labeled mental. Psychotic patients spent months of inactivity in overcrowded, closed wards in military hospitals awaiting beds in state hospitals. Divisions were combed and recombed for psychiatric defects before shipping out. Some units' training had to be extended because of unsatisfactory adjustment. Morale was so low that officers feared "psychopaths" might shoot them. In one instance, a riot occurred in camp, which ended only with tear gas. Similar incidents occurred in other ports of embarkation around the country.[27]

Still, psychiatrists successfully used preventive measures in replacement training camps such as Aberdeen Proving Grounds, Maryland. Working in mental hygiene units with social workers and psychologists from the National Committee for Mental Hygiene (NCMH), psychiatrists employed individual therapy and lectures on homesickness, fear, discipline, and the mind-body relationship to successfully reduce AWOLs, court-martials, and sick calls. By September 1942, the army expanded this program to fifteen replacement centers, and by April 1943, to thirty-three.[28]

For its part, the navy continued to concentrate on screening. One prominent example of a sailor discharged from training for psychiatric reasons was Jack Kerouac. The future author of On the Road and a Columbia College dropout, he left the merchant marine after three months to enlist in the Navy Reserves on December 8, 1942. After ten days in navy boot camp, he was referred to the Newport Rhode Island Naval Hospital and then to the Naval Hospital in Bethesda, Maryland. Qualities that would make him a fine author did not sit well with the navy. His independence, creativity, and eagerness to be left alone, plus his boredom with camp, made him suspect. Originally diagnosed "schizophrenic," his lack of respect for discipline, authority, and structure concerned the doctors. He told them he was nervous because he had overworked on his novel before enlisting, but this explanation appeared as "grandiosity." His erratic work history confirmed "impulsiveness." He was observed, analyzed, asked about his sexual history (termed "promiscuous"), and discharged in June 1943 with a diagnosis of "Constitutional Psychopathic State, Schizoid Personality." He signed a form stating that his condition was preexisting and officially received an administrative discharge "for reason of unsuitability rather than physical or mental disability." This meant no veterans benefits, including medical.[29]

In the Caribbean

During the fall of 1942, a psychiatrist sent by Frederick Osborn, then chief of the Army Morale Branch, to anonymously investigate army units in the Caribbean, found many psychopaths. Private W, for example, drank a half-pint of whiskey and "under the impulse of a characteristic paranoid fantasy, armed himself, walked into the headquarters of the commanding general, Fort Read, and not finding the general at his desk, turned and fired at the adjutant before he could be seized and disarmed." Another psychotic soldier in Trinidad killed a fellow patient. Antigua had two suicides and two homicides among ninety-five neuropsychiatric cases. Surinam and Aruba each had two suicides. The investigating psychiatrist concluded that the high casualty rate could have been avoided with more thorough psychiatric screening, including civilian histories before induction. So alarmed was Osborn that he immediately sent the report to Marshall, urging him to tighten psychiatric screening, evacuate psychiatric patients more quickly, and improve treatment.[30]

Roy Grinker, John Spiegel, Herbert Spiegel, and Frederick Hanson in North Africa

As the Allies fought strenuous tank and infantry battles in the Tunisian mountains at Kairouan and Mateur from late 1942 to May 1943, the armies experienced especially heavy losses at Faid Pass and Kasserine Pass. Psychiatric injuries accounted for 20 to 34 percent of nonfatal casualties. Only 2 percent returned to combat.[31] The enemies' powerful weaponry had devastating effects. Men cringed, wept, shook, curled up in fetal positions, and became unresponsive. Facing trained German troops, night fighting, dive bombing, and insufficient water for days on end, American soldiers near Kasserine panicked and pulled back before orders were given. One commander, a law enforcement officer in civilian life, afflicted with combat neurosis refused to leave his dugout during heavy shelling and had to be removed from command.[32]

Trained and analyzed by Sigmund Freud, the psychiatrist/psychoanalyst Roy Grinker worked closely with John Spiegel, his former resident at the University of Chicago, and with the British psychiatrist Colman Kenton, treating soldiers at the 95th British Hospital, Algiers, where more than 1,700 infantry and aviators from Tunisia were transported.[33] The hospital was at least three hundred miles from the front and 150 to three hundred miles from any air base. Patients generally arrived two to five days after breakdown.

In *War Neuroses in North Africa: The Tunisian Campaign* (1943), with 45,000 copies distributed by the army as a textbook, Grinker described caring for aviators in the army air force who were psychotic, concussed, exhausted, hysterical, amnesiac, mute, tremorous, afflicted with battle nightmares, stuttered, or were malingerers.[34] Grinker utilized narcosynthesis to enhance an aviator's recall of battle experiences to eventually resolve conflicts. He preferred sodium pentothal (popularly known as "truth serum") over sodium amytal because the latter took longer to induce and stayed longer in the system, whereas the shorter-acting pentothal allowed patients to be alert during psychotherapy. If a patient were sedated, the doctor would have him freely relate his battle experience as if he were living in the present; if not sufficiently sedated, the patient might be prompted by asking questions. During narcosynthesis, the patient's body could become tense and rigid as he relived the battle. The pupils dilated; the body sweated. The hands might seek out a weapon. The patient would talk about the explosion of shells, death of a friend, or extreme dangers. When reaching a climax, his body would drop on the bed. For severe cases plunged into terror, the psychiatrist might play the role of protector. Sometimes, a patient would need two or three sessions to relate the traumatic events. For those with serious hysteria, such as mutism or deafness, narcosynthesis generally removed the symptoms in the long run.

It was harder to cure the less serious anxiety cases, especially if the patient superficially had the malady under control. Sometimes, a psychiatrist would lack the time to reach the root of the problem, and the emotional wound would remain unsalved. Reassurance by the therapist that the battle had ended and all was safe might not convince a weak ego. The battle might continue to feel too close, in which case individual psychotherapy might be added to the narcosynthesis, for fifteen to thirty minutes over several weeks. Conditions were not ideal. New battles or new patients might interrupt therapy.

Narcosynthesis did not cure all patients, like one melancholic twenty-two-year-old who pounded the mattress with clenched fists when told he was being shelled. He looked like he would kill someone and then buried his head under a pillow. Neither psychotherapy nor a second attempt at narcosynthesis succeeded. With insufficient time to resolve conflicts, narcosynthesis, which left open emotional sores, might exacerbate fears, making a patient less willing to return to combat. The psychiatrist might then appear to be encouraging the patient to avoid combat.[35] While Grinker had little faith in convulsive shock therapy (ECT), he did use it in several clinical depression cases where narcosynthesis was unsuccessful and the cases had to be treated quickly to avoid calcification. According to an interview years later with Herbert Spiegel, a psychiatrist who also treated soldiers in North Africa, Grinker's and Spiegel's use of narcosynthesis also returned fewer to combat than originally anticipated, because after only a few days of treatment soldiers were still stunned and could not fight effectively.[36]

After North Africa, Grinker spent much of the war with the 12th Army Air Force in the Mediterranean and in 1944 became chief psychiatrist at the Don Ce-Sar Hotel, a resort turned psychiatric convalescent hospital and training center for army air force doctors in St. Petersburg, Florida. At Don Ce-Sar, Grinker and his staff had time to successfully employ narcosynthesis and other therapies, as patients generally stayed a week or more. Some doctors, including Dr. Howard Rusk, objected to a hospital solely dedicated to psychiatric rehabilitation. Rusk, who in 1950 would establish the Rusk Institute for Rehabilitation in New York City, saw rehabilitation as having both physical and psychological components and was willing to have a psychiatric wing in a hospital but not the entire institution. But Don Ce-Sar remained a psychiatric facility throughout the war thanks to Grinker's lobbying and that of his colleague at the Josiah Macy Jr. Foundation, Frank Fremont-Smith.[37]

About the same time, Herbert Spiegel (no relation to John) treated soldiers in North Africa. Years later, he recalled that he was probably "the first psychiatrist in the field in combat" in World War II. He was "so far forward in the war zone that very often casualties were taking place behind" him, he said.[38] Soon after training at St. Elizabeth's (Sullivan being one of his teachers), he was sent to Fort Meade as a psychiatrist. In May 1942, he was secretly assigned as an assistant battalion surgeon in the First Battalion, 26th Infantry Regiment of the First Division because they were "desperate to get young doctors in the infantry." Trained with his troops in Scotland, he "swam" into Africa in the invasion's second wave, treated soldiers at the front both as a surgeon and psychiatrist, and was wounded on the last day of fighting in Tunisia.

Herbert Spiegel differed significantly from Grinker and John Spiegel in the mode of treatment. Herbert Spiegel chose suggestion and hypnotism over narcosynthesis to treat his patients because of amytal's or pentothal's adverse effects on the ability of a soldier to fight. According to Spiegel, pentothal and amytal (called "blue 88s," probably after the powerful German gun) did not always work. Sometimes, pentothal was not correctly injected. Occasionally a patient was asphyxiated. When amytal was given orally, it could knock a man out.[39]

He remembered anxiety-ridden, tremulous soldiers facing "the utter finality of being killed," struggling between the obligation to fight and the wish to leave battle. In the throes of combat, where every man was needed, he tried to prevent soldiers from becoming psychiatric casualties. He told one tearful soldier in "no uncertain terms that he was letting everyone down and failing those who were continuing to fight." Then, "he ordered him to dig a foxhole and stay there until ordered otherwise." The next morning, he was fine. To suppress a soldier's fears, he would put his arm on his back to divert him from panicking or, if necessary, allow him a few hours or days of rest.[40]

Herbert Spiegel was known for his use of hypnosis. The treatment began with the doctor telling the patient he would be hypnotized if there were enough time. The patient would be asked whether he knew anything about hypnosis. If the patient objected to hypnosis, the doctor would explain why it was needed. The patient was "told repeatedly, in a low voice, that he should relax and go to sleep. Heaviness of the eyes was suggested. At times this was reinforced by a stroking of the forehead and eyes." The patient generally fell asleep in a few minutes. The doctor quieted the patient's neuroses by playing the reassuring father in the midst of a simulated combat zone "with all the stimuli of warfare." While the patient was coming through, the psychiatrist was supposed to bring the "traumatic experience back to [the patient's] consciousness" by discussing in detail the material brought out while asleep. The goal was to have the ego accept and master the traumatic combat experience.[41] Spiegel continued to utilize hypnosis in his civilian practice for many years after the war.

The neurologist and neurosurgeon Frederick Hanson also treated soldiers at the front. First serving with the Canadian army as a neurologist and neurosurgeon, he joined the American army after the United States entered the war, treating soldiers at a clearing station in Tunisia. Denying a physical cause for shell shock, he early on believed that men became emotionally exhausted by endless fighting and could be returned to combat after being given adequate rest, sleep, good food, warm clothes, supportive talks, and, if necessary, sedation, all "close to the enemies' guns." According to Hanson, approximately 30 percent of 494 patients were returned to combat after thirty hours and approximately 70 percent after forty-eight hours. Appointed later as army neuropsychiatric consultant for the Mediterranean theater, he instructed army psychiatrists in Europe and the Pacific throughout the war on treatment and prevention.[42]

The work of Hanson, Grinker, and the Spiegels was the exception, not the rule. The Army Neuropsychiatry Branch reported that as of the end of July 1943, 95 percent of army psychiatrists were stationed in general and station hospitals hundreds of miles from the front, where they often saw soldiers after their mental symptoms had calcified.[43] Except for some efforts at Guadalcanal, medical officers in the Pacific primarily evacuated psychiatric casualties and did little else.

Psychiatric Policy Making Back Home

Aware of rising psychiatric casualties overseas and disturbances in military camps at home, America's leading civilian psychiatrists campaigned for a more prominent role in the military. Assuming psychiatric casualties could be reduced through stricter psychiatric screening, they called for tougher standards and the complete restoration of the local board examination eviscerated by the army. They also called for the appointment of one of their own, a well-qualified civilian psychiatrist, to head a full-scale division of psychiatry in the Army Surgeon General's Office, with the same clout as the divisions of surgery and medicine; the recruitment of more civilian psychiatrists to positions commensurate with their expertise; and the establishment of schools to train other doctors and nondoctors in the rudiments of emergency military psychiatry.[44]

Limiting their efforts, however, were major differences in personality and medical philosophy among a widespread group of psychiatrists, including neurologists, medical school professors, private practitioners, superintendents of mental hospitals, and a small but growing cadre of psychoanalysts. That psychologists and psychiatrists in World War II did not work together as they had done in World War I was also detrimental.

In March 1942, Edward Strecker, a University of Pennsylvania professor of psychiatry who would soon become a psychiatric consultant to the army and navy, led the quest for tougher screening. Writing to Patrick Madigan in the Army Surgeon General's Office, he requested that the "examining powers and functions of Selective Service" be expanded to reduce the burden on army induction boards. Otherwise, he cautioned, the results would be "detrimental" and "felt far into the future long after the war [was] over."[45] This most likely meant that the costs of hospitalization would be staggering.

The same month, Lawrence Kubie, trained in psychiatry and neuropathology at Phipps Clinic, the Rockefeller Institute, and the London Institute of Psychoanalysis, and Tracy Putnam, a neurologist and one of the inventors of Dilantin, a drug for epilepsy, charged that neuropsychiatric screening was "less effective than in the last war," since military hospitals contained "more psychiatric casualties than any other single type." So upset were they that they threatened Winfred Overholser, chair of the National Research Council (NRC) Committee on Neuropsychiatry, to "resign from the committee . . . with a strong statement to the press" if the army and navy did not give them a more effective role.[46] Feeling it necessary to "try a little psychiatry" on his malcontents, Overholser replied: "I hope . . . you and Larry have recovered from acute anxiety. . . . Resignation with a public statement would be one of the worst things . . . a violation of our oath of office . . . unpatriotic."[47]

But Kubie and Putnam were not alone. In June 1942, the newly formed APA Special Committee on War Activities, consisting of Strecker, APA President Arthur Ruggles, and Frederick Parsons, former New York State commissioner of mental hygiene under then-governor Franklin Roosevelt, condemned excessive psychiatric casualties in training camps. A month later, Overholser relayed their message to Roosevelt's personal physician. He advised McIntire that the APA committee "may, unless matters improve, request a private interview with the President. In the meantime, it holds itself in readiness should its advice and suggestions be desired."[48]

That July, Ruggles also called for stiffer screening in his APA presidential address. Recommending a more extensive review of mental and criminal records, he highlighted the case of Joseph Leonski, who murdered three women while serving in the American army in Australia. Had his long criminal and mental health record been reviewed, Ruggles was certain the army would not have taken him.[49] At a meeting of the NRC Subcommittee on Psychiatry, Ruggles likewise called for rejecting from service those with addiction, alcoholism, personality maladjustment, psychosomatic disorder, or epilepsy, citing high rates of psychiatric discharges from army and navy training camps and large numbers of psychiatrically hospitalized soldiers.

Referring to his NRC-sponsored study of one hundred psychiatric casualties and one hundred control soldiers in the 8th Army Corps, Franklin Ebaugh, a well-known psychiatrist/researcher at the University of Colorado, also confirmed the need for more careful local board screening at a meeting of the NRC Subcommittee on Psychiatry. Soon thereafter, that committee asked Overholser to ask the Army Surgeon General to allow some of its civilian psychiatrists to tour army camps and hospitals to gain firsthand knowledge of why men were breaking down in order to refine preinduction psychiatric criteria, a request that was granted the following year.[50]

Since there were scarcely any psychiatrists overseas while battles raged, Strecker called for the recruitment of more civilian psychiatrists and their assignment to suitable positions.[51] At the beginning of the war, the army employed only thirty-five psychiatrists. Mostly assigned to hospitals, few had formal training, and only four were board certified. In February 1942, Army Surgeon General James Magee appointed Patrick Madigan, a career army psychiatrist principally involved in drafting Circular Letter No. 19, the army's preinduction psychiatric examination, to head the newly instituted Army Neuropsychiatric Branch. In April, Malcolm Farrell, formerly assistant superintendent of the Walter E. Fernald State School, Waverly, Massachusetts, and instructor in psychiatry at Boston University Medical School, joined Madigan. Assigned to the Professional Services Division (Personnel Division) of the Army Surgeon General, they had little clout when it came to requisitioning supplies or staff. According to William Menninger, their section's function was to review the papers of officers retiring for medical reasons. By way of comparison, by 1945, the Army Neuropsychiatric Consultants Division employed eleven psychiatrists, and the army as a whole employed a total of 2,402.[52]

During the spring of 1942, Overholser, who had worked closely with Sullivan in establishing the local board psychiatric examination program and had opposed its being reduced by the army to a one-minute examination, provided the Army Surgeon General with a list of civilian psychiatrists to replace Madigan. But before Overholser could win approval for his preferred candidate, he had to fend off efforts of another committee appointed by the military to select officers for the Medical Corps. Writing to Lewis Weed, director of the NRC Medical Division in July 1942, Overholser complained that this other group consisted of six to eight relatively unknown "Orthodox

Freudian analysts." "To my mind the selection of a group made up exclusively of analysts will perhaps do more to discredit psychiatry in this field than if psychiatrists had not been used at all."[53] Although there were no more than one hundred to five hundred trained psychoanalysts in the United States at the time, they were clearly beginning to have influence. But not enough: A month later, on August 17, 1942, the Army Surgeon General indeed appointed Overholser's candidate, Roy Halloran, to head the psychiatry branch, with the rank of colonel. Two days earlier, according to the army's official history, Madigan had been transferred to the AG, possibly because he was being made to take the blame for the shockingly high psychiatric casualty rates in training camps and overseas.[54] Like Overholser, Halloran had been a superintendent of a mental hospital, Metropolitan State Hospital, Waltham, Massachusetts. Halloran was also professor of clinical psychiatry at Tufts Medical School, Boston. But Halloran's tenure was short; he died of a coronary occlusion on November 9, 1943. His successor, William Menninger, was more friendly to psychoanalysis. Analyzed by the founder of the Chicago Psychoanalytic Institute, Franz Alexander, Menninger appointed among his deputies two psychoanalysts: Moe Kaufman in the Pacific and South Pacific and John M. Murray as liaison between the army and Army Air Surgeon General.[55]

But while Overholser saw his candidate, Halloran, appointed early on to replace Madigan in the Army Surgeon General's Office, neither Overholser nor any other prominent civilian psychiatrist appeared to lobby Selective Service for a successor to Sullivan in 1942 or 1943. Perhaps their aversion reflected an interest in avoiding the bitterness Sullivan had experienced in dealing with Hershey; or perhaps they revered Sullivan; or, most likely, perhaps they felt little need given the army's reduction of the local board examination to a one-minute affair. In any case, as we shall see, not until July 1943 did Selective Service appoint Raymond Waggoner of Michigan to succeed Sullivan as its psychiatric consultant, someone personally chosen by Hershey and outside the prestigious Washington/Baltimore/Boston psychiatric network.

In the meantime, to augment the number of psychiatrists in the field as combat losses steadily grew, Kubie also proposed to Overholser and Weed in June 1942 that hospitals train nonpsychiatrists and civilian psychiatrists in military psychiatry. The NRC endorsed his recommendation, referring it to the Army Surgeon General. Under Kubie's plan, military and civilian physicians would train doctors or even nondoctors with special aptitude to become psychiatrists. Depending on their ability, the training could run from two weeks to six months: in the morning in a hospital outpatient clinic learning about neuroses, and in the afternoon in a general ward focusing on psychosomatic disorders, which were of much concern to the military at the time. Doctors might also spend an additional month learning about antisocial behavior in criminal courts or criminal wards of psychiatric hospitals. Some civilian psychiatrists, Kubie remarked archly, though professionally trained, might "have more right to be shoemakers" and should be placed in other medical specialties. Others, he said, "who had real aptitudes without formal training," should be placed in psychiatric specialties.[56]

The following fall, the army schooled a limited number of physicians, psychologists, social workers, and civilian psychiatrists in basic military psychiatry at Lawson General Hospital in Atlanta, Georgia, in a four-week program. Later, it expanded the program to include a twelve-week course for medical officers who were not psychiatrists. Since even civilian psychiatrists had little prior experience diagnosing mild personality maladjustments, more than half the course work at the school focused on the detection and treatment of questionable cases.[57] The School of Neuropsychiatry was moved in October 1943 to Mason General Hospital, Long Island, New York. Its director was Colonel William Porter, a career military psychiatrist formerly at Walter Reed Hospital, Washington, DC.

Altogether, by war's end, at least one thousand men had graduated from the army programs. Columbia and New York Universities also trained an additional 227 doctors in three-month courses in military psychiatry.[58] But not until 1944 did the numbers with such training appear to satisfy the army's needs.

Since World War I, the army had placed psychiatrists in divisions, but in October 1940, the surgeon general eliminated those posts for economic reasons. Though army surgeons tried to requisition psychiatrists for divisions in the years to come, not until December 1943 were psychiatrists returned to divisions.

As early as June 1942, the APA Special Committee on War Activities recommended that the army assign psychiatrists to the front so they could immediately treat patients after the onset of illness. "There is a direct ratio," they wrote, "between the 'shellshock' recovery ratio and the elapsed time before the soldier is handled by a psychiatrist."[59] In a New York City Committee on Mental Hygiene memorandum, Kubie recognized that to treat or engage in preventive psychiatry, a psychiatrist needed to be at the front, where he could see for himself what constituted combat stress. "Experienced psychiatric observers," he wrote, must "live with . . . men in . . . army posts and vessels to experience the [psychological effects] of cramped quarters . . . boredom . . . duration of tours . . . to explore . . . the various methods for . . .

treatment of... war neuroses."⁶⁰ Kubie and Strecker also called on psychiatrists to motivate men in training camps and at the front through political and mental health lectures. To "psychologically harden" troops, Strecker suggested "reproduc[ing] in miniature ... some of the conditions which precipitated ... war neuroses in World War I"⁶¹ (indicating how unfamiliar some doctors were with the current war's travails, at a time when communications were in no way as rapid as they are today). Unfortunately, neither treatment by division psychiatrists at the front nor preventive psychiatry emerged until much later in the war.

More than anything else, psychiatrists in 1942 debated whether they should switch their focus from psychiatric screening to working with psychologists and educational specialists on assigning inductees to the most appropriate placements in the military. The British and Canadians had a system in which psychologists and psychiatrists worked together in assigning men for national service. If men could not cope with combat, they could be assigned to noncombat assignments. If they could not adjust to the military at all, they could be assigned to industry or agriculture. But after a bitter debate, prominent American civilian psychiatrists, despite the recommendations of Kubie and other neurologists, held to their belief that they should do psychiatric screening and little else. The importance of this resistance cannot be stressed enough. Had they switched to emphasizing vocational assignments more, fewer individuals might have been rejected and discharged on psychiatric grounds, which affected their lives and the lives of their families in the long run. Fewer rejections might also have postponed the need to conscript eighteen- and nineteen-year-olds and fathers into the military.

Though APA President Ruggles championed tougher psychiatric screening, he was open to alternatives. In March 1942, Ruggles and the psychologist Frederic Lyman Wells, who had been employed, like Ruggles, by a mental hospital (in Wells's case, as a psychologist at Boston Psychopathic Hospital for many years), issued an NRC report on the "Utilization of Psychiatric and Psychological Knowledge in Selecting Men for Military Service." Though the original report concluded that the two disciplines should go their separate ways, one determining emotional stability, the other cognitive ability, their supplemental report recommended that Selective Service employ both disciplines together to reclassify neuropsychiatric and physical rejectees for limited service in industry and agriculture.⁶²

About the same time, Kubie and a team of psychiatrists at the New York City Committee on Mental Hygiene prepared a thirty-page "Memorandum on the Selection Process in General and on the Role of the Psychiatrist in the Selection Process and in the Armed Forces." First issued in draft form in June 1942, it was published the following October. More traditional psychiatrists found its recommendations astounding.[63]

Kubie's memorandum called for one unified central "Selection Agency," composed of psychiatrists, psychologists, internists, psychiatric social workers, and statisticians, to coordinate all decisions on placement, rejection, and discharge in the navy, army, marines, and coast guard. No longer would there be separate Selective Service local boards and army induction centers. To eliminate conflicts between the work of psychiatrists and psychologists, each military service (army, navy, marines, and coast guard) would each transfer their section on psychopathological problems in the Adjutant General Personnel Division to their Surgeon General's Office. The new section would be called the Section on Psychology and Personnel. That section would be combined with the Surgeon General's Section on Psychiatry. Together, the two sections would become the Division of Psychiatry and Psychology. Within this division, the Section on Psychiatry would oversee treatment in hospitals and mobile units and the training of doctors and nondoctors in military psychiatry. The new Section on Psychology and Personnel would cover emotional and vocational placement of servicemen and problems of morale and be manned by psychologists, educators, and liaison psychiatrists. Behind this fusion was Kubie's basic premise that faulty vocational placement could adversely affect someone emotionally and vice versa. Often, Kubie said, the soldier's or sailor's anxieties about being in the wrong job caused his neuroses. For this reason, Kubie's memorandum advocated reclassifying men into different vocations several times before discharging them on psychiatric grounds as a last resort. Each agency was required to maintain up-to-date cumulative physiological and psychological records for each service member before and after induction and even after discharge.[64] More than seventy years before the initiation of HIPAA, the memorandum stressed that records must be kept confidential, with written permission for release required from every recruit.

For mainstream psychiatrists, Kubie's proposal seemed out of line. On the surface, the memorandum's rhetoric emphasized stricter psychiatric screening, but in reality, it promoted psychiatrists working with psychologists on vocational classification. In August 1942, Overholser wrote to Robert Yerkes, now sixty-seven years old, who had overseen the IQ program in World War I. He warned Yerkes that Kubie's proposal "would do a great deal of damage to the entire selection process." While Yerkes's response is unknown, it may well be that Overholser was warning him in order to dissuade him and other psychologists from participating in Kubie's program. In any case, no indication exists that any psychologist favored it.

Right away, the Public Health Service psychiatrist Lawrence Kolb, who had worked on designing the navy's psychiatric examination, criticized Kubie's "elaborate" and "time-consuming" plan. It would be virtually impossible, Kolb wrote, to conduct "a worthwhile follow-up . . . on the 7,000,000 soldiers."[65] Harry Steckel, chair of the APA Military Mobilization Committee, wrote Kubie, essentially calling him unpatriotic. He found Kubie's charge that the navy and army had been unprepared for war "subversive propaganda." He called Kubie's proposal to use civilian psychiatrists unrealistic, because Steckel was "personally acquainted with a number of civilian 'self-appointed' psychiatrists who [were] doing an exceedingly poor job with Selective Service."[66]

From March 1942 on, psychiatrists had been asking Overholser to persuade the president and his staff to get involved in psychiatric decision making. Now, with battle casualties mounting and leading psychiatrists back home divided over their proper role in the war, input from the top became critical.

Though Overholser had managed to quiet down Kubie in March, three months later, during the initial debate over Kubie's memorandum, the irate neurologist once more urged Overholser to give the army and navy surgeon generals "one week to act" and "if nothing happens . . . resign publicly . . . demand a Senatorial investigation." A month later, Overholser wrote Secretary of Labor Frances Perkins and Navy Surgeon General McIntire that "if matters did not improve" and psychiatrists were not given a greater role in the war, he would as secretary/treasurer of the APA request a meeting between the president and the APA Special Committee Dealing with War Activities. He enclosed a May APA resolution calling for greater use of psychiatry. Perkins spoke to Roosevelt and wrote to Roosevelt's personal secretary, Marvin MacIntyre, that psychiatrists "are very disturbed about conditions for the care of mental cases in both the Army and Navy, and . . . say that a considerable number . . . are developing as a result of actual battle duty." She asked for a meeting with the president and conveyed the psychiatrists' same concerns to Eleanor Roosevelt. "Their feeling," she said, "is . . . that a large number of cases are developing, particularly in the Navy, from men who have been in battle." "I have spoken to the President," she wrote Mrs. Roosevelt, "but I know that he is overburdened and doesn't get an opportunity to think about this. I thought perhaps you would like to look into it."[67] This episode is exemplary of the general view that the president focused more on winning the war and his wife on improving conditions for soldiers and on the home front.

On July 21, 1942, the First Lady asked McIntire to meet with psychiatrists. "On every hand," she wrote, "I hear we are not using psychiatrists to the fullest . . . they are desperately needed by both the Army and . . . Navy." She had seen "so many [boys in the military] going out to St. Elizabeth's . . . it makes my heart ache."[68]

Responding indirectly on July 31 to Eleanor Roosevelt's concerns in a letter to Perkins, McIntire as navy surgeon general somewhat chauvinistically praised the navy's comprehensive screening program for preventing psychiatric and "borderline" cases from entering service. He could not understand why Strecker's and Overholser's criticism included the navy.[69]

Two months later, on September 22, 1942, reflecting McIntire's position, Eleanor Roosevelt wrote Secretary of War Henry Stimson that leading psychiatrists had told her that the army's psychiatric work was inferior to the navy's and that the Army Surgeon General had not given psychiatry its proper status. She added that she had received many letters indicating that "there are men in the Army . . . psychologically unfit to be combat soldiers." Perhaps they should have been given psychiatric tests and assigned to other types of work. Particularly, she found this important if the draft age were lowered. She was sure it would mean "fewer mental cases as a result of the war."[70] (By "psychiatric tests," she probably meant written aptitude tests given by psychologists in conjunction with psychiatric screening, a program not universally implemented until later in the war but already occurring in the navy.)

Hence, the First Lady, like Kubie, as of September 1942 supported vocational placement rather than simple psychiatric rejection or discharge. Eleanor Roosevelt's and McIntire's opinions also reflected army-navy competition and the president's supposed preference for the navy, having been assistant naval secretary in World War I. Since McIntire examined Roosevelt several times a day, it is likely Roosevelt knew of these discussions.

Responding to Eleanor Roosevelt on October 3, Stimson defended the Army Surgeon General by noting its recent establishment of a "Division of Psychiatry" headed by a "well qualified neuro psychiatrist" and the training of several hundred medical officers in psychiatry. "This Division," he commented, "is also giving special attention to the exclusion of the mentally unsound from the military service."[71] Halloran had recently been appointed as head psychiatrist, but psychiatry was still a branch. More important, Stimson was adamant that tough psychiatric screening was the route to take.

Perhaps because of Stimson's and McIntire's pride in their service's tough psychiatric screening, Eleanor Roosevelt changed her tune in favor of stricter screening despite complaints from constituents about unfair rejections. Only three days after Stimson's letter, on October 6, she wrote in her syndicated column "My Day": "We are not giving our draftees a sufficiently careful psychiatric examination before they are taken into service . . . there seems to be a considerable number of maladjustments which may or may not become liabilities in the Army. In the Navy, too, I have seen many cases of what one might call 'nerves.'"[72]

On October 22, 1942, the Surgeon General's Office strengthened its criteria for mental and nervous fitness in the army's Mobilization Regulations, MR 1-9. It stipulated: "The objective . . . is not only to procure men who are physically fit for the rigors of general military service or limited service, but also to avoid burdening the medical facilities with unqualified personnel."

Two weeks later, on November 5, members of Kubie's NRC Subcommittee on War Neuroses, still bucking the system, again supported Kubie's vocational assignment plan, because it would allow more men to serve. They maintained that men with previous neurological histories could make good soldiers and that candidates should not be rejected on "theoretical" grounds. With the subcommittee's approval, Kubie and the neuropathologist Fremont-Smith agreed to revise the reorganization plan further.[73] (It is not known if this was done.)

Yet, contacted by Dr. Weed, on December 1, 1942, the dean of American psychiatry, Adolf Meyer, then seventy-nine years old, condemned Kubie's plan to transform "the entire personnel problem, from . . . recruiting . . . through . . . distribution . . . of . . . manpower." Describing Kubie as "a very taxed and taxing worker, with much intelligence," Meyer nonetheless wrote Weed that he found Kubie "poor in relative capacity."[74] But while he found Kubie's plan impractical, anticipating problems in the selection of eighteen- and nineteen-year-olds, who on November 11 had just been added to the draft, he called for a "a simple document for the local board" requiring information on "schooling, grades, and [the] health record" to help select teens for military service. Bemoaning the resignation of his protégé Sullivan, Meyer asked: "Who can be the best substitute of Harry Stack Sullivan in this important venture? Certainly not a '*mere* psychiatrist.'"[75] (Hence, hinting at the need for a replacement, which did not occur until seven months later.)

Agreeing with Meyer about the impracticality of Kubie's program, Weed tabled it. "Thus far," Weed assured Meyer, "Kubie has merely looked into the heavens and seen many stars. Something should be done but the great over-all plan will not be effective within this war."[76]

Adding a last word, Roscoe Hall wrote the neurologist Putnam, Kubie's associate on the Subcommittee on War Neuroses, on December 10 that Kubie's proposal was "more ideal than practical ... if carried out ... would require a set-up ... almost prohibitive in men and time," one requiring "the services of informed and not unsympathetic Army and Navy medical men," who apparently he did not believe existed.[77]

Hence, Kubie's classification program was not approved, despite similar programs in Great Britain and Canada, because of opposition from the military, Eleanor Roosevelt, and prominent civilian psychiatrists. The conscription of 2.5 million eighteen- and nineteen-year-olds began on November 11, substantially increasing the numbers available for service and making it less necessary to conserve manpower. Further, psychiatrists assigned to the Surgeon General and psychologists to the Adjutant General continued not to work together on vocational classification or other areas throughout the war. The Adjutant General, not the Surgeon General, trained clinical psychologists throughout the war. Until June 1943, psychiatrists alone determined whether a person should be rejected from service for illiteracy. Even after illiterates were able to receive psychological aptitude tests, mental deficiency was still listed as a neuropsychiatric disorder, not a learning issue.[78]

Behind the decision to toughen preinduction psychiatric screening and little else was the premise that if enough of the predisposed were eliminated from service, psychiatric casualty rates would decline. Yet while the rate of psychiatric rejection rose from 28.4 percent of medical rejections in 1942 to 42.7 percent in 1943,[79] the rate of psychiatric casualties also skyrocketed. As battles raged in the Pacific and North Africa, between February and July 1943, psychiatric casualties accounted for approximately 30 to 40 percent of all disability discharges for wounds and illnesses, by far the leading cause of medical disability. Psychiatric disorders, according to the Army's Neuropsychiatric Section annual report, were "three times as great as the next highest single cause, namely, cardiovascular disease." The army was also expelling many psychopaths and mentally deficient with Section VIII discharges for unspecified "undesirable habits and traits."[80]

Despite their reservations concerning the ability of psychiatrists to forecast mental breakdowns, pressured by the military, Selective Service representatives met with army and navy Surgeon General associates in Detroit on March 1943. The services' representatives emphasized that the rate of psychiatric discharge was much too high and urged tougher preinduction screening. Selective Service Medical Director Leonard Rowntree assured the group that more would be done to "help identify and reject those who might break down after induction." Commander Francis J. Braceland of the Navy Psychiatric Division highlighted the uniquely hazardous conditions of navy warfare, which made it particularly necessary to screen out misfits: "The constant need for teamwork, complicated machinery, irregular meals, little or no sleep." A person, he said, "could be at his battle station for hours or even days. Obviously, there is no room in the Navy for the problem child, the neurotic, the epileptic, or the psychopath."[81] This was particularly important because the navy had just converted a month earlier from voluntary enlistment to the draft.[82]

That same day, on March 25, 1943, following Army Surgeon General and War Department recommendations, the army Adjutant General officially issued Memorandum No. W 600-30-43. Noting that "too many men who are mentally unsuited for the ordinary military duties are arriving overseas," the memorandum ordered medical officers to use more care in screening at induction, training camps, and ports of embarkation.[83]

Drafting Eighteen- and Nineteen-Year-Olds

The previous fall, that of 1942, psychiatrists had debated the wisdom of extending conscription to include eighteen- and nineteen-year-olds. Leading the call for the use of eighteen- and nineteen-year-olds was Secretary of War Stimson. Writing to the chair of the Senate Committee on Military Affairs, which was holding hearings on a teenage draft, he contended that eighteen- and nineteen-year-olds would significantly contribute to service. He argued that they were more responsive to leadership than any other group, had a flair for soldiering, quickly recovered from fatigue, and seemed better suited than any other group to fight the youth of Europe and Asia. Similar arguments were made by Marshall and Hershey at the hearings.[84]

Psychiatrists, whose screening efforts had become increasingly discriminating, were now asked to relax their standards to admit eighteen- and nineteen-year-olds. Their comments before Congress and the press, for and against drafting younger men, reflected both health considerations and the needs of the war. Meyer and Overholser, among others, openly favored drafting eighteen- and nineteen-year-olds to win the war, even though they acknowledged that the medical effect on youth was uncertain.[85]

On the other hand, George Stevenson, director of the National Committee for Mental Hygiene, and the social scientist Lawrence K. Frank, an advocate of child study programs with the Rockefeller Foundation in the 1920s and 1930s and vice president of the Josiah H. Macy Foundation from 1936 through 1942, opposed drafting eighteen- and nineteen-year-olds. Speaking to the National Resources Planning Board, Frank stated that eighteen- and nineteen-year-olds had special problems of sexual adjustment, education, and employment, which older, more settled comrades did not. Some, he said, were still rebelling against their fathers or other authority figures, which might interfere with military discipline. For others, it would be their first experience away from home, having had no prior work experience or opportunity to take responsibility. Frank cited statistics showing unusually high rates of arrests and first admissions to mental hospitals for eighteen- and nineteen-year-olds.[86] Nor did Stevenson believe they would do as well in combat as their German peers, since Americans lacked the years of regimentation during childhood. He feared that sending a group straight from home to the army would later create a large group of civilians with no model for life except military totalitarianism in the immediate postwar era.[87]

Overholser and Foster Kennedy, Roosevelt's personal neurologist, were more positive about the teenage group. Recalling his experiences as a doctor with the British in World War I, Kennedy stated that the younger soldiers were more likely to take things in stride and brood less than their elders. He cited reports from doctors in England during the Blitz "that even children under heavy bombardment recovered more rapidly than grownups."[88] The navy's experience earlier in World War II taking younger men, Overholser maintained, had demonstrated "that 18- and 19-year-old men make excellent fighters and that the incidence of mental disorder had not been inordinately high in that age group." While he acknowledged that eighteen- and nineteen-year-olds in World War I had displayed a higher incidence of neuroses than their older comrades, he found the doctors now much more adept at selection. Nor did Overholser see any deleterious effects on democracy in sending eighteen- and nineteen-year-olds into service, as the army was a "citizens' army, democratically selected, where men fought side by side with others like themselves in pursuit of a wholesome ideal."[89]

In the face of such divergent medical opinion, what ultimately determined policy? It can be argued it was patriotism, not scientific data. Those in favor of screening, such as Overholser, openly admitted that medical evidence for a teenage draft was inconclusive, yet as he explained in the newspaper *PM*: "We must dispose of our manpower in the way most certain to win the war and take our chances." He continued: "War is always a destructive process and it hits all age groups. It is never a pleasant experience. Right now winning the war has a priority over everything else in the world, [and] neither psychiatrists nor any other group has any right to over-protect any particular age group." Thus, he appeared to openly concede that the obligations of the Hippocratic Oath to preserve health stood second to national security. In addition, supporters of the teenage draft professed a particular reverence for the military's opinions. "It is presumptuous," Overholser argued, "to challenge without reasonable proof to the contrary, the testimony of military leaders who have observed the relative fighting qualities of younger and older men."[90] More fundamentally, America had lost a great deal of manpower in its first year in the war and needed replenishment, and other possible sources of manpower, such as previously rejected psychiatric cases, had been turned down.

It is not clear where the Roosevelts stood. On the one hand, two of the leading advocates of the draft of eighteen-year-olds—Kennedy and Overholser—were in frequent contact with the president and First Lady. On the other, while debate in Congress raged, Eleanor Roosevelt urged Stimson to have psychiatrists transfer registrants possibly unfit for combat to other assignments, largely because of her concern about the vulnerability of younger men if the draft age was lowered. Yet, by October 15, 1942, when Stevenson, an opponent of the teenage draft, tried to see her, he found the First Lady, usually approachable, now uncharacteristically "extremely busy, with not a free minute, and will be away for the rest of the month," according to her secretary's note. On November 11, 1942, the draft age was lowered to eighteen.[91] In the end, the need to win the war overrode objection.

In 1942 and 1943, the driving factors in determining what role psychiatrists should play were the rising number of psychiatric casualties, the fear of men panicking in combat or causing trouble in their units, and mounting hospital costs. Ultimately, by late March 1943, the army and navy officially supported more screening both before induction and before assignment overseas. By the end of 1943, over 10.5 million men at Selective Service local boards and army induction centers had been examined by psychiatrists and, of these, 1.25 million, or 12 percent, rejected. In addition, 415,161 soldiers had been discharged from service for nervous or mental disorders. This represented at least 40 percent of all discharges for wounds and diseases (certificate of disability discharge) and ranked first among the reasons for medical discharge.[92] Although statistics are not available for the rejection of women soldiers during this time, we do know that neuropsychiatric disorders accounted for 44.3 percent of the 1,200 disability discharges for WACs between August 1942 and May 1943, or 532 women,[93] a rate similar to that for males. In addition to contributing to a shortage of available men and women for military service, these rejections and discharges would deeply impact the futures of 4Fs and neuropsychiatric veterans, their families, and society during a patriotic war and immediately thereafter.

5   The Public Reaction

As the number of psychiatric rejections and discharges soared, the American public wondered why so many could not play their part. Traditionally associating mental disorders with chronic cases in institutions, they found it hard to believe psychiatric 4Fs and veterans with minor maladjustments were truly sick. The war's emphasis on universal sacrifice added to public intolerance. So too did the growing need for military manpower. As civilians, they were "draft dodgers." In the military, bound up in time-honored values of bravery and masculinity, they were malingerers or cowards. While Congress held hearings on a bill to draft fathers, which eventually passed, American resentment rose. They wondered why heads of families would have to risk their lives while seemingly fit "psychoneurotic" 4Fs remained safe at home. Equally upset were the psychoneurotic 4Fs, dischargees, and their families, who voiced shame and fear at being regarded as "insane." They complained that their psychiatric label prevented them from employment. While Congress and Roosevelt called for a National Service Act to place rejectees into industrial and agricultural work, this was not passed, due in large part to opposition from organized labor and business. Minorities, particularly Blacks, also decried the bias of examiners and disproportionate rejection rates.

The Media

To understand the response to psychiatric rejections and discharges, we must first gauge the political atmosphere during the war. Whatever doubts we may have about whether everyone contributed his or her share to the war effort, advertisements, government-sponsored activities and publicity, and motion pictures aggressively promoted this message.[1]

An award-winning poster in *Life* (November 1942) showed a helmet atop a cross, with a gun impaled on the grave nearby, asking, "What have you given?"[2] The Office of Civilian Defense sloganeered: "Every time you decide not to buy something, you help to win the war." "The empty [carpool] seat is a gift to Hitler," and "Hoarders are on the same level as spies."[3] The

Mimeograph Company exhorted women, "Hang up the apron. Put on the office dress ... the nurse's uniform ... the blue khaki or forest green of our armed service auxiliaries.... Your country needs every woman who can be spared ... from her home."[4]

Hollywood, too, exhorted the public to sacrifice. RKO's "Conquer by the Clock" (1943) illustrated the disastrous impact of small lapses of time: one extra coffee break and a bad bullet produced, one ballgame during work and a strategic message lost. In a 1943 War Activities Committee film, Rosalind Russell urged workers to stay on the job. The same year, Walt Disney's "Out of the Frying Pan and into the Firing Line" featured Minnie Mouse saving her cooking fat for bullets.[5]

Little wonder that Americans in 1943 and 1944 criticized the almost one and a half million neuropsychiatric 4Fs and veterans for not doing their share, a feeling internalized by the men and women themselves. Other groups had an excuse for their draft deferments. Farmers and industrial workers were needed to produce vital food and equipment; men without arms or legs could no longer fight; children, husbands, and fathers had dependent mothers, wives, and youngsters. But the neuropsychiatric rejectee seemed without excuse. Bellyaches, nail biting, sleeplessness, temporary high blood pressure, stuttering, stammering, bedwetting: All seemed minor or imaginary complaints from men too soft or cowardly to serve.

Typical of the widespread critics was Fink J. Farrell of Georgia, who wrote his senator, Richard B. Russell: "Nearly every patriot in our country down here feels that all the deferments being granted to neurotics is a lot of hooey. Every coward going to Ft. McPherson Reception Center can qualify as a neurotic, thence is put in 4F." Russell referred this letter to Secretary of War Henry Stimson.[6] A few weeks later, the Army Surgeon General defended psychiatrists against Farrell's charge of encouraging draft evasion: "In the vast majority of cases malingering on the part of inductees being examined for induction occurs but rarely.... The psychiatric examination of selectees at induction stations is carried out by well-qualified psychiatrists who are making sincere efforts to screen out ... registrants most likely to become neuropsychiatric casualties."[7]

Farrell was but one example. In Michigan, citizens wrote their draft boards about the "brilliant" men who had done well at school and held down "responsible well-paying jobs" who seemed to be using psychoneuroses to "put something over" on the induction centers. The Michigan juvenile court justice Malcolm Hatfield, while calling for more preinduction screening, admitted that most people in his community doubted psychiatric 4Fs were sick.[8] So many men "faked" illness at the Douglas Aircraft Company in Oklahoma City that the head of the Selective Service field division claimed the employees assumed "it is not essential to be crazy, but it helps a lot in not being accepted for the armed forces."[9]

As Americans fought across difficult Italian mountain terrain in 1943 and 1944 and casualties rose, intolerance for psychiatric deferments grew. Senator Burton K. Wheeler of the Committee on Military Affairs, author of a bill to exempt fathers from the draft, remarked at hearings in 1943: "As a lawyer who has tried a good many cases, I happen to know that the easiest thing to simulate is a nervous condition.... A great many ... of those troubled with nervous conditions ... would get over [it] if they knew they were going to be inducted and then perhaps furloughed into something else."[10] In a widely read indictment of psychiatry in the *American Mercury* (July 1944), the psychologist Henry Link accused screening of giving Americans "a scientific excuse for draft evasion, and cowardice." Press reports of thirty-eight Rice and University of Tulsa football players, plus leading baseball players, jockeys, and prizefighters, rejected from service on nebulous physical and mental grounds added to public suspicion.[11]

Selective Service had its own doubts. At a hearing on the bill to exempt fathers, Hershey advised Vermont senator Warren Austin that to a layman, many of the physical and mental rejectees would be acceptable, and in some cases Selective Service would find them so later. Of particular concern for him were the psychiatric rejections "running the number one reason for rejections for whites." (For Blacks, the leading reason for rejections was inaptitude or mental deficiency, including illiteracy.) Targeting psychiatric malingering, Hershey added: "Of course ... you will get a lot of people who are going to act like the people that do break."[12]

Selective Service's Medical Division and the Army Surgeon General deplored "epidemics" of enuresis (bedwetting), epilepsy, and hypertension. "The boys go back and talk to the others. They tell them what they should do and how to get out of the service by such means as enuresis," Malcolm Farrell, assistant director in the Army Neuropsychiatric Branch, told the army committee investigating rejections in August 1943. "In one state, there was a real epidemic of epilepsy for a while," Assistant Selective Service Director Richard Eanes told the same committee. "Then the state officials started to take away the driver's license of all epileptics ... and the epidemic broke up."[13]

Selective Service officials were shocked at how many they found faked mental illness. "I can't believe," one colonel told its Directors Conference, "that 25 percent of our people are crazy.... A lot of the local boards feel that drugs have been used to produce such a situation." Many, he believed, could be saved for service if the local boards spent several days observing them before rejection.[14] But unlike the navy, the army and Selective Service did not provide for observation periods. The *Official History of Selective Service for 1943–1944* accused one man of conducting a school in New York City to teach selectees to fake mental disorders, deafness, and heart ailments. The service also charged a husband and wife with conspiring to instruct registrants by mail on how to dissemble symptoms using drugs and various physical routines.[15]

Selective Service was concerned about the adverse effect of leniency on American character. Eanes condemned psychiatrists for "coddling" young men and "encouraging [them] to look to the central Government [for] a way out of their problems."[16] A medical adviser to Hershey pointed to several well-educated graduate students in his native Baltimore rejected for psychoneuroses. Such men, he suggested in the AMA's journal *Hygeia*, could at least serve in the military in a noncombat function. Refusing to induct them encouraged evasion of responsibilities. "Our constitutional inferiors must play their part along with the rest of us," he concluded.[17] But no such plan was put into effect.

Selective Service also suspected the motives of conscientious objectors discharged on psychiatric grounds from civilian service camps. While the "peace churches" (Quakers, Mennonites, and Brethren) largely funded and operated the camps, Selective Service assigned draftees to service units and discharged them because of illness, using the army's medical criteria. By June 1944, Selective Service had discharged one thousand of the seven thousand men then in the CO camps, many on psychiatric grounds.[18] The manager of one camp believed the men had faked mental illness. The manager of another accused psychiatrists of encouraging fakery: "A good many people say you turn a psychiatrist loose in a conscientious objector camp and they will discharge all of them, and that is pretty near true." Another manager blamed the COs: "One group tried every other means, and then painted their fingernails and toenails red, and put a few flowers in their hair—and they tried to get discharged that way."[19]

Psychiatric 4Fs, veterans, and their families themselves questioned their rejections or discharges. In Oklahoma, 4Fs and their families asked the local boards every day to tell them why they had been rejected when, as far as they knew, they were physically and mentally sound.[20] In Detroit, boys became angry or broke down in tears. An army major advised psychiatrists to assign 4Fs to industrial jobs to restore their confidence in their ability to do as good a job in the war effort as those on the battlefield.[21] As to veterans at his Rhode Island psychiatric clinic, the industrial psychiatrist Temple Burling similarly noted: "They are casualties without ever having had battle experience and wonder uneasily if they may not be something like 4Fs themselves and ... one man complained that his girl would have nothing more to do with him because she regarded him the same as a 4F."[22]

Some 4Fs at psychiatric clinics expressed guilt. A forty-one-year-old man refused to accept a psychogenic interpretation for his Bell's palsy and migraine headaches because he felt ashamed of not serving and felt the rejection implied malingering. Another psychiatric 4F admitted to a case worker that "he would like to get married. However, he feels that children would feel disgraced if their father hadn't been in the Service."[23] It should be mentioned, however, that this attitude was not always prevalent. One psychiatric clinic reported that twenty neuropsychiatric 4Fs told them they were not ashamed about not participating in the war and only feared getting better, being reclassified, and being drafted.[24]

Criticism of deferments rose when Selective Service started drafting fathers in October 1942. In February 1943, the *Washington Star* reported that despite deferments for men with dependents, Long Island local boards had drafted about 30 percent of the Grumman Aircraft workforce during the past few months, many being fathers. "We couldn't honestly give assurance to a man with ten children that he wouldn't be drafted," a Grumman official told the paper.[25]

With the bloody Sicilian campaign in full swing and plans pending for the Normandy invasion, Selective Service plunged into its pool of fathers to meet monthly quotas in late 1943 and early 1944. Left with only about one million eligible after drafting nine million men, Selective Service decided to draft the four million men with dependent deferments and call up some of the five million others in essential industry, rather than take the approximately three million with physical, mental, or moral deferments. This decision fired resentment against the "privileged" 4Fs, especially the almost one million neuropsychiatric 4Fs accounting for the largest proportion of medical rejection—many with intangible disorders.[26]

Selective Service and Congress received complaints about seemingly healthy persons rejected on psychiatric grounds while fathers served. Wives and mothers wrote to North Carolina senator Robert Reynolds about neuropsychiatric youngsters mingling at drugstores and poolrooms while fathers served.[27]

According to a memorandum from the Oklahoma State Selective Service office to Richard Eanes, Oklahoma citizens complained that local boards had drafted fathers while psychiatrically rejecting healthy single men with high-paying industrial jobs. Of forty recently rejected psychiatric registrants, they had told them, sixteen were employed by the Du Pont Company at Chateau and earned between "$25 and $71 per week." "The majority admitted ... they had no desire to serve in the armed forces at $50 per month when they could draw $100 to $250 per month in war industry." Abuse of the psychiatric label was so common, the memorandum concluded, that many Oklahoma local boards decided not to draft fathers until those rejected for mental reasons had been "cleaned up."[28]

Speakers at congressional hearings on bills to draft fathers receiving nationwide media coverage similarly expressed concern that fathers would be required to serve, while seemingly normal 4Fs were allowed to stay home.[29] While Congress considered other groups that could be inducted, including occupational or physical deferments and curable cases of gonorrhea and syphilis, they were most concerned with psychoneurotic 4Fs. At the hearing on Senator Wheeler's bill, one Selective Service colonel reported that as of July 31, 1943, 875,000 of the 3,200,000 4Fs (27 percent) had been rejected for neuropsychiatric disorders. These included 297,600 for mental deficiency, or 9.3 percent; 163,700 for neurological disorders, or 5.1 percent; and 413,700 for mental disease, or 12.9 percent. The percentage for mental disease was higher than for any other subcategory of rejection. By war's end, the rejection rate for mental disease was 15.3 times higher than in World War I.[30] Anxious about the unusually large number of men in 1943 rejected for "nervous conditions," the senator maintained that many of them should be inducted to relieve the manpower crunch. When Hershey conceded to Senator Austin that many rejected on psychiatric grounds lacked serious disabilities and could have served, Austin became alarmed.[31] Other senators similarly complained about psychoneurotic 4Fs faking illness while fathers served.[32]

Throughout the hearings, the army, navy, and Selective Service pressed Congress to endorse inducting fathers instead of those deferred for medical reasons, including psychiatric. Admiral Ernest King, chief of naval operations, was certain that the navy needed all the fit men it could get and could not lower medical standards. If one man's health was below standards, he believed, he might endanger the entire team in combat.[33] On December 5, 1943, Roosevelt signed the fathers' draft act.

About the same time, a special subcommittee of the House Committee on Military Affairs began to investigate the large number of federal government employees rejected from military service on psychiatric grounds. Chaired by Congressman John M. Costello, the subcommittee reviewed case records and heard testimony from the Washington, DC, local boards, Fort Myer Induction Center, and the Army Surgeon General. When several witnesses testified that psychiatric examiners at Fort Myer had rejected many men in high federal government positions, the committee was appalled. They could not believe that such capable men were mentally ill. Though they admitted that the induction center had an unusually high rate of rejection—one out of seven on mental grounds—because of its exceptional examiners, including Overholser and Sullivan, they were concerned about the rate of psychiatric rejections nationwide and intended to investigate psychiatric records at other induction centers. Whether they did is unclear.[34]

Alarmed by the possibility of bogus medical rejections, Roosevelt and members of the Congress lobbied for mandatory service in wartime industry or the military. Representative Clare Boothe Luce (Connecticut) and others offered bills to draft 4Fs with questionable physical disorders into industrial or noncombat battalions. Senators James Wadsworth (New York) and Warren Austin (Vermont) and Roosevelt campaigned for a National (Universal) Service Act. But because of organized labor's fears that such an act would prohibit strikes, the army's fear of lowering mental and physical requirements for service, and the public's fear of "compulsory" labor as anathema to democracy, the United States, unlike England, Australia, Canada, and New Zealand, never passed a universal service act. At a time when America was fighting a war against fascism, Americans also opposed a "slave labor" bill that would prohibit the individual's right to choose where he worked and the entrepreneur's right to choose whom he hired.[35]

The importance of the proposed universal service program should not be minimized. Had it passed, the numbers placed in noncombat assignments would have been higher. The placement would have freed more able workers for military service as replacements, at a time when America was gearing up to invade mainland Europe. Rejections on psychiatric grounds would also have been lower, reducing the stigma felt by many and their problems finding civilian employment.

Criticism of Psychiatry by the Catholic Church

The Catholic Church joined the criticism of psychiatry, alleging examiners were asking intrusive questions about sex. In August 1943, an army aviator in San Antonio complained to the War Department chief of chaplains, William R. Arnold, that he was found "unfit to fly" despite passing the aviation aptitude tests after he admitted to a psychiatrist that he "had never indulged in sexual relief [despite] strong passion." Then, a second psychiatrist diagnosed him as having "signs of nervousness," discussed his sex history with him again, ordered him to lower his trousers for inspection, and sent him to the "Anthropology unit," where examiners forced him "to submit to sex pictures" and discuss sex again. The aviator maintained that psychiatrists had been questioning many others in this fashion. (This probably served several purposes: to detect homosexual proclivities, possible venereal disease, and potential general maladjustment.)

Excoriating the excessive "Freudian sex questions," Arnold referred the letter to the senior chaplain in the air force, asking him to urge the air force not to ask such questions and to revise the air force's psychiatric standards and suitability for flying section in its technical manual or there would be protests to the president and secretary of war.[36] A year later, in September 1944, Bishop John F. O'Hara, liaison between the Catholic Church and the army and later archbishop of Philadelphia, wrote Marshall that the public was complaining that "decent young soldiers who ha[d] given everything they had to their country, [were] told that . . . they are *nervous* because they are 'sex starved.'" He urged Marshall to initiate a careful, secret investigation, resulting in the "wholesale elimination of unfit practitioners."[37]

To what extent these complaints had merit is unknown. But what is known is that the top Catholic echelon was concerned. True, some leading air force psychiatrists had been trained by Freud, including Roy Grinker, known for his work with narcosynthesis in North Africa, and the air force's chief psychiatrist, John Murray, a member of the Boston Psychoanalytic Society and Institute. And all military psychiatric examinations, including the air force's, had questions about sexual activity and homosexuality. But the number of airmen who were actually subjected to such exams is unknown, and there were probably far fewer psychoanalysts in the air force than the hundred formally trained.[38] In any case, at about this time, the War Department ordered the IG to investigate psychoneuroses in the army in response to criticism from many groups. The army's chief chaplain did send Bishop O'Hara a draft copy of Grinker and Spiegel's *War Neurosis in North Africa*, the textbook most medical and psychiatric personnel used in the army, to inform him better about psychiatry. And the air force began to give every chaplain an additional two weeks of psychiatric training after completion of chaplain's school.[39]

Psychiatry and Race

The public was also concerned about bias in psychiatric treatment and examination of minorities. Charges of bias in examination of Native Americans (such as Malcolm H), as we have seen, developed even before America's entry into the war. Discrimination in the selection of African Americans was widely complained of throughout the war.

To put the matter in context, we need to look at contemporary racial attitudes and practices. It took several years for the army, Hollywood, and major Black leaders to reach sufficient consensus to produce the army's propaganda film *The Negro Soldier* (1944). While *The Negro Soldier* promoted the contributions of the Black soldier in World War II as well as appearing to favor racial toleration, critics condemned it for glossing over a rampantly segregated military and for "sugar coating . . . racial problems."[40] One million two hundred thousand Black men and women served in World War II. But they only comprised 8.4 percent of the army population, compared to 10.6 percent of the population at large.[41] America fought a war supposedly "against global injustice," but not until late 1948 did President Harry Truman sign Executive Order 9981 endorsing integration in the military. While a handful of Black officers in the army commanded Black troops, almost all commanders were white throughout the war. Most white officers had reservations about commanding Black troops, believing that Black troops did not have the ability to fight in combat. Reflecting this mindset, the War Department delayed assigning Black units to combat until very late in the war, assigning them instead, regardless of ability, to low status, support, engineering, and transportation units.[42]

At Fort Huachuca, Arizona, where the 92nd and 93rd Black infantry divisions were trained, in addition to separate officer clubs, there were two hospitals, one for Blacks with Black doctors, the other for whites with white doctors.[43] At Fort Bragg, there were all-Black wards. But the basic problem was that there just were not enough Black doctors to make all-Black wards feasible, and Eleanor Roosevelt and the NAACP grew increasingly opposed.[44] In Europe, the American army initially assigned Black nurses to treat Black patients only, but when the army found them caring for German prisoners of war because of a shortage of Black patients, the army changed its policy.[45]

Recreation and housing for Black troops was inferior to those for whites. Blacks could not live on base or in towns nearby because of segregation. At Camp Lee, in Richmond, Virginia, a theater opened for whites and Blacks, but white officers and enlisted men sat in front, while Blacks, regardless of rank, sat in the rear, behind a rope. In September 1942, Eleanor Roosevelt complained to Stimson about a Tuskegee pilot trainee who had been waiting for four months for housing facilities. One Black veteran recalled that in December 1942, Blacks were stationed in a sewage dump at Camp Claiborne, Louisiana.[46]

On May 5, 1943, Colonel William Colman, post commander at Selfridge Air Base in Michigan, for no apparent reason shot and killed his Black chauffeur, Private William McRae. Soon after, the War Department, the Army Inspector General, and the House Military Affairs Committee chaired by Congressman Paul Shafer (of Battle Creek, Michigan), all conducted investigations. Ultimately, the army air force court-martialed Colman for "careless use of weapons" and lowered his rank to captain. Assistant Secretary of War Robert Patterson privately contended much more should have been done.[47]

Executions of Black soldiers compared to whites were disproportionate. Of the ninety-six executed by the army in the European theater, 78 percent, or seventy-five, were Black. One was the father of Emmet Till, who would be lynched in Mississippi in 1955. Black soldiers constituted 8.5 percent of army strength but were accused of committing 79 percent of the capital crimes and convicted of 60 percent of the sexual offenses in Europe.[48]

Navy conditions were no better. Early in the war, no more than 2 percent of navy enlistees were Black. After a joint army-navy induction process starting February 1943, the rate rose, so that for the war in its entirety it was 5 percent. The navy segregated Blacks by occupation. Blacks worked and lived together in crowded segregated quarters. They cooked, ladled out food, served the crew, did construction, or handled ammunition. They were not assigned to combat.

Given this atmosphere, it is no surprise that one twenty-six-year-old, anticipating service, asked, "Is the kind of America I know worth fighting for?" Or that the *Pittsburgh Courier* launched a "Double V Campaign," for victory against racism at home and fascism abroad. Or that a Black lawyer stated that quite a number of Black Americans, with no personal ties to Europe, thought of it as a "white man's war."[49]

Eleanor Roosevelt; Frederick Osborn, the chief of the army's Morale Branch; Stimson; and Patterson were concerned about the state of Black morale. They tried to deal with it through more officer promotions and better housing. The Office of War Information promoted Blacks' accomplishments in athletics and culture to instill pride and motivation to fight for their country. But no one, however liberal, was able to deal with segregation.[50]

Examiners' political and racial biases influenced psychiatric screening and contributed to an underrepresentation of Blacks in the military. Reflecting an interest in promoting unity between races in the military, psychiatric examiners rejected Blacks from service who opposed segregation or expressed interest in civil rights.

Unhappy with a severe shortage of Black soldiers and sailors, Paul McNutt, director of the War Manpower Commission; the Black press; and Hershey criticized the army for limiting the number of Black units. They pressed Selective Service to abandon its practice of separately calling Blacks and instead draft all men regardless of race as their numbers came due. Though numbers increased somewhat starting in 1943, Blacks never constituted their 10.6 percent of the general population in the military, largely because of rejections.[51]

In November 1943, Representative Charles E. McKenzie of Louisiana told the House of Representatives of a "deliberate attempt" to keep single Blacks out of service while drafting white fathers. He cited an editorial from the *Morehouse Enterprise*, a Black newspaper in Bastrop, Louisiana, which charged: "There are still 267 colored men in 1-A who have not been inducted—simply because there has been no 'colored call' for them [although white husbands are being drafted]. Simply because the Government doesn't seem to want Negroes in the armed forces is no excuse.... It is race discrimination and colored men of Morehouse Parish feel that it is putting them in an inferior classification."

About the same time, Representative A. Leonard Allen of Winnfield, Louisiana, telegrammed Assistant Secretary of War Patterson about the unusually high percentage of Blacks being rejected on mental grounds. The secretary responded: "These [mental] standards are as low as the ability of men to perform the duties of a soldier."[52]

The NAACP decried the high rate of psychiatric rejection, reporting that no Blacks served on local draft boards in twenty-nine cities in seventeen states. In Oklahoma City, Black doctors only examined Black registrants. The NAACP maintained that the all-white boards rejected a higher percentage of Blacks than racially mixed boards,[53] a position also held by the National Medical Association (NMA), the leading organization of Black doctors and dentists, since the AMA was segregated. To offset criticism from the NMA's journal that draft boards in the nation's capital unfairly rejected Blacks because of a lack of Black doctors, Franklin Delano Roosevelt appointed five Black dentists and twenty-eight Black physicians to the all-Black examining board at Freedman's Hospital, Howard University, Washington, DC. But the regional army induction center subsequently rejected an additional 30 percent, mainly for mental deficiency.[54]

In mid-1943, Navy Chief Psychiatrist Francis Braceland decried the inordinate rate of psychiatric rejections of Black trainees at camps in Norfolk and Williamsburg, Virginia, especially of "colored mess attendants" in Norfolk. Stressing the urgent need for manpower, he called for a careful, thorough, practical examination before rejecting anyone. Yet, commanders at other navy training stations, such as Great Lakes, Illinois, saw things differently. One officer there accused the Mississippi induction station of sending them "unqualified Negroes," since 121 of the 360 Black recruits, mainly from Mississippi, needed to be discharged, seventy-eight for being mentally defective. The "added labor," he wrote, of "sorting out the masses of mental defective and inadequate Negroes makes it impossible to do justice to other recruits."[55]

The National Conference of Negro Educators advised Selective Service of bias in local board psychological testing. This criticism indirectly referred to psychiatric screening, because, according to Overholser, psychiatrists sometimes automatically added a rejection for inadequate personality to one for mental deficiency.[56] The conference admitted that in some cases Blacks pretended they were slow because they did not want to serve in an army that segregated and treated them poorly. But conference members stressed that many rejections stemmed from biased white psychologists who mistook reticence for dullness. The educators called on Selective Service to use Black psychologists instead, but Patterson in the War Department insisted that rejection rates were not that high and did not reflect any lack of objectivity.

Even the written aptitude tests were not without racial problems. In making assignments based on aptitude, psychologists used the Army General Classification Test (AGCT) throughout the war. That test measured inherent intelligence, occupational experience, and ability to learn. It included five categories, differentiated by number of points. Class I had the highest scores: 130 or above; II: 110 to 129; III: 90 to 110; IV: 70 to 89; and V: 69 or less. Classes I or II were likely to be assigned to the elite army air force. Blacks often received scores of IV or V and were largely relegated to service units. Part of this situation reflected poor education rather than aptitude. After the war, social scientists at Columbia University reported that almost a third of the Blacks rejected from service had been rejected largely because of poor education.[57] But regardless of cause, given a choice between an illiterate white and an illiterate Black soldier, the War Department was more likely to favor the white. While the Conference of Negro Educators decried the bias of white psychologists, the military hierarchy had no problem with it. Stimson supported a navy psychiatrist who found that Tennessee hillbillies who did not even know what countries were at war could become good soldiers given their "peculiar philosophy of life and psychological reactions." The same conclusion was not reached about poorly educated Blacks.[58]

As early as October 1942, Colonel Michael Eanes of the Army Medical Corps complained that psychiatrists at Governor's Island, New York, were rejecting Black men who said they opposed segregation in the armed forces.

A Black registrant, Eanes wrote, told him "he did not bring the subject up, but the psychiatrist asked him about it and persuaded him to speak freely on it and when he did speak freely, he received a IV-F classification." "Several local board members," Eanes said, "complained to [him about] their registrants [being rejected] for the same reason." Finding "far-fetched" the belief of psychiatrists that a "Negro" was "not mentally suited for . . . service" because of "resentment of discrimination," he said, "We are having enough trouble with real disabilities without having [this prejudice] . . . handicap[ping] . . . efforts to meet our calls in the various states."[59] In the *American Journal of Psychiatry* (1947), the Black psychiatrist Rutherford Stevens recalled that many Blacks were rejected by psychiatrists when they expressed their feelings about segregation.[60]

One of the most prominent Black men rejected for opposing segregation was the novelist Richard Wright, author of *Native Son*, published in March 1940 and circulated as a Book of the Month Club selection. In September 1941, Selective Service classified Wright 3-A, because Wright had a wife and mother who were considered dependents. In July 1942, Selective Service switched Wright's classification to 1-A, even though by then he had a wife and child. Upset that Selective Service was discriminating against him (at that time the law authorizing a fathers' draft had not yet been enacted), Wright contacted a friend, who appealed to Eleanor Roosevelt. Possibly thanks to the friend's letter, Selective Service returned Wright's classification to 3-A in October 1942, a classification he held until January 1944, when his Brooklyn draft board called him for service. This time, Wright wrote a vehement denunciation of racial segregation on his Selective Service registration form, as follows:

> The segregated units and quarters for Negroes in the armed forces violate my instincts and feelings to the degree that . . . to serve in our armed forces is to fight in defense of such a system and to give my approval to it. . . . I shall therefore render military service passively, obeying all orders automatically, strictly observing the letter of the law and obeying all demands made upon me, yet fervently hoping that any military action in which I shall be engaged and which shall extend this loathesome system of racial hate and segregation will fail, even though I shall fall before the fire of the enemy in such engagements.[61]

A week later, Wright received a 4-F classification. According to Wright's FBI file, No. 100-41674, the reason Selective Service gave was: "psychoneurosis, severe psychiatric rejection, referred to Local Board for further investigation and social investigation." The FBI agent concluded:

> It appeared from Subject's contacts with his Local Board that his interest in the problem of the Negro has become almost an obsession.... He apparently overlooks the fact that his own rise to success refutes many of his own statements regarding the impossibility of the Negro's improving his personal position.[62]

But this did not mean that other Blacks did not suffer from discrimination, as Wright was well aware. As for Wright, it was not his first wartime rejection. The previous October 1942, the Office of War Information had denied his application for a position as a public relations officer or army newspaper reporter. Although he also passed the written Volunteer Officer Entry Test and an accompanying physical, the army denied his application for that as well without any written explanation. These denials may well have occurred because Wright was considered to be a communist and had delivered a speech before the American Writer's Congress on June 6, 1941, published in *New Masses*, opposing Blacks fighting "a racist war in a segregated army." But while the Communist Party in the United States switched to wholeheartedly supporting America's entry into the war immediately after Germany's invasion of Russia in June 1941, Wright remained openly hostile to Blacks' participation in the war because of segregation.[63]

Other psychiatrists, according to Blacks, rejected them for fear they might incite riot in service. After the Detroit riot in 1943, the city's Black leaders complained that the rate of psychiatric rejection for Blacks rose.[64] In the *Autobiography of Malcolm X*, Malcolm recalled how in his hipster days, he exploited the induction board's discrimination against the Black rebel to avoid the draft: He spread the word in Harlem that he wanted to join the Japanese army, then donned a "wild zoot suit ... wore yellow knob-toe shoes ... frizzled [his] hair up into a reddish bush of conk." When he finally got to see the psychiatrist at induction, he quickly whispered to him: "Daddy-o, now you and me, we're from the North here, so don't you tell nobody ... I want to get sent down South.... Organize them nigger soldiers, you dig? Steal us some guns and kill up crackers!" Malcolm X concluded: "He stared at me as if I were a snake's egg hatching, fumbled for his red pencil.... A 4F card came to me in the mail."[65] A subsequent FBI report contained his official medical reason for disqualification: "psychopathic personality inadequate, sexual perversion, psychiatric rejection."[66]

Sensitive to possible inequities and eager to reach its induction targets, Selective Service conceded psychiatric bias against Blacks. Colonel Richard Eanes told the army committee of psychiatrists investigating rejection rates at induction: "Where psychiatry has failed has been in the fact that the psychiatrist and the registrant are not talking the same language and have not met on the same ground. Put a man trained in New England down in Arkansas, and he does not even understand the same words. The psychiatrists and psychologists do not understand the people down there—the sharecroppers and negroes."[67]

Georgia's state director for Selective Service wrote to national headquarters in June 1943: "The rejection rate is exceedingly high, and it is very difficult for Georgia to fill calls for Negroes—[the local boards] simply do not want them. For a long while they rejected the Negroes for urethritis [a venereal disease] and when we kicked so much about that they switched to inadequate personality, we kicked so much about that, and they switched to psychoneuroses." Attached to this letter was a memorandum emphasizing that another forty-four state directors "shared the same sentiment." The following November 1943, the director again complained. This time, he wrote the State Directors' Conference of Selective Service that five out of six persons rejected for mental reasons in Georgia were Negroes. "When they get back," he said, "they feel they have a license to loaf."[68]

The high rate of neuropsychiatric rejection for Blacks was indeed partly attributable to the association of mental inferiority with venereal disease, the rate of VD being higher for Blacks than whites, and the common belief that Blacks were less intelligent than whites and more likely to have a criminal bent and be promiscuous, leading to VD. Writing to Patterson, one Louisiana congressman requested that the military give Blacks who have "social diseases" proper medical treatment so their rejection rate would go down. Patterson replied that it would be done once additional medical facilities were constructed, meaning segregated ones.[69] In some cases, the military accepted Blacks even when they had VD, but they were provided with fewer days of hospitalization than whites. The Virginia deputy director of Selective Service wrote that the rate of rejection on mental grounds for Blacks could be lowered if Local Board No. 1, Hanover County, could present to the medical advisory board "some special, non-syphilitic Negro registrants who have been rejected and who the local board feels are mentally qualified."[70] According to Selective Service's chief medical officer, the rate of rejection on mental grounds was higher for Blacks than whites, especially in the eighteen- and nineteen-year-old group, partly because of educational deficiency, positive syphilis tests, psychopathic personality, and sexual psychopathy.[71] (It is a sad commentary that the prejudice of the era about Blacks and VD enabled the notorious Tuskegee Syphilis Study, conducted by the Public Health Service from 1932 to 1972, which failed to notify Black subjects who had syphilis of the specific diagnosis and, under the guise of treatment, gave them placebos or toxic medicine, leading to unfortunate deaths.)[72]

Army colonel Robert H. Owens's investigation of psychological procedures at induction centers nationwide found that rejection rates for Blacks for inadequate personality and mental deficiency were particularly high in Arkansas, because examiners were bending over backward to find Blacks mentally deficient. Since most Blacks did not attend a certified high school, the induction board examiner immediately classified them "illiterate." This meant that almost every Black had to pass a special psychological test that whites did not take. The Little Rock board also required that every person without a proper school record take the special test, since most of their schools, even when certified, did not maintain records or had poorly filled-out forms. When Owens investigated the Little Rock board, he found only two of nineteen Black registrants could produce adequate records.

Owens also found the psychiatric portion of the Little Rock induction procedures tilted against Blacks. Since the Little Rock board assumed "the Negro did not feel ... he had any part in this fight as it was not his fight and he had nothing for which to fight," the board was quick to classify Black inductees as malingerers. To this board, the term "malingerer" implied the possibility of emotional or mental problems, which might make the individual unacceptable. Therefore, the board gave each "malingerer" additional psychological tests and another psychiatric examination and from the group examined rejected even more. Not surprisingly, Owens found that in June 1943, 49 percent of Black registrants at the Little Rock induction station were rejected for psychological defects, compared to 13 percent of whites. Since the board also gave every person who failed the psychological examination the tag "inadequate personality," the psychiatric rate of rejection for Blacks was also exceedingly high.[73]

Blacks charged that the army used psychoneurotic discharges to flush out dissident Black officers. Writing to Roosevelt in February 1945 about the all-Black 93rd Division in Bougainville, Walter White of the NAACP asserted: "Another harmful practice, which steps are being taken to correct, has been the transferring out of the division [of] competent Negro officers when they expressed disagreement with anti-Negro practices or policies. In some instances, attempts were made to declare such men psychoneurotics."[74]

Twenty-six psychiatrists on the Selective Service Central Examining Board for Neurology and Psychiatry (known as the CEB) reported differences in decisions on rejections influenced by racial bias. For example, the psychoanalyst Ernest E. Hadley, who had worked closely with Sullivan on screening in 1941 and 1942, recalled that "poor cultural occupation and educational backgrounds, often made it difficult to decide whether [the Black registrant] was defective, pre-schizoid or just colored." In one case, two examiners considered an arrest record too minor to reject a Black registrant, but when a third found the man "unusually troublesome," they deferred to his decision and rejected him. In another case, an examiner wanted to reject a Black registrant for sounding "manic." In a third, a psychiatrist found a draftee acceptable given his work history, but two other doctors favored rejection, since he would have to "serve with Negro troops" and as a "Negro he might [not] qualify for limited service." A Black registrant with a tenth-grade education, religious, and with a "nervous stomach" was also rejected while a white registrant with the same qualities was accepted into service.[75]

Once in service, prejudice persisted. Statistics released after the war disclosed that Blacks had a much higher percentage of discharge for inaptitude and undesirable character, while whites had a higher percentage of psychoneuroses.[76] Indeed, it was estimated that Blacks accounted for 22 percent of the Section VIII blue discharges without honor, benefits, or hospitalization, when Blacks comprised 8.4 percent of the soldiers.[77]

In late 1944, the War Department approved clinical psychologists to work in neuropsychiatric sections of army hospitals. But while quite a few qualified Black candidates applied, the army only commissioned one, placing him not in a hospital but in the officers' pool, where his skills were not utilized. Clearly, the lack of Black clinical psychologists affected the treatment of Blacks in hospitals and their classification.[78]

Other Groups Experiencing Discrimination

Other groups also complained of psychiatric discrimination. In March 1943, the American Legion appealed "J. L. H.'s" psychiatric discharge on grounds that the navy discriminated against him because he was an "Okie." According to the American Legion, J. L. H. had served in the navy for over a year when he was admitted to the United States Naval Hospital, Pearl Harbor, where he was "routinely examined by a psychiatrist," who wrote: "This is a typical 'Okie.' He is probably too lazy to get up and go to the head. He does not like sea duty and wants to be a hospital corpsman. Says his 'stomach trouble' is okay now, since being on a diet. . . . He is an inadequate boy but should be tried at duty as he is capable." Obviously, the American Legion said, this diagnosis was unfair and "obnoxious to we 'Oklahomans,'" claiming the psychiatrist was too much influenced by John Steinbeck's *The Grapes of Wrath*, "which we in Oklahoma do not appreciate." A few days later, the assistant chief of the Navy Bureau of Medicine and Surgery apologized for J. L. H.'s rejection, "calling it "unfortunate" and "unusual."[79]

In a similar vein, a training camp psychiatrist told the army's Special Committee Investigating Psychiatric Rejections that "mountain men" were complaining about bias in psychological rejections. However, he contended that the "men from the southern mountains [have] a high degree of illiteracy and feeblemindedness." When their psychological rejections went up, he continued, "the boards and the politicians start questioning it" and changing the classification. For example, he wrote "class 1-A was changed [so] that men of 'marginal intelligence,' if compensated for by better than average stability were ... acceptable for ... military service."[80]

Psychiatric 4Fs and veterans coming home complained of problems getting jobs despite a full-employment economy. Even individuals from well-to-do families suffered. One socially prominent father complained to the Payne Whitney psychiatrist Thomas Rennie that the doctor's assessment of his son's emotional problems had led to the army induction board's rejecting him, resulting in over a year of unemployment. Only after Rennie interceded with a second letter certifying the son's fitness for civilian defense work did the son get a job, and even then only with a family friend.[81]

Psychiatric veterans and 4Fs from less influential families fared worse. Throughout Virginia, Blacks rejected for mental disabilities complained to local boards that employers refused to hire them.[82] According to G-1 (the army deputy chief of staff for personnel), by 1943, hundreds of unemployed veterans had appealed to his office to have the reasons for their discharge changed so they could get employed.[83] Similar reports came from the Illinois Department of Public Health and Welfare and Washington State.[84] Referring to complaints throughout the country, the director of the American Legion informed the Army Surgeon General that a man rejected by an induction board for "psychoneurosis" has great difficulty securing employment.[85]

Moreover, an Army Surgeon General study of 4,178 psychoneurotic veterans randomly selected throughout the country who were discharged between May 1943 and January 1944 and out for at least six months revealed that 94 percent had jobs before induction but only 86 percent afterward, in a better economy. Conducted by William Menninger and Fort Bragg's psychiatry chief, Norman Brill, the study cited a quarter of employed veterans and half unemployed, connecting problems getting employed with diagnoses. Such statements as "too nervous," "medical discharge," and "limitation of work capacity" had deleterious effects.[86]

Soon, however, psychiatrists would attempt to resolve some of these criticisms.

6 The Response of Psychiatrists

Responding to criticism, psychiatrists sought to legitimate their screening role. They participated in army, presidential, and congressional investigations of psychiatric screening. They designed new written personality tests. They inaugurated a nationwide program that gathered welfare, school, and criminal records for each registrant to improve the accuracy of their diagnoses. Sadly, however, the inability to prevent psychiatric casualties persisted.

Why, when faced with much public criticism and numerous technical obstacles, did psychiatrists not shift their focus to prevention and treatment instead? Some would attribute it to inertia and the fact that once a decision was made and money expended it was hard to reverse course. Yet, more than that, it was the hubris of certain members of the profession, their faith in their ability to predict human conduct, their belief that if only more records could be found and better tests developed, then screening would succeed and psychiatric casualties decline. The unavailability of timely hospital statistics and the lack of personal combat experience among leaders in civilian psychiatry enabled this wishful thinking to persist. While a few psychiatrists in North Africa treated soldiers at the front from late 1942 onward, 95 percent of army psychiatrists were not sent to the field until at least December 1943 and thus knew little about the war's devastating impact.[1]

Ensuring the Confidentiality of Psychiatric Records

Rather than fundamentally refocusing their role in the war, leading psychiatrists initially tried to cover up the problem by preventing 4Fs and dischargees from seeing their medical records. Initially, Section 8a of the Selective Training and Service Act (September 1940) permitted 4Fs and veterans access to their medical records. But as early as January 1941, psychiatrists proposed eliminating Section 8a at meetings of the National Academy of Sciences, National Research Council (NRC) Committee on Neuropsychiatry. Among the most active critics of Section 8a was the chair, Winfred Overholser, and the well-known Adolf Meyer.[2] A month later, William Porter, an army psychiatrist, informed the NRC Neurology Subcommittee that local social service agencies were resisting providing important records about registrants to Selective Service because of the provisions in 8a. About the same time, the psychoanalyst Karl Menninger and other psychiatrists in Kansas started calling for the use of numerical codes instead of named diagnoses because "reports are rather unpleasant reading to the individual concerned."[3] In March and April 1942, the NRC Committee on Neuropsychiatry went a step further, lobbying Congress to repeal Section 8a altogether. Representing the committee, Overholser, who was then superintendent of St. Elizabeth's Hospital, called for a return to the traditional confidential doctor-patient relationship, which prohibited psychiatric patients from seeing their records, out of concern that their health might be endangered, even to the point of suicide. In addition, he believed that closing military and Selective Service medical records would alleviate community or family disapproval of the screening program and discourage employers from discriminating against psychiatric 4Fs or those rejected for syphilis, silicosis, or inactive tuberculosis.

Accepting these arguments, Congress amended 8a in July 1942 to state that any person serving in the armed forces or rejected at induction could receive a copy of his medical record upon written request, but only provided "that such statement shall not contain any reference to mental or other conditions which in the judgment of the Secretary of War or the Secretary of Navy would prove injurious to the physical or mental health of the person to whom it pertains."[4] While this amendment closed psychiatric records to most registrants and servicemen, it did not totally resolve the problem of stigma. At times Selective Service, while not telling the individual, still provided employers with records of neuropsychiatric 4Fs. In any case, an employer could usually surmise a psychiatric rejection or discharge from the job candidate's silence or a blank space on a military or Selective Service medical report.[5]

Army and Presidential Investigations during Debate on the Fathers' Draft

Another strategy employed to offset criticism was to appoint blue-ribbon commissions to investigate. In response to public outcry during congressional debate on the fathers' draft that persons with dubious psychiatric disorders were being rejected while fathers had to serve, the War Department during the summer of 1943 appointed a special committee of leading psychiatrists to study the issue. Led by the ubiquitous Overholser, the committee included Edward Strecker and Roy Halloran, chief of the army psychiatry branch. The committee confirmed the contention of the army surgeon general that psychiatrists not only had validly rejected 4Fs but that more, not less, screening needed to be done at army induction centers and local boards.[6] After observing examinations at thirty-five army induction stations, the committee concluded: "In no case did [we] find that individuals were excluded without good reasons." Nor was there evidence of malingering "in any considerable degree." Instead, "The psychiatric rejection rate, far from being too high is actually lower than is warranted."[7] This conclusion was reached by the committee even though by July 1943 psychiatric veterans accounted for almost half of the army's medical discharges.[8]

Reviewing figures from Veterans Affairs, the committee also reported that 34 percent of total admissions to VA hospitals from December 1941 through July 1943 were mental cases, the majority found to have had conditions incurred before service, which could have been detected and eliminated before induction. Likewise, training camp psychiatrists reported to the committee that many trainees had emotional problems incurred before service, which should have been eliminated at induction stations.[9] Noting that some induction stations had no psychiatrists at all while in others psychiatrists carried a daily load of three hundred or more, the committee recommended assigning psychiatrists to each induction station, lowering loads to fifty examinees per day, using social histories "in doubtful cases," and employing such diagnostic tools as the electroencephalograph (lie detector).[10]

On December 5, 1943, the president signed the fathers' draft. In exchange for Congress's agreeing to eliminate a provision exempting pre–Pearl Harbor fathers, Roosevelt agreed to name yet another commission of physicians to review the requirements for admission to the army, navy, and marine corps. This time, the commission included Navy Surgeon General Ross T. McIntire, Dr. Strecker, and Army Surgeon General Norman Kirk.[11] Though Senator Burton Wheeler and others in Congress had hoped its review of medical standards would restore at least 500,000 4Fs to service and stall the induction of fathers, in March 1944 the study concluded otherwise. Like the investigation by the War Department's special committee, the president's commission found that examiners had not erroneously rejected 4Fs. Indeed, army and navy standards of admission, including psychiatric standards, could not be compromised. Three months before D-Day, which military leaders knew would necessitate immense manpower, the commission, like its War Department predecessor, called for more rejections and better social history and testing methods.[12]

These investigatory bodies came to their unpopular conclusions for several reasons. First, the army SG believed that 4Fs and discharged veterans were not in fact malingerers and that an investigation would demonstrate to the public the seriousness of the psychiatric problem.[13] Second, doctors on the two investigations relied almost exclusively on interviews with other doctors and government officials who felt the same way. Besides interviewing army and navy directors of personnel and army induction center and training camp psychiatrists, they spoke to VA Director Frank Hines and Paul McNutt of the War Manpower Commission, both early screening advocates. Third, they continued to believe in their predictive expertise and were averse to considering contrary views.

When, for example, John Appel, liaison between the Army Neuropsychiatric Consultants Branch and Osborn's Army Morale Branch, at the August 31 meeting of the special committee questioned whether it was really the "predisposed" who were breaking down in combat or in actuality "normal" men, making it almost impossible to screen the vulnerable, the committee disregarded his skepticism. When Richard Eanes, Selective Service assistant director, questioned the validity of psychiatric rejections and suggested that men be allowed "to try to serve" instead of being "coddled" by the government, the committee called Eanes's opinions "at great variance with the officially accepted principles of the Army and of Selective Service" and asked for his resignation in their letter the following month to Surgeon General Kirk.[14] As to the congressmen who had required a presidential commission as part of the fathers' draft bill and who could have influenced the outcome of its investigation, they ultimately deferred to the experts. The *Washington Star* reported on December 30, 1943, that while "members of the Congress ... wanted to see ... physical standards lowered to tap the pool of more than 3,000,000 4Fs ... they believed they weren't qualified to change standards themselves."[15]

Improving Screening through the Medical Survey Program

Responding to criticism of screening, psychiatrists also championed a nationwide Selective Service social history program, the Medical Survey Program (MSP), which took effect in October 1943.

Well before that date mental hygiene divisions in Connecticut, New York, New Jersey, and Pennsylvania had maintained indices of registrants previously hospitalized in mental institutions, in prisons, or on relief.[16] But a national program proved problematic since local social service agencies and juvenile courts resisted providing written records because of Section 8a.

Back in 1941, before the United States entered the war, Sullivan and Lawrence Kolb successfully petitioned the federal government for over $3 million for a "WPA Information Service of Defense Agencies." They used the funds to hire social workers and WPA clerks to gather school, court, and social service records. The NRC Committee on Neuropsychiatry, the American Psychiatric Association (APA), and the National Committee for Mental Hygiene (NCMH) recognized that more needed to be done. Putting it bluntly, the Army Planning Council maintained that without a nationwide program, registrants "were not going to disclose these black spots in their lives if they [could] help it."[17] After Congress enacted the draft of eighteen-year-olds at the end of 1942, Overholser became particularly interested in using school and employment records to ensure candidates' maturity.[18] Since local board examinations barely existed by late 1942, Selective Service's administering a nationwide social history program would revitalize Selective Service's role.

Perhaps the MSP's most ardent advocate was George Stevenson, the NCMH's head and a leader in the child guidance movement in the 1920s and 1930s, which had examined children in juvenile psychiatric clinics and given advice on education for children. In 1943, he and a team of private social workers reviewed the records of some army training camp soldiers. The records confirmed that a substantial proportion had a preinduction history of maladjustment. The study persuaded Alan Gregg, a Rockefeller Foundation psychiatrist, to fund an NCMH program coordinating the gathering of Selective Service social history data from thirty-three states, leading to the establishment of the Medical Survey Program, an ambitious undertaking, especially given the absence of computers or the internet.[19]

Secretary of War Stimson also called for a nationwide social history program. Struck by the horrendous psychiatric casualties at Guadalcanal, he complained to Selective Service Director General Lewis Hershey and War Manpower Commissioner Paul McNutt that inadequate Selective Service data had allowed numerous epileptics, alcoholics, criminals, and severely maladjusted to enter service. Responding to Stimson's letter, Colonel Lewis Renfrow of Selective Service initially proposed expanding the existing social history program and later helped design the MSP.[20]

What directly triggered the MSP's inauguration was the rising outcry as psychiatric rejections approached one million by the end of 1943. William Menninger, chief of the Army Neuropsychiatric Consultants Division, urged Selective Service to establish the program to locate all evidence of positive adjustment, enabling all capable men to serve. Probably referring to the virtual demise of the local board examination, Menninger wrote Strecker: "You know my feeling that psychiatry had nearly missed the boat in the Army. I want in every possible way to keep ourselves from getting any more of a black eye... [The Medical Survey Program would] do a tremendous service to the whole social situation throughout the country."[21]

Hershey appointed Raymond Waggoner around July 1943 to coordinate the program. Waggoner came to Selective Service almost by chance. After hearing Sullivan suggest at a seminar in Washington, DC, that a general practitioner could give a local board psychiatric examination after a mere two-week course, Waggoner wrote Selective Service Medical Chief Leonard Rowntree in January 1941 that it was almost impossible "for psychiatrists to adequately screen inductees let alone a general practitioner with two weeks psychiatric information. . . . This sort of thing would result in a lot of babies being thrown out with the bathwater." Waggoner further cautioned that "Medical Circular No. 1 might well exclude . . . many men who would be adequate or even exceptional soldiers."[22] Two and a half years later, Hershey, who must have been given the letter from Rowntree, recalled it and asked Waggoner to come to Washington and submit a proposal for a medical survey program. After examining his proposal, he appointed him head of the Selective Service Psychiatric Division.[23]

As formulated by Waggoner in Selective Service's Medical Circular No. 4, the MSP responded to public and psychiatric demands. To satisfy the public, it promised to use social histories "to accept those registrants whose previous medical . . . histories indicate their ability to adjust . . . including [the] borderline." To meet psychiatric demands, it sought to "reject those . . . whose condition positively indicates physical or mental breakdown or failure to adjust . . . [to] military service."[24] In practice, the program satisfied psychiatrists more than the public. In searching through more records, psychiatrists often found new evidence of deviance, leading to more rejections and creating more complaints of bias and invasion of privacy.

The MSP extended the government's ability to gather personal information on private individuals. In theory, a medical field agent (a local board social worker) would ensure that several forms were filled out for each registrant: a medical history by the social worker, an identity verification and education verification by the registrant, and a cooperative school report by five secondary school teachers. According to the minister Luther Woodward, who was also a social work adviser to Selective Service, field agents not only used records from state welfare exchanges but also interviewed registrants and their families, employers, physicians, law enforcement officers, and hospital staff. They reviewed the records of individuals previously committed or about to be committed to mental institutions, prisons, reformatories, or tuberculosis sanitariums. Some states accessed WPA, CCC, and National Youth Administration (NYA) records. By war's end, every state, plus Alaska, Hawaii, and Puerto Rico, had an MSP. Over nine thousand medical field agents investigated records of as many as three million registrants during the war at a cost over $1,000,000.²⁵ (Based on the Consumer Price Index calculator's assumption of a certain inflation rate, the $1 million in 1943 is equivalent to $15,410,000.)²⁶

The program greatly extended the government's reach into individuals' private affairs. What previously had been considered nobody's business, least of all the federal government's, under the aegis of medicine became part of Selective Service's standard inquiry. In addition to questions about alcoholism, addiction, or commitment to a mental institution, the medical field agent looked for "repeated marital or domestic difficulties with the family" and "excessive shyness, seclusiveness, [and] vagrancy." Besides noting obvious disorders such as epilepsy and severe head or spinal injuries, the field agents reported psychosomatic disorders such as asthma, ulcers, and behavioral problems such as bedwetting and sleepwalking. The field rep was supposed to obtain reports from five high school teachers about the former pupil's "seclusive," "moody," "suspicious," "indecisive," "effeminate," "deceptive," "nervous," "immature," or unsociable character, extending Medical Circular No. 1's existing focus on interpersonal relations.²⁷

The MSP drew much criticism. Registrants and their families complained about its criteria for rejection and invasion of their privacy. Though inductees waiting for psychiatric examinations were instructed not to look at their records, they sometimes managed to see their files anyway. At the Louisville, Kentucky, induction station, registrants not only discussed one another's records, but the examining psychiatrist also confronted them with details, subjecting them to an embarrassing and sometimes emotionally charged interview. One registrant complained that the psychiatrist had asked him in a rude and critical tone why his mother and father were separated so frequently. When a mother of another registrant learned that the same psychiatrist had asked her son: "Why can't you get along with your brother? What's wrong with you?" she told the local board the psychiatrist and social worker had no business interfering with their personal affairs and embarrassing her son in the presence of unspecified others. Other registrants appealed diagnoses on their medical social history forms. One already accepted registrant complained that his report did not contain all the information regarding his health condition.²⁸

Complaints of bias in rejections arose, including one from a Missouri family who read this Selective Service report:

> This nineteen-year-old boy is a member of a large family of farmers living in a rural community and known to be clannish, having immigrated to this state

from the mountains of Tennessee. They are a family known to be very proud and sensitive, a little hard to get along with, inclined to drinking and several of the younger generation are classified as "wild." Two members of the family are known to have been patients in a state institution for the care of mental diseases. When the term "family" is used it means not only the registrant's father and brothers but his uncles, cousins, grandparents etc. The registrant is known to be a little "wild" and occasionally gets drunk.[29]

According to Missouri's Selective Service director, after reading the report, "ten of the registrant's brothers, cousins, and male kinsmen" came to the little town of Fredericktown, threatening to sue the medical field agent. When the town's lawyers refused to take the case, the family told the local board's field agent that they "would feel disgraced if the registrant [was] not accepted" and "afflictions or misconduct on the part of relatives should not reflect on the registrant." After being contacted by the Selective Service director, the induction station reexamined the registrant and admitted him to the army.[30]

Sensitive to popular criticism, Bureau of the Budget Director Harold Smith made several recommendations before funding the MSP's continuance in July 1944. To ensure registrants did not see their forms, he suggested that the survey be "put in a separate file" away from the registrant's nonpsychiatric file, which he was entitled to see. This policy had been suggested in Medical Circular No. 4 but rarely used. At the same time, Smith recognized a registrant's right to know if Selective Service had interviewed anyone about him, except for "strictly confidential inquiries" of trustworthy sources. To further protect the individual's rights, he emphasized that individuals should be rejected only if hospital records of commitment specifically contained a diagnosis of mental disease.[31] These changes, however, may not have been implemented, because Overholser, Menninger, and Navy Chief Psychiatrist Francis Braceland objected. They saw the disclosure of the contents of interviews as against the intent of the MSP.[32]

While both Halloran and Menninger believed that using the MSP to locate favorable information was just as important as using it to find the unfavorable,[33] the program's questions and the predilections of psychiatrists often led them to ignore positive attributes. "Certain questions in Circular No. 4 might be misinterpreted and keep good material out of the army," Strecker warned Waggoner. "Too often [psychiatrists] will interpret [questions] literally and [reject registrants unnecessarily]," a complaint also raised by Selective Service in North and South Dakota. A month before D-Day, the Selective Service social work adviser Luther Woodward disclosed that the pressure to process so many men for service in such a short time had given examiners only time to read very brief histories and send psychiatrists histories with blatant pathologies. It was, he said, "somewhat regrettable" that histories with evidence of good work, good health, and social adjustment, which would have led to borderline cases being accepted, were being ignored.[34]

Information on the forms could be inaccurate or distorted. As early as September 1943, Colonel Robert Owens, originator of the MSP's educational records system, warned Selective Service: "Few people know . . . that certain records in school do not mean failure in life. Truancy, etc., does not determine that a student is emotionally unstable."[35] Nevertheless, teachers made destructive snap judgments. "It was not uncommon to receive a school form with a notation 'I don't think John would make a good soldier,'" Waggoner recalled. In fairness to the teachers, the forms' questions about misbehavior, truancy, and personal idiosyncrasies may have encouraged snap evaluations.[36] Whatever the reason, Strecker was concerned. Writing to Smith in February 1944, he called for more careful location by social workers of authentic information, in an effort to reduce public resentment. Two months later, Smith called for the discontinuance of reports from teachers.[37]

Not surprisingly, while few statistical studies compared the number of rejections with and without social histories, those that did indicated a rising rate of rejection of borderline cases. One Louisville study revealed a rejection rate of 63 percent for eight hundred men with histories and a rate of 53 percent for eight hundred men without.[38] During 1944, when the MSP was actively in force, the rate of psychiatric rejection rose from 134 per thousand (first quarter) to 227 per thousand (last quarter), by far the highest during the war.[39]

Nor did the program reach its full potential—good or bad—because of insufficient time and personnel. According to Woodward, most social workers were reluctant to leave well-paying industrial or government jobs for volunteer employment.[40] North Carolina was reported to have no experienced social workers; Oklahoma had sizable resignations because medical field agents refused to work without pay. It took as many as fifteen days for a medical field agent to fill out the forms on one registrant, according to Selective Service. In Pennsylvania, medical field agents canvassed more than 1,500 secondary school districts to fill out the data for the Cooperative School Report alone. To make matters worse, Medical Circular No. 4 stipulated that agents should not delay induction for investigations. Consequently, in Pennsylvania and elsewhere, medical field agents frequently left forms substantially incomplete. Overloaded with forms, field agents reported men "in the pen" or in TB sanitariums who were never there, Ohio's Selective Service director told directors at a Selective Service medical conference.[41] And the registrant had no way of contesting fallacious reports, because the amended Selective Service Act prohibited him from seeing his record.

Alarmed at these deficiencies, Strecker opposed funding the program for fiscal year 1945 because it was wasteful to investigate individuals only to have army induction boards later reject them. Further, he contended, it was impossible to get all the information for all forms in the time allotted. The MSP would also be taking an already severely inadequate number of psychiatrists away from their essential task of examining registrants. If the program were to continue, he concluded, Selective Service must lower the number of forms from four to one and stop investigations as soon as agents reported a previous commitment to a mental institution.[42]

Others questioned the program's capacity for data collection. Even Menninger, one of the program's advocates, admitted it was "a kind of social revolution [and] very few states in the United States [have] a central register to keep track of . . . individuals who had been in insane institutions or had difficulty in the courts. . . . So trying to get such states as Alabama or Indiana . . . to inaugurate such a complicated procedure . . . is going to be difficult."[43] In addition, only literate registrants could fill out the identity verification form.

Even when states had records, they did not always make them available. California and Louisiana prohibited the disclosure of information about present or former welfare recipients, convicts, or inmates of insane asylums to agencies without the individual's approval. Hospitals refused to give information without the patient's consent. Yet, medical field agents sometimes subverted the rules by contacting doctors. When the Iowa Psychopathic Hospital refused to give one colonel at the Camp Dodge induction station information on an ex-patient, he contacted the doctor who had referred the case to the hospital, and the doctor told him the man had dementia praecox.[44]

While agents had little trouble obtaining information on registrants in a small town where everybody knew one another, it was harder and more expensive in a large, anonymous city. The New York State Mental Hygiene Division refused to clear New York City registrants through its files. The city's welfare agencies, courts, hospitals, and prisons released information reluctantly. The city's Selective Service had a limited listing of registrants from Bellevue or Kings County Hospitals' psychiatric divisions. The cost for even this limited program came to well over $30,000 per year.[45] After inflation, the value as of 2021, according to the Consumer Price Index, would be

$462,380.⁴⁶ Though Chicago's social history effort proved more successful, Boston faced the same problems as New York. Wisconsin too reported greater difficulty getting criminal offense data from cities than from isolated rural areas. In Mississippi, where a large proportion of the population had little formal schooling, school records provided little information.[47]

From late 1943 to late 1944, the MSP faced a shortage of funds. Though nine thousand social workers volunteered, the program still needed cash for clerical workers at courts, prisons, and social agencies. Congress eventually approved $1 million for fiscal year 1945, but the victory was not won easily.[48] Strecker, originally opposed to the program's continuance, relented only after pressure from the NRC and his increasing awareness of the military's need for manpower.[49]

Yet, as the war ended, mental health specialists pressed for the program's demise. Frederick Parsons, former head of mental hygiene under then–New York governor Roosevelt, believed psychiatrists could get equally reliable data from personal interviews, especially since most information on the medical surveys was unverified.[50] Citing complaints from social workers in Cleveland, Akron, and Seattle, Woodward questioned whether induction stations were sufficiently using MSP data to warrant its continuance. By August 1945, quite a few induction centers estimated that as few as 1 to 10 percent of forms contained relevant information. By November 1945, Selective Service concluded that the time and effort spent on the MSP outweighed its benefits.[51]

The MSP in World War II established a vast personal data-gathering apparatus. According to Menninger, it led to the compilation in several states of central listings of state mental hospital commitments and court records.[52] It also expanded the role of the social worker and popular awareness of the profession. But it did not fulfill its goal of ensuring fair rejections. If there had been more time, and if computers or the internet had existed, the program might have been more thorough and objective. But as Waggoner later commented, "the American Civil Liberties Union would [have made] a fuss about collecting that much information about individuals."[53] It is not known what happened with the data. One possibility, however, is that it provided information for Eli Ginzberg's three-volume *The Ineffective Soldier*, which contained numerous case histories and statistics from Selective Service and army records.[54]

It is likely that some MSP information was referred to the rapidly growing FBI, the House Special Committee to Investigate Un-American Activities (the Dies Committee), and elsewhere. We know from Richard Wright's nonpublic FBI file that the Dies Committee also had a file on the Black author during the war.⁵⁵ As mentioned in a previous chapter, General Lewis Hershey and Harry Stack Sullivan did refer a case of a Russian-born inductee who had reservations about the draft to the FBI as part of their general policy of referring such cases.

The MSP's intrusion into the rights and privacy of Americans reflected the large expansion of federal size and power during the war. In 1939, the executive branch employed 936,000 civil servants; by 1945, it employed more than 3.8 million, almost four times as many. America interned 120,000 Japanese, at least half American citizens. The FBI reported increasing its agent and support staff from 2,400 in 1940 to 13,000 in 1945. On December 7, 1941, Roosevelt ordered the arrest of 3,800 aliens listed in Hoover's secretive "Custodial Detention Index." Within three days, they were all arrested without incident. In addition to investigating communists, Japanese, Italians, and Germans, the FBI also sought out "draft-dodgers" and suspected spies throughout the war.⁵⁶ Clearly, within this atmosphere, information from the MSP could be valuable.

Improving Written Personality Tests

Both the army and the navy developed written personality tests, but for different reasons. Though the navy had a more rudimentary neuropsychiatric examination than the army, in other ways the navy was more selective. It had its own social history gathering program, which it continued until it adopted the MSP in September 1944, and it had a week-long observation period in training camps before discharging sailors for psychiatric reasons.⁵⁷

From 1941 on, navy psychologists and psychiatrists jointly selected manpower, utilizing the Shipley Inventory (discussed in what follows). After the joint army-navy draft starting February 1943, the navy became more rigorous in testing. By August, they refined the Shipley, and by 1944, they developed the Battle Noise Test and the Cornell Selectee Index. Prompting refinements in selection was the Navy Bureau of Medicine's belief that navy working conditions were more arduous than the army's. The bureau particularly noted cramped quarters, long periods at sea without recreation ashore, and the unpredictability of enemy attack. So sure was the bureau that its standards for psychiatric selection were tougher than the army's that the navy suggested that their training stations refer navy psychiatric dischargees to the army for assignment, a suggestion not put into effect.⁵⁸ On August 8, 1945, a day before the bombing of Nagasaki, the bureau, in its continued quest for refined selection, recommended the "completion and validation of new psychological test batteries."⁵⁹ But the war soon ended.

For its part, the army developed written tests in late 1943 for two reasons: first, to eliminate those who could not fit in or would break down in combat; and second, to assuage public criticism of excessive psychiatric rejections and discharges through fairer selection. Like the MSP, the army's tests were supposed to ensure rejection only of those with definite emotional problems. But the tests led to more rejections, including false positives.

In 1941, Carney Landis and Walter Shipley, both professors of psychology, at Columbia University and Wheaton College, respectively, designed the Shipley Inventory (or Personal Inventory) to detect "troublemakers" before entering service.[60] The inventory questioned navy volunteers on attitudes toward employers, self-esteem, making friends, and fantasies and was tested on thousands of air force and navy men; adult, juvenile, and homosexual prisoners; alcoholics; addicts; and mental patients.[61]

The navy psychiatrist Cecil L. Wittson and the psychologist William Hunt developed a revised Shipley Inventory in 1944 after trying it out on thousands of navy recruits and one hundred discharged veterans. The new test included three hundred biographical items covering, among other things, a person's education, occupation, attitudes, and behavior. For the rest of the war, it was widely used by the navy, coast guard, and merchant marine.[62]

But by far the most sophisticated navy test was the Cornell Selectee Index, currently still used worldwide. The designers had distinguished civilian backgrounds: Bela Mittelman was a well-known Cornell psychoanalyst/psychiatrist, and the neurologist Harold G. Wolff had been trained by Adolf Meyer at Phipps Clinic. Arthur Weider was a psychologist at Columbia University Medical School, and David Wechsler was chief psychologist at Bellevue Psychiatric Hospital, known for the Wechsler Intelligence Test and for routine IQ testing in World War I.[63] Developed by the navy in August 1943, the Cornell Selectee Index was based on interviews with medical students, psychiatric 4Fs, and patients with psychosomatic, psychoneurotic, and psychotic disorders. The index included questions on self-confidence, interests, decisiveness, and sexual abnormalities and had three fifteen-minute subtests. The first, derived from an earlier study of the work preferences of homosexual prisoners at Riker's Island, questioned the individual about his interest in "male" or "female" employment and determined from the answers whether the individual could accept the male social pattern. The second estimated the individual's self-esteem. The third explored symptoms of psychoneuroses or psychosomatic disorders: "Are you easily discouraged?" "Do you find it hard to forget an unpleasant experience?" "Have you ever had a headache?" Every fifth item in the subtests, plus the last six, were "stop questions," any of which if answered positively could elicit further inquiry.[64]

Reflecting the navy's increasing acknowledgment of the impact of military life on personality, the navy doctors Wittson and Hunt also designed the Battle Noise Test in 1944. The outdoor version provided a recording of a simulated aircraft attack and cruiser engagement replete with human screams and groans at "intensities of 110 decibels and higher." The examiner instructed each trainee to raise his hand every time he began to sweat, have a headache, suffer stomach upset, or feel trembling or his heart pounding. The indoor version used the same recordings but added the restricted film "Raids on Wotje, Makin, and Kwajelein Harbor," which included an attack on Japanese navy ships in Kwajelein Harbor, the destruction of Makin, the disposal of the Japanese dead, and a Japanese religious service.[65]

During the fall of 1943, the Army Research Branch, part of Osborn's I&E Division, under the direction of the sociologist Samuel Stouffer, later president of the American Sociological Association, with the request and assistance of John Appel, developed the written Neuropsychiatric Screening Adjunct (NSA) to detect psychoneuroses.[66] To formulate questions for the NSA, the branch first surveyed the attitudes of a "cross section" of thousands of infantry recruits in army training camps. (In 1949 and 1950, Princeton University Press published the results of these and other surveys conducted by Stouffer and his team in the four-volume study *Studies in Social Psychology in World War II.*)[67]

After distinguishing between the normal and abnormal responses to the survey questions, the branch developed one hundred questions for its NSA—half on childhood behavior and half on adult adjustment. The branch gave the questions to normal men in sixteen army camps and psychoneurotic patients in sixteen army hospitals throughout the United States. Because the psychoneurotic patients and normal soldiers differed most in their responses to questions about psychosomatic disorders, the branch weighted these items very heavily. Yet, the Research Branch realized that the test for civilian inductees also needed to cover psychopathic and psychotic conditions, so they added stop questions in these areas.[68] The army did not adopt the test until October 1944, so it had little impact during the war and, according to some historians, "was never employed as intended."[69]

The Army Air Force, like the navy, had psychologists and psychiatrists working together. The Eighth Army Air Force, for example, gave each air force recruit twenty written aptitude and physical tests for flying plus a three-hour qualifying examination, with a composite score ranging from one (low) to nine (high). In addition, each candidate had a brief interview with a psychiatrist to evaluate family history and possible maladjustment. Word association tests and inkblot tests were also provided; all were combined together in an Adaptability Rating for Military Aeronautics (ARMA).[70]

The army and navy tests shared several advantages. Human emotion and bias could spoil the psychiatric interview but not the standardized test or composite score. "No matter how expert a psychiatrist may be, his intuitive faculties fluctuate with fatigue, with the stress of his day's work and with his own emotional involvements," Kubie wrote in June 1944. The psychiatrist's experience with "one patient [may] carry over to another [biasing his] quick appraisal of a succession of individuals."[71] The tests also reduced the time needed for psychiatric selection. A group of twenty-five to thirty examinees could be given the same fifteen-minute paper-and-pencil test at one sitting. Each test took no more than one minute to score. A clerk with a high school education could be trained to administer the test in no more than a couple of hours; not every psychiatrist had the skill to diagnose an individual in such a short time.[72] On the other hand, army and navy psychiatrists lacked sufficient confidence in the tests to use them without giving each examinee a psychiatric interview. Thus, a main advantage of the program—quicker, more efficient selection—was not fully realized.[73]

While psychiatrists hoped the tests would improve accuracy in detection, the tests were generally less accurate than face-to-face examinations. The earlier and revised versions of the Shipley Inventory as well as the Battle Noise Test detected no more than 50 to 75 percent of the men ultimately rejected by psychiatrists. Only the Cornell Selectee Index detected 80 to 90 percent.[74] But the real criterion for test success was not whether it had the same rate of acceptance/rejection as the psychiatric interview but whether it could successfully predict performance in training or, more importantly, combat. Only the air force's battery of written tests and personal interview, compiled together in one score, the ARMA, correlated closely with actual performance in training. But these tests were mainly about aptitude, not personality, and there is little indication that the ARMA correlated well with combat performance, which was much more unpredictable.[75]

Army and navy personality tests generated considerable false positives, that is, men found unsuitable on the test but healthy by psychiatrists on later examination. Most of the tests falsely labeled 5 to 8 percent of the normal population, with at least 20 percent for the NSA, and an even higher false-positive percentage for the Battle Noise Tests, as the noise disturbed even "normal" men. The rate of false positives was also higher when the Personal Inventory was tested on thousands of sixteen-year-old cadets. The rates of false positives were particularly high for the 5,660 men, 4,896 white and 764 Black, given the NSA at a New York induction center in February 1945.

Twenty-three percent of the whites and 12 percent of the Blacks rejected were false positives.[76]

The tests were limited in the types of mental illness they could readily detect. The original Shipley was better at finding psychopathy than anything else. It was based on records of Section VIII army dischargees and tested on incarcerated juvenile delinquents, homosexuals, addicts, and alcoholics.[77] The more sophisticated Cornell Selectee Index was better at locating psychosomatic conditions, as the index had been tried out on civilian hospital patients.

The tests had their own biases. Because the originators assumed a certain level of literacy, the tests discriminated against inductees in certain regions. The Office of Scientific Research and Development (OSRD) reported in August 1943 that a person needed the equivalent of a seventh-grade elementary education to adequately comprehend items on the Cornell Selectee Index but that 5 to 10 percent of the population in the northeastern United States were not sufficiently educated, and, much worse, in certain southern communities, as many as 70 percent of the Black population could not take the index.[78]

The forced-choice method of questions in the Shipley Inventory discriminated against the more intelligent. Citing data from training schools and the Adjutant General's Office, the psychologists M. A. Seidenfeld and Clarence Graham noted that because the tests made examinees choose between two alternatives, sometimes equally questionable answers, the more intelligent sometimes scored worse than others. It was hard for the more intelligent to choose between such answers as "I have felt bad more from head colds" or "I have felt bad more from dizziness," "I take life easy" or "I tend to worry," and "I have my share of lucky breaks" or "Most of my friends are luckier than I am."[79]

The basic rigidity of the Shipley and Personality Inventories contributed to their bias. Psychologists asked the same written questions nationwide based on cultural assumptions more attuned to one area of the country. Not surprisingly, the NSA had a higher rejection rate in the Southwest and Southeast than in the North. Moreover, the tests were less flexible than a personal interview. Regardless of an examinee's facial expression, tone of voice, or ability to explain extenuating circumstances, regardless of cultural background, previous experience, or knowledge of the psychiatrist, the examination gave the same weight to the respondent's answers.[80]

Because psychiatrists varied according to region in their criteria for mental illness, the results of the tests correlated better with the judgment of psychiatrists in some areas. In Chicago and Detroit, the NSA test screened out about 25 percent of the inductees, yet psychiatrists in Chicago rejected 7.6 percent of inductees, while in Detroit, they rejected almost 22 percent.[81]

Most important, the tests had problems predicting military adjustment. Because the Shipley and Personality Inventories and the Cornell Selectee Index based their questions on surveys of civilian prisoners and mental patients who told them about their civilian experiences, and because they were designed by experts with civilian experience, the tests developed civilian criteria for mental health, which did not always apply to military performance. As we shall see, sometimes men deemed deviant in civilian life who managed to slip through the screen, such as homosexuals, "psychopaths," and those with psychosomatic disorders, performed well in combat.[82]

Studies confirmed the tests' problems predicting military performance. True, a certain Personal Inventory given to several hundred submarine seamen correlated well with later performance in service: "Of those men [with scores] between 12 and 20, 24 percent were rated as undesirable by the submarine commanders ... of those [with scores] between 5 and 11, 16.2 percent were ... undesirable [and] of those [with] scores between 0 and 4, 12.3 percent ... rated undesirable." But a larger navy follow-up study of 1,466 sailors revealed more unsatisfactory results. A year after they took the test in training, discharged veterans, court-martials, officers, and enlisted men showed about the same score on the Personal Inventory. Though the Army Research Branch secured the NSA scores for five thousand soldiers from all over the country, they never got a chance to compare them with later scores in service, because the war ended.[83]

The tests had other predictive problems. Even if the tests could statistically predict breakdown, their scope seemed too limited. "Failure in one type of stressful situation does not necessarily indicate failure in another. Tests must be designed specifically to meet different types of stress," the psychologist Graham and the psychiatrist Frank Fremont-Smith reminded the NRC Subcommittee on Psychiatry in June 1944. At the same meeting, Rear Admiral Dallas Sutton, Sullivan's close associate and one of the originators of the screening program, noted the tests seemed to eliminate men who initially seemed unstable but who could have become effective soldiers after training and indoctrination; his suspicions were confirmed by at least one study after the war finding the number of false positives exceeding those classified correctly as positive. Nor could the added sophistication of the new techniques guarantee the validity of the newer tests. If the questions were based on faulty psychiatric assumptions, the tests remained invalid.[84] In the case of the ARMA, such factors as motivation, family background, and interests were difficult to quantify. Men who could do well in service were disarmed by evasive personal questions in the interview portion, making them unduly nervous, evasive, or quiet.[85]

The development of army and navy written personality tests, like the MSP, did not answer the public's objections to the screening program. Intended to make examinations fair and objective, the tests, like the MSP, created additional unfair and biased rejections and false positives. False positives frequently meant that men and women who could have performed in service adequately if given sufficient training did not get the chance. Instead, they confronted the stigma of their diagnosis, problems with employment, loss of self-esteem, and loss of respect from their community.[86] Given these deficiencies, one wonders why mental health specialists devoted so much time and energy to the programs. Three factors may contribute to the answer. First, the Mental Hygiene Movement, from which some leaders came, was comfortable using testing and gathering social data from child guidance clinics and prisons. To those from that movement, the huge pool of servicemen available for investigation and testing represented a major research opportunity. Second, many psychiatrists and allied professionals could not give up their belief in predisposition and their ability to thoroughly weed out "troublemakers" if only the proper tools were found. Third, the funding and development of most of the tests were already in full swing when the army and navy surgeon generals began to reevaluate their screening role. Therefore, it was difficult to switch. Also making it hard was just plain inertia. As we have seen in the case of the MSP, this was particularly clear.

7 The Horrors of War and Beginnings of Change

By May 1943, with Franklin Delano Roosevelt and Britain's prime minister Winston Churchill agreeing to invade Normandy the following spring, the need for manpower rose, and military leaders lost faith in psychiatry. That August, in two widely reported incidents, General George Patton slapped two psychiatric hospital patients in Sicily and ordered them to the front. While Army Chief of Staff George C. Marshall and General Dwight D. Eisenhower disapproved of his methods, they shared his concern about mammoth psychiatric casualties sapping military strength and endangering comrades under fire. In a critical memorandum leaked to the press in early January 1944, despite an official army news blackout on psychoneurosis, Marshall openly doubted the reality of psychoneurosis and the need for psychiatry altogether. Soon, Eisenhower ordered his generals to restrict psychiatric evacuations from the North African theater.

On the other hand, Franklin Delano Roosevelt's support for psychiatry did not falter. As before, he urged the military to increase its treatment efforts in order to reduce the number of psychiatric casualties and neuropsychiatric veterans plus the costs of pensions and hospitalization.

Meanwhile, the army's chief psychiatrist, William Menninger, defended his profession's expertise against mounting military skepticism. Others, like Omar Bradley, supported using euphemistic terms for mental illness, such as "combat fatigue," to quell military concerns. Leading psychiatrists also championed preventive psychiatry and psychiatric treatment. Behind this was the profession's growing acceptance of a new etiology. No longer was predisposition deemed the primary determinant of maladjustment. By mid-1944, it would become a truism of the war that "everyone has his breaking point" given the proper stress. Accordingly, psychiatrists came to believe they could minimize breakdowns and salvage psychiatric cases by modifying soldiers' environment. The views of the medical skeptics who had questioned predisposition in 1941 and favored preventive psychiatry and treatment now received rising prominence.

The Horrors of War and Beginnings of Change | 139

To understand why psychiatric policy began to change, we need to appreciate the war's calamitous conditions. Americans were being killed by the thousands on battlefields month after month, year after year. Replacements became essential but were always behind, not only in number but in training and equipment. While the Germans surrendered to the Allies in Sicily in less than six weeks, several thousand Americans were killed or missing in the campaign. On the Italian mainland, American soldiers struggled up tortuous mountains while Germans shot at them from above. In Cassino, men lay in foxholes, freezing, without taking off their shoes for as many as twenty-four days in a row. Severe frostbite on feet led to amputations. Medics, at risk to their backs, carried the wounded down steep mountains on litters.[1] By the end of the Italian campaign, Americans had suffered at least 110,000 casualties, including over 22,000 killed, 77,248 wounded, and 10,338 missing.

In January 1944, only twenty thousand American combat troops were stationed in England, despite the impending invasion. That same month, Marshall complained to Stimson that Selective Service lagged by 200,000 in supplying servicemen. On D-Day, June 6, 1944, the Allies shipped 150,000 largely inexperienced servicemen to Normandy. On the way, without escort convoys, boats were torpedoed by German submarines. Beset both by poor weather and by the inability to neutralize German defenses, 2,500 or more drowned in the sea or were killed in violent plane crashes, plus at least 8,230 Americans who were killed, wounded, or missing as they approached shore. Altogether, the Allies suffered 12,000 casualties, not to mention thousands unaccounted for. On the Normandy beaches and battling through twenty-foot-high hedgerows during the next few months, Americans suffered another 20,838 killed. The Battle of the Bulge, in December 1944 and January 1945, the war's bloodiest engagement, saw as many as 105,000 casualties, including 19,246 dead, 23,000 taken prisoner, and over 60,000 injured.[2] So many lieutenants died in combat that an emergency school for new lieutenants was opened in France near the end of the war.[3]

In the campaigns in the Solomon Islands and New Guinea, rates of evacuation and discharge were higher for psychoneurosis than for all physical wounds or disease. The exact number who contracted malaria was unknown because of a news blackout, but it seriously depleted the numbers who could engage in combat. Making matters worse were insufficient medical supplies and medical staff. With fewer men to share the burden of combat, psychiatric casualties grew as well. By July 1943, several planned actions in the New Georgia campaign were forced to cancel because of a troop shortage.[4] Though the Pacific saw one-fifth of the combat action of the European theater in 1944, because of the former's severe climatic and fighting conditions, the same rate of psychiatric breakdown prevailed. In Leyte, the Philippines, hundreds of kamikaze fighters flew right through ships, blowing themselves up. On Iwo Jima, some divisions suffered as many as 75 to 85 percent casualties. On Okinawa, Americans fought Japanese hidden deep in caves. Over 12,000 Americans were killed and 50,000 wounded. Altogether, at least 420,000 Americans died in the war.[5]

No American conflict since the Civil War had been so long or bloody. World War I began on June 28, 1914, but America did not enter the war until April 1917 or see action until at least October 1917, and the war ended slightly more than a year later, in November 1918. Thus, when Americans entered World War II, unlike the British, they had little real experience with what they would face. In contrast, by 1943, with the Germans and Japanese nowhere near giving up, it was clear that World War II would drag on, with conditions equal to or more arduous than any previous American conflict. Initially, policy makers had assumed that psychiatrists could be highly selective in their psychiatric examinations, anticipating that any war would last little more than a year. But now faced with soaring numbers of dead and wounded and with no clear end to the conflict in sight, Marshall and Eisenhower largely lost faith in the psychiatric profession. While Roosevelt favored rehabilitation, the military questioned the reality of psychoneurosis altogether.

The Patton Incident and Its Fallout

General George S. Patton's slapping of two neuropsychiatric patients in hospitals in Sicily was the most well-known instance of the military's opposition to psychiatry. Concerned about soldiers' avoiding combat by faking illness, in August 1943 the general slapped two soldiers with "nerves" in evacuation hospitals, called them "yellow belly cowards," and ordered them back to the front.

A few months earlier, Army Commanding General Alexander Patch, certain that neuropsychiatric cases at Guadalcanal were "a disgrace to the service," had threatened to court-martial them despite army regulations. But the difference between Patch and Patton was that Patch, thanks to the intercession of Martin Berezin, an army psychiatrist, did not carry out his threat.[6] More importantly, General Patton was the only officer in the military to be excoriated in the national press for months on end for actually physically assaulting soldiers hospitalized with war neuroses.

The response to the Patton incidents substantially affected psychiatric policy. It fostered two reactions: The medical reaction was that combat fatigue was a genuine disease necessitating hospitalization and that punishment was unjust and totalitarian; the military reaction was that evacuees who could not face fire were cowards who could not be tolerated in a war with so much suffering and so much need for manpower.

A career army officer, part of General John Pershing's expedition against Mexico in 1916 and thereafter part of a tank unit in World War I, Patton was wounded in battle in September 1918. A general in North Africa in World War II, he eventually commanded all American forces in the Tunisian campaign.[7] In July 1943, he became commanding general of the Seventh Army in Sicily. For at least thirty-eight days straight he led his men over rough terrain, culminating in capturing Messina from the Germans. The Germans recalled: "Americans fought during the day and marched throughout the night." Known as "Old Blood and Guts," he was reputed to get the most out of his men while subjecting himself to the same torture.

But he had a temper. He was opinionated. His views were not appealing to medical officers. One doctor recalled him saying, "If you have two wounded soldiers, one with a gunshot wound of the lung, [the] other with an arm or leg blown off, you save the sonofabitch with the lung wound . . . let the goddamn sonofabitch with an amputated arm or leg go to hell. He is no goddamn use to us anymore."[8] In his autobiography, Patton called for court-martialing soldiers with self-inflicted wounds, concluding, "Any time a soldier is shot through either [the left foot or left hand, there is] a high probability it is self-inflicted."[9]

As to a man with "nerves," he was nothing but a coward, a person who had less of a chance of staying alive in battle because fear "dulls intuition." A person "must conquer fear to continue with the scheme of God."[10] While Patton's views on combat exhaustion were hotly debated in the United States, they were gospel to the Germans, Japanese, and Russians. Many men in each of these armies were summarily shot at the front for cowardice without recourse to trial. The Germans could not understand why the American press was upset about Patton's slapping two soldiers. They suspected it was a ploy to induce the enemy into thinking Patton's military role was over.[11]

But furor there was. On August 3, 1943, "Old Blood and Guts" visited the 15th Evacuation Hospital, outside Nicosia, Sicily. He saw a soldier bandaged from head to foot from an explosive shell and another in traction, with a bandage over an eye and a broken leg and arm, caused by a land mine. Both told Patton they wanted to return to battle soon. Then he saw a patient without wounds, a "cowardly rat" who "whined . . . I just can't take it."¹² Infuriated, Patton slapped Private Charles H. Kuhl in the face with his gloves. He pushed him out of the tent with a kick in the rear. In a memorandum two days later, he ordered all commanders to court-martial soldiers with "nerves" instead of sending them to hospitals, since their stay in hospitals only brought "discredit on the army" and enabled them to "heartlessly leave their comrades to endure."

On August 10, a second incident occurred at the 93rd Evacuation Hospital. According to firsthand accounts, a battery surgeon sent a shivering soldier with a good combat record (Paul Bennett) to a hospital against his will. Patton asked the soldier why he was there. He replied, "nerves." Hearing this, Patton uttered one expletive after another and called him a "yellow belly." Patton then drew his pistol, waved it at the patient, slapped him several times across the face, and ordered him back to the front right away. "Companies," wrote Patton in his diary, "should deal with such men, and if they shirk their duty, they should be tried for cowardice and shot."¹³

The news leaked to reporters from the *Saturday Evening Post*, NBC, *Newsweek*, CBS, and *Collier's*. The reporters decided to tell Eisenhower they would kill the story if Patton were summarily fired. Eisenhower, in charge of Allied forces in North Africa and Sicily, would soon be appointed by Roosevelt as supreme commander of the Allied Expeditionary Forces, which would invade the European mainland in June 1944.

But for now, in August 1943, Eisenhower would display his already exceptional command skills. Sympathetic and tolerant of soldiers' and officers' foibles, he was personally modest yet known for his ability to plan strategy, foster Anglo-American teamwork, and make quick, sound decisions.¹⁴ Here he faced a dilemma. He needed to control Patton, but he valued the prized warrior. He did not want to fire him. To him, Patton endured the unendurable with his troops and had turned the tide of the war with wins in North Africa and Sicily. Eisenhower persuaded the reporters to drop the story in exchange for Patton's apologizing to the two soldiers and the hospital staffs. He also initiated an internal investigation.

Eisenhower had his own reservations about the medical validity of combat exhaustion but was critical of Patton's methods. He explained to a fellow officer that "in any army one-third of the soldiers are natural fighters and brave; two-thirds inherently cowards." The two-thirds had to be motivated to fight. While he found Patton's method "deplorable," he said his results were "excellent."

Ordered by Eisenhower, Patton apologized to everyone, though secretly, he entered in his diary: "It is rather a commentary on justice when an army commander has to soft-soap a skulker to placate the timidity of those above."[15]

Nevertheless, all seemed calm until someone leaked the story to Drew Pearson, known for his column "Washington Merry-Go-Round." Pearson reported Patton's actions on his national NBC radio show and harped on a secret internal investigation by Eisenhower, indications that Eisenhower was intending to banish Patton to the United States, and Patton's questionable previous socializing with the pro-Vichy element in Casablanca.[16]

In response to this information, the Senate Committee on Military Affairs conducted hearings from November 1943 through January 1944, stalling Patton's promotion. Congressmen wrote to Secretary of War Henry Stimson and Marshall, calling for his dishonorable discharge. The Senate committee received letters from families and friends of shell-shocked soldiers asking them to ensure that other officers did not mistreat their men. Nevertheless, the Republican congressman Hamilton Fish, from Hyde Park, New York, a fierce isolationist before the war and political opponent of Roosevelt's, defended Patton.[17] According to a biographer, Patton's personal mail ran 89 percent favorable. One soldier wrote the *New York Times*:

> In an all-out war we need more, not fewer, hard-boiled, tough, fighting generals. To crucify a general for telling off, even if physically, a soldier who seemingly exhibited cowardice is the worst sabotage that any Axis propaganda could possibly inflict on our Armies. Having spent a year and a half as a wounded patient in Army hospitals, I know that there must be in the hospitals even in this war many "goldbrickers" who prefer hospitalization to active service or even to the responsibilities of post-war civilian life.[18]

The mail in the Marshall Archives, however, ran two to one against Patton (52 to 26).[19] Out of fourteen letters sent to Eleanor Roosevelt, twelve opposed Patton, one was in favor, and one neutral. Those against Patton's behavior saw shell shock as a real disease requiring medical attention. At least three wondered why the United States bothered to wage war against fascism when its own officers used fascistic methods. One even called Patton "Hitler all over again." Another: "American soldiers are not lacking in courage ... hundreds ... suffer and die without a whimper.... We are fighting for democracy; what a farce! Disgraceful indeed that American soldiers can be abused by their commanding officer."[20]

Still, neither Roosevelt, Stimson, Marshall, nor Eisenhower wanted to sack Patton. Perhaps it was the manpower shortage that prompted their sympathy for Patton's actions.[21] In reports to the chair of the Senate investigative committee, Stimson extolled Patton's abilities as an officer; as Stimson put it, he was "one who successfully concluded, in record time, a complicated and important military campaign, and one whom his officers and men would again be willing to follow into battle," and one whose loss of services "would afford aid and comfort to the enemy."[22] FDR was personally interested in reading the transcript of a pro-Patton radio broadcast on November 23 by Hilmar Robert (H. R.) Baukhage on WJZ, New York. (Baukhage had been a reporter for the Associated Press in Europe and America, then on the staff of *Leslie's Illustrated Weekly*, the predecessor to *Life*.[23] He had also worked with Roosevelt's press secretary Stephen Early.)

FDR jotted down his request for Baukhage's transcript on a letter received by Eleanor from a constituent. The transcript, which the president and Eleanor Roosevelt soon obtained, plus a more extensive one from the same commentator on another station, excused Patton for having his own brand of nerves, his "fear of fear," a fear of breaking down and not being able to fight. It pointed out that "it is a common error" to believe that someone who does not appear disabled should be treated as someone who disobeys and must be punished, that without being a psychiatrist it is difficult to understand that "any kind of malingerer is in a greater or less degree a mental case."[24] A few weeks later, asked to comment on Patton at a press conference, the president recalled the story of a "former President who had a good deal of trouble in finding a successful commander . . . and one of them turned up one day, and . . . was successful. And some very good citizens went to [him]. 'You can't keep him. He drinks.' To which Lincoln replied: 'It must be a good brand of liquor.'"[25] Roosevelt likewise could forgive the "whiskey" Patton drank.

Over three-quarters of a century later, a practicing psychiatrist attempted to explain Patton's behavior in rhetoric like Baukhage's. Writing in *Psychological Reports*, after reviewing the historical record, the psychiatrist attributed Patton's "violent projections of . . . anger toward the cowardice in others" to part of the general's excessive efforts to remove the cowardice "he knew lurked within himself." Patton's "hyperkinetic enthusiasm in war" was a response to childhood dyslexia, sleeplessness, anxiety, and fear, and cowardice was anathema to his military family. At West Point, to overcompensate, he "refused . . . to acknowledge danger," placing himself and his men in extremely precarious positions. To train himself to overcome fear, during rifle practice, against all advice, he "stood up as bullets whizzed past him." In the years that followed, he continued to put his men in jeopardy and to virtually court suicide. Fearful, sweating, nervous before battle, he had no tolerance for anyone who could not control their cowardice as he did. Hence, he loathed the "combat exhausted"; even soldiers "killed in battle" were "fools who had merely failed to protect themselves adequately." Likewise, the "pitiful" concentration camp inmate.[26]

In 1943, while Eisenhower, Marshall, and even Roosevelt sympathized with Patton's skepticism about psychoneurosis, they could not accept Patton's slapping his men and drawing his pistol on them. And they knew they had to appease the press and Congress. A promotion was not approved for Patton by the Senate until August 1944. The cool-headed Bradley was chosen instead by Eisenhower to head Overlord, the Allied invasion of Europe.[27]

Meanwhile, the GI continued to confront horrors in battles overseas. Although the landing on the mainland of Italy at Salerno on September 1, 1943, was supposed to be easy because the Italian government had just surrendered, Arthur C. Wenzel, a medic veteran, recalled years later being pounded by three well-trained German panzer divisions, without any American naval or air cover:

> Around the mountains surrounding our beachhead . . . they had their 88s . . . antiaircraft guns and they were firing them pointblank at us. . . . We got wiped out. . . . Our CO . . . wasn't on the beach two minutes . . . his leg was cut right off . . . another medic ran off the boat. He was shot and killed immediately. The first one I had to treat . . . a buddy of mine. His head was so ripped back, I didn't know how to take care of it. . . . I've got some sulfa . . . loaded it into this wound . . . got a bandage and just tied his head. . . . He lived for three days. The day he died, his son was born.[28]

He described the winter of 1943–1944 as nothing but rain, snow, muck, and casualties. At Rapido, Italy, General Mark Clark ordered men to cross an eight-foot-deep, exceptionally swift river. Men crossing "were mowed down." The Germans on high ground "just picked . . . guys off."[29]

As combat stress increased, so too did army neuropsychiatric hospital admissions worldwide. Altogether, the number for 1943 was 341,087 and for 1944 was 367,815. For the entire 1942–1945 period, neuropsychiatric hospital admissions, with some repetitions, came to 1.1 million. Of these, psychoneuroses accounted for approximately 60 percent of the total. Additionally, neuropsychiatric discharges each month averaged around 20,000. By the end of the war, at least 389,000 soldiers had been discharged for neuropsychiatric disorders, almost all on certificates of disability discharge. In addition, another 163,000 were discharged administratively, coming to a total for the army of 538,000. Of these, 69.1 percent were for psychoneurosis.[30] This did not include discharges for sailors and marines.

Psychoneurosis, a diagnosis that broadly and amorphously defined maladjustment as "an inability to cope with wartime stress and strain," constituted most neuropsychiatric hospital admissions and neuropsychiatric discharges. While cases existed that resembled the shell shock of World War I (soldiers stammering, temporarily amnesiac, blind, deaf, paralyzed), these were uncommon. The vast bulk consisted of an undefined "stress reaction" previously unknown to most military. Was this really a disease, or did it constitute cowardice, or was it simply a human reaction to the stress of army life?

A News Blackout

Reacting to the serious growth in neuropsychiatric rejections, casualties, and discharges, somewhere around September 1943 the War Department imposed a blackout on all news and medical discourse about psychiatry. Despite a number of leaks, the blackout continued through the end of April 1944, and even afterward the War Department prohibited the army surgeon general from releasing any numbers. When the war ended in Europe in May 1945, the War Department and surgeon general were still wrestling with the correct dissemination of information on psychiatry. The only other known American wartime blackout was for news about malaria.[31]

Marshall's Attack on Psychiatry

On December 30, 1943, Marshall issued a "SECRET" memorandum, leaked to the *Washington Sunday Star* on January 9, 1944, despite the official blackout of all news and scientific information on psychiatry.[32] The memorandum began with Marshall criticizing the practice of evacuating psychoneurotics to hospitals. While a doctor might consider a psychoneurotic to be a hospital patient, a line officer saw him as a "malingerer . . . a man *unwilling, unable* or *slow* to adjust to . . . military life . . . someone who developed an imaginary ailment which in time bec[a]me . . . fixed." Because no doctor was willing to affirm under oath that the pain did not exist, the military had not court-martialed any malingerer. But Marshall complained that thousands of hospitalized psychoneurotics commanded expensive services, such as cooks, nurses, and doctors, and many were the fault of their line officers being "unable to make soldiers of them."

As for the doctors, he continued, they were overeager or too cautious and not sufficiently trained in psychiatry to make the right call. Hospitalized, a soldier's "value to the service is . . . destroyed." Marshall wondered whether patients were faking symptoms, especially since patients learned "from other patients the symptoms most likely to perplex the doctors." In one general hospital, he wrote, patients on light duty, who heard rumors that psychoneurotic discharges were going to be discontinued, immediately confined themselves to beds, suddenly too sick to attend meals. American education was at fault: Instead of teaching youth to endure hardships to prepare for war, as our enemies had, we had encouraged them to "expect luxuries," to depend on government largesse for livelihood, and to regard "soldiers and war as unnecessary and hateful."

In conclusion, Marshall called for a reduction in psychiatric evacuees and a military inquiry.[33] Reinforcing Marshall's plea, on January 29, 1944, in a "Dear General letter," Eisenhower ordered his commanders not to evacuate any "psychoneurotic" from the theater until they had determined by "actual test" that he was not fit for any type of duty.[34]

Psychiatrists in Charge

Responding to criticism from the top brass, leading military psychiatrists defended their expertise, proposed euphemisms to soften the blow of the psychoneurotic diagnosis, and provided limited assignments for psychoneurotics instead of discharge. By May 1944, as we shall see, at the annual convention of the American Psychiatric Association (APA), they officially endorsed preventive psychiatry and treatment at the front and largely dismissed the efficacy of screening.

Heading the campaign for change was William Menninger, who would serve as chief of the Army Neuropsychiatric Consultants Division from December 10, 1943, to June 30, 1946. Menninger was not part of Sullivan's Washington, DC/Baltimore circle. Nor had he been active in the APA or worked as a mental hospital superintendent, like Winfred Overholser; Roy Halloran, his predecessor; or Arthur Ruggles, a former APA president. A year earlier, he had been appointed a consultant by the army to the Fourth Service Command, Georgia, responsible for procurement of troops and overseeing Southern military bases.[35] On November 30, 1943, the Executive Committee of the National Committee for Mental Hygiene (NCMH), headed by Dr. George Stevenson, sent Eleanor Roosevelt a letter recommending that the army appoint Menninger chief of the Army Neuropsychiatric Consultants Division. Four days later, on December 3, Eleanor Roosevelt endorsed Menninger's appointment in a letter to Norman Kirk, the Army Surgeon General. A week later, the army appointed Menninger the chief. Again, the influence of the Roosevelts appeared.[36]

While others tended their gardens at home, Menninger made friends in the 1930s with the Canadian psychiatrist G. Brock Chisholm and the British psychiatrist John R. Rees, the director of the Tavistock Clinic and later prominent in the British army. These friendships may well have influenced his affinity for treatment at the front and for preventive psychiatry. As chief, Menninger embraced the "team approach" developed by his father at the Menninger Clinic: psychiatrists, psychiatric social workers, and psychologists working together, something the army had done little before and that had interfered with the success of psychiatric efforts.

Hailing from Topeka, Kansas—a town only eighty miles from Eisenhower's Abilene—Menninger was known for his social skills, administrative ability, flexibility, and practicality as a doctor and military commander. Early on, he had displayed organizational skills as a scoutmaster, leading seventy-five of his charges to become Eagle Scouts in nine years.[37] A stamp collector like Eisenhower and Roosevelt and an avid piano player like future president Harry Truman, Menninger used his social skills to gain approval for his division's programs.[38] Lobbying by civilian psychiatrists with Roosevelt in 1942 and early 1943, with the support of the army surgeon general, to make psychiatry a division equal in power to surgery and medicine and to raise the director's rank, providing him more influence, finally reaped success with Menninger's promotion to brigadier general. Menninger consulted his brother, the psychoanalyst Karl Menninger, about treatment. In addition to his assistant chief, Malcolm Farrell, who had been in the Army Surgeon General since early 1942, Menninger depended on deputies to carry out his program, including John Appel, director of the Army Mental Hygiene Branch; Frederick Hanson, psychiatric consultant for the Mediterranean theater; and the psychoanalysts John Murray, consultant to the army air force, and M. Ralph Kaufman, consultant to the South Pacific and Pacific areas.

Trained by Edward Strecker at the University of Pennsylvania Medical School, Appel later instructed doctors in psychiatry at the University of Pennsylvania and received psychoanalytic training after the war. In early 1942, he had asked Madigan to assign him to a position in preventive psychiatry, but Madigan had turned him down because there was "no need," given screening.[39] Only after a family friend, Harvey Bundy, interceded with Frederick Osborn, head of the Information and Education Division (I&E), did Appel become head of Mental Hygiene, first under Halloran. (Bundy was special assistant to Secretary of War Stimson and previously assistant secretary of state when Stimson headed the State Department under Hoover.)[40] Soon after, Osborn also appointed Appel liaison between Mental Hygiene and the I&E, where Appel worked closely with the sociologist Samuel Stouffer.[41]

Frederick Hanson was, as we have seen, one of the few psychiatrists to successfully treat soldiers close to the front in North Africa at the beginning of 1943. Hanson claimed he had returned 30 percent to combat within a day and 70 percent within forty-eight hours. In February 1943, Halloran appointed Hanson as psychiatric consultant to the Mediterranean theater of operations, a position Hanson held until the end of the war.[42]

Menninger's Response to Marshall's Memorandum

While the army chief of staff did not give the Surgeon General's Office a copy of Marshall's negative memorandum on psychoneuroses dated December 30, 1943, until three months later, Menninger even then could not defend psychiatry in the press, given the continuing news blackout. But he did write to Bundy on April 3, 1944, that psychoneurosis was not an "imaginary ailment" feigned by soldiers; American soldiers were not soft, and the numbers evacuated were not that large, because psychiatrists, he said, were rehabilitating substantial numbers for combat, Roosevelt's interest from early on. Rather than faulting psychiatrists, Menninger blamed America for inculcating in its young men cherished beliefs in freedom of thought and individualism, which made it difficult for soldiers to appreciate "why we fight" or to conform to regimentation, hinting ironically that it might be necessary to copy fascist methods to defeat fascism, a point similar to one made by Marshall. By May 9, with the news blackout lifted, Menninger boasted at an Army Surgeon General's press conference, "Of all psychoneurotic cases treated in the army not one has been proved a malingerer."[43]

Nomenclature

Responding to concerns about excessive numbers of psychoneurotics, some line officers and military psychiatrists favored labeling the malady in less alarming terms. Months before the Patton incident, Omar Bradley, then commander of II Corps, North Africa, approved using the term "exhaustion" for psychiatric casualties.[44] Later in 1943 and 1944, army psychiatrists used the term "combat exhaustion" or "combat fatigue," while air force psychiatrists employed "operational fatigue" or, in cases occurring after only a few missions, "lack of moral fiber." Similarly, the navy used "No Disease, Temperamentally Unqualified for Service" to administratively discharge sailors without benefits.

Psychiatrists employed the new minimalistic or administrative nomenclature not only to reduce concerns about the rising numbers but also to soften the military's fear that if the diagnosis "psychoneurosis" was real, then soldiers might well be "psychotic." Given that most Americans had not had much contact with psychiatry before the war and that psychiatric cases had previously been associated with patients in isolated mental hospitals, this was a natural concern. So, in early 1944, Menninger emphasized that "psychoneurosis" did not necessarily signify severe illness or insanity. Rather, as Assistant Director Malcolm Farrell stated, a person could develop a "minor temporary mental ill health just as he [might] have a head cold." But to leading civilian psychiatrists such as Overholser, no reason existed to use any term other than psychoneurosis; nor did he believe a mere change of nomenclature could assuage military concerns.[45]

Labor Battalions

While Overholser and Sullivan had opposed labor battalions in 1941, with the increasing number of discharges, Menninger now endorsed such assignments. In February 1944, Marshall also endorsed "limited service," emphasizing that the military had lost as many as 50,000 to 80,000 men because of its earlier abolition. For the next five months, Menninger's Neuropsychiatric Consultants Division established training battalions at Camp Lee, in Virginia, and Aberdeen Proving Grounds, in Maryland, where they retrained 1,192 "mild" psychoneurotic patients, reclassifying 65 percent "for limited assignment" in noncombat units in the Zone of Interior. But while Marshall supported these battalions, he denied Menninger's request for another larger retraining program, claiming a shortage of trainers and assignments.[46] In December 1944, the Army Surgeon General also endorsed limited service. But little more was done. After the war, Menninger asserted that if the military had used more labor battalions, they would have spared many men the stigma of psychoneurosis and problems of adjusting to civilian life.[47]

Sending Psychiatrists to Divisions

In a much more significant development, beginning in mid-1944, with the initial interest of Roosevelt and to a limited extent Eisenhower, the army's leading psychiatrists advocated a broader role, namely, treatment and prevention. Brought on in part by the previous experiences of a limited number of psychiatrists in North Africa—namely, Hanson, Roy Grinker, and John and Herbert Spiegel—it was also engendered by the dynamism, ingenuity, and flexibility of the new psychiatric leaders Menninger, Hanson, Murray, Kaufman, and Appel and by the fact that, finally, psychiatrists were being sent to the divisions, where they could see for themselves what caused combat exhaustion and treat accordingly.

Reflecting both an eagerness to economize and a fear that psychiatrists in the field might incite discipline problems, Army Surgeon General James Magee had eliminated division psychiatrists from the army's Table of Organization in October 1940, despite their use in World War I. For the most part, Roy Halloran did little to reverse this order, believing that improving morale at the front was the province not of doctors but of line officers. In fairness, Halloran also confronted a general opinion in 1942 and 1943 among the military that psychiatrists were nothing but weirdo "nut-pickers" themselves belonging in "lunatic asylums."[48] Yet, even after Roosevelt's handpicked successor to Magee, Surgeon General Norman Kirk, urged the assistant army chief of staff (G-1, Personnel) during the summer of 1943 to approve division psychiatrists, the War Department did not issue Circular No. 290 authorizing such psychiatrists until the day before Halloran died on November 9, 1943. It would be left to the dynamic William Menninger to send psychiatrists to divisions. Wasting no time, on December 11, a day after being appointed, Menninger instructed sixty-one new division psychiatrists to live with soldiers in the field, "do what [they] do, shoot their weapons, ride their vehicles, participate in their bivouacs, take their infiltration course," and thus gain firsthand knowledge of the causes of war neuroses and an ability to work with line officers.[49]

Military and Presidential Support for Treatment

As far back as 1941, Roosevelt had promoted rehabilitation when he urged Selective Service to pay private doctors to reexamine and treat 4Fs to restore them to service. In 1943, he took a similar stance, writing to VA Director Frank Hines that troops should be rehabilitated to reduce the numbers obtaining veterans' pensions and hospitalization.[50] That December, Eleanor Roosevelt complained to Stimson about excessive numbers of veterans being committed to state asylums. Possibly responding to her complaint, in January 1944, Menninger urged the army to rehabilitate psychiatric soldiers to prevent discharge, because otherwise they would be "looked upon with doubts and suspicions, often refused jobs, become pension seekers, and [be] no good to themselves." Two months later, Roosevelt urged then APA president Edward Strecker in a letter to impress on psychiatrists the need to rehabilitate soldiers so they could return to civilian life as useful members of their communities.[51] The president, himself disabled, adhered to this belief all his life.

Responding to charges by Eisenhower that the care of American airmen in American hospitals in England was deplorable and that excessive numbers of psychiatric patients were being evacuated, Roosevelt ordered the Army and Navy Surgeon Generals and Strecker to study medical facilities for airmen in England. Their report dated April 4, 1944, signed, and approved by Roosevelt, also with Eisenhower's signature, confirmed the superiority of British psychiatric care, including narcosynthesis, insulin therapy, and rest centers, and suggested that Americans emulate that model, especially given the shortage of airmen and few replacements available. The Germans were shooting down at least a quarter of the American planes flying over Germany.[52]

In the meantime, the Army Neuropsychiatric Consultants Division assigned Hanson to train psychiatrists in theaters throughout the world in treating the combat-exhausted close to the front. Hanson was also responsible for directing medical studies on the impact of the environment on combat readiness. In October 1943, Hanson claimed in a *Reader's Digest* article that the effects of his methods were profound: that psychiatrists could return thousands to combat or send them home cured of mental fixations through simple methods of rest, sleep, good food, and necessary sedation, all close to the front. Military psychiatrists adopted his methods not only in World War II but also in Korea and Vietnam. Soon after the article was published in *Reader's Digest* in November 1943, Hanson's mother sent a copy to Stimson along with a letter pleading for additional governmental recognition of her son's work. A month later, Stimson referred her letter to Eleanor Roosevelt, asking for her intervention. Whether or not Stimson's letter had any effect, the following July 1944, Marshall appointed Hanson to the office of G-1 (Assistant Army Chief of Staff, Personnel) where he could have more impact on military psychiatric policy. Hanson also retained his position as army psychiatric consultant to the Mediterranean theater.[53]

But not just pressure from the executive branch and the military influenced the evolving role of the psychiatrist. It was also a basic change in medical etiology—what causes what—that led to change. This evolution in medical philosophy is described in the next chapter.

8 From Prediction to Prevention

From 1943 through 1945, the numbers killed, wounded, and psychologically broken by battle rose substantially. Simultaneously, more and more psychiatrists began to question the validity of predisposition, prompted especially by their own experiences in the field starting in December 1943, when they were able to see for themselves the devastation of war.

Yet change did not occur overnight. Though the American military in World War I had been impressed with French and British efforts to treat soldiers close to the front, Americans had done little themselves during that war and then only shortly before the Armistice.[1] And because the War Department in World War II did not order the surgeon general to send psychiatrists to divisions until the end of 1943, the military received few direct reports from the front that might have raised doubts about the concept of predisposition until late in the war.

Further deterring change was that the concept of predisposition had been ingrained in psychology and psychiatry at least as far back as the nineteenth century. As late as February 1943, an army psychiatrist who had previously worked in the child guidance movement told the surgeon general that "a large proportion of individuals who develop frank and lasting mental diseases in combat were carrying burdensome personality problems" before the war.[2] The following October, a New Georgia (South Pacific) psychiatric report still found that most "true psychoneurotics" had histories that would have made them unsuitable for induction had they been properly evaluated.[3]

Reinforcing this adherence to "predisposition" were economic considerations. In a memorandum dated January 14, 1943, to Malcolm Farrell, assistant chief of the Army Neuropsychiatric Branch, the chief psychiatric consultant in New Guinea, Major Samuel A. Challman, cautioned that diagnoses based on the immediate traumatic events of combat ("blast concussion," bombing, strafing, small-arms fire) could place undue fiscal responsibility on the government.[4] Conversely, diagnoses that emphasized long-standing psychological weakness (that is, not service related) could significantly reduce costs for the government. Similar considerations influenced Veterans Affairs (VA) decisions on paying for hospitalization and pensions after the war.

Nor was the military particularly receptive to an environmental explanation for mental breakdown, given its tradition of soldiers "toughing it out." In Alaska, the Defense Command denied that the climate or a long tour of duty unduly stressed soldiers, since they believed the most hardy members of the human race came from the Nordic Zone and, further, that "such things take secondary importance to . . . winning the war."[5] Because officers in North Africa regarded soldiers as "cogs in the machine of war" instead of "human beings with feelings and self-respect," the psychiatrist Herbert Spiegel contended, they "hampered and sometimes stifled psychiatric attempts to improve military conditions."[6]

Yet, by late 1943 and into early 1944, change began. As reports arrived from the field depicting combat eroding the psyche, psychiatrists questioned predisposition and screening's predictive powers. One officer in the Medical Corps initially attributed "jitters" in the Tunisian campaign to men "unfit to begin with" yet ultimately found the same men "not neurotic or psychoneurotic" but "all types of people" distressed by a losing engagement.[7] Not unresolved childhood conflicts but "blast concussions" led to long-term headaches, syndromes triggered by the sound of an exploding shell, and panic episodes. By May 1943, *Time* and *Newsweek* had publicized naval psychiatric accounts asserting that the most stalwart marines had broken down at Guadalcanal. The Thirty-First Station Hospital, South Pacific, in its annual report for 1944 concluded that most of its ten thousand psychiatric casualties had not been predisposed but had crumbled under the stress of combat. Psychiatrists at Bougainville in the Solomon Islands failed to correlate combat exhaustion with any precombat insomnia, enuresis, nail biting, unexplained indigestion, or vomiting, even though Medical Circular No. 1 and the Cornell Selectee Index had earlier listed these traits as indicia of future military maladjustment.[8]

Soldiers deemed least likely to succeed often performed best in combat. The psychiatrist Marvin Plesset found that most of the 138 men in his combat unit recommended as unfit for duty overseas remained emotionally sound after 150 days of continuous combat. At the end of the war, 120 were still on duty, nine had received Purple Hearts, and another eight received Bronze Stars for heroic service.[9] Recalling his experience in North Africa, Herbert Spiegel wrote that men "labeled by some as psychopathic or psychoneurotic performed adequately in battle under good leaders. One such case, with about 250 days absence without leave against him, served so well that he was cited three times for gallantry in action."[10]

By June 30, 1943, Navy Surgeon General Ross T. McIntire cautioned hospital commanders not to discharge anyone without definite evidence of mental disturbance, since it would be difficult to explain to parents "why a patient should be discharged [for] some personality defect . . . prior to . . . service after he has completed months of satisfactory service, particularly patients . . . engaged in active combat."[11]

The high rate of mental casualties among veteran troops raised issues about screening. The chief surgeon for the North African theater found in October 1943 that 66 percent and 88 percent of the casualties in two combat-experienced divisions in the Tunisian campaign were neuropsychiatric.[12] The novel *A Walk in the Sun*, published in 1944 with a prominent film version released in 1946, portrayed a sergeant at Salerno with combat fatigue who could no longer lead his troops. A victim of simply "too much war," he trembled, cried without reason, lay down on an unprotected path, "lost all track of the platoon and the objective," and was ready "for the cleaners."[13] In the film, one soldier in the unit remarks, "He was screened like everyone else," and another responds, "I know, but once in a while they get by the screen."[14]

In July 1943, Army Surgeon General Norman Kirk refused to be swayed by rising doubts about predisposition and screening's effectiveness. Indeed, Kirk informed the press that 85 percent of psychiatric casualties had a history of instability in civilian life.[15] Consequently, he called for even tougher screening. But as battlefield losses rose higher and higher, Patton, Eisenhower, and Marshall became increasingly intolerant of psychiatric evacuations.

In November 1943, the War Department ordered psychiatrists to the front. Once they deployed, there was no denying the harsh reality of combat exhaustion.

In a landmark paper delivered in May 1944 at the American Psychiatric Association's (APA) centenary meeting, Assistant Chief Farrell and Mental Hygiene Branch Chief Appel of the Army Neuropsychiatric Consultants Division lambasted screening. Despite high psychiatric rejection rates, they stressed, discharge rates were still mounting. Most of those eliminated, they maintained, were not psychopaths, mental defectives, or psychotics who needed to be screened to preserve military unity but psychoneurotics with little or no adverse social history who could have performed well in service. Frontline reports had shown not weaklings but normal men breaking down, unhinged by stress. They questioned psychiatrists' ability to screen when "anyone" could break. "Everyone" would have to be rejected to avoid casualties. Instead, they favored working with line officers to remove environmental stress and salvage men. "Prevention," they concluded, "began where screening left off. It was necessary to find out what was causing men to break down and then attempt to eliminate these causes." Treatment, they continued, must be done at the front during early stages of ailment, away from hospitals, so symptoms did not harden, under a military environment with military discipline, returning men quickly to combat. Too many discharges had occurred under the erroneous assumption that those who broke down were "weaklings." In fact, 60 to 80 percent, they claimed, if properly treated could return successfully to combat. Since soldiers were more than anything else worn out by lack of rest and sleep, they recommended sufficient rest and sedation. For more serious cases, they approved narcosynthesis and, if psychotic, insulin or electroshock.[16]

At the same APA meeting, Herbert Spiegel, recalling his experiences in combat in North Africa, urged psychiatrists to work closely with commanding officers and advise them on good leadership and appropriate discipline, because the commander was "burdened with innumerable details of the logistics of war."[17] Spiegel's paper reaffirmed War Department Circular No. 290, which had authorized psychiatrists with divisions to spread their "professional knowledge" on discipline and morale through educational programs and to advise officers on the proper assignment of personnel.[18]

Significantly, these papers represented a change from a strictly medical diagnostic role to more of a line officer function. Line officers, as well as officers in the Information and Education (I&E) Division under Frederick Osborn, had previously been in charge of improving morale through political orientation, adequate housing, and recreation. Now psychiatrists worked with officers in combat units on improving morale or with I&E field agents on political orientation. In his memorandum at the end of December 1943, Marshall decried the inability of platoon leaders and company commanders to satisfactorily influence the attitudes of inductees.[19] This comment may have prompted the involvement of psychiatrists, particularly Appel, who served as the liaison between the Army Neuropsychiatric Consultants Division and I&E. Previously, line officers were the ones to give a recalcitrant soldier coffee, urge him to return to combat, and send him back a few hours later. Now, psychiatrists treated the soldier, ensuring he received proper rest and food, motivating him to return so he would not let his buddies down, or, if need be, employing drugs to alleviate anxiety and after a few days return him to battle.[20]

Appel's Memorandum

The seminal memorandum on the recognition of environmental stress was Appel's "Prevention of Manpower Loss from Psychiatric Disorders, May

17–July 29, 1944," based on his inspection of neuropsychiatric treatment centers, clearing stations near the front, and hospitals in the rear in the North African theater during the spring and summer of 1944, as well as on interviews with surgeons, psychiatrists, and commanders stationed with the 34th Infantry Division in combat in Italy. In it, he disputed the validity of predisposition, instead emphasizing the environment's stressful effects on even the most stalwart veteran:

> From the Sicilian Campaign onward . . . an increasing number of psychiatric patients being sent back from the lines were not weaklings . . . broken down after a short exposure to combat, but experienced veterans, strong men with excellent combat records, often including decorations. . . . By the spring of 1944, following the Volturno, Rapido, and Cassino actions, more of these old men than new . . . were coming in as psychiatric patients. Finally, the statements began to be heard: "I'm the last old man left in my platoon". . . "There's only the two of us old men left, and they're no better than I am. You'll be seeing them soon." The frequency of these statements made it difficult to doubt their credibility.[21]

Though Appel estimated that "just as a two-and one-half ton truck becomes worn out after 14–15,000 miles . . . the doughboy became worn out . . . in the region of 200–240 aggregate combat days," Fifth Army officers in Italy informed him that many men became "ineffective" after as few as 140 to 180 days in combat.[22]

On the other hand, if soldiers, like British riflemen, had four days of rest for every twelve days of combat, Appel contended, they could remain in combat for up to 400 aggregate days. A veteran of the Italian campaign told him: "I believe I'd be all right if I hadn't had to face it so long and so often. If a man were in for two weeks and then out for a week . . . a man could go indefinitely."[23]

Contributing to the problem of excessive days in combat was the perception of an endless tour of duty. Unlike the navy or the army air force, the army lacked a rotation system until the end of 1944, except for the sick and wounded. Most soldiers in combat areas were kept there indefinitely, some for three or four years. It was not uncommon to find a veteran of North Africa fighting in Sicily, Italy, or France. Based on Appel's memorandum, Menninger wrote that when a soldier saw no end to his combat tour, he had "nothing to look forward to but more fighting and an unending physical ordeal with his life in the balance twenty-four hours a day. He [was] entirely expendable and [knew] it. His only out [was] a wound, mental illness or desertion."[24]

After reading Appel's memorandum in September 1944, Marshall sent it to his generals, stating: "I am much impressed with whatever can be done to break the strain of too long employment of the individual in active operations." (It is interesting to note that Marshall's support for a limited tour occurred a month after Eleanor Roosevelt expressed the same concern to him regarding one division too long in the jungle.)[25]

Other reports reiterated Appel's contention that the longer the combat, the higher the toll of exhausted victims. According to a psychiatrist who lived and fought with marines at Bougainville in the Solomon Islands, starting with their landing at the end of 1943, the campaign had its first casualties after twenty-five days; after thirty-nine days and the arduous taking of "Hill 1,000," the psychiatric casualty rate rose; from the fortieth to the fifty-fifth day, with the end still not in sight, it was simply "a matter of who [would] break next."[26] The I&E Research Branch in February 1944 directly correlated low morale among Fifth Army soldiers in Cassino and Anzio with the duration of time spent at relief.[27]

The Air Force and Length in Combat

The helplessness and uncontrollability of air warfare necessitated shorter tours of duty, but this did not always occur. During a mission, an aviator might be virtually lulled to sleep by his engines, only to confront a quick rattling explosion, bullets tearing through the plane, arms or kneecaps being sheared off. With no means to escape during flak or fighter plane attacks, a man had to face his imminent mortality. The genteel life that the flier may have experienced on recent days off, perhaps in an idyllic British rest home/castle, made the sudden desperation even graver. Weather conditions and long waiting in plane formation added to the feeling of helplessness.[28]

In close quarters with the crew, each depending on the others for life, anyone with "operational fatigue" threatened the mission's success. If distress occurred after only a few missions, an airman might receive the humiliating diagnosis of "lacking moral fiber" (LMF) or of "poor intestinal fortitude," terms adopted from the Royal Air Force (RAF). An officer might be urged to "resign for the good of the service" or face discharge without honor or benefits. An enlisted man might be discharged or reduced to the grade of private, removed from flying, or sent for reassignment.[29]

But this solution—removing the "weak"—did not eliminate the problem. Too many consecutive missions led to excessive numbers of deaths and casualties, including psychiatric. In the Eighth Air Force, which conducted daytime bombing over Germany in early 1944 unprotected by long-range fighter escorts, a staggering 26,000 died, and total casualties rose to over 50 percent of aircrew strengths. Though the chief medical officer recommended a flight limit of fifteen missions before being rotated out, the number crept up to twenty-five, then thirty-five.[30] Only one man in four survived twenty-five missions, and only one in five reached thirty-five.[31] In the Far East, the number of flights was even higher. Bomber pilots and crews at the Bora Bora Airfield in the Society Islands, Polynesia, reported being returned to the States after forty missions because accident rates rose 40 percent thereafter.[32] (The protagonist Yossarian in Joseph Heller's *Catch-22* complained frequently about the ever-rising number of flights required and the helplessness experienced during the missions, virtually driving men to insanity.)[33] In August 1944, Chief Air Force Psychiatrist John Murray concluded that Far East pilots had little value beyond ten to twelve months; nevertheless, some flew as many as twenty months. Flight surgeons attributed deaths caused by pilot error to operational fatigue.[34]

Other Environmental Factors

In addition to length of continuous combat and term of tour, psychiatrists attributed psychiatric casualties at the front to poor leadership, isolation, severe climate and topography, excessive boredom, little or no sleep, incorrect job assignment, lack of understanding of why we fight, an absence of camaraderie, and the need for religion. While these conditions particularly took their toll at the front, the vast majority of men and women who were not in combat also suffered psychologically. Of the 16.3 million who served in World War II, probably no more than 800,000 engaged in extended combat.[35] Of those who did not see combat, soldiers in training camps, awaiting embarkation, or in replacement depots especially suffered emotionally.

Leadership

While Marshall had tried to improve leadership training in the United States in 1941 and 1942, an Army Neuropsychiatric Consultants morale survey of three battalions in the Sicilian campaign revealed that the highest psychiatric casualty rate and the lowest battle casualty rate correlated with the greatest lack of faith in commanders, as shown in Figure 5.

Psychiatrists in Sicily and the Southwest Pacific reported an increase in psychiatric casualties when officers broke down, defected, or were killed or wounded. Appel's study of the North African theater disclosed that during four weeks of heavy fighting in Sicily, a third of the total neuropsychiatric cases came from a single infantry company, whose officer "stayed in his hole

TABLE 1

CASUALTIES FOR 26TH INFANTRY, SICILIAN CAMPAIGN,
JULY 10-AUGUST 1, 1943

Battalion	I	II	III
Battle Casualties	115	88	71
Rate/1000/Annum	2110	1612	1298
Psychiatric Casualties	32	36	74
Rate/1000/Annum	579	653	1353
How many officers in your company are the kind you would want to serve under in combat?			
All or most of them are	74%	56%	40%
About half of them are	10%	17%	17%
Few or none of them are	8%	25%	40%
No answer	8%	2%	3%
How many of your officers are the kind who are willing to go through anything they ask their men to go through?			
All or most of them are	75%	48%	36%
About half of them are	3%	17%	17%
Few or none of them are	14%	33%	42%
No answer	8%	2%	5%
Which of the following statements best tells the way you feel about getting back into actual battle?			
Relatively ready for next combat	39%	23%	16%
Relatively not ready for next combat	56%	75%	79%
No answer	5%	2%	5%

Note: Morale Survey made six weeks later and psychiatric casualties not included in questionnaire.

Source: Annual Neuropsychiatric Consultants Division, Fiscal Year 1945, p. 60.

Figure 5. Psychiatric casualties, 26th Infantry, Sicilian campaign.

most of the time."[36] The psychologist Joseph Zubin recalled that his National Research Council (NRC) Committee on the Selection of Military Leaders found that being a drill martinet correlated little with effective leadership. What counted was participating with one's men: crawling on one's belly, helping one's buddies, acting like the rest of the soldiers.[37] A medical report from the New Georgia campaign found that in Bougainville almost half of the NP casualties came from one company where the men had little respect for an officer who forced an offender to "dig a foxhole a few yards in the front line ... remain there, subsisting on nothing but cold C rations for a prescribed number of days."[38]

Letting men down affected an officer's psyche as well as his men's. Years later, James Wells recalled that his men had criticized him for running "like a deer" after the first Guam attack. While minimizing the import of their comments, he admitted that "showing fear or hesitation . . . in front of your people . . . is a great fear in many officers' . . . minds."[39] After the war, another veteran officer expressed immense guilt to a VA psychiatrist for surrendering to a Nazi panzer unit and letting his men down, even though he had killed the panzer unit's commander and the tanks' guns had been pointed at the unit.[40]

Isolation

Being alone in a foxhole for days at a time adversely affected soldiers in a way little known to soldiers in trenches in World War I. In August 1943, the career military psychiatrist William Porter, an early supporter of screening, stated that many of his psychiatric patients at the School of Neuropsychiatry in Atlanta, Georgia, had broken down on Guadalcanal after being "in foxholes alone for twenty-eight days, constantly . . . under the apprehension of sniper bullet or of Japs creeping up."[41]

Medics who were isolated were particularly vulnerable. One psychiatrist for the 99th Division, active at the Battle of the Bulge, recalled that during the German breakthrough in the Ardennes in December 1944 and January 1945 medics had a psychiatric casualty rate twice that of the regiment with the highest number of mental casualties. He attributed it to a lack of a sense of group protection or group loyalty in battle, especially since many medics had only been with their units for a short time.[42]

Similar conditions affected replacements. After basic training in the States, they could be moved from one depot in Europe to another in trucks or unheated, cramped boxcars. Often after being dropped off they entered combat with little or no training and only a few days with their new unit. In Tunisia, army replacements frequently did not know the names of the American soldiers next to them in combat. In Anzio, the "old guys" who were assigned to acquaint them with the ways of combat sometimes protected one another instead by persuading the greenhorns to go first into battle. Or veterans might enflame the replacements' anxieties with tales of gore and devastation. Not surprisingly, in the 91st Infantry Division, Fifth Army, Italy, from September 16 to September 30, 1944, replacements comprised 70 percent of the 412 neuropsychiatric evacuees. A survey of three hundred soldiers in one division in Bougainville from December 1943 to April 1944 found that replacements accounted for the highest percentage of psychiatric casualties, 36 percent.[43]

Poor Job Assignment

In his battalion in North Africa, Herbert Spiegel saw an expert rifleman reassigned as a medic, a man who could barely carry anything assigned as a litter bearer, and a perfectly fit medic sent to the rear.[44] Appel attributed the high mental casualty rate among replacements to a third having been trained as cooks, clerks, or buglers and often being sent into combat after seven to thirteen weeks of training without knowing how to load and unload, fire, or clean a rifle.[45]

Political Motivation

As originally designed by Frederick Osborn, the objective of the I&E Division was to provide the "truth" about current events so servicemen and -women could appreciate why they were making sacrifices. To do so, I&E provided soldiers with their own worldwide daily newspaper, *Stars and Stripes*, which continues to this day; a monthly magazine similar to *Life*, called *Yank*, which ceased publication in December 1945; a radio station (now radio and television); a weekly, two-page *Newsmap* of news stories and maps; and reading materials for a weekly one-hour current-events discussion group. In addition, servicemen and -women were able to see Capra's Why We Fight films. Yet despite all this, psychiatrists still expressed much concern that troops were insufficiently politically motivated.[46]

In October 1944, psychiatrists in II Corps, Fifth Army, which accounted for almost half of the casualties in Italy that year, linked mental exhaustion to poor esprit de corps caused by a lack of understanding of why they fought. Likewise, in no uncertain terms, a Bougainville psychiatric report in 1944 maintained that the "greatest single long-range cause of mental breakdown in the U.S. Army is the lack of [indoctrination] in the causes for this war, principals [sic] involved, and the ideals of democracy versus fascism." As a result, "the whole war becomes ... meaningless, and the hardships, fears, and killings ... senseless."[47]

While psychiatric disorders in the American army accounted for almost half the medical discharges, according to the psychoanalyst Gregory Zilboorg, a Russian émigré and later biographer of Sigmund Freud, they accounted for only 17.5 percent in the Russian army. He attributed this to the Russian army's considering "education of the soldier in the aims of the war as important as teaching the techniques of shooting a gun."[48]

Noting the low rate of mental casualties among German prisoners of war compared to the rate in the American army, Menninger wondered whether the sophisticated system of German propaganda was responsible.[49] At the end of the war, an investigation by the Office of Scientific Research and Development (OSRD) of psychoneuroses went a step further, attributing the higher rate of psychiatric casualties among American troops in 1945, compared to that of British and Russian troops, to Americans' having little reason for revenge when, aside from Pearl Harbor, their country had not been attacked or had their families slaughtered. Many, the OSRD reported, felt they "were only doing their share in a disagreeable and dangerous task."[50]

What little "ideology" American GIs did have, the investigation continued, actually seemed to interfere with their motivation to fight. That is, Americans' traditional belief in individualism made it hard to conform to military authority, and the "cynical pacifism" cultivated in the 1920s and 1930s made it difficult to engage in combat. (Again, this cast doubts on democracy, in a war ostensibly fought to preserve democracy.)

However, the argument that lack of political motivation was "the" cause of a higher psychiatric casualty rate among Americans than among other combatants should be viewed with some skepticism. Take the Russians. While their lower rate of psychiatric casualties, according to one historian, was at least partly attributable to their being motivated by fighting on their own soil, another historian has noted that Russian psychiatrists had a different concept of mental illness. In order for a soldier to have a recognized psychiatric disorder, Russian doctors required a physiological cause and resulting physiological damage. Emotional trauma did not constitute illness. It was the normal reaction of a soldier to combat. If the soldier could not take it, something was wrong with his character. He might be sent to a "political officer" to reorient his mind. If that failed, he might be sent to a penal battalion or shot. Clearly, this view reduced the psychiatric casualty rate.[51]

In October 1944, American psychiatrists in Italy linked low morale to "a very skeptical attitude toward the present Italian Campaign and the need for it." (An important question, given that among Americans, casualties sometimes ran as high as 50 to 95 percent of all troops. By the end of the Italian campaign, Americans had suffered at least 110,000 casualties, including over 22,000 killed, 77,248 wounded, and 10,338 missing.) Psychiatrists quoted patients saying: "1. The war in Italy, particularly since the fall of Rome, has been an unnecessary waste of men and material; 2. The war in Italy at present is not worth the cost since the war with Germany will not be won here but in France and Germany. So why risk life and limb here."[52]

Psychiatrists feared that Americans' seeming lack of hatred for the enemy, particularly Germany, might interfere with their ability to fight and could increase mental breakdowns. As early as October 1943, Appel requested that Stouffer's branch investigate how attitudes toward the enemy affected "behavior in the combat zone," "susceptibility to psychiatric disorder," and "mental stamina." In part, Appel answered his own question when he heard from psychiatric patients during an observation tour in 1944. Patients told him: "I have nothing against the Germans. They are forced to fight, too." Or, "I still can't see any sense in sending American boys over here and getting them blowed up—if Germans came over to the United States, I'd fight all right."[53]

Stouffer's surveys of troops in North Africa, Sicily, and the Pacific in 1944 and 1945 confirmed that soldiers were more sympathetic to the Germans than the Japanese. In one survey, more infantrymen favored wiping out the entire nation of Japan than favored wiping out Germany.[54] The racist, dehumanizing attitudes of Americans toward the Japanese, according to one historian, propelled them to kill without rule or compassion. Early on, Americans at home had incarcerated 110,000 Japanese Americans in internment camps. Throughout the war, the military and the press equated them with "apes," "rats," and "vermin."[55] On the other hand, one historian wrote, "Americans fought German soldiers without hatred or even moral indignation, at least until their subsequent European encounters with slave labor and concentration camps."[56]

Comradeship
Stouffer's surveys plus those of other social scientists and historians concluded that teamwork motivated men in combat more than did political indoctrination.[57] An I&E Research Branch study commissioned by Appel found that "going through the worst and sticking it out together" supported a man through battle. According to the OSRD investigation conducted near the end of the war, soldier patients in military hospitals separated from buddies would sometimes go AWOL to rejoin their units.[58] One such "escapee" was the *Stars and Stripes* cartoonist Bill Mauldin.[59] On the other hand, at least one historian has recently maintained that while comradeship was a primary factor, "willingness to obey orders ultimately hinged on the group's believing, at least implicitly, in the legitimacy of the cause and the country that sent it to war."[60]

Yet despite the academic debate over what most motivated soldiers to fight, military psychiatrists and military leaders from Marshall and Menninger on down continued to express the belief that the predominant factor in motivating soldiers to fight was political orientation.

Religion
Religion too played a role in reassuring men they would be protected from death in battle. Many a man prayed or was counseled by a chaplain before

From Prediction to Prevention | 165

battle. In his oral history, the veteran Bert Manhoff recalled: "There are no atheists in foxholes.... You are appealing to something when you are in that foxhole. You may be a non-believer and you're praying to that tree in front of you or you're praying to something around you."[61] One I&E Research Branch survey found that 70 to 83 percent of veteran infantrymen believed prayer helped the most "when the going was tough," followed by 55 to 61 percent finding that the sense of "not letting men down" was most helpful, and last, 20 to 30 percent were most motivated by hating the enemy.[62] Another veteran recalled that prayer comforted the wounded.[63]

Training Camps

Even before men shipped overseas, psychiatrists recognized that training camps had their own stresses. At Aberdeen Proving Grounds, Maryland, and Fort Hood, Texas, they noted the pressure to conform to authoritarian rule anathema to an individualistic society; to accept killing and being killed, both repugnant to civilian morality; to work and live with individuals one would never come in contact with in civilian life; to be separated from wife or mother (especially hard on eighteen- and nineteen-year-olds); or to adjust to an inappropriate assignment or a poor commander.[64]

"Hit th' dirt, boys!"

"Joe, yestiddy ya saved my life an' I swore I'd pay ya back. Here's my last pair of dry socks."

Figure 6. "Hit th' dirt, boys!"

Figure 7. "Joe, yestiddy ya saved my life . . . Here's my last pair of dry socks."

"Maybe Joe needs a rest. He's talkin' in his sleep."

Figure 8. "Maybe Joe needs a rest. He's talkin' in his sleep."

"I guess it's okay. The replacement center says he comes from a long line of infantrymen."

Figure 9. "I guess it's okay. The replacement center says he comes from a long line of infantrymen."

"I'm depending on you old men to be a steadying influence for the replacements."

Figure 10. "I'm depending on you old men to be a steadying influence for the replacements."

"I feel like a fugitive from th' law of averages."

Figure 11. "I feel like a fugitive from th' law of averages."

"Everyone Has His Breaking Point"

By the middle of the war, the phrase "everyone has his breaking point" had become quite popular on the warfront. As far back as January 1941, an army air force technical manual had employed the phrase. However, the manual qualified the statement by stipulating that "individuals vary in this as in all other traits."[65] But by fiscal year 1943, the Army Neuropsychiatry Branch's annual report switched from emphasizing individuality to emphasizing the universality of mental breakdown. The report denied that "psychiatric disorders are necessarily "queer" or "a special class of people." It continued: "Anybody may have a nervous breakdown no matter who he is . . . put under strain long enough and intense enough, everybody has his breaking point."[66] That October, Army Surgeon General Circular Letter No. 176 went further, stating: "A significant proportion of the neuropsychiatric casualties are . . . individuals who give no history suggesting predisposition. Under the extremes of stress and fatigue of modern combat, the most stable individual may reach his breaking point."[67]

Put another way, in "Psychiatric Toll of Warfare," appearing in the December 1943 issue of *Fortune*, the author affirmed that "each man has his breaking point. But what the breaking point and where the threshold, no psychiatrist is able to say."[68] In October 1944, a returned flier wrote in *Woman's Home Companion* that vulnerability to breakdown did not occur on the battleground alone but extended to a "young lieutenant [who] cracked up from overwork in England,"[69] a concept to be broadened even further during and after the war.

On the other hand, within the profession, significant differences of opinion about the phrase persisted. Speaking before the Chicago Institute for Psychoanalysis on January 14, 1944, the psychiatrists Roy Grinker and John Spiegel tried to limit the phrase to those in actual combat, under bombing attack, or pilots in training, their lives in constant jeopardy. They distinguished these soldiers from those with neuroses before or during induction, in training, or in the US noncombat zones abroad. The latter categories, they maintained, had disorders attributable to "latent" or "active neuroses" incurred earlier and not to stressful conditions of military service.[70]

Yet the Army Neuropsychiatric Consultants Division, represented by Appel and Farrell at the APA Centenary Meeting in May 1944, took a broader stance. Though acknowledging that the highest rates of psychiatric disorders came from units in actual combat, they asserted that a large proportion of neuropsychiatric cases admitted to hospitals in the United States without being in combat had no history of "neuropathic traits or anything that could be taken to indicate 'predisposition.'" Instead, they maintained that the "stress of the situation," even if not combat, had engendered their disorders.[71]

The importance of this difference of opinion cannot be minimized. According to leading historians, no more than 10 percent of soldiers saw extended combat in the war.[72] Hence, to restrict "everyone has his breaking point" to those in actual combat would limit the import of the concept considerably.

Despite definitional differences, the phrase "everyone has a breaking point" caught hold and profoundly affected medical and popular perceptions during and after the war. In its broadest sense, it meant at any time, with no way of knowing, any person might crack given a particular stress, the stress itself being unpredictable. Consequently, doctors could not screen. All they could do was attempt to reduce or eliminate stress. As to soldiers, since there was no way of knowing when they might break down, they could do little about it. Consequently, they had no reason to worry. As Farrell stated, it was just like a head cold; it would happen when it happened. And since the most "normal" might break down, there was no stigma either. A person who broke was not a "creep," a "softee," a "coward," or "malingerer." But this rhetoric was not fully in line with soldiers' opinions. In surveys, the average soldier expressed more respect for the soldier who broke down after years of combat than for the soldier who was just getting his feet wet.[73] But at least to some extent, tolerance for mental breakdown was promoted by the "breaking point" concept.

Segregation and Mental Health

Some authors have asserted that psychiatrists did not consider the impact of racial segregation during the war.[74] But the record indicates otherwise. Reflecting widespread military leadership attitudes, in January 1944 Menninger maintained in a paper for Osborn's I&E Division that segregation benefited the Black GI's psyche.[75] On the other hand, Lawrence Kubie (a well-known psychoanalyst and neurologist) and M. Ralph Kaufman (a psychiatric consultant to the South Pacific and Pacific) held that segregation had detrimental psychological effects, opinions more in tune with contemporary NAACP reports. The issue was in fact considered and debated.

William C. Menninger

Menninger's positive view of segregation reflected the views of many military leaders. Secretary of War Stimson maintained that "segregation was not discrimination" and that the "war was no time for social experiments." "Negroes," Stimson told Congress, "have been unable to master efficiently the techniques of modern weapons."[76] Menninger shared Stimson's belief that Blacks, with inferior education and lower scores on army classification tests, could not keep up with whites and hence could not be integrated with white troops, an opinion affirmed by General George C. Marshall.[77] Menninger believed that integrating training units would create discipline problems. Comparing Black troops to the British Pioneer Corps for the mentally deficient, he wrote: "The British experience in this war has left little doubt that men grouped on the basis of their mental and physical capacities have a better chance to develop high morale and excellent teamwork than a mixture of personalities with widely different capacities."[78] In the same paper, he stressed that it was imperative for Blacks to have white officers because they perceived the white man as a "father figure" and the paternalistic relationship inspired the Black soldier to be more loyal and appreciative. While many line officers probably shared Menninger's belief, Truman K. Gibson Jr., the special civilian aide to the War Department for racial matters, criticized racial segregation. [79]

Though Menninger recommended recreation to improve Black mental health, he cautioned: "It is not practical to present intellectual pursuits, moving pictures, or lectures as a form of entertainment to a group who can neither understand nor appreciate them. On the contrary, the Negro's love of spontaneous music is an example of the type of specific recreation which should be provided for this group."[80] (As we will see, Menninger reversed his position on integration when the war ended.)

Lawrence Kubie's Campaign for Integration

In contrast to the wartime positions of Menninger and military leaders, Kubie contended that segregation harmed the Black soldier's fighting capability. He bolstered his position with interviews with aviators and doctors at the segregated Selfridge Airfield, near Detroit, and Oscoda Airfield, Michigan, both installations where Tuskegee Airmen trained. Aware of claims that Blacks could not withstand combat under long, heavy pounding, Kubie contended that even if true, segregation was probably the cause, since it made it difficult for Blacks to fight alongside whites. Segregation, he wrote, made Black soldiers "too sensitive to the plight of their own group" and unable to identify with the nation's larger interests in a time of war.[81] Kubie also noted that Black officers at Selfridge had to live in "Mud Town," inferior temporary barracks, and were forced to travel two to three hours each way to Detroit just to spend an hour with their wives and children because the air force refused to allow Black families to live on base.

Black officers, he wrote, faced a dilemma. On the one hand, they needed to impose the necessary discipline on their men according to air force standards; on the other, they needed to defend their men's civil rights.[82] Segregation was less painful, Kubie found, at all-Black Oscoda than at Selfridge, where white and Black servicemen lived in separate barracks, because white officers did "not feel under social pressure" from other whites to disparage their Black trainees. Still, Black servicemen at both bases suffered from segregation. In August 1943, a month before the race riot in Detroit, Kubie wrote: "Every Negro aviator and doctor with whom I spoke believed race riots in the armed forces are a direct and inevitable consequence of separate Negro units [which] breed friction." But a request by Kubie to end segregation was ignored by the military and his medical superior officers. As he told Arthur Ruggles, then APA president: "I feel badly that it has gone spinning into the gutter, without knocking down even one pin."[83]

In an oral history in 1972, Kubie recalled that he had advised the air force to gradually integrate all combat units except for training and labor battalions for the mentally deficient. But Commanding General Henry ("Hap") Arnold classified his request and did not allow anyone, including the Committee on Neuropsychiatry, to see it without his permission. Kubie asked senior members of that committee, Edward Strecker and Arthur Ruggles, for their opinions. But they felt that any protest would impede the committee's participation in the war effort. According to Kubie, John Murray, chief of army air force psychiatry, recommended that the study not proceed up the chain of command. Kubie considered appealing directly to the Roosevelts, but by that time the president was quite ill.[84] The matter went no further.

M. Ralph Kaufman

In a report in 1944 for Brigadier General Earl Maxwell of the 93rd Division, South Pacific, Dr. Kaufman likewise tied segregation to low morale. Black officers, he wrote, complained that their commanders refused to promote them and threatened to replace them with white officers once combat began. Some Black officers were so upset they "openly expressed contempt and hostility [toward] white officers and ... the white race in general." Other Black officers and enlistees seemed intent on getting rotated or reclassified; still others went increasingly to sick call for psychiatric problems or, even, it seemed, to "welcome court-martial." Like white officers in Italy who feared the 92nd Division would panic in combat, white officers commanding the 93rd contended the division was "unsuitable for almost any kind of military duty, especially combat duty," and requested transfer. Actually, the 93rd Division psychiatrist George Little noted later, when the division did go into combat and fought side by side with white combat veterans, Black morale rose. Little attributed this to the "friendliness and cooperation that the [Blacks] received from veteran troops, who have worked with white officers and troops in the past."[85] The following February 1945, the NAACP's Walter White similarly criticized the effects of segregation on the 93rd in a memorandum for Roosevelt, but nothing was done then either.[86]

Instead, through most of the war, despite serious manpower shortages, the military, imbued with skepticism about the combat readiness of Blacks, delayed assigning them to combat, placing them in low-status support, engineering, and transportation units instead. When they were finally assigned, Blacks in the 92nd in Italy and the 93rd in the Pacific fought valiantly despite insufficient, poorly trained replacements and inferior leadership.[87]

Psychiatry and the Women's Army Corps (WAC)

While WAC psychiatrists originally focused on modifying the environment to improve mental health, as the war progressed, they toughened screening, primarily in response to contemporary conservative attitudes about sexual morality and respectability. Hence, while psychiatry for most men increasingly deemphasized screening in favor of changing the environment, WAC psychiatry did the reverse.

To appreciate how the role of the WAC psychiatrist changed during the war, we first need to review some facts about women in the military. No more than 350,000 women served in the military in all branches, of which 150,000 were in the WAC, out of a total of over 16,300,000 in military service.[88] Women performed essential functions, freeing men for combat. Women soldiers were, for example, typists, clerks, drivers, instructors, intelligence agents, decipherers, and newspaper reporters. Though no woman was officially assigned to combat, women army nurses were stationed at the front, and other women were there, too. The army nurse Mary Robinson recalled in an oral history that in 1943 her unit lived in hot tents in trenches in Leyte, the Philippines. The women could often hear gunfire at night. While they did not carry weapons, they donned helmets when they anticipated bombs.[89] Late in the war, a kamikaze pilot attacked a navy hospital ship, killing at least six nurses.[90]

Many factors contributed to a change in the focus of psychiatry in the WAC from improving the environment to screening. First, no woman served in combat in World War II. Since leading military psychiatrists focused on the stress of combat, they spent less time on women's mental health. To the extent that psychiatric leadership did influence WAC policy, it was not from the military but from civilian psychiatrists who had initiated the screening program in 1940 and 1941 and persisted throughout the war in advocating tougher screening for men and women. Negative public attitudes toward women being soldiers and puritanical social mores also influenced the WAC to conduct increasingly tough psychiatric screening.

After Congress converted the Women's Army Auxiliary Corps (WAAC, a volunteer organization) into the more costly WAC (the Women's Army Corps), an official part of the army, with the same pay and benefits as men, the American public became more intolerant of women being soldiers. The WAAC had recruited women from colleges and business schools with higher educational standards than the army's, ensuring the corps' selectivity. But the WAC tended to have lower standards, leading to the need for screening.

In a predominantly puritanical society—and also one where men during the Depression had had a hard time getting jobs—Americans found it difficult to accept women taking on the traditional "male" role of soldier. Men in decent jobs at home were particularly reluctant to have women replace them while they were sent overseas to fight. A survey by the Office of Censorship of letters from soldiers revealed that 84 percent opposed women being WACs. Unaccustomed to women being soldiers, Americans questioned what type of woman would join: Were they lesbians or promiscuous or just women who could not adapt to domestic life? While the WAC and all other female military units contributed greatly to the war effort, the War Department employing them in key policy roles and Eisenhower praising their competence, the press persistently questioned WACs' respectability and the propriety of their joining the military.[91] While experts emphasized that women's roles in the military were merely temporary and that they would soon return to domesticity, still not everyone could accept them being soldiers.

To promote the respectability of the organization, WAC Director Oveta Hobby, a law school graduate, newspaper correspondent, and co-owner with her husband of the *Houston Post*, engaged in several efforts, which eventually included tough psychiatric screening. Initially, Hobby provided Congress with statistics showing exceptionally low rates of pregnancy and venereal disease among WAACs to persuade them to pass the act establishing the WAC. The WAC also conducted several well-publicized investigations of lesbians. In response to baseless charges from Robert Rutherford McCormick, editor and publisher of the archconservative *Chicago Tribune* and owner of the radio station WGN, Oveta Hobby and Franklin and Eleanor Roosevelt emphasized that the WAC, unlike the army, did not provide contraceptives to women soldiers at all and discharged any woman who became pregnant.[92]

In the beginning, the priority was not on screening. True, as early as 1942 the WAAC advised recruiters to weed out those of "doubtful reputation" and distributed a list of undesirable habits and traits of character, including homosexuality and sexual promiscuity.[93] But they scarcely employed psychiatrists at all. Instead, they emphasized through their literature the need to improve the environment to ensure mental health. In their May 1943 training pamphlet "Sex Hygiene Course for Officers and Officer Candidates," the WAAC advised officers to "keep the number of sexually undisciplined as low as possible." Fearful of pregnancy and the spread of venereal disease (before penicillin), the pamphlet described the biology of sex so that officers could educate enlistees and keep them out of trouble. Reflecting attitudes more tolerant than they became later in the war, the pamphlet noted that everyone was born with "a bisexual nature" and that sometimes "recessive traits became more evident," but this did not mean that anyone was physiologically abnormal. They reminded readers that a person "was innocent until proven guilty" and that there should be no "witch-hunts" over sexual orientation.

Dressing in a mannish fashion, according to the manual, meant little; the important thing was to control conditions, that is, have women in barracks instead of hotel rooms with only a few other women; give women enough activities to prevent boredom, which might lead to sexual contact with other women; provide wholesome social activities with men; use the example of morally upright leaders to discourage enlistees from homosexual activity; and have officers caution enlistees that homosexual activity would interfere with a future happy married family life. If this did not work, officers were to refer enlistees to psychiatrists and if still "not amenable to guidance" discharge them "as quickly as possible." As for sex with men, the manual emphasized that officers should stress that "continence is not harmful to men or women, and sublimation of the sex drive into work channels is not only possible but can give added strength . . . to the job at hand."[94]

Even after the WAAC became the WAC, it took a while until the organization really supported screening. For one thing, no more than sixteen female psychiatrists served in the army during the war. While a psychiatrist, male or female, might review the recommendations of recruiters, a psychiatrist did not generally examine each candidate. Nor were lower-level WAC officials eager to implement the screening program, given such rumors as that of one psychiatrist at Fort Oglethorpe admitting a woman who later proclaimed herself the "Duchess of Windsor." A WAC state director bemoaned the loss of nice prospects because a psychiatrist insisted on examining women in the nude, as was done for the males, and on asking embarrassing sexual questions. WACs complained that aptitude tests had gender-biased questions. Though medical instructions called for routine psychiatric examinations, many recruitment stations were still reluctant to implement them.[95]

In September 1943, the leading civilian psychiatrists Overholser and Strecker and Chief of Army Psychiatry Division Roy Halloran, among others, charged WAC induction boards with conducting inadequate or nonexistent psychiatric examinations in their "Report of the Special Committee to the Secretary of War on Induction." The doctors faulted the WAC for permitting women to enlist up to the age of fifty, the peak age for neuropsychiatric illness in women; and for lacking clear criteria for psychoneuroses.[96]

Years later, George Stevenson, head of the National Committee for Mental Hygiene (NCMH) at the time, recalled his concern about news stories that WACs were prostitutes or lesbians, which led him to urge Hobby to inspect the social, criminal, and welfare records of each enlistee. As a result, in mid-1944 the Army Surgeon General placed the psychiatrist Margaret Craighill in charge of WAC health and welfare.[97]

Still, in July 1944, Major Ivan C. Berlien of the Army Medical Corps complained that every WAC in the neuropsychiatric wards at the time of his study could and should have been rejected had there been a careful psychiatric examination and in some cases a careful social history as well. Instead, WACs who had previously been in mental institutions and others who were psychopaths, including some "sex psychopaths," had slipped in, threatening morale and incurring unnecessary expense for the government. He favored approval of a more careful psychiatric examination.[98] Little more than a week later, Craighill, newly appointed, instructed attendants, including psychiatrists at a WAC Selection Conference, to evaluate recruiters' reports before allowing a candidate to enlist and to reject applicants found promiscuous or exhibiting behavior problems.

Thereafter, the corps became more vigilant. Not only women in lesbian relationships but those who cross-dressed or acted "butch" might be rejected or discharged. The focus on mere "tendencies," short of concrete behavior, which had pervaded the men's psychiatric examinations throughout the war, now arrived in the WAC. Women were subject to investigation based on gossip and innuendo and like their male counterparts received Section VIII administrative discharges, frequently blue, that is, without benefits. At times, they were pressured to name names of other women. Years later, they discussed at length the horrors of the experience in documentaries.[99]

One WAC investigation went on for over a month and covered training camps throughout the United States. It occurred after a mother, discovering love letters from a WAC sergeant to her twenty-year-old daughter, who was in training at Fort Oglethorpe, Georgia, complained to the army AG of "widespread lesbianism and depravity." Though the mother later recanted her claims about the extent of lesbianism, at least one officer resigned "for the good of the service" without benefits, and five other WACs, including the alleged victim, were sent to a WAC hospital in Iowa for psychiatric treatment.[100]

By October 1944, the WAC psychiatric screening bulletin *TB MED 100* set standards quite difficult for women to meet, reflecting the popular confusion about the female's role in society at that time. On the one hand, a recruit was supposed to assume a traditionally male role; on the other, she was supposed to do so only temporarily and be eager to return to domesticity. Reflecting this dilemma, the bulletin found it improper to escape from a "traditional female role" yet not proper to be too conventional. This left little room for maneuver. Indeed, the bulletin suggested weeding out a wide range of applicants. In addition to urging psychiatrists to screen lesbians, alcoholics, epileptics, and women in menopause, the bulletin called for excluding the young woman fleeing parental supervision and the older woman fleeing confined domestic life, an unhappy love affair, difficult work situation, or divorce; also undesirable, the woman "heretofore living in a protected social strata" such as the housewife who had little to do "with masses of women ... or outside ... conditions."[101] Who was left?

The WAC vigilantly checked enlistees' social and criminal records. Responding to Stevenson's suggestion, Hobby instructed the WAC not to admit anyone with a criminal background, a provision not required by any other military branch. When General Lewis Hershey, in charge of Selective Service, refused Hobby's request to use the Medical Survey Program (MSP) to obtain records, the WAC turned to Dr. Lewis Weed, director of the NRC Medical Division, and to Army Surgeon General Norman Kirk, who made alternate arrangements for the WAC to obtain social histories.

By 1944, over 20 percent of WAC medical rejections and 60 percent of WAC medical discharges were on neuropsychiatric grounds, both figures higher than for men. A year later, discharges for inaptitude, unsuitability, and for "other than honorable" reasons rose to the highest level in the war.[102] However, the extent of homosexuality in the corps is unknown, since there are no known statistics specifically for discharges for homosexuality. Such discharges were probably listed under other categories. We know, for example, this was the practice in the navy. For example, Ross T. McIntire received a letter in 1944 advising him that one ensign in the Navy Women's Reserve had been discharged for "Maladjustment and

Temperamentally Unsuited for Naval Service. Real Charge sexual abnormality."[103]

The predominant thrust of psychiatric practice in the WAC in 1944 and 1945 was screening. Yet WAC psychiatrists continued to try to improve the environment to foster mental health. Craighill discussed the effects of poor job placement, extreme climates, and pressure to have sex on the female psyche. In Ceylon, a WAC psychiatrist found that Signal Corps specialists enduring irregular meals and lack of sleep showed a high rate of mental breakdown. In New Guinea, psychiatrists found that most WACs were "restricted to locked compounds," forced to live in noisy, crowded barracks with communal showers and latrines with no privacy, and denied opportunities for rest and recreation. Psychiatrists also reported that male competition for the women's attention, isolation, loneliness, and the ever-present threat of death created enormous pressure for friendship and sexual intimacy. In some cases, women could not take it and broke down.

Group cohesiveness, according to Craighill, positively influenced morale. One study followed a WAC unit in Egypt for nineteen months. All 139 women were well adjusted, which was attributed to feelings of group cohesion. On the other hand, 157 women in West Africa, overseas for three months but together for only two weeks before being shipped out, had enormous problems. When introduced into an "isolated camp of several thousand men" eager for female companionship, there was "enormous tension," a lot of drinking, and many "psychiatric conditions."[104]

American psychiatrists had come a long way from the psychiatric screening of 1940 and 1941. By late 1944, psychiatrists overseas recognized the effect of the environment on mental health in war and doubted their ability to forecast behavior. Consequently, they focused more on psychiatric treatment and prevention.

9   Limits to Prevention and Treatment

Responding to pressure from the military to conserve manpower and to a major transformation in the philosophy of what causes mental illness, military psychiatry began to switch its focus during the last year of the war. Increasingly, military psychiatrists focused not on screening but on enhancing the environment to improve mental health either through prevention or cure, including providing for rest and recuperation, limited tours of duty, and treatment at the front. But change came too little and too late, and not without flaws; its benefits were experienced more in Korea and Vietnam.

More than anything else, John Appel, chief of the Army Mental Hygiene Branch, advocated limiting tours of duty to approximately 120 aggregate combat days. He called on Frederick Hanson, the psychiatric consultant to the Mediterranean theater, the army inspector general, and Congresswoman Claire Boothe Luce of the House Committee on Military Affairs to endorse his program. However, Army Chief of Staff George Marshall did not officially implement a limited tour until May 1945, after the war in Europe had ended.[1]

Why was Marshall's rhetoric more positive than his actions? For one, Marshall feared that a limited tour would strain manpower at a point when supply was far behind demand. Draft levies had risen by the end of 1944 from sixty thousand to ninety thousand a month; by March 1945, they would go to one hundred thousand. With British manpower sorely depleted by five years of continuous warfare, the responsibility fell on America to furnish more than two-thirds of the manpower pool by the end of the war. Eisenhower sought an additional hundred thousand marines; Patton fruitlessly requested additional divisions.[2] Under these conditions, every man was needed, making limited tours of duty a luxury.

Marshall's G-1 (assistant chief of staff for personnel) claimed that shortening tours would reduce the incentive to fight. With just a month or two remaining in a tour, a soldier might grow cautious or even refuse to fight, as documented among some airmen who became afraid to fly when approaching their last mission.[3]

Appel's concept of a limited tour later proved its worth in Korea and Vietnam, with lower rates of breakdown in those conflicts. However, by Iraq and Afghanistan, a smaller all-volunteer military was forced to redeploy again and again, defeating Appel's objective and contributing to resurgent rates of mental breakdown and suicide.[4]

Rest

Appel's companion proposal for adequate rest led the Third and Twelfth Armies in Europe to establish rest camps in late 1944. Some in the Third spent time in Normandy and Paris after its liberation in August 1944. In the Twelfth Army, where most soldiers were assigned, some took ten-day stints in England. During the winter of 1944–1945, after spending four hundred days in combat in Italy and France, the 36th Infantry Division sent soldiers on six-day vacations to local French towns, featuring a hotel, hot bath, fresh clothes, souvenirs, free beer, doughnuts, waitress-served food, and dances twice a week. Rest camps also appeared in the Pacific theater.[5] Nonetheless, an Inspector General investigation in May 1945 concluded that many psychiatric casualties were still attributable to inadequate rest and called for two to four days off after every twelve days in combat.[6]

Some psychiatrists, however, contended that rest encouraged unhelpful thoughts. Roy Grinker, a Twelfth Army Air Force psychiatrist and the innovator of narcosynthesis, cautioned: "The contrast with the grim realities of combat reminds them what they must return to . . . they remain preoccupied with gloomy thoughts of flying and dying."[7] Vacations in Paris and Nancy were often too far for a combat soldier to reach on a two- or three-day pass. And once there, soldiers might find MPs governing with an iron hand.[8]

In October 1944, General Mark Clark advised Marshall that he had neither time nor replacements to relieve troops. "The decision . . . is one of halting our attack . . . to rest, or of pushing on in an all-out effort . . . before winter catches us in the Apennines and thus contribute to . . . shortening . . . the war. To me there is only one answer . . . and I am proud to . . . tell you that the Fifth Army troops have made significant advances every day for more than two weeks."[9] While Clark's policy may have been justified, other officers in France and Germany opposed R&R simply because, according to the OSRD psychiatrists Karl and William Menninger, they "treated men worse than . . . jeeps."[10]

Leadership Selection and Training

Unlike the Germans and British, American psychiatrists and psychologists had not focused on leadership selection or training. Concentrating on psychiatric screening of enlisted men, they failed to appreciate the importance of officer selection. In contrast, in the much more class-ridden British and German societies, officer candidates, especially those not born gentlemen, needed to prove their worth through extensive tests and training.

Nevertheless, changes in America's officer training slowly evolved. Before the war, training manuals stressed gentility and etiquette, but during the war, the manuals switched to emphasize motivating men to fight.[11] Based on his experience in combat in Tunisia, Herbert Spiegel instructed commanders to explain the reasons for tactics and the importance of missions. Officers, he warned, must not mince harsh realities but instead assure their men they would support them to the hilt.[12]

A psychiatric training manual for the 38th Division in New Guinea and the Philippines advised officers to use a bit of humor to buoy spirits but "never wise crack about death."[13] Other psychiatric manuals instructed officers to know their soldiers' birthdays, hobbies, and occupations; treat men equally; visit each soldier in the hospital; write to his family; and ensure he got the proper assignment, adequate food, clothes, and recreation.[14]

In designing leadership training, psychiatrists surely knew of Colonel Evans F. Carlson's command of his famed "Raiders" on Guadalcanal. Carlson encouraged men to tell him what went wrong in battle, even when it pertained to officers. He prohibited officers to order men to do anything they would not do themselves or to enjoy luxuries their men did not have. Inspired by this training, the Raiders killed as many as seven hundred Japanese after crossing 150 miles of jungle, with only seventeen dead and one neuropsychiatric casualty. But when Carlson was assigned elsewhere, the program disbanded.[15]

In his widely disseminated memorandum on preventing loss of manpower, Appel called for better officer screening and placement, for fear that weak officers could spread panic among troops. Chaired by the Columbia University psychologist Henry Garrett, a subcommittee of the National Defense Research Committee (NDRC) experimented with an officer screening test, but while successful in assessing performance in training, it could not adequately evaluate an officer's ability to command in combat.[16] Altogether, the limited involvement of psychiatrists with officer selection and training represented a missed opportunity for the profession, especially because it had been a persistent problem since the beginning of the war.

In contrast, Germany's officer selection efforts were extensive. A team of officers, psychologists, a physician, and a psychiatrist interviewed each candidate about his previous social history; judged his facial expressions, speech patterns, handwriting, and interpersonal skills; and tested his ability to complete tasks and solve problems. Afterward, they gave him a two-day "Fuhrer probe," including assessing his ability to command an unfamiliar group in unpleasant tasks.[17] Likewise, the British had a three-day officer selection program, which included intelligence, personality, and military tests. It also assessed an officer's ability to command under stress by having him participate in a "Leaderless Group" in such activities as building a bridge.[18]

Political Orientation

As to political indoctrination, while some psychiatrists had misgivings, others believed it significantly boosted morale. Based on surveys of the attitudes of thousands of soldiers toward the war conducted by the sociologist Samuel Stouffer and his team of social-scientist researchers at the Information and Education Division (I&E)'s Research Branch, with the assistance of Appel, the military concluded that most American soldiers already hated the Japanese. Hence, psychiatrists focused primarily on inspiring hatred for the Germans.[19]

Although I&E devoted substantial resources to politically orienting troops through the division's daily newspaper *Stars and Stripes* and monthly magazine *Yank*, both distributed to GIs throughout the world, plus widely listened-to radio programs and current events discussion groups—psychiatrists also played a role. Psychiatrists were more successful in indoctrinating new trainees than soldiers already overseas, where officers complained that they did not have the time. Probably the most noteworthy indoctrination effort was Dr. Julius Schreiber's at Camp Callan, an Anti-Aircraft Replacement Training Center in California. As early as June 1942, faced with soldiers' lack of understanding of "why we fight," Schreiber initiated current events groups, daily newscasts, and published weekly newspaper columns demonstrating fascism's evils as a ruthless dictatorship suppressing liberty, compared to democracy's virtues as a "government of the people, by the people, and for the people." Confronting the ironies of American society, the program assisted soldiers in resolving their conflicts between personal prejudices, for example, against Blacks or Jews, and their obligation to defend democracy against a racist Germany. After monitoring the program for a year, Osborn appointed Schreiber a psychiatrist in the I&E Division. By 1944, Osborn approved similar programs under the guidance of Schreiber by other psychiatrists in nine training installations throughout the States and central Pacific.[20]

Appel also used army media to inculcate soldiers with the harsh realities of Nazism. Referring to data from the FBI, Federal Communications Commission (FCC), and Office of War Information (OWI), Appel contended in the military press that the country was under attack by the Nazis. Years later, he recalled that he had studied "secret" maps later deposited in the National Archives. Drawing on them, he stated that he had created a map published by I&E showing that Nazi air bases in South America were aiming at the Panama Canal and the southern United States.[21] (This may have been one of I&E's weekly *Newsmaps*, consisting of about four pages of short news stories and a map.)[22]

Appel and Stouffer provided some of the content and much of the psychological theory for Frank Capra's seven Why We Fight films. Using captured enemy footage depicting stark totalitarianism, the films sought to convince Americans that democracy was worth fighting and dying for.[23] As an example, Capra's film *Prelude to War* compared the Free World's freedoms of religion, thought, and right to vote with the Slave World's regimentation, torture, and indoctrination.[24] Another, *Divide and Conquer*, detailed Nazi atrocities while invading Europe, especially the slaughter and maiming of children. Some audiences were indeed inspired to fight, one soldier proclaiming that when he watched *Divide and Conquer* he could hear "soldiers who were very low in spirit muttering and grumbling, calling Hitler all sorts of names, cursing him ... the crowd was very quiet, and the picture got under their skin." On the other hand, while finding the films informative about the political situation, I&E concluded that the movies did not effectively inspire men to fight.[25]

To ease guilt about killing, psychiatrists used group therapy.[26] This therapy also included a discussion of current events. One of the first users of group psychotherapy in the military, Samuel Paster, a military psychiatrist at Kennedy General Hospital, Memphis, Tennessee,[27] graphically described an army hospital session where several patients tried to talk a pacifist out of his reservations about killing. The soldier was particularly reluctant about fighting Germans. He began:

> When I faced the Germans, I kept saying to myself "The Germans killed Americans. They should all be killed." . . . At the same time, I thought: "Life is full of cruelty, no one seems to remember that life is sacred." And then I thought of my buddies; good boys; mothers' sons, poor fellows. My heart bled for them. I saw fellows blown up. I couldn't stand it. . . . Human beings are God's own image. . . . I was getting ready to throw a grenade. I just couldn't kill. I knew that it was best for my buddies that I leave. . . . I wished I was like other boys, but I couldn't take a human life. Then there was an explosion. My eardrums pounded. I don't remember what happened afterwards. I found myself in England in a hospital.[28]

Others told him that while they too had reservations, the need to protect America from German atrocities and Germany's invasion overrode any concerns. "I too felt terrible in having to bayonet white men like myself," a miner's son said, "but when I saw what they did to us with their devilish booby traps, I wouldn't think of retreat." A Tennessee farmer admitted he found it hard to kill Italians because they had once let him go when he was in front of their machine guns. But: "The Jerries wouldn't do it. They'd kill you." But the patient was not convinced "the Jerries" would come to his doorstep. "Anyway," he said, "I'd rather take a chance, rather than kill." "That's what many people said," another retorted, "and now they are dead." "I'd rather be dead," the patient said.

Paster suggested the therapist should have continued by emphasizing the "inalienable rights of freedom of speech, press and worship compared [to] the . . . abnegation of [all] personal liberties in Germany, where the right of the individual was completely subjugated to the welfare of the state."[29] (On the other hand, Marshall and Menninger, as we have seen, were concerned about excessive American individualism.)

In their efforts at indoctrination, psychiatrists could arguably be considered to have abrogated their medical role. According to the Hippocratic Oath, the doctor is pledged to "exercise his art solely for the cure of [his] patients." Yet, in indoctrination, the psychiatrist was advancing the military goal of defeating the enemy even at the risk of his own patients' lives. And in inspiring soldiers to hate another ethnic group, it could be said that the psychiatrist promoted an unhealthy emotional reaction that might plague the soldier for decades to come.

Looking back on the war, Appel quipped that psychiatrists had switched their "oath of allegiance from Hippocrates . . . to General Marshall."[30] The Army Surgeon General in the South Pacific in September 1944 openly asserted that "the primary duty of the psychiatrist was to the military service rather than to the individual patient; that the first responsibility . . . [was] maintenance of the fighting strength . . . and all other responsibilities . . . supported this . . . or were secondary."[31]

Nonetheless, psychiatrists often failed to see a conflict or rationalized it away. Psychiatrists in Italy cited the high correlation between poor political morale and increasing mental breakdowns to prove the medical need for political orientation.[32] Menninger and Appel believed that unlike the Russian and British soldier, the American GI had a high psychiatric casualty rate because he felt no reason to kill: "The Russians are fighting to avenge the death of their loved ones . . . the British . . . for survival. . . . The doughboy fights because he has to . . . for his buddies and because his self-respect won't let him quit. For a period this is a very strong incentive, but the time comes when it rapidly loses its effectiveness."[33] Only the perceived need to defend democracy from fascism, some doctors believed, would enable a man to withstand adverse conditions of combat, including the threat of death.

Based on input from army psychiatrists, an article entitled "Mental Breakdowns in the Army," in *Yank*, attributed the GI's inability to withstand strains of combat to such factors as eagerness to get home to a profitable job, disgust with poor military job assignments, or a lack of appreciation by the folks back home of what the soldier was doing. Only the inculcation of "why you fight," it concluded, could counteract such societal pressures. Since this article was disseminated throughout the world, it had a great effect on the military's understanding of the GI's motivations.

The Columbia University psychoanalyst Leonard R. Sillman went further. He believed that inspiring hatred for the enemy protected the individual from unconscious boiling aggression, which would otherwise spill into uncontrollable panic during combat.[34] On the other hand, while Herbert Spiegel believed indoctrination could improve mental health during military training, he did not believe it influenced men to fight. "Thoughts of the Star Spangled Banner and pristine Democracy," he wrote, could only create irritation and resentment when a soldier was tired, cold, and cynical. Hanson cautioned that attempting to prove the enemy intended to "subjugate the United States" would only lead to "derision and suspicion on the part of the average GI." Rejecting Sillman's analysis of combat motivation, the Anzio beachhead battalion surgeon and later chief division psychiatrist Raymond Sobel reported that "old sergeants" in Italy who had seen hundreds of days of combat and slews of buddies killed or wounded developed an enormous hatred for Germans, which sometimes led to seriously disabling guilt feelings.[35] (Presumably, these guilt feelings stemmed from an ingrown morality that condemned eagerness to kill.)

These concerns of American psychiatrists may explain why, unlike the British, Americans did not establish "battle schools" where psychiatrists and psychologists indoctrinated servicemen to hate or to be sadistic or bloodthirsty. Although the British also had their misgivings about the negative psychological impact of such training, their schools continued. Americans, instead, relied on officer training to inspire their men.[36]

Congressional opposition to perceived mind control also limited the extent of indoctrination at home and abroad by psychiatrists or any other group. In 1944, the Neuropsychiatry Consultants Division complained that instead of urging their soldiers to win the war or "kill some Japs for me," family and friends pressured them to come home, and such attitudes had to be changed.[37] Political indoctrination was a mammoth task, beyond the ability of the military alone, and viewed with suspicion in Congress. Years later, Appel recalled that when psychiatrists tried to use army media to persuade soldiers that the nation was under imminent Nazi attack, and when they questioned soldiers and tried to change their thinking, "then Congress got interested. . . . This got too dangerous politically, thought control."[38] In the field, I&E officers worked reluctantly at best with psychiatrists to lecture to the troops, some not understanding why psychiatrists were needed at all.[39] Nor was the work of I&E officers always appreciated. Not all field commanders allowed personnel of whatever background an hour a week to discuss current events with troops. I&E surveys of fifty-seven officers in the European, fifty in the Mediterranean, and thirty-five in the China-Burma-India theaters revealed that on average, less than a quarter had presented a lecture on politics the previous week.[40] Psychiatrists like Hanson opposed anti-German indoctrination because it might interfere with American-German efforts at postwar reconciliation.[41] Sometimes, the military preferred clergy rather than psychiatrists to persuade soldiers to kill, because clergy could invoke freedom of religion to counter congressional opposition. Despite all efforts, as of January 1945 psychiatrists still correlated the high rate of psychiatric disorder with soldiers' failure to internalize the enemy's threat to America's way of life.[42] While I&E radio programs appeared to have been more appreciated than other media, it is not known what influence they specifically had on political orientation and whether psychiatrists participated in any way.[43]

Group Cohesion

Stouffer and other sociologists and historians then and later contended that camaraderie—supporting one's buddy in combat and he supporting you—motivated a soldier even more than political indoctrination. Herbert Spiegel believed that love, not hate, motivated men to kill: love of commander, platoon, unit, and country.[44] In this, psychiatrists found group therapy to be critical. Departing from the prewar emphasis on the individual, therapists tried to convert the group's personal values into "social concerns." Howard Rome, an expert in rehabilitation, among others, stressed encouraging soldiers to work together and return to their units as cooperative men.[45]

But promoting cohesion had drawbacks. One of a soldier's cruelest experiences was witnessing the violent death of a buddy in combat. According to one psychiatrist, it led to a "great collapse of a well-regulated mental mechanism."[46] Sobel found that "old sergeants" who saw one comrade after another killed or wounded resisted making friends, hesitant to waste feelings on a marked man.[47] In July 1945, the 38th Division's psychological training manual cautioned officers not to pair a soldier with a close friend, because if one is hit, "the other will go to pieces."[48] Psychiatrists advised hospital commanders to return groups, instead of individual patients, to the front so that no GI would return alone to find most of his former comrades dead or wounded.[49] Menninger and Appel favored sending replacements to the front in groups of three to nine. Yet the army did not approve group replacements until the end of the war, in part because of the scarcity of manpower.[50] Every fighting division needed men, so the army struggled to spread meager resources equitably. In the army air force, where an entire crew could be lost at once, aviators were reluctant to get too close. For example, the air force grounded Navigator Seymour Cohen because he had contracted the flu. He missed a mission over Berlin where the Luftwaffe killed his entire crew of eleven, and it led to grief, guilt, and a fear of getting too close in the future.[51]

Reducing Fear of Combat

As in all wars, dread of death, gore, and dismemberment played on men's nerves. Many admitted being so scared "they lost control of bowels or were nauseous or experienced violent pounding of the heart."[52] To counteract fear, psychiatrists emphasized that everyone felt the same anxiety, with the same physical symptoms, but that most GIs did not lose control in battle. A 38th Infantry Division Medical Bulletin stated that "out of every 100 men, 71 were most afraid before going into combat."[53]

To motivate soldiers to engage in combat, psychiatrists used mental hygiene lectures to teach GIs how to control fear. John Dollard, an I&E consultant, wrote two pamphlets for the division, "Fear in Battle" and a shorter one, "Twelve Rules on Meeting Battle Fear."[54] The latter was particularly well known. Dollard had studied psychoanalysis at the Berlin Institute in 1931–1932. He wrote *Caste and Class in a Southern Town* (1937) and with other members of the Yale Institute of Human Relations, *Frustration and Aggression* (1939). Based on his study of three hundred veterans of the Spanish Civil War's Abraham Lincoln Brigade, he instructed soldiers in "Twelve Rules":

1. Learn to know when you are becoming afraid.
2. Figure out in advance the best ways of meeting danger.
3. Keep remembering that being scared makes you a smarter soldier—and a safer one.
4. Keep your mind on the job and do it one step at a time.
5. The enemy is scared of you—and don't forget it.

6. Remember that your life may depend on somebody else's guts—and his on yours.
7. Remember, too, if you lose the enemy wins.
8. Never show fear in battle.
9. Make a wisecrack when you can.
10. Fear wears you out. So, forget it when you can.
11. Don't hesitate to talk about being scared.
12. Have a good time when you get the chance. Fun combats fear.

The pamphlet explained that Rule 3's "fear makes you smarter" meant that "fear gets you set, ready to meet any danger, quicker and smarter." If you adhered to Rule 11 and talked to others about being scared, the pamphlet assured, you would be safer. However, Dollard's message was somewhat self-contradictory. Rules 3 and 11 applauded fear's value, but Rules 8 and 10 cautioned against it. Rule 10 advised soldiers: "Fear wears you out." Rule 8 stated: "Never show fear in battle." In other words, it was okay to admit fear before but not during combat.

As to Rule 7, "if you lose, the enemy wins," the pamphlet went on: "If you lose, the Heinee or the Jap wins the battle, with you yourself lucky if you are not a prisoner or a casualty . . . a lost war means danger and damage to you and your family and your friends." Clearly, Rule 7 did not relieve anxiety but actually raised it.[55]

In August 1942, the psychiatrist R. Robert Cohen instituted a series of lectures and pamphlets for ordnance trainees at Aberdeen Proving Grounds on homesickness, discipline, and especially fear. Cohen's pamphlet "Mack and Mike" (March 1944) probably gives the best example of his message: There was a right way to control fear—the way of Mike—and a wrong way—the way of Mack (see Figure 12).

Mack did not pay attention to training, resented the commander's instructions, hated to cooperate, whether that meant marching with others or turning off the lights at 9 PM. Instead, he brooded incessantly. As he curled into himself, he fell behind in his training, making him more anxious and a possible target for enemy fire. Mike, on the other hand, took everything in stride. He was rough, tough, and all-American. He knew how to lighten his load with a joke. He concentrated on training, made new friends, and had no time to brood or resent. By 9 PM lights out he was tired from a long day of hard but enjoyable physical labor and could easily fall asleep.[56] Cohen believed his message was effective because when he compared five hundred Aberdeen trainees who received the lectures with five hundred who did not,

Figure 12. "Mack and Mike."

he found the former had lower rates of AWOL and sick call and higher grades.[57]

Years later, Gordon F. Lewis, a University of Vermont professor of sociology, recalled a similar wartime experience. While assigned to the Aberdeen Proving Grounds, he saw an announcement for servicemen to assist a colonel, a psychiatrist (possibly Cohen), in setting up a psychiatric unit to rehabilitate Section VIII or battle fatigue cases. After being interviewed, he was hired along with Jerry Oberwager, a New York City puppeteer who had worked with the folk singer Pete Seeger and with a friend of the actor Zero Mostel. The psychiatrist gave them a script for a puppet show. The names of the hand puppets were Rufus Resentment, Freddie Fear, and Arnie (or Albie) Anger. The show took place under battle conditions, foxholes, and explosive charges. He recalled:

> One GI (puppet) would be yelling about how mad he was. The other . . . would be cowering in his slit trench, wailing, crying. Maybe the other . . . would be saying things like . . . "Why am I here and why are all those lazy 4-Fers back

home?" We . . . would emphasize . . . that these feelings were normal given the situation . . . disabuse them from thinking . . . they were cowards.

Eventually, the show became so popular that the Army Surgeon General permitted Paramount Studios in Astoria, Queens, to make it into a movie. The cameraman was Stanley Cortez (later, a well-known cinematographer), the younger brother of the film star Ricardo Cortez; the director was "Frank somebody," most likely Capra.[58]

At another camp, the Tank Destroyer Replacement Training Center, Fort Hood, Texas, Commanding Psychiatrist Samuel Kraines developed an advisor system for soldiers with personal problems. Before this, someone who needed to consult a psychiatrist had to go up the chain of command, from corporal to platoon sergeant to commander, which could take days, by which time the trauma might have grown beyond repair, leading to the trainee's discharge. But with the advisor system, Kraines removed the red tape. He selected noncommissioned officers, gave them several lectures on elementary psychiatry, and placed them in barracks to live with the platoon and treat problems as they arose. But while Herbert Spiegel had promoted the idea of psychiatrists becoming advisors, in this particular case a conference of training camp psychiatrists criticized the advisor system for establishing a separate channel of authority directly reporting to the psychiatrist. Additionally, they were concerned that advisors might spy on members of the platoon and that men with little psychiatric training would wield too much influence. (This might contribute to decisions on whether or not to court-martial, give a soldier psychiatric treatment, or recommend a medical or administrative discharge, with or without benefits.) They also thought that an advisor might prevent a man from working things out on his own. It is not known whether the program was continued.[59]

Of particular concern was infantrymen's fear of enemy weapons. In October 1943, Appel and Stouffer released a survey of the fears of German weapons experienced by seven hundred enlistees recently evacuated from North Africa. According to the survey, soldiers were most afraid of the 88 mm gun, followed by the dive bomber, mortar, horizontal bomber, and light machine gun. Stouffer and Appel recommended making the training as realistic as possible, using live ammunition. "A few will get killed but the others will learn." By 1944, basic training included crawling in the midst of machine gun and artillery fire with live ammunition overhead.[60]

Psychiatrists working with the I&E and in the navy also produced training films late in the war covering such subjects as fear of combat, regimentation, deprivation, discipline, resentment, and the effects of emotions on the body.

In addition to training staff on how to treat servicemen who had such problems, the films also assuaged anticipatory fear of combat by inductees and the trauma GIs and sailors felt from prior battle experience. By self-identifying with battle scenes, GIs could emote and eliminate some of their trauma. However, as one historian has pointed out, the scary scenes of combat could also have the opposite effect. Among the films were the army's *Combat Exhaustion* and *Returning Soldier* and the navy's *Introduction to Combat Fatigue*, *The Neuropsychiatric Patient*, and *The Inside Story of Seaman Jones*. Psychiatrists who worked on such films included Frederick Hanson; George S. Goldman, head of the army psychiatric film program; Lloyd Thompson, psychiatric consultant for the European theater; and M. Ralph Kaufman and Lindsay Beaton, both at Okinawa.[61]

Treatment

Increasingly as psychiatrists joined units at the front, they recognized the inadvisability of evacuating patients to the rear. The Army Neuropsychiatric Consultants Division report for fiscal year 1943 found that patients in hospitals far from the front became listless and disinterested in recovery or experienced guilt over letting their buddies down. Successively evacuated to as many as ten different hospitals, they became despondent, believing that "nothing could be done." A South Pacific medical circular in September 1944 instructed medical officers to transfer fewer men to psychiatric wards or hospitals because the environment "might make minimal symptoms . . . unduly important."[62]

Instead, psychiatrists began to emphasize treating at the front, providing patients with rest, warm food, emotional support, and medication, with the objective of returning them to combat in two to three days. Whereas in 1942 and 1943 most psychiatrists reported returning to combat no more than 0 to 40 percent of casualties and evacuating 60 percent or more, after 1943 they reported returning from 30 to 70 percent to combat and even more to service in general.[63] By comparison, Britain and Canada, associating breakdowns more with congenital inferiority, had lower rates of return, instead evacuating large numbers or reassigning them to noncombat positions.[64]

In March 1944, one supervising psychiatrist in New Guinea described how psychiatrists made clear to the men that they were still in the military and were only suffering a temporary setback, soon to be cured and returned to battle. A combat-exhausted soldier would be transferred to a treatment center no more than twenty miles from the combat zone in the torrid jungle, where he would enter a highly organized military routine, reveille at 5:30 AM, lights out 10 PM. In between, a normal workday with an hour or two before bed for mandatory sports and games. Psychiatrists would assure him that they were doctors with the medical expertise to cure and that he would soon be ready to fight again. A few days of adequate rest, sleep, rest, and, if need be, a sedative, then back to combat.[65]

But soldiers did not always find such "treatment" assuring, as it did not appear to them anything like what they commonly considered medicine. Nor was "fatigue" always transient. Nor was it just "fatigue" when a GI came into an aid station shaking uncontrollably, weeping continuously, disoriented, and vomiting. Frequently, hypersensitivity to noise from planes, trucks, and blasting shells interrupted sleep; sometimes, screams could be heard late at night, and attempts were made to bolt. A "whirlwind of activity" did not always diminish symptoms over time. Often the headaches and tremors, nausea, insomnia, and endless crying continued. Only a narrow border appeared to exist between neurosis and psychosis.[66]

Dr. M. Ralph Kaufman

From April to June 1945, M. Ralph Kaufman, chief psychiatrist in the Pacific and South Pacific areas, in active military combat for forty-four months, and recipient of five combat stars,[67] adopted the treatment methods of Roy Grinker to the vagaries of Okinawa. Like Frederick Hanson, Kaufman returned substantial numbers to combat. Like Grinker and John Spiegel, Kaufman used narcoanalysis. However, he was more cautious about sedation. While Grinker's text recommended several sessions of psychotherapy to uproot a problem, Kaufman shortened the therapy, focusing only on the immediate precipitant of the neurosis.

Such an approach reflected the horrendous battle conditions on Okinawa. According to the official army history, Americans on Okinawa experienced the highest casualties of any campaign against the Japanese, including probably the highest rate of psychiatric casualties in the Pacific. Soldiers fought a relentless enemy who appeared in almost all cases unwilling to stop fighting until killed. Americans sat in shallow exposed foxholes, while the Japanese hid in deep fortified caves and burial tombs, armed with mortars and artillery. Americans had a hard time finding and bayoneting their enemy; the caves could be several stories deep. Unafraid to die, Japanese launched suicide boats to drop depth charges among ships. Altogether, Americans on Okinawa incurred 49,151 in casualties, of which 12,520 were killed or missing and 36,631 wounded. Nonbattle casualties (largely psychiatric) came to 15,613 soldiers and 10,598 marines. Japanese casualties were even higher, losing 110,000 lives alone.[68]

Under these conditions, Kaufman and his team of ten psychiatrists concentrated on returning men quickly to combat. They treated patients for at most a few days in regimental clearing stations no more than five hundred yards from the battle. If needed, they transferred them to a field hospital still within hearing range of the enemy's artillery, no more than four thousand to six thousand yards from the front.

Kaufman recognized the psychological impact of warfare, especially the conflict between the soldier's desire to escape danger and to do his duty.[69] Yet his therapeutic goal was to work through the immediate traumatic experience, not to deal with long-term neurotic problems, since "from the military point of view, it was essential to return a man to duty as soon as possible."

Kaufman described soldiers he felt compelled to return to combat without being completely cured. In one case, a confused man thrashing in his litter underwent hypnosis, recalling being caught in a concentration of mortar shells. He refused to admit his fear because he would be labeled "yellow." He felt responsible for other men, forty-five of whom had been wounded. He blamed himself and, though expressing "a superficial loyalty to his officers," blamed them too. After hypnosis, his tremors began to subside. Despite several talks with psychiatrists and group therapy he continued to feel guilty. Still, psychiatrists returned him to duty, concluding: "He was certainly far from a well man, but . . . the chance was worth taking." The doctors did not explore further because they felt it might only instigate further guilt, and they had insufficient time to keep treating the man until he was completely fit to return to the line.[70]

While the circumstances of Okinawa were extreme, they were not unique. In August 1945, psychiatrists, including Karl and William Menninger, concluded in the OSRD report of its investigation in Europe that the doctor "must get his patient well promptly for return to combat if possible. He thus becomes in a sense the arbiter of life and death, or at least of health and long illness, when he sends a man back into the line . . . knowing that further breaks are due to happen."[71]

Looking back after the war, William Menninger regretted the high percentage of casualties found incapable of combat, observing that "psychiatrists had the difficult assignment of returning men to the hell of battle, knowing full well that in many instances it would make their illness worse."[72] Some OSRD psychiatrists questioned whether quick psychoanalysis did little but stir up old wounds. In the military, they found that "abreaction" (generally defined as the expression and consequent release of repressed emotion) consisted of brusquely recalling traumatic experiences without having time to resolve them. In civilian practice, the process would be more deliberate and take place over a longer timeframe, enabling the patient to relive and "digest" his clinical experience.[73]

Early on, Frederick Hanson, who had much experience in treatment from North Africa, had rationalized psychiatrists' incomplete treatment of soldiers in battle by differentiating between concepts of mental health in war and peace. Military psychiatry involved compromises made under tough conditions and severe time pressures. What was "cured" was the immediate problem, not the long-term issues, which a civilian psychiatrist might later address. On the battlefield, Hanson wrote: "Abnormal insomnia, trembling, recurrent nightmares became the norm."[74] (A far cry from the rejection of recruits with even vague potential maladjustments espoused by Sullivan before the war.)

Yet this more expansive definition of "mental health" and tolerance of "mental illness" did not mitigate doctors' ethical qualms about returning soldiers to battle incompletely cured. While recognizing that recovery in the military was defined ipso facto as returning to duty, the OSRD psychoanalysts Karl and William Menninger cautioned that from a long-range perspective true recovery meant "durability of readjustment" and "the flexible adaptability of the patient to varying situations."[75]

With these conflicts in mind, Kaufman tried to employ hypnosis and sometimes sedation to satisfy both military necessity and the medical obligation to cure. For him, hypnosis should only have been used when a soldier was likely to remain effective and not break down again after reexposure to combat. Kaufman and psychiatrists working with him preferred hypnosis without sedation, since sedation could exacerbate the patient's ongoing confusion and amnesia. "It was no uncommon sight," Kaufman wrote, "to see patients stagger about as if drunk on barbiturates, confused and with an amnesia ... fixed by ... drugs,"[76] an opinion he and his associates also expressed in their 1945 training film *Hypnosis: Okinawa*.[77] Sedation, he felt, also interfered with building the necessary reassuring father-child relationship between doctor and patient.

But regardless of whether or not drugs were used, after the war Menninger admitted that success had been exaggerated, since it counted many who were returned to noncombat assignments or whose return to combat was short-term. Some soldiers, after returning for a few days or weeks, again ended up at battalion stations or in hospitals, eventually having to be discharged.[78] A report by the First Army in Europe found that "four months after 708 combat exhaustion cases returned to their units in July and August 1944, more than 200 of the returnees were killed or wounded, 108 had been evacuated for sickness, and 278 (39 percent) had experienced a relapse of combat exhaustion."[79] A study of Eighth Air Force pilots treated with sodium pentothal found that only about 12 percent returned to combat flying.[80] A report from the 18th Station Hospital in the Pacific in March 1945 disclosed that more and more psychiatrists were reassigning the combat-exhausted to noncombat positions.

After special treatment centers were incorporated into base hospitals, doctors increasingly sent psychiatric casualties to crowded, dirty redeployment or reconditioning centers, which also housed green replacements, alcoholics, self-mutilators, and "agitators." So many received noncombat assignments that Marshall pleaded with Pacific Headquarters to stop placing combat-exhausted in noncombat assignments, for fear the numbers would severely deplete the manpower necessary for combat.[81] A study by the psychiatrist Albert Glass of 393 neuropsychiatric troops who had waged combat in the central Apennines, Italy, for seventy days found that less than a third were salvaged for effective combat duty, although the vast majority could be returned to noncombat duties. Glass concluded that four or five days of rest, sedation, and superficial psychotherapy was insufficient to alter the disposition of anyone other than those with acute cases; those who had not been caught by any psychiatric screen and had been chronically ill before battle could not be changed.[82]

Figure 13. Marines crouching behind a rock as they blow up a cave on Iwo Jima.

Figure 14. "The 2000 Yard Stare," Battle of Peleliu, Pacific.

Treatment in Hospitals Far from the Front

Not every soldier was treated at the front. Evacuations continued to hospitals further in the rear. Though not as commonly as the British, American psychiatrists used drug therapies and insulin comas in hospitals and, after April 1943, electroshock for psychotic patients and those with resistant anxiety and depression. Another modality, insulin subshock therapy with or without phenobarbital, was first introduced in the United States and later in Italy for anxiety and depression or hysteria. Treatment could last up to fourteen days. Psychiatrists could also induce prolonged sleep for the sleep-deprived for up to seven days. The drug of choice was sodium amytal, sometimes with phenobarbital. But phenobarbital, as Herbert Spiegel recalled years later, could lead soldiers to "lose all senses when fighting."[83]

Psychiatrists also used a more extensive form of hypnosis than at the front. For example, American Army psychiatrists hypnotized a 12th Infantry replacement sergeant at a station hospital in England in November 1944. Though the soldier had lost his voice in combat, he continued commanding his soldiers with grunts and signs. Still, because he remained mute and partially amnesic, psychiatrists at the hospital chose to hypnotize him to uncover the "underlying unconscious desire" to escape fighting. Under hypnosis, the man fluently elaborated his views on the war, Russia, England, and living in a foxhole; his job before the war; and his feelings about race. However, on subjects that deeply troubled him, such as combat, he writhed on the bed, wept, and stuttered. When it got bad, he was told "to draw some deep breaths, relax and try to control himself." When asked if he thought the "88" was a good weapon, still under hypnosis he said: "That's what the Germans tried to kill me with. A guy hasn't got a chance." Asked about the atrocities he experienced in battle, he talked with difficulty about the SS capturing, shooting, and killing two of his comrades who refused to answer questions and about their shooting a third in the leg, who survived to tell his unit what had happened.

After the doctor woke him up, he did not remember the interview or the questionnaire on "Fear of Weapons" he had completed, but when he received the same questionnaire to fill out, he gave the same responses, except that he did not respond emotionally to the word "88." Whether or not hypnotism eliminated his mutism is unknown.[84]

The Psychiatrist and the Clergy

One of the major functions of the psychiatrist was assuring men they were doing the right thing in combat, that the enemy was evil and had to be defeated. This function was also undertaken by clergy. Sometimes the message was conveyed in two stages: Before battle, a minister counseled the soldier not to be afraid. Then a psychiatrist, while treating a casualty, told the patient he had done nothing wrong and should return to battle. Other times the two professions might join to convey the same message. According to the OSRD, the chaplain performed an important role in "giving moral and religious sanction to the necessity for killing and destruction."[85] In the military, the chaplain had a number of advantages over a psychiatrist: A patient could divulge his secrets in complete confidence to a chaplain, while he had to be careful when he spoke to a psychiatrist, since army regulations permitted doctors to abrogate the patient-doctor privilege.[86] A sympathetic chaplain might be better able to rehabilitate a religious soldier with a psychiatric diagnosis by explaining it in religious terms. For some, the very presence of a "man of God" might overcome fear. To avoid the stigma of a psychiatric diagnosis, a soldier might also consult a minister rather than a psychiatrist. On the other hand, instructors in the army chaplain school made it clear that clergy were to defer to medical, including psychiatric, experts. But a shortage of psychiatrists would sometimes necessitate the military employing clergy in a psychiatric role.[87]

The Catholic Church

Relations between psychiatry and the clergy were not seamless. Sometimes, perhaps reflecting a degree of competition, the church made clear that it believed its methods of consolation were superior to that of the psychiatrist. In August 1944, the Roman Catholic bishop John O'Hara became concerned about a complaint in a monthly report from an army hospital priest, Louis J. Meyer, that many Protestant and Catholic patients were objecting to a psychoanalyst's using a "needle" to induce "twilight sleep." O'Hara asked the chief of chaplains for the War Department to investigate. This was followed by John F. Monahan, the army chaplain for Roman Catholic priests, asking Meyer for a written explanation. Disgusted with the "abusive" use of narcoanalysis without consent, Meyer wrote in his return letter that "all they seem to think of is SEX." Upon waking after half an hour of groggy responses to questions and half an hour of recovery, Meyer added, the patient received a diagnosis of "nervous," "criminally inclined," or "homosexual," possibly all three, a diagnosis humiliating, stigmatic, and often unjustified.

For the priest, twilight sleep without consent was an invasion of conscience, inspiring resentment, which made it difficult for the questioner to find the truth. So much better, Meyer said, was the church's use of a conscious willing confessional, a heart-to-heart talk, or communion. One nurse, he wrote, received a "ridiculous" diagnosis of "suicidal tendencies." She had to return to the States with a "stained" reputation. Her hospital records, he was sure, were open to the public, since the army nurses lived "in a glass bowl." A soldier might lose his temper, or a nurse might be labeled "rebellious" if she fell in love. Such commonplace problems would be blown out of proportion and sent to a psychiatrist. In normal times, they would have confided in a friend or changed a routine, and the problem would go away. Now, they were sent to the "nut-house" and from there "home with a life scar." "We are creating," Meyer concluded, "countless inferiority complexes" caused merely by temporary overwork in a "horrible place of isolation, unhealthy climate." Several months later, Monahan sent Meyer's letter to the Army Surgeon General.[88] What happened thereafter is unknown, although by October, as discussed in what follows, there were many IG investigations, perhaps influenced in part by Catholic criticism.

The Inspector General Investigations of Psychoneuroses and Conditions Leading Up to It

As the number of Americans killed or wounded soared from D-Day on and available manpower plunged, the military became increasingly intolerant of psychiatric casualties. In the largest challenge to psychiatry of the entire war, supported by leaders in the War Department, the army chief of staff ordered the IG to investigate psychoneuroses. The IG conducted three extensive investigations of psychoneurosis in the United States, Europe, and the South Pacific from October 1944 through May 1945. Though the IG acknowledged psychiatric efforts at prevention and treatment, the very breadth of the investigations, each taking several months, impeded the success of psychiatrists' efforts (ironically, at the very moment Marshall was praising Appel's memorandum calling for more preventive psychiatry). The IG's reports not only questioned the value of military psychiatry but suggested significant nonpsychiatric alternatives. While the reports would have little immediate impact because the war was soon to end, their general condemnation of psychiatry conveyed a message for future policy making, a message softened only by the consistent promotion of psychiatry by the president until his death. Indeed, even during the investigations Roosevelt pressed his secretary of war to assure sufficient psychiatric treatment and rehabilitation to return soldiers home healthy and self-reliant.

The IG's first investigation of the Zone of Interior (United States), concluding in December 1944, recommended that the Army Surgeon General virtually eliminate the predominant psychiatric diagnosis, psychoneurosis. The army chief of staff delayed objecting to the idea of eliminating the diagnosis for three months, until March 1945. The second investigation of the South Pacific concluded in early May 1945 that psychiatrists should assign servicemen to more suitable vocations instead of discharging them on psychiatric grounds, a role previously relegated to psychologists; the third, covering Europe, concluding a few weeks later, valued psychiatrists' efforts at treatment and prevention but still called for court-martials and even executions to avert future breakdowns.

What precipitated these investigations? The answer was a growing frustration brought on by severe manpower shortages. As supreme commander of the Allied European forces, Eisenhower faced a challenge. How could he find sufficient manpower to win the war in Europe when British and Commonwealth troops had been decimated by over five years of constant warfare, when the British Command was even contemplating refusing to attack when a division might be lost? Could America take over the burden when its supply of troops was also dwindling? By the end of 1943, according to a letter from the Army Surgeon General, 1,250,000 (12 percent of those examined) had been rejected on psychiatric grounds, the equivalent of 104 divisions. During the last six months of 1943, 20 percent of those examined were rejected on neuropsychiatric grounds. The monthly input of soldiers from Selective Service was cut even further by Marshall in late 1944. As pointed out by one historian, Marshall had a dual role: Unlike Eisenhower, who was a military commander and nothing else, Marshall represented the interests of the country in winning the war and those of his direct boss, the president and commander-in-chief. By late 1944, Roosevelt was very sensitive to the fact that Congress and the public were getting tired of the war and wanted it to end. To appease them, Marshall reduced the monthly draft quota; at the same time, troops were increasingly evading service through self-inflicted wounds or desertion. Selective Service particularly lagged in providing sufficient Black troops, because of a shortage of segregated facilities and many white commanders who continued to oppose Blacks serving in combat units.[89] As to psychiatric casualties, many of which Eisenhower found questionable, their numbers grew and grew.

While Eisenhower had previously endorsed British methods of preventive psychiatry and treatment, after D-Day his sentiments changed. His close friend Major General Howard McC. Snyder (a military surgeon, future White House physician, member of the War Department Special Staff, chief of the Inspector General's Medical Division, and soon to head the first IG investigation of psychoneurosis) had also initially favored psychiatry. At a training conference in November 1943 for the sixty psychiatrists about to be sent to divisions, Snyder had stressed the importance of conserving manpower and screening out "misfits."[90] But after the Normandy invasion, he changed his tune.

One veteran, William A. Biehler, recalled for an oral history his experience crossing the English Channel and landing on Utah Beach during the Normandy invasion. His company, originally consisting of two hundred, was down to thirty. His group of replacements declined from twelve to four. Soon after landing, an 88 blew two more men "to smithereens." In the days to come, the slim remainder confronted gruesome combat:

> The roads . . . were sunken, so you couldn't . . . fire from them. . . . A tank couldn't fire to the side . . . they were trapped. . . . We had to do hedgerow by hedgerow. . . . We took heavy casualties . . . that Battle of Beau Coudray was so fierce that the night after it was over . . . three guys in the company shot themselves in the foot. . . . That's just the coward's way out, but . . . some guys . . . went to pieces. . . . Just once in a while, some guy'd . . . say, "I can't take it

anymore"... start crying or sobbing... wouldn't get out of his foxhole. We had one lieutenant who wouldn't get out.... We never saw him again. He went back to Company Headquarters... never heard what happened.... Nobody ever told us... but they were no good in the infantry, that's for sure."[91]

By June 12, six days after D-Day, as much as two-thirds of American troop strength in Normandy had been killed or wounded. While visiting the Fifth General Hospital during the Battle of Carentan, Eisenhower expressed shock at the growing numbers avoiding combat through self-inflicted wounds or claims of psychoneurosis. Later, he recalled that Brigadier General Albert Kenner, chief medical officer for the North Africa/Italian and Normandy invasions, had told him: "Rarely do you find a case of psychoneurosis amongst [physically] wounded men." Though a few authentic cases of psychoneurosis existed, Kenner told Eisenhower, many were "merely imaginary or faked to avoid battle."[92]

During the next six months in France and Germany, Americans and their allies confronted more equipment and manpower shortages, tougher terrain, prolonged battles, and an enemy hidden in dense forests of pine and fir, ready at any moment to surprise and kill. In Hitler's last desperate counterattack, the Battle of the Bulge, at one point SS troops herded 130 American prisoners into a field and against the Geneva Convention mowed down almost all of them with machine guns and tank fire.[93]

Faced with severe losses, Eisenhower wrote Marshall in September 1944 that Kenner, "one of the finest medical officers [he had] ever met," had been "report[ing] to [him] personally about once a week [about]... facts [concerning] the evacuation system and the causes of disability,"[94] keeping him abreast of the number of psychoneurotics and other suspect categories. Other combat leaders were even more unforgiving. According to Appel's unpublished history, the military was coming to believe "that the psychiatric problem was nothing more than a concoction of psychiatrists, that if there were no psychiatrists there would be no problem." "High ranking line officers," he complained, "actually went on to the wards of army hospitals and reversed decisions made by psychiatrists, ordering men out of hospitals and back to duty against medical advice."[95]

On September 23, 1944, the *Colliers* journalist Kyle Crighton concluded in "Repairing War-Cracked Minds" that "the mental state of our fighting men is a serious problem and will be even a greater problem after the war." The article reported 85,000 being rejected as 4Fs each month, largely because of neuropsychiatric disabilities. It praised psychiatrists for their efforts to treat men close to the front but cautioned that the need for psychiatry would only increase after the war. Higher-ups in the War Department, possibly Stimson himself, were deeply troubled by the article's contents and ordered the chief of staff to look into it. (The news blackout had officially ended in April 1944, but the War Department continued to prohibit publication of psychiatric casualty statistics throughout the war, and until the end army and psychiatric leaders differed widely over the scope of publicity.)[96] Simultaneously, the army chief of staff expressed concern that the numbers discharged, largely for psychoneurosis, were as high as the numbers inducted, thwarting any increase in manpower.[97]

On September 28, 1944, the assistant deputy chief of staff requested that G-1 look into psychiatrists' alleged abuse of the diagnosis of psychoneurosis in the Zone of Interior. G-1 in turn ordered the IG to investigate why the diagnosis was rampant and whether the navy's terminology of "No disease. Temperamentally unqualified for service" should be substituted as a discharge, conferring no disability or other benefits.[98] In his unofficial history, Appel commented that psychiatrists viewed the army's interest in the navy's practice as a challenge to their authority: A "high command of laymen without medical training would be telling doctors what diagnosis they would make on army patients."

In addition to appointing Snyder to head its investigation, the IG chose a team headed by Brigadier General Elliot Cooke, a thirty-year veteran, and five civilian psychiatrists who had helped develop the screening program, including the ubiquitous Strecker.[99] Cooke's take on the investigation was described in his widely read *All but Me and Thee: Psychiatry in a Fox Hole*.

A week or two before Snyder started his investigation, Westray Battle Boyce, the WAC G-1, soon to succeed Hobby as WAC director, interviewed Snyder about his views on psychiatry. Skeptical of the profession, Snyder told her he wanted to probe whether inexperienced army psychiatrists were "experimenting with soldiers in army hospitals, using them as guinea pigs to prove or disprove their own ideas."[100] He contended that "many of the milder forms of psychoneuroses could be handled more expeditiously and effectively by a psychologist rather than a psychiatrist," since the psychiatrist might have an "unconscious tendency ... to confirm in the mind of his patient that he is a psychoneurotic, thereby delaying his recovery and in some instances ... preventing recovery." Echoing Marshall, Snyder said that line officers felt psychiatrists were "tearing down the moral fiber of the nation by 'coddling' psychoneurotics who should be handled more firmly and often through discipline."[101] Hence, even before starting his investigation Snyder concurred with critics that psychiatrists were being overused; that psychologists should be used instead, since they were more likely to reassign soldiers to other vocations rather than label them mentally ill; and that a need existed for the stricter discipline practiced in other countries. Reflecting his mindset as a physician, however, Snyder doubted that psychiatrists could really be reined in to follow War Department directives, given the conflict between their medical ethics and the army's obligation "to society in general."[102]

During the IG's first investigation, which took place in the Zone of Interior (United States) from mid-October to mid-December 1944, staff supervised by inspectors general Snyder and Elliott D. Cooke, among others, culled records of neuropsychiatric patients from the army and Veterans Affairs. They quizzed personnel at sixty army hospitals, induction stations, reception centers, replacement training centers, and redistribution centers.[103] Based on the recommendations of prominent consulting civilian psychiatrists including Strecker, the inspectors general concluded that many cases of psychoneurosis were dubious, suffering not from mental illness but from inadaptability to army life, and once more called for stricter preinduction psychiatric screening and rejection of more men. While George C. Marshall in January 1944 had found that psychiatrists excessively diagnosed psychoneurosis overseas, the IG's report that fall put the blame more on lower-level officers who abused psychiatric diagnoses to rid their units of discipline problems. While Cooke in *All but Me and Thee* also recognized the self-interest of lower-level officers in exploiting psychiatric labeling, he also concluded that psychiatrists' medical propensities had encouraged them to find illness in the most dubious cases.[104]

The IG found that from July 1943 to July 1944, one hundred thousand soldiers in the Zone of Interior had received disability discharges for psychoneurosis but that of these 83 percent had never left the United States and thus had seen no combat. Diagnoses often lacked sufficient clinical basis. Soldiers were discharged for psychoneurosis, potentially with costly VA pensions, simply because of officers' inability to "make soldiers out of them." Probably, their symptoms had existed "long before they were inducted,"[105] a conclusion much at variance with the position of Farrell and Appel at the APA meeting only about six months earlier. Half of the three thousand psychiatric casualties in one army hospital had received disability discharges "simply because they could not adjust themselves to the army." Of the 17 percent of dischargees with overseas service, less than half had seen combat, indicating that the problem may not have been "war neurosis" but simply "inadaptability." Nor were these psychiatric veterans being handled as their cohorts in previous wars. Instead, 99 percent were sent to no institution but were simply "deemed capable of taking care of themselves."[106]

The sheer fact that "the patient does not desire to get well," more than any insufficiency in facilities or staff, interfered with the efficacy of treatment the study asserted. Concluding that the diagnosis "psychoneurosis" had been abused, the IG recommended that it only apply where a likelihood of recurrence after discharge existed. Instead, the inadaptable should be discharged administratively, without benefits. Reflecting the views of the five civilian psychiatrists, the IG recommended tougher psychiatric screening at army induction centers, probably because of the psychiatric belief that symptoms existed even before induction. This recommendation contradicted the War Department's updated position in Technical Bulletin 33 (April 21, 1944), which instructed the centers to accept persons with "minor personality defects and neurotic trends."[107]

Appel recalled that on learning the army planned to strip psychiatrists of their diagnostic role when it came to discharges, Menninger, Appel, and Norman Q. Brill, a psychiatrist assigned to the army's Office of the Surgeon General, approached the surgeon general, Brigadier General Norman Kirk. They told him the War Department was about to "order doctors to no longer make a psychiatric diagnosis on anybody in the whole Army." "They can't do that," Kirk responded. He marched over to G-1 and threatened that if "you put out an order like that you're going to have every doctor resign." An "accommodation" was made several months later, in March 1945, whereby psychiatric discharges were still permitted but would hopefully be reduced by "a program of preventive psychiatry . . . based on sound principles."[108] (It may be posited that Kirk's influence was enhanced by being Roosevelt's handpicked candidate, when Stimson, Marshall, and Patton had all wanted Albert Kenner, a medical officer more skeptical of psychiatry. Roosevelt explained to them that he, Roosevelt, was "in much closer touch with the medical profession . . . than most people and [he] believe[d another] selection . . . would do more credit to . . . us.")[109]

Whether or not a dramatic confrontation occurred, G-1 incorporated the Office of the Surgeon General's suggestions in its final recommendations. Instead of eliminating the diagnosis "psychoneurosis" altogether, it allowed psychiatrists to use the diagnosis as long as it was accompanied by a specific *type* of psychoneuroses (such as "anxiety reaction") with a brief description of the stressors contributing to it. Reversing the IG's call for tougher screening, G-1 concurred with the SG that "in view of the manpower situation and the increasingly high rejection rate for neuropsychiatric disorders, registrants should be rejected only after definite evidence that they are below acceptable standards."

But this compromise did not become final until the War Department and Roosevelt had signed on. The president had been actively corresponding with Stimson about psychiatric treatment and rehabilitation since December 1944. He may have also heard from the surgeon general. Perhaps fearing Roosevelt's reaction to the G-1's criticism, Marshall instructed his staff not to let the White House see the report, including the earlier IG memorandum, until the War Department had reviewed it. But it was leaked to Roosevelt's press secretary.[110] On March 13, the War Department officially implemented G-1's recommendations in WD Circular No. 81, which replaced the general term "psychoneurosis" as a diagnosis with designated subtypes, such as "anxiety reaction" or "conversion reaction," together with a description of the ailment and its precipitating stress. According to Appel, Roosevelt approved these changes. The final report also stipulated that more efforts should be made in preventive psychiatry.

With the continuation of psychiatric diagnoses assured, the Army Neuropsychiatric Consultants Division no longer had to fear that lay officers would take over psychiatrists' functions. Coming less than two months before the end of the war in Europe, Circular No. 81 had little immediate effect. But, ultimately, nomenclature from Circular No. 81 was incorporated in *Diagnostic Statistical Manual No. 1* (1952), the original *DSM*.[111]

Following issuance of G-1's report, the Office of the Adjutant General issued a series of orders tightening the standards for psychiatric rejections and discharges. On March 31, it instructed commanding generals in the Pacific that too many white men had been rejected from service for "mild, transient psychoneurotic reactions" when such men were "even doing effective combat duty." A person should not be rejected, he wrote, for "a predisposition to disabling psychoneurosis" or for negative attitudes, such as believing "the end of the war is near." (The reference to whites alone was probably because whites had a higher rate of psychoneuroses than Blacks and because white officers were opposed to using Black infantry in combat.)[112]

Another AG order, dated March 31, 1945, prohibited officers from giving a psychiatric diagnosis based on symptoms exhibited at draft boards, because such symptoms represented normal responses to separations from home.[113] This was a far cry from Sullivan's original examination goals. But now, with a dire need for troops, standards for acceptance had to be relaxed.

Having completed its first investigation of psychoneurosis, the IG conducted two more, one in the Pacific Ocean Areas and the other in the European and Mediterranean Theaters of Operations (ETO and MTO). Based on its inquiry covering the Pacific from March through April 1945, the Office of the Inspector General, under the direction and advice of, among others, Cooke and the psychiatrist Norman Q. Brill of the Surgeon General's Office, praised the theater's psychiatric treatment program for reducing psychoneurotic casualties more than elsewhere and for psychiatrists' efforts in vocational placement. For the first time, American psychiatrists, in line with their British counterparts, were evaluating soldiers based not on the severity of symptoms but on the degree to which they could cope with a particular assignment, implying retention in service. The Inspector General's Office noted: "An infantryman with a battle-incurred neurosis would probably be diagnosed ... 'severe' if returned to duty as a rifleman; [but], if he [were placed in] noncombatant duty in the combat zone his condition would be considered 'moderate,' either 'mild' or 'slight.'" So successful was this program, it continued, that "psychiatrists in the Pacific Ocean Areas [were] rapidly becoming the recognized authorities ... on classification and reassignment." The report recommended that the approach continue and that the military include a soldier's psychiatric case history in his military service record, reminiscent of Kubie's recommendations to the NRC in 1942 as well as foreshadowing the future use of records in the computer/Internet age.[114] Hence, in the final few months of the war, the military was willing to try new ideas to ensure sufficient combat soldiers. In future wars, even more focus was placed on vocational aptitude.

The third report, issued May 26, 1945, on "Psychoneurotics in the Mediterranean and European Theaters," came to more startling conclusions. Reflecting the desperate need to finish the war in Europe and a looming massive invasion of the Japanese mainland soon thereafter, the report suggested using the threat of court-martials and executions to motivate men. For the report, a committee from the Office of the Inspector General and the Office of the Surgeon General, including Kenner and the psychiatric consultants Frederick Hanson (MTO) and Lloyd Thompson (ETO), visited over seventy general hospitals and battalion aid stations in France, Germany, Belgium, Britain, and Italy. They found records showing that from June 6, 1944, to March 31, 1945, the First Army suffered 32,928 psychiatric casualties, "more than the equivalent of one division," a rate similar to that of other armies in the theater. In the Third Army, 71 percent of psychiatric cases were returned to some duty, 55 percent to combat. While they praised line and medical officers for standardizing procedures of diagnoses, treatment, and prevention and for limiting days of continuous combat and tours of duty to avert breakdowns, they nevertheless stated:

> Most combat officers [believed] that "combat exhaustion" . . . would be greatly reduced, if severe punishment, such as death, were inflicted upon the first proven cases of malingering, cowardice, desertion, or self-inflicted wounds; that such action would serve as a powerful deterrent to the intentional quitter and serve to raise the threshold of the average soldier's breaking point in combat and salvage many men who make the minimum effort to control fear.[115]

Such measures, if imposed, would have dwarfed any discipline to date in a war where only one deserter, Eddie Slovik, was ever executed and where Patton's slapping of two soldiers caused such public controversy. But the low morale of troops in Europe after V-E Day, already at war for years and now expecting orders to invade Japan, encouraged desperate action.[116]

Roosevelt's Last Days

Until a few weeks before he died, Roosevelt continued his pattern of interceding with the military in favor of psychiatry. The president had endorsed Medical Circular No. 1, promoted rehabilitating 4Fs, and promoted rehabilitating servicemen. He had called on the armed services to emulate British preventive psychiatry and expand psychiatric treatment. He had opposed the IG's recommendation to virtually eliminate the diagnosis of psychoneurosis, contributing to the War Department's decision to retain the diagnosis in a modified form.

On December 4, 1944, Roosevelt wrote Stimson, urging him to order the military to conduct the maximum possible in-service treatment and rehabilitation before discharging anyone with a disability, be it physical or mental. Responding a few weeks later, Stimson assured the president that the military would do everything possible to return disabled soldiers to civilian life as "useful citizens." In a second letter, dated February 28, 1945, only a month and a half before Roosevelt died, Stimson again assured him that the military would not discharge any "emotionally sick" soldier "until every effort [was] made toward maximum improvement."

In the same letter, reflecting Roosevelt's deep interest in psychiatry, Stimson assured him that all was going well in many areas. The "combat exhausted," he wrote, were being treated as early as possible "within the range of the guns," most recovering and returning to combat, others to duty in the rear. Those with illnesses incurred before service or stateside received effective and practical treatment in military hospitals in the United States. None, he professed, would receive anything but a medical discharge. As to the "inapt" or" inadaptable" who had "adjusted fairly well in civil life," the military would treat and educate them and do its best through improved leadership, orientation, and motivation. If, however, this did not work "and there [was] no medical reason for a disability discharge," they would be discharged administratively (generally without benefits). Those who returned home and had difficulty readjusting to life in the States would receive psychiatric treatment, education, leadership, and job placement, so they could be "better prepar[ed] to return to civil life." (We shall see how much of this happened in the next chapter.) On March 24, 1945, Roosevelt wrote Stimson, thanking him for outlining the army's neuropsychiatric problem and for instituting a good program to readjust soldiers to civilian life.[117] But FDR had no time left to suggest anything further to Stimson. On April 12, he died.

On April 30, Adolf Hitler committed suicide. A week later, the war in Europe was over. Following two atomic bombings, on September 2, 1945, Japan officially surrendered. The war was over, but both the effects of the psychological horrors of the war and the evolution of psychiatry continued.

Part III
After the War

10   Returning to Normalcy

By the end of World War II, the United States had rejected or discharged on neuropsychiatric grounds approximately two and a half million American men and women from military service. Another one million arrived home with physical wounds, often accompanied by mental disorders.[1] After five years of war, following ten years of Depression, many families had difficulty readjusting. Before the war, psychiatric care concentrated on the chronically ill, who might remain in asylums for years.[2] After the war, psychiatry expanded to treat in private practices and clinics a broad range of individuals with everyday problems.[3] Despite a widespread medical belief that combat exhaustion was transient, such veterans frequently experienced long-term disabilities. Correspondingly, the number of psychiatrists and associated mental health professionals rose, as did the number of psychiatric hospital beds. In 1946, President Harry Truman signed the National Mental Health Act (NMHA), which authorized significant funding for psychiatric treatment, clinics, research, and training for decades to come.

What led to this massive postwar acceptance and growth of psychiatry? This chapter explores the multiple factors facilitating the change, including:

1. the psychiatric rejection and discharge of more than two and a half million individuals, many on questionable grounds, ironically leading to a rising postwar awareness and demand for psychiatry;
2. the expansion of the role of psychiatrists during the war to cover problems of everyday life;
3. an increased public understanding of the profession, arising from Americans' wartime experiences with screening and treatment, including group psychotherapy and narcoanalysis, and a widespread popular belief that "everyone has his breaking point";

4. growing coverage of psychiatry in the media (films, books, magazines, and newspapers) during and immediately after the war;
5. more advocacy of psychiatry by political and military leaders, increasing numbers of émigré and American-born psychoanalysts, and a growing demand for psychoanalysis, facilitated by the ability of Karl and William Menninger and others to adjust their philosophy to the moral compunctions of Americans, psychoanalysts' particular intellectual expertise, and contemporary social needs; and
6. most basically, America's eagerness to shake off and move beyond fifteen years of debilitating economic depression and war and return to normalcy—to successful, self-reliant lives as breadwinning fathers and nurturing wives and mothers, assisted if need be by psychiatrists and allied mental health professionals.

Ironically, the profession's wartime record could hardly have been called a success. Leading military psychiatrists had gradually concluded that screening predicated on the notion of predisposition did not work. Families legitimately questioned why some men had been rejected while others with the same characteristics were drafted. Racial and ethnic bias in examinations drew growing criticism. In a largely patriotic war, the public had little tolerance for normal-looking psychiatric 4Fs and dischargees not doing their share. Military commanders expressed skepticism about the reality of psychiatric disorders, wondering whether the men were malingering or just cowards.

But as Americans demobilized, skepticism evaporated. The sheer numbers of neuropsychiatric 4Fs and veterans; the legions of physically disabled veterans with emotional problems; the men and women with troubling Section VIII discharges, or with "combat exhaustion," or with critical problems getting employed propelled the demand for psychiatry. Veterans returned home with a new familiarity with psychiatry. Military psychiatrists had been their advisers, their guides to health through psychotherapy and group therapy, and even their educators through mental hygiene lectures on world affairs. No longer did the public consider psychiatrists "weirdos in white coats" treating psychotics in isolated mental hospitals. Now, the psychiatrist was a doctor helping everyone adjust to everyday problems. The war won, Americans sought a return to normalcy with psychiatry the facilitator.

Conditions after the War: The Department of Veterans Affairs (VA)

The expansion of psychiatric services for veterans and 4Fs did not come at once. Indeed, as of V-J Day, World War I, not World War II veterans, still occupied three-quarters of the 51,000 VA psychiatric hospital beds.[4] Upset by the large unmet demand from new veterans, President Harry Truman, just weeks after succeeding Roosevelt, told reporters, "I am trying to get this mess to operate" and called for "modernizing" the VA. Several months later, Truman replaced Frank Hines, Roosevelt's cost-conscious administrator, with the recently victorious four-star (later five-star) general Omar Bradley, chief of the European theater. "A General," Truman told the press, of "their own war." In January 1946, Truman signed a bill to establish a VA Department of Medicine and Surgery.[5] As head, Bradley chose his own former army surgeon general, Paul Hawley.

Faced with long waiting lists, Bradley and Hawley placed some veterans in army and navy hospitals, arranged for separate VA outpatient treatment for veterans with nonservice-connected disabilities, and referred others to private clinics. When Bradley took office, the VA had a total of ninety-seven hospitals and 51,000 neuropsychiatric hospital beds. When he left in 1948, the VA had a total of 126 hospitals but still just 54,790 psychiatric hospital beds.[6] (This was far from Dr. Lawrence Kubie's dire prediction of five times more psychiatric beds needed for World War II veterans than for veterans of World War I.)[7]

Instead of becoming long-term inpatients, a new group of patients, as many as 75 percent of those attending psychiatric clinics, instead required psychiatric outpatient services. Many had considered themselves normal before the war. Most, especially from the rural South, had not previously considered consulting a psychiatrist.

Before the war, most of the nation's seven hundred psychiatric clinics were devoted to child guidance. By 1949, according to the Group for the Advancement of Psychiatry (GAP), an organization led by Dr. William Menninger, the number of clinics had risen to 855, with two-thirds of the 188,443 patients now veterans and their families. Another fifty-seven VA clinics served 102,311 patients. Other public, university, and private clinics brought the total number of clinics to over one thousand.[8]

Once the government enacted the NMHA, clinics with federal subsidies could treat almost anyone, regardless of finances. Among the most prominent was Payne Whitney Psychiatric Clinic in New York City, directed by Dr. Thomas Rennie. It was so popular that it was unable to accept more than one out of four applicants. Reflecting the clinic's interdisciplinary approach, the staff included ten psychiatrists, five social workers, one psychologist, and two occupational therapists.⁹ (In this respect, it was similar to William and Karl Menninger's team approach before and during World War II.)

In response to racial discrimination and high clinic fees, the psychiatrist Fredric Wertham, a former student of Adolf Meyer and a prominent psychoanalyst, supported by the novelist Richard Wright, opened the Lafargue Clinic in a Harlem church basement in 1946, a separate psychiatric clinic to serve the Black community. In the 1940s, Wertham and Wright had bonded over their mutual interest in analyzing murderers, reflected in Wertham's 1941 novel *Dark Legend: A Study in Murder* and Wright's 1954 *Savage Holiday*.¹⁰ Though originally Wertham's clinic was supposed to be for juvenile defendants in criminal trials, it treated a sizable number of VA-referred veterans from all backgrounds. Continuing until 1958, the clinic employed at least fourteen psychiatrists and twelve social workers, including a psychiatrist and psychotherapist of color. Instead of testing, it emphasized intensive therapy. While most patients were Black, the clinic welcomed anyone in need of inexpensive care. It charged a minimal fee of 25 cents a visit or, if even that was unaffordable, no fee at all. (Wertham and his associates later did a study of segregation in Delaware public schools, which contributed to court-ordered desegregation efforts and the landmark Supreme Court ruling *Brown v. Topeka Board of Education*.)¹¹

The number of psychiatrists belonging to the American Psychiatric Association (APA) grew 80 percent from 1930 to 1940 (1,346 to 2,423) and 142 percent from 1940 to 1950 (2,423 to 5,856), the largest growth thus far in American history (see Figure 15).¹² This figure most likely did not include the war's "90-day wonders." By 1946, GAP reported that the United States had 4,010 licensed psychiatrists.¹³ As their ranks grew, so did their influence in medicine and the social sciences.

Before the war, over 80 percent of America's psychiatrists worked in mental hospitals. After the war, the majority had private practices or worked outside the hospital.¹⁴ The demand for treatment of less serious psychiatric disorders, the recognition of the environment's impact on mental health, and the belief that treatment of minor ailments could forestall more serious problems led to the profession's broad support of community mental health.¹⁵

By the end of the decade, GAP had much influence in the APA. GAP's founders included a veritable "Who's Who" of psychiatric policy makers during the war, including GAP's first president, William Menninger; Karl Menninger; M. Ralph Kaufman; Roy Grinker; Chief of Army Air Force Psychiatry John Murray; Navy Chief Psychiatrist Francis Braceland; Assistant Army Chief of Psychiatry Malcolm Farrell; and Thomas Rennie. Called the "Young Turks," they were not part of the APA establishment and were

American Psychiatric Association Membership

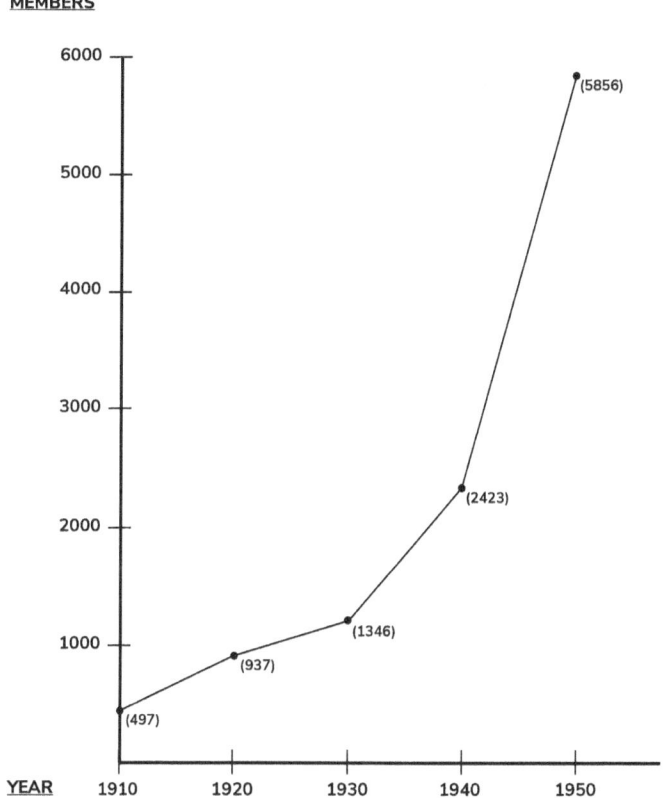

Unpublished.Table, Carolyn Gifford, American Psychiatric Association Library, Washington D.C.

Figure 15. American Psychiatric Association Membership, 1910–1950.

strongly interested in the medical and social needs of the two and a half million neuropsychiatric veterans and 4Fs and their families, which they did not feel the APA was addressing. Through lobbying and research, GAP expedited changes in APA policy, including a greater emphasis on preventive, forensic, and industrial psychiatry.[16]

Psychoanalysts

Though psychoanalysts constituted a small portion of all psychiatrists, they played a disproportionate role. By 1947, four hundred psychoanalysts were practicing in the United States, up from one hundred in 1941. Of these, fifty had emigrated from Germany, Austria, Czechoslovakia, and Hungary, many leaving by 1944, because of being Jewish.[17] Increasingly occupying prestigious faculty and medical positions in universities, institutes, and hospitals, they contributed new theories to psychiatry, to medicine, and to popular thought.

Among the émigrés were the neo-Freudians, who considered the effects of society on mental health in addition to Freudian theory. They included Karen Horney; Erich Fromm, known for *Escape from Freedom* (1941); and Frieda Fromm-Reichmann. Horney especially related women's mental health to social conditions. Fromm-Reichmann worked with Harry Stack Sullivan, also a neo-Freudian, on the causes of schizophrenia.[18]

The strict Freudian émigrés included Sandor Rado, director and founder of the Psychoanalytic Institute in Columbia University's department of psychiatry, the first of its kind; Franz Alexander, a specialist in psychosomatic medicine, who founded the Chicago Psychoanalytic Institute in 1932 and two years later analyzed William Menninger; Otto Fenichel, author of the first textbook on psychoanalysis, published by Norton in 1934; and Paul Schilder, who became a professor at New York University and director of the psychiatric division of Bellevue Hospital in 1929.[19]

But American-born psychoanalysts still had more clout. Of the seventeen psychoanalysts playing key roles in military psychiatry in World War II, only one had emigrated from Europe. The Americans included the Menninger brothers, Kaufman, Lawrence Kubie, Grinker, John Spiegel, Murray, and Martin Berezin, the only psychiatrist at Guadalcanal. After the war, these men assumed key positions in GAP, the APA, and the American Psychoanalytic Association (APsaA). William Menninger became APsaA president in 1946 and president of the APA two years later. About the same time, Kaufman became president of the APsaA. Karl Menninger followed in 1951. During the war, the Menninger Foundation staffed a 2,300-bed army hospital. *Time* named William Menninger "Man of the Year" in 1948 and featured his picture on its cover.[20] *Time* reported that the Menninger Foundation had "the largest psychiatric training center in the world, training 15 percent of all psychiatrists trained in the United States." According to one historian, this came to about one hundred residents a year.[21]

American psychoanalysts garnered popular interest in the 1940s because they provided a palatable form of treatment. Instead of focusing on an apolitical doctrinal Freudian view of mental health, the Americans stressed the effect of environment and the effect of mental health on society.

By downplaying the relationship between sex and mental illness, they calmed their religious critics.²²

Soon after the war, the Boston Reform rabbi Joshua Loth Liebman published *Peace of Mind* (1946), which remained on the *New York Times* bestseller list for over three years. In it, Liebman extolled his religion's view of God as benevolent and powerful yet promoted the use of psychoanalysis to achieve cooperation and peace among mankind by rooting out individual destructive behavior. The popular press, including *Ladies' Home Journal* and *Life*, applauded Liebman's book as well as the details about his family, including the fact that they had adopted a teenage girl who had survived Auschwitz, but other religions showed little interest in reconciling their faith with psychoanalysis.²³

Reminiscent of the views of Catholic leadership during the war, New York City's Bishop Fulton J. Sheen condemned the excessive, immoral, hedonistic focus of psychoanalysis on "SEX." He contrasted it with the confessional's purpose of recognizing sin and absolving guilt. In response, William Menninger defended psychoanalysis. He denied that analysts interpreted the unconscious purely from a sexual perspective. He stressed that, instead, analysts were interested in reducing a person's focus on sex. By 1950, a popular guide to psychoanalysis, including contributions from Kubie, Karl Menninger, and Alexander, minimized the interest of analysis in linking mental disorders to sex. By 1949, Catholic criticism had declined. Even the pope became more tolerant.²⁴ However, with émigré analysts achieving prominence in the 1950s and 1960s, the field reverted to a stricter Freudian and more sexual interpretation of the causes of maladjustments, contributing, in part, according to some historians, to the decline in popularity of psychoanalysis in America.²⁵

Unemployment

Before war's end, many Americans, including psychiatrists, the Nobel Prize–winning economist Paul Samuelson, and the sociologist Gunnar Myrdal, worried that the government's reconversion to a peacetime economy would lead to another Depression with high rates of unemployment and that returning soldiers who had been unemployed during the Depression would lack the skills or experience for work. This concern prompted passage of the GI Bill, which provided educational and housing benefits.²⁶ But while unemployment rose after the war, it scarcely approached Depression figures (a low of 3.6 percent in 1947 and a high of 6.6 percent in 1949, compared to the Depression's high of 24.0 percent in 1933).²⁷ Yet problems of unemployment disproportionately plagued psychiatric 4Fs and veterans. And they frequently expressed their concerns to mental health specialists at psychiatric clinics after the war.

With amendment of the Selective Service Act to withhold psychiatric records from 4Fs and veterans after 1942, the absence of an accessible explanation for the way they were treated by society became a problem. Without knowledge of a psychiatric classification or its basis, veterans or rejectees could not object to their diagnosis or ask for a second opinion. In the worst case, an individual might go through life being refused employment based on a fallacious psychiatric diagnosis or erroneous record, with no ability to correct it.[28]

Statistical studies confirmed that many discharged on psychiatric grounds had been employed during the Depression yet could not find work even in the full-employment economy during or after the war. Winfred Overholser, superintendent of St. Elizabeth's Hospital, expressed concern in February 1944 that thousands of psychoneurotic veterans were still unemployed.[29] While Payne Whitney's director Rennie denied that the 750 veterans and 4Fs seen at his clinic from 1943 to 1945 had problems getting jobs, he admitted that 30 percent were still unemployed as of January 1945, despite the clinic's emphasis on making discharged soldiers employable and finding them jobs.[30]

As late as 1947, a study of 493 psychiatrically discharged veterans from the Los Angeles VA clinic showed a lower rate of employment than in the 1930s. Specifically, 80 percent had been employed in the 1930s compared to less than 34 percent after the war. Further, almost 20 percent reported that a medical label had deterred employers from hiring them one or more times.[31] Columbia University School of Social Work masters theses studying psychiatric veterans at Kings County Hospital and the Vanderbilt Clinic in New York likewise reported high rates of unemployment and underemployment.[32] Reflecting the troubles returning servicemen with psychiatric discharges faced getting employed, navy and army films expressed much concern. These included the navy's *Combat Fatigue: Assignment Home* (1945) and the army's *Returning Soldier* (1945).[33]

Problems getting jobs or VA benefits and pensions were even greater for homosexuals, drug addicts, alcoholics, and Blacks. Contributing was the military's disproportionate issuance of Section VIII (blue) discharges to these groups, with mandated nonreceipt of benefits. Lobbying by the NAACP, gay rights organizations, and the CIO persuaded the army and navy in March 1945 to grant honorable discharges to homosexuals who had committed no "in-service acts," or to upgrade their blue discharges to honorable, thus allowing them to receive VA and other GI benefits. But by late 1947, with the shortage of workers easing, the military reversed its policy regarding identified homosexuals, making it virtually impossible for them to obtain honorable discharges with benefits,[34] consistent with conservatizing social attitudes toward homosexuality in the late 1940s and 1950s.

One twenty-seven-year-old Black veteran reported finally landing a job only to be fired when his employer saw his blue discharge papers. Another problem was that certificates of disability for discharge (CDDs) were sometimes confused with Section VIII discharges, though a CDD might be for either physical or mental disabilities.[35]

And yet, a Section VIII discharge was not always entirely detrimental, especially compared to a criminal alternative. Consider the case of the Academy Award–winning actor the late Sidney Poitier. Raised in the Bahamas without running water, indoor plumbing, or electricity, then moving to New York and facing a cold Harlem winter, Poitier at age sixteen pretended he was eighteen and enlisted in the army. Assigned as a soldier to care for mental patients at a VA hospital, he found the institution's treatment of psychiatric patients, the working conditions for Black soldiers, and the prejudice he encountered in the community to be deplorable. Eager to escape, having heard about Section VIIIs, he deliberately, he said, flung a chair at a commanding officer, broke a large window, and rammed into a tray of food, splattering it everywhere. The army hospitalized him at Mason General Hospital, a psychiatric facility on Long Island. Luckily, an understanding army psychiatrist psychoanalyzed him for an hour each day for three months and then discharged him with a Section VIII. For Poitier, Section VIII was a gift. Otherwise, he might well have been court-martialed and imprisoned, his future destroyed. As he later explained it, the psychiatrist had gotten him "to focus on me inside of me that no one knew,"[36] a self-understanding upon which he drew in his brilliant acting career.[37]

But for others, a psychiatric diagnosis, with or without a Section VIII discharge, could be devastating. Overholser had hoped that amending the Selective Service Act to prohibit 4Fs and veterans from seeing their own psychiatric records would protect them from stigma, but that did not happen. Employers demanded discharge information from Selective Service because they knew it was legally available. The Washington, DC, Civil Service Commission refused to employ any 4F without "a statement of diagnosis."[38] If the individual refused to disclose his psychiatric record, a doctor or dentist could obtain it.[39] Or, a suspicious employer could simply not hire him. In May 1944, the army and navy opened their medical discharge records to eight government agencies and certain individuals, increasing the possibility of discrimination. These included the War Department, Navy Department (navy, marine corps, and coast guard), the VA, Selective Service, federal and state hospitals and penal institutions, the Department of Justice, Treasury Department, Post Office Department, registered civilian physicians, and next of kin. Each agency in turn could divulge psychiatric information to another, in some cases creating a de facto blacklist.

Concerned psychiatrists unsuccessfully lobbied Congress in 1945 to enact a law guaranteeing full employment for all veterans. Menninger pointed to 1930s studies showing that a man lost a sense of purpose and self-esteem when he could not support his family; that his wife and children lost respect for him; that the family, ashamed of its poverty, withdrew from social activity; and that the children became confused and upset by the friction between father and mother. He maintained that the unemployed (contrary to the concern of Sullivan and Selective Service before the war) were not a defective group who simply did not care to work.[40] Braceland warned the Senate Subcommittee on Wartime Health and Education that unemployment was "a fertile field in which neuroses can grow. A man who is idle [can] notice little things which he wouldn't notice if he were busy. He becomes anxious and insecure. He develops a fear for his future." He urged employers not to refuse to hire a psychoneurotic veteran per se but to consider his preenlistment record.[41] The psychiatrists Malcolm Farrell and Winfred Overholser urged business leaders, academics, and clergy to hire psychiatric veterans. They emphasized that they were well trained and emotionally stable despite their discharge status.[42]

To ensure that a man got back on his feet, psychiatrists urged families and friends to encourage him to seek employment. In the *Rotarian*, the magazine of the Rotary Clubs, Farrell advised families: "Remember that just because he cracked up nervously, he is not 'yellow' . . . treat him naturally; Listen to his war stories but do not push him into telling them; Don't coddle him; Start him to think right away about getting a job, then help him land one."[43]

Families Readjusting to Civilian Life

Families had problems adjusting to the returning veteran. Some had difficulty sharing with a veteran after years of separation. A returning husband's interest in restoring his authority might collide with a wife's reluctance to drop her wartime role as breadwinner. A child raised by others might have difficulty accepting discipline from a returning father or might fear he would leave again. A husband or wife might find it hard to live up to the idealized versions of each other developed during separation. Veterans had gone through things their families could not comprehend. They had different values and attitudes than when they left for war. They faced parental responsibility for children they had not known. A child born while a veteran was gone could lead to suspicions about legitimacy. The father might be closer to a child born after he came home. He might be unduly jealous of his wife's divided attention. Extramarital relations might cause jealousy and guilt. Not surprisingly, divorce rates rose.[44] Veterans who were alcoholic or suffered combat flashbacks could turn abusive to their spouse or children. These problems were widespread. Nearly 20 percent of America's families were separated from husbands, fathers, or sons for one to four years. A total of 183,000 children lost their fathers during the war. The Servicemen's Dependency Act of 1942 provided monthly allowances, but these were insufficient to support a family. Fully 1,360,000 wives of servicemen worked; 280,000 of these had children. Public daycare for children under two years old did not exist until 1944 and then was inadequate. "Latchkey kids" spent evenings at movie theaters or afternoons at home alone. Maternity leave was rare. Women might take men's jobs, but their pay in manufacturing was only 65 percent of men's. Women with small children faced poverty. The rate of abortion, though illegal and dangerous, rose considerably during the first two years of the war, as did deaths from abortion, pregnancy, and childbirth. All this affected readjustment when fathers returned. Many children placed in orphanages were sexually abused.[45]

Physically disabled veterans and their families had particular problems overcoming their loss of pride, depression, and resentment at disfigurement. The War Department's pamphlet "He's Back" described their emotional travail: "Recognize the debt we owe to him for his sacrifice, but don't patronize or pity or fuss over him." Lawrence Kubie, secretary of the American Psychoanalytic Association, and George Stevenson, a former APA president, emphasized the need to educate families to emotionally accept their veterans' "bodily mutilations, burns, amputations, disfigurements, paralyses, deafness, and blindness."[46]

Media, Movies, and Psychiatry

The media fostered the popular interest in psychiatry. Journalists and filmmakers highlighted advances in the field, exposed poor conditions in asylums, and described the plight of returning veterans. First serialized in the newspaper *PM* in 1946, the journalist Albert Deutsch's expose of asylums was published in book form as *The Shame of the States* (1948). Mary Jane Ward's autobiographical novel on an asylum, *The Snakepit* (later a popular movie), was also influential. While old institutions were criticized, the growing new role of psychiatrists in society was applauded.

In addition to the thirty-three psychiatric training films produced by the army and navy during the war, forty-three box-office films in the 1940s with psychiatrist protagonists appeared, compared to only seventeen in the 1930s, six in the 1920s, and one between 1910 and 1920.[47] Other films portrayed the psychological effects of war, most notably the poignant, award-winning *Best Years of Our Lives*, which followed several veterans in their quest to readjust, and *Twelve O'Clock High*, depicting the terrible emotional toll on those flying bombing raids over Germany. *Pride of the Marines* depicted a war hero returning home, struggling to come to terms with the loss of his eyesight.

Reflecting the expanding role of the psychiatrist/psychoanalyst in society, films explored such themes as the relationship between love and psychiatry in Alfred Hitchcock's box-office hit *Spellbound* (1946) and a psychoanalyst's adept reading of a dream in *Lady in the Dark* (1944). When *Shock* (1946) negatively portrayed a psychiatrist—he murders his wife with a candlestick and uses an overdose of insulin to eliminate a witness—the *New York Times* critic Bosley Crowther castigated the film for "provok[ing] fear of treatment" at a time when "thousands of men who suffered shock of one sort or another in the war" needed it. Narcosynthesis, widely used by the military, was introduced to the American public in *Possessed* (1947), *Snake Pit* (1948), and *Home of the Brave* (1949). *Snake Pit* also dealt with electroshock. In *The Dark Mirror* (1946), a psychiatrist used Rorschach and lie-detector tests plus psychoanalysis to determine which of two twins had committed murder. *Home of the Brave* depicted a psychiatrist treating a Black soldier mentally distraught from racial prejudice.[48] By acquainting the public with a wide spectrum of psychiatry, these films enhanced the public's comfort with a field they had feared or barely known.

Legislation Leading to the National Mental Health Act

As early as February 1939, in response to the president's personal interest in establishing a national neuropsychiatric institute, Roosevelt's neurologist Foster Kennedy corresponded with Lawrence Kolb, director of the Public Health Service's Mental Hygiene Division, about funding. But just as a bill was about to be introduced in Congress, the United States started mobilizing for war.[49] After the war, the campaign resumed. The House and Senate each drafted separate bills to establish a National Neuropsychiatric Institute (NNI). In the Senate, Claude Pepper (Florida) chaired the hearings; in the House, Percy Priest (Tennessee).[50] Witnesses included Thomas Parran of the US Public Health Service; General Lewis Hershey; the journalist Albert Deutsch; Eleanor Roosevelt; the psychiatrists Stevenson, Kubie, Adolf Meyer, and Gregory Zilboorg; the novelist Pearl Buck; the publisher Henry Luce; and Sidney Hillman, head of the Amalgamated Clothing Workers. They supported a bill that would fund medical school and residency programs in psychiatry, psychiatric clinics, and hospital care for 4Fs, veterans, and their families; psychiatric research; the establishment of a national neuropsychiatric institute to promote research in the field; and funds for amelioration of conditions in mental hospitals. By July 1946, two separate bills were passed in the Senate and House, which were reconciled and signed by President Harry Truman into law as the National Mental Health Act.

The specter of half a million psychiatric veterans unable to find work and dependent on pensions and hospitalization prompted political leaders to support the psychiatric legislation that eventually passed. Roosevelt before his death had pressed Stimson to rehabilitate as many soldiers and sailors as possible so they could be self-sufficient in civilian life, but this did not occur. At Senate hearings, Chair Pepper called for more psychiatrists to help neuropsychiatric veterans.[51] He placed in the *Congressional Record* letters from prominent practitioners endorsing the need for care. The director of the San Francisco Veterans Rehabilitation Clinic estimated that the vast numbers of neuropsychiatric veterans would require twenty thousand psychiatrists, compared with the current three thousand available, and that training facilities could turn out no more than fifty to two hundred new psychiatrists annually.[52] Menninger called for making psychiatry a basic subject in medical school, since many doctors during the war had found it difficult to treat the emotional problems accompanying physical disabilities.[53]

Fear of crime by returning veterans also motivated legislation. Statistics pointed to a growing rate of postwar criminality. The Justice Department reported an average increase of 8.1 percent in crime during the first nine months of 1946. Robberies rose by 19.1 percent, murders 15.3 percent, and burglaries 11.3 percent. Psychologically related incidents abounded. First-time admissions for alcoholic psychosis climbed from 4,651 in 1933 to 5,036 in 1943; the number of drug-addicted patients rose from 1 per 1,900 admissions (1928–1937) to 1 per 1,600 (1940–1947). Metropolitan Life Insurance reported a sharp rise in suicides among its white male policyholders, from 7.9 per 100,000 (1945) to 12.0 per 100,000 (1946). Of special concern was the high rate of crime among males age eighteen to twenty-four, the age of many veterans. The FBI reported an increase in crime during the first nine months of 1946 of 21.5 percent for males eighteen to twenty and 69.7 percent for those twenty-one to twenty-four, the very people who had served in the military.[54]

Leaders demanded psychiatric services to protect society from alleged criminally insane veterans. Claiming that fifty mentally deranged veterans were supposedly at large in New York City, one otolaryngologist urged medical officers at a Selective Service conference to refer all dangerous veterans to facilities instead of returning them home or helping them get employed. The American Legion, supported by Congressman Philip J. Philbin of Massachusetts, asked the Army Surgeon General to release records to the local police or refer deranged veterans to psychiatric facilities. But the surgeon general objected that this would violate the confidential doctor-patient relationship. Moreover, he assured them, the military was extremely careful to discharge possibly dangerous individuals only to the care of institutions or individuals.[55]

Nonetheless, reports of crime by psychoneurotic veterans abounded. *PM*'s columnist Deutsch told a Senate hearing about the number of untreated psychoneurotic cases in trouble with the law, specifically in Westchester County, New York. One twenty-three-year-old medically discharged navy veteran mentioned by Deutsch had no idea why he had stabbed his mother.[56] In another case, a woman wrote Senator Pepper about a psychoneurotic army veteran who "came back to the farm [where] he had worked and in a short time killed the young woman of the family, the father and himself and wounded the mother." "Another young man I knew of is acting strangely, found in out-of-the way places and can't hold a job," the same correspondent noted. "He needs medical attention, but will not get it until he commits some awful thing."[57]

Fear of social chaos pervaded the hearings and media. Echoing the psychiatrist Pearce Bailey's apprehensions after World War I, Overholser told the army's newspaper, *Stars and Stripes*, in 1945: "A period of lax morals and unrest exceeding even the riotous living of the Roaring Twenties will follow this war." The Senate report on the act to establish the NNI warned that immediate vigorous action was needed to avert a sharp rise in delinquency, suicide, and alcoholism, all symptomatic of postwar psychiatric disorders.[58]

The horrors of Nazi extermination camps sensitized Americans to the similarities between those camps and America's hospitals for the chronically ill. Prominent citizens like Eleanor Roosevelt, Pearl Buck, Henry Luce, Sidney Hillman, and Dr. Meyer formed a National Mental Health Foundation to lobby Congress to enact a National Mental Health Act, after reviewing 1,400 complaints of deplorable conditions in a quarter of the nation's mental hospitals.[59] Newspapers reported on overcrowding, use of straps and handcuffs, inadequate or nonexistent treatment, and immense shortages of staff depleted by the military's needs during the war. In one public psychiatric hospital, one attendant was responsible for twelve to thirty patients, a nurse for 176 patients, and a psychiatrist for 250 to five hundred.

Abysmal conditions pervaded private and public mental hospitals nationwide. At the Senate's NNI hearings, witnesses testified about deaths caused by institutional negligence or beatings in Illinois, Arkansas, North Carolina, Oregon, Pennsylvania, and Washington, DC; insane individuals kidnapped and placed in institutions; insufficient, unpalatable food, crowded sleeping quarters, forced labor, and inmates clothed in rags. In the autobiographical novel *The Snake Pit*, the author described incompetent administrators, arbitrary nurses, and overcrowding. The movie based on the book depicted, with vivid sound and visual effects, a grotesque and ineffective electroshock treatment and a contraption forced into a patient's mouth.[60]

Deutsch testified about the horrendous conditions he had observed in psychiatric hospitals.[61] The worst psychiatric hospital, he said, was "Byberry," the Philadelphia State Hospital for Mental Diseases. Supposedly adhering to Dr. Benjamin Rush's time-honored cures, in reality it had vastly deteriorated after staff had been transferred to military service and suffering a severe decline in funding. He wrote:

> I entered the buildings swarming with naked humans herded like cattle and treated with less concern, pervaded by a fetid odor so heavy, so nauseating that stench seemed to have an almost physical existence of its own. I saw hundreds of patients living under leaking roofs, surrounded by moldy, decaying walls, and sprawling on rotten floors for want of seats or benches.

Broken windows contributed to health hazards. Vagrants were assigned as attendants instead of being sent to jail; when drunk, they brutally assaulted patients. Because of a shortage of tableware, patients often ate with their hands. APA standards required that Byberry house no more than 3,400 patients, 1,100 attendants, two hundred nurses, and ninety physicians. In actuality, it held 6,100 patients, 75 percent above capacity, 180 attendants, forty-one nurses, and fourteen doctors. After seeing photos of Byberry, Eleanor Roosevelt aggressively supported the NNI legislation.[62]

Deutsch also testified about offensive conditions at the well-known Manhattan State Hospital on Ward's Island, New York City, earlier exposed by the intrepid female reporter "Nelly Bly" (Elizabeth Cochran Seaman) in 1887. Though doctors were required to examine patients twice a year, many patients had not been examined for five years. In April 1946 alone, twelve patients suffered serious accidents, four leading to death.[63]

Aware of the deterioration of asylums and the onslaught of veterans and families with mental problems, psychiatrists lobbied Congress to fund community outpatient clinics. Stevenson wrote Pepper about the severe shortage of adequate VA outpatient facilities for psychoneurotic veterans.[64] The VA's Dr. Daniel Blain stressed the enormous federal savings from veterans attending clinics instead of occupying hospital beds. Surgeon General Thomas Parran told senators that the future earning power of a person admitted to a mental institution for the first time declined on average 60 percent, while others emphasized that persons attending clinics would avoid the stigma of mental hospitalization.[65] Enhanced worker productivity and an increase in average lifespan were also cited as reasons for additional government funding of psychiatry.[66]

A few, not psychiatrists, expressed reservations about federal spending for mental health. For example, the editor of the *Fitchberg Sentinel* (Massachusetts) wondered whether the scourge of mental illness had been exaggerated, since the criteria for military mental health differed significantly from that for civilians. Were not the discharges and rejections, he asked, based on a military definition of mental health, one of regimentation, discipline, and the ability to kill without emotion? Was this really the civilian definition of health? Or were these requirements anathema to America's peacetime democratic society? The *Sentinel* asked: "General Hershey reveals that 75 percent of the million mental rejectees were first thought to be sound, but later showed that 'their emotions were in such a state that they could not stand modern war.' Isn't that rather a condemnation of war than of a democracy's neglect?"[67] In a similar vein, Colonel Julien E. Benjamin at the Lowell General Hospital in Massachusetts asserted: "It is true that a large number of apparently healthy young men, from a physical point of view, lack mental stability, but in many instances, only insofar as this dreadful type of war is concerned, and the lack of mental preparation for a war which has for them at least, indefinite aims and fought at remote areas."[68] And at the House hearings, the Citizens Medical Reference Bureau, a conservative lobbying group, worried that funding psychiatric care would facilitate extreme mental regimentation and experimentation on asylum residents and that branding large numbers as psychoneurotic might lead to more mental disturbance than it would cure.[69]

Despite this limited skepticism, the House and Senate each passed their own versions of an act to fund a National Neuropsychiatric Institute. Reconciled, they were signed into law as the National Mental Health Act in July 1946. The law provided for nationwide funding for psychiatric research, training, and treatment, plus $7.5 million (over $203,925,000 in today's dollars) for equipment and construction of hospital and laboratory facilities at the National Institute of Mental Health (NIMH), Washington, DC.[70]

The Social Role of the Psychiatrist

Looking back in 1948, William Menninger opined that one of the key contributions to American psychiatry in World War II was the recognition that environmental stresses could affect the personality and that such knowledge could be applied to civilian life.[71] Hence, he pressed for an expanded role for psychiatry beyond the medical. At an APA Council meeting, Menninger urged psychiatrists to get involved in vocational training and placement for returning veterans, improving industrial conditions and labor relations to reduce absenteeism, selecting teachers and advising on teaching methods, and giving advice on reducing racial strife.[72] Later, as head of the APA Committee on Preventive Psychiatry, John Appel, formerly the director of the Mental Hygiene Branch during World War II, supported civilian psychiatrists' efforts to prevent labor strikes, eliminate unemployment, clear slums, and improve the quality of education by joining school boards, city councils, and church vestries. But his committee had little success and soon disbanded. Years later, Appel commented that civilian society was not a total institution that could be controlled like the military. In 1946, Kubie too advocated psychiatric involvement in improving worker productivity by increasing work hours, speeding production, giving personality and aptitude tests to workers, and providing therapy for maladjusted workers. But his methods, he admitted, might not garner much support from labor unions.[73] This reflected another element of the return to normalcy, namely, the emphasis on self-reliance and individual productivity without assistance, and also the growing popular reservations about unions, reflected in passage of the Taft-Hartley Act the following year.

Psychiatrists continued to use the individual and group psychotherapy techniques developed during the war.[74] Some used milieu therapy—helping the patient and his family create the proper environment for mental health, with healthy foods and sufficient leisure, rest, and recreation. Psychiatrists also referred patients to occupational and recreational activities, corrective therapy, psychodrama, and educational and vocational courses.[75] While these techniques reflected preventive psychiatry in World War II, they also stemmed from the practices in place in mental hygiene clinics before the war.

As part of their social role, psychiatrists also advocated for the rights of Blacks. During the summer of 1945, after the war in Europe had ended, psychiatrists testified in favor of several Black servicemen accused of murder in the European theater.[76] They argued that defendants lacked the mental capacity to understand what had happened, had low IQs, or could not distinguish right from wrong. But their testimony had little weight, and almost all the men were executed.

Reversing his earlier stance during the war, William Menninger, in *Psychiatry in a Troubled World*, saw "no basis from a scientific standpoint" for finding the capabilities of Blacks different from any others, and he criticized his hometown of Topeka for not permitting "the Negro (or the Mexican) . . . to stay in the two first-class hotels or to sit on the ground floor of the main theaters." Recognizing that "prejudice is . . . a kind of neurosis" that "warp[s] the personalities of both the prejudiced people and their victims," he wrote that not only did it apply to Blacks but also to Jews, Catholics, Japanese, and Mexicans. Germany's extermination of Jews represented "the psychopathic extent to which a nation may go." Now, he called on the United States to accept displaced persons.[77]

Led by Menninger, GAP unanimously passed a resolution in November 1947 endorsing *To Secure These Rights: The Report of the President's Committee on Civil Rights*. In doing so, GAP recognized "that the protection of civil rights is vital to the mental health of our citizens." They also endorsed the specifics in the report, including ending the poll tax, passing antilynching legislation, continuing the Federal Employment Practices Commission's (FEPC) ban on employment discrimination in government contracts, and integrating troops. In 1948, President Truman signed an executive order ending military segregation.[78]

Psychiatrists' role in the international arena grew as well. During the war, such psychiatrists as Alexander M. Leighton had worked with psychologists on studies of Japanese and German character and how to influence enemy morale. Others, like Richard Brickner in *Is Germany Incurable?* (1943), had raised questions about how to treat the "dangerous mental trend" among Germans.[79] That same year, the psychoanalyst Walter Langer, trained under Anna Freud, authored a study, *The Mind of Adolf Hitler*, for the Office of Strategic Services (OSS), the predecessor of the CIA. Later commercially published with notes and an afterword, it became a bestseller in 1972.

Beyond this, the psychiatrist Douglas Kelley and the psychologist Gustave Gilbert evaluated prisoners at the Nuremberg war crimes trials to assess whether they were suicidal and could stand trial and to assist in developing trial strategy. Among the prisoners examined were Rudolph Hess and Hermann Göring. Daniel Jaffe, who examined defendants at the Tokyo war crimes trials from 1946 through 1948, found one of the defendants unfit to stand trial. Similarly, under Overholser's direction, a team of psychiatrists examined the poet, Fascist sympathizer, and antisemite Ezra Pound, finding him mentally unfit for trial for treason, resulting in his commitment to St. Elizabeth's Hospital from 1946 to 1958.[80]

At a time when world peace was of utmost importance, exemplified by the establishment of the United Nations in October 1945, psychiatrists saw themselves playing a central role in promoting global understanding to prevent war. Lecturing to the William Alanson White Psychiatric Foundation, the Canadian psychiatrist G. Brock Chisholm, future head of the World Health Organization, championed this goal. So too did Harry Stack Sullivan when he attended an International Conference of Mental Health in London in 1948, soon thereafter dying of a heart attack.[81]

Psychiatric Nomenclature

Not only did the social role of the psychiatrist expand but also the definition of mental illness, as propounded in the army's and VA's nomenclatures on mental disorders, namely, *War Department Technical Bulletin, Medical 203* (October 19, 1945) and Veterans Administration TB 10A-78, *Nomenclature of Psychiatric Disorders and Reactions* (1947). The APA's *Diagnostic and Statistical Manual of Mental Disorders (DSM-I)* (1952) drew on these military publications. Whereas before the war the focus had been on chronic psychoses and neurological disorders, after the war the definition of mental illness expanded to include widespread problems in adjusting to stress. Both *Medical 203* and *DSM-I* divided nonphysiological disorders into neurotic, psychotic, and character disorders. *Medical 203* referred to a psychological "reaction" to stress such as "combat exhaustion" as a "transient reaction" that could range from neurosis to psychosis. It identified "acute situational maladjustment" as a temporary reaction to a trying situation manifested, for example, by anxiety or alcoholism.[82] Though *DSM-I* did not utilize the term "combat exhaustion," it included a reaction to combat as one example of "Gross Stress Reaction," a reaction to a civilian catastrophe being another. While posttraumatic stress disorder (PTSD) was not recognized as a disorder until 1980, *DSM-I* foreshadowed its use by including combat exhaustion as a category of Gross Stress Reaction. *DSM-I* defined stress as the "immediate emotional, economic, environmental, or cultural situation which is directly related to the reaction manifested in the patient."[83] Influenced by *Medical 203*, it departed from the traditional prewar diagnostic system, which had emphasized the psychological influence of early personality development almost to the exclusion of environment.

"Momism"

In another controversial way, psychiatry expanded its postwar role by creating a need for psychiatric assistance in childrearing through the concept of "Momism." Focusing on the 2.5 million rejected or discharged "neuropsychiatrics" plus another five hundred thousand "draft dodgers," the psychiatrist Edward Strecker in *Their Mother's Sons* (1946) criticized the overprotective mother who emotionally crippled her son: a mother who for her own emotional needs would not let go, tied her son to her apron strings, instilling guilt and separation anxiety. Curiously, Strecker seemed to forget that the military had blamed not the mothers but the psychiatric profession for being overzealous in their excessive screening, implying that many of the 4Fs and veterans with psychiatric diagnoses were for that reason suspect. Nor did he recall that the army had placed another part of the blame on lower-level officers exploiting psychiatric evacuations to rid themselves of troublemakers and to prevent criticism of their ineffective leadership from higher-ups. During the army's investigation of psychoneuroses in the Zone of Interior the previous year, Strecker and other psychiatric consultants had concluded that most of the psychiatric cases in the military in the United States had preexisting neuroses. Perhaps, it was this view that shaped Strecker's shameless faulting of mothers for the psychiatric disabilities of their veteran sons, with the exception of the true cases of war neuroses brought down by actual combat.[84] To Philip Wylie, the popular writer of *Generation of Vipers* (1942), a collection of essays, "Momism" (a term he coined) was a unique American pathology, threatening the nation's security. Endorsing Strecker's theory that mothers were weakening their veteran sons' psyches by interfering with their ability to be independent, the psychiatrist George Pratt recalled one scar-faced veteran welcomed home by an overreaching mother. "Tiptoe[ing] about the house, shushing everyone who talked loudly . . . fuss[ing] over him [with] tears of silent pity." Likewise, a *Psychiatric Primer for the Veteran's Family* condemned another mother for being so upset, shushing, questioning, peering around the hospital, to the point the hospital did not know who the patient was; perhaps it was the mother.[85]

Extending the contentions of Army Chief of Staff George C. Marshall during the war, "Momists" blamed New Deal largesse for "coddling" future soldiers and sailors by conveying the message that government was always there for them, instead of insisting on self-reliance. Maybe not coincidentally, Momism was a way of attributing psychological illness to prewar conditions, which meant it was not service connected and therefore not grounds for a veteran's pension.

At a time when William Bradford Huie, author of a book on the execution of the deserter Eddie Slovik, accused psychiatrists of "abolish[ing] cowardice" and relieving American soldiers of their "individual responsibility to fight," "Momism" enabled psychiatrists to shift blame elsewhere, that is, to America's mothers, in a way calling them unpatriotic.[86] It also harkened back to the philosophy of the child guidance clinics tracing adult behavior to childhood socialization.[87] In 1948, the psychoanalyst Frieda Fromm-Reichmann also coined the term "schizophrenogenic mothers" for mothers whose rejection and warping of their child contributed to schizophrenia.[88] "Momism" also propelled families to attend clinics for training in childrearing skills or to self-help with such well-known "How to" books, as Dr. Benjamin Spock's *The Common Sense Book of Baby and Child Care* (1946), which has sold more than 50 million copies and continues to be used to this very day.[89]

The Wife at Home

Along with "Momism" came the belief that the wife or sweetheart who worked during the war should now relinquish her job. Psychiatrists and sociologists, as well as the popular press and government literature, stressed that women were only taking a break from domesticity to work during an emergency while the men fought. When the men returned home, women were supposed to be there for them, leaving their jobs to help them get back on their feet as sole breadwinners, fathers, and mates.[90]

Plotlines of the popular 1946 film *The Best Years of Our Lives* reflect this message. A veteran army air force flyer with flashbacks of bombing raids can only manage to reclaim his prewar job as a soda jerk. He needs a wife to help him forget his worries, support his readjustment, and help him find a better job. He no longer appreciates the wife he has, who had a good job she wants to keep and male friends she made during the war years. She looks down on him for his lowly job and for not being the same as before the war. On the other hand, another returning veteran, ashamed of his prosthetic steel hooks for hands, is fortunate to have the girl next door eagerly awaiting him, wanting to resume their relationship, supporting him 100 percent despite his injury, and marrying him at the film's end.[91] In *Pride of the Marines*, the fiancée of the real-life war hero Al Schmid welcomes him home and assures him that it does not matter to her that he is now blind. All she wants is to be with him and care for him.

"Let There Be Light" versus "Shades of Gray"

In the military as well, psychiatric philosophy shifted emphasis from believing in "everyone has his breaking point" to "Momism." This is best reflected in a comparison of the publicly restricted army medical training film *Let There Be Light* with its more militarily accepted *Shades of Gray*. In *Let There Be Light*, the director John Huston filmed on site an actual eight-week course of treatment of seventy-five mental patients, from their initial interviews to discharge at Mason General Hospital, the army's largest neuropsychiatric hospital on the East Coast. But as he prepared to screen the film privately at the Museum of Modern Art, before commercial distribution to cinemas throughout the country, the army confiscated the film. Not until 1980 was Jack Valenti, president of the Motion Picture Association of America, able to convince Vice President Walter Mondale to order the army to release the film to the general public. Before that, its use was restricted by the military to training purposes and to viewing by specially approved private groups.[92]

According to Menninger, *Let There Be Light* was commissioned to demonstrate to mothers throughout the country that the army was properly treating neuropsychiatric soldiers, after complaints from mothers to the top brass. According to Huston, the War Department wanted to demonstrate that the neuropsychiatric casualties "were not lunatics, because at the time these men weren't getting jobs."[93]

Huston filmed real patients with tics, paralysis, depression, and psychosis. He filmed actual treatments with narcosynthesis, hypnosis, and group psychotherapy. In one case, as the cameras rolled, a psychiatrist persuaded a paralyzed soldier to walk again through use of narcosynthesis. In another, a patient regained his speech through a similar treatment. An amnesic patient, after reliving a battle on Okinawa under hypnosis, regained his memory. The narrator distinguished between physical and "spiritual" wounds. "These," he said, "are the casualties of the spirit . . . men who are damaged emotionally. Born and bred in peace, educated to hate war, they were overnight plunged into sudden and terrible situations. Every man has his breaking point, and these, in the fulfillment of their duties as soldiers, were forced beyond the limit of human endurance." All the patients, the narrator explained, experienced the "fear of death." At the end of the film, before the army discharged them, the men were reminded that "everyone has a breaking point," that what happened to them could happen to anyone, and that they might have problems getting hired given their diagnoses but that they should work to sell themselves anyway. The film did not avoid depiction of depression and weakness—some soldiers whimpered, others wept. It presented patients with forms of hysteria similar to shell shock of World War I. Atypically, in an army whose hospitals were just beginning to integrate, the hospital unit in the film contained both Black and white patients.[94]

But before public release, the army confiscated the film, alleging it violated patients' privacy. Huston maintained he had obtained written permissions from the patients, which had been lost, and offered to obtain new forms, but the army showed no interest. Huston claimed the army really suppressed the film because it wanted to portray returning soldiers as warriors, not weaklings.[95] There were also disagreements about the benefits of narcosynthesis and whether *Let There Be Light* had exaggerated it. But as to the concern about confidentiality among the military, one historian has pointed out that around this time *Life* was permitted to include in its magazine photos of patients at Mason General.[96]

Soon thereafter, the army filmed *Shades of Gray* (1948), which to avoid privacy issues used actors instead of patients. While the actors exhibited many of the same symptoms and expressed the same words under narcosynthesis and hypnosis as in *Let There Be Light*, the message differed. *Shades of Gray* stressed that while everyone harbors seeds of mental illness, just as everyone harbors germs, some mental problems are more severe than others, darker shades of gray. Making a soldier's shade particularly dark might be his childhood socialization. The film looked at "Joe Smith," for example. His mother had been overprotective, anxious, and afraid, interfering with Joe's independence. Joe grew up fearful and dependent. He could not socialize with anyone outside his immediate family. Probably influenced by Strecker's *Their Mothers' Sons*, the filmmakers attributed Smith's "borderline personality" not to the war experience but to an overprotective mother. The film did acknowledge, however, that even the "cream of the crop" could reach a breaking point in combat. More comprehensive than *Let There Be Light*, *Shades of Gray* described the full gamut of military psychiatry, from preinduction screening to training camp mental hygiene, morale boosting, and leadership training, to treatment at the front and behind the lines. Unlike *Let There Be Light*, the film did not show treatment in an actual mental hospital; nor did it portray a group therapy session where problems finding employment were discussed.

In addition to portraying a wider spectrum of military psychiatry, *Shades of Gray* largely supplanted the message that "everyone has his breaking point" with the message that quite a number of neuropsychiatric cases were their mother's fault. The army seemed to suppress *Let There Be Light* because it wanted a film less critical of war neuroses, one that did not upset the public by showing soldiers weeping, stuttering, or worrying about getting employed. *Let There Be Light* was finally released in 1980 in the more antiwar climate after Vietnam, when the lasting effects of post-traumatic stress disorder (PTSD) were beginning to be recognized.

11

From "War Man" to "Peace Man"

The dramatic postwar growth of psychiatry did not benefit all veterans equally. Unfortunately, there were blind spots. The issue of converting a man psychologically from an engine of war to an engine of peace was one. The condition later termed post-traumatic stress disorder (PTSD) was another. Neither was adequately identified or addressed by the profession, leaving many veterans and their families to suffer unnecessarily.

Of course, not everyone was permanently scarred by the war. Some were able to resume tranquil civilian lives after killing in battle. They were able to rationalize their brutality as necessary acts for their country, a matter of obeying orders or of protecting their buddies.[1] But others were conflicted, ashamed about killing, guilty about their dead buddies left behind. They did not want society to know what was irking them and what society did not seem to care about. They wanted to appear normal. Others felt guilt about killing or failing to kill. Still others suffered from a fear of their own aggression.[2]

During the war, soldiers built mental walls around themselves. One veteran, who became a psychologist, recalled: "The wall let in certain things. You don't get yourself killed. You see an enemy, you kill him. You eat as much as you can because you never know when you're going to get your next meal. You keep moving. You don't go by yourself anywhere."[3] There was the numbing effect of a soldier becoming "a killing machine." Years later, it still plagued Bert Manhoff, a veteran. He told an oral historian about the original 82nd Airborne, General Jim Gavin's troop. Some "guy" in town one day

> teased them about their cravat. . . . They walked over to the telegraph pole and broke his back on . . . the pole . . . [they] fixed their cravats and went . . . on. See, they were taught the same as we were, that you were a war machine and human life meant nothing to you under certain circumstances. We were trained the same way. . . . I found no problem ordering . . . having to administer death to Germans or anything like that . . . not a problem . . . because we were taught . . . we were a war machine.[4]

A veteran who had been a marine at Guadalcanal similarly remembered about killing:

> We were trained to respond to directions or orders and the Marine Corps did that. . . . War is psychological. You've got to do whatever someone else tells you to do. . . . To kill in war is not something that you think about as killing. It is something you have to do. That's what you are there for. It is not civilized stuff. . . . You don't have any control in it. The other thing is, when you see your very close friend who you live with and depend on for your own survival, killed, you get angry. You lose it. It's very difficult to explain to people, you aren't sorry you killed somebody. You did it because you had to.[5]

In a foreword to *Breakdown and Recovery*, one of three volumes of Eli Ginzberg's *The Ineffective Soldier* (1959), Howard McC. Snyder, President Dwight D. Eisenhower's personal physician, attributed to pride and shame the reluctance of some mentally disabled veterans to seek help from Veterans Affairs (VA).[6] In New York City after the war, only ten thousand of an estimated 38,000 neuropsychiatric veterans requiring treatment actually sought it out. (To this day, many soldiers of the Iraq and Afghanistan wars view psychological/psychiatric counseling as a sign of weakness.)[7]

Many had difficulty readjusting to civilian society without their buddies. The "group" had allowed them to repress anxiety and hostility, which they now could not escape. In the service, the soldier or sailor had relinquished his civilian morality; now he was expected to regain it. He was supposed to come home a hero, a strong man. Society did not want to hear about his worries; these he had to repress.[8]

News reports expressed concern about returning "criminally insane" veterans who committed crimes as serious as murder, affirming public worries that men in combat for years might become freaks or killers. They wondered how to protect civilian society. But little therapy was available to reconvert the human psyche from wartime killer to peacetime civilian. The recruit in training, opined one soldier, is taught to "Kill, Kill, Kill," but nothing is done to untrain him. Even dogs trained to kill, he said, were retrained better than soldiers.[9]

Even before the war ended, the issue of how to reconvert a "war man" back to a "peace man" was raised with Eleanor Roosevelt by Rabbi Stanley Brav of Anshe Chesed Congregation, Vicksburg, Mississippi. A politically active Reform Jewish rabbi, Brav was known for his 1940s Vicksburg radio broadcasts, reprinted in the local press. In November 1944, he sent Eleanor Roosevelt his article in *Survey Midmonthly* entitled "Basic Training for

Homecoming." Eleanor Roosevelt mailed it to the army and navy psychiatric consultant Edward Strecker. Strecker dismissed it, advising her that an agency already existed to do rehabilitation. But Brav's article is pertinent for its proposal of a special federal agency to help veterans relinquish the military ethic of killing in favor of a peacetime ethic of abhorring violence and appreciating family life. As he wrote, "the Joe" who comes home will "not be quite the same as the Joe they used to know." He had had "a dirty job to do." He had "learned commando tactics . . . dipped his hands in the blood of his fellowman." He had been trained in "discipline . . . drill, maneuvers, and actual battle." Brav continued:

> The scars of battle may have spared their bodies, but not their souls. . . . On the one hand, they . . . suffered unnatural unhealthy repressions. On the other, they [had become] over-expressed in certain "instincts" civilization usually seeks to bridle. They ha[d] been taught to look on the immorality of taking a human life as temporary morality. Their nerves ha[d] been strained beyond what mortals . . . believed possible. . . . They [had] been subjected to a life that is sexually abnormal."

How, then, to make a "war man" into a "peace man"? Mustering-out pay, education, bonuses, pensions, and employment services were insufficient. The GI could not be "dumped unceremoniously into a way of life from which he is alienated," Brav concluded. Reorientation was necessary.[10] But reorientation to peacetime morality was second in policy makers' minds to reducing the cost of VA benefits and getting men employed. Right after the war, in a time of rising unemployment, they did not want to repeat the clamor for benefits of the veterans' "Bonus Army" in Washington, DC, in the 1930s or the high cost of VA hospitalization after World War I. Therapy at VA hospitals and clinics in the 1940s usually lasted no more than twelve weeks. Sometimes the very same doctor who determined the percentage of disability for pensions also treated the veteran, a clear conflict of interest. Instead of treating a disability, the emphasis was mainly on getting jobs. Even the director's full title announced the importance of employment: "Administrator of Veterans Affairs and Administrator of Retraining and Reemployment."[11]

The Forgotten or Mistreated

While the war led to an expansion in funds for mental health professional training, research, and clinic and hospital beds and to a changing social role, certain groups, such as psychotics, were ignored or mistreated. The severity of combat exhaustion was minimized; PTSD was not recognized in the United

States as an official psychiatric diagnosis until 1980. For both psychiatrists and the populace at large, veterans were supposed to return home resilient to change. The atrocities of war, society generally assumed, would soon evaporate from combat-exhausted veterans' minds, leaving them independent, resourceful breadwinners. Little tolerance existed for anyone who could not fit in. Without recognition of PTSD as a medical disability, little treatment was available for the broken veteran. Nor was there much diagnostic connection drawn between the experiences of war and a rise after in homicides and suicides, particularly among males in their twenties to late thirties. Not only Americans but Europeans as well barely acknowledged PTSD. Germans, for example, had assumed that returning warriors, similar to civilians who had adjusted to the ravages of defeat, would be able to forget their battle traumas and move on. But case studies soon indicated otherwise. German veterans, like their peers in other countries, suffered long-term PTSD.[12]

Psychoses

Some psychiatric casualties faced an especially grim path. For the 6 to 8 percent of servicemen diagnosed as psychotic, their treatment in the military had been harsh. Overseas and in the States, psychotics, potential suicides, and psychopaths were often placed in locked wards with little occupational therapy, since it was assumed they would quickly be separated from service.[13] (An exception was St. Elizabeth's in Washington, DC, where the First Lady frequently visited soldiers and sailors, taking particular interest in their occupational therapy.)[14] While homosexual soldiers, epileptics, neurotics, and bedwetters were generally placed on open wards, they too were sometimes punished by being locked up on closed wards.[15]

Because the military feared psychotics would be disruptive, they shipped some of them home in wire cages, no more than six feet by three feet by three feet, that is, so cramped that a person could not sit up or attend to sanitary needs. While the Army Transportation Office issued a circular letter in March 1943 abolishing cages, some were used as late as June 1945. Generally, patients came home on ships equipped with electric shock equipment, drug therapy (in some cases, morphine), hydrotherapy, and physical restraints. Later, VA hospitals would use electric shock and insulin therapy as well as individual and group therapy.[16] Those on ships wore badges marked "NP," for neuropsychiatric. Among 2,980 mental patients shipped from the Pacific to San Francisco from April to October 1944, eighteen of the nineteen who died en route were psychotics. Of those, nine drowned, one hanged himself, and one died of diphtheria, three of cardiac arrest, one from severe kidney infection, and one from malnutrition.[17]

Psychoneurosis and Combat Exhaustion

From the beginning, psychiatrists minimized the severity of psychoneurosis. Faced with the dilemma of wanting to prove that the maladjustment was real, not a form of malingering, they were nonetheless reluctant to be too explicit for fear the description might stigmatize the victim. Hence, psychiatrists including Winfred Overholser, Harry Stack Sullivan, and Karl Bowman sidestepped the problem by defining it as "non-adjustment" to military life. (As the Cornell psychiatrist Carl Binger explained, a person became ill because the service could not accommodate his idiosyncrasies, analogizing his maladjustment to an otherwise successful salesman unable to travel by bus but only by train.)[18] But this message did not remove the stigma.

Along the same lines, the navy and army chiefs of psychiatry Francis Braceland and William Menninger maintained that combat exhaustion, like civilian trauma, was transient. Many combat exhausted, Menninger wrote, were capable citizens before service and would be afterward. While Howard P. Rome acknowledged to APA members that "life on a combat ship or raft or in a jungle foxhole makes ordinary traumatic situations seem relatively benign," he still assured them time would heal the wounds of combat.[19]

By late 1944, Menninger remembered from experience at the front the ferocity of battle but still contended combat exhaustion was transient. As he accepted the Lasker Award for Excellence in Mental Hygiene in Michigan, he recalled a clearing station at the German front within earshot of artillery, with "row after row of stretchers of psychiatric casualties, directly in from the fighting front a few miles distant. A sergeant . . . running around dispensing 'blue heaven' sodium amytal." They had seen hell, their comrades maimed and killed. Yet 60 percent would return to their foxholes after forty-eight hours "only to take it again." Postwar, they continued to believe their "combat exhaustion" would be short-term. In 1948, in *Psychiatry in a Troubled World*, he wrote that "probably the great majority, of combat psychiatric casualties, responded sufficiently under appropriate treatment to permit them to carry on. . . . Their experiences left scars . . . no doubt, but certainly, in many men, those scars are not sufficient to disable them seriously or permanently."[20]

PTSD

As did Menninger, many psychiatrists shied away from recognizing that soldiers with war experience might sustain long-term, even permanent debilitating illness, despite significant numbers exhibiting symptoms later termed PTSD. First enumerated in the third edition of the APA's *Diagnostic and Statistical Manual of Mental Disorders* (1980), or *DSM-III*, the criteria included a "stressor," that is, a traumatic occurrence beyond the individual's usual experiences. The stressor had to be a rape, torture, a natural disaster, an airplane crash, or, in the case of veterans, combat. The stressor would cause symptoms within six months of the date of trauma ("acute") or later on ("chronic or delayed"). The primary symptoms included reliving the traumatic past in one's mind through flashbacks, dreams, or an association with a similar, current incident and withdrawal from social or sexual activity, along with other possible symptoms, including difficulty sleeping, exaggerated startle reaction, guilt about surviving, the death of someone close, memory impairment, avoiding events that reminded him or her about the trauma or, on the other hand, intensifying the symptoms by exposure to events that resembled the original stressor.[21]

Many from World War II had characteristics of PTSD, though it was not then recognized: They withdrew from social or sexual contact, especially in their first year home. They replayed the trauma in their minds continuously. They carried guns or knives as if still in combat. They avoided memories of combat by binging on drugs or, more frequently, alcohol. (Over 750,000 veterans were alcoholics, at a treatment cost of $750 million annually by 1947, according to Menninger. Two years later, it came close to $780 million.)[22] They had suicidal or homicidal thoughts. Noise, smells, or food could trigger recollection of the trauma.[23]

The first studies of prisoners of war returning from Japan pointed to detachment and loss of sexual interest. By 1947, extensive psychiatric examination of thirty-five Americans subjected to three years of torture in Japanese prison of war camps found widespread mental changes. Half had impaired memory. Eight were psychopathic. Follow-ups six months and a year later revealed continuing alarm reactions, nightmares, and, particularly, distrust of others. A six-year study in 1954 found continuing psychoneuroses and psychosis among thousands of Pacific POWs, with symptoms resembling PTSD. Robert Keehn's 1974 study of almost ten thousand psychoneurotic veterans and ten thousand controls found that psychoneurotics, twenty-six to thirty years old in 1944, who had served at least ninety days, had higher rates of homicide, suicide, alcoholism, and suicide-prone accidents, especially accidental drowning, than their normal counterparts.[24] Though PTSD was not yet an official diagnosis, the media recognized behavior resembling PTSD. In one episode of the television series *Streets of San Francisco* (1973), a police detective, played by a young Michael Douglas, sympathetically protected a reclusive "schizoid" navy veteran, who suffered with a disability incurred from seeing all his men go down during the Japanese bombing of the battleship *Oklahoma* at Pearl Harbor.[25]

Once PTSD became official, World War II veterans were diagnosed, and, forty, fifty, even sixty or seventy years after the war, new cases continued to come to the VA, especially among POWs and veterans of long-term severe combat. For many, PTSD was coupled with alcohol used to self-medicate.[26] A widespread characteristic continued to be obtrusive memories and an inability to forget. A patient in a 1995 study wrote:

> Wheat fell headless in the field
> Till Death did reap enough.
> We seek to bury the revealed
> No earth is deep enough.
> You cannot wash the stains from minds.
> No one can weep enough.
> No night has sleep enough.[27]

The film *The Best Years of Our Lives* described several veterans who had PTSD-like symptoms. The bombardier returned home with frequent flashbacks of air battles; he had a hard time sleeping; he had nightmares; he lost his temper without reason. The father of his girlfriend came home an alcoholic after being in battle. The combat veteran who lost his arms was afraid that no one would accept him.

In *Unbroken*, an award-winning book and movie, the author Laura Hillenbrand described the PTSD of Louis Zamperini, an American distance runner at the 1936 Olympics who had shaken the hand of Hitler in Munich. He had later enlisted in the army air force, and his plane had crashed into the ocean. Zamperini and one of his comrades managed to survive two and a half months on a raft in the Pacific, existing on fish and bird meat. Afterward, they became POWs at a series of Japanese camps, during which time Zamperini was often tortured by a sadistic prison commander. Several years after returning home, he still had terrible flashbacks and nightmares. Binging on alcohol to forget, his wife about to divorce him, he was saved not by VA therapy but by the evangelist Billy Graham. Detoxed, he became a professional inspirational speaker into his late nineties.[28]

Others suffered as well, as documented by the historian Thomas Childers. Michael Gold, a Jewish air force bombardier, experienced the fear that Jewish American aviators held in common when the Germans imprisoned him for eighteen months in a German war camp for Allied flyers, Stalag Luft I, near Barth, on the Baltic Sea.[29] For the last six months, he was transferred to an isolated, ramshackle, "Jews only" barracks surrounded by its own wire fence. There he suffered untold miseries, was given virtually nothing to eat, and was shriveling away when, luckily, the war ended. Gold came home to become a talented engineering student, then a doctor, yet he was beset with crippling nightmares and flashbacks and frequently got into fights for little reason. Another soldier, Willis Allen, lost his legs in battle in Germany in December 1944; he and his wife had problems adjusting to his disability for years to come. A third, Childers's father, seemingly had it easy in a support unit for two years in England, never seeing combat, but seeing the loss of many friends, including his best friend; fliers who did not return from missions; blood splattered on planes; "headless bodies"; "scraps of tissue"; and "fragments of bone" got to him. "He came home not the same man, saddened, unable to talk about it, a businessman, there were times he just could not handle it."[30] Arthur "Dutch" Schultz, a hero paratrooper of the 82nd Airborne, memorialized by Stephen Ambrose and Steven Spielberg, landed in Normandy on D-Day, fought at the Battle of the Bulge, but spent years after the war reliving in his mind the scourge of combat.[31]

Veterans with symptoms of what would later be termed PTSD, or with a drug or alcohol addiction, or a Section VIII discharge generally did not receive pensions, especially if the discharge was deemed not service connected.[32] A patient might be considered to have a non-service-connected disability when his symptoms or the bulk of them were attributable to a mental condition from before military service or, if in service, were deemed a transient phenomenon. Often, the VA decision could be quite arbitrary. Some with worse histories got no pensions. Some psychiatrists generally disfavored pensions. Menninger, for one, opposed them, because they would pay a man "to maintain his illness."[33]

In an oral history, Thomas Calderone recalled that although he had been a Japanese prisoner of war, the VA refused his pension several times before finally granting it. Enlisting in the army at the end of the 1930s, assuming America's engagement in the war would be brief, he ended up serving until 1946, more than seven years. At Bataan and Corregidor, he endured insufficient food, malaria, and dysentery. He recalled an especially jarring experience on a burial detail in a POW camp:

> So, we used to go every morning to the "zero ward" and pick up these poor [dead] GIs and we walked carrying them for about a mile to the cemetery. When we picked them up their skin would come off in your hand ... and they had a big trench. They put twenty guys in at a time. So, when we would go there the next day, they didn't cover the holes that we put guys in ... and the dogs, wild dogs, would come and eat them.

The VA denied his petition for a PTSD pension multiple times despite its having assured prisoners of war that 75 percent would receive pensions. Only through his wife's insistence that he try just one more time did he finally receive a pension. Except for one Black female psychiatrist, the VA was blasé and would not help him. Some examiners insisted that he provide "the morning report" from the Japanese to prove his story. But "the Japs didn't have no morning report on any of us guys, because that would have been against them," he explained.[34]

Another former POW, also a veteran of the Philippines, Albert Senna, who enlisted in 1941 and was discharged in 1946, did not receive any pension for PTSD. He attributed the resistance he received to the VA's failure to recognize PTSD as an illness, though they did treat him for beriberi. Like Calderone, he was deprived of food and medicine in the POW camps, where he was imprisoned for three and a half years. Afflicted with diphtheria and temporary blindness, he was treated in a Japanese hospital, only to return to the camp to find that nine of his barracks mates had been forced to dig their own graves while he was away. In that respect he was lucky. Returning to the States, he spent over a year in a military hospital at Valley Forge before discharge, during which time he found it "terrible to see all those people with arms and legs missing." For a long time afterward, he sought a pension but was turned down and gave up, though he worked for fifteen years at the Lyons VA Hospital in New Jersey. The problem, as he saw it, was that from the time POWs came home, America ignored their suffering. "They never did come out with the truth, all the tortures and heads cutting off." Then there were "those fellows committing suicide." The husband of a friend of his "just drove the car up on the railroad [tracks] and shut off the keys . . . the train . . . smashed him all to pieces."[35]

The veteran Bert Manhoff recalled that his VA pension was reduced time and again as his disability percentage declined, though he had been diagnosed "psycho-neurotic-moderate severe." He suffered from panic attacks about planes flying overhead—memories of D-Day and combat—and from seeing skeleton-like dead piled up in Buchenwald. Finally, he met a Rutgers University basketball player whose father, a VA doctor, told him: "Look, they will keep calling you back, cutting . . . I'll make yours a permanent disability, at twenty percent." Manhoff agreed. Dr. Reuben Levinson, who helped liberate Nordhausen concentration camp, was likewise afflicted by long-running memories of the camps, which negatively affected his family. Other liberators suffered similarly.[36]

Survivors of German POW camps were often permanently emotionally debilitated. Timothy Dyas, after surrendering with his parachute troops to

Germans in 1943, spent over two years in POW camps. He lost so much weight he could barely crawl. Plagued by PTSD, especially after surrendering to the Germans and feeling he had let his men down, he suffered anxiety attacks and was "very much depressed at times." The VA informed him he had PTSD and granted him a pension, despite the fact that he had successfully held a position as a high school vice principal, in opposition to the VA's prerequisite that a claimant demonstrate his or her inability to work.[37]

It took thirty-five years after the war ended for the American Psychiatric Association (APA) to include PTSD as a diagnosis in *DSM-III* (1980). It occurred after the VA had rejected applications for pensions for psychiatric disabilities from many veterans of World War II, Korea, and finally, a new group beset by harrowing experiences in Vietnam. Initially, psychiatrists had assumed that combat exhaustion was transient. But the anti-Vietnam analyst Robert Jay Lifton, among other American psychiatrists, gradually began to notice that symptoms from Vietnam did not evaporate, that many months and even years later, veterans still suffered from nightmares, flashbacks, insomnia, and difficulty determining what was past and what present. Simultaneously, Holocaust survivors seeking pensions from the German government complained of similar emotional difficulties, a chorus also joined by victims of Hiroshima. Cumulatively, they were successful in lobbying the APA to include PTSD as a disorder in its *DSM-III*, despite continuing questions raised by some psychiatrists about the link between past traumatic incidents and recent disablement.[38]

Since then, regardless of the previous debate, the Veterans Administration has approved many pensions for PTSD for American veterans of the wars in Vietnam, Korea, and World War II. In 1983, a congressionally ordered study of the prevalence of PTSD among 1,450 veterans, known as the National Vietnam Veterans Readjustment Study (NVVRS), confirmed that as many as 15 percent had PTSD. In 2013, a follow-up study of the same 1,450, known as the National Vietnam Veterans Longitudinal Study (NVVLS), confirmed that among those who had served in the Vietnam theater forty years earlier, 11 percent of the males and 7 percent of the females still had PTSD. Of those with PTSD, the study also found, 37 percent had major depression.[39]

Eisenhower

As late as 1948, former supreme allied commander Dwight D. Eisenhower continued to wonder whether psychiatry had taken the right path. Addressing labor leaders and industrialists as the newly inaugurated president of Columbia University, he recalled how the military in the crucial months of the European campaign had become desperate for infantry replacements after Selective Service had rejected so many for psychiatric disorders or mental deficiency. He remembered that a sufficient manpower pool was unavailable and that the military had no choice but to take "drastic measures" to pull "men out of the service of supply . . . comb the air forces, anything to get replacements." He informed his audience that over two million had been rejected for mental illness and disorders. He wondered how those numbers could have been reduced, since manpower "is one of our most treasured assets." He recalled the military "overflowing" with "psychiatric cases."

He remembered men at the front "blue, cold, muddy . . . undergoing everything" but nevertheless assuring him, "Everything's all right, General—don't worry about us." In contrast, the psychiatric cases were "cleaned up, shaved . . . look[ing] strong." On several occasions, he sat at the bedside of a psychiatric patient, put his hand on his shoulder, and talked to him, the soldier responding, "General, get me out of here—I want to join my outfit." Perhaps "direct human contact," he suggested, treating the man as a human being, talking to him about his problems, could have cured many cases and sent them back to the front. Tempering his earlier skepticism of psychoneurosis, he recognized that some people "definitely break" and that these individuals cannot be dismissed as unfortunate "wanderers" as "they are one of you." He recalled, for instance, a "Major General, one of the finest athletes of his time," who "could not talk . . . without shaking [and] had to go home." He "broke . . . because he could no longer sustain the agonies of combat."[40]

Eisenhower's wartime experience led to his quest to reduce mental illness in war and peace. Two years later, in 1950, while still at Columbia, at a time when the Korean War was just beginning, he commissioned the Conservation of Human Resources Project, supervised by the sociologist/economist Eli Ginzberg, to study the military selection process in World War II in order to understand why so many had been rejected or discharged on neuropsychiatric grounds and aptitude and how it might affect postwar industrial productivity. The project drew experts from disparate academic disciplines as well as from the federal government, business, and labor unions. Experts included the well-known forensic psychiatrist Nolan D. C. Lewis, who had been involved in planning the use of psychiatry in World War II. Subsidized and sponsored by the Ford Foundation and companies such as DuPont, General Electric, RCA, and Standard Oil, it reflected the nation's concern that the GIs of World War II might not be productive workers. Ultimately in 1959, the project issued its three-volume *The Ineffective Soldier*, which not only dealt with why so many were rejected or discharged on neuropsychiatric grounds and how their performance could have been improved but also why so many Blacks had been rejected and discharged for inaptitude and undesirable character. Reflecting the evolving ethos of the time, expounded most prominently in the Supreme Court decision in *Brown v. Topeka*, the volume of *The Ineffective Soldier* entitled *The Lost Divisions* recognized the detrimental effects of poor education and racial segregation on Black self-esteem and mental aptitude,[41] also discussed in Ginzberg's earlier *The Uneducated* (1953) and *The Negro Potential* (1956).

Lessons from the War: Korea and Vietnam

Within six years of ending World War II, the United States entered the Korean War (June 1950 through July 1953). Called the "Forgotten War," it nevertheless resulted in 54,000 American deaths and one hundred thousand wounded. We provide here a mere thumbnail sketch of how lessons learned by American psychiatry in World War II were applied in Korea and Vietnam.[42]

After World War II, America's troops gradually became racially integrated in the Korean War.[43] It was fought by soldiers confronting the harshest cold weather in the toughest terrain; initially, North Korea had the upper hand. Active combat ended in an unofficial armistice. Figures on psychiatric casualties were much lower in Korea than World War II. Benefiting from its experience with psychiatry in World War II, the American army did not routinely give inductees psychiatric examinations. Instead, they referred to a psychiatrist those who had definite psychiatric symptoms or documentation of a mental condition. Hence, the rate of psychiatric rejection dropped to 2.0 percent. On the other hand, the military was much more interested in screening the potentially untrainable by expanding and toughening the standards of its Armed Forces Qualification Test (AFQT). As a result, the rate of rejection on psychological grounds during the Korean War rose to 7.9 percent compared to 4.3 percent in World War II. Hence, the combined figure for psychiatric disorders and mental deficiency came to about the same percentage in both the Korean War and World War II.[44]

As to psychiatric hospital admissions, the rate was much lower in the Korean War than in World War II, partly because of increasing treatment at the front soon after the appearance of symptoms. Unlike World War II, the army rotated troops in groups every twelve months, relieving stress before it could show up. (Sending in replacements alone or in small groups had been a major problem in World War II.) On the other hand, the severe Korean winters contributed to mental stress.[45] As on the domestic front in America, on the war front in Korea psychiatrists used outpatient care as much as possible. In this way, they were able to catch patients with symptoms at a much earlier stage. Whereas in World War II some of the training camps had psychiatric consultation services, in the Korean War, they all did. These services oriented soldiers to the problems they would most likely face in military service and provided them with information on how to cope.[46]

From 1963 to 1975, the United States engaged in the Vietnam War.[47] Altogether, more than 58,000 Americans lost their lives during this war. Unlike previous wars, American soldiers in Vietnam largely engaged an unseen civilian enemy and encountered growing political opposition back home. A disproportionate number of those serving came from lower-income families. For 1961–1968, the Black rate of combat deaths was 13.7 percent, considerably higher than their percentage in the military and in the general population.[48] While the military no longer denied Blacks the right to serve in combat, new racial and ethical issues emerged, including claims that the burden and danger of combat fell inordinately on the poor and on Blacks.

As in the Korean War, the army focused on aptitude testing instead of psychiatric screening. Again, doctors only referred inductees to examining psychiatrists if they appeared blatantly ill or had sufficient documentation of mental disorders. However, unlike Korea, given the desperate need for manpower, the bar for intelligence testing was much lower, admitting individuals into the military with IQs as low as 62. While there was no routine psychiatric screening, there was a de facto form of psychiatric screening outside the military. Similar in a way to the purchasing of substitutes by prospective soldiers in the Civil War, Americans with sufficient means could now consult private psychiatrists who could write letters for them to their draft boards if they diagnosed them unfit. Facilitating this practice was the expansive definition of mental illness developed in World War II but now utilized in a realm external to the military institution.[49]

On the surface, there appeared to be a low percentage of psychiatric casualties in Vietnam, much lower than even Korea. Psychiatric casualties were ten times less than the rate in World War II and three times less than in Korea.[50] Accounting for this, as in Korea, was widespread, immediate front-line psychiatry. Stress was also alleviated by a tour of duty of no more than 365 days, ample rest and recreation during the tour, and battles much shorter in length, all recommendations previously made during World War II. But the numbers from Vietnam were in part illusory. They did not account for widespread drug, largely heroin, addiction. In 1971, more soldiers were evacuated from Vietnam for drug use than for wounds. Nor did the rate of psychiatric casualty include "behavior" or "character" disorders. Rather, continuing a practice begun in World War II, such men and women received administrative discharges, in many cases without benefits and without honor. It is possible that the psychiatric casualty rate was also low because soldiers were leery of seeing psychiatrists who would administer such powerful medications as Thorazine and Mellaril. Nor did limiting tours to 365 days always have a positive effect. Similar to the concerns in World War II, while soldiers less often developed "old sergeant's syndrome" from too many months of steady combat, they tended to lose their feeling of unit cohesion and obligation to others when they knew that they had only a few weeks left on their tour ("short timer's syndrome").[51] Since Vietnam, however, the opposite has occurred: soldiers in Iraq and Afghanistan being worn down by repeated consecutive tours. Once home, as in World War II, soldiers in the Vietnam War were advised to forget and move on. But by 1980, psychiatrists added the diagnosis PTSD in *DSM-III*, recognizing its debilitating effects on Vietnam veterans years afterward.

In *War and the Rise of the State*, the political scientist Bruce D. Porter recognized that

> wars are not mere intermissions in a human drama of relentless progress. . . . It is instead a powerful catalyst of change, the direction of which is always morally problematic. . . . Regardless of whether a war is just or unjust, positive or negative in its long-term consequences, military conflict tends to unleash the most primitive human passions, often with enduring consequences for the moral fabric of societies that wage it.[52]

Certainly, Franklin Roosevelt had hoped to eliminate the psychological scourge of war. And Dwight D. Eisenhower sought to understand why American psychiatry had largely failed in World War II. But for the individual veteran and his family, it was more than an academic exercise. World War II had a profound psychological, economic, and social impact for decades to come.

Conclusion

In 1938, at a time when American youth was exhausted physically and mentally by the Great Depression and imbued with pacificism and isolationism, the psychiatrist Harry Stack Sullivan and his associates began to design a universal psychiatric examination for Selective Service, which ultimately became Selective Service Medical Circular No. 1. Approved by President Franklin Delano Roosevelt, the circular's ambitious objective was to eliminate from service all those who might in any way have difficulty in interpersonal relations in the military and even in civilian life thereafter. Faced with the reluctance of an isolationist Congress to fund preparations for war and an economy reeling from the Depression, Roosevelt and his team were persuaded that such an examination could minimize VA psychiatric hospital costs should America enter the war by eliminating from service most of those who might break down. Later, the army and navy introduced their own universal psychiatric examinations, focusing more narrowly on gross neurological impairments and potential disciplinary problems that might interfere with the regimentation needed to defeat fascism. Nothing on the scale of these massive screening programs had been implemented in the United States before (or since). As a result, the military rejected and discharged from military service at least 2.5 million in World War II.

Once the United States entered the war to defeat fascism, other leading civilian psychiatrists began to discuss alternatives to psychiatric screening. They considered plans to jointly work with psychologists in assigning the maladjusted to noncombat positions in the military or in industry or agriculture. To forestall mental breakdowns, they discussed treating psychological issues at the front and quickly returning the patients to combat and attempted to reduce the stresses of the conditions of military life to the extent possible (preventive psychiatry). But even as reports emerged of severe breakdowns of discipline in training camps and embarkation centers, as well as overseas, and of psychiatric casualties climbing while soldiers fought abortive battles in the Pacific and North Africa, military leaders and prominent civilian psychiatrists by late 1942–early 1943 embraced stricter screening and little else.

By late 1943, however, as the numbers of psychiatric 4Fs and psychiatric discharges continued to rise precipitously, military and civilian leaders—and the latter's constituents—had lost their patience for psychiatry. Accustomed to associating mental disorders with the chronically insane or severely disabled, they puzzled over the new diagnoses of intangible maladjustments encompassed in the examinations. Faced with the reality of eighteen-year-olds and fathers with young children being drafted while more than a million outwardly healthy men were being rejected on vague suspicions of neuropsychiatric problems, Americans accused psychiatric 4Fs, in numerous congressional hearings and complaints to Selective Service, of being unpatriotic draft dodgers. And many rejectees and their families expressed shame at not doing their part and objected to perceived racial and regional biases of psychiatric examiners. Yet despite intense criticism, many civilian psychiatrists, to the very end of the war, called for more, not less, screening and sought to develop new tests and social histories to improve their ability to forecast behavior. In the end, however, none of these refinements really worked.

Making matters worse, there was never really a consensus among psychiatrists as to diagnoses, treatment methods, or prevention techniques. To the end of the war, mental hospital superintendents, career military psychiatrists, neurologists, psychoanalysts, and private practitioners continued to disagree. Only a few months before the war ended, leading civilian psychiatrists were still calling for tougher preinduction screening, even when the military psychiatric establishment was definitely opposed. Nor was there ever a unified psychiatric classification system. This did not occur until 1952, with the publication of the first edition of the *Diagnostic and Statistical Manual of Mental Disorders*. With such divergence in psychiatric opinion, military commanders, such as Army Chief of Staff George C. Marshall, found it difficult to respect the field.

Added to this were the mounting battlefield deaths and casualties. By late 1943, infantry numbers had been seriously depleted, and psychiatric casualties had risen to unprecedented levels. Never comfortable with what they termed "nut-pickers," military leaders accused psychiatrists of sapping manpower while encouraging cowardice and malingering. General George Patton caused an uproar when he slapped in the face two psychiatric patients in military hospitals and sent them back to the front, finding nothing wrong with them except abject cowardice. Though Marshall and Commander Dwight D. Eisenhower deplored Patton's behavior, they shared his concerns.

Despite an official War Department news blackout of psychiatry that lasted for almost a year, Marshall's staff leaked his memorandum condemning psychiatry to the press at the end of December 1943. By October 1944, the army IG began three separate, months-long investigations of psychoneurosis, which lasted until May 1945 and criticized every psychiatric method, recommending alternatives including even threats of court-martial and execution.

Leading military psychiatrists sought unsuccessfully to appease the military. Mindful of the need to conserve manpower, responding to their own growing doubts about their ability to forecast behavior, and recognizing the impact of stressful environmental conditions on mental health, they, unlike their civilian counterparts, began to develop a new strategy involving preventive psychiatry and treatment at the front. But the reluctance of quite a few within their own ranks to abandon the time-honored doctrine of predisposition, plus the military's resistance to limiting tours of duty and increasing rest and recuperation (R&R), with a war still to be won, topped off by the IG's caustic investigations, limited psychiatrists' efforts significantly.

Soon after the war, studies of psychiatric rejectees who were later accepted by the army found that the vast majority performed satisfactorily, leading psychiatrists to conclude that many rejectees were "false positives" who could have performed well in service had they been given the chance. Whereas other combatant nations had placed individuals deemed unfit for combat into noncombat military, agricultural, or industrial assignments, America's business and organized labor interests successfully stymied passage of a National Service Act.

Eliminated from service, often with questionable stigmatic diagnoses, many American psychiatric 4Fs and veterans confronted problems getting jobs in a full-employment economy. Others, with psychiatrically related Section VIII blue discharges, many of whom were Black or homosexual, received no veterans' benefits. The exigencies of war pressured psychiatrists, despite the Hippocratic Oath, to return men to combat before they were psychologically ready, contributing to long-lasting psychological illness. Despite the common belief among the medical profession that combat exhaustion would be transient, many suffered persistent, long-lasting symptoms, later termed post-traumatic stress disorder (PTSD). Not until 1980 did psychiatrists officially recognize PTSD as a disorder to be diagnosed and treated. This meant that many veterans' ailments were largely ignored for generations to come and that current knowledge about PTSD suffered from years of ignorance.

If there is a lesson to be learned in this book, it is the value of compromise and flexibility. Had psychiatrists not been so intransigent about screening and had the army been more flexible about preventive psychiatry and treatment at the front, fewer men and women might have been stigmatized, fewer possibly might have died, and fewer might have broken down in combat. But the desperation to win the war deterred compromise.

Yet screening did have important positive effects. It served to unify the will to fight by eliminating from service, among others, cynics, malcontents, and those expressing reservations about the war. Hence, it was able at times to fill the role played in other societies by propaganda, imprisonment, and execution, which, if implemented in the United States, could have torn the fabric of democracy apart. In addition, screening largely promoted the medicalization of certain categories previously considered matters for court-martial and imprisonment, such as alcoholism and addiction. For the most part, this was a humanitarian advance in World War II, though psychiatric diagnosis and discharge could still lead to discrimination and abuse of rights. But the "medicalization" of homosexuality did not go far enough. Only in 1973 did the American Psychiatric Association officially remove homosexuality as a diagnosis from the second edition of its *Diagnostic and Statistical Manual of Mental Disorders (DSM-II)*. More recently, the military, recognizing that homosexuality is neither a crime nor a medical condition, no longer disqualifies anyone who is homosexual from military service.

Despite the debates, tensions, and missed opportunities, by the end of World War II American psychiatry had blossomed, witnessing a major expansion in popularity, numbers of patients, research, training, and funding. How can we reconcile this dramatic change with the skepticism and scorn of the profession during the war? In part, this was a self-fulfilling prophecy. Many of the men and women rejected or discharged on psychiatric grounds had never had contact with psychiatry before. Now, they had become personally familiar with the methods of psychiatry. Some became genuinely attracted to analysis. Though presented in abbreviated form in the military, they liked learning about who they really were. No longer a profession primarily caring for the chronically insane in isolated institutions, it was now perceived as a profession caring for everyone. Fifteen straight years of the Great Depression and devastating global war had germinated in many a need for psychiatry. In addition to those rejected or discharged, 1.2 million psychiatric casualties were treated in army hospitals while in military service; many endured PTSD for years afterward, though their illnesses were yet to be formally recognized. At least a million more veterans had physical disabilities, large numbers with emotional components. Added to this were families simply stressed out by the Depression, by wartime separations, and by spouses and fathers with emotional and physical disabilities. Husbands and wives returned home to a cult of normalcy: the husband the breadwinner, the wife the nurturer. Some who could not readjust also sought assistance from psychiatrists.

Expansion of the concept and nomenclature of psychiatric illness, largely as a byproduct of the screening examinations and particularly the broad catch-all term "psychoneurosis," plus the wartime belief that "everyone has a breaking point," led to a growing public perception of the need for psychiatry. In the military, psychiatrists in part adopted roles previously reserved for line officers, including lecturing on fear, anxiety, and current events and advising on improvements in living conditions. As one priest at the front noted, individuals who may have previously sought advice from friends or gone to clergy with their everyday concerns now turned to psychiatrists instead.

Nor can the profession's hubris be ignored. Unlike military psychiatrists stationed overseas, many civilian psychiatrists retained their belief to the end in the value of screening, despite its major weaknesses, so much so that Edward Strecker, who never abandoned his belief in predisposition, popularized a new iteration of this concept called "Momism." Psychiatrists accused mothers of having psychologically crippled their sons, making them cowards and weaklings, which contributed to the millions of psychiatric rejections, discharges, and draft dodgers during the war. "Momism" attempted to roll back the war's evolution in thinking. During the war, military leaders had accused psychiatrists of overzealousness in screening; military psychiatrists themselves had acknowledged that sufficient stress could cause anyone to break. Now, disavowing these lessons, some psychiatrists argued that the fault lay largely with America's mothers, a belief suggested in the army's descriptive tale of soldiers' psychiatric disabilities in the training film *Shades of Gray*, issued as a replacement for the suddenly withdrawn *Let There Be Light*. Accompanying the theory of "Momism" came a growing popular demand for childrearing training and literature, also prompted by the call for female nurturing during an age of normalcy.

On the other hand, military psychiatrists who founded the Group for Advancement of Psychiatry (GAP) took a more progressive route. Soon to become major formulators of American Psychiatric Association (APA) policies, the psychiatrist-founders of GAP applied lessons learned at the front to postwar psychiatry. Continuing their espousal of the need to modify the environment to improve mental health, they supported efforts in forensic and industrial psychiatry. Exhibiting an interest cultivated during the war in treatment close to the front, they endorsed the opening of community clinics, which were provided for in the National Mental Health Act (1946) and even more so in the Community Mental Health Act (1963).

While after the war psychiatrists began to focus on instilling in the average person the will to become self-sufficient, their efforts did not extend to everyone. For many years, those troubled with combat exhaustion (PTSD) were overlooked or dismissed. Even today, the focus on enabling individuals in industry and the military to become more resilient has left behind those with chronic afflictions who cannot return to normal living. As to screening, never before or since has there been such a program conducted by the military. In the Korean and Vietnam wars, Americans focused much more on aptitude tests. Still, some researchers today are discovering genetic predispositions to developing PTSD.[1] In the end, the transformation of American psychiatry in the "Good War" influenced the philosophy and direction of mental health in subsequent wars and domestically for decades to come. This, however, is another book to be written.

Acronyms and Abbreviations

Absence Without Leave—AWOL
Adaptability Rating for Military Aeronautics—ARMA
Adjutant General—AG
American Civil Liberties Union—ACLU
American General Classification Test—AGCT
American Medical Association—AMA
American Psychiatric Association—APA
American Psychoanalytic Association—APsaA
American Student Union—ASU
Army Information and Education Division—previously Army Morale Branch and then Army Special Services Division, referred to as I&E Division
Army Mobilization Regulations—MR
Assistant Army Chief of Staff for Personnel—G-1
Boston Psychoanalytic Society and Institute—BPSI
Certificate of Disability for Discharge—CDD
Civilian Conservation Corps—CCC
Civilian Public Service—CPS
Conscientious Objector—CO
Diagnostic and Statistical Manual—DSM
Displaced Person—DP
Electroconvulsive Therapy—ECT
European Theater of Operations, United States of America—ETOUSA
Fair Employment Practice Committee—FEPC
Federal Communications Commission—FCC
Group for the Advancement of Psychiatry—GAP
Henry Phipps Psychiatric Clinic, Baltimore, MD—Phipps Clinic
Inspector General—IG
Intelligence Quotient—IQ
Joint Army Navy Selective Service Committee—JANSSC
Judge Advocate General—JAG

Medical Survey Program—MSP
Mediterranean Theater of Operations, United States Army—MTOUSA, formerly NATOUSA
National Academy of Sciences—NAS
National Association for the Advancement of Colored People—NAACP
National Committee for Mental Hygiene—NCMH
National Defense Research Committee—NDRC
National Medical Association—NMA
National Mental Health Act—NMHA
National Neuropsychiatric Institute Act—NNIA
National Research Council—NRC
National Vietnam Veterans Longitudinal Study—NVVLS
National Vietnam Veterans Readjustment Study—NVVRS
National Youth Administration—NYA
Neuropsychiatric Screening Adjunct—NSA
New York Psychoanalytic Association—NYPA
North African Theater of Operations, United States Army—NATOUSA
Office of Civilian Defense—OCD
Office of Scientific Research and Development—OSRD
Office of Strategic Services—OSS
Office of War Information—OWI
Post-Traumatic Stress Disorder—PTSD
Prisoner of War—POW
Rest and Recuperation—R&R
Selective Service Medical Advisory Board—MAB
Selective Training and Service Act of 1940—Selective Service Act
Supreme Headquarters Allied Expeditionary Force—SHAEF
Surgeon General—SG
United Nations—UN
United States Public Health Service—PHS
War Manpower Commission—WMC
William Alanson White Psychiatric Foundation, Washington, DC—WAWPF
Women's Army Auxiliary Corps—WAAC
Women's Army Corps—WAC
Works Progress Administration—WPA
World Health Organization—WHO

Principal Physicians and Social Scientists

Karl Abraham—German protégé of Sigmund Freud, attributed mental maladjustment, including war neuroses in World War I, to problems originating largely in infant sexuality. This view is discussed in *Psychoanalysis and the War Neuroses* (1921), edited by Karl Abraham et al.

S. Spafford Ackerly—As an American soldier in France in World War I, suffered a leg wound, which despite numerous surgeries never properly healed, plaguing him the rest of his life. After the war, studied medicine at Yale Medical School and trained as a psychiatrist in Vienna. As a member of the Selective Service Psychiatric Advisory Committee, 1940–1941, assisted in drafting and implementing Selective Service Medical Circular No. 1, a routine psychiatric examination for military service. Served as a psychiatrist at the University of Louisville Medical School, Kentucky, 1932–1947.

Franz Alexander—Émigré psychiatrist from Hungary, specialist in psychosomatic medicine, founder of the Chicago Psychoanalytic Institute in 1932. Analyzed William Menninger.

John Appel—Director of the Lancaster Pennsylvania Child Guidance Clinic before World War II and continued his interest in preventive psychiatry as chief of the Army Mental Hygiene Branch, Army Neuropsychiatric Consultants Division, starting 1943. With the sociologist-psychologist Samuel Stouffer, designed the army's NSA, a routine written personality test for military service. Also assisted Stouffer in drafting questions for surveys distributed by the Army Research Branch to as many as half a million soldiers on issues related to morale; advised Frank Capra on his seven Why We Fight films.

Pearce Bailey—Before World War I, director of the Neurological Institute, New York City. Headed the Army's Neurology and Psychiatry Division in the United States during World War I.

Clifford Beers—Founder and first director of the National Committee for Mental Hygiene (NCMH). Wrote about his devastating personal experiences as a patient in a mental hospital in *A Mind That Found Itself* (1921).

256 | Principal Physicians and Social Scientists

Martin Berezin—Trained as a psychoanalyst and served as a division surgeon, director of the Army Medical Corps, and sole psychiatrist at Guadalcanal in 1943. Persuaded Commanding General Alexander Patch in Guadalcanal not to court-martial soldiers diagnosed with neuropsychiatric disorders.

Ivan C. Berlien –Member of William Menninger's staff in the Army Neuropsychiatric Consultants Division; wrote a critical memorandum in 1944 on the inadequacy of WAC psychiatric selection. Along with Malcolm Farrell, deputy chief of the division, reported to Menninger on conditions in the Southwest Pacific in 1944.

Karl Birnbaum—Noted forensic psychiatrist and chief physician in the Berlin Institute for Mental Diseases. Immigrated to the United States in 1939, assisted by Clifford Beers, NCMH, interceding on his behalf with the State Department.

Daniel Blain—Director of the Veterans Administration Psychiatry and Neurology Division, 1946–1948. As first medical director of the APA, 1948–1958, he was principally involved in efforts to improve mental hospital conditions.

Karl Bowman—Member of the Selective Service Psychiatric Advisory Committee, 1940–1941; chief psychiatrist at Bellevue Hospital, New York University, New York City, 1936–1941; on the special committee appointed by the Secretary of War to investigate rejections of mental cases at induction stations (August–September 1943). Also consultant to the Office of the Inspector General in its inquiry regarding the diagnosis, treatment, and disposition of psychoneurotics in the Zone of Interior. Became the APA's president in 1946.

Francis Braceland—Chief of psychiatry in the navy in World War II and protégé of psychiatrist Edward Strecker. Dean of the Loyola University School of Medicine starting in 1941.

Carl Brigham—Prominent psychologist who originally promoted the widespread use of the psychologist Robert Yerkes's IQ test; by 1930, he became one of its major critics. Also principal designer of the Scholastic Aptitude Test (SAT) introduced in 1926.

Norman Brill—Chief psychiatrist at Fort Bragg, North Carolina, during World War II; conducted Office of the Surgeon General study in 1944, with William Menninger, of 4,178 psychoneurotic veterans randomly selected throughout the country who were discharged between May 1943 and January 1944 regarding receipt of employment. Starting in 1926 he chaired the Department of Neurology, Georgetown University, Washington, DC, and from 1953 on, the Department of Psychiatry, University of California, Los Angeles.

Temple Burling—Industrial psychiatrist employed by R. H. Macy & Co., 1937–1940; director of the Psychiatry Program at the Cornell School of Industrial and Labor Relations, 1948–1964.

Charles Burlingame—Psychiatric consultant to Secretary of War, 1944–1945; consultant to the Office of the Inspector General in its investigation of the diagnosis, treatment, and disposition of psychoneurotics in the Zone of Interior. Psychiatrist-Director, Institute for Living, Hartford, Connecticut, 1931–1950.

C. MacFie Campbell—Trained future Selective Service and Army preinduction examiners in diagnoses at Selective Service seminars, 1940–1941. Born in Scotland, studied psychiatry with Emil Kraepelin in Germany and, after immigrating to the United States, with Adolf Meyer at the New York Psychiatric Institute. Director of the Boston Psychopathic Hospital and professor of Psychiatry at Harvard Medical School, 1920–1943, APA president, 1936–1937.

John Cathcart—Medical officer in the Canadian army in World War I. Chief psychiatrist, Canadian Department of Pensions, 1939–1940. Advocated the military's employing the term "Below Standard" instead of "shell shock" to reduce the number of psychiatric patients; in favor of treating close to the front.

G. Brock Chisholm—Canadian World War I veteran, director of Medical Services and chief of Personnel Selection in the Canadian Army in World War II, and the Canadian deputy minister of health starting 1944. Friend of William Menninger in the 1930s, director of World Health Organization (WHO), 1948–1953.

R. Robert Cohen—Psychiatrist at Aberdeen Proving Grounds Ordnance Replacement Training Camp during World War II. Author of widely distributed army pamphlet entitled "Mack and Mike" contrasting the right and wrong way for a soldier to adjust to military life.

Martin Cooley—Veterans Affairs (VA) psychiatrist starting in 1919. While still at the VA, served on the Selective Service Psychiatric Advisory Committee in 1941, training attendees at Selective Service Seminars to become Selective Service and Army Induction Board examiners; advocated tough psychiatric screening to reduce the cost of hospitalizing psychiatric veterans.

Margaret Craighill—Chief WAC psychiatrist in World War II and first female commissioned officer (lieutenant colonel) in the US Army. Dean of the Women's Medical College of Pennsylvania, Philadelphia, before the war. After the war, consultant to General Omar Bradley at the VA on medical care for women veterans.

Joseph de Jarnette—Eugenicist/psychiatrist, superintendent of Western State Hospital, Staunton, Virginia, 1905–1943. Conducted hundreds of forced sterilizations on primarily Black and Native American women who were considered mentally disabled, epileptic, alcoholic, or promiscuous. Vocal on issues of Selective Service selection criteria.

J. Paul de River—Navy psychiatrist in World War I; head of the Los Angeles Sex Offender Bureau in the 1930s and psychiatric consultant to the Los Angeles Superior Court. Author of *The Sexual Criminal* (1950) and *Crime and the Sexual Psychopath* (1958). Advocated stricter rejection of homosexuals from military service in a letter in October 1941 to President Franklin Delano Roosevelt's personal secretary.

Harry Deutsch—Oklahoma psychiatrist. Criticized excessive rejection from military service on psychiatric grounds in 1941 of Native Americans in Oklahoma by army and Selective Service psychiatrists.

John Dollard—Psychologist/psychoanalyst, known for *Caste and Class in a Southern Town* (1937); with other Yale psychologists, for *Frustration and Aggression* (1939); and for his widely disseminated pamphlet for soldiers published in *Infantry Journal* (1944) entitled "Twelve Rules on Meeting Battle Fear."

George Draper—President Franklin Delano Roosevelt's personal polio specialist. Head of Columbia University's Constitutionalism Clinic (a field related to eugenics) for thirty years, researching alleged relationships between individuals' physical characteristics, personality, and susceptibility to diseases.

Franklin Ebaugh—Professor of psychiatry, University of Colorado Medical School, starting in 1925; did a major study for the NRC Committee on Neuropsychiatry in 1942 comparing the backgrounds of one hundred psychiatric casualties and one hundred soldier controls, concluding that more careful screening would have avoided such casualties occurring in the army.

Principal Physicians and Social Scientists | 259

Erik Erikson—German psychoanalyst and psychologist. Analyzed by Anna Freud, immigrated to the United States in 1933, taught at Harvard Medical School, and wrote many well-known books focusing on psychosocial personality development, including *Childhood and Society* (1950).

Malcolm Farrell—Assistant chief of the Army Psychiatry section, later branch and then division, in World War II under chiefs Patrick Madigan, Roy Halloran, and William Menninger. After the untimely death of Halloran, became acting chief of psychiatry from November 10, 1943, until December 17, 1943, when Surgeon General Norman Kirk appointed Menninger.

Lawrence Frank—Social scientist specializing in child welfare. Opposed drafting eighteen- and nineteen-year-olds into military service in 1942. Director of the Laura Spelman Rockefeller Memorial Foundation and the Rockefeller Foundation Child Development Program, 1929–1942; also on the Social Science Research Council.

Frank Fremont-Smith—Psychiatric director of the Josiah H. Macy Foundation during World War II. Consultant to the Office of the Inspector General in its investigation of the diagnosis, treatment, and disposition of psychoneurotics in the Zone of Interior.

Erich Fromm—German émigré psychoanalyst with a doctorate in sociology. A challenger of some of Freud's theories, known for examining the social forces generating authoritarianism and alienation from democracy in his influential bestseller *Escape from Freedom* (1941).

Frieda Fromm-Reichmann—German psychoanalyst who immigrated to the United States in 1935 with her then husband, Erich Fromm. Worked with Harry Stack Sullivan on the etiology of schizophrenia, connecting schizophrenia with inadequate early child nurturing. Analyst at Chestnut Lodge, Maryland, 1926–1948; also employed as a training analyst at the Washington Psychoanalytic Society.

Clements Fry—Psychiatrist and head of the Department of Mental Hygiene, Yale University, 1930–1955. Surveyed the military performance of many former student/patients at the Yale clinic, including those identified as homosexual, finding scarcely any correlation between performance and sexual identification.

Henry Garrett—Columbia University professor of psychology, 1920–1956. President of the American Psychological Association in 1946; worked on developing a written test for officer selection as head of a subcommittee of the National Defense Research Committee.

R. D. Gillespie—British psychiatrist. With psychiatrist David Kennedy Henderson, wrote a psychiatry textbook widely used by medical students throughout its thirty-three editions (1932–1978). Chief psychiatrist of the Royal Air Force (RAF); delivered lectures at the New York Academy of Medicine and in Chicago on the psychological effects of the blitz and of combat on British soldiers, published as *Psychological Effects of War on Citizen and Soldier*.

Albert J. Glass—Army division psychiatrist, 1944–1949; chief psychiatric consultant to Far East Command, 1950–1951; known for applying his experience with treating psychiatric casualties in World War II to combat exhaustion cases in the Korean War. Editor of volume 1 of US Army Medical Department, *Neuropsychiatry in World War II* 1 (1966).

Bernard Glueck—Criminal psychiatrist and psychoanalyst. Treated residents at St. Elizabeth's Hospital in 1909; examined immigrants at Ellis Island, 1912–1913, and prisoners at Sing Sing, 1918. Served in the Army Medical Corps in World War I.

Roy Grinker—Neurologist and psychoanalyst analyzed by Sigmund Freud. His neurology textbook was published in 1933. He and his residents at the University of Chicago Medical School, John Spiegel, treated Army Air Crew and infantry at a British military hospital in Algiers, 1942–1943, working closely with their British colleagues, early on recognizing the effects of environment on mental health. Grinker and Spiegel authored *War Neuroses in North Africa: The Tunisian Campaign* (1943), widely used as a textbook by doctors throughout the army in World War II, and *Men under Stress* (1946), on soldiers and veterans. Professor of psychiatry at the University of Chicago, Northwestern, and the University of Illinois.

Martin Grotjahn—Trained by the Berlin Psychoanalytic Society, immigrated to the United States in 1936, and worked with Karl Menninger in Topeka, Kansas, and Franz Alexander in Chicago before enlisting in the army from 1943 through 1945. Thereafter was a training analyst in Los Angeles and an early advocate of the benefits of group therapy.

Ernest Hadley—Psychiatrist at WAWPF, where he worked closely with Sullivan, particularly in the design and implementation of Medical Circular No. 1.

Principal Physicians and Social Scientists | 261

Roy Halloran—Chief, Army Neuropsychiatry Branch, from August 1942 until his sudden death of a coronary occlusion on November 9, 1943. Appointed by the surgeon general as head of the neuropsychiatric branch with a rank of colonel after an extensive search of civilian psychiatrists led by Dr. Winfred Overholser, superintendent of St. Elizabeth's Hospital. Before his military service, he was superintendent of Metropolitan State Hospital, Waltham, Massachusetts, and professor of clinical psychiatry at Tufts College Medical School.

Samuel Hamilton—Member of the Selective Service Psychiatric Advisory Committee and of the APA Military Mobilization Committee and mental hospital adviser to the US Public Health Service (PHS) in 1941.

Frederick Hanson—Neurologist and neurosurgeon. Known for returning a high percentage of men to combat at the front after a few days of rest. Appointed neuropsychiatric consultant to the Mediterranean theater and trained military psychiatrists around the globe in treating soldiers at the front and returning them quickly to combat. Assigned to the staff of the assistant chief of staff, G-1, in July 1944. Appointed to accompany the inspector general's team throughout their investigation of treatment and disposition of psychoneurotics in the Mediterranean Theater of Operations (MTO). Hanson's treatment methods were widely used by psychiatrists in the Korean War.

Heinz Hartmann—Last psychoanalyst trained by Freud in Austria in 1934–1935. Served in the Austrian Army in World War I. Immigrated to the United States in 1941 with the assistance of Lawrence Kubie and the State Department.

Karen Horney—Neo-Freudian analyst. Trained in Berlin, immigrated to Chicago in 1932, worked with Harry Stack Sullivan. Known for relating social conditions to the mental health of women.

William A. Hunt—Professor of psychology at Northwestern University and, later, Loyola University. Designed with the psychiatrist Cecil Wittson in World War II the revised Shipley Inventory, a written personality test used by the navy.

Daniel Jaffe—Division psychiatrist in the Pacific and psychiatrist at the War Crimes Trials in Tokyo.

Ernest Jones—British psychiatrist/psychoanalyst. Protégé of Freud and author of a three-volume biography of Freud. Assisted in the escape of Freud and his daughter Anna from Vienna to England as well as the emigration from central Europe of Jewish analysts to England and the United States.

Carl Jung—Swiss analytic psychologist. Analyst of George Draper, Roosevelt's polio physician. Specializing in theories of the unconscious, at the turn of the twentieth century he worked with the psychologist and classifier of mental illness Eugen Bleuler at the Burghölzli Asylum in Zurich.

Abram Kardiner—Based on his experiences as a VA psychiatrist in the 1920s, told members of the NRC Committee on Neuropsychiatry in 1941 that he doubted the ability of psychiatrists to forecast human military behavior through psychiatric screening and urged military psychiatrists to instead treat at the front. Analyzed by Freud for six months in Vienna (1921–1922). Among the books he authored was *Mark of Oppression: Explorations in the Personality of the American Negro* (1951) with Lionel Ovesey.

Moses (Moe or M. Ralph) Kaufman—Trained at the Vienna Psychoanalytic Institute in 1929 and a founding member of the BPSI. Worked with the psychoanalyst Lawrence Kubie in persuading the State Department to admit émigré psychiatrists to the United States before America's entry into World War II. Served forty-four months as the psychiatric consultant to the South Pacific and Pacific theaters, including treating soldiers at the front in Okinawa in 1945. Awarded two Bronze Stars. In 1948, he became president of the American Psychoanalytic Society.

Foster Kennedy—President Roosevelt's personal neurologist and close family friend. President of the American Neurological Association in 1940 and professor of psychiatry at Cornell Medical Center during World War II. Supervised a French military hospital in World War I; wrote article equating shell shock with hysteria.

Albert Kenner—Chief medical officer for the North Africa, Italy, and Normandy invasions, reporting directly to General Dwight D. Eisenhower. Participated in conferences with the IG and other army officers during their investigation of treatment and disposition of psychoneurotics in the MTO and European Theater of Operations (ETO).

Norman Kirk—Army Surgeon General starting June 1943; on Commission of Physicians appointed by the president and authorized by Public Law 197 to examine requirements for admission to the army, navy, and marine corps (March 1944). Career army doctor beginning 1910, credited with having treated at least a third of the major amputations in World War I; Chief Surgeon, Letterman Hospital, San Francisco, and Walter Reed Hospital, Washington, DC, 1930s–early 1940s.

Lawrence Kolb—Psychiatrist in the US Public Health Service before and during World War II. Helped design a separate psychiatric examination for the navy in World War II, became member of the newly formed NIMH staff in 1946, and specialist in drug addiction and alcoholism.

Emil Kraepelin—German psychiatrist trained at the end of the nineteenth century in psychology and physiology in the laboratory of Wilhelm Wundt; known for developing a system of classification of mental disorders based on patterns of symptoms.

Samuel Kraines—Army psychiatrist at Tank Destroyer Replacement Training Camp, TC, Camp Hood, Texas, where he devised the psychiatrist adviser system.

Lawrence Kubie—Harvard College and Johns Hopkins Medical School graduate. Trained as a neurologist and as a psychiatrist/psychoanalyst at Phipps Clinic, Baltimore; employed as a neuropsychiatrist at the Rockefeller Institute, New York City; president of the New York Psychoanalytic Institute in 1938 and secretary of the American Psychoanalytic Association (APsaA); head of the APsaA's Emergency Committee on Relief and Immigration; and head of the New York City Committee for Mental Hygiene. As a member of the NRC Committee on Neuropsychiatry, Kubie played a leading role in the development of military policy on the prevention and treatment of psychiatric casualties and on the training of military psychiatrists; also advised military leaders against segregating troops as detrimental to troops' performance and mental health.

Frank H. Lahey—Surgeon-in-chief, Lahey Clinic, Boston, founded 1923; major in Army Medical Corps in World War II; appointed by the president to serve as a physician on the commission of physicians charged with examining the requirements for admission to the army, navy, and marine corps, March 1944. President, AMA, 1941–1942.

Carney Landis—Psychologist, researcher at New York Psychiatric Institute, and professor of psychology at Columbia University. With Shipley, designed the Shipley Inventory. Also authored a textbook in abnormal psychology published in 1951; known for studies of facial responses to stimuli.

Walter Langer—OSS psychoanalyst in World War II, during which time he wrote a study entitled *The Mind of Adolf Hitler*, which became a bestseller in 1972.

Aubrey Lewis—Psychiatrist. Clinical director of the Mill Hill Emergency Hospital (EMS), London; served on British commission established in World War II to advise on the role of psychologists and psychiatrists; civilian consultant to Royal Air Force (RAF); made key recommendation to War Office in May 1941 that soldiers' abilities should be assessed for assignment to proper jobs to reduce the numbers breaking down and discharged from service.

Nolan D. C. Lewis—Criminal psychiatrist. As member of the NRC Committee on Neuropsychiatry, he provided his opinions on the criteria for psychiatric selection for service, including a definition of malingering. Served as a soldier in World War I. Consultant, Nuremberg War Crimes Trials, 1945–1946.

Patrick Madigan—Member of Sullivan's WAWPF and of the Selective Service Psychiatric Advisory Committee. Career army medical officer between the wars and head of the Psychiatry Branch in the Army's Office of the Surgeon General, February 1942–August 1942. Principally involved in drafting the army's routine preinduction psychiatric examination, Circular Letter No. 19.

James C. Magee—Army Surgeon General, June 1939–June 1943, succeeded by Norman Kirk. Career army medical doctor; served in army medical corps in France in World War I with American Expeditionary Force; recipient of Purple Heart.

Ross T. McIntire—Navy eye surgeon under Assistant Secretary of the Navy Franklin Delano Roosevelt, 1917. Protégé of Woodrow Wilson's White House physician Admiral Cary Grayson. White House physician and confidant to President Franklin Delano Roosevelt, also Navy Surgeon General in World War II. As member of the Federal Board of Hospitalization, played a large role in persuading Roosevelt to approve Selective Service Medical Circular No. 1; in 1944, appointed by Roosevelt to be the chair and a physician on the commission of physicians appointed to examine requirements for admission to the U.S. Army, Navy, and Marine Corps.

Hugo Mella—Medical officer in army in World War I, VA psychiatrist from the 1920s through the 1950s, and served on the Selective Service Psychiatric Advisory Committee, 1940–1941.

Principal Physicians and Social Scientists | 265

Karl Menninger—The first American psychoanalyst to be analyzed by a psychoanalytic institute in the United States, namely, the Chicago Psychoanalytic Institute. With his brother William, their father, and their descendents, starting in the 1920s established and maintained the Menninger Clinic and, later, the Menninger Foundation, Topeka, Kansas. Well-known for many popular books, including *The Human Mind* (1930), Karl was a member of the Committee for National Morale, formed in July 1940 to advise the president on German psychological warfare and American national character. Besides Menninger, the committee included Edward Strecker, the anthropologists Ruth Benedict and Margaret Mead, and the psychologist Robert Yerkes. Member of the Psychiatric Mission of the Office of Field Services (OFS), OSRD, which investigated combat exhaustion and related aspects of military psychiatry in the ETO in 1945; APsaA president, 1951.

William Menninger—Trained as a psychiatrist at St. Elizabeth's Hospital in 1927 and analyzed by Franz Alexander. Chief of the Army Neuropsychiatric Consultants Division, December 1943–June 1946, with the rank of brigadier general. President of GAP in 1946–1951, APsaA president in 1946, and APA president in 1948. Author of the widely consulted *Psychiatry in a Troubled World* (1948). Instrumental in major psychiatric policy-making decisions in the war and, with his brother, played a central role in promoting the profession of psychiatry from the 1940s through the 1960s.

Adolph Meyer—Swiss-born American psychiatrist; first professor of psychiatry at Johns Hopkins University Hospital, 1908–1941; founder/director of the Henry Phipps Clinic, Baltimore, Maryland, starting 1913; APA president, 1927–1928. Known for employing detailed case studies and for developing the concept of psychobiology, which tied psychological, biological, and social symptoms together in diagnosing and treating the patient. Lobbied for enactment of the NMHA and institution of the NIMH in 1946.

C. S. Meyers—Based on his experience with the British Expeditionary Force treating victims of shell shock in World War I at a front-line hospital in France, he concluded that victims of shell shock were not malingerers or cowards but men predisposed to breakdown. Also supported treating soldiers as close to the front as possible so that they could be returned soon to combat.

Emilio Mira y Lopez—Leading Spanish psychiatrist, professor of psychiatry at the University of Barcelona, appointed in 1938 by the Republican government to head the Department of Psychiatric Services. With Franco's takeover in 1939, Mira left for London, where Maudsley Hospital, known for its care of psychiatric veterans in World War I, appointed him a fellow. In 1942, the New York Academy of Medicine invited him to deliver its Thomas Salmon lectures on his experiences in Spain and in Great Britain, which were subsequently published in 1943 as *Psychiatry in War*.

Bela Mittelman—Cornell psychiatrist/psychoanalyst. Worked on designing the Cornell Selectee Index in 1943, used by the navy to sift out enlistees unable to adjust. Published textbook on abnormal psychology in 1941; founding member of the Association for Psychoanalytic Medicine, New York.

F. W. Mott—British psychiatrist in World War I. He first associated shell shock with the physical impact of exploding shells on the brain but later attributed it to a soldier's predisposition.

John Murray—Chief of Army Air Force Psychiatry under Roy Halloran and William Menninger, liaison between the air surgeon general and the army surgeon general, 1942–1945. BPSI president, 1942–1943, 1946–1949, and 1954–1955; professor of clinical psychiatry at Boston University School of Medicine, 1945–1962.

Douglas Orr—Psychiatrist at the Menninger Clinic, Topeka, Kansas; psychoanalyst in Chicago; and naval medical officer in World War II. In 1941, he questioned in the *Menninger Clinic Bulletin* why psychiatric rejections from military service could not be given a vocational classification instead of a psychiatric one. Author, with Jean Walker, of *Health Insurance with Medical Care: The British Experience* (1935) and of a chapter on "Antisemitism and the Psychopathology of Everyday Life" in *Anti-Semitism: A Social Disease* (1946), edited by the psychiatrist Ernst Simmel.

Frederick Osborn—Successful businessman appointed by his fellow Hudson Valley squire President Franklin Roosevelt to head the Selective Service Psychiatric Advisory Committee, where he worked closely with Harry Stack Sullivan in the design and implementation of Medical Circular No. 1. Appointed by Roosevelt to head the Army Morale Branch, which later became the Information and Education Division (I&E). Carried out many missions for the president, with whom he had much influence. A career-long eugenicist.

Henry Fairfield Osborn (1857–1955)—Paleontologist, first president of the American Museum of Natural History, well-known eugenicist, uncle of Frederick Osborn.

Winfred Overholser—A graduate of Harvard College with an MD from Boston University, Overholser was a psychiatrist on the front in France in

World War I, treating American soldiers. Returning home, he was director of the Massachusetts Commissioners' Department of Mental Diseases, Division for Examining Prisoners. In 1937, he succeeded William Alanson White as superintendent of St. Elizabeth's Hospital, Washington, DC, a position Overholser held until 1962. In World War II, he chaired the NRC Committee on Neuropsychiatry. Overholser also chaired and was a special consultant on the committee appointed by the secretary of war to study procedures at induction centers pertaining especially to rejections for mental causes (August–September 1943). President of the APA, 1947–1948. Among his famous patients at St. Elizabeth's Hospital was the controversial poet Ezra Pound, who resided there from 1945 through 1958.

Frederick Parsons—NYS commissioner of mental hygiene under Governor Franklin D. Roosevelt in the 1930s. Served on the APA Special Committee Dealing with War Activities; also appointed by the secretary of war to serve on the special committee that investigated rejections of mental cases at induction stations.

Samuel Paster—Army psychiatrist stationed in World War II at Kennedy General Hospital, Memphis, Tennessee. Early practitioner of group psychotherapy in the military.

William Porter—Career army psychiatrist, in the army's Office of the Surgeon General and a psychiatrist at Walter Reed Hospital beginning in 1941. Member of the NRC Committee on Neuropsychiatry, Subcommittee on War Neuroses throughout the war; as of 1943, head of the School of Military Neuropsychiatry, Lawson General Hospital, Atlanta, Georgia, its location later changed to Mason General Hospital, Long Island. The school trained doctors in psychiatry in ninety-day programs.

Tracy Putnam—Professor of neurology at Harvard Medical School and chief of neurology, Boston City Hospital, 1934–1939, during which time he and Dr. H. Houston Merritt invented Dilantin, a drug for controlling epilepsy. Director, New York Neurological Institute, Columbia University, 1939–1947, and member of the NRC Subcommittee on War Neuroses, Committee on Neuropsychiatry, where he participated in policy discussions of psychiatric selection and other issues. During his tenure at Columbia, Putnam employed several prominent Jewish refugee neurologists, including Otto Marburg, who had emigrated from Austria to England with Sigmund Freud.

John R. Rees—Medical officer in the army in World War I; psychiatrist/director of the Tavistock Clinic, a well-known psychiatric outpatient clinic in London; consultant on psychiatry to the British Army at home in World War II; and author of *The Shaping of Psychiatry by War* (1945).

Thomas Rennie—Psychiatrist at Phipps Clinic, 1931–1941, and associate professor of psychiatry at Cornell Medical School during the war; also director of Payne Whitney Psychiatric Clinic, New York City, and a founding member of GAP.

Leonard Rowntree—Chief, Medical Division, Selective Service, through World War II.

Arthur Ruggles—Trained as a psychiatrist, did graduate work with Emil Kraepelin at the University of Munich, Germany, and supervised a base hospital in France during World War I. Superintendent of Butler Hospital, Providence, Rhode Island, 1922–1948; APA president in 1942 and a member of the NRC Committee on Neuropsychiatry.

Benjamin Rush (1745–1813)—Called the "Father of American Psychiatry," Rush maintained that mental illness was not an affliction of the devil but an actual disease that should be treated as humanely as possible in a hospital setting. In 1783, he joined the staff of Pennsylvania Hospital and established a separate wing for mental patients with severe disorders.

Howard Rusk—A specialist in rehabilitative medicine for patients with both mental and physical disorders with the objective of returning them to the community. First applied his methods in the army air force at Jefferson Barracks, St. Louis, during World War II. After the war, founded the Rusk Institute for Rehabilitation at NYU in 1951.

Thomas William Salmon—As an assistant surgeon in the US Public Health Service at Ellis Island starting in 1903, Salmon and a small team of doctors inspected thousands of immigrants each day for physical and mental disorders with the objective of possibly deporting them or placing them in institutions. As chief consultant in psychiatry for the American Expeditionary Force in World War I, he directed the military's efforts to medically examine recruits for military service and to work on new procedures to treat victims of shell shock. A few years before the war, in 1912, Salmon surveyed conditions in state and local mental institutions for the NCMH. In 1915, the NCMH appointed him its first medical director, a position he held until 1925. At the same time, Salmon was a professor of psychiatry at Columbia University, starting in 1921, and president of the APA in 1923.

Julius Schreiber—While an army air force psychiatrist at the Anti-Aircraft Replacement Training Camp, Camp Callan, California, Schreiber developed political orientation programs. So successful was he at motivating troops with his programs that Frederick Osborn appointed him to establish similar programs in other camps as well and made him an I&E psychiatrist.

Sidney Schwab—As a doctor in the American Expeditionary Force in World War I, treated victims of shell shock in base hospitals. On the faculty of the Department of Neurology and Psychiatry, Washington University, St. Louis, 1918–1938. Member of the NRC Committee on Neuropsychiatry, Subcommittee on War Neuroses in World War II.

Walter Shipley—Professor of psychology at Wheaton College from 1941 until his death in 1966, Shipley along with Landis designed the Shipley Inventory in World War II, a routine written personality test for use in the military. Later, Shipley also designed the Shipley Institute of Living Scale to determine cognitive dysfunction using nonverbal block patterns.

Ernst Simmel—A protégé of Sigmund Freud, Simmel treated soldiers with war neuroses in World War I, was trained in psychoanalysis by Karl Abraham, and was one of the editors of *Psychoanalysis and the War Neuroses* (1921).

Howard McC. Snyder—Member of the War Department Special Staff and chief of the Office of Inspector General Medical Division, which conducted investigations of psychoneuroses in 1944–1945 in the Zone of Interior, the ETO, MTO, and Pacific Ocean areas. Confidant and personal physician to President Dwight D. Eisenhower during both his terms.

Raymond Sobel—Soon after receiving his medical degree from NYU, angered by Nazi oppression of European Jews, Sobel enlisted in the army as a first lieutenant in the army medical corps. Starting in 1942, he served forty-one months at the front, including thirty-three months in North Africa and Italy. Awarded a Bronze Star for heroic achievement in battle. While chief division psychiatrist and battalion surgeon at Anzio Beachhead, Italy, Sobel coined the term "Old Sergeant Syndrome."

Harry C. Solomon—A soldier in World War I; psychiatrist at Boston Psychopathic Hospital, 1917, where he worked with Dr. Elmer E. Southard on studying the syphilitic nervous system. In 1943, Solomon became director at Boston Psychopathic. Served on the NRC Committee on Neuropsychiatry throughout the war and was one of the five civilian psychiatrists consulted by the Office of the Inspector General during its investigation of the treatment and disposition of psychoneurotics in the Zone of Interior.

Herbert Spiegel—Trained as a psychiatrist at St. Elizabeth's Hospital, Spiegel was nevertheless assigned by the military as a battalion surgeon in North Africa, 1942–1946. While in combat, he suffered a shrapnel wound and was awarded a Purple Heart. As early as 1942, he treated psychiatric soldier patients close to the front. Throughout his career, starting in the military and in later civilian life as well, he used hypnosis to treat psychiatric patients effectively.

John Spiegel—Psychiatric resident at the University of Chicago, where he worked with Dr. Roy Grinker. Medical officer with Grinker in North Africa. The two authored *War Neuroses in North Africa*, which the army used as a textbook throughout the world. In 1946, Grinker and Spiegel authored their second book together, *Men under Stress*, based on their experiences with soldiers and veterans during the war.

Harry Steckel—A division psychiatrist in World War I, Steckel was on the NRC Committee on Neuropsychiatry in World War II. As chair of the APA Military Mobilization Committee from 1940 through 1941, he was responsible for compiling a list of civilian psychiatrists available for military service.

George S. Stevenson—APA president in 1940, director of the NCMH in 1943, and medical director of the NCMH in 1949. Directed NCMH psychiatric treatment efforts on the domestic front as well as political orientation and group therapy programs in army training camps. After the war, he championed the establishment of the NIMH. Under Stevenson's guidance, the NCMH's study of training camp records revealed that many soldiers had preexisting psychiatric disorders, convincing the Rockefeller Foundation to fund the Medical Survey Program (MSP). He also criticized the lack of sufficient screening in the WAC.

Samuel Stouffer—Social psychologist and head of the Army Research Branch in Osborn's I&E. Responsible for designing the surveys of attitudes of over half a million soldiers about their experiences in the military in order to aid military efforts to improve morale so as to win the war. Stouffer and his team of experts compiled the results in a multivolume study for the army entitled *Social Psychology in World War II*. After the war, Princeton University Press published it in four volumes, *The American Soldier: Adjustment during Army Life*; *The American Soldier: Combat and Its Aftermath*;

Experiments on Mass Communication; and *Measurement and Prediction*. Stouffer and John Appel also advised Frank Capra, producer of the Why We Fight film series.

Edward Strecker—Army division psychiatrist in World War I; APA president in 1944; psychiatrist on the special committee appointed by the secretary of war to investigate rejections of mental cases at induction stations; physician on the president's commission of physicians that examined requirements for admission to the army, navy, and marine corps; consulting psychiatrist for the investigation by the Office of the Inspector General of the treatment and disposition of psychoneurotics in the Zone of Interior. Known for his best-selling book *Their Mothers' Sons* (1946), advancing "Momism," Strecker was also a professor of psychiatry at Yale University, 1925–1931, and at the University of Pennsylvania, 1931–1953.

Harry Stack Sullivan—Author of the Selective Service psychiatric examination in World War II, Medical Circular No. 1, which he developed during 1938–1941. In charge of the implementation of the Selective Service psychiatric screening program for all registrants until November 1941, when he resigned. Influenced by the theories of William Alanson White and Adolph Meyer, he developed his own well-known concept of interpersonal relations in the 1920s and 1930s, departing from the Freudian emphasis on childhood sexuality. Applying his theory on interpersonal relations in the 1920s at Sheppard and Enoch Pratt Hospital in Baltimore, Sullivan treated male schizophrenics. After leaving Selective Service, Sullivan treated patients at Chestnut Lodge, Maryland. He died in 1948 soon after attending an international conference on mental health in London.

Dallas Sutton—Navy psychiatrist. Worked with Sullivan at the WAWPF in the 1930s and served on the Selective Service Psychiatric Advisory Committee.

Lloyd Thompson—Professor of psychiatry at Yale University, 1930–1942, colonel in the Army Medical Corps, and psychiatric consultant to the ETO. Accompanied the inspector general and his team during the investigation of policies in the ETO concerning psychoneurotics, March–May 1945.

Raymond Waggoner—Psychiatrist and neurologist. Chair of the Department of Psychiatry, University of Michigan, 1937–1970, and director of the University of Michigan Psychiatric Clinic in the late 1930s and 1940s. Successor to Sullivan as psychiatric consultant to Selective Service; appointed by the secretary of war to serve on the special committee investigating rejections of mental cases at induction stations (August–September 1943). After the war, the Office of the Surgeon General appointed Waggoner to advise the army on the psychological effects of the Allied occupation of Germany and Japan. APA president, 1969–1970.

Bettina Warburg—As a psychoanalyst and member of the NYPI, worked with Kubie in assisting analysts from Europe in immigrating to the United States to escape Hitler.

David Wechsler—Chief psychologist at Bellevue's Psychiatric Division. Known for designing the Wechsler Intelligence Test, used routinely to determine the IQ of World War I soldiers. Also contributed to developing the Cornell Selectee Index in World War II.

Lewis Weed—Director of the NAS, NRC Division of Medical Sciences (the Division), which encompassed fourteen committees and forty-two subcommittees, including the NRC Committee on Neuropsychiatry. The Division, along with the Committee on Medical Research (CMR), recommended medical projects to the OSRD for its approval as well as doing some of the actual planning.

Arthur Weider—Columbia University psychologist. Helped design the Cornell Selectee Index, a written test to screen persons with personality defects from navy service. On the faculty of Columbia University Medical School and on cable television as "The People's Psychologist."

Frederic Lyman Wells—A captain in the Army Signal Corps in World War I, he was head psychologist at Boston Psychopathic Hospital, 1921–1938, before becoming a consultant to the army's Office of the Adjutant General. In 1942, Wells and Ruggles collaborated in two studies for the NRC Committee on Neuropsychiatry on the use of psychologists and psychiatrists in the war.

Fredric Wertham—Psychiatrist. Mentored by Adolf Meyer and Emil Kraepelin. Founded the LaFargue Clinic in Harlem, which operated from 1946 to the late 1950s. Known for criticizing the violent psychological effect of comics on America's youth and for supporting civil rights.

William Alanson White—Superintendent of St. Elizabeth's Hospital from 1903 to his death in 1937. Proponent of "habit theory," which connected predisposition to conditions in the family and the larger society. White's theories significantly influenced Sullivan's own conceptualizations. White's textbook, *Outlines of Psychiatry* (1907), had much influence in the field for the next thirty years.

John Clare Whitehorn—Successor to Adolph Meyer as head of Phipps Clinic, Baltimore, Maryland, he was also a professor of psychiatry at Washington University Medical School, St. Louis, 1938–1941, and at Johns Hopkins University Medical School, 1941–1960. One of the founders of GAP; APA president, 1950–1951; and a member of the psychiatric mission of the Office of Field Services (OFS), OSRD, which investigated combat exhaustion and related aspects of military psychiatry in the ETO in 1945.

Frankwood Williams—Chief of the division of neurology and psychiatry in the US Surgeon General's Office in World War I; medical director of the NCMH, 1922–1931. One of the authors of the *Medical Department of the United States Army in the World War*, vol. 10, *Neuropsychiatry* (1929); among his private patients was Harry Hopkins.

Cecil Wittson—While commander of US Navy Research in World War II, he and the psychiatrist William A. Hunt designed the revised Shipley Inventory, a routine navy written personality test. Served as director of the University of Nebraska Medical Center's psychiatric institute, 1950–1964, as well as president of the APA in 1980.

Harold Wolff—Neurologist; helped design the Cornell Selectee Index. Earlier, he studied in Russia under Ivan Pavlov and in the United States with Adolf Meyer at Phipps Clinic.

Luther Woodward—Awarded a divinity degree from Gettysburg Theological Seminary and an MSW from New York University, Woodward worked as a psychiatric social worker for the New York City Schools' Bureau of Child Guidance, 1932–1943. As social work adviser for Selective Service, 1943–1944, Woodward applied his experience with the school system to his recommendations concerning the gathering of educational records of prospective draftees in the Medical Survey Program.

Gregory Zilboorg—Specialist in Russian psychiatry for the army during World War II. Born in Kiev, Russia, immigrated to the United States in 1919, received a medical degree from Columbia University, and wrote a *History of Medical Psychology* (1941) as well as other works, including *Psychology of the Criminal Act* (1950) and a biography of Sigmund Freud. Among his patients was George Gershwin.

Appendix A: Medical Circular No. 1

Medical Circular No. 1 REVISED, Minimum Psychiatric Inspection (May 1941)

This circular instructs Selective Service physicians, many of whom are not psychiatrists, on how to detect indicia of mental illness in Selective Service registrants. Revised in May 1941 to conform with the criteria in the Army's own psychiatric examination, Circular Letter No. 19 (Appendix B), it still contains major differences in medical interpretations, briefly described below.

Initially designed by the well-known civilian psychiatrist, Harry Stack Sullivan, the revised Medical Circular No. 1 still focuses on histories of poor interpersonal relations which may possibly lead to future maladjustment. Examiners are told to follow-up on "suspicions." The very first sentence recognizes that it is providing "methods whereby [examiners] may suspect the existence of incapacitating ... factors." To detect what might otherwise be concealed by a registrant, the examiners are instructed to ask questions "outside of easy hearing of other men" to facilitate a man's disclosing his "peculiarity." If they "suspect" an incapacity, they may either "eliminate such individuals" or "refer them to the psychiatrist at the medical advisory board."

The key determinant is a history of problems in interpersonal relations. For example, an examiner might ask a machinist about a scar on his finger. From there, he might go on to inquire if the man likes his work, if his employer is fair, if he gets along with others, men, women ...

While originally Medical Circular No. 1 did not list "chronic inebriety," the revised circular does so; in the case of alcoholism, focusing not on physical signs but poor interpersonal relations, e.g., "loss of jobs, repeated arrests ... repeated hospital treatment ... institutional care."

While Circular Letter No. 19 focuses on physical signs of epilepsy, Medical Circular No. 1 makes certain judgment calls: "The personality type is not diagnostic but the epileptic individual may be egocentric, selfish, rigid, and irritable with a tendency to excessive religiosity."

While both Circular Letter No. 19 and the revised circular conclude with a list of neurological disorders, the revised Circular says nothing about them, whereas Circular Letter No. 19 describes physical symptoms at length.

Finally, for the first time, Medical Circular No. 1 REVISED ends with a paragraph listing certain "personality deviations" starting with "instability, seclusiveness, and sulkiness" and ending with "homosexual proclivities." This listing can also be found in Circular Letter No. 19 but on the first page.

Medical Circular No. 1 REVISED can be accessed by clicking on download at https://research.library.fordham.edu/history/20/.

Appendix B: Circular Letter No. 19

Army Circular Letter No. 19, Neuropsychiatric Examination of Applicants for Voluntary Enlistment and Selectees for Induction (March 1941)

Army Circular Letter No. 19's psychiatric examination instructs medical officers to look for certain behavior in volunteers and draftees. Designed by career military medical officer, Patrick Madigan, it particularly refers to specific medical diagnoses rather than a history of poor interpersonal relations, thereby differing from Medical Circular No. 1 REVISED.

Circular Letter No. 19 focuses on locating those who might disrupt discipline and morale in the military, interfere with military training, or become a fiscal burden on the government through undue hospitalization.

Reflecting public criticism of the initial Selective Service psychiatric examination program and the growing need for soldiers as entry into World War II became imminent, Circular Letter No. 19 emphasizes that the information in the letter is solely "a practical guide" to be applied with "discretion and mature judgment." At the end, it adds that men should not be "lightly rejected" but rather only when "unfit" and not when they are "capable of satisfactorily performing the duties of warfare."

Recognizing that not everyone can adjust to the restrictions of military life, which unlike civilian life, cannot be escaped, it calls on physicians to especially look out for those who have such personality deviations, in paragraph 5 on the front page, as "instability, seclusiveness, sulkiness" and ending with "homosexual proclivities." The same list is in the revised Medical Circular No. 1 but hidden in the last paragraph.

Additionally, though not mentioned in revised Medical Circular No. 1, Circular Letter No. 19 also instructs physicians to look out for "homosexual persons," among its list of *Psychopathic Personality Disorders*. The others include: "grotesque and pathologic liars, vagabonds ... petty offenders, swindlers, kleptomaniacs ..."

Confronting the imminence of war, No. 19 emphasizes that the Army is "in no sense a social service or a curative agency ... neither a haven of rest for wanderers nor a corrective school for misfits ... nor a psychiatric clinic for proper adjustment to adult emotional development." (A position which would somewhat change as the war progressed.)

Like Medical Circular No. 1 REVISED, it also includes a Group VI on chronic inebriety. But instead of emphasizing a history of poor interpersonal relations from alcoholism, it focuses on physical signs of such addiction, e.g., "suffused eyes, prominent superficial blood vessels of the nose and cheek ..."

As in previous Army neuropsychiatric examinations, the circular ends by describing certain symptoms of serious diseases of the nervous system.

Army Circular Letter No. 19 can be accessed by clicking on download at https://research.library.fordham.edu/history/21/.

Appendix C: Key Investigations of Military Psychiatry

Special Committee Appointed by the Secretary of War to Investigate Rejections of Mental Cases at Induction Stations, August–September 1943

Physicians Appointed by President Franklin Delano Roosevelt to Investigate Hospitalization of American Fliers in England, February 1944–April 1944

Commission of Physicians Appointed by the President Pursuant to Public Law 197 of the 78th Congress to Examine the Requirements for Admission to the Army, Navy, and Marine Corps, March 1944

Office of the Inspector General, War Department, Inquiry Regarding Diagnosis, Treatment and Disposition of Psychoneurotics in Zone of Interior, October 10, 1944–December 15, 1944

———, Inquiry Regarding Psychoneurosis in the Pacific Ocean Areas, March and April 1945

———, Study of Policies Regarding Psychoneurotics in the European Theater of Operations and Mediterranean Theater of Operations (ETO and MTO), March 30, 1945–May 13, 1945

Psychiatric Mission of the Office of Field Service (OFS), Office of Scientific Research and Development (OSRD) to Investigate Combat Exhaustion and Related Aspects of Military Psychiatry, ETO, April 16, 1945–July 16, 1945

Acknowledgments

This book grew from my Columbia University doctoral dissertation, "The Role of the Psychiatrist in World War II." Growing up during the Korean and Vietnam wars, with a father who had served in the infantry in World War II, I found it hard to understand how American history as taught in college tended to neglect the two world wars. So, asked by my dissertation adviser, the late professor David Rothman, for a topic, I suggested something on World War II and American society to partially fill the gap. Rothman suggested one segment—psychiatry in World War II—because the Second World War had profoundly transformed the profession. Though it was not my idea originally, I am very happy I pursued it. I also wish to express my gratitude to him for instilling in me an appreciation of the difference between rhetoric and reality and of the importance of asking "why," of placing events within their socioeconomic context, and of exploring the history of those from the bottom up, which I learned as his research assistant.

I wish to also thank the late Lehman College professor Davis Ross, author of *Preparing for Ulysses*, on the GI Bill, for his valuable advice on my topic and on archival research in general. Professor Ross suggested I contact Columbia University Professor William Leuchtenburg about funding, who referred me to Professor Norman Dain, at Rutgers, Newark, a member of Cornell Medical School's Section on Psychiatric History. He in turn referred me to its director, the late Dr. Eric T. Carlson. Appointed by Carlson a Josiah Macy historical research fellow, I was fortunate not only to receive a stipend but to meet with him monthly to discuss my ongoing research, present several papers to the section, take courses with the residents in psychiatry, and even be granted access to a ward at Payne Whitney. I also wish to thank the psychoanalyst Jacques Quen, professor emeritus of clinical psychiatry at Cornell, for several valuable discussions and for providing me, along with Dr. Carlson, with the names of leading World War II psychiatrists to interview.

I wish to thank the many leading psychiatrists who gave generously of their time in interviews, including the late Abram Kardiner, Herbert Spiegel,

John Appel, M. Ralph Kaufman, George S. Stevenson, and Raymond Waggoner. Additionally, I interviewed Frederick Osborn, a friend of Franklin Delano Roosevelt and head of the Army Information and Education Division, and corresponded with General Lewis Hershey, director of the Selective Service System from 1941 to 1970.

When I started my research, few books were concerned with psychiatry in World War II other than William Menninger's *Psychiatry in a Troubled World* (1948), Eli Ginzberg's three-volume *The Ineffective Soldier* (1959), and the US Army's two-volume *Neuropsychiatry in World War II*, the second volume of which had just come out. Less than thirty years had transpired since the end of the war, and many records had not yet been released, including the papers of Sigmund Freud in the Library of Congress, which would not be opened until much later. As for the records on psychiatry in World War II that were available, scarcely anyone, as far as I knew, had looked at them. I owe special thanks to the many archivists who plowed through catalogs and record groups to assist me in finding the pertinent military, Selective Service, and scientific records, especially Charles Dewing, James Miller, James Hastings, and Dorothy Provine at the National Archives; Jean Jones, librarian, American Psychiatric Association; Verne B. Horne, archivist, Menninger Foundation; Roderick Engert, chief, Research Division, US Army Medical Division Historical Unit; and Jean St. Clair, archivist at the National Academy of Sciences. I also wish to thank the archivists at the US Army Historical Research Collection, Carlisle Barracks, Pennsylvania, where the Hershey Papers were housed; and the archivists at the George C. Marshall Research Library, Virginia Military Institute, Lexington, Virginia. The Marshall papers gave me unique insight into the attitudes of military leadership toward psychiatry, not always accepting, and their discourse with the chief military psychiatrists on policy, widening the scope and point of view of my book. I wish to also thank the chief archivist at the Franklin Delano Roosevelt Library, where I reviewed the Eleanor and Franklin Roosevelt Papers, for pointing out Roosevelt's statement to the press excusing George Patton's behavior toward shell-shocked patients by alluding to Lincoln's remark about General Grant's "brand of liquor." Also, my thanks to the archivists at the American Philosophical Society, Philadelphia, for access to the papers of Frederick Osborn, which included information on the relationship between psychiatry and the I&E Division and on why the psychiatrist Harry Stack Sullivan resigned from Selective Service. And to Cecily Dyer, archivist at the S. Spafford Ackerly Papers, Brooklyn Historical Center, Brooklyn Public Library, my thanks for scanning documents for me during the pandemic, when many archives were closed, including her own.

I wish to thank the members of my doctoral dissertation committee for their insightful contributions, particularly Professor Rothman, for his careful reading of my manuscript and for asking critical questions. I want to also thank the late Professor Walter Metzger, Columbia History Department; Dr. Carlson; the late Columbia University professor of sociology Allan Silver; and Barnard College professor of History John Chambers, currently distinguished emeritus professor of history at Rutgers, New Brunswick, an authority on the history of Selective Service, military history, and American history. I also wish to thank Professor Chambers for assisting me in assembling a panel on World War II at the Organization of American Historians as well as one at the American Association for the History of Medicine.

Soon after receiving my doctorate, I received a postdoctoral grant from the National Institutes of Health. I am grateful to the late professor of history of medicine at the University of Maryland John Duffy for advising me on how to apply for this grant while I taught history of religion and history of psychiatry there.

About ten years ago, I had the good fortune to reconnect with Professor Chambers at a Rutgers University D-Day Celebration in New Brunswick. At that time, he fondly remembered my dissertation, urged me to publish it, and referred me to Fordham University Press. I am so happy he did so. All the editors at Fordham have been tremendous. I wish particularly to thank Fredric Nachbaur, director, for his patience and wisdom in helping me make the manuscript as good as it possibly could be and for his tremendous organizational and political skills. Above all, I owe much gratitude to Professor of History G. Kurt Piehler, Florida State University director of the Institute on World War II and the Human Experience and series editor at Fordham for spending considerable time and energy reading and rereading my manuscript as it progressed. To the very end of the revision process, he was asking new questions and providing me with new information. This was a monumental task for both of us, as years had passed since I first did research on the subject, with much new scholarship emerging. Professor Piehler made it easy for me to delve into a daunting task by taking one step at a time, starting with reviewing the dissertation. He never lost confidence or enthusiasm for the project. I also want to thank the Press's two anonymous peer reviewers for providing me with valuable comments, which greatly enhanced the book's focus and content, as well as Fordham's developmental editor Andrea Chapin, a well-known novelist in her own right, for being so interested in the subject, giving me much support, and advising me on how to make the book more appealing to a larger, general audience. In addition, I want to thank Will Cerbone, editor and rights and permissions manager at

Fordham; Kem Crimmins, project editor at Fordham; Robert Fellman, copy editor; and all the supporting staff at Fordham who have had to work on a much larger and more complex manuscript than usual. I wish too to express my gratitude to Professor Noah Tsika for his excellent foreword and to Rachel Freeman for her excellent graphics.

Initially, I thought I would publish a book right after writing the dissertation, but for economic and other reasons, it occurred later. However, I am in no way saddened by this. The extra span of time facilitated the publication of many new excellent works about the war, which I drew on for a better understanding of the context in which psychiatry grew and flourished. Additionally, I believe my own personal experiences away from the ivory tower as a government and legal services attorney provided me with particular understanding of how government works. And I was able to see records that had previously been closed, such as the records of the army air force psychiatrist John Murray, which contained correspondence from the notable psychoanalyst/neurologist Lawrence Kubie. In no way can I individually thank the many recent authors whose works have given me additional insights. However, I would like to say in general that I appreciate what they have done.

I am truly indebted to Seton Hall University for facilitating my success in this project. Six years ago, I lost my son Ethan Frederick Greene, an assistant professor of music theory and electronic music at Stetson University, Florida, who died at the age of thirty-two, thirteen days after being diagnosed with AML leukemia. Needless to say, my husband, Peter Alan Greene, and I and the rest of our family were devastated. There was no way I could stay home and write a book. I contacted Nathanial Knight, professor of Russian history at Seton Hall and chair of the History Department, who generously found a carrel for me in the university's library, where I could work away from my troubles, and referred me to professor Larry Greene, who specializes, among other subjects, in World War II. Professor Greene invited me to attend his graduate seminar on World War II, where I presented a paper. He and I had several rewarding conversations about my topic, and he referred me to several important books. Recently, during COVID, I faced a second challenge. On a happier note, my older son, Abraham Greene, his wife, and my granddaughter moved back to South Orange, New Jersey, but for about three weeks they needed to stay with us before closing on their house. Once more, Professor Knight came to the rescue, generously arranging with Lisa De Luca, librarian, for me to get another carrel and Seton Hall University library privileges.

I am particularly grateful to Michael Pucci, acquisitions librarian at South Orange Public Library. During the past months when time pressures from the publisher mounted and my need to review books accelerated, Mr. Pucci always came through. Without his efforts, the book would not be as good.

And I wish to thank Alfred Donnarumma, director of litigation and appeals at Central Jersey Legal Services, for whom I worked for years as a senior attorney, for advancing my ability to coherently and briefly elucidate my arguments based on sufficient adequate evidence, as well as for giving me the opportunity to try many cases in court. Undeniably, arguing a case before a judge, in the face of an adversary, promotes intellectual accuracy and honesty. All these skills I believe have enhanced the writing of this book.

Ironically, the pandemic in one way proved beneficial, enabling me to Zoom in on valuable lectures at the Cornell Medical Center Section on History of Psychiatry (now the Institute on the History of Psychiatry, Policy, and the Arts) organized under its adept director Dr. George Makari.

I have been encouraged in my pursuit by the example of others. Specifically, I want to acknowledge the efforts of the late John McLaughlin, a Short Hills, New Jersey, bankruptcy attorney who went on to earn a Drew University PhD in history and to publish a book on World War II general Albert C. Wedemeyer. In addition, he established the New Jersey World War II Book Club, where members can hear key historians each month talk about their books, now in its eleventh year. I want to also thank Richard Cohen for inviting me to speak about the process of writing my book to our minyan, Kol Rina.

Many years ago, a young girl played with "toys" in a bedroom. Those toys consisted of her father's and his dead buddy's helmets, their khaki caps, their mess kits, canteens, and jackets. Outside, the nation's economy and prestige flourished, but in the apartment, the vestiges of the war persisted. That girl was me. It was my parents' reminiscences, their symbols from World War II, and their continuing friendships with comrades who had fought the war with them and been with them in postwar Berlin that piqued my early curiosity. Although they are both no longer here, I wish to thank my parents, David and Anita Schwartz, for teaching me the values of hard, thorough research; for setting priorities (which I did not always keep); for inculcating in me the value of academic integrity; saying what you know and not what you do not; and for making clear to me their faith in my ability to create.

I want to thank my brother, Joseph Schwartz, professor emeritus of political science and theory at Temple University, for encouraging me to write this book and for giving much advice on how to proceed; my brother-in-law Benjamin Greene, for his interest in the history of the IQ and for lending me his copy of Stephen Jay Gould's *The Mismeasure of Man*; my son Abraham Greene, for his pride and faith in his mother and for being a great father and husband; my daughter-in-law Susan Nakley, professor of English and Chaucer scholar at St. Joseph's College, for giving me valuable advice about publishing; my daughter-in-law Alma Lagarda, Esq., for being a great mother and fighting against the death penalty in Texas; my sister Adina Beth Schwartz, professor emeritus at John Jay College, for instructing me in essential computer skills, so necessary for this endeavor; my brother-in-law Andrew Greene, for sharing with me insights from his own experience in publishing; and, most important, my two wonderful grandchildren, Mateo Lagarda Greene and Shulamit Nakley-Greene. My only regret is that my son Ethan is not here. A beautiful writer in his own right, he wanted to read my manuscript and offer editing suggestions; however, that could not be . . . .

But most of all, I want to thank my life partner and closest friend, my husband, Peter Alan Greene. We have experienced much joy and overcome much sorrow. He has stopped me from worrying unnecessarily and encouraged me to appreciate the bright side of life, including its comedy. Over the years he has read many versions of this book over and over and made many valuable editorial suggestions on substance and style, contributing his skills as an attorney with a masters in journalism from Columbia University and his sense of humor. Without him, my life and the lives of my children and grandchildren would have been much different and decidedly less good.

Notes

Foreword

1. Colonel Walter S. Jensen, "Neuropsychiatric Problems in Aviation Medicine," Box 20, Folder 13, John M. Murray Papers, Sigmund Freud Collection, Manuscript Division, Library of Congress, Washington, DC.

2. Eric Jaffe, *A Curious Madness: An American Combat Psychiatrist, a Japanese War Crimes Suspect, and an Unsolved Mystery from World War II* (New York: Scribner, 2014), 248.

3. Abram Kardiner and Herbert X. Spiegel, *War Stress and Neurotic Illness* (New York: Paul B. Hoeber, 1947), 44.

4. William C. Menninger, "Education and Training," in *Neuropsychiatry in World War II*, Vol. 1: *Zone of Interior*, ed. R. S. Anderson, A. J. Glass, and R. J. Bernucci (Washington, DC: US Government Printing Office, 1966), 53–66 [65].

5. William C. Menninger, *Psychiatry in a Troubled World: Yesterday's War and Today's Challenge* (New York: Macmillan, 1948), 157.

Introduction

1. A number of key works contribute significantly to an understanding of wartime psychiatry, including its statistics. These include William C. Menninger, *Psychiatry in a Troubled World* (New York: Macmillan, 1948); Eli Ginzberg's three-volume *The Ineffective Soldier: Lessons for Management* (New York: Columbia University Press, 1959), including *The Lost Divisions*, *Breakdown and Recovery*, and *Patterns of Performance*; and the brief but illuminating Eli Ginzberg, *Psychiatry and Military Manpower Policy—A Reappraisal of the Experience in World War II* (New York: Columbia University Press, 1953). Additionally, the US Army Medical Department produced two comprehensive volumes: *Neuropsychiatry in World War II*, ed. Albert J. Glass, MC, USA (Ret.) and Lt. Col. Robert J. Bernucci (Washington, DC: US Government Printing Office, 1966); and *Neuropsychiatry in World War II*, ed. William S. Mullins, MSC, USA and Albert J. Glass, MC, USA (Ret.) (Washington, DC: US Government Printing Office, 1973).

Regarding the 18 million screened for military service, see Ginzberg, *Patterns of Performance*, 314. Describing the establishment of the navy examination, see C. L. Wittson, H. I. Harris, W. A. Hunt, P. S. Solomon, and M. M. Jackson, "The Neuropsychiatric Selection of Recruits," *American Journal of Psychiatry* 99, no. 5

(March 1943): 639. Except for Richard Gabriel, historians have generally estimated that neuropsychiatric rejections accounted for anywhere between approximately 1.8 million and 2.0 million. For 1,846,000, see Menninger, *Psychiatry in a Troubled World*, 587; for 1,992,950, J. R. Eagan, L. Jackson, and R. H. Eanes, "A Study of Neuropsychiatric Rejectees," *Journal of the American Medical Association* 145, no. 7 (February 1951): 466–69 (Eanes was the assistant executive director of Selective Service in World War II); also, citing 1,992,950, Albert E. Cowdrey, *Fighting for Life: American Military Medicine in World War II* (New York: Free Press, 1994), 27. On the other hand, Ginzberg cites a figure of 1,773,000 (including 87,000 nonmedical, administrative) in *The Lost Divisions*, 36. All these figures, however, may be low, as the army and navy had separate induction systems until February 1943, and the sources do not specifically mention any navy numbers. On the other hand, Richard Gabriel, *The Painful Field: The Psychiatric Dimension of Modern War* (New York: Greenwood, 1988), 74n17, states that the "United States ... rejected 970,000 men for neuropsychiatric disorders and other emotional problems." He bases his number on Ginzberg, *The Lost Divisions*, 35, which refers to Table 8, p. 36. That table, however, states that the 970,000 was for emotional disorder alone. Ginzberg's "neuropsychiatric rejections," however, included the other items in Table 8, which are mental or educational deficiency, 716,000; and nonmedical, administrative, 87,000. Together, all three come to 1,773,000. Thus, all figures discovered by this author on psychiatric rejections fall between 1.77 and 1.99 million. Again, since these numbers are drawn exclusively from Selective Service data, it is possible that some navy figures may have been omitted.

As to neuropsychiatric discharges, see Ginzberg, *The Lost Divisions*, 61, which, totaling army, navy, and marines' figures, comes to 754,000, including psychiatric, inaptitude, and undesirability. According to *Neuropsychiatry in World War II*, 1: Appendix A, 771, neuropsychiatric discharges come to 375,333 plus administrative separations for inaptitude or unsuitability and unfitness of 163,119, for a total of 538,452. This, however, does not include navy discharges. Francis J. Braceland, head of Navy Psychiatry, states in "Psychiatric Lessons from World War II," *American Journal of Psychiatry* 103, no. 5 (March 1947): 587, that between January 1, 1942, and July 1, 1945, 149,281 were admitted as patients for psychiatric reasons to naval hospitals; of these 76,721 were discharged. But he also points out that another 91,565 recruits were separated (discharged) from naval training stations for neurological and psychiatric reasons. Adding 76,721 to 91,565 comes to 168,286. Adding the navy's 168,286 to the army's 538,452 comes to 706,738. The total figure rises to 713,286 if we use Menninger's 545,000 army neuropsychiatric discharges instead. See *Psychiatry in a Troubled World*, 589.

2. Other historians have written about American psychiatry in World War II, but none with the depth or outlook of this book. Ben Shepherd's *A War of Nerves: Soldiers and Psychiatrists, 1914–1994* (Cambridge, MA: Harvard University Press, 2001) and Edgar Jones and Arthur Wessely's *From Shell Shock to PTSD: A Century*

of Invisible War Trauma (New York: Psychology Press, 2005) cover British and American military psychiatry throughout the twentieth century, each giving a brief description of American psychiatry in World War II. More extensive is Richard Gabriel's *No More Heroes* (New York: Hill & Wang, 1987) and *The Painful Field*. In *Fighting for Life*, Cowdrey deftly describes the evolution of military psychiatric policy but as a small segment of the larger history of medicine. Gerald Linderman's *The World Within War: America's Combat Experience in World War II* (Cambridge, MA: Harvard University Press, 1999) provides an excellent social history of the GI, although little specifically on psychiatry. While John C. McManus's graphic descriptions of combat exhaustion in Europe and Asia in *The Deadly Brotherhood* (San Francisco: Presidio, 1998) and *Fire and Fortitude: The U.S. Army in the Pacific War, 1941–1943* (New York: Penguin, 2019) are illuminating, they are but small statements in a very extensive description of major military campaigns. Nathan G. Hale, *The Rise and Crisis of Psychoanalysis in the United States: Freud and the Americans, 1917–1985* (New York: Oxford University Press, 1995), vol. 2, contains an excellent chapter on psychoanalysis in World War II. But what is left out is that psychoanalysts were not always in the ascendency in the war. Especially in the first few years, American psychiatry was dominated by the superintendents of mental hospitals, such as Winfred Overholser, and to the extent a shift occurred, it was hampered by the exigencies of the war, namely, that soldiers had to be returned as soon as possible to combat, limiting severely the time for successful analysis.

3. "Editorial," *Psychiatry*, February 1938, 1; *Psychiatry*, February 1940, 87, 142; Harry Stack Sullivan, "Editorial," *Psychiatry*, May 1940, 296; "President's Statement Special Meeting, 6 June 1940," William Alanson White Psychiatric Foundation Archives, hereafter referred to as WAWPF; "Southern Psychiatric Association Report," *Psychiatry*, November 1940, 622; Medical Circular No. 1 (Washington, DC: US Government Printing Office, November 1940).

4. Depending on whether we use the figures of Ginzberg or Menninger, cited in note 1, neuropsychiatric rejections accounted for between 35 to 38 percent of all medical rejections. As to discharges, based on the figures of the Army Surgeon General's Office, Medical Statistics Division, Menninger, *Psychiatry in a Troubled World*, Appendix D, 587–89, arrives at a figure of 545,000, accounting for 49 percent of all mental and physical discharges. Of the 545,000, 47 percent were for psychoneuroses; 10 percent for psychoses, 30 percent psychopaths and mentally deficient, including 163,000 administrative discharges for inaptness and lacking adaptability; 9 percent neurological; and 4 percent other psychiatric disorders.

5. Edgar Jones and Simon Wessely, *Shell Shock to PTSD* (New York: Psychology Press, 2005); Mark Wells, *Courage and Air Warfare: The Allied Aircrew Experiences in the Second World War* (London: Routledge, 1995); Paul Lerner, *Hysterical Men: War, Psychiatry, and the Politics of Trauma in Germany, 1890–1930* (Ithaca, NY: Cornell University Press, 2003).

6. Jones and Wessely, *Shell Shock to PTSD*, xvii, 73, 75, 79, 89.

7. Sullivan, "Editorial," *Psychiatry*, May 1940, 296; A. D. MacLeod, *Shell Shock Doctors: Neuropsychiatry in the Trenches, 1914–1918* (Cambridge: Cambridge Scholars, 2019), 59. Sandor Ferenczi, ed., *Psychoanalysis and the War Neuroses* (New York: International Psychoanalytic Press, 1921); Selective Service Medical Circular No. 1, November 1940, 622, File, RG 147, Washington National Records Center, Suitland, MD, hereafter referred to as WNRC; Letter, R. W. Moyer, Clerk, Local Board No. 1, Oklahoma City to Fred Shaw, Delivery and Induction, Selective Service, Oklahoma City, March 27, 1941, 622 Okl. 1941, RG 147, WNRC; Miriam Kleiman, "Hit the Road Jack," *Prologue Magazine* 43, no. 3 (Fall 2001): 1–15.

8. Selwyn Raab, "John Franzese, Mafioso Who Consorted with Celebrities, Dies at 103," *New York Times*, February 24, 2020, https://www.nytimes.com/2020/02/24/nyregion/john-franzese-dead.html.

9. According to Menninger, *Psychiatry in a Troubled World*, 277, 287, psychiatrists sometimes also asked: "How are you?" "Have you any complaints?" "Have you visited a doctor often—and for what?" "Have you ever had a nervous breakdown?" But he acknowledges that hardly anything could be asked because psychiatrists often saw hundreds in one day. Ginzberg, *The Lost Divisions*, 38, states that such questions could be asked but then comments: "Many selectees reported that the sole question they were asked by the examining psychiatrist was 'Do you like girls?'" Also reported in Allan Bérubé, *Coming Out under Fire: The History of Gay Men and Women in World War II*, foreword by John D'Emilio and Estelle Freedman (Chapel Hill: University of North Carolina Press, 2012), 21.

10. Ginzberg, *The Lost Divisions*, 38; William Menninger, "The Psychiatrist in Relation to the Examining Board," *Menninger Clinic Bulletin*, September 1941, 134, 137; "Southern Psychiatric Association: Report of Its Committee on Psychiatry and the National Defense," *Psychiatry*, November 1940, 620; "Selective Service Psychiatry," *Psychiatry* 4 (August 1941): 448–51; Proceedings, Selective Service Seminar for Medical Advisory Board and Army Induction Board Psychiatrists, January 2–3, 1941, Washington, DC, 622 S1 c.1, pp. 73, 74, Lewis Hershey Papers, United States Army Military History Research Collection, Carlisle Barracks, PA; hereafter referred to as Proceedings and as USAMHRC.

11. While Ellen Herman's chapters on psychologists in World War II in *The Romance of American Psychology* (Berkeley, CA, 1995) are excellent, she may be overemphasizing the degree of cooperation between psychologists and psychiatrists. Admittedly, as Herman shows, they worked together on studies of national character and on the mindset of the enemy. Yet, as discussed by Donald Napoli in *Architects of Adjustment* (New York: National University Publications, 1981), 88–90, their efforts faltered in the Second World War because psychologists' leadership persuaded the military in 1938 to assign them to the Army Adjutant General instead of the Army Surgeon General, where they had been in World War I. According to Napoli, they did so because they believed they could have a greater role in classification in the Adjutant General and felt psychiatrists had frustrated their efforts at psychological testing in World War I. As a result, psychologists did

not refer suspect cases to psychiatrists for reevaluation at induction centers in World War II. Clinical psychologists had their own separate training programs, and they were not transferred to the Surgeon General until the war came to a close, making it more difficult for psychiatrists and psychologists to work together in hospitals. See *Neuropsychiatry in World War II*, 1:584–94.

12. Paul Starr, *The Social Transformation of American Medicine* (New York: Basic Books, 1982), 4, 8, 9, 15, 18, 22.

13. Hans Pols, "The Tunisian Campaign: War Neuroses and the Reorientation of American Psychiatry during World War II," *Harvard Review of Psychiatry* 19, no. 6 (2011): 313–20.

14. See, e.g., S. Alan Challman MD and Henry A. Davidson MD, "Southwest Pacific Area," in *Overseas Theaters, Neuropsychiatry in World War II*, 2:513–77.

15. Dr. Herbert Spiegel, interview by Rebecca Greene, December 18, 1975, New York City; Spiegel, "Psychiatry with an Infantry Battalion," undated unpublished paper, 11–13, private papers of Dr. Herbert Spiegel; WAWPF, Report of Executive Director, February 14, 1942, p. 2, WAWPF.

16. Dr. John Appel, interview by Rebecca Greene, December 23, 1975, Philadelphia.

17. Dr. M. Ralph Kaufman, interview by Rebecca Greene, January 5, 1976, New York City.

18. Statement by Gen. Norman Kirk, Surgeon General, US Army at Press Conference, including portion from Menninger, May 9, 1944, 702, RG 112, WNRC. See also *Neuropsychiatry in World War II*, 1:134–39.

19. Samuel Stouffer, *The American Soldier: Combat and Its Aftermath* (Princeton, NJ: Princeton University Press, 1949), 11, 12. Memoranda from Marshall to FDR, September 6, 1941, File 30; November 30,1942, File 38, Box 80, George C. Marshall Research Library, Lexington, VA; "Attitudes of Troops towards War," Drawer 920, GCMRL. See also 69, 70. Altogether during the war, Stouffer's group gave out at least two hundred questionnaires to half a million soldiers in over ten thousand classroom sessions.

20. Letter, Hanson to Appel, October 4, 1944, Surgeon General's Office, NATOUSA, ED 730 (NP), Letter, Hanson to Appel, October 4, 1944, Surgeon General's Office, NATOUSA, ED 730 (NP), both from US Army Medical Division Historical Unit, Ft. Detrick, Frederick, MD, hereafter referred to as USAMDHU.

21. Menninger, *Psychiatry in a Troubled World*, 421–24. William Menninger, "The Mental Health of the Negro," January 28, 1944, prepared for I&E Division, 1944, Papers and Speeches of Dr. William Menninger, 1942–1947, Menninger Foundation Archives, Topeka, KS.

22. *Neuropsychiatry in World War II*, 1:432, 434; Judith A. Bellafaire, "The Women's Army Corps: A Commemoration of World War II Service," *CMH Publication* 72-15, http://history.army.mil. In addition to the 150,000 in the WAC, at least 80,000 served in the navy WAVES, 13,000 in the coast guard SPARS,

60,000 in the Army Nurse Corps, 14,000 in the Navy Nurse Corps, and 1,000 as volunteer civilian pilots with the Women's Air Service.

23. Also see Herman, *The Romance of American Psychology*, 34, 35.

24. Menninger, *Psychiatry in a Troubled World*, xiii, 41, 47, 417–37.

25. *Neuropsychiatry in World War II*, 2:5–9; *Neuropsychiatry in World War II*, 1:393. Also, Jones and Wessely, *Shell Shock to PTSD*, 85–87.

26. Jones, *Shell Shock to PTSD*, 88.

27. Gerald Grob, "World War II and American Psychiatry," *Psychohistory Review 19* (Fall 1990): 41–69.

28. Andrew Scull, "Richardson Seminar on *Psychiatry and Its Discontents*," presentation, New York Hospital–Cornell Medical Center, Institute of History of Psychiatry and Policy, October 21, 2020; Andrew Scull, *Psychiatry and Its Discontents* (Berkeley: University of California Press, 2019).

29. General Peter Chiarelli, Vice Chief of Staff of Army, *Army Health Promotion Risk Reduction Suicide Prevention (2010)*. See also David Finkel, *The Good Soldiers* (New York: Farrar, Straus and Giroux, 2009); and David Finkel, *Thank You for Your Service* (New York: Farrar, Straus, and Giroux, 2013), following the personal psychiatric travails of soldiers of one combat unit in Iraq. For a description of the mental health problems among American soldiers and veterans of the Iraq and Afghanistan—blast concussions, trauma, and suicide—and recent military efforts to treat them, see also David Kieran, *Signature Wounds: The Untold Story of the Military's Mental Health Crisis* (New York: New York University Press, 2019).

30. Jones and Wessely, *Shell Shock to PTSD*, 107–9.

1. Mobilizing for War

1. Figures on the number rejected on neuropsychiatric grounds range from, on the low end, 1,773,000 (including 87,000 administrative), in Eli Ginzberg, *The Lost Divisions* (New York: Columbia University Press, 1959), 36; to 1,846,000, in William C. Menninger, *Psychiatry in a Troubled World* (New York: Macmillan, 1948), 588; to 1,992,950, in J. R. Eagan, L. Jackson, and R. H. Eanes, "A Study of Neuropsychiatric Rejectees," *Journal of the American Medical Association* 145, no. 7 (February 1951): 466–69, which may have included navy rejections. The army and navy had separate induction systems until February 1943; thereafter, they were supposed to coordinate their systems, although this did not always occur. Therefore, estimates may not include all the figures from the navy. However, since Eanes was assistant executive director of Selective Service, his figures should be credible. As to discharges, army, navy, and marine figures together come to 754,000 discharges, including psychiatric, inaptitude, and undesirability. Ginzberg, *The Lost Divisions*, 61. US Army, Medical Department, *Neuropsychiatry in World War II*, ed. Albert J. Glass, MC, USA (Ret.) and Lt. Col. Robert J. Bernucci (Washington, DC: US Government Printing Office, 1966), 1:Appendix A, 771, reported that army neuropsychiatric discharges came to 375,333 plus administrative separations for inaptitude or unsuitability and unfitness of

163,119, for a total together of 538,452. This, however, did not include navy discharges. Francis J. Braceland, head of Navy Psychiatry, stated in "Psychiatric Lessons from World War II," *American Journal of Psychiatry* 103, no. 5 (March 1947): 587, that between January 1, 1942, and July 1, 1945, 149,281 were admitted as patients for psychiatric reasons to naval hospitals; of these 76,721 were discharged. But he also wrote that another 91,565 recruits were separated (discharged) from naval training stations for neurological and psychiatric reasons, including the mentally deficient and patients with epilepsy and other nervous diseases. Adding 76,721 to 91,565 comes to a total of 168,286. Adding the navy's 168,286 to the army's 538,452 comes to a total of 706,738. The total figure rises to 713,286 if we use Menninger's 545,000 army neuropsychiatric discharges instead. See *Psychiatry in a Troubled World*, 589. Hence, an estimate of at least 700,000 discharges.

2. Menninger, *Psychiatry in a Troubled World*, 587, 588. According to Menninger, 1,846,000 were rejected on psychiatric grounds including mental deficiency; 1,846,000 comes to 38 percent of all the 4,828,000 medical rejections. On the other hand, when we use the figure of 5,250,000 for all the medical rejections, cited in Ginzberg, *The Lost Divisions*, 36, we come to 35 percent. Menninger also states (541) that 12 percent of all those examined were rejected on psychiatric grounds. This is based on 15,000,000 examined. When we use Ginzberg's figure of 18,000,000 examined with the 1,846,000, we get 10 percent. Another 4.4 million between 18 and 37 years of age received nonagricultural, agricultural, and dependency deferments. Adding the 4.4 million to the 18 million examined, we arrive at 22.4 million men between 18 and 37 years of age living in the United States during the war. Ginzberg, *The Lost Divisions*, 35.

3. Winfred Overholser, Paper for Selective Service Seminar, National Research Council (NRC), MED: Committee on Neuropsychiatry: General, 1940–1941, Archives of the National Academy of Sciences (NAS); Memorandum, Adjutant General to Surgeon General, "Mentally Unfit in Replacement Troops," July 22, 1918, Misc. Div., 201.6, or 702.4, Surgeon General's Office (SGO), Record Group (RG) 112, Washington National Records Center, Suitland, MD (WNRC).

4. See, e.g., Letter, Dr. Dabney, Surgeon General's Office, Medical Corps, to Dr. H. H. McClellan, San Antonio, Texas, January 17, 1939, 710 (Insanity), SGO, RG 112, WNRC.

5. A very limited number, at most 14.2 per 100,000, were examined at Ellis Island between 1906 and1910. Report, State Charities Aid Association, 1–10, 1917 Folder, Thomas Salmon Papers, ODHL; E. H. Mullan, "Mental Examination of Immigrants," Reprint No. 398 from the Public Health Reports, US Public Health Service (Washington, DC: Government Printing Office, 1917), 3, 4; also in File 702.3 (Neuropsychiatry, 1917–1927), SGO, RG 112, WNRC; Vincent J. Connato, *American Passage: The History of Ellis Island* (New York, 2009).

6. See esp. Bernard D. Karpinos and Albert Glass, "Disqualifications and Discharges for Neuropsychiatric Reasons, World War I and World War II (A

Comparative Evaluation)," in *Neuropsychiatry in World War II*, 1:Appendix A, 761–73, esp. 766–67. Records for those examined were incomplete, especially where Americans overseas were treated in European military hospitals. Also see *The Medical Department of the US Army in the World War*, ed. Pearce Bailey; Frankwood Williams and Paul O. Komora, *Neuropsychiatry in the United States*; and Thomas Salmon and Norman Fenton, eds., *Neuropsychiatry in the American Expeditionary Forces* (Washington, DC: US Government Printing Office, 1929), 10:157, 305, 306.

7. Princeton-educated Carl Brigham led the criticism of the IQ in the 1930s. Brigham also designed the Scholastic Aptitude Test. Stephen Murdoch, *IQ: A Smart History of a Failed Idea* (New York: Wiley, 2007), 80–90, 92, 98; Stephen Jay Gould, *The Mismeasure of Man* (New York: Norton, 1996), 224, 227–30, 235, 248–53. The level of intelligence was reported to be lower among Southeastern Europeans as compared to Nordics, while the average intelligence for Blacks was measured as 10.4, with 89 percent under 13. This compared with the standard of 16 as normal by the well-known psychologist Lewis Terman. See page 227, and on cultural biases, 230. Donald S. Napoli, *Architects of Adjustment* (New York: Kennikat, 1981), 25, 50, 88; Franz Samelson, "From Race Psychology to 'Studies in Prejudice,'" *Journal of the History of the Behavioral Sciences* 14, no. 3 (July 1978): 265–78. For description of the Army General Classification Test (AGCT), see John McCollins, "World War II: NCOs," http://www.ausa.org.publications; also Thomas Harrell, "Some History of the Army Classification Test," *Journal of Applied Psychology* 77, no. 6 (December 1993): 875–78.

8. Reports, NCMH Division on the Prevention of Delinquency, December 1921, November 1923, Spelman Rockefeller folder, NCMH, Rockefeller Foundation Archives, New York City; Frankwood Williams, "Finding a Way in Mental Hygiene," *Mental Hygiene* 14 (April 1930): 225–27, 232. On mental hygiene clinics, see also Gerald Grob, *The Mad among Us* (New York, 1994), 152–58. Albert Deutsch, *The Mentally Ill in America* (New York, 1946), 323. In addition to 159 child guidance clinics, Deutsch wrote there were 427 clinics that did some child guidance work. Also see George Pratt, "Twenty Years of Mental Hygiene," *Mental Hygiene* 14 (1930): 405–6.

9. Clifford Beers, *A Mind That Found Itself* (New York: Longmans, Green, 1921).

10. Ian Dowbiggin, *The Quest for Mental Health* (New York: Cambridge University Press, 2011), 93–95; Announcement, Washington School of Psychiatry, 3, 1936, Archives of the William Alanson White Psychiatric Foundation (hereafter referred to as WAWPF); William Alanson White, "Childhood: The Golden Period for Mental Hygiene," *Mental Hygiene* 4 (April 1920): 264–66; Marvin Perkins MD, "Preventive Psychiatry during World War II," chapter 6, History of the Office of Medical History, Office of Medical History website. *William Alanson White: The Washington Years, 1903–1937*, ed. Arcangelo R. T. D'Amore (Washington, DC, 1976), 12–15.

11. Stevenson contributed significantly to group therapy and political orientation in army training camps. John C. Whitehorn, Director of Phipps Clinic, Baltimore, following Adolf Meyer, participated in the investigation of army psychiatry by the Office of Scientific Research and Development at the end of the war. The University of Michigan's clinic annually examined all entering college students, referring them for psychiatric clinic treatment if necessary. By the end of the 1930s, the University of Michigan clinic had seen about 5,000 persons with about eight interviews per student. Psychoneurosis was by far the most frequent diagnosis both at the University of Michigan and in World War II. Theophile Raphael, "Four Years of Mental Hygiene Work at the University of Michigan," *Mental Hygiene* 20 (1936): 218–31.

12. Frederick W. Mott, *The Effects of High Explosives upon the Central Nervous System* (London: Harrison and Sons, 1916), 1–5; Mott delivered these lectures before the Medical Society of London in February and March 1916. Psychiatry file, National Association of Mental Health Papers, Oscar Diethelm Historical Library, Cornell Medical Center, New York City, hereafter referred to as ODHL; also E. E. Southard, "The Effects of High Explosives upon the Central Nervous System," *Mental Hygiene*, July 1917, 397–405; Dowbiggin, *The Quest for Mental Health*, 61–63, 89, notes that the concept of railway spine went even further back, to the late nineteenth century. At first, it was thought to be a nervous disorder brought on by a physical trauma derived from the jerking motion of a train. But by the 1880s, it was tied to a particular psychological vulnerability. Paul Lerner, *Hysterical Men: War, Psychiatry, and the Politics of Trauma in Germany, 1890–1930* (Ithaca, NY: Cornell University Press, 2003), 2, 8, 9; also on railway spine, Jones and Wessely, *Shell Shock to PTSD*, 15.

13. Thomas Salmon, "Mental Diseases and War Neuroses," *Mental Hygiene*, October 1917, 509–47; Report, "War Neuroses and Their Lessons," 1919 folder, Salmon Papers, ODHL; E. Murray Auer, "Some of the Nervous and Mental Conditions Arising in the Present War," *Mental Hygiene*, July 1917, 383–88; Pearce Bailey, "Care and Disposition of Military Insane," *Mental Hygiene*, July 1918, 358. See also Jones and Wessely, "Battle for the Mind: World War I and the Birth of Military Psychiatry," *Lancet* 384 (2014):1,708–14. This is not to say that belief in predisposition was universal. As in World War II, there were those in the First World War such as Gordon Morgan Holmes, a British consultant neurologist, who thought of shell shock without an injury "as a form of character weakness." He believed that giving a medical diagnosis for a personality trait "legitimized a lack of determination and encouraged invalidity." Additionally, the belief that some malingered to escape combat "seemed to legitimize the use of brutal forms of treatment, such as electric shock." Jones and Wessely, "Battle for the Mind," 1,711. Shell shock could include shortness of breath, palpitations, joint and muscle pains, tremors, dizziness, nightmares, and difficulty going to sleep. After F. W. Mott studied soldiers in the field, he came to favor predisposition as the cause.

14. Edward Strecker, "Experiments in the Immediate Treatment of War Neuroses," *American Journal of Insanity* 76 (July 1919): 45–69.

15. Thomas Salmon, "War Neuroses and Their Lesson," Mary Scott Newbold Lecture delivered to the Philadelphia College of Physicians, April 3, 1919, 1919 folder, Salmon Papers, ODHL; Pearce Bailey, "Applicability of Findings of Neuropsychiatric Examinations in Army to Civil Problems," *Mental Hygiene* 4, no. 301 (April 1920): 304, 305.

16. Sandor Ferenczi, ed., *Psychoanalysis and the War Neuroses* (New York: International Psychoanalytic Press, 1921), 19, 23–26.

17. Lerner, *Hysterical Men*, 1–10.

18. Nathan Hale, *Freud and the Americans* (New York: Oxford University Press, 1971), 454; Douglas Thom, "Child Management," U.S. Department of Labor Child's Bureau Publication No. 13 (Washington, DC, 1925).

19. S. D. Lamb, *Pathologist of the Mind* (Baltimore, MD: Johns Hopkins University Press, 2014); Announcement, WAWPF, 1936.

20. Letters, Harry Stack Sullivan to Adolf Meyer, September 12, 1930, and Meyer to Sullivan, September 15, 1930. In the latter letter Meyer wrote Sullivan: "The problem of psychiatry and its relation to the social sciences is by no means 'finished.' . . . The Freudian conceptions have taken such strong literary hold on the social sciences that investigations in connection with nursery schools by competently trained persons would mean a great deal. That is where association with Gesell and May could be most telling." In a second letter from Sullivan to Meyer dated April 8, 1932, Sullivan asked Meyer for comments on Sullivan's manuscript on *Psychopathology*, specifically regarding his use of Meyer's terms for schizophrenia as opposed to Bleuler's and whether the manuscript conformed enough to Meyer's principles of psychobiology. (Bleuler had studied with Freud and was a believer in sterilizing those with schizophrenia.) All from Series I, Correspondence S, Unit 1/3736, Correspondence Harry Stack Sullivan, Alan Mason Chesney Medical Archives, JHMA, Baltimore, Maryland, JBox. I am indebted to Professor Lamb for pointing out to me the correspondence with Sullivan in the Adolf Meyer Collection.

21. Patrick Mullahy, *The Beginnings of Modern American Psychiatry* (New York: Houghton Mifflin, 1973), 1–8; Sullivan's book *Schizophrenia as a Human Process* (New York: Norton, 1974) contained an introduction and commentary by Helen Swick Perry.

22. Harry Stack Sullivan, *Conceptions of Modern Psychiatry* (New York: Norton, 1953). Harry Stack Sullivan, *Personal Psychopathology* (New York: Norton, 1984); Harry Stack Sullivan, *Schizophrenia as a Human Process* (New York: Norton, 1974).

23. Lutz Kaelber, "Eugenics," http://www.uvm.edu; Dowbiggin, *The Quest for Mental Health*, 101–10; Mark H. Haller, *Eugenics: Hereditarian Attitudes in American Thought* (New Brunswick, NJ: Rutgers University Press, 1963). On sterilization in Germany and England, see Greg Eghigian, *From Madness to*

Mental Health (New Brunswick, NJ: Rutgers University Press, 2010), 294–310; Michael Burleigh, *Death and Deliverance* (London: Cambridge University Press, 1994). On army medical statistics, see *Neuropsychiatry in the United States*, 10:200–20.

24. Interview, Frederick Osborn by Rebecca Greene, April 4, 1980, Garrison, New York; *New York Times*, August 20, 1941, 1:8; Frank Lorimer and Frederick Osborn, *Dynamics of Population* (1934); Frederick Osborn, *Preface to Eugenics* (New York, 1940); Keith E. Eiler, *Mobilizing America* (Ithaca, NY: Cornell University Press, 1997), 106, 260. Abstract, Frederick H. Osborn Papers, American Philosophical Society, https://search.amphil.soc.org. Dowbiggin, *The Quest for Mental Health*, 101–10; Elazar Barkan, *The Retreat of Scientific Racism: Changing Concepts of Race in Britain and the United States between the World Wars* (London: Cambridge University Press, 1992), 282, 283, 328.

25. Sarah W. Tracy, "An Evolving Science of Man: The Transformation and Demise of American Constitutional Medicine, 1920–1950," in *Greater Than the Parts: Holism in Biomedicine, 1920–1950*, ed. Christopher Lawrence and George Weisz (New York: Oxford University Press, 1998), 160–74.

26. Thomas Salmon and Norman Fenton, *Neuropsychiatry in the American Expeditionary Force*, 10:57–59; referred to in Marvin Perkins, "Preventive Psychiatry during World War II," in US Army Medical Department, *Preventive Medicine in World War II*, vol. 3: *Personal Health Measures and Immunization*, ed. John Boyd Coates Jr. and Ebbe Curtis Hoff (Washington, DC: Office of the Surgeon General, Department of the Army, 1955), 174; also https://apps.dtic.mil/dtic.

27. US Army, *Handbook for the Medical Soldier* (1927).

28. Letter, Hershey to Rebecca Greene, March 30, 1974. Lewis Hershey, "Fear in War as Seen by Hershey," abstract of paper to Army Command and General Staff School, 1933; *New York Times*, September 27, 1942, 36; "General Hershey Dead at 83," *New York Times*, May 21, 1977, 1.

29. George Q. Flynn, *Lewis B. Hershey, Mr. Selective Service* (Chapel Hill: University of North Carolina Press, 1985), 61, 62, 67, 69, 75, 76. Also see Flynn, *The Draft, 1940–1973* (Lawrence: University of Kansas Press, 1993).

30. Flynn, *Lewis B. Hershey*, 69.

31. Harold J. Laski, "Letter to MacLeish," *New Republic* 103 (September 2, 1940): 299–300; Mortimer J. Adler, "This Prewar Generation," *Harper's*, October 1940, 524, 525; "American Soldier, Shell Shocked—and After," *Atlantic Monthly* 128 (December 1921): 738–44; W. Merlin Jones, "Beating Shell Shock with a Canoe," *Outing* 75 (March 1920): 340–41; in the *Kalamazoo (Michigan) Gazette*, September 28, 1939, the Society for the Psychological Study of Social Issues also decried shell shock.

32. US Senate, Committee on Military Affairs, *Hearings on S. 4164*, July 10, 1940, 172, 173; see also Gordon W. Allport, "Liabilities and Assets in Civilian Morale," *Annals of the American Academy of Political and Social Science*, July 1941, 89; Arthur Link, *American Epoch* (New York, 1963), 491.

33. Franklin Delano Roosevelt, "Campaign Address at Boston, Massachusetts (October 30, 1940)," American Presidency Project, https://www.presidency.ucsb.edu/documents/campaign-address-boston-massachusetts. The debate on a peacetime draft appeared in such articles as John T. Flynn, "Compulsory Service," *New York World Telegram*, June 18, 1940; "On the German Model," *Washington Post*, June 20, 1940; "Best Use of Manpower," *New York Post*, June 14, 1940; "Sugar Coated!" *Cincinnati Times-Star*, June 19, 1940; all in Box 1, New Deal File, Perkins Collection, E. Roosevelt Papers, Hyde Park, New York, hereafter referred to as FDRL.

34. Flynn, *Lewis B. Hershey*, esp. 70–72, 77; Nicholas A. Krehbiel, *General Lewis B. Hershey and Conscientious Objection during World War II* (Missouri, 2011).

35. Charles Spruit, "Medical Participation in Selective Service," *Journal of the American Medical Association* 115, no. 13 (September 28, 1940): 1,105–7.

36. Helen Swick Perry, *Psychiatrist of America: The Life of Harry Stack Sullivan* (Cambridge, MA: Harvard University Press, 1982); A. H. Chapman, *Harry Stack Sullivan: His Life and Work* (New York, 1976); Ralph Crowley, "On Sullivan: I," *William Alanson White Newsletter*, hereafter referred to as *WAWN* (Summer 1970); Crowley, "On Sullivan: II," *WAWN* (Winter 1971); *Current Biography* (New York, 1940), 209.

37. Interview, Frederick Osborn by Rebecca Greene, April 4, 1980, Garrison, New York.

38. For relations between Harry Stack Sullivan and leading contemporary social scientists and neo-Freudians, see also Lawrence Friedman, assisted by Anke Schreiber, *The Lives of Erich Fromm: Love's Prophet* (New York: Columbia University Press, 2013). In addition to those mentioned in this text, the book states that his circle also included Clara Thompson, the anthropologists Margaret Mead and Edward Sapir, and members of a Monday-evening discussion group conducted by Sullivan, including Abram Kardiner and Frieda Fromm-Reichmann. See esp. 76–78 and, on Sullivan's advocacy of Fromm's *Escape from Freedom* in Sullivan's reviews of Fromm's book, 87.

39. "Editorial," *Psychiatry* 1 (February 1938); Harold Lasswell, "What Psychiatrists and Political Scientists Can Learn from One Another," *Psychiatry* 1 (February 1938): 35–37; "Southern Psychiatric Association: Report," *Psychiatry* 3 (November 1940): 621–23; "Editorial," *Psychiatry*, August 1938, 119. Newspaper reports referred to Sullivan's concern about antisemitism. Thomas R. Henry, *Washington Star*, January 22, 1939: "Dr. Sullivan describes 'a strange, weird hate disease that is afflicting the mind of Christendom.'" On Lasswell's views in the 1930s on emotional disturbances and antisemitism, see also Ellen Herman, *The Romance of American Psychology* (Berkeley: University of California Press, 1995), 49.

40. *Psychiatry*, February 1940, 87, 142; "Southern Psychiatric Association Report," *Psychiatry*, November 1940, 622; "President's Statement Special Meeting, 6 June 1940," WAWPF.

41. Sullivan, "Editorial," *Psychiatry* 3 (May 1940): 290, 296.

42. The fear in America of the defeatist effects of German propaganda on France in May 1940 was also expressed by Edmond Taylor, *The Strategy of Terror: Europe's Inner Front* (New York, 1940), virtually predicting the surrender of France. Roosevelt, "Fireside Chat," May 26, 1940, *The Public Papers and Addresses of FDR*, 9:230–31; for concerns of Roosevelt about the propaganda of Goebbels, see "White House Press Conference, March 1941," *The Public Papers and Addresses of FDR*, 9:62, 63; Frank Hines and McIntire echoed the sentiments of Roosevelt. See Address, Brig. Gen. Hines, American Legion, August 16, 1940; Address, McIntire before American College of Surgeons, October 1940, FDRL.

43. Link, *The American Epoch*, 471. It is interesting to note too that the concern of Sullivan about communists was expressed about six months after the passage of the Smith Act, which outlawed the instruction or advocacy by any group or person in support of the violent overthrow of government. Link, *The American Epoch*, 497.

44. Harold Lasswell, "The Volume of Communist Propaganda in Chicago," *Public Opinion Quarterly*, January 1939, 63–78.

45. J. E. Wallace Wallin, "Letter to Editor," *Readers' Forum: Psychological Exchange* 2 (October–November 1933): 199–200.

46. Philip Eisenberg and Paul F. Lazarsfeld, "The Psychological Effects of Unemployment," *Psychological Bulletin* 35 (1938): 360–65, 380, 381; here, Eisenberg and Lazarsfeld mention, for example, E. A. Rundquist, *Personality in the Depression* (Minneapolis, 1936), 3, 4, 369; N. Israel, "Distress in the Outlook of Lancashire and Scottish Unemployment," *Journal of Applied Psychology* 19 (1935): 67–69; F. E. Williams, *Russia, Youth, and the Present-Day World* (New York, 1934), 270; M. Lazarsfeld-Jahoda and H. Zeisl, *Die Arbeitlosen von Marienthal, Psychologische Monograph* V (1933); E. W. Bakke, *The Unemployed Man* (London, 1933); L. Brandt, "An Impressionistic View of the Winter of 1930–1931 in New York City," New York, 1932; *Children, Young People, and Unemployment* (Geneva, 1933); M. Elderton, *Case Studies of Unemployment* (Philadelphia, 1931).

47. Sullivan, "Editorial," *Psychiatry*, May 1940, 296.

48. E. W. Bakke, *The Unemployed Worker* (New Haven, 1940), 324.

49. "Southern Psychiatric Association Report," *Psychiatry*, November 1940, 623–24.

50. Letter, Harry Stack Sullivan to Dorothy Blitsten, November 27, 1940, Sullivan-Blitsten Correspondence, ODHL.

51. Ernest Jones, *The Life and Work of Sigmund Freud*, vol. 3 (New York, 1957). For mention of Freud's safety, see *AJP* 95 (1938): 228; on Hitler, *AJP* 96 (1939): 1–2.

52. I am indebted to the late historian Norman Dain for referring me to two letters about the NCMH's negotiations with the federal government to bring Karl Birnbaum over from Germany. Letters, Clifford Beers to Dr. Vance Murray, US Public Health Service, May 2, 1939; G. Howland Shaw, American Foreign Service (as of 1941 Assistant Secretary of State) to Beers, May 8, 1939. As to Kubie's

actions regarding Hartmann, see Letters, Eliot B. Coulter, Acting Chief Visa Division, State Dept. to Mr. Arthur Sweetser, League of Nations, August 10, 1940; Heinz Hartmann to Sweetser, October 11, 1940; Kubie to Coulter, October 17, 1940; Kubie to Coulter, October 29,1940; Kubie to Mrs. Franklin D. Roosevelt, November 22, 1940; Mrs. Roosevelt to Cordell Hull, Secretary of State, November 26, 1940, from File 70, Box 781, Eleanor Roosevelt (ER) Papers, FDRL. See also Nellie Thompson, "The Transformation of Psychoanalysis in America: Émigré Analysts and the New York Psychoanalytic Society and Institute, 1935–1961," *Journal of the American Psychoanalytic Association* 60, no. 1 (March 16, 2012): 9–44. The Emergency Committee also included Helene Deutsch from BPS; Bertram Lewin, Sandor Rado, Monroe Meyer, and George Daniels from the NYPI; Franz Alexander and Thomas French from the Chicago Psychoanalytic Association; and Lewis Hill from the Washington Baltimore Psychoanalytic Association. Other psychiatrists who were assisted by Kubie in emigrating included the German psychiatrist Helmut Baum. Initially, Baum obtained a position at Hillside Hospital in New York, later at the Mitchell Sanitarium in Peoria, Illinois, followed by military service in the army. Kubie also assisted the Hungarian analyst Dr. George Gero and the Viennese analyst Dr. Josef Breuer. During this time too, the Austrian psychoanalysts Robert Waelder and Edward Bibring became BPS members. And the Los Angeles Psychoanalytic Study Group, forerunner of the Los Angeles Psychoanalytic Society and Institute (LPSI), invited Otto Fenichel to come over. See also "Boston Psychoanalytic Society and Institute," https: bpsi.org/who-we-are-2/history. Edward Shorter, *A History of Psychiatry: From the Era of the Asylum to the Age of Prozac* (New York: John Wiley & Sons, 1997), 167–68.

53. "Winfred Overholser," *Current Biography* (New York, 1954); Overholser, "Mental Disease—a Challenge," *Scientific Monthly* 48 (March 1939): 203–9; Overholser, untitled paper for Selective Service Seminar, NRC, MED: Committee on Neuropsychiatry: General, 1940–1941, NAS.

54. Interview with Osborn by Rebecca Greene; Frances Perkins, *The Roosevelt I Knew* (New York, 2011); David Roll, *The Hopkins Touch* (New York: Oxford University Press, 2013), 26. Ross T. McIntire, *The White House Physician* (New York, 1946); William Leuchtenburg, *Franklin Delano Roosevelt and the New Deal* (New York, 1963), 120.

55. Profile, Edward A. Strecker (1886–1959), webpage, Department of Psychiatry Penn Behavioral Health; Letters, Secretary to Mrs. Roosevelt to Dr. Edward Strecker, September 9, 1942; Mrs. Roosevelt to Strecker, April 21, 1944; Strecker to Mrs. Roosevelt, April 27, 1944, File 100; Anonymous to Mama, File 170, Box 2610; Strecker to Mrs. Roosevelt, May 27, 1944; Mrs. Roosevelt to Strecker, June 5, 1944, File 100; Strecker to Betty , June 7, 1944; Strecker to Mrs. Roosevelt, June 7, 1944, File 100; Strecker to Mrs. Roosevelt, June 19, 1944, File 100; Strecker to Bill, June 13, 1944, File 100; Strecker to Mrs. Roosevelt, June 13, 1944; Mrs. Roosevelt to Strecker, June 22, 1944; all in Box 1747, E. Roosevelt

Papers, FDRL; *New York Times*, January 7, 1943, 15:7; June 10, 1943, 14:7; June 12, 1943, 18:8, and June 16, 1943, 23:3; "Dr. Edward A. Strecker: A Psychiatrist, 72," *New York Times*, January 3, 1959, 17:3. Herman, *The Romance of American Psychology*, 49; also Strecker, *Their Mothers' Sons* (New York, 1946), 5, 6. Letter, Kubie to Mrs. A. Roosevelt, October 3, 1951, Eleanor Roosevelt Papers, FDRL.

56. McIntire, *The White House Physician*, 53.

57. Letter, Isabel Butterfield, daughter of Dr. Foster Kennedy, to Rebecca Greene, April 8, 1979; Letter, Katherine Kennedy Montor, widow of Dr. Kennedy, to Rebecca Greene, April 17, 1979.

58. Her father, Elliott, also used laudanum and morphine. One servant girl claimed she was carrying his child and pressed for $10,000; a settlement was reached. Eventually, Theodore Roosevelt, Elliott's brother, and Eleanor's mother reluctantly brought suit to have Elliott declared insane and place his property in trust for his wife and children. Elliott settled by agreeing to spend a year at a center for alcoholism, put a large part of his property in trust for his children and wife, and, as probation, worked for his brother-in-law on his estate in Abingdon, Virginia, for approximately two years. Jean Smith, *FDR* (New York: Random House, 2008), 41–43; Blanche Wiesen Cook, *Eleanor Roosevelt*, vol. 1: *1884-1933* (New York: Penguin, 1992), 4, 39, 59–69. Also see *The Autobiography of Eleanor Roosevelt* (Boston, 2000).

59. Cook, *Eleanor Roosevelt*, 1:4, 8, 23, 39. See also Ward and Burns, *The Roosevelts: An Intimate History*, film, http://usualhistoricals.blogspot.com; Resa Willis, *FDR and Lucy* (New York, 2004). On alcoholism of brother, effects of Franklin's polio on children, and Eleanor's activities at St. Elizabeth's in World War I, see Geoffrey Ward and Ken Burns, *The Roosevelts: An Intimate History* (New York: Knopf Doubleday, 2014), 204, 249, 390. And in general, on Eleanor and Franklin, Joseph Lash, *Eleanor and Franklin* (New York, 1971), 57, 61, 71, 77, 87, 362, 364, 369.

60. Letters, Franklin Delano Roosevelt to Dr. Foster Kennedy, regarding establishing neuropsychiatric institute, December 12, 1938, 103-C, OF FDR; Mrs. Roosevelt corresponded with the public about their problems with psychiatry. For example, Mrs. S. to Mrs. Roosevelt, March 10, 1942, about revoking naval commission of son because of diagnosis of psychoneurosis; Secretary to Mrs. Roosevelt to Mrs. S., March 18, 1942; Mrs. S. to Secretary to Mrs. Roosevelt, April 8, 1942, Sti-Sz Folder, Box 377, E. Roosevelt 70, 1942 Smith Papers; FDR to Secretary of War Stimson, March 24, 1945, on rehabilitating combat exhausted soldiers, OF FDR; Letter, Stimson to Mrs. Roosevelt, November 27, 1942; Mrs. Roosevelt to Stimson, November 25, 1942, Mrs. Roosevelt to Strecker, December 8, 1942, regarding medical discharge, Sti-Sz Folder, 100, E. Roosevelt White House Papers; Mrs. Ittleson, Executive Committee National Committee of Mental Hygiene, November 30, 1943, recommending William Menninger; Mrs. Roosevelt to Major General Norman Kirk, Surgeon General USA, recommending Menninger, December 3, 1943, File 100, B. 1687, E. Roosevelt Papers. All from

FDRL. This footnote represents but a sample of the involvement of Eleanor Roosevelt in psychiatric policy.

61. "Selective Service Psychiatry," *Psychiatry* 4 (August 1941): 444–53; Harry Stack Sullivan, *The Fusion of Psychiatry and Social Science* (New York, 1964), 122. Letter, Eleanor Roosevelt to Frank Hines, Director of Veterans Affairs, May 28, 1940; Letter, Hines to Mrs. Roosevelt, June 4, 1940; Letter, Secretary to Mrs. Roosevelt to Hines, June 12, 1940; Letter, Hines to Mrs. Roosevelt, July 20, 1940, File 70, Box 777, E. R. Papers, FDRL. Mrs. Roosevelt also tried to help some psychiatrists get visas. For example, in August 1941, she asked Mayor La Guardia to ask the State Department to issue a passport to the child psychiatrist Viola Bernard. Bernard was at that time interested in surveying the psychological impact of bombing and evacuation on children in Great Britain and hoped to use her study in advising the Board of Education of New York City on contingency plans. La Guardia refused, believing the project unnecessary. Letter, Bernard to Mrs. Roosevelt, August 6, 1941, and attached memorandum; Letter, Mrs. Roosevelt to La Guardia, August 15, 1941, both in Box 1608, Eleanor Roosevelt Papers, FDRL.

62. Testimony of Mayor Fiorello La Guardia before US House of Representatives Committee on Military Affairs, *Hearings on H.R. 10132*, 224, 225.

63. H. W. Brands, *Traitor to His Class: The Privileged Life and Radical Presidency of Franklin Delano Roosevelt* (New York: Random House, 2008).

64. Roosevelt spent a large proportion of his income on Warm Springs. He used his funds to persuade the orthopedic surgeon Leroy Hubbard, who headed rehabilitation for New York State, to come there with a trained nurse and physiotherapist, Helena Mahoney. He and his foundation also paid for a dozen physical education graduates to take care of patients. Patients could come to Warm Springs for $42 a week, which included the magnesium-laden pool waters, board and lodging, therapy, and medicine. No one was turned away. If need be, FDR paid the bill himself. In 1938, the March of Dimes was started, which paid for the expenses of Warm Springs and also for polio research, ultimately leading to the Salk vaccine in 1955. The abject poverty in Warm Springs, Georgia, meant that there was no electricity or running water, no shoes for the kids, not even grade-level education. The farms there were totally unprofitable. Smith, *FDR*, x, 216–20.

65. Smith, *FDR*, 193–96, 209, 220; James Tobin, *The Man He Became: How FDR Defied Polio to Win the Presidency* (New York: Simon and Schuster, 2014), 119, 120, 130–32.

66. Brands, *Traitor to His Class*, 146–48.

67. Curtis Hart, MD, "Franklin Delano Roosevelt: A Famous Patient," *Journal of Religion and Health* 53 (2014): 1,102–11; also, Ward and Burns, *The Roosevelts*, 259.

68. Tobin, *The Man He Became*, 305–10.

69. Ross T. McIntire, *The White House Physician* (New York, 1946), 55, 56.

70. Letter, Hatfield to Roosevelt, June 1, 1940, National Research Council (hereafter referred to as NRC) Neuropsychiatric Committee (hereafter referred to

as NP Committee), Morale folder, Overholser Papers, St. Elizabeth's Hospital Records, RG 418, National Archives, Washington, DC, hereafter referred to as NA. Hatfield was known for his book on *Children in Court* and for his weekly column on juvenile delinquency, which appeared in five hundred newspapers and magazines throughout the country. See "Judge Malcolm Hatfield," Iowa Digital Library, University of Iowa Libraries, http://digital.lib.uiowa.edu/cdm/ref/collection/tc/id/21213.

71. Address, Brig. Gen. Hines, Administrator VA, 22nd Annual Convention, American Legion, Pa., August 16, 1940; Albert J. Glass, "Army Psychiatry before World War II," 20–22, US Army Medical Department, Office of Medical History. During this time, there was also correspondence between Mrs. Roosevelt and Overholser about the conditions in mental hospitals. Letter, Overholser to Mrs. Roosevelt, February 1, 1940; Mrs. Roosevelt to Overholser, February 5, 1940, both in Personal Letters, Os-Pz File, Box 1,569, and attached; Overholser, "The Desiderata of Central Administrative Control of State Mental Hospitals," *AJP* 96, no. 3 (November 1939); Overholser, "Mental Disease—a Challenge," *Scientific Monthly*, Memorandum for General Hines from FDR, November 16, 1939, Hines to FDR, November 15, 1939, occupational therapy in neuropsychiatric hospitals, VA 1939 Folder, Box OF 8, OF FDR, FDRL.

72. Memorandum to the President from John Blandford, Acting Director, Bureau of the Budget, stamped September 26, 1940, and Memorandum to Federal Board of Hospitalization regarding Possible Future Hospital Needs for Veterans Suffering from Nervous and Mental Diseases, from Overholser, August 19, 1940, OF 8b, Veterans Administration, Federal Hospitalization Board, 1940, FDRL; Overholser, Paper for Selective Service Seminar, file MED: Committee on Neuropsychiatry, General, 1940–1941, NAS. Ironically, as mentioned in Ellen Herman, *Romance of American Psychology*, 344, citing Jeanne Brand, "The National Mental Health Act of 1946," *Bulletin of the History of Medicine* 39 (May–June 1965): 236–37, the cost after the Second World War actually came to $40,000 per patient, with 60 percent of all Veterans Administration hospital cases being psychiatric. And as of June 1947, each month neuropsychiatric veterans of World War I and World War II were receiving $20 million in pensions.

73. Telegram, Sullivan to Overholser, September 8, 1940, WAWPF Folder, Office Files of Superintendent Overholser, 1937–1955, Records of St. Elizabeth's Hospital, RG 418, NA; *Bulletin from the William Alanson White Psychiatric Foundation*, September 11, 1940, WAWPF folder, Official Files Superintendent Overholser, 1937–1955, RG 418, NA.

74. John O'Sullivan and Adam M. Meckler, eds., *The Draft and Its Enemies* (Chicago, 1974), 177, 178, 180. *Selective Training and Service Act*, 54 Stat. 885 (September 16, 1940).

75. Memorandum to the President from Blandford, stamped September 26, 1940, and Memorandum to Federal Board of Hospitalization; Address, McIntire,

Surgeon General of Navy, before American College of Surgeons, October 1940, FDRL.

76. Letter, Roosevelt to Osborn, September 27, 1940, Harold Smith file, Collection 24, Osborn Papers, APS.

77. Reports, George C. Marshall to Henry Stimson, July 1, 1939, to June 30, 1941, Folder 26–3, Austin Papers, University of Vermont, Burlington, hereafter referred to as Austin Papers, esp. 13, 16. Forrest Pogue, *Ordeal and Hope*, foreword by General Omar N. Bradley (New York: Viking, 1968), 113; Mark S. Watson, *Chief of Staff, Prewar Plans and Preparations* (Washington, DC: Department of the Army Historical Division, 1949), 16, 23, 30–34, 185, 187, 188, 208, 209, 231, 234; Arthur Link, *The American Epoch*, 485, 478; US Senate, Committee on Military Affairs, *Hearings on S. 4164, to Protect the Integrity and Institutions of the United States through a System of Selective, Compulsory Military Training and Service*, 76th Cong., 3d Sess., 1940, 160–62. Eiler, *Mobilizing America*, 106. "Biographical Data on Frederick H. Osborn," January 28, 1948, Collection 24, Osborn Papers, APS.

78. Other members of the committee were: Samuel W. Hamilton, Hugo Mella, Roscoe Hall, Howard W. Potter, Lauren H. Smith, William Porter, Patrick Madigan, Martin Cooley, S. Spafford Ackerly, and Karl M. Bowman.

79. Allan Bérubé, *Coming Out under Fire: The History of Gay Men and Women in World War II*, with a new foreword by John D'Emilio and Estelle Freedman (Chapel Hill: University of North Carolina Press, 2012), 8. The number here is 6,400. For 6,403, see "American Psychiatric Association Military Mobilization Committee Questionnaire," *American Journal of Psychiatry* 97 (September 1940): 477.

80. WAWPF, Report of Executive Director, February 14, 1942, 2, WAWPF; Letter, Harry Stack Sullivan to Dorothy Blitsten, November 27, 1940, Sullivan-Blitsten Correspondence, ODHL. Sullivan, "Selective Service Psychiatry," *Psychiatry* 4, no. 3 (August 1941): 444–53.

81. Selective Service System, cover letter to State Directors of Selective Service, State Medical Officer, Chairman of Boards, Chairman of Medical Advisory Boards, Chairman of Local Boards, Examining Physicians, and Members of Medical Advisory Boards, plus National Headquarters, Selective Service System, Washington, DC, Medical Circular No. 1 (Washington, DC: Superintendent of Documents, November 7, 1940), 1–7. Hereafter referred to as "Medical Circular No. 1" (November 7, 1940).

82. Harry Stack Sullivan, "A Seminar on Practical Psychiatric Diagnosis," *Psychiatry* 4 (May 1941): 269, 270.

83. Medical Circular No. 1, November 1940, 1.

84. "Selective Service Psychiatry," *Psychiatry*, February 1940, 118–21.

85. Medical Circular No. 1, November 1940, 4.

86. Medical Circular No. 1 (November 1940), 1.

87. Medical Circular No. 1 (November 1940), 4.

88. Spruit, untitled paper, September 1940, Hershey Papers, USAMHRC.

89. Interview by telephone with Dr. Dexter Bullard by Rebecca Greene, May 29, 1975, Washington, DC.

90. Robert P. Knight, "Recognizing the Psychoneurotic Registrant," *Bulletin of the Menninger Clinic* 5 (1941): 161–66, esp. 164. The paper was read before the Chicago Seminar on Practical Psychiatric Diagnosis for Selective Service Registrants, May 19, 1941. After the war, Knight became medical director of the Austen Riggs Center, Stockbridge, MA. He was also a psychoanalyst. https://prabook.com.

91. Selective Service Medical Conference at National Headquarters, June 5 and 6, 1944, RG 147, WNRC. Of the 12,000 assigned to CPS, some worked in camps on conservation projects, others in 41 mental hospitals and 17 schools for the mentally deficient, where residents were kept in the worst living conditions. Six thousand men who did not pass the religious test and refused to register for the draft ended up in prison. These included the civil rights activist and pacifist Bayard Rustin. At least another 25,000 COs were assigned to noncombat positions in the military (especially medics). Adding the 25,000 to the 12,000 and the 6,000 comes to a total of 43,000 COs. See Scott H. Bennett, "American Pacifism, 'The Greatest Generation,' and World War II," in *The United States and the Second World War: New Perspectives on Diplomacy, War, and the Home Front*, ed. G. Kurt Piehler and Sidney Pash (New York: Fordham University Press, 2010), 260, 269, 274. Bennett derives his numbers from Mulford Q. Sibley and Philip E. Jacob, *Conscription of Conscience* (New York: Cornell University Press, 1952), 86–87, 124, 354–55. Also Steven J. Taylor, *Acts of Conscience: World War II, Mental Institutions, and Religious Objectors* (Syracuse, NY: Syracuse University Press, 2009). On Bayard Rustin's experience, John D'Emilio, *Lost Prophet—The Life and Times of Bayard Rustin* (New York: Free Press, 2003). Also see Krehbiel, *General Lewis B. Hershey*, 3, 22.

2. Military Necessity Overrides Psychiatric Skepticism

1. Drs. William Sargant and Eliot Slater, *Lancet*, July 6, 1940, 1. Ben Shephard, *A War of Nerves* (Cambridge, MA: Harvard University Press, 2001), 204, 205. Edgar Jones and Simon Wessely, *Shell Shock to PTSD* (New York, 2005), esp. 72, 73. F. A. E. Crew, *The Army Medical Services* (London: Her Majesty's Stationery Office, 1957), 2:461–65, 467. Likewise, an investigating British army consultant discovered that a stressful two-year tropical service tour from 1939 to 1941, including insufficient rest, incompetent leadership, insufficient weaponry, and large numbers with fatal wounds, rather than predisposition, contributed to breakdown.

2. Jones and Wessely, *Shell Shock to PTSD*, xvii, 71, 73, 75, 89.

3. Letter, Dr. John Cathcart to Dr. Harry Steckel, October 2, 1940, Cathcart to Steckel, NRC Neuropsychiatry File, Revision of MR 1-9, Winfred Overholser Papers, St. Elizabeth's Hospital Records, RG 418, National Archives, Washington, DC, hereafter referred to as NA.

4. Letter, Aubrey Lewis to Steckel, December 20, 1940, p. 6, NRC Neuropsychiatry File, Revision of MR 1-9, Winfred Overholser Papers, St. Elizabeth's Hospital Records, RG 418, NA.

5. Roscoe Hall, "Report of an Observation Trip to Canada from April 7th to April 18, 1941," War Neuroses Minutes and Reports File, Archives of the National Academy of Sciences, Washington, DC, hereafter referred to as NAS.

6. Emilio Mira y Lopez, "Psychological Work during the Spanish War," *Occupational Psychology* 13 (1939): 168–70; also *Psychiatry in War* (New York: Norton, 1943), http://pep.gvpi.net/documents.

7. Report, Conference on the Neurotic Soldier, December 14 and 15, 1940, p. 20, NRC Division of Anthropology and Psychology, Committee on Problems of Neurotic Behavior File, NAS. Altogether, 2,500 Scots died from German aerial bombings beginning in March 1940 and continuing into 1943. See "New Book Lifts Lid on Why Scotland Was Top of Hitler's Air-Raid List," *Daily Record*, https://www.dailyrecord.co.uk/news/new-book. Les Taylor, *Luftwaffe over Scotland* (Scotland: Whittles, 2010). American psychiatrists were also probably well aware of the British psychiatric studies during the Blitz that reported a surprisingly high level of civilian morale and attributed it to a communal spirit of self-sacrifice. Altogether, 43,000 British civilians died during German bombings of London, Liverpool, Coventry, and Birmingham from September 1940 through May 1941. On the psychological impact of the Blitz, see Edgar Jones et al., "Civilian Morale during the Second World War: Responses to Air-Raids Re-examined," *Social History of Medicine* 17, no. 3 (2004). For recent opinion on the psychological virtues of the Blitz, Sebastian Junger, *Tribe: On Homecoming and Belonging* (New York, 2016).

8. "Proceedings Selective Service Seminar for Medical Advisory Board and Army Induction Board Psychiatrists, January 2–3, 1941," Washington, DC, 622 S1 c.1, p. 100, Hershey Papers, United States Army Military History Research Collection, Carlisle Barracks, PA; hereafter referred to as Proceedings and as USAMHRC.

9. Bernard Glueck, "A Note on War Psychiatry," *Bulletin of the New York Academy of Medicine* 18 (February 1942): 141. He spoke to the annual meeting of the New York Society of Psychotherapy and Psychopathology.

10. Proceedings, January 2–3, 1941, p. 100, Hershey Papers, USAMHRC.

11. Abram Kardiner, "The Neuroses of War," *War Medicine* 1 (March 1941): 219–26. For more discussion, also see "The Traumatic Neuroses of War," *Psychosomatic Medicine Monograph* (Washington, 1941); Interview, Rebecca Greene with Dr. Kardiner, October 26, 1974, New York City.

12. Kardiner, "The Neuroses of War," 224, 223; also see Minutes, NRC, Neurology subcommittee, January 13, 1941, p. 8, 040.9–10, RG 112, Washington National Records Center, Suitland, MD (WNRC); Report, "Meeting at the Metropole," 622, RG 147, WNRC.

13. This quote is cited in Letter, Major A. J. Fletcher, Army Planning Board to Colonel Langston, April 7, 1941, 333, RG 147, WNRC.

14. Harry Stack Sullivan, "A Seminar on Practical Psychiatric Diagnosis," *Psychiatry* 4 (1941): 275; Proceedings, p. 55, USAMHRC; Alexander Simon, R. W. Hall, and Margaret Hagan, *War Medicine* 1 (1941): 387; this is the St. Elizabeth Hospital study. Seminar for Medical Advisory Board and Army Induction Board Psychiatrists, January 2–3, 1941, p. 35d, Hershey Papers, USAMHRC.

15. Franklin Delano Roosevelt, "Speech to White House Correspondents, March 1941," in *The Public Papers and Addresses of Franklin D. Roosevelt*, ed. Samuel I. Rosenman et al., vol. 10 (New York: Random House, 1941); Forrest C. Pogue, *Ordeal and Hope, 1939–1942* (New York, 1973), 2:118; Richard W. Steele, "Preparing the Public for War: Efforts to Establish a National Propaganda Agency, 1940–41," *American Historical Review* 75, no. 6 (October 1970): 1,642, 1,643.

16. Joseph W. Ryan, *Samuel Stouffer and the GI Survey: Sociologists and Soldiers during the Second World War* (Knoxville: University of Tennessee Press, 2013), x, xi. Also, discussion of I&E functions in Frederick Osborn, Address before the School for Special Services Graduation, Fifth Session, September 8, 1942; Address before 11th Session, Lexington, Va., in Addresses before Special Service Officers, 1942–1943 file, Collection 24, Frederick Osborn Papers, American Philosophical Society, Philadelphia, hereafter referred to as APS. The emphasis on print matter was particularly great because whereas in World War I, 9 percent had been high school or college educated, in World War II, it was 39 percent. Also see Frederick Osborn, "Morale Services in the Zone of the Interior," Talk to Service Command, Conference, July 28, 1944, Fort Leonard Wood, MO, and his Diary, January 5, 1944, both in Collection 24, Osborn Papers, APS. For the administration's policies on truth in propaganda, see John Morton Blum, *V Was for Victory* (New York, 1976), 20–39.

17. Joseph McBride, *Frank Capra: The Catastrophe of Success* (Tuscaloosa: University of Mississippi Press, 2011), 475, states that two of the *Why We Fight* films were shown in public theaters, those being *Prelude to War* and *Battle of Russia*. In contrast, Ellen Herman, *The Romance of American Psychology* (Berkeley: University of California Press, 1995), 70; Frank Capra, *The Name above the Title* (New York: Da Capo, 1997), 336; and James E. Combs and Sara T. Combs, *Film Propaganda and American Politics* (New York: Garland, 1994), 70, state that only one film, *Prelude to War*, was shown in theaters, Combs and Combs maintaining that Roosevelt was so "impressed" with *Prelude* that he "ordered it shown to civilian groups as well as military inductees." However, the eligibility rules of the Academy of Motion Picture Arts and Sciences require that a nominated film must be shown in a public theater for paid admission for at least one week, implying that *Battle for Russia* was publicly released. In contrast, Capra states that all the films in the *Why We Fight* series were shown in British theaters (336). On Roosevelt and propaganda, see Roosevelt, "Speech to White House Correspondents, March 1941," in *The Public Papers and Addresses*, vol. 10; Pogue, *Ordeal and Hope*, 2:118; Blum, *V Was for Victory*, 8–11; Steele, "Preparing the Public for War," 1,642, 1,643.

18. NRC, Committee on Neuropsychiatry, Minutes, November 11, 1940, Neuropsychiatry File, NAS; "Proceedings: Selective Service System Seminar," January 1 and 2, 1941, Washington, DC, pp. 5, 6, General Lewis Hershey Papers, USAMHRC, hereafter referred to as "Proceedings: Selective Service System"; *1940 Supplement to Code of Federal Regulations*, Title 32, National Defense, Selective Service System, Section 606.613, Limited Services; Correspondence, Eleanor Roosevelt, 1942, File, Smith, Harold, Box 377, E. Roosevelt 70, 1942, Franklin Delano Roosevelt Library, Hyde Park, New York, hereafter referred to as FDRL. The Selective Service Act for World War I was in part a reaction to the wrong men volunteering for the army, leaving the more skilled at home. The thought was that a Selective Service System would scientifically place the person best suited for either a civilian or military position. While this was also a concept in World War II, it did not work out. John Whiteclay Chambers II, *To Raise an Army: The Draft Comes to Modern America* (New York, 1987).

19. See Minutes, NRC Neurology Subcommittee, p. 7, January 13, 1941, NAS, for a description of the military's disinterest in treatment.

20. Maury Klein, *A Call to Arms: Mobilizing for World War II* (New York, 2013), 56; Letter sign-stamped Franklin Delano Roosevelt to Frank Hines, Veterans Affairs, VA, 1940 Folder, Official File FDR, FDRL. George C. Marshall, "Biennial Request of Chief of Staff U.S. Army to the Secretary of War," July 1, 1939 to June 30, 1941, 2–11, Folder 26–3, B-26, Senator Warren R. Austin Papers, University of Vermont, Burlington, hereafter referred to as UV.

21. Patrick Madigan, "Military Neuropsychiatry, Discipline and Morale," *Journal of Criminal Law* 32 (1941): 492.

22. Selective Service Medical Circular No. 1 (Washington, DC: US Government Printing Office, 1940), 622 file, Selective Service Records, RG 147, WNRC; revised and published as "Selective Service System, Medical Circular No. 1, Minimum Psychiatric Inspection," revised, May 1941, *Journal of American Medical Association* 116 (May 3, 1941): 2,060; War Department, Office of the Surgeon General, Washington, DC, March 12, 1941, Circular Letter No. 19, NRC, Committee on Neuropsychiatry, Revision MR 1-9, Records of St. Elizabeth's Hospital, Official Files of Superintendent Winfred Overholser, 1937–1955, RG 418, NA; also published as "Neuropsychiatric Examination of Applicants for Voluntary Enlistment and Selectees for Induction," *JAMA* 116, no. 22 (May 31, 1941): 2509–11; Edward G. Billings, "Recognition, Prevention, and Treatment of Personality Disorders in Soldiers," *Army Medical Bulletin No. 58* (October 1941), 1–37.

23. Proceedings, 100, USAMHRC; for description of Navy examination: C. L. Wittson, "The Neuropsychiatric Selection of recruits," *AJP* 99 (1943): 639–49. Memorandum, Howard Montgomery to Surgeon General Ross T. McIntire, April 8, 1943, General Correspondence, Bureau of Medicine and Surgery, P3-1/P19-1 1945, Navy Records, RG 52, NA. For World War I examination by way of comparison, see "Examinations in Nervous and Mental Diseases," August 1, 1917,

Circular No. 22, 702.3, Neuropsychiatric Examinations File, Records of the Surgeon General's Office, RG 112, WNRC.

24. For more biographical information on the Menningers, see American Psychiatric Association, "Contributions of Organized Psychiatry in World War II," *Psychiatry Online*; Henry W. Brosin MD, "A Biographical Sketch," and Bernard H. Hall MD's introduction to *A Psychiatrist for a Troubled World: Selected Papers of William C. Menninger MD*, ed. Bernard H. Hall MD (New York: Viking, 1967).

25. For the actual text of the revised Selective Service Medical Circular No. 1 and Army Circular Letter No. 19, see Appendices A and B.

26. "Neuropsychiatric Examination of Applicants for Voluntary Enlistment and Selectees for Induction."

27. "Colonel Patrick Madigan, 1887–1944," Madigan Army Center, https://www.mamc.health.mil/about/colonel.

28. War Department, Office of the Surgeon General, Washington, DC, March 12, 1941, Circular Letter No. 19, NRC, Committee on Neuropsychiatry, Revision MR 1-9, Records of St. Elizabeth's Hospital, Official Files of Superintendent Winfred Overholser, 1937–1955, RG 418, NA.

29. Edward G. Billings MD, "The Recognition, Prevention, and Treatment of Personality Disorders in Soldiers," *Army Medical Bulletin* 58 (October 1941).

30. War Department, Office of the Surgeon General, March 12, 1941, Circular Letter No. 19, NRC, Committee on Neuropsychiatry, Revision MR 1-9, Records of St. Elizabeth's Hospital, Official Files of Superintendent Winfred Overholser, 1937–1955, RG 418.

31. Madigan, "Military Neuropsychiatry, Discipline and Morale."

32. Of those on the MABs, 315 were APA members, and 149 belonged to the AMA. Sullivan, "Selective Service Psychiatry," *Psychiatry*, August 1941, Selective Service System file, Collection 24, Osborn Papers, APS.

33. Miriam Ottenberg, "How Navy's Mind Detectives Seek Men of Sound Nerve for Warfare," *Sun Star* (Washington, DC), January 10, 1943. The process, according to Memorandum, Montgomery to McIntire, April 8, 1943, continued after February 1943 because the navy was not satisfied with the cursory psychiatric examination at the induction stations and was concerned that men with more than ninety days in service would continue in service, requiring veterans' hospitalization and benefits, when they should have been detected at the training camps.

34. Terry Copp and Bill McAndrew, *Battle Exhaustion: Soldiers and Psychiatrists in the Canadian Army, 1939–1945* (Montreal: McGill University Press, 1990), 15, 27–45; Jones and Wessely, *Shell Shock to PTSD*, 84, 92, 94.

35. Copp and McAndrew, *Battle Exhaustion*, 13; Jones and Wessely, *Shell Shock to PTSD*, 139.

36. Richard J. Evans, *The Coming of the Third Reich* (New York: Penguin, 2003); Richard J. Evans, *The Third Reich in Power* (New York: Penguin, 2005); Shephard, *A War of Nerves*, 299–306. Shephard discusses how psychiatrists such

as Karl Bonhoeffer and the psychoanalyst C. G. Jung succumbed to Nazi ideology or adopted elements of that philosophy (301–2). Also, Ian Dowbiggin, *The Quest for Mental Health* (New York: Cambridge University Press, 2011), 97, 100, 103, 108, 109, 135; Paul Lerner, *Hysterical Men: War, Psychiatry, and the Politics of Trauma in Germany* (Ithaca, NY: Cornell University Press, 2009), 1:3. Michael Burleigh, *Death and Deliverance* (London: Cambridge University Press, 1994), 11, 29–34. Janice Matsumura, "State Propaganda and Mental Disorders: The Issue of Psychiatric Casualties among Japanese Soldiers during the Asia-Pacific War," *Bulletin of the History of Medicine* 78, no. 4 (Winter 2004): 806, citing Shephard, *A War of Nerves*, 299–303.

37. Paul Warnke, "Inevitably Every Man Has His Threshold: Soviet Military Psychiatry during World War II—A Comparative Approach," *Journal of Slavic Military Studies* 16 (2003): 89–92. Richard Gabriel, *The Painful Field: The Psychiatric Dimension of Modern War* (New York: Greenwood, 1988), 73, 77–79, 88, 89.

38. Matsumura, "State Propaganda and Mental Disorders."

39 Akihito Suzuki, "A Brain Hospital in Tokyo and Its Private and Public Patients, 1926–45," *History of Psychiatry*, 2003, 349. It is interesting to note that the Chinese likewise appear to have kept patients in mental hospitals in the 1930s for no longer than a couple of months, returning them to families for further care. In some cases, families sent loved ones back to hospitals several times when they could not satisfactorily care for them, but the actual stays each time were quite brief. Emily Baum, "The Psychiatric Hospital in Modern Chinese History," unpublished paper, March 17, 2021, Dewitt Wallace Institute of Psychiatry: History, Policy, and the Arts, Weill Cornell Medicine; see also Emily Baum, *The Invention of Madness: State, Society, and the Insane in Modern China* (Chicago: University of Chicago Press, 2018). The similarity in disposition may indicate a difference in the American and Japanese/Chinese attitude toward caring for the mentally disabled in the late 1930s at the beginning of World War II.

40. Matsumura, "State Propaganda and Mental Disorders," 816–18, 829.

41. Matsumura, "State Propaganda and Mental Disorders," 805, 814, 816, 819, 822, 825, 828. On pensions in general, see Eri Nakamura, "Psychiatrists as Gatekeepers of War Expenditures: Diagnosis and Distribution of Military Pensions in Japan during the Asia-Pacific War," *East Asian Science, Technology, and Society*, https://read.dukeupress.edu/easts/article-pdf.

42. Matsumura and Diane Wright, "Japanese Military Suicides during the Asia-Pacific War: Studies of the Unauthorized Self-Killings of Soldiers," *Asia-Pacific Journal* 13, issue 24, no. 3 (June 22, 2015).

3. Debating Screening's Viability

1. American Psychiatric Association Military Mobilization Questionnaire, *American Journal of Psychiatry* 97 (September 1940): 477.

2. "Southern Psychiatric Association: Report of Its Committee on Psychiatry and the National Defense," *Psychiatry*, November 1940, 619. On the shortage of psychiatrists in Virginia and the suggestion that one physician be designated for each of four Medical Advisory Boards as a psychiatrist, see Letter, Dr. Robert A. Bier, Medical Advisor to Virginia Selective Service to Lieutenant Colonel Ernest Trice, December 14, 1940, 54.5 Virginia File, RG 147, Washington National Records Center, Suitland, MD (WNRC).

3. William Menninger, "The Psychiatrist in Relation to the Examining Board," *Bulletin of the Menninger Clinic*, September 1941, 134, 137; Memorandum, Major Brainerd to Colonel Rowntree, Selective Service, October 7, 1941, 622 File, RG 147, WNRC; *Neuropsychiatry in World War II*, prep. and dir. Lt. Gen. Leonard D. Heaton, the Surgeon General, US Army, and ed. Col. Robert S. Anderson, MC, USA, Col. Albert J. Glass, MC, USA (Ret.), and Lt. Col. Robert J. Bernucci, MC, USA (Ret.) (Washington, DC: US Government Printing Office, 1966), 1:42.

4. "Selective Service Psychiatry," *Psychiatry*, August 1941, 488; Roscoe Hall, "Report on an Observation Trip," War Neuroses—Minutes and Reports File, National Research Council, Committee on Neuropsychiatry, National Academy of Sciences records, Washington, DC, hereafter referred to as NAS; Arthur Ruggles, "The Effective Use of Psychiatric and Psychological Knowledge Applicable in Selecting Men for Military Service," National Research Council (NRC) Study (July 31, 1942), 622 General File, RG 147, WNRC.

5. Eli Ginzberg, *Lost Divisions* (New York, 1959), 38.

6. On asking one question, see Ginzberg, *Lost Divisions*, 38; Allan Bérubé, *Coming Out under Fire: The History of Gay Men and Women in World War II* (Chapel Hill: University of North Carolina Press, 2012), 8. Also recollections by veteran soldiers, sailors, and WACs in the film, *Coming Out under Fire*, dir. Arthur Dong and Allan Bérubé. See also Stephen Holden, "Film Review; Gay in World War II: Abuse by the Military," *New York Times*, July 8, 1994, https://www.nytimes.com/1994/07/08/movies; "Coming Out under Fire: The Story of Gay and Lesbian Service Members [review]," National World War II Museum, June 25, 2020, https//www.nationalww2museum.org/war/articles/gay-and-lesbian-service-members. Also, Leisa Meyer, *Creating GI Jane: Sexuality and Power in the Women's Army Corps during World War II* (New York: Columbia University Press, 1998), 157. On the examination process in general, see also Menninger, "The Psychiatrist in Relation to the Examining Board," 137; "Southern Psychiatric Association: Report of Its Committee," 620.

7. Report, Dr. Samuel Hamilton, "Conference on the Neurotic Soldier," November 23–24, 1940, Committee on Military Psychiatry File, American Psychiatric Association Archives, Washington, DC, hereafter referred to as APA. "Meeting of the Special Committee Appointed to Investigate the Rejection of Mental Cases at Induction Stations," August 31, 1943, Winfred Overholser Papers, Library of Congress, hereafter referred to as LC. The committee included Winfred Overholser, Raymond Waggoner, and Edward Strecker.

312 | Notes to pages 47–50

8. Harry Stack Sullivan, "Selective Service Psychiatry," *Psychiatry* 4 (August 1941): 448–51; Proceedings, Selective Service Seminar for Medical Advisory Board and Army Induction Board Psychiatrists, January 2–3, 1941, Washington, DC, 622 S1 c.1, pp. 73, 74, Lewis Hershey Papers, US Army Military History Research Collection, Carlisle Barracks, PA, hereafter referred to as "Proceedings" and as USAMHRC.

9. Sullivan, "Selective Service Psychiatry," 448–51.

10. John Aita, "Neurological and Psychiatric Examination during Military Mobilization: Results and Suggestions Derived from a Study of 9,652 Men," *War Medicine* 1 (November 1941): 775, 776.

11. "Proceedings," 58–60, USAMHRC.

12. Douglass Orr, "Objectives to Selective Service Psychiatric Classification," *Bulletin of the Menninger Clinic* 5 (September 1941): 133. See also obituary, HistoryLink.org.

13. Eli Ginzberg, *Psychiatry and Military Manpower Policy* (New York, 1953), 11.

14. Sullivan, "Selective Service Psychiatry," 448, 451.

15. Letter, General Lewis Hershey to Rebecca Greene, March 30, 1974.

16. Sullivan, "Selective Service Psychiatry," 450, see n6.

17. "Proceedings," 15, USAMHRC. Minutes, NRC neurology subcommittee, January 13, 1941, p. 9, 040.9–10, RG 112, WNRC; Minutes, NRC neurology subcommittee, February 3, 1941, p. 2, RG 52, NA; Letter, Colonel C. C. Hillman, Medical Corps to Dr. Lewis H. Weed, Division of Medical Science, National Research Council, April 21, 1941, 040.9–10, RG 112, WNRC; Henry Stimson Diaries, XLI, p. 119, Yale University Sterling Memorial Library; hereafter referred to as YUSML.

18. Letter, Dr. Raymond Waggoner to Dr. Leonard Rowntree, Selective Service, January 27, 1941, 622, RG 147, WNRC.

19. Letter, Major US Army Field Division, William S. Iliff to Major Brainerd, April 3, 1941, 622, RG 147, WNRC.

20. "Report on Psychiatric Meeting, January 2–3, 1941," Helen F. Kerins, member of Selective Service Medical Division, Selective Service File 622, Selective Service, RG 147, WNRC.

21. "Editorial," *Psychiatry*, August 1941, 453.

22. Letter, Dr. Raymond Waggoner to Dr. Leonard Rowntree, Selective Service, Medical Division, January 27, 1941, 622, S.S., RG 147, WNRC.

23. Interview by telephone, Rebecca Greene with Dr. Raymond Waggoner, May 27, 1974.

24. Ginzberg, *Psychiatry and Military Manpower Policy*, 33.

25. US Army Medical Department, *Neuropsychiatry in World War II* (Washington, DC, 1973), 2:551.

26. The widespread employment of a uniform classification of mental illness did not occur immediately after the war, as the American Psychiatric

Association's *Diagnostic Statistical Manual (DSM)* I and II were not routinely used. Only *DSM* III in 1980 and later, IV and V, with the advent of the computer and internet, led to a global use of a routine definition of illness. Hannah Decker, *The Making of DSM-III: A Diagnostic Manual's Conquest of American Psychiatry* (New York: Oxford University Press, 2013), xvii, xviii.

27. US Army Medical Department, *Neuropsychiatry in World War II*, 1:196. Gerald F. Linderman, *The World within War* (New York: Free Press, 1997), 217.

28. William Porter, a psychiatrist at Walter Reed, complained to the NRC Subcommittee on Neurology of the Committee on Neuropsychiatry in February 1941 about the fact that Section 8a permitted registrants to see their files, thereby inhibiting juvenile courts and social agencies from providing records. Minutes, Neurology Subcommittee, February 3, 1941, p. 2, NRC Neurology File, RG 52, National Archives, Washington, DC, hereafter referred to as NA.

29. Harry Stack Sullivan, "Psychiatry and the National Defense," *Psychiatry* 4 (1941): 201–12; "Proceedings," 40, 133, 134, USAMHRC. Further complicating the determination of psychopathy was that even when records were studied, it was not certain whether heredity could be considered a factor; Kerins, File 622, Selective Service, RG 147, WNRC. On Bowman, see *New York Times*, March 4, 1973.

30. Revised Selective Service Medical Circular No. 1, May 3, 1941, 2,060; also see Karl Menninger, "Recognizing and Renaming Psychopathic Personalities," *Bulletin of the Menninger Clinic* 5 (1941): 152, 154.

31. Edward Billings, "Recognition, Prevention, and Treatment of Personality Disorders in Soldiers," *Army Medical Bulletin* 58, October 1941, 1–37; "Neuropsychiatric Examination of Applicants for Voluntary Enlistment and Selectees for Induction," Surgeon General's Office Circular Letter No. 19, 2,509.

32. See also Army Surgeon General, Circular Letter No. 176, October 20, 1943, 3, which defines psychopathic personality to include homosexuality, emotional instability, or asocial and amoral trends and states that "they are not caused by the stress of battle" and are "more likely to become psychiatric casualties than are 'normal' individuals." From G-1 file, RG 165, WNRC.

33. *Neuropsychiatry*, 1:752. William Menninger, *Psychiatry in a Troubled World* (New York, 1948), 193.

34. M. Ralph Kaufman, "The Problem of the Psychopath in the Army," *Proceedings of the 1942 Congress of the American Prison Association.* G. Kurt Piehler and Sidney Pash, eds., *The United States and the Second World War* (New York: Fordham University Press, 2010), 228, 229. Charles Glass, *The Deserters: A Hidden History of World War II* (New York, 2013). US Army Medical Department, *Neuropsychiatry in World War II*, 1:196. Linderman, *The World within War*, 217.

35. US Army Medical Department, *Neuropsychiatry in World War II*, 1:216, also states that 1,295 soldiers were admitted to psychiatric military hospitals for drug addiction; Menninger, *Psychiatry in a Troubled World*, 22, 189.

36. A. D. MacLeod, *Shell Shock Doctors: Neuropsychiatry in the Trenches, 1914–1918* (Cambridge: Cambridge Scholars, 2019), 59. Sandor Ferenczi, ed.,

Psychoanalysis and the War Neuroses (New York: International Psychoanalytic Press, 1921).

37. Minutes, NRC Committee on Neuropsychiatry, Subcommittee on Neurology, February 3, 1941, p. 3, NRC Neurology File, RG 52, NA; Letter, McIntire to Charles H. Voelker, Director of the Speech Clinic, Oklahoma Agriculture and Mechanics College, December 31, 1941, P8-2/1 16-1 (123) Folder, Med: Committee on Neuropsychiatry General File, NAS.

38. Douglass Thom, "Schizoid and Related Personalities," *War Medicine* 1 (1941): 412, 415.

39. Dexter Bullard, "Selective Service Psychiatry: Schizoid and Related Personalities," *Psychiatry* 4, no. 2 (1941): 231.

40. War Department, Mobilization Regulations, No. 1-9, Standards of Physical Examination during Mobilization, August 31, 1940, Section XXI, "Notes on Malingering," Appendix B, US Army Medical Department, *Neuropsychiatry in World War II*, 1:780–82.

41. "Proceedings," 150, USAMHRC. "Guide to the Papers of S. Spafford Ackerly," Center for Brooklyn History, Brooklyn Public Library, http://dlib.nyu.edu/findingaids/htlml/bhs/arms. I am indebted to Cecily Dyer for scanning forty pages of documents regarding Dr. Ackerly's activities in World War I, the 1930s, and 1940s during a time when the center was totally closed to scholars due to coronavirus.

42. William Menninger and Edward D. Greenwood, "The Psychiatrist in Relation to the Examining Board," *Bulletin of the Menninger Clinic* 5 (September 1941): 135; Minutes, NRC Committee on Neuropsychiatry, Subcommittee on Psychiatry, May 5, 1941, 3, NRC Subcommittee Psychiatry File, RG 52, NA.

43. An indication of the medicalization of other categories that used to be considered subject to punishment was the letters Eleanor Roosevelt received. As early as 1939, when Eleanor Roosevelt wrote to Surgeon General Thomas Parran about employing a doctor with the Public Health Service who had been an alcoholic and drug addict, Parran responded by saying the doctor should probably be treated for psychoneurosis. A few years later, Dr. E. H. Sutton sent Mrs. Roosevelt his proposal for treating bedwetters and then accepting them in service instead of rejecting them on psychiatric grounds, but the surgeon general denied it. About the same time, a mother wrote to Mrs. Roosevelt about a son in service who had gone AWOL and was in a "wrecked nervous condition and not right mentally." She requested he be returned to her care instead of being imprisoned or hospitalized. Letter, Mrs. P to Mrs. Roosevelt, May 10, 1942, and Secretary to Mrs. Roosevelt to Mrs. P, May 13, 1942; Pa-Ph File, Eleanor Roosevelt White House Papers, 70; Letter, Parran to Mrs. Roosevelt, November 7, 1939; Letters, James Anderson, Colonel, Medical Corps, Office of the Surgeon General to Dr. E. H. Sutton, Clarksburg, WV, September 12, 1942; Sutton to Mrs. Roosevelt, September 14, 1942, and Secretary to Mrs. Roosevelt to Sutton, September 19, 1942, all in Sti-Sz 1942 File, E. Roosevelt White House, 70, FDRL.

44. US Army Medical Department, *Neuropsychiatry in World War II*, 1:239.

45. Minutes, Subcommittee on Psychiatry, April 30, 1941, 2, 040.9–10 File, RG 112, WNRC; the psychiatrist Nolan D. C. Lewis would later be a consultant to Dr. Eli Ginzberg's Conservation of Human Resources project, Columbia University, during the time it was working on the three-volume study *The Ineffective Soldier*, which came out in 1959.

46. Selective Service Medical Circular No. 1, November 1940, 622, File, RG 147, WNRC.

47. Sullivan, "Selective Service Psychiatry," 453.

48. "Proceedings," January 2–3, 1941, 53–55, USAMHRC; Letter, Dr. Paul de River to Stephen P. Early, October 25, 1941, 250.1, File, RG 112, WNRC.

49. Letter, Temple Fay, Temple University Medical School, to William Lewis, Director of Pennsylvania Selective Service, January 7, 1941; Letter, Lewis to Hershey, February 4, 1941; Letter, Hershey to Lewis, February 11, 1941; Letter, Sullivan to Honorable Edward A. Tamm, Assistant Director of the FBI, February 18, 1941; Letter, J. Edgar Hoover to Clarence Dykstra, March 6, 1941; all in 622 Pa. 1941 File, RG 147, WNRC.

50. Letter, Raymond Waggoner to Selective Service Medical Director Leonard Rowntree, January 27, l941, 622, S.S., RG 147, WNRC.

51. "Proceedings," 55–58, USAMHRC; Roscoe Hall, "Peculiar Personalities: Disorders of Mood, Psychopathic Personality," *War Medicine* 1 (1941): 386.

52. William H. Dunn, "The Psychopath in the Armed Forces," *Psychiatry* 4 (May 1941): 251–59.

53. E. L. Dravo, "The Problem of the Psychopath in Recruit Training of the U.S. Navy," *Journal of the Indiana Medical Association* 33 (September 1940): 451.

54. "Proceedings," 59, 60, USAMHRC; Roscoe Hall, "Report of Observation Trip to Canada, April 7th to 18th, 1941," War Neuroses—Minutes and Reports File, NRC Committee on Neuropsychiatry, NAS.

55. Circular No. 22, August 1, 1917, *Examinations in Nervous and Mental Disease*, War Department, Office of the Surgeon General, August 1, 1917, in Pearce Bailey, Frankwood Williams, and Paul O. Komora, *Neuropsychiatry in the United States*; Thomas Salmon and Norman Fenton, *Neuropsychiatry in the American Expeditionary Forces*, vol. 10 of the US Army Medical Department, *The Medical Department of the U.S. Army in the World War* (Washington, DC, 1929), 66–71. Also in 702.3, Neuropsychiatric Examinations File, Records of the Surgeon General's Office, RG 112, WNRC. From September 1917 to November 1918, out of 1,787 neuropsychiatric rejections at Camp Devens, MA, only four were sexual psychopaths. At Camp Upton, NY, out of 1,050 recruits rejected on neuropsychiatric grounds during four months, 50 were rejected for constitutional psychopathy, sex perversion being one of three subcategories. An Army Adjutant General report revealed that in April 1918 only one person was excluded for sexual psychopathy out of those rejected for psychological reasons in Ohio. Bailey, *Neuropsychiatry*, 76–82; Margot Canaday, *The Straight State* (Princeton,

NJ: Princeton University Press, 2009), 65, citing Adjutant General to Surgeon General, April 16, 1918, file no. 702, box 1090, central decimal files 1917–1972, AGO, RG 407.

56. "Military Sodomy Laws," *Human Rights Watch*, http://hrw.org/reports/2000.

57. Bérubé, *Coming Out under Fire*, 129.

58. Between the two world wars, American military psychiatrists began to question whether discipline or treatment within military service should be used to eradicate homosexuality. Concerned that "sodomists" in barracks or in military prisons might disturb fellow servicemen, they considered using psychiatry to treat or discharge servicemen instead. Reflecting prevailing psychoanalytic theory, the Navy Bureau of Medicine in 1924 attributed homosexuality to stalled psychological development. It urged the department to hire psychiatrists to examine sailors charged with sodomy before the navy brought them to trial. But navy administrators declined, alleging insufficient resources. The army, on the other hand, employed psychiatrists to testify at court-martial but not in other capacities. For a discussion of psychoanalytic theories concerning homosexuality, see Kenneth Lewes, *The Psychoanalytic Theory of Male Homosexuality* (New York: Simon and Schuster, 1988); Lillian Faderman, *Odd Girls and Twilight Lovers: A History of Lesbian Life in Twentieth-Century America* (New York: Columbia University Press, 2011). Faderman refers to an excellent discussion by A. A. Brill, a student of Freud's in "The Psychiatric Approach to the Problem of Homosexuality," *Lancet* 55.

59. On the history of sodomy laws in the United States, see William N. Eskridge Jr., *Dishonorable Passions: Sodomy Laws in America, 1861–2003* (New York: Viking, 2008). On the domestic side, between the world wars the press waged a campaign against purported rampant homosexual activity in male social organizations. In response, the navy launched widespread investigations to find out who had enticed its men, including a very controversial investigation of the YMCA of Newport, RI, in 1919, at a time when Franklin Roosevelt was assistant navy secretary and Josephus Daniels secretary. Resulting in congressional hearings, it involved the navy ordering an "entrapment operation in which enlisted men allowed civilians to perform sexual acts on them." This resulted in a number of civilians being imprisoned and tried and in the ministers of Newport retaliating by charging that the navy "had made its men 'perverts by official order'" and "fostered indignities on the citizens of Newport." See Margot Canaday, *The Straight State*, esp. 72. For other military attempts to control homosexual activities in the service between the wars, including psychiatric examinations, see 65, 68–71, 77, 85–87. The Newport investigation occurred the same year as the Palmer Raids, when intolerance against many groups was quite prevalent. Similar intolerance of gays occurred in the late 1940s and 1950. For more on Roosevelt's involvement in the Newport investigation, see Bérubé, *Coming Out under Fire*, 134.

60. *Neuropsychiatry in World War II*, 1:236–39; Menninger, *Psychiatry in a Troubled World*, 228–35.

61. Meyer, *Creating GI Jane*, 9, 160–75.

62. Helen Swick Perry, *Psychiatrist of America: The Life of Harry Stack Sullivan* (Cambridge, MA: Harvard University Press, 1990). See also discussion by Naoko Wake, "The Military, Psychiatry, and 'Unfit' Soldiers, 1939–1942," *Journal of the History of Medicine and Allied Sciences* 62, no. 4 (2007): 463, 475–77.

63. Harry Stack Sullivan, *Personal Psychopathology: Early Formulations* (New York, 1972), 171, 169–70. Wake, "The Military, Psychiatry, and Unfit Soldiers," 475.

64. "Proceedings," January 2–3, 1941, 131, 132, 150, USAMHRC. Decker, *The Making of DSM III*.

65. "Proceedings," January 2–3, 1941, 131, 132, USAMHRC.

66. Considerable discussion has occurred over Sullivan as a doctor and his homosexuality. See, e.g., Naoko Wake, *Private Practices: Harry Stack Sullivan, the Science of Homosexuality, and American Liberalism* (New Brunswick, NJ: Rutgers University Press, 2011); and Wake, "The Military, Psychiatry and Unfit Soldiers."

67. Wake, "The Military, Psychiatry, and Unfit Soldiers," 474–84. Included here is the author's contention that Sullivan's failure to oppose discrimination based on homosexuality in selection was partly out of a fear of disclosure of his own sexual preference.

68. Wake, *Private Practices*, 168.

69. "Neuropsychiatric Examination of Applicants for Voluntary Enlistment and Selection for Induction," *Journal of the American Medical Association* 116, no. 22 (May 1941): 2,509; "Minimum Psychiatric Inspection," Medical Circular No. 1 REVISED, *Journal of the American Medical Association* 116, no. 19 (May 1941): 2,061. For the complete examinations, see Appendices A and B, at the end of this book.

70. Wake, *Private Practices*, 166, 168, 170.

71. Minutes, NRC Committee on Neuropsychiatry, Subcommittee on War Neuroses, April 24, 1941, 16, NRC Psychiatry File, RG 52, NA.

72. M. Ralph Kaufman, "The Problem of the Psychopath in the Army," f. 1–20, M. Ralph Kaufman Papers, 1928–1971, Boston Psychoanalytic Society and Institute.

73. Interview with Lionel Greer by G. Kurt Piehler, New York City for Veteran's Oral History Project, Center for the Study of War and Society, Department of History, University of Tennessee, Knoxville, November 13, 2003, 52, http://csws.utk.edu/wp-content/uploads/2013/04/2003-Greer-Lionel-Transcript.pdf.

74. Joseph Cotton, "Nerves and the Military, Either Hurts the Other," speech before Public Health Section, Commonwealth Club, San Francisco, 1942.

75. Letter, Dr. Paul de River to Honorable Stephen P. Early, Secretary to President Roosevelt, October 25, 1941, 250.1, File, RG 112, WNRC. De River published *The Sexual Criminal* (Illinois, 1950) and later *Crime and the Sexual*

Psychopath (Illinois, 1958). Letter, Madigan to de River, November 17, 1941, 250.1-1 File, RG 112, WNRC. Also see reports of admissions from the Civilian Conservation Corps to the Boston Psychopathic Hospital of individuals who were allegedly made emotionally distraught in the camps by homosexual practices or advances. These may have also persuaded the military to reject homosexuals in World War II. John B. Dynes, "Mental Disorders in the CCC Camps," *Mental Hygiene* 23 (July 1939): 365.

76. Minutes, NRC War Neuroses subcommittee, March 27, 1941, 5, 7, 8, NRC War Neuroses Subcommittee file, RG 52, NA.

77. Memorandum for General Allen W. Gullion, Maj. Gen. the JAG from Ernest H. Burt, Lt. Col., JAGD, Chief, Military Justice Section, May 14, 1941; Memorandum from Gullion to the AG, May 14, 1941; Memorandum from Maj. Gen. the AG to the Commanding Generals, Subject: Sodomists, July 15, 1941, all in 250.1-1, RG 112, NA. Bérubé, *Coming Out under Fire*, 128–32.

78. Minutes, NRC Committee on Neuropsychiatry, Subcommittee on War Neuroses, March 27, 1941, 5, 7, 8, NRC Subcommittee on Neuroses File, RG 52, NA; Memorandum, NRC Committee on Neuropsychiatry to Chief of the Bureau of Medicine and Surgery, Navy, through Chairman of the Division of Medical Sciences, NRC, Re: Thomas D., apprentice seaman, US Navy general court-martial prisoner, January 13, 1942, Homosexuality 1942 File, Overholser Papers, RG 418, NA. Bérubé, *Coming Out under Fire*, 133.

79. Letter, Winfred Overholser, Chair, Committee on Neuropsychiatry, and John C. Whitehorn, Secretary, Committee on Neuropsychiatry, to Capt. Forrest M. Harrison, Bureau of Medicine and Surgery, November 3, 1942, National Research Council, Committee on Neuropsychiatry, NAS.

80. For a survey of the policy changes, see especially Bérubé, *Coming Out under Fire*, 128–43, including mention that Roosevelt himself commuted the sentence of a navy officer convicted of sodomy in August 1942 only a few days after McIntire indicated his approval to Overholser of his position (134). This, however, did not lead to a formal change of AG policy. Letter, J. E. Moore, Chairman, Subcommittee on Venereal Diseases, National Research Council, to Dr. Winfred Overholser, Chairman, Committee on Neuropsychiatry, December 23, 1942, and Letter, Overholser to Dr. J. E. Moore, Baltimore, MD, December 26, 1942, both in National Research Council, Committee on Neuropsychiatry, Homosexuality File, Winfred Overholser Papers, St. Elizabeth's Hospital Records, RG 418, NA.

81. Bérubé, *Coming Out under Fire*, 147.

82. *Coming Out under Fire*, dir. Arthur Dong.

83. Wake, *Private Practices*, 174; Bérubé, *Coming Out under Fire*, 52, 180, 186. See also Rhonda Evans, *US Military Policies Concerning Homosexuality: Development, Implementation, and Outcomes* (University of California, Santa Barbara: Center for the Study of Sexual Minorities in the Military), 19, 20.

84. Studs Terkel, *The Good War* (New York, 1984), 180, 182.

85. See "Ask and Tell: Gay Veterans, Identity, and Oral History on a Civil Rights Frontier," *Oral History Review* 32, no. 2 (2005): 31. On increasing discharges of homosexuals from 1947 through 1950, see Bérubé, *Coming Out under Fire*, 261, 262. However, on the positive side, also see the recollection of Paul Jordan, whose service in the army spanned from the early 1930s through the end of the war in Europe. Jordan recalled no prejudice in the military, attributing it to his being as masculine as anyone else, just "one of the boys." Also, Bill Taylor, an aircraft gunner in World War II from Bowling Green, TN, did not remember any intolerance either. Steve Estes, *Ask and Tell: Gay and Lesbian Veterans Speak Out* (Chapel Hill: University of North Carolina Press, 2007), 5–28.

86. Herbert Spiegel, "Psychiatry with an Infantry Battalion," undated, US Army Medical Division Historical Unit, Fort Detrick, MD. Interview, Rebecca Greene with Dr. Spiegel, December 18, 1975, New York City; Clements Fry and Edna Rostow, "Some Observations on Homosexuals in Military Service," unpublished paper, April 1, 1945, 62–66, Committee on Medical Research of OSRD, Neuropsychiatry Reports File, NAS. Herbert Greenspan and John D. Campbell, *American Journal of Psychiatry* 101 (March 1945): 685; Lewis Loeser, "The Sexual Psychopath in the Military," *American Journal of Psychiatry* 102 (July 1945): 92–101, cited in Josephine Callisen Bresnahan, "Dangers in Paradise: The Battle against Combat Fatigue in the Pacific War," PhD diss., Harvard University, 1999, 158.

87. Bérubé, *Coming Out under Fire*, 256 and foreword; John D'Emilio, *Sexual Politics, Sexual Communities* (Chicago: University of Chicago Press, 1983).

88. Bérubé, *Coming Out under Fire*, 147.

89. US Army Medical Department, *Neuropsychiatry*, 1:237, 487; Menninger, *Psychiatry in a Troubled World*, 225, 227. On the navy, Bérubé, *Coming Out under Fire*, 147. Regarding discharges from the army, they are based on the number of men admitted to hospitals with the diagnosis "pathological sexuality," primarily "homosexuality" (*Neuropsychiatry*, 1:237), with an assumption by William Menninger that less than one thousand might have been able to be salvaged for further duty. However, this figure may be high, as War Department, *Technical Manual: Outline of Neuropsychiatry in Aviation Medicine*, No. 8-325 (Washington, DC, December 12, 1940), 34–36, includes, among others, fetishism, masturbation, bestiality, necrophilia, plus "sexual inversion," which refers to homosexuality, as forms of "sexual psychopathies."

90. Menninger, *Psychiatry in a Troubled World*, 227.

91. The number of rejections cited by Bérubé, *Coming Out under Fire*, 33, 297n72, is based on his referral to Memorandum, Statistics on Army Homosexuals Furnished by the Surgeon General's Office, June 22, 1950, and on a Memorandum for the Record, Subject: Information on Homosexuals, June 23, 1950, by Arthur J. McDowell, Assistant Chief, Medical Statistics Division, Army Surgeon General, which Bérubé says is from Record Group 407, either from NA or WNRC. However, the Army Surgeon General usually had statistics

on discharges, not rejections. Statistics on rejections would more likely have come from Selective Service.

92. An indication that in the navy, administrative discharges were used on women suspected of homosexuality, is found in Summary of Letter from Estelle R. Stevens, Referred to Admiral McIntire, June 20, 1944, Box 1789, Papers of Eleanor Roosevelt, FDRL. One ensign in the Navy Women's Reserve had been discharged for "Maladjustment and Temperamentally Unsuited for Naval Service. Real Charge sexual abnormality." For more on psychiatry policy toward WACs in World War II, including treatment of suspected lesbians, see Chapter 8.

93. Selective Service Medical Circular No. 1, 622, RG 147, WNRC; Memo, Dr. Richard Eanes to General Lewis Hershey, November 10, 1942, "Conference on Psychiatry conducted by Dr. Emilio Mira," p. 1, 622 General, RG 147, WNRC.

94. Ginzberg, *Psychiatry and Military Manpower Policy*, 14.

95. Letter to Rebecca Greene from General Hershey, March 30, 1974.

96. Letter, R. W. Moyer, Clerk, Local Board No. 1, Oklahoma City to Fred Shaw, Delivery and Induction, Selective Service, Oklahoma City, March 27, 1941.

97. Letter, Lieutenant Colonel F. H. Hollingsworth, District Recruiting Office, to Fort Sam Houston, May 21, 1941; Letter, Dr. Harry L. Deutsch to Selective Service Oklahoma State headquarters, April 3, 1941, Letter, Stanley Koch, Acting Assistant Adjutant General, Fort Sam Houston to AGO, October 1941; all these letters are in 622 Okl. 1941, RG 147, WNRC. Before becoming Roosevelt's secretary of war, Stimson had been secretary of war under William Howard Taft and secretary of state under Herbert Hoover. Godfrey Hodgson, *The Colonel: The Life and Wars of Henry Stimson, 1867–1950* (New York: Knopf, 1990).

98. US House of Representatives, Committee on Interstate and Foreign Commerce, Hearings on HR 2550, to . . . Establish a National Neuropsychiatric Institute, 79th Cong., 1st Sess., 1945, Appendix, 117; here, Selective Service figures for November 1940–September 1941 show 23.7 per 1,000 of all registrants, all races, rejected for mental disease. I have assumed about the same rate were rejected at army induction boards.

99. *Statistical Abstract* (Washington, DC, 1960), 30, 32. Page 30 shows that 63,357 persons in Oklahoma in 1940 were from "other races," that is, not white or Black.

100. Letter, Dr. Deutsch to Selective Service Oklahoma State headquarters, April 3, 1941, 622 Okl. 1941, RG 147, WNRC.

101. Letter, General Hershey to Secretary of War Stimson, May 5, 1941; Letter, Secretary Stimson to General Hershey, May 13, 1941; Letter, Lieutenant Colonel Carlton S. Dargusch, JAG, to Director of Oklahoma Selective Service Murray, April 24, 1941; Letter, AGO to Commanding General 8th Corps Area, Fort Sam Houston, Texas, May 19, 1941; all in 622 Okl. 1941, RG 147, WNRC.

102. Letter, Colonel Louis H. Ritzhaupt to "Dear Dr.," July 21, 1941, 622 Okl. 1941, RG 147, WNRC; Letter, Colonel Hollingsworth to District Recruiting Officer, Fort Sam Houston, Texas, May 21, 1941, 622 Okl. 1941, RG 147, WNRC.

103. Letter, Dr. Sullivan to Colonel Eanes, April 14, 1941, 622 Okl. 1941, RG 147, WNRC; Letter, Dr. Sullivan to Colonel Brainerd, March 26, 1941, 622 General, RG 147, WNRC.

104. Memorandum, F. H. Hollingsworth, Lt. Col., Field Artillery, District Recruiting Officer to Commanding Gen., Eighth Corps Area, Fort Sam Houston, Texas, May 31, 1941, 622 Okl. 1941, RG 147, WNRC.

105. "Examinations of Indians under the Selective Service Act," US Public Health Service Report No. 1, January 2, 1942, USAMHRC.

106. Alison Bernstein, *American Indians and World War II* (Norman: University of Oklahoma Press, 1999); *Statistical Abstract* (Washington, DC, 1960), 32.

107. Martin Gilbert, *The Second World War* (New York, 1991), 110–80; James McGregor Burns, *Roosevelt: The Soldier of Freedom (1940–1945)* (New York: Harcourt Brace Jovanovich, 2012), 9–15, 140–65; Craig L. Symonds, *Neptune* (New York: Oxford University Press, 2014), 18.

108. By October 1941, half (50 percent) of the 2,000,000 called-for inducted were rejected on medical grounds. *New York Times*, October 4, 1941, 8:4; *New York Times*, October 11, 1941, 1:4, "Forty Per Cent Rejected in Tests," *New York Times*, April 6, 1941.

109. George Flynn, *Lewis B. Hershey: Mr. Selective Service* (Chapel Hill: University of North Carolina, 1985), 42.

110. Lewis B. Hershey, "The Health of Registrants as Revealed by Selective Service and Inferences Therefrom," before College of Physicians, Phil., 102 (Conferences), RG 147, WNRC; *Complete Presidential Press Conferences of Franklin Delano Roosevelt* (New York, 1972), 17:774. On Roosevelt's concern about the state of American youth health reflected in high medical rejections, see *Complete Presidential Press Conferences of Franklin Delano Roosevelt* (November 7, 1941), 241, 242. La Guardia also supported Hershey's rehabilitation plan. *New York Times*, May 13, 1941, 7:4; also, Letter, Hershey to Stimson, May 27, 1941, USAMHRC. And about concern among policy makers and in the press about the state of youth health as reflected in Selective Service rejections, see discussion by Charles P. Taft, Assist. Coordinator of Health, Welfare and Related Defense Activities (Federal Security Administration) and Gov. Robert Blood (NH), who was also a physician. *New York Times*, April 21, 1941, 3:8; *New York Times*, July 2, 1941, 13:1; *New York Times*, October 4, 1941, 8:4; *New York Times*, October 11, 1941, 1:4; "Forty Per Cent Rejected in Tests," *New York Times*, April 6, 1941. The American College of Physicians' President Roger I. Lee favored programs to reduce the numbers rejected, as did the Commission on Physical Rehabilitation, *Journal of the American Medical Association*, November 1941, 1540.

111. *Psychiatry*, August 1941, 454.

112. Diary, Henry Stimson, 35:153, 154, Stimson Papers, YUSML; Doris Kearns Goodwin, *No Ordinary Time* (New York, 1994), 10; interview, Rebecca Greene with Frederick Osborn, Garrison, NY, April 4, 1980.

113. Letter, Osborn to Overholser, October 10, 1941, Selective Service System Folder, Overholser Papers, RG 418, NA.

114. Col. Leonard Rowntree, "Groups of Diseases Unfavorable for Rehabilitation for the Army," December 1, 1941, speech at a Meeting of the Organized Medical and Dental Professions of Greater New York, Hershey Papers, 336.1, USAMHRC. Here he announced that no attempt would be made to rehabilitate psychiatric 4Fs.

115. Letter, Overholser to Sullivan, April 10,1941; Letter, Overholser to Osborn, September 25, 1941; Letter, Overholser to Osborn, October 8, 1941; Letter, Osborn to Overholser, October 10, l941; all in Selective Service System Folder, Overholser Papers, RG 418, NA.

116. "Aspects of Morale," *American Journal of Sociology*, November 1941, 293, 294; *Complete Presidential Press Conferences of Franklin Delano Roosevelt* (New York, 1972), vol. 17; Minutes, NRC Psychiatry Subcommittee, September 30, 1941, 040.0-10 File, RG 112, WNRC; "The Future of Medicine in Selective Service," undated, Hershey Papers, 636.1-12 p V. f, USAMHRC; *Psychiatry*, August 1941, 448; editorial, *Psychiatry*, February 1942, 105; Menninger, *Psychiatry in a Troubled World*, 282. For some, however, Roosevelt's one-minute examination appeared insufficient. McIntire believed that reducing the effectiveness of the preinduction psychiatric examination might lead to more psychiatric discharges, with high rates of hospitalized veterans and pensioners. Letters, Overholser to McIntire, November 2, 1941; McIntire to Overholser, November 10, 1941, Overholser Papers, St. Elizabeth Hospital Records, RG 418, NA.

117. Letter, Gen. Lewis Hershey to Secretary of War Henry Stimson, May 27, 1941, USAMHRC; Letter, Stimson to Hershey, July 9, 1941, USAMHRC; Letter, Frederick Osborn to Hershey, July 15, 1941, USAMHRC. In November 1941, Selective Service psychiatrists heard Dr. R. D. Gillespie, a British psychiatrist, discuss the Pioneer Corps as a "very successful group and these men are very happy in their jobs." "Report on Dr. Gillespie," November 24, 1941, 622 (1941), RG 147, WNRC. Menninger, *Psychiatry in a Troubled World*, 208.

118. *Federal Register* 6 (August 23, 1941): 4,319.

119. *Time*, August 18, 1941.

120. Forrest Pogue, *Ordeal and Hope* (New York, 1973), 148–53. Undersecretary of War Robert Patterson relayed his fears about soldier morale to Stimson; see Memorandum, Under Secretary of War Patterson to Stimson, August 14, 1941, Letters, Volume I, Patterson Papers, LC; Memorandum for General Haislip from Marshall, August 18, 1941, Marshall Papers, George C. Marshall Library, Lexington, VA, hereafter referred to as GCMRL. On Roosevelt's action, *New York Times*, August 20, 1941, 1:8.

121. Osborn replaced James A. Ulio, who became the army adjutant general. Letter, Osborn to Sen. William Jenner, Subcommittee Senate on Internal Security, August 10, 1954, US Army—I & E Division folder, Frederick Osborn Papers 24, American Philosophical Society, Philadelphia, hereafter referred to as APS.

122. *Life*, August 18, 1941; *Time*, August 18, 1941; Anonymous, "An Army Fit to Fight?" October 1941, scheduled to be published in *Readers Digest*; Hilton Howell Railey, "Morale of the U.S. Army: An Appraisal," intended to be published in the *New York Times*, October 1941, 7, 16, 353.8 File, Serials of Army Adjutant General's Office, RG 407, NA. Railey visited Fort Meade, MD; Camp Lee, VA; Fort Bragg, NC; Camp Croft, SC; Camp Stewart, GA; the Presidio, San Francisco; Fort Lewis, Olympia, WA; and wide areas of the Second Army in Arkansas and the Third Army in Louisiana.

123. Railey, "Morale of the U.S. Army," 65.

124. Linderman, *The World within War*, 186, 187.

125. Railey, "Morale of the U.S. Army," 16.

126. Memorandum, Lieutenant General Lesley McNair to General George C. Marshall, October 14, 1941, 353.8 File, RG 407, NA.

127. Railey, "Morale of the U.S. Army," 5, 6, 99, 100; *Life*, August 18, 1941, 17; Interviewed by *Life*, McNair acknowledged that the "principal weakness" with the training maneuvers for the 350,000 soldiers in Louisiana in September 1941 was "a deficiency in small unit training due fundamentally to inadequate leadership." For concerns of Marshall about report, see *Ordeal and Hope*, 82. Even before Marshall heard of the Railey report, the War Department's concern about morale led it to announce it would send home all men over twenty-eight after a year of service as well as hardship cases. After the report came out, Patterson and McNair suggested to Marshall an officer training school for enlistees and better methods of officer selection. Insufficient outmoded equipment was a particular problem. *Life*, October 6, 1941, 33, reported that most men in the 27th Division "never shot a trench mortar and get to shoot a Springfield rifle rarely." This depressed the men. Simulating, according to Railey, made the men feel that they were wasting time. Memorandum, McNair to Marshall, October 14, 1941, 353.8 File, RG 407, NA. Paul L. Savage and Richard A. Gabriel, "Cohesion and Disintegration in the American Army," *Armed Forces and Society*, Spring 1976, 345. Another report by an anonymous writer in the National Guard that was scheduled for *Reader's Digest* entitled "An Army Fit to Fight?" (October 1941) was refused publication by Surles and Osborn after they advised Undersecretary of War Robert Patterson that the article "raises questions in the soldiers' minds which would otherwise not be there." Letters, Patterson to the Secretary of War, September 27, 1941; Patterson to McCloy, September 27, 1941; Osborn to Patterson, September 25, 1941; Patterson to Osborn, September 22, 1941; "An Army Fit to Fight?" all in Selective Service Act, 1941, Patterson Papers, LC.

128. NRC Committee on Neuropsychiatry, Subcommittee on War Neuroses, September 12, 1941, Minutes, US Navy Records, RG 52, NA. Lewis P. Rowland, *The Legacy of Tracy J. Putnam and H. Houston Merritt* (New York: Oxford University Press, 2009), 62–72.

129. NRC Committee on Neuropsychiatry, Subcommittee on War Neuroses, September 12, 1941. Overholser and William Porter of Walter Reed Hospital

were also involved in the exchange about the role of Osborn and civilian and military morale. On August 19, 1941, the Subcommittee on Neurology read a letter from Dr. Edith Klemperer suggesting a Fear Institute "to investigate persons in important positions who might panic in an emergency." NRC Division of Medical Sciences, Subcommittee on Neurology, Minutes, 040.9–10 File, RG 112, WNRC. There were also other offices dealing with morale during the war, including Elmer Davis's Office of War Information (OWI), the Office of Censorship, the Office of Civilian Defense (under La Guardia and Mrs. Roosevelt), and the Committee for National Morale, headed by Arthur Upham Pope and including Karl Menninger, Erik Erikson, Erich Fromm, Edward Strecker, Yerkes, the child psychiatrist David Levy, and Foster Kennedy. The September 12 meeting mentioned earlier noted that little was being done by the Pope Committee because of a lack of funds. However, the committee did study German psychological warfare, and Erikson analyzed Hitler's speeches. Ellen Herman, *The Romance of American Psychology* (Berkeley, CA, 1995), 44, 48.

130. Samuel Stouffer, *The American Soldier: Combat and Its Aftermath* (Princeton, NJ: Princeton University Press, 1949), 11, 12. Memoranda from Marshall to FDR, September 6, 1941, File 30; November 30, 1942, File 38, Box 80, George C. Marshall Research Library, Lexington, VA; "Attitudes of Troops towards War," Drawer 920, GCMRL. See also Herman, *The Romance of American Psychology*, 69, 70. Altogether during the war, Stouffer's group gave out at least 200 questionnaires to half a million soldiers in over 10,000 classroom sessions.

131. Letter, Hershey to Osborn, July 21, 1941, Hershey Papers, USAMHRC.

132. Letter, Sullivan to Stimson, November 4, 1941, copy of which was sent to Osborn, Selective Service System File, Collection 24, Osborn Papers, APS.

133. Letter, Sullivan to Hershey, November 9, 1941, Selective Service System file, Collection 24. For Sullivan's concerns, see also Harry Stack Sullivan, "A Year of Selective Service Psychiatry," *Mental Hygiene* 26, no. 3 (January 1942): 7–15, esp. 13–14.

134. Osborn also had his reservations about Sullivan's personality, criticizing the "sarcastic" tone in his "A Year of Selective Service Psychiatry" article. Letter, Osborn to Sullivan, October 14, 1941, Selective Service System folder, Manuscript Collection No. 24, Osborn Papers, APS. On other views as to what occurred: William Alanson White Psychiatric Foundation (WAWPF), Report of Executive Director, February 14, 1942, 2, WAWPF; Letter, Waggoner to Rowntree, January 27, 1941, 622 File, RG 147, WNRC; interview (Taped Telephone), Rebecca Greene with Dr. Waggoner, May 27, 1974, in which Waggoner states that Sullivan was an isolated man. Interview, Rebecca Greene with Crowley, October 31, 1974, New York City. Letter, Gen. Hershey to Rebecca Greene, April 19, 1974. *American Journal of Psychiatry* 99 (September 1942): 295. Ralph Crowley, *William Alanson White Psychoanalytic Foundation Newsletter*, Winter 1971, 2; interview, Rebecca Greene with Dorothy Blitsten, New York City, November 21, 1974; Leonard Rowntree, "Selective Service and Psychiatry," *Danville State Hospital Mental*

Health Bulletin 20 (October 8, 1942): 3. Oral History, McKinzie with Osborn, Garrison, NY, 1974, Truman Library, https://www.trumanlibrary.gov/library/oral-histories/osbornf.

135. Sullivan, "A Year of Selective Service Psychiatry," 12.

136. Interview, Rebecca Greene with Dorothy Blitsten, November 21, 1974, New York City.

4. Psychiatric Policy Making in the Throes of War

1. Albert A. Rosner, "Neuropsychiatric Casualties from Guadalcanal: I. Persistent Symptoms in These Cases," *American Journal of the Medical Sciences* 207 (June 1944): 770–76, esp. 770. In Tunisia at that time, only 3 percent of the psychiatric casualties were returned to combat duty. *Neuropsychiatry in World War II*, prep. and dir. Lt. Gen. Leonard D. Heaton, The Surgeon General, US Army, and ed. Col. Robert S. Anderson, MC, USA, and eds. for Neuropsychiatry Col. Albert J. Glass, MC, USA (Ret.), Lt. Col. Robert J. Bernucci, MC, USA (Ret.) (Washington, DC: US Government Printing Office, 1966) 1:8. On 35 percent, see also Hans Pols, "The Tunisian Campaign, War Neuroses, and the Reorientation of American Psychiatry during World War II," *Harvard Review of Psychiatry* 105, no. 1 (2011): 314. On the figure of 20 to 34 percent of all patients being neuropsychiatric during the North African campaign, see also Nathan G. Hale, *The Rise and Crisis of Psychoanalysis in the United States: Freud and the Americans, 1917–1985* (Oxford, 1995), 189.

2. William Manchester, *Goodbye Darkness: A Memoir of the Pacific War* (New York, 1979), 39–41.

3. Martin Gilbert, *The Second World War* (New York, 1989), 275, 278.

4. Interview of Thomas Calderone by Shaun Illingworth, Sarah Rose, and Erik Coccia at Browns Mills, New Jersey, pp. 14–22, https://oral history.rutgers.edu/interviewees/30-interview-html-text/668-calderone-thomas-g.

5. Interview by telephone of Everett D. Reamer, Arizona, Corporal-US Army, Battery F, Corregidor, Japanese POW, by Richard Misenhimer, November 5, 2002, National Museum of the Pacific War (Admiral Nimitz Museum), https://digitalarchive.pacificwarmuseum.org/digital/collection/p16769coll/search.

6. Ozatwar.com.

7. Gilbert, *The Second World War*, 272, 275, 282, 302, 316; Michael Norman and Elizabeth M. Norman, *Tears in the Darkness* (New York, 2009), 4.

8. Norman and Norman, *Tears in the Darkness*, 335.

9. Laura Hillenbrand, *Unbroken: A World War II Story of Survival, Resilience, and Redemption* (New York, 2014).

10. Lt. Commander Robert S. Schwab, NC, Chelsea US Naval Hospital, to Rear Admiral Dallas J. Sutton, "Disposal of U.S. Marines Evacuated from Guadalcanal with War Neurosis," P3-1/P19-1, 1943 folder, RG 52, National Archives, Washington, DC, hereafter referred to as NA.

11. Richard Tregaskis, *Guadalcanal Diary* (New York, 1943), 79, 143.

12. On Dr. Martin Berezin, see Mary Ellen Condo-Rall and Albert E. Cowdrey, *The Medical Department: Medical Service in the War against Japan* (Washington, DC: US Army Center of Military History, 1998), 24. *Neuropsychiatry in World War II*, 2:458n15.

13. Rosner, "Neuropsychiatric Casualties from Guadalcanal," 770.

14. Lt. Commander E. Rogers Smith, "Guadalcanal Neurosis: A Study of 500 Psychiatric Evacuees from the Solomon Islands Campaign," unpublished paper, USN/MC, May 10, 1943, 3, 99th Annual Convention of the American Psychiatric Association, Detroit, MI, May 10–13, 1943, publicized in "Guadalcanal Neurosis," *Time*, May 24, 1943, 39. "What Happened to the Marine Heroes of Guadalcanal," *Newsweek*, May 29, 1943; also E. Rogers Smith, *American Journal of Psychiatry*, July 1943, 94.

15. For statistics, see Condo-Rall and Cowdrey, *The Medical Department*, 147; Josephine Callisen Bresnahan, "Dangers in Paradise: The Battle against Combat Fatigue in the Pacific War," PhD diss., Harvard University, May 1999, 176–81 (on Guadalcanal); Frank O. Hough, *Pearl Harbor to Guadalcanal: History of the U.S. Marine Corps Operations in World War II* (Washington, DC, 1958), 1:235; Irving Werstein, *Guadalcanal* (New York, 1963).

16. Condo-Rall and Cowdrey, *The Medical Department*, 404.

17. Norman and Norman, *Tears in the Darkness*, 105, 155, 156.

18. Akihito Suzuki, "Psychiatry in the Land of Suicide: Medicalization of Self-Killing in Early 20th Century Japan," 9, 10, http://jsmh.umin.jp/journal/59.pdf.

19. Cecil Brown, "How the Japanese Wages War," *Life*, May 11, 1942, 105. Lesley J. McNair, "The Struggle Is for Survival," *Vital Speeches*, December 1, 1942, 112, 113.

20. Condo-Rall and Cowdrey, *The Medical Department*, 90, 109; *Neuropsychiatry in World War II*, 2:433, 449.

21. Condo-Rall and Cowdrey, *The Medical Department*, 109.

22. *Neuropsychiatry in World War II*, 2:461, 462.

23. Annual Report FY 1943, Professional Service—Medical Division, Neuropsychiatric Branch, Surgeon General's Office, July 1943, pp. 14, 25, HD 319.1-2, US Army Medical Division, Historical Unit, Surgeon General's Office Archives, Fort Detrick, Frederick, MD, hereafter referred to as USAMDHU.

24. South Pacific Area, Base Surgeon's Report—Annual, 1943, p. 3, Box 676, 710 (NP), SGO Record Group 112 (1945–1946), Washington National Records Center, Suitland, MD, hereafter referred to as WNRC. See also Albert E. Cowdrey, *American Military Medicine in World War II* (New York: Free Press, 1998), 138.

25. Josephine Bresnahan, "Dangers in Paradise," 130, 131, 134, 135, referring to Major Merrill Moore MC, "Care of Neuropsychiatric Patients in the South Pacific Area: Report to the Chief Surgeon, Theater Headquarters, 12 July 1943," in RG 112, E 31 (ZJ) Box 1335, National Archives, College Park, MD, hereafter referred to as NACP; Lt. Col. Samuel A. Challman MC to Surgeon General,

Washington, DC, "Memo: Treatment of Mental Disorders," in SWPA, January 26, 1943, 3, RG 112, E31 (ZI), Box 1335, NACP.

26. Forrest Pogue, *George C. Marshall: Ordeal and Hope, 1939–1942* (New York: Viking, 1968), 82, 334, 335, 402, 403, 424, 425; Forrest Pogue, *George C. Marshall: Organizer of Victory, 1943–1945* (New York: Viking, 1973), 111, 191. John Morton Blum, *V Was for Victory* (Boston: Houghton Mifflin Harcourt, 1976), 16.

27. *Neuropsychiatry in World War II*, 1:326–32.

28. Annual Reports, Fiscal Years 1943 and 1944, Neuropsychiatry Branch, Professional Services—Medical Division, Surgeon General's Office, HD:319.1–2, USAMDHU.

29. Miriam Kleiman, "Hit the Road Jack," *Prologue* 43, no. 3 (Fall 2001): 1–15.

30. Memorandum for Chief of Staff Osborn, "Psychiatric Services for Overseas Bases," December 3, 1942, including Tabs A, B, and C; Memorandum, G. S. McCullough to Col. Reynolds, February 16, 1943, Headquarters of the Army Services Forces, 711 Folder, RG 160, NA.

31. Cowdrey, *Fighting for Life*, 136, 137, 140–45; Ben Shephard, *A War of Nerves* (Cambridge, MA: Harvard University Press, 2001), 211–14; Hale, *The Rise and Crisis of Psychoanalysis in the United States*, 189.

32. Hale, *The Rise and Crisis of Psychoanalysis in the United States*, 189.

33. After the war, John Spiegel became a member of the American Academy of Psychoanalysis, a president of the APA, and a professor of social psychiatry at Brandeis University; *Neuropsychiatry in World War II*, 2:5–9. Pols, "The Tunisian Campaign," 313–20.

34. Roy Grinker, *War Neurosis in North Africa: The Tunisian Campaign, January–May 1943* (Josiah Macy Jr. Foundation, 1943), 1–10, 156–80, 210–20; "Roy Richard Grinker, 92, Educator in Psychiatry," *New York Times*, May 11, 1993; "John P. Spiegel, 80, Expert on Violence and Combat Fatigue," *New York Times*, July 19, 1991; Grinker and Spiegel also authored *Men under Stress* (Philadelphia: Blakiston, 1945) on their experience with men in combat and veterans.

35. Grinker, *War Neurosis in North Africa*, 1–10, 156–80, 210–20; Shephard, *A War of Nerves*, 213–17.

36. Interview, Rebecca Greene with Dr. Herbert Spiegel, New York City, December 15, 1975.

37. Letters, Edwin N. Bingham, Lt. Air Corps, Assistant Chief Staff, January 9, 1946; Grinker to Bingham, January 12, 1946, Papers of John Murray, Library of Congress, Washington, DC, hereafter referred to as LC. Grinker also thought that Eleanor Roosevelt may have intervened. Obituary, *New York Times*, March 1, 1974.

38. Interview, Rebecca Greene with Dr. Herbert Spiegel.

39. Interview, Rebecca Greene with Dr. Herbert Spiegel.

40. Herbert Spiegel, "Psychiatry with an Infantry Battalion in North Africa," undated unpublished paper, 11–13; interview, Rebecca Greene with Dr. Herbert Spiegel.

41. For example: Interview with Patient under Hypnosis in NP Hospital, Interviewed by Capt. Wallace and M/Sgt Yoswein at the 312th Station Hospital in England, November 1, 1944, Research Branch, I&E Div., ETO B-20, RG 330, NA.

42. *Neuropsychiatry in World War II*, 2:5–9, regarding the fact that Hanson and Grinker appeared to have similar assignments in North Africa, with Hanson eventually getting the upper hand in being appointed assigned consultant to the Mediterranean theater. See also *Neuropsychiatry in World War II*, 1:393. British and Canadian psychiatry, on the other hand, emphasized assignment to noncombat positions as opposed to returning to combat. Terry Copp and Bill McAndrew, *Battle Exhaustion: Soldiers and Psychiatrists in the Canadian Army, 1939–1945* (Montreal: McGill University Press, 1990), 153. On Grinker and Hanson, see Edgar Jones and Simon Wessely, *Shell Shock to PTSD: Military Psychiatry from 1900 to the Gulf War* (New York: Psychology Press, 2005), 85–87.

43. Annual Report FY 1943, Professional Service—Medical Division, Neuropsychiatric Branch, July 1943, p. 25, USAMDHU.

44. Leading civilian psychiatrists in the United States campaigned for a more influential role in military psychiatric policy making despite the fact that statistics on the numbers hospitalized for psychiatric reasons were not available until at least mid-1943, most likely because they were able to gain knowledge from working in military or veterans' hospitals or from conversing with American and European doctors returning from overseas or at professional conferences. There was no cross-ocean telephone service at the time, news was censored particularly about psychiatry starting in mid-1943, and photographs of battle dead were not permitted in the press. See John Appel, unpublished paper, "Cause and Prevention of Psychiatric Disorders in the US Army in World War II," chap. 1, 5–6, Appel Personal Papers, wherein he states that until the spring of 1943, the only source of information on the number of neuropsychiatric casualties was "Med Rept Form 52 card," filled out at the time the soldier was discharged, and that the Medical Statistics Division of the Surgeon General was two to three years behind in tabulating the data. Med. Rept. Form 86, which reported injury and disease, had no place for nervous or mental disease. *Neuropsychiatry in World War II*, 1:16–20, 27–33.

45. Letter, Edward Strecker to General Charles C. Hillman and Colonel Patrick Madigan, Surgeon General's Office, March 9, 1942. General Hillman was head of the Professional Services Division, which reported to the Army Surgeon General. Madigan reported to Hillman. Profile, Edward A. Strecker (1886–1959), Department of Psychiatry, Penn Behavioral Health, https://www.med.upenn.edu/psychiatry/streckerbio.html. "Dr. Edward Strecker: A Psychiatrist 72," *New York Times*, January 3, 1959.

46. Letter, Putnam to Dr. Overholser, March 19, 1942, NRC Committee on Neuropsychiatry, War Neuroses Subcommittee folder, Overholser Papers, St. Elizabeth's Hospital, RG 418, NA.

47. Letter, Overholser to Tracy Putnam, March 24,1942, NRC Committee on Neuropsychiatry, War Neuroses Subcommittee folder, War Neuroses, Overholser Papers, St. Elizabeth's Hospital, RG 418, NA.

48. Meeting, Special Committee Dealing with War Activities, June 16, 1942, Letter, Overholser to McIntire, July 22, 1942, both in American Psychiatric Association Archives, hereafter referred to as APA.

49. Ruggles was superintendent of Butler Hospital, Rhode Island, from 1922 on, had studied with Emil Kraepelin at the University of Munich, and had supervised an American base hospital in France in World War I; Arthur Ruggles, "Presidential Address," *American Journal of Psychiatry*, July 1942.

50. Minutes, NRC Subcommittee on Psychiatry, Committee on Neuropsychiatry, July 10, 1942, and July 11, 1942, NAS; Letter, Overholser to Surgeon General James Magee, US Army Surgeon General, August 3, 1942, MED: Committee on Neuropsychiatry General, 1942–1943 file, NAS.

51. Letter, Edward Strecker to General Charles C. Hillman and Colonel Patrick Madigan, Surgeon General's Office, March 9, 1942.

52. *Neuropsychiatry in World War II*, 2:23, 3; William Menninger, *Psychiatry in a Troubled World* (New York: Macmillan, 1948), 12, 14, 35, 238, 241–43. Gerald Grob, "Origins of DSM-1: A Study in Appearance and Reality," *American Journal of Psychiatry* 148 (1991): 421–31, estimates that a third of the 2,400 physicians in the military assigned to psychiatry near the end of the war were previously trained as psychiatrists. This means that two-thirds were not. The others most likely either received on-the-job training (OJT) and/or a few months of psychiatric training at the army's Lawson General Hospital, Atlanta, Georgia, or at Columbia University or New York University. Many, according to Menninger, took residencies in psychiatry and/or psychoanalytic training after the war.

53. Letter, Overholser to Weed, July 6, 1942, National Academy of Sciences, Washington, DC, hereafter referred to as NAS.

54. *Neuropsychiatry in World War II*, 1:28, 29. Madigan was transferred to the Army Adjutant General during a time when Overholser was campaigning with the Adjutant General for the use of administrative discharges instead of court-martials for most purported homosexuals. Allan Bérubé, *Coming Out under Fire*, 135–40. As we have seen, early on Madigan clearly supported rejecting those with homosexual proclivities.

55. Hale, *The Rise and Crisis of Psychoanalysis in the United States*; Rebecca Jo Plant, "William Menninger and American Psychoanalysis, 1946–48," *History of Psychiatry* 16, no. 2 (2005): 181–202; Army Surgeon General, Neuropsychiatric Division, Fiscal Year 1943 Report, p. 38, USAMDHU. On Halloran, *Neuropsychiatry in World War II*, 1:29.

56. Memorandum from Dr. Kubie to Dr. Weed, June 9, 1942, attached to Letter to Overholser, Subcommittee on War Neuroses, General, MED: Com on NP, 1942–1943, NAS; NYC Committee on Mental Hygiene, "A Memorandum on the

Selection Process in General"; Letter, Overholser to Gen. Magee, Office of the Surgeon General, December 23, 1942, MED: Committee on N.P., 1942–1943 General, NAS.

57. *Neuropsychiatry in World War II*, 1:47, 57.

58. *Neuropsychiatry in World War II*, 1:43, 55, 57, 58; Menninger, *Psychiatry in a Troubled World*, 28.

59. Report, Meeting of the Special Committee on Wartime Activities," June 16, 1942, APA Special Committee File, APA.

60. New York City Committee on Mental Hygiene, "A Memorandum on the Selection Process in General and on the Psychiatrist in the Selection Process and in the Armed Forces," *American Journal of Mental Deficiency* 47 (October 1942): 136–47.

61. "A Memorandum on the Selection Process in General," 139–47. Letter, Strecker to General Charles C. Hillman and Colonel Patrick Madigan, March 9, 1942.

62. "Frederic Lyman Wells," htttp://www.springerreference.com; "Preliminary Report upon the Utilization of Psychiatric and Psychological Knowledge in the Selection of Men for Military," by Ruggles and Wells, March 27, 1942; Supplementary Report, July 31, 1942, especially in latter, pp. 25–26, both in NAS; also, supplement from 622 Gen., NA; Donald S. Napoli, "The Mobilization of American Psychologists, 1938–1941," *Military Affairs*, February 1978, 32–36; Donald S. Napoli, *Architects of Adjustment: The History of the Psychological Profession in the United States* (New York: Kennikat, 1981), 32–35, 94, 95. Psychologists administered a battery of army tests including the Army General Classification Test (AGCT) and Wechsler-Bellevue Intelligence Scale for intelligence, personality tests, an arithmetic test, mechanical aptitude test, radio code aptitude test, clerical aptitude, driving test, electrical and radio information test, and typing test. The AGCT placed recruits in categories according to their ability to be trained. Napoli, "The Mobilization of American Psychologists," 33.

63. "A Memorandum on the Selection Process in General," 139–47. The subcommittee that worked on the report with chair Kubie came from the New York City Committee on Mental Hygiene of the State Charities Aid Association and the Emergency Committee of Neuro-Psychiatric Societies of New York City. They included Richard M. Brickner MD, Lawson G. Lawry MD, Marian McBee, John A. P. Millet MD, and George S. Stevenson MD. Dr. Stevenson was also the director of the National Committee for Mental Hygiene. See "A Memorandum on the Selection Process in General," 132.

64. "A Memorandum on the Selection Process in General," 132–47.

65. Letters, Overholser to Robert Yerkes, August 29, 1942, and Lawrence Kolb to Kubie, August 19, 1942, NYS Charities Aid Association folder, Overholser Papers, RG 418, NA.

66. Harry Steckel to Lawrence Kubie, August 30, 1942, NYS Charities Aid Association folder, NA.

67. Letter, Kubie to Overholser, via Lewis Weed, Chair, Medical Sciences Division NRC, June 9, 1942, NRC Committee on NP, Overholser Papers, St. Elizabeth's Hospital, RG 418, NA; Letters, Frances Perkins to Marvin McIntyre, Roosevelt's personal secretary, July 15, 1942, Perkins to Eleanor, same day, Perkins Folder, 100 File, E. Roosevelt Papers, FDRL; Letter, Overholser to McIntire, July 22, 1942, APA.

68. Letter, Mrs. Roosevelt to McIntire, July 21, 1942, Mc-Mi Folder, 100 File, E. Roosevelt Papers, Hyde Park, New York (hereafter referred to as FDRL). Eleanor Roosevelt also suggested that women could be used "with great success" in this "area." Mrs. Roosevelt was probably reflecting the recommendation of Stevenson, director of the National Committee on Mental Hygiene, to employ women in civilian clinics and mental hospitals so men in the mental health field could serve in the army and navy. "In the year after Pearl Harbor," according to James McGregor Burns, *Roosevelt: The Soldier of Freedom (1940–1945)* (New York: Harcourt Brace Jovanovich, 2012), "women workers increased by almost two million" (262); Summary Report of Stevenson, Medical Director, National Committee for Mental Hygiene, Annual Meeting, November 12, 1942, NRC, Committee on Neuropsychiatry, III, Overholser Papers, St. Elizabeth's Hospital Records, RG 418, NA.

69. Letter, McIntire to Perkins, July 31, 1942, Mental Diseases, OF 103-3, FDRL. It should be noted that the navy at that time took only volunteers. In addition, it employed routine psychiatric examinations with psychological testing at recruiting stations and in training camps, gathered social histories, observed questionable candidates for two weeks, and had a board review psychiatrists' decisions. It should be noted that after the navy and army induction processes were merged in February 1943 and draftees were taken by the navy in certain cases, its rejection rate increased.

70. Letter, Mrs. Roosevelt to Stimson, September 22, 1942, 70 file, ER Papers, FDRL.

71. Letter, Stimson to Mrs. Roosevelt, October 3, 1942, 70 file, ER Papers, FDRL.

72. Eleanor Roosevelt, "My Day," *New York World Telegram*, October 6, 1942; October 7, 1942, 25.

73. Minutes, Subcommittee on War Neuroses, November 5, 1942. War Neuroses—Minutes and Reports file, NAS. Besides Putnam and Kubie, the subcommittee also included the neurologist Sidney Schwab, known for the treatment of shell shock victims in World War I, and the career army psychiatrist William Porter, head of psychiatry at Walter Reed Hospital, Washington, DC. Schwab particularly believed that men with past histories of neurological disorders might make good soldiers and Porter that "rejection should not be based on theoretical grounds."

74. Letter, Adolf Meyer to Lewis Weed, December 1, 1942, MED: Committee on Neuropsychiatry, General, 1942–1943 file, NAS.

75. Letter, Adolf Meyer, Johns Hopkins Hospital, to Dr. Lewis Weed, December 1, 1942, MED: Committee on Neuropsychiatry, General, 1942–1943 file, NAS.

76. Letters, Weed to Meyer, December 3, 1942, Weed to Overholser, December 3, 1942, MED: Committee on Neuropsychiatry, General, 1942–1943 file, NAS.

77. Letter, Roscoe Hall to Tracy Putnam, December 10, 1942, MED: Committee on 1942–1943: Subcommittee on War Neuroses General file, NAS.

78. *Neuropsychiatry in World War II*, 1:37, 570–97, 768. See specifically 596, wherein Menninger states that in August 1942, the army's policy changed to admit 10 percent of Blacks and 10 percent of whites who were classified as illiterate, provided they could understand verbal instructions. Only 5 percent were allowed in from February 1943 to June 1943. The separation between psychologists and psychiatrists began as early as 1939 when the American Association of Clinical Psychologists successfully campaigned to be part of the Adjutant General instead of the Surgeon General, because psychologists recalled psychiatrists interfering with their psychological testing program in World War I. As a result, the Army Neuropsychiatric Consultants Division did not have a Psychological Branch until after the war ended in September 1945. Nor did the Army Surgeon General train any clinical psychologists before then. Rather, the Adjutant General had a school to train psychologists, the curriculum of which included information on medical standards, and arranged for visits by students to observe psychiatrists in the field. Napoli, "The Mobilization of American Psychologists, 1938–1941," 32–36.

79. *Neuropsychiatry in World War II*, 1:167; Menninger, *Psychiatry in a Troubled World*, 282.

80. Annual Report for 1943 of the Army Surgeon General's Neuropsychiatry Section, p. 13, USAMDHU; This report says 30 percent of the Certificates of Disability for Discharges (CDD) were psychiatric. On the other hand, the US Army "Report to Investigate the Rejection of Mental Cases at Induction Centers" (August 31, 1943), only about a month later, says that 41.9 percent of the CDDs for the first six months of 1943 were psychiatric. The report's authors were Drs. Overholser, Ruggles, Waggoner, Parsons, Strecker, Bowman, and Titus H. Harris. In Overholser Papers, Library of Congress, Washington, DC, hereafter referred to as LC.

81. Meeting, Michigan Society of Neurology and Psychiatry, March 25, 1943, p. 10, US Army Military History Research Collection, Carlisle Barracks, PA. The medical director of Selective Service was Leonard Rowntree.

82. *Neuropsychiatry in World War II*, 1:173.

83. Memorandum, Major General J. A. Ulio, Adjutant General, "Mental Condition of Men Ordered Overseas," Memorandum No. W600-30-43, March 25, 1943, W600 Series, NA.

84. US Senate, Committee on Military Affairs, Hearings on S. 2748, A Bill to Extend Liability for Service, 77th Congress, 2nd Session, 1942. See also Richard

Polenberg, *War and Society: The United States, 1941–1945* (Philadelphia: Lippincott, 1972), 84, 97, 193.

85. In addition to Meyer and Overholser, others in favor included Kennedy (Roosevelt's doctor and president of the American Neurological Association) and C. MacFie Campbell (head of the Boston Psychopathic Hospital, trained by Kraepelin and Meyer). Also Drs. Oskar Diethelm; Tracy Putnam; Charles C. Burlingame, Institute for Living, Hartford, CT; Bernard Wortis; and Edwin G. Zabriskie and the analysts Joseph Wortis, Judah Marmor, and Stephen Jewett. See Letter in the *Journal of the American Medical Association*, October 31, 1942. The navy psychiatrists Forrest M. Harrison and Gregory Zilboorg echoed similar opinions in Albert Deutsch, *PM*, October 31, 1942, Box 24, Scrapbook, Overholser Papers, LC.

86. See Lawrence Frank to National Resources Planning Board, "18–19 Year Youths," paper, November 30, 1942, 622 (1942), File RG 147, WNRC. The National Resources Planning Board oversaw economic, medical, and welfare planning for the war and its immediate aftermath. Richard Polenberg, *War and Society*, 84, 97, 193. Also, on the background of Frank, see "Biographical Description," Papers of Lawrence K. Frank, part of the Merrill-Palmer Collection, 1922–1968, Archives of Labor and Urban Affairs, Walter P. Reuther Library, Wayne State University, Detroit.

87. Besides Stevenson, those opposed included the criminal psychiatrist Nolan D. C. Lewis, Thomas V. Moore, and William L. Russell. US Senate, Committee on Military Affairs, Hearings on S. 2478, A Bill to Extend Liability for Service, 77th Congress, 2nd Session, 1942, 88, 89.

88. Albert Deutsch, *PM*, October 19, 1942, Scrapbook, Box 24, Overholser Papers, LC.

89. Letter, Overholser to Honorable Frances P. Bolton, House of Representatives, October 23, 1942, William Alanson White Correspondence File, Overholser Papers, RG 418, NA; *PM*, October 19, 1942, in Scrapbook, Box 24, Overholser Papers, LC.

90. Albert Deutsch, in *PM*, October 19, 1942, Box 24, Overholser Papers, LC.

91. Letter, Secretary to Mrs. Roosevelt to Dr. Stevenson, October 15, 1942, 170 File, Eleanor Roosevelt Papers; Letter, Secretary to Eleanor Roosevelt to Secretary of War Stimson, including three letters responding to article in *Ladies Home Journal*, White House Correspondence, Gov't Dept. 1942, Smith-Ty, 70 File, E. Roosevelt Papers, FDRL. In the *Ladies' Home Journal* of December 1942, the First Lady fretted over "untrained boys being sent to the front" and wrote Stimson, who assured her that was not the case. Report, Lewis Hershey, "Health of Registrants Revealed by Selective Services and Inferences There-from," undated, 102, Conferences, Selective Service, RG 147, WNRC; *Complete Presidential Press Conferences of Franklin Delano Roosevelt* (New York: Da Capo, 1972), 17:74.

334 | Notes to pages 100–2

92. "Discharges of Inducted and Enlisted Men from Army for Physical and Mental Reasons," Box 124, RG 147, WNRC. Also, the US Army Report to Investigate the Rejection of Mental Cases at Induction Stations (August 31, 1943), Overholser Papers, LC, says that 41.9 percent of the CDDs for the first six months of 1943 were psychiatric. The authors included Drs. Overholser, Ruggles, Waggoner, Strecker, and Karl Bowman.

93. *Neuropsychiatry in World War II*, 1:436, 437.

5. The Public Reaction

1. Gordon F. Lewis, a veteran, recalled that "unlike the present widespread antipathy to our involvement in Iraq . . . the country in general was solidly behind this war effort and people were willing to jump in and make sacrifices." Gordon F. Lewis, interviewed by Elaine Blatt and Shaun Illingworth, July 24, 2006, Rutgers Oral History Archives, hereafter referred to as ROHA, https://oralhistory.rutgers.edu/images/PDFs/lewis_gordon.pdf. Hollywood emphasized national unity in movies with Black protagonists, such as Paul Robeson. This does not mean that there were no race riots or desertions. According to a memorandum from Assistant Secretary of War John J. McCloy, head of the War Department's advisory body on racial matters, by mid-1943, there had been race riots at Camp Van Dorn, MS; Camp Stewart, GA; March Field, CA; Fort Bliss, TX; Camp San Luis Obispo, CA; and Camp Breckinridge, KY. Bernard C. Nalty, *Strength for the Fight: A History of Black Americans in the Military* (New York: Free Press, 1986), 154, 156, 195. Also see Charles Glass, *The Deserters: A Hidden History of World War II* (New York, 2013), 1. For an in-depth look at the culture and attitudes in the 1940s, see William Graebner, *The Age of Doubt: American Thought and Culture in the 1940s* (Boston: Twayne, 1991).

2. *Life*, November 6, 1942, 11.

3. Richard Polenberg, *War and Society* (Philadelphia, 1972), 133–36.

4. *Newsweek*, February 1944, 32. In *Good Housekeeping*, February 1943, 27, the Armour Company declared that they "not only suppl[y] America's fighting men with millions of pounds of . . . body building meat . . . but also with many byproducts . . . Wool and Leather, Oils and Soap. . . . That is why Americans at home are not only asked to share meat but to share many other things as well." Even Cadillac, luxury of all luxuries, tried to prove its practical contribution to America's impending victory: "In the vanguard of the fighting craft that track the U-boat down are fighter planes powered by Allison. . . . During five years of intervention millions of Allison parts . . . have 'gone to war' bearing the imprint of Cadillac's precision workmanship." *Good Housekeeping*, May 8, 1944, 23.

5. *On the Homefront 1941–1945: Films at the Archives* (Washington, DC, 1975).

6. Letter, Fink J. Farrell to Senator R. B. Russell, March 15, 1944, File 327.02-1 (Draft or Conscription), S.G.O., RG 112, Washington National Records Center, Suitland, MD, hereafter referred to as WNRC; Letter, Russell to Secretary of War, March 18, 1944, 327.02-1, RG 112, WNRC.

7. Memorandum, for the Surgeon General from Robert J. Carpenter, Lieut. Colonel Medical Corps, Executive Officer to the Adjutant General, March 30, 1944, 327.02-1, RG 112, WNRC.

8. Letter, Judge Malcolm Hatfield to Major General Lewis B. Hershey, April 24, 1944, P. 710, Surgeon General's Office, RG 112, 1, WNRC; Anonymous Letter to Administrator Frank T. Hines, Veterans Affairs, January 1, 1944, and Letter, Hines to Hershey, January 12, 1944, both in 621 (Mental Age Limits), Selective Service, RG 147, WNRC. Report, Annual Meeting of the Michigan Society of Neurology and Psychiatry, March 25, 1943, testimony by Clarence I. Owen, director of the Michigan State Selective Service, pp. 13, 14, S.S., RG 147, WNRC.

9. Memorandum, Colonel Carlton S. Dargusch, Oklahoma Selective Service to Colonel Richard Eanes, August 19, 1943, 622, S.S., RG 147, WNRC. In a personal interview this author had in 1974 with the late psychiatrist Eric T. Carlson, director, Cornell Medical Center Section on Psychiatric History, Carlson recalled that the public attitude toward him in World War II somewhat resembled the attitude toward the neuropsychiatric 4F. As a chemist on the Manhattan Project, Carlson was not allowed to explain what he did or why he was a civilian, and people wondered what was wrong with him and why a healthy young man could not serve in the war.

10. US Senate, Committee on Military Affairs, Hearings on S. 763, *Exempting Certain Married Men Who Have Children from the Liability under Selective Service Training and Service Act*, 78th Cong., 1st Sess., 1943, 298.

11. Henry Link, "The Errors of Psychiatry," *American Mercury*, July 1944, 72, 74, 76, 77; Elliot Cooke, *All but Me and Thee: Psychiatry at the Fox Hole Level* (Washington, DC, 1945), 64–84.

12. US Senate, Committee on Military Affairs, Hearings on H.R. 1730, Amendment of Selective Service Act Regarding Deferment of Certain Categories, 78th Cong., 1st Sess., 1943, 8–10.

13. "Meeting Special Committee Appointed to Investigate the Rejection of Mental Cases at Induction Stations," August 31, 1943, Overholser Papers, Library of Congress, Washington, DC, hereafter referred to as LC. See esp. 7, 9, 11, 6. A year later, Leonard Rowntree, the director of the Selective Service Medical Division, recalled an epidemic of hypertension in South Dakota in his speech to the Selective Service Medical Conference in June 1944. Report, "Medical Conference at National Headquarters," June 5, 6, 19, 1944, RG 147, WNRC.

14. "Confidential Report of State Directors' Conference," November 11, 1943, 25, 27, 105, RG 147, WNRC.

15. *Selective Service as the Tide of War Turns: The 3rd Report of the Director of Selective Service, 1943–1944* (Washington, DC, 1945), 220–26.

16. "Meeting of the Special Committee Appointed to Investigate the Rejection of Mental Cases at Induction Stations," esp. 3.

17. Amos Koontz MD, *Hygeia*, May 1943, 494.

18. Richard Polenberg, *America at War: The Home Front, 1941–1945* (New Jersey: Prentice-Hall, 1968), 115. Steven Taylor, *Acts of Conscience: World War II, Mental Institutions, and Religious Objectors* (Syracuse, NY: Syracuse University Press, 2009). Also, Leslie Eisan, *Pathways of Peace: A History of the Civilian Public Service Program Administered by the Brethren Service Committee* (Elgin, IL, 1948), 368–76. The peace churches and Selective Service worked with such technical agencies as the National Park Service and Forest Service in planning and supervising work programs. Selective Service and the peace churches were responsible for discipline, at times disagreeing on methods. There were about 151 CO camps. Those entering the camps were classified by the local boards as 1-E, i.e., fit for military service but barred because of conscientious objections. COs doing civilian public service were not paid. Scott H. Bennett, "American Pacifism, the 'Greatest Generation,' and World War II," in *The United States and the Second World War*, ed. G. Kurt Piehler and Sidney Pash (New York: Fordham University Press, 2010), 259–92. Kurt Piehler, *A Religious History of the American GI in World War II* (Lincoln: University of Nebraska Press, 2021), 37–42.

19. Report, "Medical Conference at National Headquarters," June 5, 6, 1944, 29, 30.

20. Memorandum, Colonel Carlton S. Dargusch, Oklahoma Selective Service to Colonel Richard Eanes, August 19, 1943, 622, S.S., RG 147, WNRC.

21. Report, Michigan Society of Neurology and Psychiatry, March 25, 1943, 15, 20.

22. Temple Burling MD, "Community Organization for Meeting Problems of Psychiatric Disabled Veterans," *American Journal of Orthopsychiatry* 17, no. 4 (October 1944): 684; "Guide to the Temple Burling Audio-Visual Materials," http://rmc.library.cornell.edu.

23. Leon Luchansky and James R. Mann, "The Meaning of Disability Payments in the Treatment of Patients in a Veterans' Mental Hygiene Clinic," unpublished MSW thesis, Columbia University School of Social Work, March 1948, 26. Ashamed of receiving a blue discharge without honor and without benefits, a returning veteran did not tell his wife about his discharge. See Winfred Dean, "Casework with the Emotionally Disturbed Veteran," unpublished MSW thesis, Columbia University School of Social Work, September 1945, 54.

24. Morris Riemer, "Effects of the 4F Classification on Psychoneurotics under Treatment," *Mental Hygiene* 30 (1946): 452, 453.

25. "Many Fathers Already Drafted Even from Essential Jobs: Navy Yards, Plane Factories and Other Plants Report Losing Workers in Droves," *Washington Star*, February 22, 1943. The article also refers to a similar rise in the number of drafted workers with families at the Boston Navy Yard and Bethlehem Steel Yards in Quincy and Hingham, MA. This was about the same time that Selective Service began to induct eighteen- and nineteen-year-olds.

26. US Senate, Committee on Military Affairs, Hearings on H.R. 1730, Amendment of Selective Service Act Regarding Deferment of Certain Categories,

78th Cong., 1st Sess., 1943, 5, 8, 15, 16, 35; US Senate, Committee on Military Affairs, Hearings on S. 763 . . . 78th Cong., 1st Sess., 1943, 2, 5, 15, 16; *Selective Service as the Tide of War Turns*, 53.

27. US Senate, Committee on Military Affairs, Hearings on H.R. 1730, 7.

28. Memorandum, Carlton Dargusch to Richard Eanes, Selective Service, August 19, 1943, 622, RG 147, WNRC.

29. There were two bills, that of Senator Burton Wheeler and of Congressman Paul Kilday (TX). Wheeler's bill exempted fathers married before Pearl Harbor. Kilday's milder bill called for their induction after single men and husbands without children had been drafted. After extensive hearings, on December 5, 1943, Congress passed Public Law 78-197, *An Act Amending the Selective Training and Service Act of 1940, As amended, and for other Purposes, United States Statutes at Large* (Washington, DC, 1944), 57:596–99. US Senate, Committee on Military Affairs, *Hearings on H.R. 1730, Amendment of Selective Service Act Regarding Deferment of Certain Categories*, 78th Cong., 1st Sess., 1943; US Senate, Committee on Military Affairs, Hearings on S. 763 . . . 78th Cong., 1st Sess., 1943. As will be discussed in the following chapter, Wheeler agreed to withdraw his provision exempting fathers married before Pearl Harbor from the draft in the final act, in exchange for Roosevelt agreeing to establish a committee to review the military requirements for admission to service. Significantly, 950,000 fathers were drafted in World War II. National Park Service, http://irma.nps.gov/DataStore/Download file/465955, p. 21.

30. *Neuropsychiatry in World War II*, prep. and dir. Lt. Gen. Leonard D. Heaton, the Surgeon General, US Army, and ed. Col. Robert S. Anderson, MC, USA, Col. Albert J. Glass, MC, USA (Ret.), and Lt. Col. Robert J. Bernucci, MC, USA (Ret.) (Washington, DC: US Government Printing Office, 1966), 1:769. A year later, Selective Service came out with even more startling figures divided into white and Black; white neuropsychiatric defects accounted for 49.3 percent of the total white Selective Service rejections, physical rejections only coming to 49.9 percent. The 49.3 percent included 33.1 mental disease, 10.3 intelligence tests, 2.7 mental deficiency, and 3.4 neurological. The percentages for mental disease and intelligence testing were by far higher than the highest physical category, musculoskeletal coming to only 8.4 percent. The figures for Blacks included 19 percent mental disease, 44.5 percent intelligence tests, 8.8 mental deficiency, and 2.0 neurological. "Defects of Selective Service Registrants Examined during July 1944–Dec. 1944," Selective Service System, Box 124, RG 147, National Archives, Washington, DC, hereafter referred to as NA.

31. US Senate Committee on Military Affairs, Hearings on H.R. 1730, 7; US Senate, Committee on Military Affairs, Hearings on S. 763, 448, 298; also see US Senate, Committee on Military Affairs, Hearings on H.R. 1730, 8–10.

32. For example, *Washington Star*, December 30, 1943; *Washington Post*, July 28, 1943; "Break for Dads," *Business Week*, December 18, 1943, 100; "Fathers and Goals," *Newsweek*, December 20, 1943, 42; "Draw for Fathers," *Time*, December 20,

1943, 15; "Manpower Problem over the Hump, but Fathers Face Heavy Draft," *Newsweek*, January 10, 1944, 37–38; "Threat of National Service Act Hangs over Fathers—Draft Debate," *Newsweek*, September 27, 1943, 41–42; also, "Congress and the Fathers' Draft," *Scholastic*, October 1943, 15; "Directives Regarding Draft of Fathers," *Monthly Labor Review*, September 1943, 472; "Army's Mental Casualties Vital Drain on Manpower," *United States News*, January 14, 1944, 16.

33. US Senate, Committee on Military Affairs, Hearings on S. 763 . . . 78th Cong., 1st Sess., 304–5.

34. The subcommittee of the House Committee on Military Affairs chaired by Rep. Costello also included John J. Sparkman (AL), E. C. Gathings (AR), Philip J. Philbin (MA), Leslie C. Arends (IL), Charles H. Elston (OH), and Forest A. Harness (IN); *Washington Post*, February 17, 1944; *Washington Post*, July 28, 1943, 12H; *Selective Service as the Tide of War Turns*, 82; Report, Hearing Held before Special Committee of Committee on Military Affairs, February 14, 1944, *US House of Representatives Report of Proceedings*, 54:2489, in Selective Service file, Overholser Papers, RG 418, NA. Also see *Guide to Senate Records*, chapter 4, section 4.22, on Senate hearing of *Report of President's Commission on the Deferment of Federal Employees*, http://www.archiveds.gov/legislative/guide/senate/chapter-04.

35. Diary, Henry Stimson, March 29, 1944, 46:136; March 30, 1994, 46:142, April 4, 1944, 46:153, Yale University Sterling Memorial Library, New Haven, CT, hereafter referred to as YUSML; Hearings, U.S. House Committee on Military Affairs, Special Committee on Draft Deferments, March 15, 1944, 1, 2, 35, 119, 120, 130; US Senate, Committee on Military Affairs, Hearings on S. 763, 43; John Chambers, *Draftees or Volunteers* (New York, 1975), 306–7; "Sen. Austin Backs FDR's Plea for National Service Act," *Montpelier Argus*, January 9, 1945, 3, 6; Editorial, *Herald Tribune*, January 8, 1945. Of course, not all military leaders were equally opposed to a National Service Act. Patterson testified in favor of the act at the Special Committee's hearings in March 1944, but his superior Stimson was opposed. Probably the military leader most against a service act was George C. Marshall. See Forrest C. Pogue, *George C. Marshall: Organizer of Victory, 1943–1945* (New York: Viking, 1973); see esp. the chapter on "Crisis in Manpower," 3:488–593. Also see Statement, President William Green of the American Federation of Labor, on the Austin-Wadsworth Bill before the Senate Military Affairs Committee, February 16, 1944, National Service No. 1, Robert Patterson Papers, Library of Congress, Washington, DC, hereafter referred to as Patterson Papers, LC. Industrial and labor organizations opposed to the National Service Act included the US Chamber of Commerce, the National Association of Manufacturers, the National Grange, the AFL, and the CIO.

36. Letters, Eugene F. McCahey, Chaplain First Lt., San Antonio, Texas, August 5, 1943, to Chief Chaplain (Brig. Gen) Wm. R. White, USA; Aviator S. Joseph Gordon White, San Antonio, Texas, to Chief Chaplain William R. Arnold, August 5, 1943; Arnold to Chaplain Charles I. Carpenter, Pentagon Building,

Washington, DC, August 12, 1943, all from Army Chaplaincy Records, RG 47, NA. While Dr. Harry Benjamin, an endocrinologist and sexologist, gave a lecture before the Association for the Advancement of Psychotherapy in April 1943 on the health value of not suppressing the libido in the military and engaging in sex, for the most part, therapy in the military centered not on sexual problems but on the immediate incident in combat precipitating stress. Harry Benjamin, "Morals versus Morale in Wartime," in *Morals in Wartime*, ed. Victor Robinson (New York, 1943). It should be noted that this predated the prevalent use of penicillin to treat syphilis, which began in 1943.

37. Letter, Bishop John F. O'Hara, Liaison between the Catholic Church and the Army, to Marshall, September 29, 1944, from Army's Chaplaincy records, RG 112, E 31 (ZJ), Box 1335, National Archives, College Park, MD, hereafter referred to as NACP.

38. Nathan Hale, *The Rise and Crisis of Psychoanalysis in the United States* (New York: Oxford, 1995), 190, states that in 1941 there were at most one hundred trained psychiatrists with psychoanalytic institutional affiliations and training; *Neuropsychiatry in World War II*, 1:85, states that the number of psychoanalysts during the war was around five hundred, without defining the term. Also see Ben Shephard, *A War of Nerves* (Cambridge, MA: Harvard University Press, 2001), 213. John M. Murray Papers, Library of Congress, biography of Murray, http://rss.locgov/service/mss. Mark K. Wells, *Courage and Air Warfare* (London, 1995), 90, 95, citing Douglas D. Bond, "A Study of Successful Airmen with Particular Respect to Their Motivations for Combat Flying and Resistance to Combat Stress," January 27, 1945, 520.7411-1, Air Force Historical Research Agency, Maxwell, AL, hereafter referred to as AFHRA.

39. Letters, O'Hara to Marshall, September 29, 1944; Arnold to Bishop William T. McCarty (in same office as O'Hara), October 28, 1944, enclosing Grinker and Spiegel, draft, "War Neuroses in North Africa"; and McCarty to Arnold, November 3, 1944, thanking him; from Army's Chaplaincy records, NACP. Also, see *Neuropsychiatry in World War II*, 1:699. I am indebted to Professor G. Kurt Piehler, Florida State University, for sharing these records with me as well as his chapter on "The Wounded" before publication of his book, *A Religious History of the American GI in World War II*. See esp. 226–27 on the Catholic Church's attitudes toward military psychiatry.

40. On movies, see Thomas Cripps, *Making Movies Black: The Hollywood Message Movie from World War II to the Civil Rights Era* (New York: Oxford University Press, 1993), 104–5, 110–14. See also Piehler, *A Religious History of the American GI in World War II*, chap. "The Wounded."

41. Bernard Nalty, *Strength for the Fight: A History of Black Americans in the Military* (New York: Free Press, 1986), 190; Helen K. Block and William H. Thompson, "A War within a War: a World War II Buffalo Soldier's Story," *Journal of Men's Studies* 20, no. 1 (2012): 34. Philip McGuire, ed., *Taps for a Jim Crow Army: Letters from Black Soldiers in World War II* (Kentucky, 1983), 145,

comes to a lower figure of 6.5 as the percentage of Blacks in the armed forces. This was because he included the navy, which had a lower percentage than the army.

42. Nalty, *Strength for the Fight*, 172–74. Memorandum for Under-Secretary of War from McNair, Subject: 93rd, and attached Memorandum from Edward S. Greenbaum, Colonel, Ord. Dept., regarding the reluctance of white officers to command Blacks because of the "question as to whether the division will ever be able to perform combat service." On the 92nd Division, Memoranda for the Inspector General, August 7, 1943, from Benjamin O. Davis Sr., Brig. Gen., US Army, Patterson Papers, Negroes, March 9, 1942 File, Container 151, LC. Davis was the first African American general in the US Army.

43. Nalty, *Strength for the Fight*, 164, 181.

44. Albert E. Cowdrey, *Fighting for Life: American Military Medicine in World War II* (New York: Free Press, 1994), 110–12.

45. Nalty, *Strength for the Fight*, 179–81. When Augusta Chiwy, a Black Belgian nurse, went to the front to treat soldiers during the Battle of the Bulge, a doctor had to get around the American practice of having white soldiers treated only by white nurses by reminding the soldiers, "You either let her treat you or you die." In 2011, Chiwy was honored for saving several hundred lives during the month she was there. "Augusta Chiwy Dies at 94: Forgotten Wartime Nurse," *New York Times*, August 26, 2015.

46. Letters to Stimson and Stimson to Eleanor Roosevelt, September 2, 1942, Eleanor Roosevelt Papers, Stimson File, Box 851, Franklin Delano Roosevelt Library, Hyde Park, NY, hereafter to be referred to as FDRL; Studs Terkel, *"The Good War": An Oral History of World War II* (New York: Ballantine, 1984), 261.

47. Memorandum for the Under Secretary of War, from Julius H. Amberg, Special Assistant to the Secretary of War, September 22, 1943, "Court-martial of Colonel Colman Selfridge Field," Memorandum for the Under Secretary of War from Julius H. Amberg, May 7, 1943, "Investigation at Selfridge Field," Memorandum to Judge Patterson (Under Secretary of War) from Edward S. Greenbaum, Brig. Gen., USA, "Selfridge Field Investigation, May 11, 1943, Memorandum for the Secretary of War from Robert Patterson, September 24, 1943, "Court-Martial of Colonel Colman, Selfridge Field," Memorandum for the Under Secretary of War from Julius H. Amberg, "House Military Affairs Committee Investigation-Colman Trial, September 23, 1943, Letter, Patterson to Oscar R. Ewing Democratic National Committee, June 13, 1943, Memorandum for the Under Secretary of War from Julius H. Amberg, "Selfridge Field Inquiry," May 13, 1943, all in Investigations March 9, 1942 file, Container 137, Patterson Papers, LC.

48. French L. MacLean, *The Fifth Column* (Atglen, PA: Schiffer, 2013), 263. For statistics on charges and convictions, see Alice Kaplan, *The Interpreter* (New York: Free Press, 2005).

49. S. Matthew Delmont, "Why African-American Soldiers Saw World War II as a Two-Front Battle," *Conversation*, August 24, 2017, http://www.smithsonianmag

.com/history; Lauren Rebecca Sklaroff, "Constructing GI Joe Louis: Cultural Solutions to the Negro Problem during World War II," *Journal of American History* 89, no. 3 (2002): 963. The jazz critic John Hammond was astounded with the state of segregation, which he found as "complete as anything one might find in fascist countries" when he was escorted out of a Black dance hall near a Black army training camp in Oklahoma by four white MPs who warned him to "stay away from 'knife wielding Niggers.'" See also Sklaroff, "Constructing GI Joe Louis," 964.

50. Letter ER to Osborn, February 6, 1943, requesting that a Black man referred to her by Mary McLeod Bethune, adviser to Roosevelt on minority affairs, be appointed a Morale Officer, and memorandum, Bethune to ER, which was sent by ER to FDR regarding Bethune's proposing integration of all federal service agencies, which was ignored; File 100.1, Box 1789, ER Papers. Also see Sklaroff, "Constructing GI Joe Louis," esp. 965–77.

51. Ulysses Lee, *US Army in World War II Special Studies: The Employment of Negro Troops* (Washington, DC, 1966), 110–12; James M. McPherson et al., *Blacks in America: Bibliographical Essays* (New York, 1971), 235; *The Christian Century*, April 12, 1944, 451. In *The Lost Divisions* (New York: Columbia University Press, 1959), 120–21, Eli Ginzberg states that the rate of rejections for Blacks versus whites was respectively 47 percent to 27 percent; Paul T. Murray: "Blacks and the Draft: A History of Institutional Racism," *Journal of Black Studies* 2, no. 1 (September 1971): 62.

52. Lee, *The Employment of Negro Troops*, 412; Letter, Assistant Secretary of War Patterson to Representative A. Leonard Allen, Winnfield, LA, September 4, 1943, Surgeon General's Office File 291.2, RG 112, WNRC.

53. Roy Wilkins, "No Negro Draft Board Members in Many States, Says N.A.A.C.P. Survey," *Crisis* 48, no. 22 (1941).

54. Ellen Dwyer, "Psychiatry and Race during World War II," *Journal of the History of Medicine and Allied Sciences* 61, no. 2 (April 2006): 126. For more information on the NMA, see https://www.nmanet.org/page/About_Us#. Also, Thomas J. Ward, *Black Physicians in the Jim Crow South* (University of Arkansas Press, 2003), 195–96, where it states that the National Association of Colored Physicians, Dentists, and Pharmacists was first formed in 1895, renamed NMA in 1903, and its journal issued starting 1909. The NMA promoted the professional interests of doctors and dentists as well as seeking parity for the health treatment of Blacks. Efforts at desegregating the AMA occurred in the 1950s and 1960s with significant resistance from local southern chapters. The NMA supported Medicare and Medicaid before the AMA.

55. Memorandum, Braceland to McIntire, "Visit to Norfolk Area and Camp Perry, Williamsburg for the purpose of Inspecting Neuropsychiatric Activities," June 17, 1943, P3-1/P19-1(1923–40), RG 52, NA; Memorandum, Lt. H. S. B. Cummings Jr. to Senior Medical Officer, USNTC, Great Lakes, IL, December 13, 1944, P3-1/P19-1, General Correspondence 41–46 folder, RG 52, NA.

56. Memorandum, Col. Campbell C. Johnson to Hershey, "Conference with Negro Educators on the High Rejection Rates of Negro Selectees for Mental Deficiency," 102, Selective Service, RG 147, WNRC; "Meeting Special Committee Appointed to Investigate the Rejection of Mental Cases at Induction Stations," August 31, 1943, Overholser Papers, LC. See also Ginzberg, *The Lost Divisions*, which includes tables showing higher rates of mental deficiency and inadequate personality for Blacks than whites in service.

57. Ginzberg, The *Lost Divisions*, 120–21. For a description of AGCT, see John McCollins, "World War II: NCOs," http://www.ausa.org.publications; also, Thomas Harrell, "Some History of the Army General Classification Test," *Journal of Applied Psychology* 77, no. 6 (December 1993): 875–78.

58. Dwyer, "Psychiatry and Race During World War II," 129.

59. Letter, Michael Eanes to Medical Corps, October 13, 1942, 291.2-1 (1941–1942), S.G.O., RG 112, WNRC.

60. Rutherford B. Stevens, "Racial Aspects of Emotional Problems of Negro Soldiers," *American Journal of Psychiatry*, January 1947, 495. During the war, Winfred W. Lynn, a Black man, was refused induction because of attitudes toward racial segregation. While he lost the case, it engendered much sympathy in the Black community. Manning Marable, *Malcolm X: A Life of Reinvention* (New York: Viking, 2011), 59.

61. Hazel Rowley, *Richard Wright: The Life and Times* (New York: Holt, 2001), 271–72, 285.

62. Rowley, *Richard Wright*, 285–86.

63. Rowley, *Richard Wright*, 252, 271–72; FBI File No. 100-41674, "Richard Nathaniel Wright," July 8, 1944, 28, 29, http://vault.fbi.gov/Richard%20Nathaniel%20Wright. Also, Gabriel Mendes, *Under the Strain of Color: Harlem's LaFargue Clinic and the Promise of Antiracist Psychiatry* (New York: Cornell University Press, 2015), 21.

64. Memorandum, Col. Campbell C. Johnson, Infantry to General Pearson, State Director of Selective Service, Lansing, MI, August 1943, 170 Gen., RG 147, WNRC.

65. Malcolm X, *The Autobiography of Malcolm X* (New York: Grove, 1964), esp. 104–7.

66. Marable, *Malcolm X*, 59, 60.

67. Report, "Meeting Special Committee Appointed to Investigate the Rejection of Mental Cases at Induction Stations," August 31, 1943, Overholser Papers, LC. In fairness, Selective Service psychiatrists knew they had to consider cultural mores when deciding on an individual's state of mental health. For example, in August 1943, Captain Rak of Camp Dodge told a conference of Selective Service doctors in Iowa: "I can very well recall a time when I worked and lived in Iowa City about nine or ten years ago. I had a patient under observation in the psychopathic hospital who talked in terms of corn eighteen feet high. I was a newcomer in Iowa. Why that man must be a bit balmy, I

thought. Let's wait and let's check. And sure enough, it turned out to be there was 18-foot corn. Afterwards, I had the case of an aviator who talked in terms of having to fly over corn twenty-five feet high. All I could do was scratch my head and say, 'Well, I'll be damned!'" (29). Minutes, Conference on Physical and Mental Qualifications for Armed Services for Physicians and Dentists of Local Boards and Medical Advisory Boards and Local Board Members in State of Iowa, August 26, 1943, Lewis Hershey Papers, US Army Military History Research Collection, Carlisle Barracks, PA, hereafter referred to as USAMHRC.

68. Lee, *The Employment of Negro Troops*, 411; originally from Letter, James N. Keelin, Col., to Col. C. G. Parker, Selective Service headquarters, June 1943, SGO file 291.2, RG 112; "Confidential Report State Directors' Conference," November 11, 1943, 105 (Conferences), 1943, RG 147, WNRC; Letter, W. C. Alexander, Orange, NJ, to Judge Hastie, Stimson's troubleshooter for Black affairs, showing that the problem of rejecting Blacks for venereal disease started very early. In particular, there were large numbers rejected for gonorrhea, when further examination "under white and colored physicians . . . revealed that a larger percentage . . . are free from this infection." See file 290.1–2, RG 112, WNRC. Rowntree, McGill, and Edwards, "Causes of Rejection and the Incidence of Defects among 18- and 19-Year-Old Selective Service Registrants," *JAMA*, 1943, 123, 181.

69. Letter, Assistant Secretary of War Patterson to Representative A. Leonard Allen, Winnfield, LA, September 4, 1943, Surgeon General's Office file 291.2, RG 112, WNRC. Brandt, *No Magic Bullet*, 116–17.

70. Letter, July 1943, Colonel C. G. Parker, Deputy Director of Selective Service to Col. Neal, director Virginia Selective Service, 622, RG 147, NA.

71. Dwyer, "Psychiatry and Race during World War II," 125, citing Rowntree, McGill, and Edwards, "Causes of Rejection."

72. Brandt, *No Magic Bullet*, 157–58.

73. Robert H. Owens particularly investigated psychological procedures at induction centers in New York City; Louisville, KY; Columbus, OH; Cincinnati, OH; and Little Rock, AR. See Colonel to Colonel Parker, "Report of Observations of Psychological Procedures at the Armed Forces Induction Stations," August 25, 1943, file 622, RG 147, WNRC.

74. Memorandum, White to Roosevelt, "93rd Division and Other Negro Combat Units," February 12, 1945, Hollandia, Dutch New Guinea, Negroes 3/9/42 file, Patterson Papers, LC.

75. Dwyer, "Psychiatry and Race during World War II," 127, 128.

76. According to Ginzberg, *The Lost Divisions*, 121, "60 percent of all white ineffectives were psychoneurotic; 53 percent of all Negro ineffectives were inapt." On the degree to which segregation and lack of schooling or inferior education were found to affect behavior and mental aptitude, see 122–25.

77. Nalty, *Strength for the Fight*, 190; Philip McGuire, ed., *Taps for a Jim Crow Army: Letters from Black Soldiers in World War II* (Kentucky, 1983), 145.

78. *Neuropsychiatry in World War II*, 1:577; Dwyer, "Psychiatry and Race during World War II," 121–30.

79. Letter, T. O. Kraabel, National Director of the American Legion, National Rehabilitation Committee, to Rear Admiral L. Sheldon, Assistant Chief Bureau of Medicine and Surgery, Navy, March 4, 1943, file P3-1/P19-1 (1943), Navy Bureau of Medicine and Surgery, RG 52, NA.

80. Report, "Meeting Special Committee with Psychiatrists from Replacement Training Centers (one of the reports of the Army Committee investigating rejections at induction centers), 8, Overholser Papers, LC.

81. Letter, James's father to Dr. Thomas Rennie, August 31, 1942; Letter, Rennie to James's father, September 2, 1942; Letter, James's father to Rennie, undated; Letter, Rennie to Induction Board, August 5, 1941; Letter, Rennie to another psychiatrist, August 10, 1942; all from Dr. Thomas Rennie Papers, Cornell University Medical Center, Section on Psychiatric History, New York City, hereafter referred to as Rennie Papers, Cornell.

82. Letter, Col. Mills F. Neal, Director of Virginia Selective Service, to Hershey, June 19, 1943, 346.3 file, Selective Service, RG 147, WNRC; Letter, Col. C. G. Parker, Deputy Director of Selective Service, to Neal, July 1, 1943, 346.3 file, Selective Service, RG 147, WNRC.

83. Memorandum, Brigadier General I. Kemper Williams, US Army to Chief of Staff through Deputy Chief of Staff, G-1, "Education Campaign on Psychoneuroses," March 16, 1945, RG 165, WNRC. Elliot, *All but Me and Thee*, 198.

84. Letter, Lewis Weed to Winfred Overholser, January 16, 1943; Letter, Overholser to Weed, January 18, 1943; Letter, Weed to Rodney Brandon, January 19, 1943 (this was a copy of a letter composed by Overholser); all from MED: Committee on Neuropsychiatry General file 1942–1943, NA.

85. Letter, Pearl Wanamaker to the Army Surgeon General, June 20, 1944, 220.811-1, Surgeon General's Office records, RG 112, WNRC; Letter, T. O. Kraabel to Norman Kirk, Surgeon General Army, September 9, 1944, 220.811, RG 112, WNRC.

86. Norman Q. Brill, Mildred Tate, and William Menninger, "Enlisted Men Discharged from the Army because of Psychoneuroses: A Follow-up Study," *Journal of the American Medical Association* 128, no. 9 (June 30, 1945): 633–37; 6,000 persons were sent questionnaires, of which 4,178 replied. All the men were discharged between May 1943 through January 1944 and were out at six months when surveyed. "Dr. Norman Brill, Standard-setter for Military Psychiatric Care and Founding Director of UCLA Neuropsychiatric Institute, Dies at 89," *UCLA Newsroom*, April 16, 2001, http://www.newsroom.ucla.edu.

6. The Response of Psychiatrists

1. Annual Report FY 1943, Professional Service-Medical Division, Neuropsychiatric Branch, July 1943, 25, US Army Medical Division Historical Unit, hereafter referred to as USAMDHU.

2. Letter, Frank Fremont-Smith to Winfred Overholser, January 21, 1941, and Overholser to Fremont-Smith, January 23, 1941, Winfred Overholser Papers, Selective Service Record Group, RG 418, National Archives, Washington, DC, hereafter referred to as NA. Other psychiatrists on the NRC Neuropsychiatry Committee lobbying for 8a's repeal included Foster Kennedy, Franklin Ebaugh, Tracy Putnam, Harry Steckel, and John C. Whitehorn.

3. Memorandum for Major Omer from Captain Robert Bier, Selective Service Medical Division, "Subject: Diagnosis of mental cases on Form 200, 150 and others," January 29, 1941, 346.3 Gen., Selective Service Records, RG 147, Washington National Records Center, Suitland, MD, hereafter referred to as WNRC; Captain Robert Bier, Selective Service Medical Division, wrote Maj. Omer: "Instead of using the word 'mentally deficient' or 'defective,' [examiners should for example record] medical C #1—Type IV"; 622, RG 147, Lt. Colonel Seth Hammel, State Medical Officer, Kansas Selective Service, "Memorandum, All States Local Boards," August 29, 1941, 622 Kansas, 1941, RG 147, WNRC.

4. US Senate, Committee on Military Affairs, Hearings on S. 2368 . . . to . . . Remove the Requirement That Medical Statements Shall Be Furnished to Those Persons Performing Military Service Thereunder," 77th Cong., 2nd Sess., March 20, 1942, 11, 25, 30, 31. US Senate Committee on Military Affairs, Report No. 1262 on Medical Statements, 77th Cong., 2nd Sess., 1942, 3. An Act to Amend the Joint Resolution Approved August 27, 1940 (54 Stat. 858), as Amended, and the Selective Training and Service Act of 1940 (54 Stat. 858), as Amended, so as to Remove the Requirement that Medical Statements Shall Be Furnished to Those Persons Performing Military Service Thereunder; 56 *Stat.* 723, 77th Cong, 2nd Sess., July 28, 1942; *Public Law* 681, p. 723.

5. As we shall see in later chapters, psychiatrically diagnosed soldiers began to express fear in psychotherapy sessions that the label would stigmatize them, and employers, it was reported, when suspecting a job candidate of a diagnosis, would say they could not handle the job or just throw them out of the office. "Army Psychiatrist Asks Industry's Help in Employment of Psychiatric Casualties," September 1944, release for *PM*, 710 (Diseases), War Department General Staff, G-1 (Personnel), RG 165, WNRC; "Give Us a Break," *Reader's Digest*, November 1944, 9, 10. M. Grotjahn, "Experiences with Group Psychotherapy as a Method of Treatment for Veterans," *American Journal of Psychiatry* 103 (1947): 640.

6. The other special consultants appointed by the War Department to the investigating committee were Raymond Waggoner, director of Selective Service psychiatry; Karl Bowman, an original member of the Selective Service Psychiatric Advisory Committee in 1940; Frederick Parsons, head of the New York State Department of Mental Hygiene under Roosevelt; and Titus Harris, chair of the Department of Psychiatry, University of Texas; Report, "Meeting, Special Committee Appointed to Investigate the Rejection of Mental Cases at Induction Stations," August 31, 1943 (Special Committee), Overholser Papers, Library of Congress, Washington, DC, hereafter referred to as LC. Also, Memo from Col. H. T.

Wickert, Assistant to Chief Surgeon, to Col. R. D. Halloran, June 30, 1943, 1–2, E 31, Box 1297, RG 112, E 31 (ZJ), Box 1335, National Archives, College Park, MD, hereafter referred to as NACP. Cited in Josephine Callisen Bresnahan, "Dangers in Paradise: The Battle against Combat Fatigue in the Pacific War," PhD diss., Harvard University, May 1999.

7. Letter, Special Committee to Surgeon General Norman T. Kirk, September 21, 1943, 6, Overholser Papers, LC. Among the induction centers visited were those in Boston, New York City, Buffalo, Newark, Baltimore, Philadelphia, Washington, DC, Detroit, Dallas, San Francisco, Salt Lake City, Oklahoma City, and Omaha.

8. The Special Committee also found that World War II's figures were higher than in World War I. By July 1943, 40 out of 1,000 servicemen in the United States were in military hospitals for psychiatric reasons in contrast to only 30 out of 1,000 in World War I. In overseas army hospitals, the discrepancy was larger. In World War II, 60 out of every 1,000 servicemen were neuropsychiatric patients compared to only 16.5 out of 1,000 in World War I.

9. "Meeting Special Committee with Psychiatrists from Replacement Training Centers," September 1, 1943, Overholser Papers, LC. The training camp psychiatrists were Oscar B. Markey, Headquarters Branch Immaterial RTC, Camp Joseph T. Robinson, AR; Maj. Harry L. Freedman, Signal Corps RTC, Fort Monmouth, NJ; Maj. Joseph L. Knapp, Infantry RTC, Camp Croft, SC; Maj. Alfred Abrams, Field Artillery RTC, Fort Bragg, NC; Maj. Samuel Kraines, Tank Destroyer RTC, Camp Hood, TX; Maj. Robert Cohen, Ordnance RTC, Aberdeen Proving Grounds, MD; Maj. Julius Schreiber, Anti-Aircraft RTC, Camp Callan, CA; Maj. Bernard A. Cruvant, Engineering RTC, Fort Belvoir, VA.

10. Letter, Committee to Surgeon General Norman Kirk, September 21, 1943, 2, 5.

11. 36 Public Law 78-197, 58 *Statute* 596, at 598. Other members of the committee were Frank H. Lahey, surgeon-in-chief, Lahey Clinic; and Alan C. Woods, an ophthalmologist at Johns Hopkins University; US Senate, Committee on Military Affairs, Hearings on H.R. 1739, 39; US Senate, Committee on Military Affairs, Hearings on S. 763, 04–305, 448, 449; Letter, Pres. Franklin Roosevelt to Admiral Ross T. McIntire, December 28, 1943, Official File 1413-3, "Commission of Doctors" (Selective Service), Franklin Delano Roosevelt Library, Hyde Park, NY, hereafter referred to as FDRL; "Report of the Commission of Physicians Appointed to Examine the Requirements for Admission to the Army, Navy, and Marine Corps" ("Commission of Physicians"), March 30, 1944, 4–18, Official File 1413, FDRL.

12. "Report, "Commission of Physicians," March 30, 1944, esp. 10, 14, 5–9, 13, 16, 18, OF 1413, FDRL.

13. Memorandum, Brig. Gen. George F. Lull, Deputy Surgeon General to the Comm. Gen. Army Serv. Forces, August 18, 1943, requesting an investigation into the huge rate of neuropsychiatric hospitalizations and discharges and denying

that any of the cases were attributable to malingering. "In view of the above," he noted, "this office has been considering the advisability of increasing rather than decreasing, the stringent neuropsychiatric induction [screen]." From Army Serv. Forces file, 710, RG 160, NA.

14. Report, "Meeting of Special Committee Appointed to Investigate the Rejection of Mental Cases at Induction Stations," August 31, 1943, 3, 44, 4, 23; Letter, Special Committee to Kirk, September 21, 1943, 5, 6; both in Overholser Papers, LC.

15. *Washington Star*, December 30, 1943.

16. Leonard Rowntree, "Selective Service and Psychiatry," *Danville State Hospital Mental Health Bulletin* 20, no. 4 (October 8, 1942): 4–6; *Selective Service Medical Circular No. 4* (Washington, DC: US Government Printing Office, October 1943), 622, RG 147, WNRC. Luther Woodward, "The Value of Social Histories in Selection for the Armed Forces," 1943, 622, RG 147, WNRC.

17. Letter, Waggoner to Rowntree, January 27, 1941, 622, S.S., RG 147, WNRC; Letter, Colonel Fletcher to Langston, April 25, 1941, 333, RG 147; Minutes, NRC Neurology subcommittee, January 13, 1941, 6, 040.9–10, S.G.O., RG 112, WNRC; "Psychiatric Examinations in the Armed Forces," *War Medicine* 1 (1941): 217–18; Minutes, War Neuroses subcommittee, March 27, 1941, RG 52, NA.

18. Letter, Overholser to Paul McNutt, December 3, 1942, MED: Comm. on NP General, 1942–1943, National Academy of Sciences, Washington, DC, hereafter referred to as NAS. As we have seen, this was two days after Adolf Meyer wrote to Dr. Lewis Weed, NRC Medical Division, proposing that records be gathered to ascertain the mental health of eighteen- and nineteen-year-olds before screening.

19. Stevenson was a psychiatrist in World War I and trained at the Vineland Training School for the Mentally Defective in the 1920s. In an interview with Rebecca Greene, May 10, 1974, Red Bank, NJ, Stevenson recalled that he had convinced Colonel Wolfson at Governor's Island to send Stevenson the name of any person discharged from Fort Dix for mental disorders. Later, other army training camp officials in New York, New Jersey, and Connecticut gave Stevenson the names of neuropsychiatric dischargees, and social workers who worked with Stevenson in the child guidance movement in the 1920s voluntarily checked the criminal and medical records of soldiers. Part of this effort may have also been to prevent neuropsychiatric discharges from trying to get into the army again. Stevenson to Dr. Alan Gregg, September 22, 1942, Rockefeller Foundation Archives, New York City; "Project for the Improvement of Psychiatric Selection of Men for the Armed Forces," February 15–August 15, 1943, 622, RG 147, WNRC.

20. Renfrow's proposal suggested a social history questionnaire with questions on alcoholism, drug addiction, institutionalization, arrests, jobs, and reasons for leaving, and whether other members of the family were mentally ill. Letter, Hershey to Stimson, February 4, 1944, 622, RG 147, WNRC; here Hershey quotes from the letter Stimson sent him on January 20, 1944, "Attached Letter from Honorable H. L. Stimson to Governor Paul V. McNutt on Gathering

Psychiatric Information by Local Boards"; Memorandum, Col. L. H. Renfrow to Col. Eanes, January 30, 1943, "Special Investigation Confidential Report," 622, RG 147, WNRC.

21. Memorandum, Ivan C. Berlien, Captain Medical Corps, Assistant to William Menninger, to Col. Richard Eanes, Selective Service, April 5, 1944, 622 Gen., RG 147, WNRC; "Confidential Report of State Directors Conference," November 13, 1943, 53; Conferences, 105, RG 147, WNRC; Letter, Menninger to Strecker, April 3, 1944, Selective Service Medical Circular No. 4 File, Overholser Papers, St. Elizabeth's Hospital Records, RG 418, NA.

22. Letter, Waggoner to Rowntree, January 27, 1941, 622, S.S., RG 147, WNRC.

23. Telephone interview, Waggoner with Rebecca Greene, March 27, 1974.

24. *Medical Circular No. 4*, October 18, 1943, 622, RG 147, WNRC.

25. *Medical Circular No. 4*, 4–7; Luther Woodward, "The Operation of the Medical Survey at the National and State Levels," unpublished paper, May 24, 1944, National Conference of Social Work, Cleveland, National Committee for Mental Hygiene (NCMH)—Psychiatric Consultant, 1942–1943 folder, Medical Sciences, 200A, Rockefeller Foundation Archives, New York, hereafter referred to as Rockefeller; "Final Report of the Project for the Improvement of Psychiatric Selection of Men for the Armed Forces," February 15, 1943–February 15, 1944, NCMH—Psychiatric Consultant, 1942–1944 folder, 200A, Rockefeller; Selective Service, *Physical Examination of Selective Service Registrants* (Washington, DC, 1945), 153, indicates that 17,684,700 persons during the war were examined for induction and enlistment. Of these, about 13,000,000 received first examinations before the Medical Survey Program began in October 1943. Therefore, roughly 5,000,000 were examined during the period when the Medical Survey Program was in operation. Since we know that some type of medical survey was given to approximately 65 percent of the registrants receiving preinduction examinations according to the "Final Report of the Project for the Improvement of Psychiatric Selection of Men for the Armed Forces," we can calculate that about 3,000,000 had their records checked under the Medical Survey Program. Selective Service Medical Conference, June 5–6, 1944, 44–45, Conferences, 102, RG 147, WNRC; "Report of the Medical Survey Program, Selective Service System Alabama," July 1944, 622, RG 147, WNRC.

26. This is based on the Consumer Price Index and an inflation rate of 3.67 percent. See https://www.dollartimes.com/calculators/inflation.htm.

27. *Medical Circular No. 4*, 4–7, 13, 17, 23; "Confidential Report," Conferences, 105 file, RG 147, WNRC, 81, 79.

28. There were complaints in other states as well. See Letter, Woodward to Rowntree, February 29, 1944, 622 Gen., RG 147, WNRC, where he wrote: "There is still difficulty at a number of induction stations on account of the incomplete use of historical material or improper channeling which exposes the material to the possible review by registrants. When I was in Ohio there was complaint from three of the induction stations and I have received inquiry from Louisiana." At

the Selective Service Medical Conference, June 5–6, 1944, Conferences, 102, RG 147, WNRC, Rowntree noted: "Any procedure that might make this information available to the man would be very dangerous. We have had some very sad things happen to a man who has been able to see his own record and has gone home and raised hell about it. In one or two places it has been kind of rough— for instance, Arizona and Alabama" (58). Helen Perkinson, Field Worker, Trimble County, KY, to Helen C. Beauchamp, Director of the Division of Public Assistance, Frankfort, KY, December 11, 1944. This was attached to Letter, Frank D. Rash, Kentucky State Director of Selective Service, to Gen. Hershey, December 22, 1944, 622, RG 147, WNRC.

29. Letter, Col. W. L. Gist, Missouri Selective Service State Medical Officer, to Hershey, September 23, 1944, 622 No., RG 147, WNRC.

30. Letter, Gist to Hershey, September 23, 1944, 622 No., RG 147, WNRC.

31. Letter, Hershey to Stimson, February 4, 1944, 622, RG 147, WNRC; "Recommendation of the Bureau of the Budget with Respect to Selective Service Medical Circular No. 4, April 13, 1944," 2, 3, 622, RG 147, WNRC; *Medical Circular No. 4*, 5, 6, 2; Letter, Hershey to Smith, Director of the Bureau of the Budget, April 26, 1944, 622, RG 147, WNRC.

32. Report, "Comments on the Recommendations of Selective Service to the Bureau of the Budget," April 13, 1944, 622 Gen., Selective Service, RG 147, WNRC.

33. Selective Service MSP Director Renfrow shared this opinion. See "Conference for the Inauguration of the Medical Survey Plan by Selective Service," September 10, 1943, 13, 622, RG 147, WNRC; also later on Selective Service Medical Conference, June 5–6, 1944, 57, 102, RG 147, WNRC.

34. Letter, Strecker to Waggoner, April 7, 1944, 622, RG 147, WNRC; Memorandum, Col. Brainerd to Renfrow, June 9, 1944, "South Dakota," 622 South Dakota, RG 147, WNRC; Letter, Harry A. Jager, Director, US Office of Education to Renfrow, October 3, 1944, 622 N. Dakota, RG 147, WNRC; Paper, Woodward, "Operation of the Medical Survey at the National and State Levels," May 24, 1944, Medical Sciences, NCMH-Psychiatric Consultant 200A, Rockefeller.

35. Owens had done the legwork for the use of school records. During the summer of 1943, he contacted state educational officials and the director of the US Office of Education, Harry A. Jager, to see if Selective Service could use school records. See "Report Conference on Neuropsychiatry," July 6, 1943, conferences, 102, RG 147, WNRC.

36. "Confidential Report of State Directors Conference," November 13, 1943, 77–78, Conferences, 102, RG 147, WNRC; "Conference for the Inauguration of the medical survey plan by Selective Service," September 10, 1943, 27, 622, RG 147, WNRC; *Neuropsychiatry in World War II*, prep. and dir. Lt. Gen. Leonard D. Heaton, the Surgeon General, US Army, and ed. Col. Robert S. Anderson, MC, USA, Col. Albert J. Glass, MC, USA (Ret.), and Lt. Col. Robert J. Bernucci, MC, USA (Ret.) (Washington, DC: US Government Printing Office, 1966), 1:178.

37. Memorandum, Strecker, "Suggestions Concerning Proposed Medical Survey by Selective Service," February 15, 1944, Selective Service 622, RG 147, WNRC; "Recommendations of the Bureau of the Budget with Respect to Selective Service System Medical Circular No. 4," April 13, 1944, 622, RG 147, WNRC.

38. Memorandum, Strecker, "Suggestions Concerning Proposed Medical Survey by Selective Service," February 15, 1944, Selective Service 622, RG 147, WNRC; "Recommendations of the Bureau of: The Budget with Respect to Selective Service System Medical Circular No. 4," April 13, 1944, 622, RG 147, WNRC.

39. Annual Report, Neuropsychiatric Consultants Div., Fiscal Year 1944," 17; Annual Report, Neuropsychiatric Consultants Division, Fiscal Year 1945, 21, 22, 33.

40. Letter, Woodward to Rowntree, February 29, 1944, 622, RG 147, WNRC.

41. "Confidential Report of State Directors Conference," November 23, 1943, 81, Conferences, 105 file, RG 147, WNRC; Memorandum, Col. Gareth Brainerd, Oklahoma to Renfrow, August 23, 1944. In Oklahoma, 40 out 505 medical field agents resigned. Col. Louis Ritzhaupt in Oklahoma had asked for 25 paid supervisors, but Brainerd had to turn him down, from 622 Okl., RG 147, WNRC; Memorandum, Brainerd to Rowntree, "Pa. State Headquarters," March 7, 1944, 622 Pa., RG 147, WNRC; Medical Circular No. 4, 5; Report, Selective Service Medical Conference, June 5–6, 1944, 60–63, 102 file, RG 147, WNRC.

42. Memorandum, Strecker to R. D. Vining, Assistant Chief, Estimates Division, Bureau of the Budget, "Selective Service System-Medical Survey Program," February 11, 1944, 622, RG 147, WNRC.

43. Selective Service Medical Conference, June 5–6, 1944, 44, 45, Conferences, 102 file, RG 147, WNRC; "Report of the Medical Survey Program, Selective Service System Alabama," July 1944, 622, RG 147, WNRC; Menninger, Braceland, and Waggoner, "Psychiatric Selection of Men for the Armed Forces," 6, 622 W 1, Hershey Papers, USAMHRC.

44. Letter, Woodward to Rowntree, February 29, 1944, 622 General, RG 147, WNRC; "Conference on the Physical and Mental Qualifications for the Armed Services for Physicians and Dentists of Local Boards and Medical Advisory Boards and Local Board Members in the State of Iowa," August 26, 1943, Hershey Papers, USAMHRC; Woodward, "Operation of the Medical Survey at National and State Levels," 6, Medical Sciences, NCMH-Psychiatric Consultant 1942–1944, 200A folder, Rockefeller; "Conference for the inauguration of the medical survey plan by Selective Service," September 10, 1943, 41, 622 Gen., RG 147, WNRC.

45. Memorandum, Eanes to Hershey, "Traveling to New York City to Discuss Available Personnel Data," December 3, 1942, 622, RG 147, WNRC; Selective Service Medical Conference, June 5–6, 1944, 63, Conferences, 102, WNRC; Col. Samuel J. Kopetzky, "Validity of Psychiatric Criteria for Rejection for Services with the Armed Forces," *War Medicine* 6 (December 1944): 357, 360; "Confidential Report of State Directors Conference," November 13, 1943, Conferences, 105, RG

147, WNRC. Col. Kopetzky, who was in the Army Medical Corps, was most concerned with the unreliability of some of the New York City records. At the Selective Service Medical Conference, June 5–6, 1944, 102, RG 147, WNRC, Kopetzky noted: "I just want to say that in the large metropolitan area, one has to be extremely cautious about sanity. We had gone on the theory that there is an employee relationship between the man who signs the certificates. 4,000 were found not to be accurate . . . when we took the certificate of a private physician . . . 4 out of 5 certificates I have investigated [were] not substantiated" (12).

46. This is based on the *Consumer Price Index*. See https://www/dollartimes.com/inflation.

47. Memorandum, Eanes to Hershey, December 3, 1942, 1, 622, RG 147, WNRC; Letter, Milton Lozoff to Dr. Waggoner, December 12, 1944, 2, 622 Wisc., RG 147, WNRC.

48. US Congress, Digest of Appropriations (Washington, DC, 1944), 206; Overholser, Menninger, and Braceland were on the NRC's Advisory Committee on the Medical Survey.

49. In February 1944, Strecker tried to persuade Vining of the Bureau of the Budget not to fund the Medical Survey because of its serious bureaucratic deficiencies. But after Waggoner, Menninger, Overholser, and Stevenson wrote to Strecker and Selective Service, he reversed his stance and asked Vining for a six-month trial period. Memorandum, Strecker to Vining, February 11, 1944; Letter, Waggoner to Strecker, April 1944; Letter, Stevenson to Rowntree, March 14, 1944; Letter, Strecker to Overholser, March 31, 1944; Letter, Strecker to Waggoner, April 1, 1944; Strecker to Waggoner, July 4, 1944; Strecker to Vining, July 4, 1944, all in 622, RG 147, WNRC. Also see Letter, Overholser to Honorable Harold D. Smith, March 21, 1944, Selective Service System folder, Overholser Papers, RG 419, NA.

50. Letter, Parsons to Overholser, May 4, 1944, Selective Service Medical Circular No. 4 folder, Overholser Papers, RG 418, NA.

51. *Neuropsychiatry in World War II*, 1:180–84; "Confidential Report of State Directors Conference, November 7, 8, 9, 10, 1945," 50, 102, RG 147, WNRC; Letter, Hartman, Acting Director of Selective Service for Pa. to Hershey, August 10, 1945, 22 Pa., RG 147, WNRC.

52. William Menninger, *Psychiatry in a Troubled World* (New York: Knopf., 1948), 280–81. *Neuropsychiatry in World War II*, 1:184–85.

53. Interview, Rebecca Greene with Dr. George S. Stevenson, Red Bank, NJ, May 10, 1974; Telephone interview, Rebecca Greene with Waggoner, March 24, 1975.

54. Eli Ginzberg, *The Ineffective Soldier: Lessons for Management and the Nation*, foreword by Howard McC. Snyder, Major General, MC, USA, 3 vols. (New York: Columbia University Press, 1959).

55. FBI File No. 100-41674, "Richard Nathaniel Wright," July 8, 1944, 258, http://vault.fbi.gov/Richard%20Nathaniel%20Wright.

56. "World War, Cold War, 1939–1953," http://fbi.gov/history/brief-history; Athan G. Theoharis and John Stuart Cox, *The Boss: J. Edgar Hoover and the Great American Inquisition* (Philadelphia: Temple University Press, 1988), 157, 169, 170–73; Bruce D. Porter, *War and the Rise of the State: The Military Foundations of Modern Politics* (New York: Free Press, 1994), xv. It is interesting to note that the numbers of FBI employees vary considerably. For example, Theoharis has a much lower number—898 in 1940 and 4886 in 1945—as compared to the FBI's 2,400 in 1940 versus 13,000 in 1944.

57. This was done in at least the navy discharge centers. Letter, Hershey to the Hon. Secretary of the Navy, September 8, 1944, 622 General, S.S., RG 147, WNRC.

58. Memorandum, Howard Montgomery to Surgeon General McIntire, April 8, 1943, P3-1/P19-1, RG 52, N.A.

59. Memorandum, Acting Chief of the Bureau W. J. C. Agnew to Chief of Naval Personnel, August 8, 1945, Psychiatric Screening of Enlisted Personnel Returning from Overseas Duty, P3-1/P19-1 (1945), RG 52, NA.

60. Both the psychologist Carney Landis and the psychologist Walter Shipley were on the NRC Committee on Problems of Neurotic Behavior. For more biographical information, see "In Memoriam: Carney Landis," *American Journal of Psychiatry*, http://ajp.psychiatryonline.org; and on Shipley, see *New York Times*, http://timesmachine.nytimes.com; and Shipley Institute, https://www.stoelting.com/shipley-institute-of-living-scale.

61. "Interim Report of the Personal Inventory Project," June 25, 1941, NRC Division of Anthropology and Psychology, Committee on Problem of Neurotic Behavior, Subcommittee on Personal Inventory. NRC Committee, Neuropsychiatry, II folder, Overholser Papers, RG 418, NA; "Summary of Final Report," Sept. 29,1941, NRC Committee on Problems of Neurotic Behavior, Subcommittee on Personal Inventory folder, Overholser Papers, St. Elizabeth's Hospital Records, RG 418, NA; "Summary of Conference on Personal Inventory, NRC," July 25, 1942, NRC Committee on Problems of Neurotic Behavior, Subcommittee on Personal Inventory, Overholser Papers, RG 418, NA. Earlier, during World War I, Robert Woodworth designed a simple personal data sheet, which did not work well. It was a forerunner of the Minnesota Multiphasic Personality Inventory (MMPI) currently in use. See E. Jones, K. C. Hyams, and S. Wessely, "Screening for Vulnerability to Psychological Disorders in the Military: An Historical Survey," *Journal of Medical Screening* 10, no. 1 (2003): 40–46.

62. Report, Subcommittee on Psychiatry, NRC Committee on Medical Research, June 29, 1944, 11, Project N113 P. I, Serial 173 file, Office of Scientific Research and Development Records, RG 227, NA; Charles Bray, *Human Factors in Military Efficiency* (Princeton, NJ, 1948), 1:40, 75–79; Hunt and Wittson first tried out the new version of the Personal Inventory on thousands of recruits and over one hundred dischargees at the New London, CT, submarine base and

at the Newport Naval training station. Oral History of Wittson, December 6, 1979, http://digitalcommons.unmc.edu.

63. For more information on the inventors, see Minutes, Association for Psychoanalytic Medicine, http://theapm.org/cont; Obituary, Arthur Weider, http://www.legacy.com/obituaries. David Wechsler was known for developing the Wechsler Intelligence test for adults as well as children. See https://www.intelltheory.com/wechsler.shtml. And see Marlon Brando, *Songs My Mother Taught Me* (1994), 150, on Bela Mittleman and Brando's rejection from military service in the Korean War.

64. "The Selectee Index: A Method for Quick Testing of Selectees for the Armed Forces," August 31, 1943, Committee on Medical Research, Office of Scientific Research and Development; Arthur Weider, "The Cornell Selectee Index: A Method of Quick Testing of Selectees for the Armed Forces," *Journal of the American Medical Association* 144 (1944); Arthur Weider, "Cornell Selectee Index," *War Medicine* 7 (April 1945): 209–13.

65. "Selection of the Emotionally Unstable Personnel by Battle Noise Equipment," February 10, 1945, Project N 113 Contract, Office of Scientific Research and Development, OEMsr-834, RG 227, NA. Altogether, Wittson and Hunt gave a trial run of the test to 1,582 men at the Newport Rhode Island training station, half given indoor and half outdoors.

66. The designers of the NSA also included, from the I&E Division's Army Research Branch, Louis Guttmann, a sociology professor at Cornell University during the war; the sociologist Edward Suchman, later a professor at the University of Pittsburgh; Paul Lazarsfeld, founder of the Columbia University Bureau of Applied Social Research; the researcher Shirley A. Star; and John A. Clausen, professor of sociology at Berkeley.

67. The four volumes of Stouffer's *Studies in Social Psychology in World War II* include *The American Soldier: Adjustment during Army Life* (Princeton, NJ: Princeton University Press, 1949); *The American Soldier: Combat and Its Aftermath* (Princeton, NJ: Princeton University Press, 1949); *Experiments on Mass Communication* (Princeton, NJ: Princeton University Press, 1949); and *Measurement and Prediction* (Princeton, NJ: Princeton University Press, 1950).

68. Stouffer, *The American Soldier: Combat and Its Aftermath*, 412, 413. Stouffer notes (413) that altogether 803 infantry recruits were tested, of which 73 were considered "psychoneurotic" and the remaining 730 normal; also, Stouffer, *Measurement and Prediction*, 488, 489, 492–500, 502–12.

69. Edgar Jones et al., "Screening for Vulnerability to Psychological Disorders," *Journal of Medical Screening* 10, no. 1 (February 2003): 40–46.

70. Mark K. Wells, *Courage and Air Warfare: The Allied Aircrew Experience in the Second World War* (London: Frank Cass, 1995), 7–11.

71. Report, Subcommittee on Psychiatry, NRC, Committee on Medical Research, June 29, 1944, 12, Project N113 P.1. Serial 173 file, RG 227, NA.

72. W. A. Hunt and C. L. Wittson, "The Screening Test in Military Selection," *Psychological Review* 51, no. 1 (January 1944): 37–46; Weider, "The Cornell Selectee Index," 225.

73. Hunt and Wittson, "The Screening Test in Military Selection," 43; Charles Bray, *Human Factors in Military Efficiency* (Princeton, 1948), 1:78.

74. Weider, "The Cornell Selectee Index," 224; "Summary of Final Report," September 30, 1941, NRC Committee on Problems of Neurotic Behavior, Subcommittee on Personal Inventory folder, Overholser Papers, RG 418, NA.

75. Wells, *Courage and Air Warfare*, 6–12.

76. "Summary of Final Report," September 30, 1941, NRC Committee on Problems of Neurotic Behavior, Subcommittee on Personal Inventory folder, Overholser Papers, RG 418, NA; Report, Subcommittee on Psychiatry, NRC Committee on Medical Research, June 29, 1944, 11, Project N113 P.1. Serial 173 file, RG 227, NA; Weider, "The Cornell Selectee Index," 224; "Selection of the Emotionally Unstable Personnel by Battle Noise Equipment," February 10, 1945, Project N113 Contract Office of Scientific Research and Development, OEMsr-834 file, RG 227, NA. See Report Subcommittee Psychiatry, June 2, 1944, 8. In Memorandum for Stouffer, "Operation of the NSA, New York Armed Forces Induction Station," March 5, 1945, HD:730 (NP) Induction Data NP Screening Adjunct file, USAMDHU; also see "Neuropsychiatry Screening Adjunct," Commanding General 8th Service Forces, Dallas, TX, April 9, 1945, RG 165, WNRC; "Memorandum to Major Devinney, Stouffer, Dr. Guttmann, and Major Appel, "Some Field Experience with the NSA," April 4, 1945, HD:730 (NP), USAMDHU; US Army Medical Department, *Neuropsychiatry in World War II*, 1:186–88.

77. Dr. Shipley's sample included over 500 Air Force pilots and sailors; about 1,000 NYA men between the ages of eighteen and twenty-five; about 150 youth prisoners from the Lewisburg and Chillicothe federal penal institutions; about 100 "troublemakers" at the Rikers Island Correctional Facility; 78 prison "psychopaths" at the US Medical Center in Springfield, MO; 53 "drunkards" at Rikers Island; about 120 "passive" homosexuals at Rikers Island; 26 "active" homosexuals at Rikers Island and the State Reformatory in Concord, MA; 36 drug addicts at Hart Island Jail, New York City; 82 prisoners at the US penitentiary in Terre Haute, IN; 53 hospital patients at a mental hospital; and 27 psychoneurotic inpatients and outpatients. "Interim Report of the Personal Inventory Project," June 25, 1941, NRC Division of Anthropology and Psychology, Committee on Problems of Neurotic Behavior, Subcommittee on Personal Inventory, NRC Committee Neuropsychiatry II folder, Overholser Papers, RG 418, NA.

78. Bray, *Human Factors in Military Efficiency*, vol. 1.

79. Report, Subcommittee on Psychiatry, NRC Committee on Medical Research, June 29, 1944, 11–12, Project N113p.1. Serial 173 file, RG 227, NA; Seidenfeld specialized in work on the effects of blindness and polio on children's psychological and cognitive development. Graham explored the visual aspects of

gunfire control, selection of specialized military personnel, and psychiatric screening. M. A. Seidenfeld, "Behavior of Post-Polio School Children on the California Test of Personality, Abstract," *American Psychologist* 2 (1947): 274. On Graham, see Lorrin A. Riggs, National Academy of Sciences, *Clarence Henry Graham: 1906–1971: A Biographical Memoir* (Washington, DC, 1975).

80. Hunt and Wittson, "The Screening Test in Military Selection," 39–40.

81. Stouffer, *Measurement and Prediction*, 4:506.

82. Interview, Rebecca Greene with Dr. Herbert Spiegel, December 18, 1975, New York City; Annual Report, 31st Station Hospital, 43 SP Area, 710, RG 112, WNRC; H. Spiegel, "Psychiatry with an Infantry Battalion," undated manuscript, USAMDHU; H. Spiegel, "Psychiatric Observations in the Tunisian Campaign," *American Journal of Orthopsychiatry* 14 (1944): 381–85; William L. Sharp MD, "Stress versus Predisposition in Combat Psychiatry," *Journal of the Indiana Medical Association*, December 1947.

83. Bray, *Human Factors in Military Efficiency*, 1:81; Report, Subcommittee on Psychiatry, NRC Committee on Medical Research, June 29, 1944, 8, 12, NAS; Stouffer, *Measurement and Prediction*, 4:506.

84. Report, Subcommittee on Psychiatry, NRC, June 29, 1944, 8, 12. For a study on false positives, see Edgar Jones and Simon Wessely, *Shell Shock to PTSD* (New York: Psychology Press, 2005), 107, citing A. Ellis and H. S. Conrad, "The Validity of Personality Inventories in Military Practice," *Psychological Bulletin* 45 (1948): 420.

85. Wells, *Courage and Air Warfare*, 9.

86. Jones and Wessely, *Shell Shock to PTSD*, 107–13.

7. The Horrors of War and Beginnings of Change

1. Report, "Observations from Patients Returning from Overseas on Hospital Ships Algonquin and Acadia," about March 1944, 710 (Neuropsychiatry), SGO 112, National Archives, Washington, DC, hereafter referred to as NA; Ernie Pyle, *Brave Men* (New York: Grosset & Dunlap, 1944), 103. Interview, Arthur C. Wenzel by Shaun Illingworth and Patrick Clark-Barnes, April 11, 2005, Rutgers Oral History Archives, hereafter referred to ROHA, https://oralhistory.rutgers.edu/image/PDFS/wenzel_arthur.pdf.

2. Annual Report, 1944 Headquarters II Corps, Office of the Surgeon, Excerpt, 27, Psychiatry, CMR General Files 1940, RG 226, NA; Craig L. Symonds, *Operation Neptune: The D-Day Landings and the Allied Invasion of Europe* (New York: Oxford University Press, 2014), 122; Stephen E. Ambrose, *D-Day: The Climactic Battle of World War II* (New York: Simon and Schuster, 1994), 151; http://www.history.army.mil.com; Rick Atkinson, *The Guns at Last Light* (New York: Henry Holt, 2013), 85–87, 488–91.

3. Memorandum, Lt. Col. Burgess L. Gordon, Hospital Division, to Neuropsychiatry Division, "Psychoneuroses among Service of Supply Troops, February 6, 1945, 1–2, HD:730 (NP), ETMD's Extracts on NP, US Army Medical

Division Historical Unit, Fort Detrick, Frederick, MD, hereafter referred to as USAMDHU.

4. Josephine Bresnahan, "Dangers in Paradise: The Battle against Combat Fatigue in the Pacific War," PhD diss., Harvard University, 1999, 128, referring to unpublished paper, Neuropsychiatric Disability, New Georgia, Solomon Islands, July 29, 1943, 2, Surgeon General's Office Records, RG 112, E 31, Box 452, National Archives, College Park, MD, hereafter referred to as NACP.

5. Roy E. Appleman, James M. Burns, Russell A. Gugeler, and John Stevens, *Okinawa: The Last Battle* (Washington, DC: US Army Center for Military History, 1993), 60, 102, 143, 384–86, 398, 441, 447, 454–56, 473. James Wells interviewed by Shaun Illingworth and Spencer Scheffling, ROHA, 19, 24, https://oralhistory.rutgers.edu/image/PDFs/wells_james.pdf; William C. Schnorr interviewed by S. Illingworth and Jared Kosch, ROHA, 23, https://oralhistory.rutgers.edu/image/PDFs/schnorr_william.pdf.

6. *Neuropsychiatry in World War II*, prep. and publ. under dir. Lt. Gen. Hal B. Jennings, the Surgeon General, US Army, ed. Col. William S. Mullins, MC, USA, ed. Col. Albert J. Glass, MC, USA (Ret.) (Washington, DC: US Government Printing Office, 1973), 2:461. As to officers, Patch still insisted that they should be court-martialed for psychoneurosis, but Berezin wrote that he got around this threat by diagnosing suspected officers with an organic disorder, such as blast concussion.

7. Patton came from a long-time distinguished Southern military family. At least four of his ancestors had attended Virginia Military Institute (VMI) in Lexington, Virginia. At least sixteen fought for the Confederacy. Patton himself transferred from VMI to West Point in New York, graduating in 1909. Carlo D'Este, *Patton: A Genius for War* (New York: Harper, 1995), 10–50, 500–50. Stimson Diary, Biographical Notes on General G. S. Patton Jr., April 1947, Xerox 3153, Drawer 920, George C. Marshall Research Library, Lexington, VA, 24450, hereafter referred to as GCMRL.

8. Albert E. Cowdrey, *Fighting for Life: American Military Medicine in World War II* (New York: Free Press, 1994), 118.

9. George Patton, *The War as I Knew It* (1947), 236.

10. D'Este, *Patton*, 545.

11. D'Este, *Patton*, 545.

12. D'Este, *Patton*, 544, 545, 533–38.

13. Gerald W. Grumet, "General George S. Patton, Jr. and the Conquest of Fear," *Psychological Reports* 105 (2009): 334.

14. Russell F. Weigley, *Eisenhower's Lieutenants* (Bloomington: Indiana University Press, 1981), 37; Goronwy Rees, "Supreme Commander," *Spectator*, January 7, 1949; Paul Johnson, *Eisenhower: A Life* (New York: Penguin, 2015), 138. Eisenhower grew up in Abilene, Kansas, one of seven sons of a strict father of German Mennonite descent who worked in a local creamery. He graduated West Point in 1915 and was an aide to Pershing in World War I and to MacArthur in the Philippines in the 1930s. He was a member of the War Plans Division

under Marshall as of December 18, 1941, assistant chief of staff of the Operations Division by March 1942, and by late June 1942 commander of the European theater of operations.

15. Grumet, "General George S. Patton, Jr. and the Conquest of Fear," 335.

16. Drew Pearson, "The Washington Merry-Go-Round," Drawer 920, GCMRL.

17. Hamilton Fish wrote several books criticizing Roosevelt for America's entry into the war. For example, Hamilton Fish, *FDR, the Other Side of the Coin: How We Were Tricked into World War II* (New York, 1976).

18. "Patton Struck Ailing Soldier, Apologizes to Him and Army," *New York Times*, November 24, 1943, 1:5, 6:2. See also *New York Times*, November 5, 1943, 7:1; *New York Times*, December 16,1943, 7:1; *New York Times*, November 26, 1943, 12:1; *New York Times*, November 27, 1943, 3:1; *New York Times*, November 28, 1943, 54:2; "Comment on the Patton Case," *New York Times*, November 26, 1943, 22:6, 7.

19. Letters about Patton, Patterson-Pershing file, Pentagon, Box 79, Marshall Papers, GCMRL.

20. For correspondence on Patton in Mrs. Roosevelt's file, see Letters, Harold C. Lewis, Coyne Electrical School, to Mrs. Roosevelt, November 25, 1943; Mrs. Edward Adams to Mrs. Roosevelt, December 21, 1943; John Wayne to Mrs. Roosevelt, November 26, 1943; W. B. Sigmund to Mrs. Roosevelt, November 25, 1943; J. J. Roland to Mrs. Roosevelt, December 15, 1943; J. Johnson to Mrs. Roosevelt, November 27, 1943; Mrs. A. M. Lottie to Mrs. Roosevelt, November 26, 1943; Mrs. Mary A. Kafahl to Mrs. Roosevelt, November 25, 1943; Mrs. Frank Goddard to Mrs. Roosevelt, November 24, 1943; James P. Griffin to Mrs. Roosevelt, November 23, 1943; Nora B. Beyer to Mrs. Roosevelt, November 23, 1943; William Murphy to Mrs. Roosevelt, November 25, 1943; Mrs. Charles W. Horr Jr. to Mrs. Roosevelt, November 24, 1943. Especially see Letters from Beyer, Kafahl, and Adams, all in Box 1778, Eleanor Roosevelt Papers, Franklin Delano Roosevelt Library, Hyde Park, NY, hereafter referred to as FDRL.

21. Ben Shephard, *A War of Nerves* (Cambridge, MA: Harvard University Press, 2001), 219. For Omar Bradley's views on the slapping incidents, Steven L. Ossad, *Omar Nelson Bradley: America's GI General, 1893–1981* (Columbia: University of Missouri Press, 2017), 142–43.

22. Letters from Stimson to members of the Senate Committee on Military Affairs, November and December 1943; Letter, Stimson to Representative Robert A. Grant, House of Representatives, December 8, 1943; and Report to Senate Committee from Eisenhower, Drawer 920, GCMRL.

23. Old Time Radio Downloads, http://Oldtimerradiodownloads.com.

24. Letter, John Rogers, DuPont & Co., 342 Madison Avenue, NYC, to Mrs. Roosevelt, November 30, 1943; Letter, Pauline Frederick Baukhage, the Blue Network, to Miss Dorothy Dow, Mrs. Roosevelt's Office, December 2, 1943, containing transcripts of radio broadcasts, Davis, Elmer file, ER 70, 1943 Box, ER White House Correspondence, FDRL.

25. D'Este, *Patton*, 546; *Complete Presidential Press Conferences of Franklin Delano Roosevelt*, 22:226–28 (New York, 1973).

26. Grumet, "General George S. Patton, Jr. and the Conquest of Fear," 314, 320, 322, 334–36. Dr. Grumet is a long-time practicing psychiatrist in Rochester, NY, with a residency in psychiatry from the University of Rochester, internship at Philadelphia General Hospital, and MD from New York University.

27. D'Este, *Patton*, 549–55. Ossad, *Omar Nelson Bradley*, 142–43.

28. Arthur C. Wenzel with Shaun Illingworth and Patrick Clark-Barnes, Tinton Falls, New Jersey, April 11, 2005, ROHA.

29. For the hearing of the House Committee on Military Affairs on Rapido, which eventually dismissed charges that Clark had shown poor judgment, see Lee Carraway Smith, *A River Swift and Deadly: The 36th "Texas" Infantry Division at the Rapido River* (Austin: Eakin, 1989), 97.

30. *Neuropsychiatry in World War II*, prep. and dir. Lt. Gen. Leonard D. Heaton, the Surgeon General, US Army, and ed. Col. Robert S. Anderson, MC, USA, Col. Albert J. Glass, MC, USA (Ret.), and Lt. Col. Robert J. Bernucci, MC, USA (Ret.) (Washington, DC: US Government Printing Office, 1966), 1:136, 376–86.

31. *Neuropsychiatry in World War II*, 1:129–48.

32. On the leakage of the memorandum to the press, see esp. *Neuropsychiatry in World War II*, 1:137–39.

33. *Neuropsychiatry in World War II*, 1:131–39.

34. Letter, "Dear General," signed Eisenhower, dated January 29, 1944, copy: Marshall, Box 67, Folder 1, Marshall Papers, GCMRL. In fairness to the generals, many soldiers, according to surveys by Stouffer for I&E, little tolerated comrades who appeared to use "combat exhaustion" to avoid combat, since everyone was supposed to try to overcome fear and fight. Michael Doubler, *Closing with the Enemy: How GIs Fought the War in Europe, 1944–1945* (Kansas, 1994), 244. For more on the attitudes of soldiers about combat exhaustion, see Paul M. Johnson, "Every Man Has His Breaking Point: The Attitudes of American Infantrymen towards Combat Fatigue in World War II," final paper, University of Wisconsin, Eau Claire, Wisconsin, 2006.

35. "4th Service Command and the Army Service Forces," http://schistory.net; *Neuropsychiatry in World War II*, 1:72.

36. Letter, Mrs. Ittleson, Executive Committee of the National Committee for Mental Hygiene, November 30, 1943; Letter, Eleanor Roosevelt to Norman Kirk, Army Surgeon General, December 3, 1943, Eleanor Roosevelt Papers, FDRL.

37. Menninger's having been a scout leader probably endeared him to FDR, whose eldest son was a scout. FDR wanted all his sons to be scouts and possibly contracted poliomyelitis on a trip with the Scouts. James Tobin, *The Man He Became: How FDR Defied Polio to Win the Presidency* (New York: Simon and Schuster, 2013), 5.

38. Menninger received his MD from Cornell and interned at Bellevue Hospital in the 1920s. Stamp Collectors, http://www.pinterest.com; Henry W.

Brosin, "A Biographical Sketch"; and *A Psychiatrist for a Troubled World: Selected Papers of William C. Menninger, MD*, ed. Bernard H. Hall (New York: Viking, 1967). Lawrence Friedman, *Menninger: The Family and the Clinic* (New York: Knopf, 1990).

39. Interview, John Appel with Rebecca Greene, Philadelphia, December 23, 1975.

40. Harvey Bundy graduated from Yale with high honors, attended Harvard Law School, and was a law clerk to Supreme Court Justice Oliver Wendell Holmes, liaison to the OSRD during World War II, and father of McGeorge Bundy, who was active in the Kennedy administration, as well as William Bundy. David Halberstam, *The Best and the Brightest*, foreword by John McCain (New York: Modern Library, 2001), 54–57.

41. Frederick Osborn, Address to Special Service Division, January 20, 1943, Addresses to Special Service Officers 1942–1943, Manuscript Collection 24, American Philosophical Society, Philadelphia, hereafter referred to as APS.

42. Cowdrey, *Fighting for Life: American Military Medicine in World War II*, 140–44; *Neuropsychiatry in World War II*, 1:108, 393, 409.

43. Statement by Gen. Norman Kirk, Surgeon Gen., US Army, at Press Conference, including portion from Menninger, May 9, 1944, 702, RG 112, WNRC. See also *Neuropsychiatry in World War II*, 1:134–39. Similar concern about the education of American youth was indicated in an Annual Report, 9th Station Hospital (Pacific), December 30, 1943, 1, in RG 112, E 31, Box 1312, NACP, cited in Bresnahan, "Dangers in Paradise," 144–45. Specifically, it stated: "Twenty years of cynicism and isolationism have done little to provide a basis for understanding the meaning of the vast conflict in which the country is engaged. . . . Many soldiers do not have sufficient will to fight to protect them against psychiatric breakdown under stress."

44. Terry Copp and Bill McAndrew, *Battle Exhaustion: Soldiers and Psychiatrists in the Canadian Army, 1939–1945* (Montreal, 1990), 50; *Neuropsychiatry in World War II*, 2:11.

45. Memorandum, "Publicity on Psychoneuroses," 710, RG 112, Statement, Gen. Norman Kirk (with portion by) U.S. Army at Press Conference, May 9, 1944, 702, RG 112; Press Release, "Army Psychiatrist Says Public Needs Better Understanding of Mental Illness," June 24, 1944, War Dept. Gen. Staff, G-1, RG 165. Letter, Overholser to Menninger, April 5, 1944; Menninger to Overholser, March 30, 1944, "Memorandum Soliciting Opinions Regarding Psychiatric Nomenclature," March 27, 1944, all from Surg. Gen. Div. of Psychiatry, Overholser Papers, St. Elizabeth Hospital, RG 418, NA. Before the war, Farrell had been an instructor in psychiatry at the Boston University Medical School. He was appointed as assistant first to Madigan in early 1942 when Madigan oversaw psychiatry for the surgeon general, and for a month between the death of Halloran and succession of Menninger, Farrell oversaw the psychiatry division. *Neuropsychiatry in World War II*, 1:27, 33. Letter, T. O. Kraabel, National Director

of the American Legion, to Maj. Gen. Norman T. Kirk, Surgeon Gen., September 9, 1944, 220.811, RG 112, WNRC, in which Kraabel stated, "From time to time . . . the diagnosis of psychoneurosis [has been] indiscriminately used . . . when there were other conditions . . . for which the veteran could have been discharged. . . . [We advise that] if there are other causes sufficient for discharge . . . they be used instead." The response to this statement is not known.

46. Memorandum, Surgeon General Kirk to Commanding General Headquarters Fifth Service Command, Columbus, OH, "Retraining Psychoneurotic Patients," January 28, 1944, 701.7—(Insanity), Surgeon General's Office Records, RG 112, Washington National Records Center, Suitland, MD, hereafter referred to as WNRC; "Report Developmental Battalions," undated, 1, 3, HD:730 (NP) Circulars, Armed Service Forces Circulars 1944, USAMDHU; Memorandum to the Director, Personnel Affairs Division, "Red Cross," signed Joe N. Dalton, Major General GSC Director of Personnel, 080 Red Cross, War Department Special and General Staff, G-1 Personnel, RG 165, NA; Memorandum, Dr. William Menninger to Col. C. E. Nixon, Director of Military Personnel Division, Pentagon, about May 1944, 701.7; Insanity, Surgeon General's Office, RG 112, WNRC.

47. Memorandum, Deputy Chief of Staff to Chief of Staff G-1, "Retraining Soldiers Previously Disabled by Psychoneurotic Disorders," September 1944, War Department 353.9, RG 165, NA.; Memoranda, Surgeon General Kirk to Assistant G-1, "Psychoneuroses," December 7, 1944, 710 (Insanity), G-1, RG 165, WNRC. William Menninger, *Psychiatry in a Troubled World* (New York: Macmillan, 1948), 285, 286.

48. *Neuropsychiatry in World War II*, 1:409.

49. Speech, William Menninger to the 61 Division Psychiatrists, December 11, 1943, Conference of Psychiatrists, Army Medical Center, DC, Papers and Speeches by Menninger, Menninger Foundation Archives, Topeka, KS, hereafter referred to as Menninger Foundation Archives; Eric Jaffe, *A Curious Madness: An American Combat Psychiatrist, a Japanese War Crimes Suspect, and an Unsolved Mystery from World War II* (New York: Simon & Schuster, 2014), 137; *Neuropsychiatry in World War II*, 1:33, 47, 408–10. Nathan Hale, *The Rise and Crisis of Psychoanalysis in the United States: Freud and the Americans, 1917–1985* (New York: Oxford University Press, 1995), 187–90; Rebecca Jo Plant, "William Menninger and American Psychoanalysis, 1946–48," *History of Psychiatry* 16, no. 2 (2005): 181–202. While the Papers from the Menninger Foundation Archives would indicate that a conference in Washington, DC, occurred on December 11, there is some discrepancy, as *Neuropsychiatry in World War II*, 1:409, refers without citation to a three-day conference in Washington, DC, in November 1943, after Halloran died, to train division psychiatrists, which included presentations by Appel, Hanson, and the inspector general, Howard McC. Snyder. *Neuropsychiatry in World War II*, 1:33.

50. Hines was also concerned about insufficient personnel in VA hospitals and urged Roosevelt to have the army staff VA hospitals. In this correspondence,

Roosevelt denied his request, suggesting instead that non-service-connected cases should not be hospitalized by the VA and that the VA should increase its patient-to-staff ratio and employ more female workers and volunteers. Dir., Bur. of Budget, Memo for Pres. January 7, 1943; Letter, Roosevelt to Hines, January 8, 1943, Vet Ad, Fed Hosp, VA1943–1944, Box 5, OF8b, FDRL.

51. Letter, Pres. Franklin D. Roosevelt to Edward Strecker, President American Psychiatric Association, March 14, 1944, PPF 7131 (American Psychiatric Association), FDRL; Memorandum, Menninger to Hillman, "Plans for Salvage of Psychoneurotic Patient," January 18, 1944, 701–7 (Insanity), RG 112, WNRC; Menninger, "The Responsibility of Neuropsychiatry for Rehabilitating Veterans," unpublished speech delivered to Michigan Society of Neurology and Psychiatry, September 1944, 10, 11, Menninger Foundation Archives.

52. The Army Surgeon General was Norman Kirk, Navy Surgeon General Ross T. McIntire, and Army Air Force Surgeon General David Grant. Memorandum for General Marshall, February 26, 1944, White House, Washington, signed FDR, Box 81, Folder 9, Marshall Papers, GCMRL; Letter from Secretary of War Henry Stimson to the President, March 29, 1944, signed and approved by the President on April 4, 1944 regarding report of physicians appointed by Franklin Delano Roosevelt to Investigate hospitalization of American fliers in England, February 1944–April 1944, Drawer 920, GCMRL. Donald L. Miller, *Masters of the Air: America's Bomber Boys Who Fought the Air War against Nazi Germany* (New York: Simon and Schuster, 2016), 127, 278–79. The manpower pressure pending D-Day was so great that crewmen could be flying as many as twenty missions in two months. Malcolm Grow, the 8th's Chief Medical Officer, reported an increase of flight fatigue and mental breakdown in seventy-three crews (127).

53. Cowdrey, *Fighting for Life*, 140–44; *Neuropsychiatry in World War II*, 1:108, 393, 409; Shephard, *A War of Nerves*, 212–17.

8. From Prediction to Prevention

1. *The Medical Department of the U.S. Army in the World War*, ed. Thomas Salmon and Norman Fenton, *Neuropsychiatry in the American Expeditionary Forces*, vol. 10 (Washington, DC: US Government Printing Office, 1929), 277, 278, 309, 325, 328, 343–45.

2. Roy R. Grinker MD and John Spiegel MD, *War Neuroses in North Africa, January–May 1943* (New York: Josiah Macy Jr. Foundation, 1943), 133, 134; "Neuropsychiatric Survey of the American Division, Bougainville," December 25, 1943–April 12, 1944, 26–28, American Division (SWPA), Neuropsychiatric Survey file, US Army Medical Division Historical Unit, Fort Detrick, MD, hereafter referred to as USAMDHU.

3. Excerpt Report New Georgia Campaign, October 31, 1943, HD:730 (NP) Neuroses—War Neuroses, USAMDHU.

4. Memorandum, Major Samuel A. Challman, MC to Lt. Col. Malcolm J. Farrell, NP/Assistant to the Surgeon General, Memo, January 14, 1943, 1, in

Surgeon General's Office Records, Record Group (RG) 112, E 31 (ZI) Box 1318, National Archives, College Park, MD, hereafter referred to as NACP; cited by Josephine Bresnahan, "Dangers in Paradise: The Battle against Combat Fatigue in the Pacific War," PhD diss., Harvard University, 1999.

5. Memorandum, E. D. Post, Col. Gen. Staff, Chief of Staff to Headquarters, Alaska Defense Command, November 30, 1942, to Surgeon General, US Army, "Existing Neuropsychiatric Problems in Alaska Defense Command," HD 730, NP, Alaska, USAMDHU.

6. Abram Kardiner and Herbert Spiegel, *War Stress and Neurotic Illness* (New York: P. B. Hoeber, 1947), vi.

7. Anonymous interview with Col. Raymond R. Scott, Medical Corps, August 1943, HD 730 (NP) CORRESPONDENCE Headquarters, NATOUSA, USAMDHU. Letter, Halloran to Foster, July 1, 1943, HD; 730 (NP) Correspondence NP Consultants Division, US Army, USAMDHU, cf. Memorandum, John A. Rogers to Commanding General Armed Service Forces for the Surgeon General, August 7, 1943, "Deficient Mental Toughness of Military Personnel," Army Service Folder, 710, RG 165, National Archives, Washington, DC, hereafter referred to as NA.

8. See earlier discussion in Chapter 4 of Navy Commander Smith's memorandum on Guadalcanal and its publication in *Time* and *Newsweek* at the end of May 1943; Bresnahan, "Dangers in Paradise," 147; for descriptions of the effect on mental breakdown of tropical climate, malaria, typhus, and medicines for malaria such as atabrine and racist fears of the Japanese, see 148–51. Report, Essential Technical Medical Data (ETMD) Far East, October 1944, HD:730 (NP) ETMDs NP Excerpts SWPA and FE, USAMDHU; Annual Report 1944, Headquarters II Corps Office of the Surgeon, Excerpt, CMR General Files 1940 Psychiatry, Records of the Office of Strategic Services, NA.

9. Marvin R. Plessset MD, "Psychoneurotics in Combat," *American Journal of Psychiatry* 103 (July 1946): 87–90.

10. Herbert Spiegel MD, "Psychiatry with an Infantry Battalion," undated, USAMDHU; also "The Prediction of Neuropsychiatric Breakdown in Combat," MTO-62, Attitude Surveys Relating to Neuropsychiatric Cases, Research Branch, Information and Education Division, US Army, RG 330, NA. William L. Sharp MD, "Stress versus Predisposition in Combat Psychiatry," *Journal of the Indiana Medical Association* (December 1947): 1,234–39.

11. Memorandum, The Chief of the Bureau of Medicine and Surgery to Commanding Officers, Naval Hospitals in United States and US Naval Convalescent Hospitals, "Origin of Neuropsychiatric Disorders in Patients Who Have Been Exposed to Combat Conditions," June 30, 1943, P3-1AP19-1 (123–40), RG 52, NA.

12. Memorandum, Brig. Gen. F. A. Blesse, Surgeon of Headquarters, North Africa, to the Surgeon General, US Army, "Neuropsychiatric Report," October 14,

1943, HD:730 (NP), USAMDHU; also in Excerpt Report, New Georgia Campaign (October 31, 1943), the doctors clearly revealed their belief in the mental superiority of veterans: "This division, the twenty-fifth, had been 'blooded' during the GUADALCANAL campaign, and was better prepared to meet combat conditions than divisions going into their first combat," 5, HD:730 (NP) Neuroses—War Neuroses, USAMDHU.

13. Harry Brown, *A Walk in the Sun* (Lincoln: University of Nebraska Press, 1944), 77–79, 117–40.

14. The reference to screening is the only such reference in a commercial film known to this author. It appears in the film but not in the original novel. The screenplay was written by Robert Rossen, probably in 1944. This was the timeframe in which psychiatric theory was evolving from predisposition to "everyone has his breaking point." The soldier's comment indicates continuing belief in screening, but attitudes were changing.

15. Bresnahan, "Dangers in Paradise," 185. Also see 181–85 for concerns about screening expressed by both Roy Halloran and William Porter, chief of the Army School of Neuropsychiatry.

16. M. J. Farrell and John Appel, "Current Trends in Military Neuropsychiatry," *American Journal of Psychiatry* 101 (July 1944): 12–19.

17. Herbert Spiegel, "Preventive Psychiatry with Combat Troops," *American Journal of Psychiatry* 101 (1944): 314.

18. *Neuropsychiatry in World War II*, prep. and dir. Lt. Gen. Leonard D. Heaton, the Surgeon General, US Army, and ed. Col. Robert S. Anderson, MC, USA, Col. Albert J. Glass, MC, USA (Ret.), and Lt. Col. Robert J. Bernucci, MC, USA (Ret.) (Washington, DC: US Government Printing Office, 1966), 1:408.

19. *Neuropsychiatry in World War II*, 1:131–36.

20. Earlier in the war, Marshall and Eleanor Roosevelt had also been very much involved in morale. On Marshall's contacting the president about films to motivate soldiers politically, see memoranda from Marshall to FDR, September 6, 1941, File 30; November 30, 1942, File 38, Box 80, George C. Marshall Research Library, Lexington, VA, hereafter GCMRL; on ribbons for men serving in isolated areas, September 28, 1942, File 35, Box 80; Letter, May 9, 1942, Mrs. Roosevelt to Under Secretary of War Robert Patterson regarding communications between families and soldiers overseas and proposal for using shortwave radio facilities; letter, Patterson to Mrs. Roosevelt, April 10, 1942, regarding bill to provide monthly family allowances for dependents of enlisted men. This occurred after Eleanor Roosevelt had heard from nurses in hospitals that wives who could not work were having abortions because they were not receiving income from their husbands overseas in service. In Box 187, White House 3/9/42, Patterson Papers, Library of Congress, Washington, DC, hereafter referred to as LC. "Attitudes of Troops towards War," Drawer 920, GCMRL; Richard W. Steele, "American Popular Opinion and the War against Germany," *Journal of American History* 65, no. 3

(December 1978): 704–9. Eleanor Roosevelt continued to express her concerns after psychiatrists became more involved.

21. John Appel, "Prevention of Manpower Loss from Psychiatric Disorders, May 17–July 29, 1944," 2, 710 (Psychoneuroses), War Department General Staff G-1, RG 165, Washington National Records Center, Suitland, MD, hereafter referred to as WNRC.

22. "Prevention of Manpower Loss from Psychiatric Disorders, May 17–July 29, 1944"; "Sample N-P Cases Seen in the Vth Army," Appel, HD:730 (NP) Fifth Army Case Histories John W. Appel-Reporting, MTO, USAMDHU. An ETMD for the Far East for October 1944 also noted the cumulative effects of combat exhaustion: HD:730 (NP) ETMDS NP Excerpts SWPA and FE, 3, USAMDHU. See also Ernie Pyle, *Brave Men* (New York, 1943), 58; Samuel Stouffer, *The American Soldier: Combat and Its Aftermath* (Princeton, NJ: Princeton University Press, 1949), 286–88.

23. Memorandum, "Prevention of Manpower Loss from Psychiatric Disorders," 3. *Neuropsychiatry in World War II*, 1:824; Interview, Greene with Appel, Philadelphia, December 23, 1975; William C. Menninger, *Psychiatry in a Troubled World* (New York, 1948), 333; Stouffer, *The American Soldier*, 325, 455–57. Years later, Bert Manhoff would tell a Rutgers University oral history interviewer that after landing in Normandy his unit was "in direct contact with the enemy for over 100 days, which is not supposed to be." Bert Manhoff, interviewed by Kurt Piehler and Jeff Schneider, April 11, 1995, ROHA, https://oralhistory.rutgers.edu/images/PDFs/manhoff_bert.pdf.

24. Report on European Theatre of Operations, Col. William Menninger, Tab C-2 attached to Memorandum from Surgeon General Norman Kirk, to Army Chief of Staff, G-1, December 7, 1944, War Department General Staff G-1, RG 165, WNRC. See also Stouffer, *The American Soldier*, 88–89, 325. An Army Research Branch survey by Stouffer and his team of 2,507 soldiers in the South Pacific revealed that in early 1944, 75 percent found "'no reason' why the army could not send all men home after two years of service," and 66 percent believed a "man overseas for 18 months has done his full share in the war and deserves to go home." Stouffer, *The American Soldier*, 187.

25. Letter, Marshall to Eisenhower, September 22, 1944, Eisenhower, D. D., George C. Marshall Papers, GCMRL; the same letter was sent to generals MacArthur and Clark. On Eleanor Roosevelt's concern about inadequate rest and too long a tour for the 37th Division, fighting in the Pacific jungle, letter, Mrs. Roosevelt to Marshall, August 1944; letter, Marshall to Mrs. Roosevelt, August 17, 1944, both in File 100.1, Box 1789, ER Papers, Franklin Delano Roosevelt Library, Hyde Park, NY, hereafter FDRL.

26. E. W. Cochran MD, "Genesis of Combat Fatigue," *Diseases of the Nervous System* 7 (July 1946): 211–15.

27. Frederick Osborn, "Morale Services in the Zone of the Interior," talk given to Service Command, Conference, Fort Leonard Wood, MO, July 28, 1944,

manuscript collection 24, Osborn Papers, American Philosophical Society, Philadelphia, hereafter referred to as APS.

28. Donald L. Miller, *Masters of the Air* (New York, 2016), 124, states that in Curtis LeMay's 305th Group almost half of the crews were lost by late winter 1943. On other conditions, see 130, 131, 317.

29. Mark K. Wells, *Courage and Air Warfare* (London, 1995), 70,161, 169, 197, 201, 202, 206, 207, 212. Wells states on 174 that three out of four of those charged with LMF (Lack of Moral Fiber) in the combined British/American bomber offensive received an "other than honorable" discharge; 95 percent of the officers, he said, were separated from the Army Air Force. On LMF, see Miller, *Masters of the Air*, 124–27.

30. *Neuropsychiatry in World War II*, 1:865; Wells, *Courage and Air Warfare*, 2, 101–4; Miller, *Masters of the Air*, 127.

31. Miller, *Masters of the Air*, 7, 124, 127; 225,000 airmen flew combat missions for the 8th. See Miller, *Masters of the Air*, 49. Psychiatric symptoms included an inability to concentrate, irritability, insomnia, weight loss, sexual impotence, binge drinking, screaming nightmares, and getting into fights. Miller, *Masters of the Air*, 125.

32. Frederick Osborn, Diary, January 13, 1944, Diaries December 1943–February 1944 file, Frederick Osborn Papers, APS.

33. Joseph Heller, *Catch-22* (New York: Simon and Schuster, 1955), esp. 142–44. On 142, he particularly notes: "Heavy flak was everywhere! He had been lulled, lured and trapped, and there was nothing he could do but sit there like an idiot and watch the ugly black puffs smashing up to kill him."

34. John Murray, "Operational Fatigue in Far East Air Forces," 1–4, Folder 9, Box 12, John Murray Collection, LC. Aircrew in the 13th Air Force, fighting the Japanese in the sparsely populated, uncomfortably humid Solomon Islands, likewise suffered from excessive operational fatigue caused by the unexpectedly high number of combat missions, inadequate replacements, distasteful food, and boredom. *Neuropsychiatry in World War II*, 1:894.

35. For statistics, see esp. Gerald F. Linderman, *The World within War* (New York: Free Press, 1997), 1. However, the term "in combat" was defined in different ways, e.g., "in a combat zone," in actual contact with the enemy, or within range of the enemy.

36. Appel, "Prevention of Manpower Loss from Psychiatric Disorders, May–July 1944," 11, RG 165, WNRC.

37. Interview, Rebecca Greene with psychologist Joseph Zubin, July 10, 1975, New York City; Obituary, http://www.nytimes.com/1990/12/22.

38. Excerpt of Report, New Georgia Campaign, October 31, 1943, 4, HD:730 (NP) USAMDHU. "When asked whether the noncommissioned officers they were serving under were the kind they would like to serve under in combat, 60 percent of two Infantry divisions in the advanced stage of training chose the least favorable reply . . . 'only a few.' Just 30 percent answered that 'most' of their

non-commissioned officers were men they would like to serve under in combat." Memorandum, Col. Roy Halloran, Director of the Psychiatry Division to Army Chief of Staff, August 1943, 702, RG 112, WNRC.

39. James Wells, interviewed by Spencer Scheffling, ROHA, 19, 24, https://oralhistory.rutgers.edu/images/PDFs/wells_james.pdf.

40. William C. Schnorr, interviewed by Shaun Illingworth and Jared Kosch, ROHA, 23, https://oralhistory.rutgers.edu/images/PDFs/schnorr_william.pdf.

41. William Porter, "Functional Nervous Disorders in the Last War," *Transactions of the American Neurological Association* 69 (1943): 79–83.

42. Sharp, "Stress versus Predisposition in Combat Psychiatry," 1235.

43. Stouffer, *The American Soldier*, 275, 277, 283, 284; Report, "Observations from Patients Returning from the Hospital Ships *Algonquin* and *Acadia*," 710, 112, WNRC; A Neuropsychiatric Survey of the American Division on Bougainville, BSI, December 25, 1943–April 12, 1944; also, American Division (SWPA) Neuropsychiatric Survey of December 1943–April 1944, esp. 11. Also, Annual Report 1944, Headquarters II Corps Office of the Surgeon General, Patterson, RG 226, NA. According to an American Research Branch study, 11 percent of the 1,766 infantry in four divisions in Italy (April 1945) spent three or more months in a replacement camp, and 30 percent spent a month to three. Michael D. Doubler, *Closing with the Enemy: How GIs Fought the War in Europe, 1944–1945* (Lawrence: University Press of Kansas, 1995), 26–28, 245–50; Bill Mauldin, *Up Front* (New York: Henry Holt, 1945), 125–27.

44. Herbert Spiegel, "Observations and Impressions of Battalion Surgeon with Combat Infantry Unit North Africa," 3, 4, Personal Papers, Spiegel.

45. "Prevention of Manpower Loss from Psychiatric Disorders," 8, 710, RG 165, WNRC. Also, Memorandum, Brig. General F. A. Blesse, Surgeon General USA to the Surgeon General US Army (Attention: Consultant Psychiatrist), "Neuro-psychiatric Report," October 14, 1943, 2, 730.M, USAMDHU.

46. "Attitudes of Troops towards War," Drawer 920, GCMRL; Steele, "American Popular Opinion and the War against Germany," 704–9; Kurt Piehler, forthcoming article for the American Soldier website.

47. Annual Report 1944, Headquarters II Corps, Office of the Surgeon, Excerpt, 26, CMR General Files 1940, Psychiatry, RG 226, NA; "Neuropsychiatric Survey of the Americal Division on Bougainville, BSI, December 25, 1943–April 12, 1944, 28, 29, USAMDHU.

48. Annual Report 1944, Headquarters II Corps, Office of the Surgeon, Excerpt, 26, CMR General Files 1940, Psychiatry, RG 226, NA. Obituary of Gregory Zilboorg, *Chicago Tribune*, September 19, 1959.

49. "Factors in the German Army Concerned with Incidence of Neuropsychiatric Casualties," October 28, 1944; "Status of Neuropsychiatric Casualties in the German versus United States Army," October 28, 1944; "Evidence of Psychiatric Casualties in German Army," October 28, 1944; all in 710 (Neuropsychiatry), Surgeon General's Office, RG 112, WNRC.

50. "Report of Psychiatric Mission, O.F.S. O.S.R.D.," April 16, 1945–July 16, 1945, 9, RG 46, NA; see also Memorandum, Col. Roy Halloran to the Acting Chief of Staff, August 1943, 702 (Insanity), RG 112, WNRC. The same concern about cynical attitudes toward war was expressed in a Memorandum from John A. Rogers, Colonel, Medical Corps to the Commanding General, Army Service Forces, "Deficient Mental Toughness of Military Personnel," August 1943: "There is reason to believe that the present high rate of neuropsychiatric casualties may be one of the prices the Army is paying for the twenty years of cynicism and pacifism which flooded this country following the last war," 4, 702 (Insanity), RG 112, WNRC. For general attitudes of the American soldier toward the political significance of war and their will to fight, see Stouffer, *The American Soldier*, 460, 433–35, 438; J. R. Rees, *The Shaping of Psychiatry by War* (New York: Norton, 1945), 107.

51. Paul Wanke, "Inevitably Every Man Has His Threshold," *Journal of Slavic Military Studies* 16, no. 1 (March 2003): 93–96; Richard Gabriel, *The Painful Field: The Psychiatric Dimension of the Modern War* (New York: Greenwood, 1988), 76–80.

52. Annual Report, 1944 Headquarters II Corps, Office of the Surgeon, Excerpt, 27, Psychiatry, CMR General Files 1940, RG 226, NA.

53. Memorandum for the Director, Morale Services ASF (Attention: Research Branch) from Lt. Col. Robert J. Carpenter, Medical Corps, and Appel, NP Branch SGO, Liaison to Special Service Division (Morale Service), October 27, 1943, 710 (Psychoneuroses), RG 112, WNRC; "Sample N-P Cases Seen in the Army," Appel, HD:730 (NP) Fifth Army Case Histories John W. Appel, Reporting NTO, USAMDHU.

54. Stouffer, *The American Soldier*, 114, 158, 177.

55. John W. Dower, *War without Mercy: Race and Power in the Pacific War* (New York: Pantheon, 1986), 5, 9, 70. On the dehumanization of the Japanese by Americans, see also Gerald Linderman, *The World within War* (New York: Free Press, 1997), 161–73.

56. Linderman, *The World within War*, 96.

57. Linderman, *The World within War*, 265. The army psychologist David Marlowe and the military historian S. L. A. Marshall also expressed this opinion. While Marshall's ideas about the percentage of soldiers who actually fired their rifles in combat have been largely discredited, his point that teamwork, fighting "to keep face and share in the common endeavor," was more important than lofty ideals has been made by many others. S. L. A. Marshall, *Men against Fire* (Washington, DC, 1947), 150–55.

58. Stouffer, *The American Soldier*, 136. According to the OSRD investigation of psychoneuroses "Report Psychiatric Mission, O.F.S. O.S.R.D., European Theatre of Operations, April 16, 1945–July 16, 1945," 13–16, RG 46, NA, group unity plus a disapproval of quitting at the cost of their fellow soldiers supported men through combat. The OSRD also included as contributors to war stress political

motivation, fear of mines, 88 mm shells and flak, fear of one's own aggression, lack of confidence in one's leaders, resentment toward comrades who let others down, guilt after killing or failing to kill, horror and grief over the murder of buddies, and "the all-pervading physical and mental exhaustion of continuous fighting" (29). See also Minutes, NRC Committee on Psychiatry, July 18, 1945, Psychiatry-Numbered Abstracts and Reports, National Academy of Sciences, Washington, DC, hereafter referred to as NAS.

59. Bill Mauldin, *Up Front*; Eli Ginzberg, *Psychiatry and Military Manpower Policy* (New York: Columbia University, 1953), 49.

60. Peter Kindsvatter, *American Soldiers: Ground Combat in the World Wars, Korea, and Vietnam* (Lawrence: University Press of Kansas, 2003), 136.

61. Interview of Manhoff by Piehler and Schneider, ROHA, https://oralhistory.rutgers.edu/images/PDFs/manhoff_bert.pdf. G. Kurt Piehler, "The Role of Military Clergy," podcast, *Midday Magazine*, WAMC, http://www.wamc.org. John McManus, *The Deadly Brotherhood: The American Combat Soldier in World War II* (California: Presidio, 2003), 234–37.

62. Stouffer, *The American Soldier*, 174, 175.

63. Kurt Piehler, *A Religious History of the American GI* (Lincoln: University of Nebraska Press, 2021), 212.

64. R. Robert Cohen, "Mental Hygiene for the Trainee," *American Journal of Psychiatry* 100 (July 1943): 62–71; Harry L. Freedman, "Services of the Military Mental Hygiene Unit," *American Journal of Psychiatry* 100 (July 1943): 35, 36; Marvin E. Perkins, "Preventive Psychiatry during World War II," in *Personal Health Measures and Immunization*, ed. John Boyd Coates Jr., in *Preventive Medicine in World War II* (Washington, DC, 1955), 6:206–7.

65. *Notes on Psychology and Personality Studies in Aviation Medicine*, Technical Manual No. 8-320 (Washington, DC: War Department, January 27, 1941), 150.

66. Report, HD:319.1-2 (Professional Services–Medical Division) Neuropsychiatry Branch-SGO-1943 F/Y, 23, 37 File, USAMDHU.

67. Army Service Forces, Office of the Surgeon General, Washington, DC, Circular Letter No. 176, October 20, 1943, G-1, RG 165, WNRC.

68. "Psychiatric Toll of Warfare: Why Breakdowns Are Higher Than Expected and What Is Being Done to Prevent and Cure Them," *Fortune*, December 1943, 143.

69. A Returned Flier, "Give Us a Break," *Woman's Home Companion*, October 1944, 8.

70. Roy R. Grinker and John P. Spiegel, "Brief Psychotherapy in War Neuroses," *Psychosomatic Medicine* 6, no. 2 (April 1944): 123.

71. Malcolm J. Farrell MC and Captain John W. Appel MC, "Current Trends in Military Neuropsychiatry," 12, 13.

72. Linderman, *The World within War*, 1; unpublished paper, Paul M. Johnson, "Every Man Has His Breaking Point: The Attitudes of American Infantrymen Towards Combat Fatigue in World War II," November 28, 2006, 7.

73. Johnson, "Every Man Has His Breaking Point."

74. Margarita Aragon, "Deep-Seated Abnormality: Military Psychiatry, Segregation, and Discourse of Black 'Unfitness' in World War II," *Men and Masculinities* 20, no. 10 (2017): 1–20.

75. William Menninger, "The Mental Health of the Negro," January 28, 1944, prepared for Information and Education Division, 1944, Dr. Menninger's papers and speeches 1942–1947, Menninger Foundation Archives, Topeka, KS.

76. Ellen Dwyer, "Psychiatry and Race during World War II," *Journal of the History of Medicine and Allied Sciences* 61, no. 2 (2006): 123; William L. O'Neill, *A Democracy at War: America's Fight at Home and Abroad in World War II* (Cambridge, MA: Harvard University Press, 1998), 237.

77. Bernard Nalty, *Strength for the Fight: A History of Black Americans in the Military* (New York: Free Press, 1986), 146, 147, quoting Marshall as saying the "level of intelligence and occupational skills of the negro population is considerably below that of the white."

78. Richard Dalfiume, *Fighting on Two Fronts: Desegregation of the US Armed Forces, 1939–1953* (Columbia: University of Missouri Press, 1969), 46, 47; Menninger, "The Mental Health of the Negro." The degree to which the Negro press was critical of racial segregation in the military is described in Ethan Michaeli, *The Defender* (New York: Houghton Mifflin Harcourt, 2015); and in Brent Staples, "A 'Most Dangerous' Newspaper," *New York Times Book Review*, January 10, 2016, 12.

79. Nalty, *Strength for the Fight*, 157.

80. Menninger, "The Mental Health of the Negro," January 1944. See also Nalty, *Strength for the Fight*, 185, where he quotes Roosevelt as suggesting in September 1941 that as a first step to integration, the navy assign "good Negro bands" to improve relationships between Black and white sailors.

81. Kubie, "The Negro Troops and Negro Physicians in the Armed Services," August 1943, 1–10, NRC Morale, Overholser Papers, St. Elizabeth Hospital Records, RG 418, NA.

82. Kubie, "The Negro Troops and Negro Physicians in the Armed Services," 3.

83. Kubie, "The Negro Troops and Negro Physicians in the Armed Services," 3.

84. Interview, Captain Alan M. Osur with Lawrence Kubie, July 5, 1972, Towson, MD, Kubie file, Papers of John M. Murray, LC.

85. *Neuropsychiatry in World War II*, prep. and pub. under dir. Lt. Gen. Hal B. Jennings Jr., Surgeon General, US Army, and ed. Col. William S. Mullins, MSC, USA and Col. Albert J. Glass, MC, USA (Ret.) (Washington, DC: US Government Printing Office, 1973), 2:452–54.

86. Memorandum to the President from Walter White, "93rd Infantry Division and Other Negro Combatants," February 12, 1945, 1–12, file Negroes 3/9/42, Container 151, Robert Patterson Papers, LC.

87. Nalty, *Strength for the Fight*, 172–74. Memorandum for Under-Secretary of War from McNair, Subject: 93rd, and attached Memorandum from Edward S.

Greenbaum, Colonel, Ord. Dept., regarding the reluctance of white officers to command Blacks because of the "question as to whether the division will ever be able to perform combat service." Also, on the 92nd Division, Memoranda for the Inspector General, August 7, 1943, from Benjamin O. Davis Sr., Brig. Gen., US Army, Patterson Papers, Negroes, March 9, 1942, File, Container 151, LC. Davis was the first African American general in the US Army.

88. World War II Database, http://ww2db.com. Judith A. Bellafaire, "The Women's Army Corps: A Commemoration of World War II Service," *CMH Publication* 72–15, http://history.army.mil. There were at least 80,000 women in the navy WAVES, 13,000 in the coast guard SPARS, 60,000 in the Army Nurse Corps, 14,000 in the Navy Nurse Corps, 1,000 volunteering as civilian pilots with the Women's Air Service, and at least 150,000 in the WAC and WAAC together. Linderman, *The World within War*, 1.

89. Mary Robinson interviewed by G. Kurt Piehler, Linda Lasko, and Bruce Chadwick, 30–40, 41, 42, ROHA, https://oralhistory.rutgers.edu/images/PDFs/robinson_mary.pdf. Robinson also used the GI Bill to attend the University of Chicago and then the London School of Economics. Thereafter, she worked at the US Department of Education. Robinson also discussed racial tensions at her training camp (21); Memoranda for General Marshall, November 30 and December 1, 1944, from Brehon Somervell, Lt. Gen. Commanding, Folder 20, Box 65, 01 Marshall Papers, Folder 20, Box 65, GCMRLS. The Rutgers Oral History Project interviewed quite a few women who served in World War II in some capacity. Carol Levin, in the WAC for about a year, interviewed by Chris Hillary and Laura Micheletti, April 1, 1998, 8, 16, 21, 11–15, ROHA, https://oralhistory.rutgers.edu/images/PDFs/levin_carol.pdf. Jean O'Grady Sheehan, interviewed by Sandra Holyoak, September 21, 2006, 7, ROHA, https://oralhistory.rutgers.edu/images/PDFs/sheehan_jean.pdf. Ms. Sheehan, in the WAVES, recalled that during her youth in New Brunswick, NJ, the Ku Klux Klan hung "wooden crosses on the fence of the nearby Catholic school and [set] them on fire so that her room was lit up."

90. Christopher Klein, "When a US Hospital Ship Was Attacked by a Kamikaze Pilot during World War II," History.com, May 1, 2020, https://www.history-com/news/hospital_ship_uss_comfort.

91. Leisa Meyer, *Creating GI Jane: Women Serving in World War II* (New York: Columbia University Press, 1998), 160–76; Richard Polenberg, "The Good War: A Reappraisal of How World War II Affected American Society," *Virginia Magazine of History and Biography* 100, no. 3 (July 1992), citing Susan M. Hartmann, *The Home Front and Beyond* (Boston: Twayne, 1982), 21. Allan Bérubé, *Coming Out under Fire: The History of Gay Men and Women in World War II* (Chapel Hill: University of North Carolina Press, 2012), 31. Eleanor Roosevelt also received complaints from women. On the other hand, while Meyer paints a picture of intolerance of gays, Yellin mentions that Eisenhower dropped an investigation when the staff in his office informed him that they were all lesbians. Emily Yellin,

Our Mothers' War: American Women at Home and at the Front During World War II (New York: Free Press, 2004), 321.

92. *Neuropsychiatry in World War II*, 1:432, 434. Robert R. McCormick was the grandnephew of Cyrus McCormick, inventor of the reaper. He inherited the *Chicago Tribune* from his mother and saw FDR as a "dangerous threat to individual liberty and free enterprise." Stevenson Swanson, *Tribune* staff writer, "The Colonel Takes Charge," http://www.chicagotribune.com.

93. Meyer, *Creating GI Jane*, 157.

94. "Sexual Hygiene Course for Officers and Officer Candidates in the WAAC," May 27, 1943 (Washington, DC: US Government Printing Office, 1943), 24–28, NA.

95. Mattie E. Treadwell, *The Women's Army Corps* (Washington, DC, 1954), 177–79. Bérubé, *Coming Out under Fire*, 150; *Neuropsychiatry in World War II*, 1:423, 431.

96. *Neuropsychiatry in World War II*, 1:803; Letter, Committee Psychiatrists Appointed to Investigate Rejections of Mental Cases at Induction Stations, to Norman Kirk, Army Surgeon General, September 21, 1943, 8–10, Overholser Papers, LC. Other psychiatrists on the committee were Waggoner, Karl Bowman, Frederick W. Parsons, Ruggles, and Titus Harris, the first professor and chair of the Department of Neurology and Psychiatry at the University of Texas Medical Branch.

97. Interview of George Stevenson MD by Rebecca Greene, Red Bank, NJ, May 10, 1974.

98. Mem., Ivan C. Berlien, Maj. Med. Cps, Assist to Col. J. F. Lieberman MD, Physical Standards Div., "Physical Rejections-ALP WAC Recruiting Memorandum"; Lieberman to AGO, Attn: Maj. C. W. Ardery, July 18, 1944, 7 Q2File, RG 112, WNRC.

99. Documentary film, Arthur Dong and Allan Bérubé, *Coming Out under Fire*.

100. Bérubé, *Coming Out under Fire*, 31; Bellafaire, "The Women's Army Corps"; Meyer, *Creating GI Jane*, 160–76.

101. *War Department Medical Technical Bulletin* 100 (October 1944): 1–5.

102. *Neuropsychiatry in World War II*, 1:432, 434.

103. Summary of Letter from Estelle R. Stevens, Referred to Admiral McIntire, June 20, 1944, re: letter from Estelle R. Stevens, Pittsburgh, about Ensign C. E., Box 1789, Papers of Eleanor Roosevelt, FDRL.

104. Bellafaire, "The Women's Army Corps"; *Neuropsychiatry in World War II*, 1:445, 449–52; Treadwell, *The Women's Army Corps*, 436, 435, 449, 450, 460.

9. Limits to Prevention and Treatment

1. John W. Appel and Gilbert W. Beebe, "Preventive Psychiatry," *Journal of the American Medical Association*, August 31, 1946, 1474–75; Letter, Dr. John W. Appel to Dr. Frederick R. Hanson, January 19, 1945, and attached *Washington Times Herald* article, "GI's IN LINE 400 DAYS SAYS CLARE," HD 730 (NP)

Combat Psychiatry, US Army Medical Division Historical Unit, Ft. Detrick, Frederick, MD, hereafter referred to as USAMDHU. Memorandum, Inspector General to Deputy Chief of Staff, "Psychoneuroses May 26, 1945," 333.9 Psychoneuroses, War Department General Staff, G-1, RG 165, National Archives (NA). Congresswoman Luce was married to *Life* magazine's publisher, Henry Luce.

2. Rick Atkinson, *The Guns at Last Light: The War in Western Europe, 1944–1945* (New York: Henry Holt, 2013), 491. David Eisenhower, *Eisenhower at War: 1943–1945* (New York: Random House, 1986), 375.

3. Memorandum, Assistant G-1 to Chief of Staff, "Prevention of Manpower Loss from Psychiatric Disorder," October 20, 1944, G-1, War Department General Staff, G-1 Records, RG 165, Washington National Records Center, Suitland, MD, hereafter referred to as WNRC; *Neuropsychiatry in World War II*, prep. and pub. under dir. Lt. Gen. Hal B. Jennings Jr., Surgeon General, US Army, and ed. Col. William S. Mullins, MSC, USA and Col. Albert J. Glass, MC, USA (Ret.) (Washington, DC: US Government Printing Office, 1973), 2:894; Ronald J. Glasser, *Three Hundred Sixty-Five Days* (New York: George Braziller, 1971). Rotation of troops was more advanced in other countries, including Germany and England; Gerald F. Linderman, *The World within War* (New York: Free Press, 2013), 45.

4. *Neuropsychiatry in World War II*, 2:1002; "Repeated Deployments Weigh Heavily on US Troops," *USA Today*, January 14, 2010, https://www.pressreader.com/usa/usa-today-international-edition/20100114/281547992017193. General Peter Chiarelli, Vice Chief of Staff of Army, *Army Health Promotion Risk Reduction Suicide Prevention* (2010), i. See also David Finkel, *The Good Soldiers* (New York: Farrar, Straus and Giroux, 2009) and *Thank You for Your Service* (New York: Farrar, Straus and Giroux, 2013), chronicling the service and aftermath of a combat unit in the Iraq War, including a burgeoning rate of mental illness and suicide.

5. Neuropsychiatric History for Third Army, II (November 1944), 1; Report, Surgeon 12th Army, "Conservation of Manpower," January 3, 1945, HD 730 NP, MTO Gen., USAMDHU; *Infantry Journal*, May 1945, 40, 41; Memorandum, Inspector General to Deputy Chief of Staff, "Psychoneuroses," May 26, 1945, 333.9 Psychoneuroses, War Department General and Special Staffs, G-1, RG 165, WNRC; *Neuropsychiatry in World War II*, 2:866; Samuel Stouffer, *The American Soldier: Combat and Its Aftermath* (Princeton, NJ: Princeton University Press, 1949), 356, 353, 355; Letter, Dr. F. M. Harrison to Dr. George Stevenson, August 31, 1942, P 8-2/A 16-1 (064-39), US Navy Bureau of Medicine and Surgery, RG 52, NA; Mark Wells, *Courage and Air Warfare: The Allied Aircrew Experience in the Second World War* (London: Frank Cass, 1995), 80. The Eighth Air Force had fifteen rest homes where officers and enlisted men could enjoy leisure activities without military duties and with rank and uniforms discouraged. The camps had a popularity rating of over 90 percent.

6. Memorandum of the Deputy Chief of Staff, Subject: Psychoneurotics, May 26, 1945, War Department Office of the Inspector General, Washington, G-1, RG

165, NA. Also on the team was Lloyd Thompson, psychiatric consultant for the European theater. Other psychiatrists participating in the investigation included Hanson, Karl Bowman, C. Charles Burlingame, Frank Fremont-Smith, and Harry C. Solomon.

7. Roy R. Grinker, *Men under Stress* (Philadelphia, 1945), 156; on 157, Grinker also stated that once flyers exhibited "serious neurotic symptoms," the rest camps could make things worse. Stouffer, *The American Soldier*, 370; Ben Shephard, *A War of Nerves: Soldiers and Psychiatrists in the Twentieth Century* (Cambridge, MA: Harvard University Press, 2001), 213. Dr. John Murray in "Psychiatry in the Army Air Forces," *American Journal of Psychiatry* 100 (July 1943): 23, similarly cautioned: "Rest camps must be provided for these men far enough away from the scene of operations to be free from tension and danger in an operating area, yet not so far distant as to make the flyer feel he has been evacuated because he has cracked." Recalling his experience as a psychiatrist in the Korean War for this author, Dr. Jacques Quen, Cornell Medical Center, New York City, noted that some soldiers sent on vacations to quiet areas far from combat missed their companions, the daily routine, and the sense of mission and had too much time to worry.

8. Requirements for proper uniforms and spotless shoes at rest locations scared away grimy, tired combat soldiers, as the cartoonist Bill Mauldin observed in *Up Front* (New York: Henry Holt, 1944); Ernie Pyle, *Here Is Your War* (New York: World, 1945).

9. Letter, Lt. Gen. Mark Clark to Gen. George C. Marshall, October 6, 1944, Clark File: Marshall Papers, George C. Marshall Research Library, Lexington, VA, hereafter referred to as GCMRL.

10. Report of Psychiatric Mission of the Office of Field Service (OFS), Office of Scientific Research and Development (OSRD), European Theater of Operations, April 16, 1945–July 16, 1945, 71, Legislative Branch, NMHA Records, Records on National Neuropsychiatric Institute Act, S. 1160, RG 46, NA. The OSRD was the chief scientific policy-making agency during the war. The National Academy of Sciences (NAS) reported to the OSRD. Dr. Leo Bartemeier headed the OSRD's team of psychiatrists on the mission, which included Karl Menninger, Lawrence Kubie, John Romano, and John Whitehorn. The OSRD also consulted British psychiatrists R. D. Gillespie and J. R. Rees of the Royal Air Force, William Menninger, and Maj. Gen. Paul R. Hawley, chief surgeon, European theater of operations (ETO). Linderman, *The World within War*, 354.

11. Adjutant General School Bulletin, "Don't Be Like That!" February 1943, 1, 2, Adjutant General Records, RG 407, WNRC.

12. Interview, Herbert Spiegel with Rebecca Greene, New York City, December 18, 1975; Herbert Spiegel, "Preventive Psychiatry with Combat Troops," *American Journal of Psychiatry* 101 (November 1944): 310–15; Herbert Spiegel, "Psychiatric Observations in the Tunisian Campaign," *American Journal of Orthopsychiatry* 14 (October 1944): 381–85. S. L. A. Marshall, *Men against Fire* (New York, 1947),

143–46, states on the basis of interviews with combat veterans late in the war that the leaders must "cut through" their men's fear and remind them "what is required." They must also continue to be vigilant even when their men relax after an initial victory.

13. "Psychiatric Toll of Warfare," *Fortune*, December 1943; Reports, 38th Infantry Division, "Conference of the Orientation Officers," March 9, 1944, HD:730 (NP)SWPA, USAMDHU.

14. Reports, 38th Infantry Division, "Conference of the Orientation Officers, Believing in the Army's Concern for the Welfare of the Individual," March 9, 1944; Psychiatric Training Aid No. 1, July 17,1945, Psychiatric Training Aid No. 2, "Combat Leadership," August 6, 1945, all in HD:730 (NP) Southwest Pacific Area, USAMDHU.

15. Linderman, *The World within War*, 230–31. Figures on how many Raiders were killed differ. Charles W. Lindberg, who was a member of Carlson's Raiders on Guadalcanal, remembered killing 480 Japanese. He stated: "We landed at Aola Bay on Guadalcanal . . . about 40 to 50 miles from Henderson Field. We went into the jungle and stayed behind enemy lines for 32 days. They called it the Long Patrol. We took a toll on the enemy of about 480 Japanese. We lost 17 men." Interview of Charles W. Lindberg by Richard Misenhimer, Richfield, MN, January 26, 2007, 13, National Museum of the Pacific War, Center for Pacific War Studies, Fredericksburg, TX, https://www.pacificwarmuseum.org.

16. Appel, "Prevention of Manpower Loss from Psychiatric Disorders," 10; Charles Bray, *Psychology and Military Proficiency: A History of the Applied Psychology Panel of the National Defense Research Committee* (Princeton, NJ, 1948), 65–71. A subcommittee of that committee observed two classes of officer candidates at the Fort Benning, Georgia Officer Candidate School, each numbering two hundred, and two classes of artillery officer candidates, one numbering eighty and another eighty-two, both at the Fort Sill Field Artillery School. The subcommittee then compared their personality scores with the efficiency ratings of 176 overseas company officers in combat. See also Memorandum, Subcommittee on Leadership to Applied Psychology Panel National Defense Research Council, October 13, 1943, Anthropology and Psychology, Emergency Committee in Psychology: Subcommittee on Problems of Leadership, National Academy of Sciences, Washington, DC, hereafter referred to as NAS.

17. Emilio Mira y Lopez, *Psychiatry in War* (New York: Norton, 1943), 59, 60.

18. Shephard, *A War of Nerves*, 192–96. Ironically, in the last desperate months of the war, German leadership, despite special officer tests, failed in certain strategic decisions. See, e.g., Ken Hechler, *The Bridge at Remagen* (New York: Ballantine, 1957).

19. Princeton University published the results of Stouffer's American Research Branch surveys in four volumes entitled S*tudies in Social Psychology in World War II.* The first volume was *The American Soldier: Adjustment during*

Army Life (Princeton, NJ: Princeton University Press, 1949); the second, *The American Soldier: Combat and Its Aftermath* (Princeton, NJ: Princeton University Press, 1949); the third, *Experiments on Mass Communication* (Princeton, NJ: Princeton University Press, 1949); and the fourth, *Measurement and Prediction* (Princeton, NJ: Princeton University Press, 1950). On attitudes toward the Japanese, see esp. Stouffer, *The American Soldier: Combat and Its Aftermath*, 164, 165, 454.

20. Julius J. Schreiber, "Psychological Training and Orientation of Soldiers," *Mental Hygiene* 28 (October 1944), 537–38, 540–54.

21. Interview, Rebecca Greene with Dr. John Appel, December 23, 1975, Philadelphia; Annual Report Neuropsychiatric Consultants Division, Fiscal Year 1945, 79, HD3I9.1-2, USAMDHU.

22. For more description of what I&E did, see the forthcoming article by Kurt Piehler on the *American Soldier* website.

23. The seven films were *Prelude to War, The Nazis Strike, The Battle of Britain, Divide and Conquer, Battle of Russia, Battle of China*, and *War Comes to America*.

24. Interview, Greene with Appel, December 23, 1975; Annual Report, Neuropsychiatric Consultants Division, Fiscal Year 1945, 79, HD 319.1-2, USAMDHU; Frank Capra, *The Name above the Title* (New York, 1971), 326–28, 332, 334–35; Richard Glatzer and John Raeburn, eds., *Frank Capra: The Man and His Films* (Ann Arbor: University of Michigan Press, 1971), 151–54.

25. Interview, Greene with Appel, December 23, 1975; Stouffer, *The American Soldier*, 1:50, 461–64. Stouffer, aided by Appel, studied the effects of Capra's films on a group of soldiers and a control group and then resurveyed both. They looked at how the films affected the political interests of soldiers in general and in groups. They particularly looked at what in the films affected soldiers' opinions. They found that specific facts in films were more effective in shaping opinions than messages in general.

26. Annual Report, Neuropsychiatric Consultants Division, Fiscal Year 1945, 77, HD 319.1-2, USAMDHU.

27. US Army, Medical Department, *Neuropsychiatry in World War II*, ed. Albert J. Glass, MC, USA (Ret.) and Lt. Col. Robert J. Bernucci (Washington, DC: US Government Printing Office, 1966), 1:289, 236.

28. Samuel Paster, "Combat Neuroses: Group Psychotherapy," *American Journal of Orthopsychiatry* 15 (July 1945): 477–78. Orthopsychiatry is the branch of psychiatry concerned with the study and prevention of mental and behavioral disorders, with emphasis on child development and family life.

29. Samuel Paster, "Combat Neuroses: Group Psychotherapy," 481, 479. War Department Technical Bulletin 103 (October 10, 1944) noted: "Where guilt feelings exist over having killed enemy troops, motivation may be defective. Frank discussion of the need to kill is generally sufficiently reassuring."

30. Interview, Greene with Appel, December 2, 1975.

31. Report, Army Surgeon General Office, APO No. 502, Headquarters South Pacific Base Command, September 28, 1944, HD:730 (NP) CORRESP, Headquarters USAFSPA, USAMDHU.

32. Annual Report 1944, Headquarters II Corps Office of the Surgeon Excerpt, MR Gen. Files 1940, Psychiatry, Records of the Office of Strategic Services, RG 226, NA.

33. Appel, "Prevention of Manpower Loss from Psychiatric Disorders," 3.

34. Leonard R. Sillman, "Morale," *War Medicine* 3 (May 1943): 498–500. For discussion by others, see Appel, "Prevention of Manpower Loss from Psychiatric Disorders," 3, 4; Memorandum, J. A. Ulio, Adjutant General, to all Medical Officers, "Deficient Mental Toughness of Military Personnel," 702 Insanity, Surgeon General's Office, RG 112, WNRC; Julius Schreiber, "Psychological Training and Orientation of Soldiers," *Mental Hygiene* 28 (October 1944), 544; and Julius Schreiber, "Morale Aspects of Military Mental Hygiene," *Diseases of the Nervous System* 4 (July 1943): 197–201.

35. Herbert Spiegel, "Preventive Psychiatry with Combat Troops," 310–15; Herbert Spiegel, "Psychiatric Observations in the Tunisian Campaign," *American Journal of Orthopsychiatry* 14 (July 1944): 381–85; Letter, Hanson to Appel, October 4, 1944, Surgeon General's Office NATOUSA, HD 730 (NP), USAMDHU; Frederick Hanson, *Combat Psychiatry: Experiences in North Africa and the Mediterranean Theater* (Washington, DC,1949), 44. In *Men under Stress*, Grinker expresses the same skepticism about the use of hatred to inspire fighting (43). The same de-emphasis on hatred is noted on page 73 of the OSRD Report of the Psychiatric Mission, April–July 1945, National Neuropsychiatric Act, RG 46, NA.

36. Joanna Bourke, "Psychiatry, Hate Training, and the Second World War," *Journal of Social History* 52, no. 1 (2018): 116.

37. Annual Report, Neuropsychiatric Consultants Division, Fiscal Year 1944, HD 319.1-2, 9, 10, USAMDHU.

38. Interview, Greene with Appel, December 23, 1975; Capra, *The Name above the Title*, 336. Ellen Herman, *The Romance of American Psychology* (Berkeley, CA: University of California Press, 1995), 70.

39. For I&E's reluctance to follow neuropsychiatrists' suggestions on instructions on politics, see Annual Report, Neuropsychiatric Consultants Division, Fiscal Year 1945, 77, HD 319.1-2, USAMDHU. According to Schreiber in *Mental Hygiene*, October 1944, 552, even before Pearl Harbor the Army Bureau of Public Relations had developed an orientation course consisting of fifteen lectures to be sent to troops all over the world. In early 1943, the I&E took over the army orientation course, later with the help of psychiatrists.

40. Stouffer, *The American Soldier*, 1:468–69.

41. Letter, Hanson to Appel, October 4, 1944, Surgeon General's Office, NATOUSA, ED 730 (NP), USAMDHU.

42. Annual Report, NP Consultants Division, FY 1945, 146, HD319.12, USAMDHU.

43. In the India-Burma theater in April 1945, more soldiers used the army's radio station than any other medium to get news about the war. In 1944, scarcely anyone was acquainted with *Newsmaps*, which presented in two brief pages maps and news articles, but by April 1945, four out of five soldiers used this medium. On the other hand, scarcely anyone participated in any current events discussion groups. See "A Study of Orientation Media in the India-Burma Theater," April 30, 1945, Records of the Secretary of Defense, RG 330, NA.

44. Linderman, *The World within War*, 230–31. In the 1970s, the psychiatrist David Marlowe also found a high correlation between group cohesion and less drug use in the military. "David Marlowe Dies at 83: Helped Army Nurture Bands of Brothers," *New York Times*, January 13, 2015; G. Kurt Piehler and Sidney Pash, eds., *The United States and the Second World War* (New York: Fordham University Press, 2010), 228. Spiegel, "Preventive Psychiatry with Combat Troops," 310–15; Spiegel, "Psychiatric Observations in the Tunisian Campaign," 381–85.

45. Howard P. Rome, "Military Group Psychotherapy," paper for presentation at APA meeting, May 1944, Psychiatry Gen. Files, CMR, RG 227, NA.

46. Josephine Bresnahan, "Dangers in Paradise: The Battle against Combat Fatigue in the Pacific War," PhD diss., Harvard University, 1999, 226, citing Maj. William Swainer, MC, 14th Station Hospital/Case Histories, September 3, 1944, 3, RG 112, E. 31, Box 1349, National Archives, College Park, hereafter referred to as NACP. Also Bresnahan, "Dangers in Paradise," 227–28; Report, Committee on Neuropsychiatry, Subcommittee on Psychiatry, July 18, 1945, Psychiatry-Numbered Abstracts, NAS; Report, Psychiatric Mission of the OFS, OSRD; Hanson, *Combat Psychiatry*, 42.

47. *Neuropsychiatry in World War II*, 2:48–53, 58, 62, 73. On Sobel's background, see "Dr. Raymond Sobel," https://www.vnews.com/Archives/2014/01/Raymond; Medical History 38th Infantry Division, July 9, 1945, Annex No. 1, HD730 (NP), USAMDHU.

48. Headquarters 38th Infantry Division, APO 38, Psychological Training Aid No. 1, July 17, 1945, HD:730(NP) Division, SWPA, USAMDHU.

49. Appel, "Prevention of Manpower Loss from Psychiatric Disorders," 9; "Observations of a General Hospital Psychiatrist," January 1945, First US Army ETO, Gen. Files Psychiatry, CMR, RG 227, NA. For suggestions on sending replacements in groups, see Spiegel, "Preventive Psychiatry with Combat Troops," 312; and Report, Psychiatric Mission of the OFS, OSRD, 18.

50. Appel and Beebe, "Preventive Psychiatry," 1475; Clark to Marshall, October 6, 1944, Clark File, Marshall Papers, GCMRL.

51. Stuart J. Wright, *An Emotional Gauntlet: From Life in Peacetime America to the War in European Skies* (Madison: University of Wisconsin Press, 2004), 167–70.

52. John C. McManus. *The Deadly Brotherhood: The American Combat Soldier in World War II* (California: Random House, 1998), 249.

53. Medical Bulletin 17, 38th Infantry Division, May 3, 1944, Surgeon General's Office, HD 730 (NP), USAMDHU; Psychological Training Aid No. 1, Battle Course Syllabus for Regimental Medical Officers, 3rd Infantry Division, July 17, 1945, HO 730 (NP) SWPA, USAMDHU. The Neuropsychiatric Consultants Division developed a film, "Introduction to Combat Fatigue," demonstrating how the army and navy psychotherapy encouraged the patient to express his feelings of anxiety and tension during psychotherapy. See Annual Report, Neuropsychiatric Consultants Division, Fiscal Year 1945, HD 319.1-2, USAMDHU.

54. These appeared in *Infantry Journal*, May 1944.

55. John Dollard, "Twelve Rules on Meeting Battle Fear," *Infantry Journal*, May 1944, 36–38. Also, Chris Chamberlain, PhD, "The Antiracist Clinic," unpublished paper, Weill Cornell Medical Center, Dewitt Wallace Institute of Psychiatry, History, Policy, and the Arts, January 20, 2021.

56. Pamphlet, R. Robert Cohen, "Mack and Mike," 1–21, Committee on Neuropsychiatry, Winfred Overholser Papers, St. Elizabeth Hospital Records, RG 418, NA; also see R. Robert Cohen, "Mental Hygiene for the Trainee," *American Journal of Psychiatry* 100 (July 1943): 62–71.

57. Annual Report, Neuropsychiatric Consultants Division, Fiscal Year 1943, 27, HD 319.1-2, USAMDHU.

58. Gordon F. Lewis, interviewed by Shaun Illingworth, July 24, 2006, 30–35, Rutgers Oral History Archives, hereafter ROHA, http://www.rutgers.edu. Dr. Gordon Lewis died on March 18, 2014; "In Memoriam," http://www.uvm.edu.

59. Report, Samuel Kraines, "The Adviser System," July 15, 1943, 730, Surgeon General's Office, RG 112, WNRC; Report, Major O. B. Markey, Medical Corps, "Conference on Advisor System, as Observed and Studied at North Camp Hood," TDRTC, March 15–18, 1944, 337(Camp Hood), Surgeon General, cited in Marvin E. Perkins, "Preventive Psychiatry during World War II," in *Personal Health Measures and Immunization*, ed. John Boyd Coates Jr. (Washington, DC, 1955), chap. 5, 204–5.

60. Report, 38th Infantry Division, Psychiatric Training Aid, July 9, 1945, Annex No. 1, HD:730 (NP) SWPA; USAMDHU; "Fear of German Weapons," October 1, 1943, Joint Study by Neuropsychiatry Branch, Surgeon General's Office and Research Branch, Special Services Division, Personal Papers of John Appel MD, 12–13. A third of the seven hundred North African theater soldiers favored live ammunition in training. The army historian S. L. A. Marshall contended in 1947 that only one out of four men used his weapon in combat in World War II. Marshall's evidence, however, has since been widely disputed. Marshall, *Men against Fire*; John Whiteclay Chambers II, "S. L. A. Marshall's *Men against Fire*: New Evidence Regarding Fire Ratios," *Parameters* 33, no. 3 (Autumn 2003): 113–21.

61. Noah Tsika, *Traumatic Imprints* (Oakland: University of California Press, 2018), 2, 3, 13–17, 35, 175–76, 191–93. *Neuropsychiatry in World War II*, 1:66.

62. Annual Report, Neuropsychiatric Consultants Division, Fiscal Year 1943, 41, HD 319.1-2, USAMDHU; Lloyd J. Thompson, Memorandum, "Psychiatric Services in the US Army NATOUSA," December 31, 1943, 710, RG 112, WNRC. E. W. Cochran, "Genesis of Combat Fatigue," *Diseases of the Nervous System* 7 (July 1946): 211–15.

63. Annual Report of the Surgeon General, Fiscal Year 1943, 15, HD 319.12, USAMDHU; Memorandum for Assistant Chief of Staff G-1, "Psychoneuroses," December 18, 1944, Psychoneuroses 33.9, RG 165, WNRC; Section III, Pacific Ocean Areas and Middle Pacific, Vol. 1 (January 1945), Office of the Center for Military History, Washington, DC; Excerpt Report, New Georgia Campaign, October 31, 1943, War Neuroses (NP), HD:730, USAMDHU; Report, "Observations of the Medical Department Activities in the South Pacific Area," August 20, 1943, HD:730 (NP) Correspondence Headquarters USAFISPA, USAMDHU. While Hanson's figures for returning men to combat in North Africa were between 30 percent, after one day, and 70 percent, after two, his figures for returning to service were much higher. Shephard, *A War of Nerves*, 217.

64. Indeed, Edgar Jones and Simon Wessely, *Shell Shock to PTSD* (East Sussex: Psychology Press, 2005), 84, estimate that after D-Day, the British rate of psychiatric casualties returning to combat duty was about 10 percent. Further, the high number of evacuees was believed attributable to men from North Africa, the Middle East, and India, often proving to be "men with long-standing temperamental instability and poor intellect" (92–94). Likewise, Terry Copp and Bill McAndrew, *Battle Exhaustion: Soldiers and Psychiatrists in the Canadian Army, 1939–1945* (Montreal: McGill-Queen's University Press, 1990), 153n, state that because of the belief that they could not convert the constitutionally inferior into fighting material they transferred them to noncombat assignments. See also Mark Wells, *Courage and Air Warfare* (London: Frank Cass, 1995), 211.

65. Bresnahan, "Dangers in Paradise," 209–12, citing Samuel Joel, MC, Supervising Psychiatrist, 18th Station Hospital, New Guinea, draft manuscript for Surgeon General's view, article for public, March 18, 1944, 6, RG 112, Entry 31, Box 1347; Lt. Col James Cromwell, MC, "Staff Study Report on Special Treatment Center Informational Materials: Letters to Patients," May 14, 1944, 3, RG 112, Entry 30, Box 1348, both in NACP; Mortimer E. Shapiro MC, "17th Station Hospital NP Treatment Center Guidelines for Patients," April 25, 1944, 10, Entry 31, Box 841, RG 112, NA; "Lecture Scripts for Patients," 12th Station Hospital, SWPA, May 1944, RG 112, E30, Box 977, NACP.

66. William Bleckwenn MC, "Functional Disorders in the Forward Area," paper presented at the 105th Base Hospital Conference on Combat Psychiatry, May 6, 1944, 3, RG 112, E31 (ZI) Box 1347, NACP; Lt. Col. L. P. Gundry, MC, "Okinawa Campaign: Phase II Planning Committee Report," April 20, 1945, 3, RG 112, Entry 31, Box 1770, NACP; both cited in Bresnahan, "Dangers in Paradise," 214–18.

67. Kaufman later became chief of the Mount Sinai Psychiatry Department, New York City, and president of the American Psychoanalytic Association. "Obituary, M. Ralph Kaufman," *New York Times*, May 21, 1977.

68. Roy E. Appleman, James M. Burns, Russell A. Gugeler, and John Stevens, *Okinawa: The Last Battle, the War in the Pacific* (Washington, DC: US Army Center for Military History, 1960), 60, 102, 143, 384–86, 398, 441, 447, 454–56, 473.

69. M. Ralph Kaufman and Lindsay E. Beaton MD, "A Psychiatric Treatment Program in Combat," *Bulletin of the Menninger Clinic* 11, no. 1 (January 1947): 412–13. Interview, Rebecca Greene with Kaufman, January 5, 1976, New York City; *Yank* wrote of a fictitious Corporal Jones: "He is not a coward. . . . He starts a personal war within himself, his conscience on one side and his instinct for self-preservation on the other . . . a tug of war. . . . He starts trembling . . . he can't hold his rifle. . . . Involuntarily he becomes physically incapable." McManus, *The Deadly Brotherhood*, 163–67; Albert Cowdrey, *Fighting for Life: American Military Medicine in World War II* (New York: Free Press, 1994), 144–45.

70. Kaufman and Beaton, "A Psychiatric Treatment Program in Combat," 414–15.

71. Report of Psychiatric Mission of the OFS, OSRD, 52–57. Interview, Greene with Appel, December 23, 1975. See also Annual Report, NP Consultants Div., FY 1944 and 1945, 24, 134, HD 319.1-2, USAMDHU; Elliot Cooke, *All but Me and Thee: Psychiatry at the Foxhole Level* (Washington, DC: Infantry Journal, 1946), 180; OSRD Investigative Report, FORM, 27.

72. William Menninger, *Psychiatry in a Troubled World* (New York: Knopf, 1948), 308.

73. Roy Grinker, "Brief Psychotherapy in War Neuroses," *Psychosomatic Medicine* 6 (April 1944): 129. Grinker cautioned: "Many [soldiers] with severe ego breakdowns were not greatly improved by reliving situations of battle which initiated the collapse. They revealed old anxieties and resentments dating back to civilian life." Cf. Kaufman and Beaton, *Bulletin of the Menninger Clinic*, January 1947.

74. Cowdrey, *Fighting for Life*, 143–45.

75. Report of Psychiatric Mission of the OFS, OSRD, 57, 58.

76. Kaufman and Beaton, "A Psychiatric Treatment Program in Combat," 414–15.

77. Tsika, *Traumatic Imprints*, 185–86.

78. Hans Pols and Stephanie Oak, "War and Military Mental Health," *American Journal of Public Health* 97, no. 12 (December 2007), citing Menninger, Brill, and Beebe, http://www.ncbi.nlm.nih.gov/pmc.

79. Michael Doubler, *Closing with the Enemy; How GIs Fought the War in Europe, 1944–1945* (Lawrence: University of Kansas Press, 1994), 245.

80. Wells, *Courage and Air Warfare*, 81, citing Douglas Danford Bond, *The Love and Fear of Flying* (International Universities Press, 1952).

81. Bresnahan, "Dangers in Paradise," 233–35, citing Conference Report, 22nd General Hospital, January 29, 1945, 4, in RG 112, E 30, Box 289, NACP; Memo, Marshall to CO/HQ Pacific Ocean Areas, February 15, 1945, in RG 330, E 97, Box 1330, NA.

82. Jones and Wessely, *Shell Shock to PTSD*, 88; Albert Glass, "Effectiveness of Forward Neuropsychiatric Treatment," *Bulletin of the US Army Medical Department* 7 (1947), esp. 1,038–40.

83. *Neuropsychiatry in World War II*, 2:249, 261, 265, 337. Interview, Rebecca Greene with Herbert Spiegel, New York City, December 15, 1975. According to the British historian Elizabeth Roberts-Pedersen, in addition to treating soldiers close to the front with simple rest and sedation, the British army engaged in physical treatments that were not just for the psychotic but also for the neurotic. Elizabeth Roberts-Pedersen, "The Hard School: Physical Treatments for War Neurosis in Britain during the Second World War," *Social History of Medicine* 29, no. 3 (2016): 612.

84. Interview with Patient under Hypnosis in NP Hospital, Interviewed by Capt. Wallace and M/Sgt Yoswein at the 312th Station Hospital in England, November 1, 1944, Research Branch, I&E Div., ETO B-20, RG 330, NA. Although the focus of the interview under hypnosis was clearly on the battle experience, the psychiatrist did ask questions about the patient's political and racial views, which could be divulged to the military authority, since there was no confidentiality in the military between a military patient and his doctor.

85. Report of Psychiatric Mission of the OFS, OSRD, 65.

86. *Neuropsychiatry in World War II*, 1:696, 697.

87. G. Kurt Piehler, "The Wounded," in *A Religious History of the American GI in World War II* (Lincoln: University of Nebraska Press, 2021), 222–27. In one case, a Protestant minister in a military hospital in St. Lo, France, gave patients psychiatric diagnoses (222, 223).

88. Letters, John Monahan, Office of Chief of Chaplains to Father Meyer, August 9, 1944; Bishop O'Hara to William Arnold, Chief of Chaplains, August 5, 1944; Monahan to Meyer, November 6, 1944; Meyer to Monahan, undated; Box 335, Army's Chaplaincy Records, RG 247, NACP. There were also problems in Aberdeen. Interview, Gordon F. Lewis by Shaun Illingworth, July 24, 2006, 31–32. In this interview, Lewis recalled soldiers at the Aberdeen Training Camp being given what were probably depressants (Blue Heavens) and becoming addicted to them. On definition of "Blue Heavens," see GINAD, http://www.ginad.org/en/search.

89. David Eisenhower, *Eisenhower at War* (New York: Random House, 1986), 375, 484, 524–25. Memorandum, Army Surgeon General Norman Kirk to Charles Hillman, June 15, 1944, Chief Professional Services Division, Surgeon General; Paul T. Murray, "Blacks and the Draft: A History of Institutional Racism," *Journal of Black Studies*, September 1971, 57–68.

90. *Neuropsychiatry in World War II*, 1:312, 408–9.

91. Interview, Shaun Illingworth with William A. Biehler, Palm Desert, CA, August 18, 2007, ROHA, https://oralhistory.rutgers.edu/images/PDFs/biehler_william.pdf. Hedgerows were at least fifteen to twenty feet high. They used a special "rhinoceros" tank to cut down the hedges. "Hedgerow Warfare during the Battle of Normandy," DDay Overlord, https://www.dday-overlord.com/en/battle-of-normandy/tactics/hedgerow-warfare.

92. Will Alexander, "The Battle of Carentan," https://prezi.com/rtdz-6qzqzke/the-battle-of-carentan/. The battle led to the consolidation of the Utah and Omaha beachheads and forestalled a German counterattack. For a description, see John C. McManus, "Battle to Control Carentan during World War II," *World War II Magazine*, July/August 2006, 2.

93. Alex Kershaw, *The Liberator: One World War II Soldier's 500-Day Odyssey from the Beaches of Sicily to the Gates of Dachau* (New York: Broadway, 2013), 158–64.

94. *My Three Years with Eisenhower: The Personal Diary of Captain Harry C. Butcher, USNR: Naval Aide to General Eisenhower, 1942 to 1945* (New York: Simon and Schuster, 1946), 645. Cowdrey, *Fighting for Life*, 94. Letter, September 28, 1944, from Eisenhower to "Dear General," copy Gen. George C. Marshall, Folder 13, Box 67, 01 Marshall Papers, GCMRL.

95. John W. Appel, "Cause and Prevention of Psychiatric Disorders in the US Army in World War II," chap. 1, Draft #2, 5–16, Historical Division of the Office of the Surgeon General, Department of the Army, from the Personal Papers of Appel. Another example Appel gave was of the commander of the Italian Peninsular Base Command ordering that "no man . . . be evacuated to the United States as a psychiatric patient until he personally had examined the man's medical record and given his approval."

96. *Neuropsychiatry in World War II*, 1:144–51.

97. Kyle Crichton, "Repairing War-Cracked Minds," *Collier's*, September 23, 1944, 22–23. Cooke, *All but Me and Thee*, 10.

98. Memorandum, O. L. Nelson, Brig. Gen. GSC, Assist. Dep. Ch. Staff, September 28, 1944, for the AC of S, G-1, Subject: Psychoneurotics, Memorandum, "Psychoneurotics," October 12, 1944, Drawer 920, GCMRL. In 1943, Congress passed the Veterans' Vocational Rehabilitation Act. This act conferred more generous educational benefits than the GI Bill passed in 1944. However, veterans had to be honorably discharged with a medical disability of at least 10 percent, and education had to be deemed necessary to overcome their handicap. Mark D. Van Ells, *To Hear Only Thunder Again* (New York: Lexington, 2001), 137.

99. The other psychiatrists appointed as consultants in September 1944 to the IG Investigation of Psychoneurotics were Karl Bowman, APA president; C. Charles Burlingame, president, Institute of Living, Hartford, CT; Frank Fremont-Smith, director, Josiah Macy Jr. Foundation, New York City; and Harry C. Solomon, director, Boston Psychopathic Hospital.

100. Memorandum for Colonel Collier from W.B.B., War Department General Staff, Personnel Division G-1, Washington, DC, October 7, 1944, RG 165, WNRC; Manuscripts Auction Catalog, Catalogue No. 6019, Correspondence Eisenhower to Snyder, 1947 to 1970, No. 35165.

101. Memorandum for Colonel Collier from W.B.B., October 7, 1944.

102. Curiously, this seemed opposite to the feeling reported in the past that line officers were using psychiatrists to give medical diagnoses so they would not be blamed by their superiors for being poor commanders.

103. Memorandum for the Assistant Chief of Staff, G-1 (Through: The Deputy Chief of Staff), Subject: Psychoneurotics, December 18, 1944, War Department, Office of Inspector General, RG 165, WNRC (Memorandum, Psychoneurotics, December 1944). The investigation focused on the diagnosis, treatment, and disposition of psychoneurotics in the Zone of Interior.

104. Cooke, *All but Me and Thee*, 10, 20, 49–51, 147, 178–80, 188, 196, 209–12. The other civilian psychiatrists consulted by the Office of Inspector General were Karl M. Bowman, president, American Psychiatric Association; C. Charles Burlingame, president, Institute of Living, Hartford, CT; Frank Fremont-Smith, director, Josiah Macy Jr. Foundation; and Harry C. Solomon, director, Boston Psychopathic Hospital. See Memorandum, Psychoneurotics, December 18, 1944, 1.

105. Memorandum, Psychoneurotics, December 18, 1944, 6–8, 14; Marshall also noticed an article entitled "Give Us a Break," *Reader's Digest*, which dealt with the stigma of a psychiatric label on employment. Memorandum for A.C. of S., G-1 from George C. Marshall, November 1, 1944, regarding "Give Us a Break, *Reader's Digest*," November 1, 1944, Drawer 920, GCMRL.

106. Memorandum, Psychoneurotics, December 18, 1944, 6–8. In *All but Me and Thee*, 209–10, Cooke states that 40 to 50 percent with combat-engendered disturbances were returned to duty within two days, another 10 to 15 percent after two weeks, and 30 percent to noncombat jobs, and some of the rest just stayed in service.

107. Memorandum, Psychoneurotics, December 18, 1944, 21; Cooke, *All but Me and Thee*, 212–13. Cooke also noted on 106 that in one case, the army sent one thousand men, all diagnosed psychopaths, to be replacements overseas.

108. Interview, Rebecca Greene with Dr. John Appel, December 23, 1975, Philadelphia; Appel, "Cause and Prevention of Psychiatric Disorders in the U.S. Army in World War II," chap. 1, Private Papers of John Appel MD.

109. Cowdrey, *Fighting for Life*, 92–93. Kirk succeeded James C. Magee as Army Surgeon General in May 1943. According to Cowdrey, Roosevelt agreed to not reappoint Magee because of opposition principally from Army Chief of Staff George C. Marshall, partly because of Magee's failure to abide with Marshall's rules about the chain of command. Also, Magee favored a policy of segregated hospitals with Black doctors and Black nurses treating Black patients in conformity as much as possible with the customs in the South, which the NAACP and Eleanor Roosevelt opposed. Cowdrey, *Fighting for Life*, 111, 92–93.

110. On February 10, 1945, six days before the G-1 report was issued, the Deputy Army Chief of Staff advised Assistant Secretary of War John J. McCloy that a copy of the final report, which the War Department had "inadvertently" received from Boyce, had been leaked to Jonathan Daniels, Roosevelt's press secretary. Daniels was the son of Josephus Daniels, who had served as secretary of the navy when Roosevelt was assistant secretary in World War I. Memorandum for McCloy, February 10, 1945, from Deputy Chief of Staff Thomas Handy, Drawer 920, GCMRL.

111. "Jonathan Daniels Is Dead at 79," *New York Times*, November 7, 1981. Memorandum, Assistant Chief of Staff, G-1 for the Deputy Chief of Staff, February 16, 1945, Drawer 920, GCMRL; Appel, Unpublished History of Psychiatry in World War II, 20, Appel Personal Papers. *Neuropsychiatry in World War II*, 1:104–7, 755–56, referring to nomenclature of anxiety reaction or conversion reaction approved in WD Circular No. 81, issued March 13, 1945.

112. Memorandum, Adjutant General J. A. Ulio, "Psychoneurotics," March 31, 1945, to the Commanding Generals, RG 160, Records of Army Service Forces (710), NA.

113. Memorandum, Adjutant General Ulio to Commanding Generals US Army, March 31, 1945, Army Chief of Staff, G-1, RG 165, WNRC.

114. Memorandum for the Deputy Chief of Staff from Virgil L. Peterson, Major General, Acting The Inspector General, War Department, Subject: Psychoneurosis in the Pacific Ocean Areas, May 8, 1945, 1–4, G-1, RG 165, WNRC. Also directing the inquiry were Inspector General Gen. Phillip E. Brown and Dr. William H. Powell of the Office of the Air Surgeon.

115. Memorandum for the Deputy Chief of Staff from Virgil L. Peterson, Major General, Acting The Inspector General, War Department, Subject: Psychoneurotics, May 26, 1945, 1, 5–7, GCMRL. While Hanson was not a consultant in the initial stages of the investigation, his views probably had weight as he was on the G-1's staff. A few weeks before the investigation started, Hanson suggested to Appel that the army exclude from the number of days of service before rotation any day a soldier spent in custody because of AWOL or other misbehavior. In this way, Hanson hoped, soldiers would be dissuaded from going AWOL, such figures being high.

116. Charles Glass, *The Deserters: A Hidden History of World War II* (London: Penguin, 2013), introduction, citing William Bradford Huie, *The Execution of Private Slovik* (Pennsylvania, 1954).

117. Letter, Stimson to Roosevelt, February 28, 1945, referring to Roosevelt letter, December 4, 1944, War Department General and Special Services, WD 333.9 File, RG 165, NA; Shephard, *A War of Nerves*, 272; *Neuropsychiatry in World War II*, 1:108.

10. Returning to Normalcy

1. At the low end, Eli Ginzberg reports a figure for neuropsychiatric rejections of 1,773,000, including 87,000 nonmedical, administrative. Eli Ginzberg, *The Lost*

Divisions (New York: Columbia University Press, 1959), table 8, 36. At the high end, J. R. Eagan, L. Jackson, and R. H. Eanes report 1,992,950 rejected in "A Study of Neuropsychiatric Rejectees," *Journal of the American Medical Association* 145, no. 7 (February 1951). Eanes was Selective Service assistant executive director during World War II. William Menninger, on the other hand, states that 1,846,000, including for mental deficiency, were rejected, in *Psychiatry in a Troubled World* (New York: Knopf, 1948), 587. Most likely, the number rejected was somewhere in between. The low figure of 1,773,000 may not have included the navy's figures, since Ginzberg et al. derived their figures from Selective Service records, and the navy and army did not have a fully operating joint induction system until at least February 1943. As to discharges, Ginzberg et al., *The Lost Divisions*, 60, gives a figure of 754,000. On the other hand, the US Army, Medical Department, in *Neuropsychiatry in World War II*, ed. Albert J. Glass, MC, USA (Ret.) and Lt. Col. Robert J. Bernucci (Washington, DC: US Government Printing Office, 1966), 1:771, gives a figure of 538,452, including administrative separations for inaptitude or unsuitability but does not include the navy's figures. Adding 76,721 discharged from the navy after being hospitalized plus 91,565 separated from naval training stations for neurological and psychiatric reasons comes to 168,286. Adding 168,286 to the army's 538,452 comes to 706,738. The navy's figures are based on Francis J. Braceland, Chief Navy Psychiatry, "Psychiatric Lessons from World War II," *American Journal of Psychiatry* 103, no. 5 (March 1947): 587. The total figure rises to 713,286 if we use Menninger's 545,000 army neuropsychiatric discharges instead. See *Psychiatry in a Troubled World*, 589. Hence, an estimate of at least 700,000 discharges. On the other hand, Edward Strecker, *Their Mothers' Sons: A Psychiatrist Examines an American Problem* (New York, 1946), 18, states that rejections come to 1,825,000, plus 600,000 discharges, plus an undefined 500,000 "draft dodgers." As to the numbers discharged for physical disabilities, according to William Menninger, *A Psychiatrist for a Troubled World: Selected Papers of William C. Menninger, M.D.* (New York, 1967), 545, as of January 1946, 1,000,000 veterans were discharged from hospitals as of January 1946 for "crippling disability" or illness, including an unspecified number for cardiovascular disorders, arthritis, diabetes, tuberculosis, peptic ulcers, and neurological disorders; 15,000 with major limb amputations; 8,400 who had received treatment for deafness; 1,200 blind or nearly totally blind in both eyes; and 1,400 paralyzed in both limbs from spinal injuries. On impact of psychiatry after the war, see also Mark D. Van Ells, *To Hear Only Thunder Again: America's World War II Veterans Come Home* (New York, 2001), 96–107.

    2. According to Gerald Grob, *The Mad among Us* (New York: Free Press, 1994), 166, by 1939, mental hospitals "cared for nearly 425,000 persons or about 92 percent of the total number of inpatients; the remainder were in private facilities (2.8 percent) and veterans' hospitals (5.6 percent)."

    3. While the focus of mental health shifted soon after World War II from institutionalization to clinics and private practices, the reverse had occurred after

the Civil War, when the states established increasing numbers of mental institutions, responding in part to increasing cases of homelessness and to maltreatment in prisons and almshouses. See R. Gregory Lande, *Madness, Malingering, and Malfeasance: The Transformation of Psychiatry and Law in the Civil War Era* (Washington, DC, 2005), 195. As for World War II, *Neuropsychiatry in World War II*, 1:85; Nathan G. Hale Jr., *The Rise and Crisis of Psychoanalysis in the United States: Freud and the Americans, 1917–1985* (New York: Oxford University Press, 1995), 187–95.

4. Testimony of Colonel John Baird, Chief, Neuropsychiatry, Veterans Administration, before Congressman Percy Priest, September 1945, 64, US House of Representatives, *Hearings on H.R. 2550 to Establish a National Neuropsychiatric Institute*, 79th Cong., 1st sess., 1945.

5. The President's News Conference, May 15, 1945, #7 Question, and The President's News Conference, June 7, 1945; "Letter to General Omar Bradley Regarding the Establishment of a Department of Medicine and Surgery in the Veterans Administration," January 3, 1946, Public Papers of the Presidents, Harry S. Truman, 1945–1953, Harry S. Truman Library, Independence, MO, http://trumanlibrary.org/public papers.

6. *The Mental Health Programs* (Chicago, 1950), 32. Figures on the number of VA hospitals are contradictory. Those cited in the text are derived from the VA History in Brief, 15 and 16, http://www.va.gov/opa/publications. On the other hand, Hines told the Council of Social Agencies, Washington, DC, on December 11, 1944, that the VA had 94 hospitals with a total of 89,000 beds and was planning to construct facilities for another 21,000 beds, for a total of 110,000 beds. VA 1943–1944 file, OF8, VA, Franklin Delano Roosevelt Library, Hyde Park, NY, hereafter referred to as FDRL. The New York Academy of Medicine reported in its *70th Anniversary of D-Day History of Medicine* that there were almost 100 VA hospitals by the late 1940s. http://www.nyamcenterfor history.org/tag. For criticism of Hines, see "Brig. Gen. Hines Ex-VA Head, Dies," *New York Times*, April 5, 1960. Van Ells in *To Hear Only Thunder Again*, 122, 123, notes that Congress with the support of Truman passed a law that allowed for the hiring of doctors and nurses outside civil service. The bill also provided for the affiliation of the VA with top medical schools. As to patients in civilian hospitals and asylums, 490,000 were hospitalized in 1941. By 1951, 577,246 were hospitalized, a growth of 17.8 percent, compared to a growth of 28.5 percent from 1933 to 1943, from 389,500 to 500, 564. US House of Representatives, Committee on Interstate and Foreign Commerce, Hearings on the Causes, Control, and Remedies of the Principal Diseases of Mankind, 83rd Cong., 1st Sess., 1953, 1092; *The Mental Health Programs of the Forty-Eight States: A Report to the Governors' Conference* (1950), 32.

7. Letter, Lawrence Kubie to Mrs. Franklin Delano Roosevelt, March 30, 1945; and Secretary to Mrs. Roosevelt to Kubie, April 4, 1945, plus paper attached, "A Program to Break the Bottleneck of the Rehabilitation Program," File 90, Eleanor Roosevelt Papers, Box 1185, FDRL.

8. Albert Deutsch, *Mentally Ill in America* (New York: Columbia University Press, 1946), 323. There were also four army, one navy, and three public health clinics treating another 19,923 veterans, as well as 72 university clinics. Of the 398 state, 324 treated children; of the 91 private, 37 treated children. Hospital Committee, "Statistics Pertinent to Psychiatry in the United States," *Group for the Advancement of Psychiatry Report No. 7* (March 1949), 4, 6. Sol Ginsburg MD estimated a shortage of psychiatric clinic services in New York City for 8,000 veterans in 1945. Sol Ginsburg, "Community Responsibility for NP Discharges," *Mental Hygiene*, 1945, 25.

9. *Payne Whitney Clinic Annual Reports* for 1943 through 1946. Eli Ginzberg, *Lost Divisions* (New York: Columbia University Press, 1959), 62; *Neuropsychiatry in World War II*, 1:771.

10. Hazel Rowley, *Richard Wright: The Life* (New York: Henry Holt, 2001), 257, 258; *Richard Wright: Writing America at Home and from Abroad*, ed. Virginia Whatley Smith (Jackson: University Press of Mississippi, 1998), 121–22. Initially, Richard Wright came in contact with the German-born American psychoanalyst Fredric Wertham when Wertham mailed Wright a complimentary copy of Wertham's novel, *Dark Legend*, which concerned an Italian immigrant's murder of his promiscuous mother to avenge the honor of his dead father. About the same time, Wright had become interested in the case of Clinton Brewer, a Black man who had been serving since age seventeen for nineteen years at Trenton State Prison, New Jersey, for murdering a woman who refused to marry him. During this time, Brewer had been an exemplary prisoner and musician. Brewer gave Wright one of his compositions, which Wright gave to Count Basie, who had it performed. Wright also got the record producer John Hammond interested in Brewer's case. Then, Wright, Count Basie, and Hammond all wrote a letter to the governor of New Jersey asking that Brewer be paroled, which the governor did. Three months later, to Wright's surprise, Brewer murdered a second woman when she refused to marry him. Wright then persuaded Dr. Wertham to examine Brewer. Dr. Wertham did so, accompanied by a lawyer he had hired. Afterward, Dr. Wertham served as an expert witness at Brewer's trial. Convicted of second-degree murder, Brewer was spared from the electric chair by the expert testimony of Wertham proving Brewer was insane. Thereafter, Wright and Wertham continued to be friends. In 1954, Wright completed his novel *Savage Holiday*, the main character of which, Erskine Fowler, was largely based on Brewer.

11. Gabriel Mendes, *Under the Strain of Color: Harlem's LaFargue Clinic and the Promise of Antiracist Psychiatry* (New York: Cornell University Press, 2015), 30–70. Wertham was also known for his work on the adverse psychological effect of cartoons on children, particularly their violence.

12. Carolyn Gifford, Unpublished Table, APA Membership, American Psychiatric Association Library, American Psychiatric Association Archives, Washington, DC, hereafter referred to as APA. The APA's membership included Fellows, Members, Associate Members, Life Members, Honorary Members,

Corresponding Members, and Inactive Members. Gifford's report covered 1906 through 1965. *U.S. News and World Report*, July 10, 2015, 1960: 11,637; 1970: 19,037.

13. Report, "Psychiatry for 20,000,000 Veterans and Its Impact on the National Picture," 11, Daniel Blain Papers, APA Archives. GAP estimated that in 1946, another 1,302 residents were trained as psychiatrists. This would be lower than the APA figures. Hospital Committee, "Statistics Pertinent to Psychiatry in the United States," *Group for the Advancement of Psychiatry Report No. 7* (March 1949), 6.

14. GAP, "Statistics Pertinent to Psychiatry in the United States," 5.

15. Gerald Grob, "World War II and American Psychiatry," *Psychohistory Review*, Fall 1990, 41–67; Grob, "The Lessons of War, 1941–45," in *From Asylum to Community: Mental Health Policy in Modern America* (Princeton, NJ, 1991); Hans Pols, "War Neurosis, Adjustment Problems in Veterans, and an Ill Nation: The Disciplinary Project of American Psychiatry during and after World War II," *Osiris* 22, no. 1 (2007): 72–92.

16. Albert Deutsch, *The History of the Group for Advancement of Psychiatry* (Washington, DC: GAP, 1959), 8–183; Arnold A. Rogow, *The Psychiatrists* (New York, 1970), 32.

17. Hale, *The Rise and Crisis of Psychoanalysis in the United States*, 189; Roy Menninger and John C. Nemiah, eds., *American Psychiatry after World War II, 1944–1994* (Washington, DC: American Psychiatric Press, 2000), 81. Edward Shorter, *A History of Psychiatry: From the Era of the Asylum to the Age of Prozac* (New York: Wiley, 1998), 167.

18. Menninger and Nemiah, *American Psychiatry after World War II*, 83. Dagmar Herzog, *Cold War Freud: Psychoanalysis in an Age of Catastrophes* (Cambridge: Cambridge University Press, 2017), 23, 24.

19. Edward Shorter, *How Everyone Became Depressed: The Rise and Fall of the Nervous Breakdown* (Oxford: Oxford University Press, 2013), 115. Shorter, *A History of Psychiatry*, 167–69, 171. Roy Menninger, *American Psychiatry after World War II*, 83. Sanford Gifford, "The Psychoanalytic Movement in the United States, 1906–1991," in *History of Psychiatry and Medical Psychology*, ed. Edwin R. Wallace and John Gach (Springer Science, 2008), 638–39, 655. Rebecca Jo Plant, "William Menninger and American Psychoanalysis, 1946–48," *History of Psychiatry* 16, no. 2: 185. By 1943, half of the analysts in Boston were Europeans. See Boston Psychoanalytic Society and Institute, https://bpsi.org/about-bpsi/. On Otto Fenichel, see Edward Shorter, *How Everyone Became Depressed*, 115; on Heinz Hartmann and Martin Grotjahn, among others, see Shorter, *A History of Psychiatry*, 168–70.

20. Herzog, *Cold War Freud*, 33. Plant, "William Menninger and American Psychoanalysis," 184. Shorter, *A History of Psychiatry*, 173. Pols, "War Neurosis," 89.

21 Herzog, *Cold War Freud*, 46. Gifford, "The Psychoanalytic Movement in the United States, 1906–1991," 641.

22. Herzog, *Cold War Freud*, 11, 12, 22, 23.

23. Herzog, *Cold War Freud*, 37.

24. Herzog, *Cold War Freud*, 39–42, 48, 50, 51. Also reflective of the improved relationship between psychiatry and religion was the growth of the pastoral counseling movement. Kurt Piehler, *A Religious History of the American GI in World War II* (Lincoln: University of Nebraska Press, 2021), 228.

25. Shorter, *A History of Psychiatry*, 165, 168, 170. It would seem that the rise of psychopharmaceuticals also played an important role.

26. William Tuttle, *Daddy's Gone to War: The Second World War in the Lives of American Children* (New York: Oxford University Press, 1993), 235; David A. Gerber, "Heroes and Misfits: The Troubled Social Reintegration of Disabled Veterans in *The Best Years of Our Lives*," *American Quarterly* 46, no. 4 (December 1994): 545–74. US Senate Committee on Banking and Currency, S.380, 79th Cong., 1st Sess., 1945, 436–39. Cecil Bohanon, "Economic Recovery: Lessons from the Post-World War II Period," Mercatus Center, George Mason University, https://www.mercatus.org/publications/economic-history/economic-recovery-lessons-post-world-war-ii-period.

27. The Balance, http://www.thebalance.com/unemployment-rate-by-year.

28. Memorandum, "Joint Statement of Policy on the Release of Information from Medical Records of Members and Former Members of the Armed Service," May 25, 1944, signed Secretary of War Henry Stimson and Secretary of the Navy James Forrestal, RG 165, Suitland, MD, hereafter referred to as WNRC. Today, this does not appear to be the case, as the veteran currently can obtain his discharge form, DD-214, including psychiatric documents. "Veterans Affairs Research Communications," *Science Daily*, March 1, 2017, http://www.sciencedaily.com/releases/2017; Veterans Service Records, http://www.archive.gov/veterans/military.service.records.

29. Dr. Lewis Weed to Dr. Winfred Overholser, January 1944, in MED: Committee on Neuropsychiatry, Gen. File 1942–1943, National Academy of Sciences, hereafter referred to as NAS; *Washington Star*, February 13, 1944, Dr. Winfred Overholser Papers, Library of Congress, Washington, DC, hereafter referred to as LC.

30. Thomas Rennie, "Psychiatric Rehabilitation Therapy," *American Journal of Psychiatry* 101, no. 4 (January 1945): 479.

31. S. Futterman, F. J. Kirkner, and Mortimer H. Meyer, "First Year Analysis of Veterans Treated in a Mental Hygiene Clinic of the Veterans Administration," *American Journal of Psychiatry* 104, no. 5 (November 1947): 298–305.

32. Abraham Zukerman's thesis revealed that 33 out of 77 veterans at the Kings County Hospital psychiatric clinic were unemployed. Further, "most of the men within the group had worked or were working at jobs requiring little specialized training—messengers, truck drivers, sewing machine operators, clerks." Abraham Zukerman, "Ten World War II Veterans with Psychoneurotic Disabilities Selected for Treatment at the Veterans Rehabilitation Clinic, Kings

County Hospital, Psychiatric Division" (1947). Likewise, Laura Bierstein's thesis at Columbia (1944) showed that of 42 neuropsychiatric veterans at the Vanderbilt clinic, the numbers in white-collar professions fell from 12 during the height of the Great Depression to 8 in 1944, from 10 in skilled occupations in the 1930s to 3 after discharge. During the same time, the numbers unemployed rose from 0 to 18.

33. Noah Tsika, *Traumatic Imprints* (Oakland: University of California Press, 2018), 191–93.

34. Allan Bérubé, *Coming Out under Fire: The History of Gay Men and Women in World War II* (Chapel Hill: University of North Carolina Press, 2012), 230–43, 229–30. The army refused to pay soldiers for time lost from duty caused by drugs, alcohol, or venereal disease. See *Neuropsychiatry in World War II*, 1:485n21, referring to A.R. 35-1440, revised November 17, 1944; and *Manual for Court-Martial* (1928). Those with blue discharges were ineligible for disability pensions and also for federally subsidized home, college, or farm loans; job training and placement programs; burial allowances; subsidized life insurance; disability pensions; insurance; and hospital care.

35. Temple Burling MD, "Community Organization for Meeting Disabled Veterans," *American Journal of Orthopsychiatry* 14, no. 4 (October 1944): 694; Winifred Dean, "Casework with the 'Emotionally Disturbed Veteran,'" MSW, Columbia University School of Social Work, September 1945, 54.

36. Sidney Poitier, *This Life* (New York: Knopf, 1980).

37. Sidney Poitier, *The Measure of a Man* (New York: Harper Collins, 2000), 2, 13, 52–55.

38. Report, "Medical Conference at National Headquarters," June 5–6, 1944, 102, RG 147, WNRC; *Psychiatry*, August 1943, 325, 326.

39. Examiner Shane at the Camp Dodge induction station, Iowa, noted: "Any doctor can always go to the local board and find out why registrants have been rejected. The files are open to doctors and dentists." Conference on the Physical and Mental Qualifications for the Armed Services for Physicians and Dentists of the Local Boards and Medical Advisory Boards and Local Board Members in the State of Iowa, August 26, 1943, 10, US Army Military Research Collection, Carlisle Barracks, PA, hereafter referred to as USAMHRC.

40. Hearings on Full Employment Act, S.380, 436–39. The bill, which did not pass, would have ensured federal employment to anyone denied by private industry.

41. US Senate, Comm. on Educ and Lab., Subcommittee on Wartime Health and Education Hearings on Sen. Res. 74, *A Resolution Authorizing Investigation of the Educational and Physical Fitness of the Civilian Population*, 78th Cong., 2nd Sess., July 10, 1944, 1709, 1710.

42. Press Release, "Army Psychiatrist Asks Industry to Help in Employment of Psychiatric Casualties," September 18, 1944, Psychoneuroses, War Department General Staff, G-1, RG 165, WNRC; *Washington Sunday Star*, February 13, 1944; *Times Herald*, March 12, 1944; *Washington Daily News*, April 12, 1944; Overholser

Papers, LC; Letter, Overholser to McIntire, May 20, 1943, Surgeon General, US Navy file, Overholser Papers, St. Elizabeth Hospital, RG 418, National Archives, Washington, DC, hereafter referred to as NA. Hearings on Full Employment Act, S.380, 436–39.

43. Farrell, "Plain Truths about the N.P.S.," *Rotarian* 65 (October 1944): 19, 57, 56. William Menninger, *Psychiatry in a Troubled World* (New York: Macmillan, 1948), 367, 376.

44. Menninger, *Psychiatry in a Troubled World*, 367–76; Norman Cameron, "The Socially Maladjusted Veteran," in *Annals of the American Academy of Political and Social Science* (Philadelphia, 1945), 29–37; S. Futterman, 299, 300; *PM* (October 6, 1946), 10; Burling, "Community Organization for Meeting Disabled Veterans," 680–98; William Menninger, "The Responsibility of Neuropsychiatry for Rehabilitating Veterans," unpublished speech delivered to Michigan Society of Neurology and Psychiatry, September 1944, 10, 11, Menninger Foundation Archives, Topeka, KS, hereafter referred to as Menninger Archives; US Senate, Committee on Education and Labor, *Report on Neuropsychiatric Institute*, Sen. Rept. 1353, 1946; "Statistics Pertinent to Psychiatry in the United States," 2. In 1946, the Los Angeles neuropsychiatric veterans clinic reported a significant rise in the number of divorces and separations at the time of intake. Tuttle, *Daddy's Gone to War*, 220.

45. Tuttle, *Daddy's Gone to War*, 31–35, 40–42, 44–48, 71–73, 79, 83, 215, 218–23.

46. G. Stevenson and L. Kubie, "Fourteen Point Program on Rehabilitation," Writers' War Board, NYC. War Department Staff, G-1 Records, RG 165, 710, WNRC; War Department Pamphlet, "He's Back," 7–11. Menninger, *Psychiatry in a Troubled World*, 376–80; According to Menninger, by 1947, the VA had awarded pensions to 3,000,000 physically disabled veterans.

47. Krin Gabbard and Glen O. Gabbard, *Psychiatry and the Cinema* (Chicago: University of Chicago Press, 1987). The book's full list of films with psychiatrists includes *His Girl Friday* and *My Favorite Wife* (1940); *King's Row, Shining Victory, That Uncertain Feeling* (1941); *The Cat People, Lady in a Jam, Now Voyager* (1942); *Crime Doctor* and *The Seventh Victim* (1943); *Arsenic and Old Lace, Dark Waters, Lady in the Dark,* and *Since You Went Away* (1944), *Bewitched, Conflict, Murder, My Sweet, The Seventh Veil,* and *Spellbound* (1945); *Bedlam, The Dark Mirror, Dead of Night, The Locket, She Wouldn't Say Yes,* and *Shock* (1946); *The Bachelor and the Bobby Soxer, Dark Delusion, Dishonored Lady, The Guilt of Janet Ames, High Wall, Miracle on 34th Street, Nightmare Alley,* and *Possessed* (1947); *The Dark Past, The Gay Intruders, Hollow Triumph (The Scar), Let's Live a Little, Sleep, My Love,* and *The Snake Pit* (1948); and *The Accused, Caught,* and *Home of the Brave* (1949). Glen Gabbard is a trained psychiatrist who has written several books on aspects of the profession.

48. Gabbard and Gabbard, *Psychiatry and the Cinema*, 6, 7–12, 19, 24, 36, 39, 68–72.

49. Letter, Franklin Delano Roosevelt to Dr. Foster Kennedy, regarding establishing neuropsychiatric institute, December 12, 1938, 103-C, OF FDR, FDRL; Letter, Assistant Surgeon General Public Health Service Lawrence Kolb to Dr. Foster Kennedy, February 17, 1939, 0875-132 Gen., NA; Robert Felix, *Mental Illness: Progress and Prospects* (New York, 1967), 44.

50. US Senate Committee on Education and Labor, *Hearings on S.1160, to Establish a National Neuropsychiatric Institute*, 79th Cong., 2nd Sess., 1946. The Senate committee that heard testimony on the proposed act included, besides Pepper, Elbert D. Thomas, Utah; James E. Murray, Montana; Lister Hill, Alabama; James M. Tunnell, Delaware; Robert M. LaFollette, Wisconsin; Robert A. Taft, Ohio; George D. Aiken, Vermont; and H. Alexander Smith, New Jersey. US House of Representatives, *Hearings on H.R. 2550*, 79th Cong., 1st Sess., 1945. The House committee, in addition to Priest, included Alfred Bullwinkle, North Carolina; Virgil Chapman, Kentucky; Vito Marcantonio, New York; Clarence Brown, Ohio; Thomas D. Winter, Kansas; and Wilson D. Gillette, Pennsylvania.

51. Letter, Franklin D. Roosevelt to Secretary of War Henry Stimson, December 4, 1944, RG 165, WNRC; Letter, Stimson to Roosevelt, February 23, 1945, WDSIG 333.9 Psychoneurotics, WD General and Special Staffs, RG 165, NA; Menninger, *Psychiatry in a Troubled World*, 296–98; Ginzberg, *Lost Divisions*, 83. A month before Roosevelt died, Kubie sent Eleanor two articles he had received permission from Congress to publish about rehabilitation for veterans and about how medical care for veterans should be organized, the latter containing the valuable advice that a doctor treating a patient should not be the one who determines the extent to which one gets a pension, a problem at the VA later on. Letters, Mrs. Roosevelt to Kubie, March 17 and March 26, File 100, Box 1760; to Kubie, April 4, File 90; Box 1185; ER to McIntire, March 19, 1945, File 100.1 (in which she wondered whether Kubie's letter of March 8 should be referred to committee in Congress amending GI Bill). Kubie to Mrs. Roosevelt, March 26 and March 30, 1945, File 90, Box 1185, plus papers attached to April 4, all from ER Papers, FDRL.

52. The numbers varied between 2,400 and 3,000, depending on how a psychiatrist was defined.

53. Letter, Dr. J. S. Kasanin, V.A. to Senator Pepper, October 5, 1945, Records U.S. Senate Committee on Education and Labor, Subcommittee on Health and Education, National Neuropsychiatric Act, S.1160, RG 46, NA; Letter from resident, 64th Street, New York City, to Pepper, March 8, 1946, Records on S.1160, RG 46, NA; Senate Hearings on S.1160, 61. As early as August 1944, Menninger had been campaigning for training facilities for psychiatrists and psychiatric training for medical students. See William Menninger, "Neuropsychiatry: Its Place in Undergraduate and Graduate Medical Education," *Journal of the American Medical Association* 125 (August 19, 1944): 1,103–5.

54. Hospital Committee, "Statistics Pertinent to Psychiatry in the United States," *Group for the Advancement of Psychiatry*, Report No. 7 (March 1949), 3;

Press Release, Department of Justice, November 10, 1946, Albert Deutsch Papers, Crime File, APA Archives. It should be noted that according to Joanna Bourke, *An Intimate History of Killing* (New York: Basic Books, 1999), veterans did not have higher rates of crime. Her sample, however, is drawn from diverse countries: the United States, Australia, and England.

55. Report, Selective Service Medical Conference, June 5–6, 1944, 6, 7, 102 (Conferences), Selective Service, RG 147, WNRC; *Wisconsin Blue Book* (1946), 160, on role of Selective Service System in working with veterans on getting reemployed. Memorandum, W.B.B. to Col. Collier, War Department General Staff Personnel Division G-1, "Psychoneuroses," October 7, 1944, RG 165, 710 Psychoneuroses, WNRC; Letter, Adjutant Lyman W. Whitcomb to Thomas F. Mackey Commander Massachusetts American Legion, June 6, 1945, 292, RG 112, WNRC. This letter was from Newton Post No. 48. The letter was copied and sent by Mackey to Surgeon General US Army Norman Kirk; Letter Rep. Philip J. Philbin, to Ross T. McIntire, Surgeon General, Navy, September 30, 1945, P3-1/P19-1 (1945–1946), Bureau of Medicine and Surgery, RG 52, NA, also in same file; Letter, McIntire to Philbin, September 30, 1945; Letter, Deputy Surgeon General Army George F. Lull to Philbin, US House of Representatives, October 9, 1945, 710 (Psychoneuroses), Surgeon General's Office records, RG 112, WNRC.

56. US Senate Committee on Education and Labor, *Hearings on S. 1160, to Establish a National Neuropsychiatric Institute*, 105–6.

57. Report from the Society for the Prevention of Crime, December 1945, Soldier File, Albert Deutsch Papers, APA Archives.

58. *Stars and Stripes*, January 17, 1945, Scrapbook Box 25, Overholser Papers, LC; Senate Report 1353, 3; US House of Representatives, Committee on Interstate and Foreign Commerce, *Hearings on H.R. 2550*, 68.

59. In May 1946, retired Supreme Court Justice Owen Roberts formally announced the establishment of the National Mental Health Foundation; besides the members previously mentioned, its sponsors included Bess Truman, Pastor Harry Emerson Fosdick, the actress Helen Hayes, the former surgeon general Thomas Parran, the labor leader William Green, the author Thomas Mann, the actress Helen Gahagan Douglas, the criminologist Sheldon Glueck, the theologian Reinhold Niebuhr, the physicist J. R. Oppenheimer, the labor leader Walter P. Reuther, and the psychiatrist Gregory Zilboorg. *New York Times*, May 6, 1946, 13.

60. *Hearings on S.1160, to Establish a National Neuropsychiatric Institute*, 91; Senate Report 1353, 3, 4; Albert Deutsch column, *PM*, October 7, 1946, 12; Mary Jane Ward, *The Snake Pit* (New York: Random House, 1946); Gabbard and Gabbard, *Psychiatry and the Cinema*, 69–71.

61. For Deutsch's description at the hearing of the deplorable conditions in mental hospitals and the need for greater psychiatric treatment facilities for veterans, see, e.g., *Hearings on S.1160, to Establish a National Neuropsychiatric Institute*, 5, 103–5. These descriptions were derived from his serialized *PM*

articles, then published as *The Shame of the States* (New York: Harcourt Brace, 1948), 10, 18, 40, 42, 43, 48, 57.

62. *Hearings on S.1160, to Establish a National Neuropsychiatric Institute*, 5, 103–5; Deutsch, *Shame of the States*, 10, 18, 40, 42, 43, 48, 57. Steven Taylor, *Acts of Conscience: World War II, Mental Institutions, and Religion* (Syracuse, NY: Syracuse University Press, 2009), 287.

63. Deutsch, *Shame of the States*, 10, 18, 40, 42, 43, 48, 57.

64. Appendix, 1865, to US Senate, Committee on Education and Labor, Subcommittee on Wartime Health and Education, Hearings on Sen. Res. 74, A Resolution Authorizing Investigation of the Educational and Physical Fitness of the Civilian Population, 78th Cong., 2nd Sess., 1944.

65. US Senate hearings on S. 1160, 28, 29, 9; Ellen Herman, "Nervous in Service," in *The Romance of American Psychology* (Berkeley: University of California Press, 1995), 344. While Overholser had estimated in 1940 that the cost of hospitalizing psychiatric patients would come to $30,000 per patient, in actuality the cost came to $40,000 per patient, and 60 percent of the VA hospital beds were occupied by psychiatric cases.

66. *Hearings on S. 1160, to Establish a National Neuropsychiatric Institute*, 61; US Senate, Comm. on Educ. and Labor, Report on a National Neuropsychiatric Institute, Sen. Report 1353, 1946.

67. "Here and There," *Fitchburg Sentinel*, July 19, 1944, RG 112, WNRC.

68. Letter, Julien E. Benjamin, Colonel, Chief of the Medical Service, First Service Command Lowell General Hospital Mass. to Maj. Gen. George F. Lull, July 20, 1944, 702.1 (Medical Examinations), RG 112, WNRC.

69. The Citizens Medical Reference Bureau, active since the 1920s, had lobbied in Congress against, inter alia, federal aid to states for maternity and infancy care and against compulsory vaccination. Its leader was Harry B. Anderson. See Vaccine Liberation, http://www.vaclib.org.

70. "Appropriation Language: National Institutes of Health, National Institute of Mental Health," http://www.nimh.nih.gov. National Institute of Mental Health: Authorization of Appropriation, 42 *U.S.C.* 232, http://www.law.cornell.edu. US Inflation Calculator, htttp://usinflationcalculator.com.

71. Menninger, *Psychiatry in a Troubled World*, xiii, 41, 47, 417–37.

72. Menninger, "Presentation to American Psychiatric Association Council," December 18, 1944, Menninger unpublished papers, 1945–1947, Menninger Archives.

73. Interview, Dr. John Appel with Rebecca Greene, December 23, 1975, Philadelphia. The APA Committee on Preventive Psychiatry included Appel, Alfred Ludwig, Leon Saul, Frederick Hanson, and Sidney K. Smith. Annual Report, Preventive Psychiatry Committee, APA, 1949, from Personal Papers of Appel; Minutes, APA Preventive Psychiatry Committee, February 8, 1950; Appel and Gilbert Beebe, "Preventive Psychiatry," *JAMA*, August 31, 1946, 1474. C. C.

Burlingame and Lawrence Kubie also supported industrial psychiatry. Lawrence Kubie, "The Psychiatrist and Industry," *Personnel Journal*, 1946, 52; C. C. Burlingame, "Mental Health in Industry," *Digest of Neurological Psychiatry*, August 1948, 462–76.

74. Among those who early on started using group therapy were the psychoanalysts Paul Schilder, Fritz Redl, Elvin Semrad (in the military), and Martin Grotjahn. Gifford, "The Psychoanalytic Movement in the United States, 1906–1991," 646.

75. Daniel Blain, "Private Practice of Psychiatry," *Annals of the American Academy of Political and Social Science* 186 (March 1953): 138–39.

76. Colonel French L. MacLean, *The Fifth Column* (Atglen, PA: Schiffer, 2013), 184, 208–9, 223.

77. Menninger, *Psychiatry in a Troubled World*, 422–25. Ruth Feldstein, *Motherhood in Black and White: Race and Sex in American Liberalism, 1930–1965* (New York: Cornell University Press, 2000), 75–77.

78. Menninger, *Psychiatry in a Troubled World*, 422. Feldstein, *Motherhood in Black and White*, 75–77.

79. Herman, *The Romance of American Psychology*. Leighton headed OWI Foreign Morale Division, where he focused on the psychiatric approach to community management (22); worked with psychologists on enemy morale at such agencies as the Office of Facts and Figures, Office of Strategic Services, and OWI (31); and headed a research team at the Boston Relocation Center for Japanese Americans (22). On Brickner, see 35.

80. Obituary, Dr. Walter Langer, *New York Times*, July 10, 1981; Leon Goldensohn, *The Nuremberg Interviews: An American Psychiatrist's Conversations with Defendants and Witnesses*, ed. Robert Gellateley (New York: Viking, 2004); Joel E. Dimsdale, *Anatomy of Malice* (New Haven, CT: Yale University Press, 2016), 28, 47, 50, 56, 58–59; Eric Jaffe, *A Curious Madness* (New York, 2014), 1–10; Alec Marsh, *Ezra Pound* (London: Reaktion, 2011). See also E. Fuller Torrey MD, *The Roots of Treason* (Kansas: Lucas, 1984); Francis Braceland, interviewed by Dr. David Musto, June 29, 1973, 20–25, RG 147. Braceland recalled taking on a sensitive task for Dr. McIntire, Roosevelt's physician, in 1944 or 1945, in which Braceland was ordered to go to a secretive place by train, which turned out to be the Atomic Energy Commission, Knoxville, TN, and then ordered to examine a navy engineer who had been stopped from flying a plane that had its "four motors running . . . ready to take off to go tell Hitler to get the hell out of this." Braceland determined that the man was schizophrenic, and the military had "a shock machine" sent down from Cincinnati.

81. Pols, "War Neurosis," 73.

82. Arthur C. Houts, "Fifty Years of Psychiatric Nomenclature: Reflections on the 1945 War Department Technical Bulletin Medical 203," *Journal of Clinical Psychology* (July 2000): 935–47, including reprint of Bulletin.

83. *Diagnostic Statistical Manual–I* (Washington, DC, 1952), 47, 48.

84. Edward Strecker, "Psychiatry Speaks to Democracy," Menas Gregory Memorial Lecture, *Mental Hygiene* 29 (October 1945): 591–605; Edward Strecker, "What's Wrong with American Mothers," *Saturday Evening Post* 21 (October 26, 1946): 14–15, 83–104; Edward Strecker, *Their Mothers' Sons: The Psychiatrist Examines an American Problem* (Philadelphia: Lippincott, 1946). Sometimes, the onus was placed on the father. In a VA psychotherapy session in 1948, reported as part of a large study of VA clinics throughout the United States, a therapist noticed one patient with severe neurosis mainly caused by "an emotionally dependent, ambivalent attitude toward his excessively demanding, over-emotional father." Once he was able to express hostility toward the doctor, his relationship with his real father improved. Florence Powdermaker, "Group Psychotherapy with Neurotics," *American Journal of Psychiatry* 105, no. 6 (December 1948): 449, 454.

85. Hans Pols, "The Repression of War Trauma in American Psychiatry after World War II," *Clio Medicine* 1 (1999): 253–58; Hans Pols, "The Tunisian Campaign, War Neuroses, and the Reorientation of American Psychiatry during World War II," *Harvard Review of Psychiatry* 19 (2011): 318–19; Rebecca Jo Plant, *Mom: The Transformation of Motherhood in Modern America* (Chicago: University of Chicago Press, 2010), 105–6, citing George K. Pratt, *Soldier to Civilian: Problems of Readjustment* (New York: McGraw Hill, 1944), 3–6; Alexander G. Dumas and Grace Graham Keen, *A Psychiatric Primer for the Veteran's Family and Friends* (Minneapolis: University of Minnesota Press, 1945), 143.

86. Charles Glass, *The Deserters: A Hidden History of World War II* (London: Penguin, 2013), 101, citing William Bradford Huie, *The Execution of Private Slovik* (Pennsylvania, 1954).

87. Pols, "War Neurosis," 91, 92.

88. Shorter, *A History of Psychiatry*, 177.

89. Eric Pace, "Benjamin Spock, World's Pediatrician, Dies at 94," *New York Times*, March 17, 1998. Also very widely consulted were Arthur Gesell, *Infant and Child in the Culture Today: The Guidance of Development in Home and Nursery School* (New York, 1943); and Arthur Gesell, *The Child from Five to Ten* (New York: Harper & Brothers, 1946).

90. Plant, *Mom*, 105, citing Susan Hartmann, regarding experts instructing women on how to leave their jobs and become traditional women, in "Prescriptions for Penelope: Literature on Women's Obligations to Returning World War II Veterans," *Women's Studies* 5, no. 3 (1978): 223–39; also see Rebecca S. Greene, "The United States: Women in World War II," *Trends in History: A Review of Current Periodical Literature in History* 2, no. 2 (Winter 1981): 74–75.

91. For an analysis of this film with a focus on the physically disabled veteran, see Gerber, "Heroes and Misfits," 545–74.

92. Tsika, *Traumatic Imprints*, 175–77.

93. Tuttle, *Daddy's Gone to War*, 216; Lawrence Grobel, *The Hustons: The Life and Times of a Hollywood Dynasty* (New York: Scribner, 1989), 274.

94. Grobel, *The Hustons*, 138–40, 269–74.

95. Grobel, *The Hustons*, 141; Ben Shephard, *A War of Nerves* (Cambridge, MA: Harvard University Press, 2000), 277.

96. Tsika, *Traumatic Imprints*, 182–85, 193.

11. From "War Man" to "Peace Man"

1. Joanna Bourke, *An Intimate History of Killing: Face-to-Face Killing in Twentieth Century Warfare* (New York: Basic Books, 2000), maintains that soldiers enjoyed killing but were able to reconvert to the mores of peacetime society afterward. Bourke's study was based on British, American, and Australian veterans over three wars, World War I, World War II, and Vietnam, and therefore may not be entirely representative of Americans in World War II. Peter Kindsvatter, *American Soldiers: Ground Combat in the World Wars, Korea, and Vietnam* (Kansas, 2003), 183–84, finds that a minority enjoyed killing in World War II and other wars. He, too, points to loyalty to country as a motivating factor.

2. Report of Psychiatric Mission of the OFS, OSRD, European Theater of Operations, April 16, 1945–July 16, 1945, 71, Legislative Branch, National Mental Health Act (NMHA) Records, RG 46, National Archives, Washington, DC, hereafter referred to as NA.

3. Melvin Silverman, interviewed by G. Kurt Piehler and Travis Richards, November 9, 1994, 45, Rutgers Oral History Archives, Rutgers University, New Brunswick, NJ, hereafter referred to as ROHA, https://oralhistory.rutgers.edu/images/PDFs/silverman_melvin.pdf.

4. Bert Manhoff, interviewed by G. Kurt Piehler and Jeff Schneider, 42, ROHA, https://oralhistory.rutgers.edu/images/PDFs/manhoff_bert.pdf.

5. Interview of Arthur Pendleton, USMC, Guadalcanal, World War II, by Cork Morris, Nimitz Museum, Fredericksburg, TX, October 25, 2003, 9, Oral Histories of the National Museum of the Pacific War, http://digitalarchive.pacificwarmuseum.org/digital/collection/p167698/coll/id/10457.

6. Eli Ginzberg et al., *The Ineffective Soldier*, vol. 1, *Breakdown and Recovery* (New York: Columbia University Press, 1959), xiv. Also see Mark D. Van Ells, *To Hear Only Thunder Again: America's World War II Veterans Come Home* (New York, 2001), 9; Judith Herman, *Trauma and Recovery* (New York: Basic Books, 1997).

7. A 1946 New York City Committee on Mental Hygiene study found that out of 314 rejected on psychiatric grounds, only a small fraction who actually needed it showed any interest in receiving treatment, and only 19 percent received it. Statement of Michael J. Shortley, Director of the US Office of Rehabilitation to Priest hearings, US House of Representatives, *Hearings on H.R. 2550*, 79th Cong. 1st Sess., 1945, 79. On Iraq, see David Finkel, *Thank You for Your Service* (New York: Farrar, Straus and Giroux, 2013).

8. Hans Pols, "The Repression of War Trauma in American Psychiatry after World War II," *Clio Medicine* 55 (1999): 262.

9. Gerald Linderman, *The World within War* (New York: Free Press, 1997), 359.

10. Letters, Rabbi Brav to Mrs. Roosevelt, November 16, 1944; Dr. Edward Strecker to Eleanor Roosevelt, December 19, 1944, ER to Strecker, December 20, 1944, article on "Basic Training for Homecoming," ER 100, Box 816, Edward Strecker file, Franklin Delano Roosevelt Library, Hyde Park, NY, hereafter referred to as FDRL. Brav later moved to a Cincinnati pulpit.

11. Lawrence Kubie to Mrs. Roosevelt, March 26 and March 30, 1945, File 90, Box 1185, ER Papers, FDRL. Van Ells, *To Hear Only Thunder Again*, 118–20; Frank Hines, "The Role of Social Agencies in the Vocational Adjustment of Veterans," before the Council of Social Agencies, Washington, DC, December 11, 1944, VA 1943–1944 file, OF Franklin Roosevelt 8B, FDRL.

12. T. J. M. Romero, "German Military Psychiatry in the Second World War. Historical Article," *Rev. Sanid. Milit. Mex.* 72 (2018): 3–4; Svenja Goltermann, *The War in Their Minds: German Soldiers and Their Violent Pasts in West Germany*, trans. Philip Schmitz (Ann Arbor: University of Michigan Press, 2017).

13. US Army, Medical Department, *Neuropsychiatry in World War II*, ed. Albert J. Glass, MC, USA (Ret.) and Lt. Col. Robert J. Bernucci (Washington, DC: US Government Printing Office, 1966), 1:257.

14. For example, see Letter, CAH to Ms. Thompson, Secretary to Mrs. Roosevelt, July 20, 1944, in which CAH wrote that Dr. Overholser had informed him over the phone that Mrs. Roosevelt had recently visited St. Elizabeth's and seen the Occupational Therapy section and had been particularly impressed by one boy's wood carvings. Overholser further told him that the boy had done a wood bust of the president and wanted to present it to him, which would do him "untold good." CAH informed him that Mrs. Roosevelt was away for the summer, at which point Overholser asked if it would be possible for Mrs. Roosevelt to "write a note . . . saying she would accept the gift, so that he might receive it before being released [to the California authorities]." It is not known what happened. Eleanor Roosevelt Papers, File O, Box 2618, FDRL. According to Francis Braceland, "Psychiatric Lessons from World War II," *American Journal of Psychiatry* (March 1947): 587–93, 4,538 navy patients were hospitalized at St. Elizabeth's during the war.

15. On the experience of homosexuals, see esp. the reminiscences of veterans in *Coming Out under Fire* based on Allan Bérubé, *Coming Out under Fire: The History of Gay Men and Women in World War II* (Chapel Hill: University of North Carolina Press, 2012).

16. Van Ells, *To Hear Only Thunder Again*, citing Samuel Paster and Saul C. Holtzman, "A Study of One Thousand Psychotic Veterans Treated with Insulin and Electric Shock," *American Journal of Psychiatry* 105 (1949); Bérubé, *Coming Out under Fire*, 211–16; *Neuropsychiatry in World War II*, 1:342, for conditions on ships.

17. *Neuropsychiatry in World War II*, 1:336–38.

18. Karl Bowman, "Psychiatric Examinations in the Armed Forces," *War Medicine*, February 4, 1941, 213–17; "No Stigma on Men Rejected as Emotionally," *Boston Post*, February 1, 1941; "Draft Rejection Holds No Stigma Says Dr. Sullivan," *Boston Globe*, February 1, 1941, both from Sullivan's Scrapbook, Luce's Press Clippings Bureau, William Alanson White Psychiatric Foundation, Washington, DC, hereafter referred to as WAWPF. Sullivan conveyed the same message at the Annual Meeting of the National Committee for Mental Hygiene in 1942; see Harry Stack Sullivan, "A Year of Selective Service Psychiatry," *Mental Hygiene*, 1942, 7–15. Also see Overholser, speech at Washington, DC, seminar, January 2–3, 1941, MED: Committee on Neuropsychiatry General file, National Academy of Sciences, Washington, DC, hereafter referred to as NAS; Winfred Overholser, "Contributions to National Defense," *American Journal of Orthopsychiatry*, October 1941, 636; "Proceedings Selective Service Seminar," January 2–3, 1941, 38, US Army Military History Research Collection, Carlisle Barracks, PA, hereafter referred to as USAMHRC. Bulletin No. 89, May 15, 1943, Selective Service, New York City, 4.

19. Howard P. Rome, "Military Group Psychotherapy," paper for presentation at the APA, May 1944, Psychiatry General Files, CNR, Records of Office of Scientific Research and Development, R.G. 227, National Archives, Washington, D.C., hereafter referred to as NA. See especially page 5.

20. "The Responsibility of Neuropsychiatry for the Rehabilitation of Veterans," Michigan Society for Neurology and Psychiatry, September 1944, Menninger Foundation, Topeka, KS, hereafter referred to as Menninger Archives; William C. Menninger, *A Psychiatrist for a Troubled World: Selected Papers of William C. Menninger, M.D.* (New York, 1947), 563–65. William C. Menninger, *Psychiatry in a Troubled World* (New York: Macmillan, 1948), 151–52.

21. American Psychiatric Association, *Diagnostic and Statistical Manual of Mental Disorders*, 3rd ed. (Washington, DC, APA, 1980), 236–38, hereafter referred to as *DSM-III*.

22. Menninger, *A Psychiatrist for a Troubled World*, 611; Paul M. Kersten, "Changing Concepts in Alcoholism and Its Management," *American Journal of Psychotherapy* 3 (1949): 522; Van Ells, *To Hear Only Thunder Again*, 119.

23. Gerald Goldstein PhD, "Survivors of Imprisonment in the Pacific Theater during World War II," *American Journal of Psychiatry* 144 (September 1987): 1210; Van Ells, *To Hear Only Thunder Again*, 107–27.

24. Robert Keehn et al., "Twenty-Four Year Mortality Follow-Up of Army Veterans with Disability Separations for Psychoneurosis in 1944," *Psychosomatic Medicine* 36, no. 1 (January/February 1974): 27–46.

25. *Streets of San Francisco*, Season 1, Episode 22, "House on Hyde Street," 1973.

26. Goldstein, "Survivors of Imprisonment in the Pacific Theater during World War II," 1,210; Patricia Sutker, "Psychopathology and Psychiatric

Diagnoses of World War II Pacific Theater Prisoner of War Survivors and Combat Veterans," *American Journal of Psychiatry* 150, no. 2 (February 1993): 240. *Recent Developments in Alcoholism: An Official Publication of the American Medical Society on Alcoholism, the Research Society on Alcoholism, and the National Council on Alcoholism* (1988), 6:89–101; Edgar Jones, "Alcohol Use and Misuse within the Military," *International Review of Psychiatry* 23 (April 2011): 166–72; Sol Ginsburg, "Community Responsibility for Neuropsychiatric Discharges," *Mental Hygiene*, 1945, 26; John C. Kluznik, "Forty-Year Follow-up of United States Prisoners of War," *American Journal of Psychiatry* 143, no. 11 (December 1986): 1443–46, citing H. J. Morgan et al., "Health of Repatriated Prisoners of War from the Far East," *Journal of the American Medical Association* 130 (1946): 995–99; Stewart Wolf and Herbert S. Ripley, "Reactions among Allied Prisoners of War Subjected to Three Years of Imprisonment and Torture by the Japanese," *American Journal of Psychiatry* 104 (1947): 180–93; Bernard M. Cohen, *A Follow-up Study of World War II Prisoners of War*, Veterans Administration Medical Monograph (Washington, DC, 1954); G. W. Beebe, "Follow-up Studies of World War II and Korean War Prisoners, II: Morbidity, Disability, and Maladjustments," *American Journal of Epidemiology* 101 (1975): 400–22.

27. Kimberly A. Lee et al., "A 50-Year Prospective Study of the Psychological Sequelae of World War II Combat," *American Journal of Psychiatry* 152 (1995): 516–22. Author of poem unknown.

28. Laura Hillenbrand, *Unbroken: A World War II Story of Survival, Resilience, and Redemption* (New York, 2014), 230, 232, 291, 298, 351.

29. Stuart J. Wright, *An Emotional Gauntlet: From Life in Peacetime America to the War in European Skies* (Madison: University of Wisconsin Press, 2004), 167–70.

30. Thomas Childers, *Soldier from the War Returning: The Greatest Generation's Troubled Homecoming from World War II* (New York: Houghton Mifflin Harcourt, 2009), 8, 28, 44, 78–85, 136, 170, 248.

31. Carol Schultz Vento, *The Hidden Legacy of World War II: A Daughter's Journey of Discovery* (Pennsylvania: Sunbury, 2011). See also Craig Van Dyke MD, "Posttraumatic Stress Disorder: A Thirty-Year Delay in a World War II Veteran," *American Journal of Psychiatry* 142, no. 9 (September 1985): 1,070–73. Also experiencing PTSD, among others, were New York City's mayor Bill de Blasio's father; the husband of Bess Myerson, a former Miss America; and Lucinda Franks's father, Tom Franks, a spy impersonating a Nazi in World War II and part of the first American liberation of a Nazi concentration camp, Ohrdruf, north of Frankfurt. Javier C. Hernandez, "From His Father's Decline, de Blasio 'Learned What Not to Do,'" *New York Times*, October 13, 2013; "Bess Myerson, New Yorker of Beauty, Wit, Service, and Scandal Dies at 90," *New York Times*, January 5, 2015; Lucinda Franks, *My Father's Secret War: A Memoir* (New York: Miramax, 2007), 22–23.

32. Letter, Rodney Brandon to Dr. Lewis Weed, January 13, 1943, NED: Committee on Neuropsychiatry General file 1942–1943, NAS; Letter, Dr. Overholser to Dr. Weed, January 18, 1943, Letter, Dr. Weed to Rodney Brandon, Jan. 19, 1943; both in same NAS file; Letter, Senator C. Wayland Brooks, US Senate, Committee on Appropriations, to Surgeon General Ross T. McIntire, US Navy, July 18, 1944, US Navy Bureau of Medicine and Surgery, RG 52, File P3-1/P19-1, 123–40, NA. About the same time, the secretary to President Roosevelt wrote a claimant that the VA had denied his pension request because of insufficient evidence of "service connection for pharyngitis or a mental condition." Letter, Edwin M. ("Pa") Watson, Major General, US Army, Military Advisor and Appointment Secretary to the President to Mr. Clark, February 11, 1944, Pensions Nervous Condition 2/44 Folder, Box 8-E, Roosevelt Papers, FDRL.

33. Statement by Gen. Norman Kirk, Surgeon Gen., US Army at Press Conference, May 9, 1944, which contains portion by William Menninger, May 9, 1944, Neuropsychiatry, 702, SGO, RG 112, WNRC. Menninger, *A Psychiatrist for a Troubled World*, 549–53.

34. Thomas G. Calderone, interviewed by Shaun Illingworth, February 24, 2006, 5–6, 18–26, ROHA, https://oralhistory.rutgers.edu/images/PDFs/calderone_thomas.pdf; Ginzberg, *Breakdown and Recovery*, 17–19, describes one veteran with a history of alcoholism before and during service who ended up dying soon after of heart disease. His wife was denied a VA pension for their child because his discharge was without honor.

35. Albert J. Senna, interviewed by Shaun Illingworth, October 17, 2005, 6–7, ROHA, https://oralhistory.rutgers.edu/images/PDFs/senna_albert.pdf.

36. Interview, Manhoff, 32–33; Leila Levinson, *Gated Grief: The Daughter of a GI Concentration Camp Liberator Discovers a Legacy of Trauma* (Wisconsin, 2011).

37. Interview, Timothy Dyas, interviewed by Shaun Illingworth and Elaine Blatt, July 23, 2008, 28, ROHA, https://oralhistory.rutgers.edu/images/PDFs/days_timothy.pdf. While Native Americans were known for their bravery as scouts in the military, some still experienced PTSD. One soldier of Apache background, torn with nightmares of his buddy blown up in combat, did not seek help until 2008, when his marriage was breaking up. David Freed, "War Leaves PTSD Scars on Native American Vets," Center for Health Reporting, May 30, 2012, http://centerforhealthreporting.org.

38. Ben Shephard, *A War of Nerves* (Cambridge, MA: Harvard University Press, 2000), 357–67, points out that not all American psychiatrists supported Lifton's position. Those in favor, he maintained, generally were "doves" when it came to Vietnam, and those opposed, "hawks." Even more disagreement arose among German psychiatrists, Israeli psychiatrists, and Americans led by the émigré analyst William Niederland concerning Holocaust survivors. German psychiatrists testified in cases in Germany brought by Holocaust-survivor

claimants that it was "common knowledge that all psychic traumata, of whatever degree or duration, lose their effects when the psychologically traumatizing event ceases to operate." Shephard, *A War of Nerves*, 359–60. On the other hand, Dr. Niederland in 1961 coined the term "survivor syndrome," based on 800 cases he had seen of Holocaust survivors who exhibited "survivor guilt," had difficulty expressing normal emotions, became old prematurely, and had mistaken events of the past for current events (360). Israeli psychiatrists took a middle position, believing that the victims' claims were somewhat exaggerated, since "the vast majority of the large survivor population in Israel had not become psychiatric patients." Further, the Israeli psychiatrist Shamai Davidson said that focusing on PTSD "obscured the remarkable potential for new adaptation, recovery and reintegration through the life span" (360). For a recent history on this matter, see Dagmar Herzog, *Cold War Freud* (Cambridge: Cambridge University Press, 2017), 89–90, 94–96; Dagmar Herzog, "Post-Holocaust Trauma and the Creation of PTSD," unpublished paper, June 6, 2019, Weinmann Lecture, US Holocaust Museum, Washington, DC, esp. 8–20.

39. "PTSD and Vietnam Veterans: A Lasting Issue 40 Years Later," US Department of Veterans Affairs, https://www.publichealth.va.gov/exposures/publications/agent-orange/agent-orange-summer-2015/nvvls.asp.

40. D. D. Eisenhower, Remarks at Luncheon Given by International Committee for Mental Hygiene at the University Club, New York City, May 5, 1948; and Eisenhower paper, "Mental Health: Key to World Peace," both in 411/4 Folder, 411 Box, Dwight D. Eisenhower, Central Files, Rare Book and Manuscript Library, Columbia University, New York City; *New York Times*, May 6, 1948, 22:1; May 19, 1948, 24:7; June 26, 1948, 30:7; August 23, 1948, 20:1; August 19, 1948; September 13, 1948, 44:3; September 21, 1948, 24:8.

41. Eli Ginzberg, *The Lost Divisions* (New York: Columbia University Press, 1959), esp. the charts on 117–25; Eli Ginzberg, *The Negro Potential* (New York: Columbia University Press, 1956). See also Dr. Abram Kardiner and Lionel Ovesey's study on the impact of culture on the black psyche, in *The Mark of Oppression: Explorations in the Personality of the American Negro* (New York: Norton, 1951).

42. The Korean War started when North Korea's People's Army invaded South Korea at the South Korean 38th Parallel. Supporting the Americans were UN forces under the command of Commanding General Douglas MacArthur. Nearly 5 million people died in the Korean War altogether, mostly civilians, including 10 percent of Korea's prewar population. For works on the Korean and Vietnam wars, see, e.g., Meghan Fitzpatrick, *Invisible Scars: Mental Trauma and the Korean War* (Canada: UBC Press, 2017); Norman M. Camp MD, *US Army Psychiatry in the Vietnam War: New Challenges in Extended Counterinsurgency Warfare* (Washington, DC: Department of Defense, Department of the Army, Army Medical Department, 2014).

43. Jonathan Dahms, "Army Commemorates 60th Anniversary of Armed Forces Integrated," July 24, 2008, http://army.mil; "Army Integrated July 26, 1951," http://americaninthekoreanwar.weebly.com. In 1948, President Harry Truman ordered the integration of the nation's armed forces. However, the army began the Korean War with segregated troops. On July 26, 1951, the army ordered the integration of all troops in the Korean War following the acceptance by some units of Black replacements given the dire shortage of manpower. Gradually, throughout the war, more and more units became integrated, but it was not until September 30, 1954, that the army announced that the last Black unit had been abolished.

44. US Army Medical Department, *Neuropsychiatry in World War II*, 1:741–45.

45. Edgar Jones PhD and Lt. Col. Ian P. Palmer, RAMC, "Army Psychiatry in the Korean War: The Experience of a Commonwealth Division," *Military Medicine* 165, no. 4 (April 2000): 256–60.

46. *Neuropsychiatry in World War II*, 1:746–56.

47. Alternatively, America's involvement in Vietnam can be considered to have occurred from the Gulf of Tonkin Resolution passed by Congress in August 1964 to President Richard Nixon's signing the Paris Peace Accords in January 1973 or to the fall of Saigon on April 30, 1975.

48. "African Americans in the Vietnam War," part 4 of 4, United States of America Vietnam War Commemoration, https://www.vietnamwar50th.com/assets/1/7/African_Americans_in_the_Vietnam_War.pdf.

49. Shephard, *A War of Nerves*, 344.

50. Edgar Jones and Simon Wessely, *Shell Shock to PTSD: Military Psychiatry from 1900 to the Gulf War* (New York: Psychology Press, 2005), 121, 130.

51. Shephard, *A War of Nerves*, 351, 347–49.

52. Bruce Porter, *War and the Rise of the State: The Military Foundations of Modern Politics* (New York: Free Press, 1994), xv.

Conclusion

1. "Researchers Identify Specific Genetic Vulnerabilities to PTSD among US Veterans," *Scienmag*, https://scienmag.com/researchers-identify-specific-genetic-vulnerabilities-to-ptsd-among-us-veterans/; David Kieran, *Signature Wounds: The Untold Story of the Military's Mental Health Crisis* (New York: New York University Press, 2019).

Select Works

Manuscript Collections

I. ARCHIVES

Alan Mason Chesney Medical Archives, Johns Hopkins Medical Institutions, Baltimore, MD, Papers of:
    Dr. Adolf Meyer

National Academy of Sciences, Archives, Records of:
    National Research Council, Committee on Anthropology and Psychology
    National Research Council, Committee on Neuropsychiatry
    National Research Council, Committee on Personnel and Training

National Archives, Washington, DC, Records of:
    Office of Scientific Research and Development, Record Group 227
    Public Health Service, Record Group 90
    St. Elizabeth's Hospital, Record Group 418
    US Army, Adjutant General, Record Group 407
    US Army, War Department General Staff, G-1 (Personnel), Record Group 165
    US Navy, Bureau of Medicine and Surgery, Record Group 52
    US Senate Committee on Education and Labor, Subcommittee on Health and Education. National Neuropsychiatric Institute Act, S.1160, Record Group 46
    Works Progress Administration, Record Group 69

National Archives Division, College Park, MD, Records of:
    Army Chaplaincy, Record Group 247

National Archives Division, Washington National Records Center, Suitland, MD, Records of:
    Selective Service System, Record Group 147
    US Army, Surgeon General's Office, Record Group 112
    US Army, War Department General Staff, G-1 (Personnel), Record Group 165

Rockefeller Foundation Archives, Records of:
    Laura Spelman Rockefeller
    National Committee for Mental Hygiene

US Army Medical Division, Historical Unit, Surgeon General's Office Archives, Fort Detrick, Frederick, MD
US Army Military History Research Collection, Carlisle Barracks, PA, Records of: General Lewis Hershey
William Alanson White Psychiatric Foundation Archives, Washington, DC

II. LIBRARIES

American Philosophical Society, Philadelphia, Papers of:
  Osborn, Frederick
American Psychiatric Association Museum and Library, Washington, DC, Papers of:
  Blain, Daniel
  Committee on Military Psychiatry
  Committee on War Psychiatry
  Deutsch, Albert
  Overholser, Winfred
  Stevenson, George
Brooklyn Historical Society, Brooklyn Public Library, Brooklyn, NY, Papers of:
  Ackerly, S. Spafford
Columbia University, Rare Book and Manuscript Library, Butler Library, New York City, Papers of:
  Dwight D. Eisenhower
Eisenhower Presidential Library, Abilene, KS, http://www.eisenhowerlibrary.gov.
Franklin D. Roosevelt Library, Hyde Park, NY, Papers of:
  McIntire, Ross
  Roosevelt, Eleanor
  Roosevelt, Franklin D.
  Smith, Harold
Harry S. Truman Library and Museum, Independence, MO, http://www.trumanlibrary.org
Library of Congress, Manuscript Division, Washington, DC, Papers of:
  Kubie, Lawrence
  Overholser, Winfred
  Murray, John
  Patterson, Robert P. (Under Secretary of War)
Marshall Research Foundation, Lexington, VA, Papers of:
  Marshall, George C.
Menninger Psychiatric Foundation Archives, Topeka, KS, Papers of:
  Menninger, William
National Library of Medicine, Bethesda, MD, Papers of:
  Gregg, Alan
Oscar Diethelm Historical Library, New York Hospital–Cornell Medical Center, New York City, Papers of:
  Rennie, Thomas

Select Works | 407

　　　Salmon, Thomas
　　　Stevenson, George S.
University of Vermont Library, Burlington, VT, Papers of:
　　　Austin, Warren R.
Yale University, New Haven, CT, Papers of:
　　　Stimson, Henry

III. PERSONAL PAPERS
Appel, John
Kaufman, M. Ralph
Spiegel, Herbert

IV. OTHER SOURCES

Interviews
Dr. John Appel with Rebecca Greene, December 23, 1975, Philadelphia, PA
Dr. Dorothy Blitsten with Rebecca Greene, November 21, 1974, New York City
Dr. Dexter Bullard with Rebecca Greene, May 29, 1975, Washington, DC (taped telephone)
Dr. Ralph M. Crowley with Rebecca Greene, October 31, 1974, New York City
Dr. Oscar Diethelm with Rebecca Greene, July 24, 1975, New York City
Dr. Abram Kardiner with Rebecca Greene, October 26, 1974, New York City
Dr. M. Ralph Kaufman with Rebecca Greene, January 5, 1976, New York City
Frederick Osborn with Rebecca Greene, April 4, 1980, Garrison, NY
Dr. Winfred Overholser Jr. with Rebecca Greene, July 6, 1976, Washington, DC (taped telephone)
Dr. Herbert Spiegel with Rebecca Greene, December 18, 1975, New York City
Dr. George S. Stevenson with Rebecca Greene, May 10, 1974, Red Bank, NJ
Dr. Raymond Waggoner with Rebecca Greene, May 27, 1974 (taped telephone)
Dr. Joseph Zubin with Rebecca Greene, July 10, 1975, New York, NY

Letters
General Lewis Hershey to Rebecca Greene, March 30, 1974; April 19, 1974
Dr. Nolan D. C. Lewis to Rebecca Greene, May 15, 1974

Interviews by Other Historians
Dr. Francis Braceland with Dr. David Musto, parts 2–4, June 29, 1973, RG 147, WNRC
Frederick Osborn with Richard D. McKinzie, July 10, 1974, Garrison, NY, http://www.trumanlibrary.org

Oral Histories
William A. Biehler with Shaun Illingworth, August 18, 2007, Palm Desert, CA, Rutgers Oral History Archives, http://oralhistory.rutgers.edu

Thomas Calderone with Shaun Illingworth, February 24, 2006, Rutgers Oral History Archives, http://oralhistory.rutgers.edu

Timothy Dyas with Shaun Illingworth, July 23, 2008, Rutgers Oral History Archives, http://oralhistory.rutgers.edu

Gordon F. Lewis with Elaine Blatt and Shaun Illingworth, July 24, 2006, Rutgers Oral History Archives, http://oralhistory.rutgers.edu

Charles W. Lindberg, Member of Carlson's Raiders, with Richard Misenhimer, January 26, 2007, Richfield, MN, National Museum of the Pacific War, Center for Pacific War Studies, Fredericksburg, TX, https://www.pacificwarmuseum.org

Bert Manhoff with Kurt Piehler and Jeff Schneider, April 19, 1995, Rutgers Oral History Archives, http://oralhistory.rutgers.edu

Everett D. Reamer with Richard Misenhimer, November 5, 2002, Fredericksburg, TX, National Museum of the Pacific War, Center for Pacific War Studies, Fredericksburg, TX, https://www.pacificwarmuseum.org

Albert Senna with Shaun Illingworth, October 17, 2005, Rutgers Oral History Archives, http://oralhistory.rutgers.edu

Raymond Taub with Kurt Piehler, June 29, 1994, Rutgers Oral History Archives, http://oralhistory.rutgers.edu

James T. Wells with Shaun Illingworth and Spencer Scheffling, April 23, 2004, Rutgers Oral History Archives, http://oralhistory.rutgers.edu

Arthur C. Wenzel with Shaun Illingworth and Patrick Clark-Barnes, April 11, 2005, Tinton Falls, NJ, Rutgers Oral History Archives, http://oralhistory.rutgers.edu

Printed Primary

I. PUBLIC DOCUMENTS

Report of the President's Committee on Deferment of Federal Employees. Washington, DC: US Government Printing Office, 1943.

Selective Service. Medical Circular No. 1. Washington, DC: US Government Printing Office, November 7, 1940.

———. "Medical Circular No. 1, Minimum Psychiatric Inspection, REVISED." *Journal of the American Medical Association* 116 (May 3, 1941): 2060.

———. Medical Circular No. 4. Washington, DC: US Government Printing Office, 1943.

Selective Service as the Tide of War Turns: Third Report of the Director of Selective Service, 1943–1944. Washington, DC, 1945.

Selective Training and Service Act. Public Law 783, 76th Cong. In *US Statutes at Large*, 54:885.

US Congress. Amendment to Selective Training and Service Act 1940. Public Law 197, 78th Cong.

Select Works | 409

———. *National Mental Health Act.* Sen. Report No. 1353. May 16, 1946.

US House of Representatives. *Conference Report—Exempting Fathers, 1943.* Report No. 870. 78th Cong., 1st Sess., November 17, 1943.

———. *Conference Report—National Mental Health Act.* Report No. 2350. June 26, 1946.

———. *Hearings on H.R. 2550 to . . . Establish a National Neuropsychiatric Institute.* 79th Cong., 1st Sess., 1945.

———. *Report Accompanying H. Res. 330. Exempting Fathers.* Report No. 789. 78th Cong., 1st Sess., October 25, 1943.

———. *Report Accompanying S. 763.* Report No. 787. 78th Cong., 1st Sess. October 21, 1943.

US House of Representatives, Committee on Military Affairs. *Hearings on H.R. 7528, Lowering the Draft Age to Eighteen Years.* October 14, 1942.

———. *Hearings on H.R. 10132, to Protect the Integrity and Institutions of the United States through a System of Selective Compulsory Military Training and Service.* 76th Cong., 3rd Sess., July 10, 1940.

———. *Hearings before Special Committee on Draft Deferments Pursuant to H.R. 30, Investigations of the National War Effort.* March 15, 16, 24, 27, 28, 30 31, 1944.

———. *Hearings on S. 763, Amending the Selective Training and Service Act.* 78th Cong., 1st Sess., October 12, 1943.

US Senate. *Report Accompanying Hearings Lowering Draft Age to Eighteen Years.* Report No. 1644. 77th Cong., 2nd Sess., October 15, 1942.

———. *Report Accompanying S. 763, Exempting Fathers.* Report No. 384. 78th Cong., 1st Sess., May 24, 1943.

US Senate, Committee on Banking and Currency. *Hearings on S. 380: A Bill to Establish a National Policy and Program for Assuring Continual Full Employment in a Free Competitive Economy.* 79th Cong., 1st Sess., 1945.

US Senate, Committee on Education and Labor. *Hearings on S. 1160, to . . . Establish a National Neuropsychiatric Institute.* 79th Cong., 2nd Sess., 1946.

US Senate, Committee on Education and Labor, Subcommittee on Wartime Health and Education. *Hearings on Sen. Res. 74, A Resolution Authorizing Investigation of the Educational and Physical Fitness of the Civilian Population.* 78th Cong., 2nd Sess., 1944.

US Senate, Committee on Military Affairs. *Hearings on H. R. 1730, Amendment of Selective Service Act Regarding Deferment on Certain Categories.* 78th Cong., 1st Sess., 1943.

———. *Hearings on S. 763 . . . Exempting Certain Married Men Who Have Children from the Liability under Selective Training and Service Act.* 78th Cong., 1st Sess., May 5 and September 15–17, 20–23, 1943.

———. *Hearings on S. 2368 to . . . Remove the Requirement That Medical Statements Shall Be Furnished to Those Persons Performing Military Service Thereunder.* 77th Cong., 2nd Sess., 1942.

———. *Hearings on S. 2748, Lowering the Draft Age to Eighteen Years.* 77th Cong., 2nd Sess., October 14–15, 1942.
———. *Hearings on S. 4164, to Protect the Integrity of Institutions of the United States through System of Selective Compulsory Military Training Service.* 76th Cong., 3d Sess., July 3, 5, 10–12, 1940.
US War Department. Circular No. 81 [on psychoneurosis]. Washington, DC, March 1945.
———. Circular No. 164 [on utilization of manpower based on physical capacity]. Washington, DC, April 26, 1944.
———. Circular No. 293 [on conservation of manpower]. Washington, DC, November 11, 1943.
———. Medical Technical Bulletin No. 28 [on treatment of psychiatric patients]. Washington, DC, April 1, 1944.
———. Medical Technical Bulletin No. 33 [on induction neuropsychiatric examinations]. Washington, DC, April 21, 1944.
———. Medical Technical Bulletin No. 94 [on neuropsychiatry for the medical officer]. Washington, DC, September 21, 1944.
———. *Notes on Psychological and Personal Studies in Aviation Medicine.* Technical Manual No. 8-320. Washington, DC: War Department, June 27, 1941.
———. *Psychological Examinations in the United States Army.* Washington, DC, 1921.
WAAC. *Sexual Hygiene Course for Officers and Officer Candidates in the WAAC.* Washington, DC: US Government Printing Office, May 27, 1943.

II. ARTICLES

Addison, Duval. "Psychoses in Officers in World War II." *War Medicine* 4 (1944): 1–6.
Adler, Mortimer. "This Pre-War Generation." *Harper's,* October 1940.
Aita, J. "Efficiency of Brief Clinical Interview Method in Producing Adjustment." *Archives of Neurology and Psychiatry* 61 (1949): 170–76.
———. "Neurologic and Psychiatric Examination during Military Mobilization; Results and Suggestions Derived from a Study of 9,652 Men." *War Medicine* 1 (November 1941): 769–80.
Allport, Gordon. "Liabilities and Assets in Civilian Morale." *Annals of the American Academy of Political and Social Science,* July 1941.
"American Psychiatric Association Military Mobilization Committee Questionnaire." *American Journal of Psychiatry* 97 (September 1940).
"American Soldier: Shell-Shocked and After." *Atlantic Monthly* 128 (December 1921): 738–49.
Appel, John W. "Comparative Incidents of Neuropsychiatric Casualties in World War I and II." *American Journal of Psychiatry* 103 (September 1946): 196.
———. "Current Trends in Military Neuropsychiatry." *American Journal of Psychiatry* 101 (July 1944).

———. "Morale and Preventive Psychiatry." *Bulletin of the Menninger Clinic* 8 (September 1944): 150–52.
———. "Preventive Psychiatry." *Journal of the American Medical Association*, August 31, 1946, 1474–75.
Bailey, Pearce. "Applicability of Findings of Neuropsychiatric Examinations in Army to Civilian Problem." *Mental Hygiene* 4 (1920): 301–11.
———. "Care and Disposition of Military Insane." *Mental Hygiene*, July 1918, 345–58.
Bartemeier, Leo H. "Schizoid Personality and Schizophrenia." *War Medicine* 1 (1941): 675–81.
Benjamin, Harry. "Morals vs. Morale in Wartime." *Clinical Medicine*, December 1942.
Billings, Edward G. "Recognition, Prevention, and Treatment of Personality Disorders in Soldiers." *US Army Medical Bulletin* 58 (October 1941): 1–37.
Binger, C. "How We Screened Out the Psychological 4–Fs." *Saturday Evening Post* 206 (January 8, 1944): 19.
Bingham, Walter V. "The Army Classification System." *Annals of the American Academy of Political and Social Science* 220 (March 1942).
Blain, Daniel. "The Neuropsychiatric Program of the Veterans Administration." *American Journal of Psychiatry* 103 (January 1947): 463.
———. "Preparedness: The Lesson of Germany." *New Republic*, November 11, 1940, 649–51.
Bowman, Claude C. "Hidden Valuations in the Interpretations of Sex and Family Relationships." *American Sociological Review*, October 1946.
Bowman, Karl. "Psychiatric Examinations in the Armed Forces." *War Medicine* 1 (1941): 213–17.
———. "Report of the Examination of the — Regiment, U.S. Army, for Nervous and Mental Diseases." *Mental Hygiene* 3 (April 1918): 555–59.
Braceland, Francis J. "Psychiatric Lessons from World War II." *American Journal of Psychiatry*, March 1947.
"Break for Dads." *Business Week*, December 18, 1943, 100.
Brickner, R. M. "Who Are the Psychiatric 4F's?" *Mental Hygiene* 26 (October 1942): 641–45.
Brill, Norman. "Enlisted Men Discharged from the Army Because of Psychoneuroses, a Follow-up Study." *Journal of the American Medical Association* 128 (June 30, 1945): 633–37.
Brill, Norman, and Gilbert W. Beebe. "Some Applications of Follow-up Study to Psychiatric Standards for Mobilization." *American Journal of Psychiatry* 109 (December 1952): 401–10.
Brooke, Eileen M. "Battle Exhaustion: Review of 500 Cases from Western Europe." *British Medical Journal* 2 (October 5, 1946): 491–93.
Brown, Cecil, "How the Japanese Wages War." *Life*, May 11, 1942, 98–108.
Brown, Warren T. "Soldiers Who Breakdown in Battle: Predisposition Factors." *Military Surgeon*, March 1944, 160–61.

"Bulletin: A Minimum Psychiatric Inspection of Registrants." *Psychiatry* 3 (November 1940): 625–27.
Burling, Temple. "Community Organization for Meeting Problems of Psychiatric Disabled Veterans." *American Journal of Orthopsychiatry* 14 (October 1944): 680–98.
Burlingame, C. C. "Mental Health in Industry." In *Twentieth-Century Mental Hygiene*, ed. Maurice J. Shore. New York, 1950.
Burns, George C. "Neuropsychiatric Problems at an Aleutian Post." *American Journal of Psychiatry* 102 (September 1945): 205–13.
Burton, Irving. "Incidents of Neuropsychiatric Disease in the Demobilization of the Veteran." *American Journal of Psychiatry* 103 (September 1946): 165.
Campbell, C. MacFie. "Personality Factors in Relation to Health of the Individual Worker." *Mental Hygiene* 13 (July 1929): 485–87.
———. "Selective Service and Psychiatric Issues." *Journal of the American Medical Association* 106 (April 26, 1941).
Cantril, Hadley. "America Faces the War." Report No .1, Princeton Public Opinion Research Project, May 22, 1940.
Chisholm, G. B. "Factors in the High Rate of Neuropsychiatric Casualties." *Bulletin of the Menninger Clinic* 8 (March 1944): 36–38.
———. "Psychological Adjustment of Soldiers to Army and to Civilian Life." *American Journal of Psychiatry* 101 (November 1944).
Clement, Rufus E. "Problems of Demobilization and Rehabilitation of the Negro Soldier." *Journal of Negro Education* 12 (1943): 542.
Cohen, Bernard M. "A Follow-up Study of World War II Prisoners of War." Veterans Administration Medical Monograph. Washington, DC, 1954.
Cohen, Edna. "Adjustment of Former Child Guidance Patients to Military Service." *Smith College Studies in Social Work* 16 (1945–1946).
Cohen, R. Robert. "Factors in the Adjustment to Army Life." *War Medicine*, February 1944, 83–91.
———. "Mental Hygiene for the Trainee." *American Journal of Psychiatry*, July 1943, 62–71.
Cohen, Samuel. "The Army Medical Officer Looks at Psychiatry." *War Medicine* 1 (February 4, 1941): 205–12.
"College Students and the War." *New Republic*, July 15, 1940, 79–80.
"Common Sense on Conscription." *New Republic*, August 12, 1940, 206–7.
"Completing Our Mobilization." *Psychiatry* 5 (May 1942): 263–82.
Cooley, Martin. "Economic Aspects of Psychiatric Examinations of Registrants." *War Medicine*, 1941, 372–82.
Craighill, Margaret. "Psychiatric Aspects of Women Serving in the Army." *American Journal of Psychiatry* 104 (October 1948): 226–30.
Crichton, Kyle. "Repairing War-Cracked Minds." *Collier's*, September 23, 1944, 22–24, 54.
Curran, D. "Wartime Psychiatry and Economy in Manpower." *Lancet*, December 14, 1940, 738–43.

Davenport, Charles B. "Heredity of Constitutional Mental Disorders." *Psychological Bulletin*, September 1920, 300–10.
Davenport, Walter. *Colliers*, May 10, 1941.
De Voto, Bernard. "The Easy Chair." *Harper's* 186 (1944): 541–53.
Diethelm, Oskar. "The Diagnostic Use of Psychological Tests from the Psychiatrist's Standpoint." In *Relation of Psychological Tests to Psychiatry*, ed. Paul H. Hoch, 73–85. New York, 1952.
Dillon, F. "Neuroses among Combatant Troops in the Great War." *British Medical Journal* 2 (July 8, 1939): 63–66.
Dollard, John. "Twelve Rules on Meeting Battle Fear." *Infantry Journal*, May 1944: 36–38.
Dos Passos, John. "The People at War: I. Downeasters Building Ships." *Harper's* 186 (March 1943).
Draper, George. "The Relationship of Human Constitution to Disease." *Science* 61, no. 1586 (May 22, 1945): 525–28.
Dravo, E. L. "Problems of the Psychopath in Recruit Training for the U.S. Navy." *Journal of the Indiana Medical Association* 33 (September 1940).
Dunn, William H. "The Psychopath in the Armed Forces." *Psychiatry* 4 (May 1941).
Dynes, John B. "Mental Disorders in the CCC Camps." *Mental Hygiene* 23 (July 1939): 363–70.
Eagan, J. R., L. Jackson, and R. H. Eanes. "A Study of Neuropsychiatric Rejectees." *Journal of the American Medical Association* 145, no. 7 (February 1951).
Ebaugh, F. G. "The Role of the Psychiatrist in National Defense." *Journal of the American Medical Association* 117 (July 26, 1941): 260–64.
"Editorial." *Psychiatry*, February 1942, 102–5.
"Editorial Notes: Ages 18 and 19." *Psychiatry* 5 (1942): 597–600.
Eisenberg, Philip, and Paul F. Lazarsfeld. "The Psychological Effects of Unemployment." *Psychological Bulletin* 35 (1938): 358–90.
Eisendorfer, A. "Internal and External Causes of Anxiety in Returning Veterans." *Journal of Nervous and Mental Diseases* 103 (1946): 137–43.
"Enlistment, Health, and Discharge of the WAC." *Bulletin of US Army Medical Department* 6 (September 1946): 276–87.
Eysenck, H. J. "Types of Personality Factors in Study of 700 Neurotics." *Journal of Mental Science* 90 (October 1944): 851–61.
Falk, I. S. "Social Security Measures as Factors in Mental Health Programs." In *Mental Health*, ed. Forest Ray Moulton and Paul O. Komora. Lancaster, PA: Science Press, 1939.
Farr, M. J. "Psychiatry in Training Centers." *Bulletin of the Menninger Clinic* 8 (September 1944): 133–35.
Farrell, M. J. "Plain Truths about the Neuropsychiatrics." *Rotarian* 65 (October 1944): 19, 56, 57.
———. "Will the Battle-Shocked Come Home Cured?" *Woman's Home Companion* 71 (April 1944): 33.

Faulkner, Alex. "How Tough Is American Censorship? The Treatment of Outgoing News." *Harper's*, March 1943.

Federn, Paul. "Some Suggestions on Mental Hygiene for Soldiers." *Mental Hygiene* 26 (October 1942): 554–59.

Fifield, William. "Report from a Conscientious Objector." *Harper's* 190 (January 1945).

"Four F Mentals." *Psychiatry* 6 (August 1943): 325–26.

Freedman, Harry. "The Mental Hygiene Approach to Reconditioning Neuropsychiatric Cases." *Mental Hygiene* 29 (April 1945): 269–302.

———. "Services of the Military Mental Hygiene Unit." *American Journal of Psychiatry* 100 (July 1943): 34–40.

Fromm, E. "Individual and Social Origins of Neurosis." *American Sociological Review*, August 1944.

Furnas, J. C. "Meet Ed Savickas, a Victim of Combat Fatigue." *Illustrated Ladies Home Journal* 62 (February 1945): 141–44.

Futterman, S. "First Year Analysis of Veterans' Treatment in a Mental Hygiene Clinic of the Veterans Administration." *American Journal of Psychiatry*, November 1947, 298–301.

Ginsburg, Sol. "Community Responsibility for Neuropsychiatric Discharges." *Mental Hygiene*, 1945, 20–32.

"Give Us a Break." *Readers Digest*, November 1944.

Glueck, Bernard. "Psychiatric Aims in the Field of Criminology." *Mental Hygiene* 2 (October 1918): 546–56.

———. "War Psychiatry." *Bulletin of the New York Academy of Medicine* 18 (February 1942): 137–49.

Goldstein, Gerald. "Survivors of Imprisonment in the Pacific Theater during World War II." *American Journal of Psychiatry* 144 (September 1987): 1,213.

Grinker, Roy R. "The Interrelationship of Neurology, Psychiatry, and Psychoanalysis." *Journal of the American Medical Association* 116 (May 17, 1941): 2,236–41.

Grinker, Roy R., and John P. Spiegel. "Brief Psychotherapy in War Neuroses." *Psychosomatic Medicine* 6 (April 1944): 123–31.

Gundlach, Ralph H. "Emotional Stability and Political Opinions as Related to Age and Income." *Journal of Social Psychology* 10 (1939): 577–90.

Hadley, Ernest. "An Experiment in Military Selection." *Psychiatry* 5 (August 1942): 371.

———. "Unrecognized Antagonisms Complicating Business Enterprises." *Psychiatry* 1 (February 1938): 31.

Hall, J. K. "Presidential Address." *American Journal of Psychiatry*, July 1942, 3.

Hall, Roscoe W. "Peculiar Personalities: Disorders of Mood; Psychopathic Personality." *War Medicine* 1 (1941): 383–86.

Hauptmann, Alfred. "Group Therapy for Psychoneuroses." *Diseases of the Nervous System* 4 (January 1943): 22.

Hawley, Paul R. "The Place of Psychiatry in the Veterans Administration's Medical Program." *American Journal of Psychiatry* 104 (July 1947): 16.

"He Who Gets Slapped—Victims of Disagreements of Draft Board Doctors and Camp Doctors." *Nation*, May 3, 1941.

Helton, Roy. "The Inner Threat: Our Own Softness." *Harper's*, September 1940, 337–43.

Hershey, Lewis B. "Fear in War—as Seen by Hershey." *New York Times Magazine*, September 27, 1942.

Hester, H. "Nerves in Wartime; Interview with Dr. H. R. Viets." *Hygeia* 22 (March 1944): 174–75.

Hogan, R. W. "Psychiatric Observations of Senior Medical Officer on Board Aircraft Carrier USS *Wasp* during Action in Combat Areas." *American Journal of Psychiatry* 100 (July 1943): 91–93.

Hohman, L. B. "Combat Fatigue." *Ladies' Home Journal* 62 (February 1945): 146–47.

"A Homecoming Congressman Finds His People Badly Muddled about the War." *Life*, September 1, 1941, 26.

"Hope for Sanity." *Time* 35 (February 5, 1940), 58.

Horney, Karen. "What Is a Neurosis?" *American Journal of Sociology* 45 (November 1939): 426–32.

"How Men Behave in Crisis." *Harper's* 190 (December 1944): 57.

Huffman, Robert E. "Which Soldiers Break Down: A Survey of 610 Psychiatric Patients in Viet Nam." *Bulletin of the Menninger Clinic* 34 (November 1970): 346–47.

Hughes, Joseph. "Psychiatric Treatment of the Veteran Outpatient." *American Journal of Psychiatry*, March 1948, 549–55.

Humphreys, Edward J. "Editorial Comment on 'A Memorandum on the Selection Process in General and on the Role of the Psychiatrist in the Selection Process and in the Armed Forces.'" *American Journal of Mental Deficiency* 47 (October 1942): 131.

Hunt, W. A., C. I. Wittson, and H. L. Harris. "The Screening Test in Military Selection." *Psychological Review* 51 (January 1944): 37–46.

Hyde, Robert W., and Roderick M. Chisholm. "Relation of Mental Disorders to Race and Nationality." *New England Journal of Medicine*, November 2, 1944, 612–16.

Jones, Carter Brooke. "Military Psychiatric Sessions to Be Held by Selective Service: Designed to Bring Uniformity in Fixing Mental Qualifications." *Washington Post*, December 28, 1940.

Kardiner, Abraham. "The Neuroses of War." *War Medicine* 1 (March 1941): 219–26.

———. "The Traumatic Neuroses of War." Psychosomatic Medicine Monograph 2–3. Washington, DC, 1941.

Kasinin, J. S. "Neuroses of War Wives." *Transactions of the American Neurological Association* 70 (1944): 176.

Kaufman, M. Ralph. "The Problem of the Psychopath in the Army." *Proceedings of the 1942 Congress of the American Prison Association*, 1942.

Keehn, Robert J. "Twenty-Four Year Mortality Follow-up of Army Veterans with Disability Separations for Psychoneuroses in 1944." *Psychosomatic Medicine* 36 (January/February 1974): 27–46.

———. "Follow-up Studies of World War II and Korean Conflict Prisoners." *American Journal of Epidemiology* 111 (1980): 194–211.

Kennedy, F. "Functional Nervous Disorders in the Last War, Spanish War and Now." *Transactions of the American Neurological Association* 69 (1943): 79–83.

Kline, Nathan S. "Group Psychotherapy in the Veterans Administration's Hospital." *American Journal of Psychiatry* 104 (April 1948): 618.

Klonoff, H. "The Neuropsychological, Psychiatric, and Physical Effects of Prolonged and Severe Stress: Thirty Years Later." *Journal of Nervous and Mental Diseases* 163 (1976): 246–52.

Kluznik, John C. "Forty-Year Follow-up of United States Prisoners of War." *American Journal of Psychiatry* 143, no. 11 (December 1986): 1,443–46.

Koontz, A. R. "Rejections in Selective Service." *Hygeia* 20 (July 1942): 494–95.

Kopetzky, Samuel J. "Validity of Psychiatric Criteria for Rejection for Service with the Armed Forces." *War Medicine* 6 (December 1944): 357–68.

Kris, E. "Problems of Propaganda; Note on Propaganda New and Old." *Psychoanalytic Quarterly* 12 (July 1943): 381–99.

Kubie, L. S. "The Detection of Potential Psychosomatic Breakdowns in the Selection of Men for the Armed Forces." *Annals of the New York Academy of Science* 44 (December 22, 1943): 605–24.

———. "A Program of Training in Psychiatry to Break the Bottleneck of Rehabilitation." *American Journal of Orthopsychiatry* 16 (1946): 447–54.

———. "Psychiatry and Industry." *Personnel Journal*, 1946, 50–54.

Landis, Carney, and James Page. "Magnitude of the Problem of Mental Disease." In *Mental Health*, ed. Forest Ray Moulton and Paul O. Komora. Lancaster, PA: Science Press, 1939.

Laski, Harold J. "Letter to MacLeish." *New Republic*, September 2, 1940, 299–300.

Lasswell, Harold D. "What Psychiatrists and Political Scientists Can Learn from One Another." *Psychiatry* 1 (February 1938): 33–40.

Lee, K. A. "A 50-Year Prospective Study of the Psychological Sequelae of World War II Combat." *American Journal of Psychiatry* 152, no. 4 (April 1995): 516–22.

Leigh, A. D. "Neuroses as Viewed by the Regimental Medical Officer." *Lancet* 1 (March 22, 1941): 394–96.

Link, H. C. "Errors of Psychiatry: Are We Making Mental Cases Wholesale through the Army?" *American Mercury* 59 (July 1944): 72–78.

Lurie, Louis A. "Military Adjustment of Former Problem Boys." *American Journal of Orthopsychiatry* 14 (July 1944): 400–5.

Lyman, Rick. "Gunman Had Clean Record." *New York Times*, April 4, 2014.

Lynd, Helen Merrell. "Must Psychology Aid Reaction?" *Nation*, 1947.

Madigan, P. S. "Military Neuropsychiatry: Discipline and Morale." *Journal of Criminal Law and Criminology* 32 (1941–1942).

———. "Military Psychiatry." *Psychiatry* 4 (May 1941): 225–29.
Maisel, Albert Q. "Out of Bed—Into Action." *Reader's Digest*, December 1943.
Malamud, W. "A Socio-Psychiatric Investigation of Schizophrenia Occurring in the Armed Forces." *Psychosomatic Medicine* V (1943): 364–75.
"Mama's Boys." *Time* 48 (November 25, 1946): 80.
"Manpower Needs and Negro Soldiers." *Christian Century*, April 12, 1944.
"Manpower Problem over the Hump, but Fathers Face Heavy Drafts." *Newsweek*, January 10, 1944.
Manson, Morse. "Why 2,276 American Soldiers in the Mediterranean Theatre of Operations Were Absent without Leave." *American Journal of Psychiatry*, July 1946, 50–54.
"Many Fathers Already Drafted Even from Essential Jobs: Navy Yards, Plane Factories, and Other Plants Report Losing Workers in 'Droves.'" *Washington Star*, February 22, 1943.
McNair, Lesley. "Struggle Is for Survival." *Vital Speeches*, December 1, 1942, 111–14.
Mead, Margaret. "Democracy's Scapegoat: Youth." *Harper's*, January 1941, 132–36.
"Memorandum from the William Alanson White Psychiatric Foundation on the Utilization of Psychiatry in the Promotion of National Security." *Psychiatry*, 1940, 483–92.
Menninger, K. "How Crazy Are Americans?" *Christian Century* 61 (August 23, 1944): 978.
———. "The New Role of Psychological Testing in Psychiatry." *American Journal of Psychiatry* 103 (July 1946–May 1947): 473.
———. "Recognizing and Renaming 'Psychopathic Personalities.'" *Bulletin of the Menninger Clinic* 5 (1941): 150–55.
Menninger, William. "Lessons from Military Psychiatry for Civilian Psychiatry." *Mental Hygiene* 30 (October 1946): 571–89.
———. "The Mental or Emotional Handicapped Veteran." *Annals of the American Academy of Political and Social Science* 239 (May 1945): 228.
———. "Neuropsychiatry: Its Place in the Undergraduate and Graduate Medical Education." *Journal of the American Medical Association* 125 (August 19, 1944): 1,103–5.
———. "Nomenclature of Psychiatric Disorders—Adopted by the Army." *US Army Medical Technical Bulletin* 203 (October 19, 1945): 203.
———. "Psychiatric Experience in the War, 1941–1946." *American Journal of Psychiatry* 103 (1947): 577–86.
———. "Psychiatric Problems in the Army." *Journal of the American Medical Association* 123 (1943).
———. "The Psychiatrist in Relation to the Examining Board." *Menninger Clinic Bulletin* 5 (September 1941): 134–38.
———. "Psychiatry and the War." *Atlantic Monthly* 176 (November 1945): 101–14.
———. "The Role of the Psychiatrist in the World Today." *American Journal of Psychiatry* 104 (August 1947): 157–58.

Menninger, William, Francis Braceland, and Raymond Waggoner. "Psychiatric Selection of Men for the Armed Forces." Report of the AMA Section on Mental and Nervous Disease, June 15, 1944.

Meyer, Adolf. "What Do Histories of Cases of Insanity Teach Us Concerning Preventive Mental Hygiene during the Years of School Life?" *Psychological Clinic* 2 (June 15, 1908): 89.

Miller, Delbert C. "The Measure of National Morale." *American Sociological Review*, August 1941, 487–98.

———. "National Morale of American College Students in 1941." *American Sociological Review*, August 1942.

Minski, L. "Mental Disorder Associated with Recent Crisis." *British Medical Journal* 1 (January 28, 1939): 163–64.

Mira, Emilio. "Psychiatric Experience in Spanish War." *British Medical Journal* 1 (June 17, 1939): 1,217–20.

———. "Psychological Work during the Spanish War." *Occupational Psychology* 13 (1939): 165–77.

Morgan, H. J., et al. "Health of Repatriated Prisoners of War from the Far East." *Journal of the American Medical Association* 130 (1946): 995–99.

Murray, John M. "Psychiatry in the Army Air Forces." *American Journal of Psychiatry* 100 (July 1943): 21–24.

"Neuropsychiatric Examination of Applicants for Voluntary Enlistment and Selectees for Induction." *Journal of the American Medical Association* 116 (May 31, 1941): 2,509–11.

"New Type of Psychiatrist Seeks Cause to Cure Society's Illness." *Washington Star*, January 22, 1939.

New York City Committee on Mental Hygiene. "A Memorandum on the Selection Process in General." *American Journal of Mental Deficiency* 47 (October 1942): 132–47.

O'Neil, William. "750,000 Unwanted Men." *Hygeia* 21 (September 1943): 650–52.

Orr, Douglass W. "Objectives of Selective Service Psychiatric Classification." *Menninger Clinic Bulletin* 5 (September 1941): 131–33.

Overholser, Winfred. "Are Mental Disorders Increasing?" *Science Monthly* 50 (June 1940): 559–61.

———. "The Desiderata of Central Administration Control of State Mental Hospitals." *American Journal of Psychiatry*, September 1939, 517–34.

———. "Psychiatric Contributions to National Defense." *American Journal of Orthopsychiatry* 11 (October 1941): 634–37.

———. "Review of Psychiatric Program 1942." *American Journal of Psychiatry* 99 (July 1942): 589.

———. "Women and Modern Stress." *Mental Hygiene* 30 (October 1946).

Owens, R. H. "Sample Study of Pre-Induction School Records and Postservice Records of Men Discharged from Army Because of Nervous or Mental Conditions." *Mental Hygiene* 29 (October 1945): 666–76.

Painton, F. C. "There Is No Such Thing as Shell Shock; Soldiers Mentally Shaken by War's Ordeal Are Being Cured and Restored to Duty by Army Psychiatrists." *Reader's Digest* 43 (October 1943): 59–63.
Parsons, Frederick. "War Neuroses." *Atlantic Monthly* 123 (March 1919): 335–38.
Paster, S. "Combat: Neuroses: Group Psychotherapy." *American Journal of Orthopsychiatry* 15 (July 1945): 472–82.
Peterson, Ralph M. "Neurotic Reactions in Wives of Servicemen." *Diseases of the Nervous System* 6 (1945): 50–52.
Plesset, M. R. "Psychoneurotics in Combat." *American Journal of Psychiatry* 103 (July 1946): 87–90.
Pollock, Horatio. "Eugenics as a Factor in the Prevention of Mental Disease." *Mental Hygiene* 5 (October 1921): 807–12.
Porter, William C. "Military Psychiatry." *War Medicine* 2 (July 1942): 543.
———. "Military Psychiatry at Work." *American Journal of Psychiatry* 98 (November 1941): 317–23.
———. "What Has the Psychiatrist to Learn during the Present War." *American Journal of Psychiatry* 99 (May 1943).
Pratt, Dallas. "Reemployment of the Psychoneurotic Ex-Soldier." *Psychiatry* 8 (February 1945): 3–8.
Preston, George. "Psychiatry and Demobilization." *Archives of Neurology and Psychiatry* 53 (1945): 396.
"Problem of Morale." *Time*, August 18, 1941, 36.
"Psychiatric Toll of Warfare." *Fortune* 28 (December 1943): 141.
"Psychiatry and the Army." *Oakland California Tribune*, June 18, 1941.
"Psychiatry, the Army, and the War." *Psychiatry*, 1942, 435–42.
Raleigh, John McCutcheon. "Your Son Will Not Return! Heil Hitler! The Way a Blitzkrieg Works." *Saturday Evening Post* 212 (June 15, 1940): 27, 40.
"Realistic Combat Training: British Army's Blood and Sweat Course." *Reader's Digest* 41 (July 1942): 96–97.
"Rejection or Discharge for Psychiatric Reasons." *Journal of the American Medical Association* 121 (March 27, 1943): 1,095–96.
"Report of the Military Mobilization Committee." *American Journal of Psychiatry* 97 (July 1940–May 1941): 475–80.
Rennie, T. A. C. "Needed: 10,000 Psychiatrists." *Mental Hygiene* 29 (October 1945): 644–49.
———. "Psychiatric Rehabilitation Therapy." *American Journal of Psychiatry* 101 (January 1945): 476–85.
Riemer, Morris D. "Effects of the 4F Classification on Psychoneurotics under Treatment." *Mental Hygiene* 30 (1946): 451–55.
Rioch, David McKenzie. "Consideration of the Registrant as a Personality by Members of the Local Boards." *Psychiatry*, August 1941, 331–36.
Ripley, Herbert. "Mental Illness among Negro Troops Overseas." *American Journal of Psychiatry*, January 1947, 499–512.

"Rise in Insanity in 'Psychiatric War' Predicted." *Herald Tribune*, November 15, 1940.

Robertson, Priscilla. "Housekeeping after the War." *Harper's*, April 1944.

Rome, Howard P. "Psychiatry as Seen in the Advanced Mobile Base Hospital." *American Journal of Psychiatry* 100 (July 1943): 85–89.

Roosevelt, Eleanor. "What Is Morale?" *Saturday Review*, July 4, 1942.

———. "My Day." *New York World Telegram*, October 6, 1942.

———. "My Day." *New York World Telegram*, October 7, 1942.

Roosevelt, Franklin Delano. "Fireside Chat [May 26, 1940]." In *The Public Papers and Addresses of Franklin Delano Roosevelt*, vol. 9. New York, 1938–1950.

———. "North African Strategy." *Vital Speeches* 9 (March 1, 1943): 289–94.

Rosner, Albert. "Neuropsychiatric Casualties from Guadalcanal." *American Journal of the Medical Sciences*, June 1944, 770.

Rowntree, Leonard. "Causes of Rejection and the Incidence of Defects." *Journal of the American Medical Association* 123 (September 25, 1943): 181–85.

———. "Health of Registrants and President's Plan of Rehabilitation: Abstract." *Science*, December 12, 1941.

———. "Health of Registrants and Rehabilitation of Rejectees." *Annals of the American Academy of Political and Social Science*, 1947, 81.

———. "Selective Service and Psychiatry." *Danville State Hospital Mental Health Bulletin* 20 (October 8, 1942).

Ruggles, Arthur. "Presidential Address." *American Journal of Psychiatry* 100 (July 1943): 1–8.

Russel, C. K. "Nature of War Neuroses." *Canadian Medical Association Journal* 41 (December 1939): 549–54.

Salmon, Thomas. "Care and Treatment of Mental Diseases and War Neuroses." *Mental Hygiene*, October 1917, 509–47.

Sapir, Edward. "Why Cultural Anthropology Needs the Psychiatrist." *Psychiatry* 1 (February 1938).

Sargant, William. "Treatment of War Neuroses." *Lancet*, January 25, 1941, 1–6.

Schneider, Alexander, and Cyrus W. Lagrone. "Delinquency in the Army: A Statistical Study of 500 Rehabilitation Center Prisoners." *American Journal of Psychiatry* 102 (July 1945): 85–90.

Schreiber, J. "Interdependence of Democracy and Mental Health." *Mental Hygiene* 29 (October 1945): 606–21.

———. "Morale Aspects of Military Mental Hygiene." *Diseases of the Nervous System* 14 (July 1943): 197–201.

———. "Psychological Training and Orientation of Soldiers." *Mental Hygiene* 28 (October 1944): 537–54.

Schreuder, B. J. "Nocturnal Re-experiencing More Than 40 Years after War Trauma." *Journal of Traumatic Stress* 13 (2000): 453–63.

"Selective Service Psychiatry." *Psychiatry* 4 (August 1941): 439–64.

"Selective Service Psychiatry." *Psychiatry* 6 (May 1943): 215–16.

"Selective Service System Psychiatry." *Psychiatry* 4 (February 1941): 118–21.
"Selective Service System: A Seminar on Practical Psychiatric Diagnosis." *Psychiatry* 4 (1941): 265–83.
"Senator Austin Backs FDR's Plea for National Service Act." *Montpelier Argus*, January 9, 1945.
Sharp, William L. "Stress versus Predisposition in Combat Psychiatry." *Journal of the Indiana State Medical Association*, December 1947.
Sheps, Jack C. "A Psychiatric Study of Successful Soldiers." *Journal of the American Medical Association* 126 (September 30, 1944).
Sillman, Leonard R. "Morale." *War Medicine* 3 (May 1943): 498–502.
Simon, Alexander. "A Study of Special Data in the Lives of the 183 Veterans Admitted to the St. Elizabeth's Hospital." *War Medicine* 1 (May 1941): 387–91.
Sinai, Nathan. "Physical Fitness and the Draft." *Harper's*, 1941.
"Six Months Was Plenty." *Newsweek* 26 (October 8, 1945): 110.
Smith, Alson. "Alcoholics Are People." *Harper's* 190 (January 1945): 151–53.
Smith, Bruce Lannes. "Literature on Propaganda Techniques and Public Opinion." *Psychological Bulletin* 38 (1941): 469–83.
Smith, E. Rogers. "Neuroses Resulting from Combat." *American Journal of Psychiatry* 100 (July 1943): 94–97.
Smith, Lauren. "Treatment Activities in War Psychiatry." *American Journal of Psychiatry* 101 (November 1944).
Southard, E. E. "The Effects of High Explosives upon the Central Nervous System." *Mental Hygiene*, July 1917, 397–405.
"Southern Psychiatric Association Report." *Psychiatry*, February 1940.
"Southern Psychiatric Association Report of Its Committee on Psychiatry and the National Defense." *Psychiatry*, November 1940, 619–24.
Spiegel, Herbert. "Preventive Psychiatry with Combat Troops." *American Journal of Psychiatry* 101 (November 1944): 310–15.
———. "Psychiatric Observations in the Tunisian Campaign." *American Journal of Orthopsychiatry* 14 (1944): 381–85.
Steckel, Harry. "Psychiatric Aspects of a National Defense Program." *Mental Hygiene* 25 (January 1941): 13–16.
———. "Report of Military Mobilization Committee." *American Journal of Psychiatry* 99 (September 1942): 295–96.
Stevens, Alden. "Morale in the Camps." *Survey Graphic*, October 1941, 513–19.
Stevens, Rutherford B. "Racial Aspects of Emotional Problems of Negro Soldiers." *American Journal of Psychiatry*, January 1947.
Stevenson, George S. "Mental Hygiene and Public Health." *American Journal of Orthopsychiatry* 18, no. 4 (October 1948).
———. "The National Committee's Part in the War Effort." *Mental Hygiene* 27 (January 1943): 33–42.
———. "The Prevention of Personality Disorders." In *Personality and the Behavioral Disorders*, ed. J. V. McHunt. New York, 1944.

Stimson, Henry. "Our Army and Its Purpose." *Vital Speeches of the Day* 215:357–60.
Strecker, Edward A. "Experiences in Immediate Treatment of War Neuroses." *American Journal of Insanity* 76 (1919): 45–69.
———. "Mental Hygiene and the Mass Man." *Mental Hygiene* 25 (1941): 2–5.
———. "Presidential Address." *American Journal of Psychiatry* 101 (July 1944–May 1945).
———. "Psychiatry Speaks to Democracy." *Mental Hygiene* 29 (October 1945): 591–605.
———. "What's Wrong with American Mothers." *Saturday Evening Post*, October 26, 1946, 14–15, 83–104.
Sullivan, Harry Stack. "Editorial." *Psychiatry*, February 1939.
———. "Leadership, Mobilization, and Postwar Change." *Psychiatry*, 1942, 263–82.
———. "Psychiatric Aspects of Morale." *American Journal of Sociology*, November 1941, 277–301.
———. "Psychiatry and the National Defense." *Psychiatry*, 1941, 201–12.
———. "Psychiatry in the Emergency." *Mental Hygiene* 25 (1941): 5–10.
———. "Psychiatry: Introduction to the Study of Interpersonal Relations: Chapter I." *Psychiatry* 1 (February 1938): 121–34.
———. "Selective Service Psychiatry." *Psychiatry*, November 1943, 443–44.
———. "A Seminar on Practical Psychiatric Diagnosis." *Psychiatry*, 1941, 277.
———. "Southern Psychiatric Association: Report of Its Committee on Psychiatry and National Defense." *Psychiatry*, November 1940, 619–24.
———. "A Year of Selective Service Psychiatry." *Mental Hygiene* 26 (1942): 7–15.
Sutherland, John D. "A Survey of 100 Cases of War Neuroses." *British Medical Journal*, September 13, 1941, 365–70.
Sutker, Patricia. "Psychotherapy and Psychiatric Diagnoses of World War II Pacific Theater Prisoner of War Survivors and Combat Veterans." *American Journal of Psychiatry* 150, no. 2 (February 1993): 240.
Sutton, Dallas. "The Utilization of Psychiatry in the Armed Forces." *Psychiatry* 2 (February 1939).
Tennant, Christopher, and Kerry Goulson. "The Psychological Effects of Being a Prisoner of War Forty Years after Release." *Psychiatry* 143 (May 1986): 5.
Thom, Douglas A. "Schizoid and Related Personalities." *War Medicine* 1 (1941): 410–17.
Thompson, Lloyd J. "Neuropsychiatry in the European Theater of Operations." *New England Journal of Medicine* 235 (July 4, 1946): 7–11.
"Threat of National Service Act Hangs over Fathers Draft Debate." *Newsweek*, September 27, 1943, 42–43.
Trager, F. N. "Some Don't Wear the Purple Heart." *Nation* 161 (October 6, 1945): 335–37.

Tredgold, R. B. "Invalidism from the Army Due to Mental Disabilities: The Aetiological Significance of Military Conditions." *Journal of Mental Science* 88 (1942): 444–48.
Ulio, J. A. "Military Morale." *American Journal of Sociology* 47 (November 1941): 321–30.
Van Dyke, Craig, and Nathan J. Zilberg. "Posttraumatic Stress Disorder: A Thirty-Year Delay in a World War II Veteran." *American Journal of Psychiatry* 142 (September 1985): 9.
Viets, Henry. "Shellshock." *Journal of American Medical Association*, November 24, 1917.
Walsh, M. N. "Aspects of Aviation Medicine." *Archives of Neurology and Psychiatry* 49 (January 1943): 147–49.
"War and Jap Nerves." *Newsweek* 28 (December 16, 1946): 64.
Weider, Arthur, Keeve Brodman, Bela Mittelman, David Wechsler, and Harold G. Wolff. "The Cornell Selective Index: A Method of Quick Testing of Selectees for the Armed Forces." *Journal of the American Medical Association* 124 (1944): 224.
White, William Alanson. "Childhood: The Golden Period for Mental Hygiene." *Mental Hygiene* 4 (April 1920): 257–67.
Wilson, Mitchell. "DSM-III and the Transformation of American Psychiatry." *American Journal of Psychiatry* 150, no. 3 (March 1993).
Williams, Frankwood E. "Finding a Way in Mental Hygiene." *Mental Hygiene* 14 (April 1930): 225–57.
———. "Mental Hygiene: An Attempt at a Definition." *Mental Hygiene* 11 (July 1927): 482–93.
Wilkins, Roy. "No Negro Draft Board Members in Many States, Says NAACP Survey." *Crisis* 48 (1941).
Wittkower, E., and J. P. Spillane. "Neuroses in War." *British Medical Journal*, February 10, 1940, 223–310.
Wittson, C. L., H. I. Harris, and W. A. Hunt. "The Neuropsychiatric Selection of Recruits." *American Journal of Psychiatry* 99 (1943): 639.
Wolf, Stewart. "Reactions among the Allied Prisoners of War Subject to Three Years of Imprisonment by the Japanese." *American Journal of Psychiatry* 104 (September 1947): 180–93.
Woolston, Howard. "Free Speech in Wartime." *American Sociological Review*, August 1942.
Woltman, Adolf G. "Johnny Doughboy Adjusts to England." *American Journal of Orthopsychiatry* 14 (1944): 731–33.
Zeiss, R. "PTSD 40 Years Later." *Journal of Clinical Psychology* 45, no. 1 (1989): 80–87.
Zilboorg, Gregory. "Psychiatry as a Social Science." *American Journal of Psychiatry* 99:585–91.

———. "Some Aspects of Psychiatry in the USSR." *American Review of Soviet Medicine*, August 1944.

Zolotow, M. "Doctors of Dilemmas." *Colliers*, September 9, 1944, 73.

III. BOOKS

Bakke, E. W. *The Unemployed Worker*. New Haven, 1940.

Brown, Harry. *A Walk in the Sun*. Nebraska, 1944.

Brill, Norman Q., and Gilbert W. Beebe. *A Follow-up Study of War Neuroses*. Washington, DC, 1955.

Butcher, Harry. *My Three Years with Eisenhower: The Personal Diary of Capt. Harry C. Butcher (USNR): Naval Aide to General Eisenhower, 1942 to 1945*. New York, 1946.

Cooke, Elliot. *All but Me and Thee: Psychiatry at the Fox Hole*. Washington, DC, 1945.

De River, J. Paul. *Crime and the Sexual Psychopath*. Illinois, 1958.

———. *The Sexual Criminal*. Illinois, 1950.

Deutsch, Albert. *The Shame of the States*. New York, 1948.

Dollard, John. *Fear in Battle*. New Haven, CT, 1943.

Dumas, Alexander G., and Grace Graham Keen. *A Psychiatric Primer for the Veteran's Family and Friends*. Minnesota: University of Minnesota Press, 1945.

Eisan, Leslie. *Pathways of Peace: History of Civilian Public Service Program Administered by the Brethren Service Committee*. Elgin, IL, 1948.

Eisenhower, D. D. *Dear General: Eisenhower's Wartime Letters to Marshall*. Baltimore, MD: Johns Hopkins University Press, 1971.

Farago, Ladislas, ed. *German Psychological Warfare*. New York: G. P. Putnam's Sons, 1941.

Ferenczi, S., K. Abraham, E. Simmel, and E. Jones. *Psychoanalysis and the War Neuroses*. New York: International Psychoanalytic Press, 1921.

Gesell, Arthur. *The Child from Five to Ten*. New York, 1940.

———. *Infant and Child in the Culture of Today*. New York, 1943.

Gillespie, R. D. *Psychological Effects of War on Citizen and Soldier*. New York: Norton, 1942.

Glueck, Eleanor, and Sheldon Glueck. *Juvenile Delinquents Grown Up*. New York, 1940.

———. *One Thousand Juvenile Delinquents*. New York, 1934.

Great Britain, Ministry of Pensions. *Neuroses in War Time: Memorandum for the Information of the Medical Profession*. London: His Majesty's Stationery Office, 1940.

Grinker, Roy R. *Men under Stress*. Philadelphia, 1945.

———. *War Neuroses in North Africa*. New York, 1943.

Group for the Advancement of Psychiatry. *An Outline for the Evaluation of Community Programs in Mental Hygiene*. New York, 1949.

———. *Emotional Aspects of School Desegregation*. New York, 1957.

———. *Statistics Pertinent to Psychiatry in the United States.* New York, 1949.
Hanson, Frederick. *Combat Psychiatry: Experiences in North Africa and the Mediterranean Theater.* Washington, DC, 1949.
Hastings, D. W., D. G. Wright, and B. C. Glueck. *Psychiatric Experiences of the Eighth Air Force: First Year of Combat.* New York, 1944.
Horney, Karen. *The Neurotic Personality of Our Time.* New York: Norton, 1937.
Kardiner, Abram, and Lionel Ovesey. *The Mark of Oppression: Explorations in the Personality of the American Negro.* New York, 1951.
Langer, Walter. *The Mind of Adolf Hitler.* New York: Basic Books, 1972.
Lasswell, Harold D. *Psychopathology and Politics.* Chicago, 1930.
———. *World Politics and Personal Insecurity.* New York, 1935.
Liebman, Joshua, Rabbi. *Peace of Mind.* New York: Simon & Schuster, 1946.
Mauldin, Bill. *Up Front.* New York: Henry Holt, 1944.
McIntire, Ross T. *White House Physician.* New York, 1946.
Marshall, S. L. A. *Men against Fire.* New York, 1947.
Mead, Margaret. *And Keep Your Powder Dry.* New York: William Morrow, 1942.
Medicine and the Neuroses: Report of the Hershey Conference on Psychiatric Rehabilitation. New York: National Committee for Mental Hygiene, 1945.
Menninger, William. *Psychiatry in a Troubled World.* New York: Macmillan, 1948.
———. *A Psychiatrist for a Troubled World: Selected Papers of William C. Menninger, MD.* New York, 1967.
Michener, James A. *Tales of the South Pacific.* New York, 1946.
Mira, Emilio. *Psychiatry in War.* New York: Norton, 1943.
Myers, Charles. *Shell Shock in France, 1914–1918.* London, 1940.
Patton, George. *The War as I Knew It.* New York: Bantam War Book, 1947.
Perkins, Frances. *The Roosevelt I Knew.* New York: Viking, 1946.
Pershing, John. *General Pershing's Own Story of the Victorious American Army.* Baltimore, MD, 1918.
Pratt, George. K. *Soldier to Civilian: Problems of Readjustment.* New York: McGraw-Hill, 1944.
Pyle, Ernie. *Brave Men.* New York: Grosset and Dunlap, 1943.
———. *Here Is Your War.* New York: World, 1945.
Rees, J. R. *The Shaping of Psychiatry by War.* New York: Norton, 1945.
Rennie, Thomas A. C., and Luther E. Woodward. *Mental Health in Modern Society.* New York: Commonwealth Fund, 1948.
Rennie, Thomas A. C., Walter Bauer, et al. *Teaching Psychotherapeutic Medicine.* New York, 1947.
Remarque, Erich Maria. *All Quiet on the Western Front.* Trans. 1929.
Roosevelt, Eleanor. *The Autobiography of Eleanor Roosevelt.* New York: Da Capo, 2000.
Roosevelt, Franklin D. *Complete Presidential Press Conferences.* New York: Da Capo, 1972.

———. *The FDR Memoirs.* New York, 1973.
———. *Franklin Delano Roosevelt: His Personal Letters.* New York, 1947.
———. *The Public Papers and Addresses of Franklin Delano Roosevelt.* New York: Random House, 1938–1950.
———. *The War Messages of Franklin Delano Roosevelt.* Washington, DC, 1945.
Spock, Benjamin. *The Common Sense Book of Baby and Child Care.* New York: Duell, Sloan and Pearce, 1946.
Stouffer, Samuel, and Edward Suchman. *The American Soldier.* Vol. 1: *Adjustment during Army Life.* Princeton, NJ: Princeton University Press, 1949.
———. *The American Soldier.* Vol. 2: *Combat and Its Aftermath.* Princeton, NJ: Princeton University Press, 1949.
———. *The American Soldier.* Vol. 3: *Experiments on Mass Communication.* Princeton, NJ: Princeton University Press, 1949.
———. *The American Soldier.* Vol. 4: *Measurement and Prediction.* Princeton, NJ: Princeton University Press, 1950.
Strecker, Edward A. *Fundamentals of Psychiatry.* Philadelphia, 1942.
———. *Psychiatry in Modern Warfare.* New York: Macmillan, 1945.
———. *Their Mothers' Sons: The Psychiatric Examinations of an American Problem.* New York, 1946.
Sullivan, Harry Stack. *Conceptions of Modern Psychiatry.* New York: Norton, 1954.
———. *The Fusion of Psychiatry and Social Science.* New York: Norton, 1964.
———. *The Interpersonal Theory of Psychiatry.* New York: Norton, 1954.
———. *Personal Psychopathology.* New York, 1972.
Taylor, Edmond. *The Strategy of Terror: Europe's Inner Front.* Boston: Houghton Mifflin, 1940.
Tregaskis, Richard. *Guadalcanal Diary.* New York: Random House, 1943.
Ward, Mary J. *Snake Pit.* New York, 1946.
Wexler, Milton. *An Investigation of Psychiatric Screening Tests in the US Army.* New York, 1948.
White, Robert. *The Abnormal Personality: A Textbook.* New York, 1948.
White, William Alanson. *Thoughts of a Psychiatrist on the War and After.* New York: P. B. Hoeber, 1919.
Wylie, Philip. *Generation of Vipers.* New York, 1946.
Yerkes, Robert. *Psychological Examining in the United States Army.* Washington: Government Printing Office, 1921.

Films

Let There Be Light. YouTube. Various versions available at https://www.youtube.com/results?search_query=let+there+be+light+war+film.
Shades of Gray. YouTube. Various versions available at https://www.youtube.com/results?search_query=shades+of+gray+war+film.

Social Work Master's Theses

Dean, Winfred. "Casework with the Emotionally Disturbed Veteran." New York School of Social Work, Columbia University, 1948.

De Beauchamp, David G. "Are There Distinguishing Factors in the Social Backgrounds of Improved and Unimproved Schizophrenia Patients?" New York School of Social Work, Columbia University, 1948.

Helfat, Lucille Podell. "An Analysis of the Records of Fifty-Three Veterans Known to the Psychiatric Clinic of the Manhattan Chapter of the American Red Cross." New York School of Social Work. Columbia University, 1944.

Luchansky, Leon, and James Mann. "The Meaning of Disability Payments in the Treatment of Patients in a Veterans' Mental Hygiene Clinic." New York School of Social Work, Columbia University, 1948.

Wilcox, Wilma. "Human Contacts with Men Rejected or Discharged by the Armed Services as Psychoneurotic." New York School of Social Work, Columbia University, 1948.

Zukerman, Abraham. "Ten World War II Veterans with Psychoneurotic Disabilities Selected for Treatment at the Veterans Rehabilitation Clinic, Kings County Hospital Psychiatric Division." New York School of Social Work, Columbia University, 1947.

Unpublished Papers

Cotton, Joseph. "Nerves and the Military: Either Hurts the Other." Paper presented before Public Health Section, Commonwealth Club, California, 1942.

Mayer, William E., Major, US Army. "Brainwashing: The Ultimate Weapon." Paper presented to officers, San Francisco Naval Shipyard, October 4, 1950.

Printed Secondary

I. ARTICLES

Aragon, Margarita. "'Deep-Seated Abnormality': Military Psychiatry, Segregation, and Discourses of 'Black' Unfitness in World War II." *Men and Masculinities* 20, no. 10 (2017): 1–20.

Beebe, G. W. "Follow-up Studies of World War II and Korean War Prisoners, II: Morbidity, Disability, and Maladjustments." *American Journal of Epidemiology* 101 (1975): 400–22.

Bennett, Scott H. "American Pacifism, the 'Greatest Generation' and World War II." In *The United States and the Second World War: New Perspectives on Diplomacy, War, and the Homefront*, ed. Kurt Piehler and Sidney Pash, 260. New York: Fordham University Press, 2010.

Black, Helen K., and William H. Thompson. "A War within a War: A World War II Buffalo Soldier's Story." *Journal of Men's Studies* 20, no. 1 (Winter 2012): 32–46.

Bourke, Joanna. "Psychiatry, Hate Training, and the Second World War." *Journal of Social History* 52, no. 1 (Fall 2018): 101–20.

Brand, Jeanne. "The National Mental Health Act of 1946." *Bulletin of the History of Medicine* 39 (May–June 1965).

Brody, E. B. "Lawrence Kubie's Psychoanalysis." *Psychological Issues* 11 (1978): 1–40.

Buchanan, R. D. "Legislative Warriors: American Psychiatrists, Psychologists, and Competing Claims over Psychotherapy in the 1950s." *Journal of the History of the Behavioral Sciences* 39, no. 3 (Summer 2003): 225–49.

Burnham, John C. "History of Personality." In *Handbook of Personality Theory and Research*, ed. Edgar F. Borgatta and William W. Lambert. Chicago: Rand McNally, 1968.

———. "The New Psychology: From Narcissism to Social Control." In *Change and Continuity in Twentieth Century America: The 1920's*. Ohio, 1968.

Canaday, Margot. "We Colonials: Sodomy Laws in America." *Nation*, September 22, 2008.

Crowley, Ralph. "On Sullivan: I." *William Alanson White Newsletter* 4 (Summer 1970).

———. "On Sullivan: II." *William Alanson White Newsletter*, Winter 1971, 2, 3.

———. "Sullivan on Social Issues." *William Alanson White Newsletter* 7 (Summer 1973): 1–2.

Dwyer, Ellen. "Psychiatry and Race during World War II." *Journal of the History of Medicine and Allied Sciences*, 2006.

Gerber, David. "Heroes and Misfits: The Troubled Social Reintegration of Disabled Veterans in 'The Best Years of Our Lives.'" *American Quarterly* 46, no. 4 (December 1994): 545–74.

Goldstein, Gerald. "Survivors of Imprisonment in the Pacific Theater during World War II." *American Journal of Psychiatry* 144 (September 1987): 1,210.

Grob, Gerald. "Origins of DSM-1: A Study in Appearance and Reality." *American Journal of Psychiatry* 148 (April 1991): 427–30.

———. "World War II and American Psychiatry." *Psychohistory Review* 19 (Fall 1990): 41–69.

Grumet, Gerald. "General George S. Patton, Jr. and the Conquest of Fear." *Psychological Report* 105, no. 1 (August 2009): 314–18.

Haulman, Daniel L. "The Tuskegee Airmen in Combat." *Air Power History*, Fall 2010, 16–21.

Hart, C. W. "Franklin Delano Roosevelt: A Famous Patient." *Journal of Religious Health* 53, no. 4 (August 2014): 1102–11.

Houts, Arthur. "Fifty Years of Psychiatric Nomenclature: Reflections on the 1943 War Department Technical Bulletin of Medicine 203." *Journal of Clinical Psychology* 56, no. 7 (2000): 935–67.

Jones, Edgar. "Alcohol Use and Misuse within the Military." *International Review of Psychiatry* 23 (April 2011): 166–72.

———. "Army Psychiatry in the Korean War: The Experience of 1 Commonwealth Division." *Military Medicine* 165, no. 4 (April 2000): 256–60.
———. "Civilian Morale during the Second World War: Responses to Air Raids Re-Examined." *Social History of Medicine* 17, no. 3 (2004).
Jones, Edgar, and Simon Wessely. "Battle for the Mind: World War I and the Birth of Military Psychiatry." *Lancet* 384 (2014): 1708–14.
Keane, Judith. "Lost to Public Commemoration: American Veterans of the 'Forgotten Korean War.'" *Journal of Social History* 44, no. 44 (Summer 2011): 1,095–1,113.
Kleiman, Miriam. "Hit the Road Jack." *Prologue* 43, no. 3 (Fall 2001): 1–15.
Krylova, Anna. "Healers of Wounded Souls: The Crisis of Private Life in Soviet Literature, 1944–1946." *Journal of Modern History*, June 2001, 307–31.
Matsumura, J. "State Propaganda and Mental Disorders: The Issue of Psychiatric Casualties among Japanese Soldiers during the Asia-Pacific War." *Bulletin of the History of Medicine* 78, no. 4 (Winter 2004): 804–35.
McGuire, Phillip. "Desegregating the Armed Forces: Black Leadership, Protests, and World War II." *Journal of Legal History* 68, no. 2 (1983): 147–58.
Murray, Paul T. "Blacks and the Draft: A History of Institutional Racism." *Journal of Black Studies* 2, no. 1 (September 1971): 57–76.
Nagata, Donna K. "The Japanese American Internment: Exploring the Transgenerational Consequences of Traumatic Stress." *Journal of Traumatic Stress* 3, no. 1 (1990).
Perkins, Marvin. "Preventive Psychiatry during World War II." In *Personal Health Measures and Immunization*, ed. John Boyd Coates Jr. Washington, DC: Surgeon General's Office, 1955.
Piehler, Kurt. "Review of Charles Glass, *The Deserters*." *Journal of Military History* 78 (June 2014).
Plant, Rebecca Jo. "William Menninger and American Psychoanalysis, 1946–1948." *History of Psychiatry* 16, no. 2 (2005): 181–202.
Polenberg, Richard. "The Good War: A Reappraisal of How World War II Affected American Society." *Virginia Magazine of History and Biography* 100, no. 3 (July 1992).
Pols, Hans. "The Repression of War Trauma in American Psychiatry after World War II." *Clio Medicine* 55 (1999): 251–76.
———. "The Tunisian Campaign, War Neuroses, and the Reorientation of American Psychiatry during World War II." *Harvard Review of Psychiatry* 19 (2011): 313–20.
———. "Waking Up to Shell Shock: Psychiatry in the US Military during World War II." *Endeavor* 30, no. 4 (2006): 144–49.
———. "War Neurosis, Adjustment Problems in Veterans, and an Ill Nation: The Disciplinary Project of American Psychiatry during and after World War II." *Osiris* 22 (2007): 72–91.

Pols, Hans, and Stephanie Oak. "War and Military Mental Health." *American Journal of Public Health* 97, no. 12 (December 2007).

"PTSD and Vietnam Veterans: A Lasting Issue 40 Years Later." Public Health, US Department of Veterans Affairs, Summer 2015. https://www.publichealth.va.gov/exposures/publications/agent-orange/agent-orange-summer-2015/nvvls.asp.

Roazen, Paul. "Book Review of the Correspondence of Edward Glover and Lawrence S. Kubie." *Psychoanalysis and History* 2, no. 2 (September 2000): 162–88.

Roberts-Pedersen, Elizabeth. "The Hard School: Physical Treatments for War Neuroses in Britain during the Second World War." *Social History of Medicine* 29, no. 3 (August 2016): 611–32.

Rollins, Peter. "Frank Capra's Why We Fight Film Series and Our American Dream." *Journal of American Culture*, Winter 1996.

Sabshin, M. "Turning Points in Twentieth-Century American Psychiatry." *American Journal of Psychiatry* 147, no. 10 (1990): 1267–74.

Sinclair, G. Dean. "Homosexuality and the Military: A Review of the Literature." *Journal of Homosexuality* 56, no. 6 (2009): 701–18.

Sklaroff, Lauren Elizabeth. "Constructing GI Joe Louis: Cultural Solutions to the 'Negro Problem' during World War II." *Journal of American History* 89, no. 3 (2002): 958–83.

Staples, Brent. "A Most Dangerous Newspaper." *New York Times Book Review*, January 10, 2016, 12.

Starr, Paul. "American Military Psychiatry and Its Role among Ground Forces in World War II." *Journal of Military History* 63 (January 1999): 127–46.

———. "Inevitably Every Man Has His Threshold: Soviet Military Psychiatry during World War II—A Comparative Approach." *Journal of Slavic Military Studies* 16, no. 1 (March 2003): 84–104.

Stone, Martin. "Shell Shock and the Psychologists." In *The Anatomy of Madness*, vol. 2. London, 1988.

Thalassis, Nafsika. "Useless Soldiers: The Dilemma of Discharging Mentally Unfit Soldiers during the Second World War." *Social History of Medicine* 23, no. 1 (2010): 98–115.

Thompson, Nellie L. "The Transformation of Psychoanalysis in America: Émigré Analysts and the New York Psychoanalytic Society and Institute, 1935–1961." *Journal of the American Psychoanalytic Association* 60, no. 1 (March 6, 2012): 9–44.

Van Dyke, Craig. "Posttraumatic Stress Disorder: A Thirty-Year Delay in a World War II Veteran." *American Journal of Psychiatry* 142, no. 9 (September 1985): 1,070–73.

Wake, Naoke. "The Military, Psychiatry, and 'Unfit' Soldiers, 1939–1942." *Journal of the History of Medicine* 62 (October 2007).

Wilson, Dale E. "Recipe for Failure: Major General Edward M. Almond and the Preparation of the United States 92nd Infantry Division." *Journal of Military History* 56, no. 3 (1992).

II. BOOKS

Abrams, Ray H. *Preachers Present Arms: Role of American Churches and Clergy in World War I and II*. Repr. Oregon, 2009.

Ambrose, Stephen. *Band of Brothers*. New York, 1992.

———. *D-Day, June 6, 1944: The Climactic Battle of World War II*. New York, 1994.

Appleman, Roy E., James M. Burns, Russell A. Gugeler, and John Stevens. *Okinawa: The Last Battle*. Washington, DC: US Army Center for Military History, 1993.

Atkinson, Rick. *The Guns at the Last Light: The War in Western Europe: 1944–1945*. New York: Holt, 2013.

Bailey, Pearce, Frankwood E. Williams, and Paul Komora. *Neuropsychiatry in the United States*. Vol. 10 in *The Medical Department in the United States Army in The World War*. Washington, DC: US Government Printing Office, 1929.

Bard, Mitchell G. *Forgotten Victims: The Abandonment of Americans in Hitler's Camps*. Boulder, CO: Westview, 1994.

Barkan, Elazar, *The Retreat of Scientific Racism: Changing Concepts of Race in Britain and the United States between the World Wars*. London: Cambridge University Press, 1992.

Bassett, Richard M., with Lewis H. Carlson. *And the Wind Blew Cold: The Story of an American POW in North Korea*. Kent, OH: Kent State University Press, 2002.

Bernstein, Alison. *American Indians and World War II*. Norman: University of Oklahoma Press, 1999.

Bérubé, Allan. *Coming Out under Fire: The History of Gay Men and Women in World War II*. Foreword by Estelle Freedman and John D'Emilio. Chapel Hill: University of North Carolina Press, 2010.

Blum, John Morton. *V Was for Victory*. New York, 1976.

Bond, Earl. *Thomas W. Salmon, Psychiatrist*. New York: Norton, 1950.

Bourke, Joanna. *An Intimate History of Killing*. New York: Basic Books, 1999.

Brands, H. W. *Traitor to His Class: The Privileged Life and Radical Presidency of Franklin Delano Roosevelt*. New York: Doubleday, 2008.

Brandt, Allan. *No Magic Bullet: A Social History of Venereal Disease in the United States since 1880*. New York: Oxford University Press, 1987.

Burleigh, Michael. *Death and Deliverance: "Euthanasia" in Germany, 1900–1945*. Cambridge: Cambridge University Press, 1994.

Canaday, Margot. *The Straight State: Sexuality and Citizenship in Twentieth-Century America*. Princeton, NJ: Princeton University Press, 2009.

Cannato, Vincent. *American Passage: The History of Ellis Island.* New York: Harper Collins, 2009.

Capra, Frank. *The Name above the Title.* Intro. Jeanine Basinger. New York: Da Capo, 1997.

Capshew, James. *Psychologists on the March: Science, Practice, and Professional Identity in America, 1929–1999.* Cambridge: Cambridge University Press, 1999.

Carlson, Lewis H. *Remembered Prisoners of a Forgotten War: An Oral History of Korean War POWs.* New York: St. Martin's, 2003.

Chambers, John. *Draftees or Volunteers: A Documentary History of the Debate over Military Conscription.* New York, 1975.

———. *To Raise an Army.* New York, 1987.

Chapman, A. H. *Harry Stack Sullivan: His Life and Work.* New York, 1976.

Chiarelli, Peter, Vice Chief of Staff, Army. *Army Health Promotion, Risk Reduction, Suicide Prevention.* 2010. https://nation.time.com/wp-content/uploads/sites/8/2011/11/hp-rr-spreport2010.pdf.

Childers, Thomas. *Soldier from the War Returning: The Greatest Generation's Troubled Homecoming from World War II.* New York, 2009.

Combs, James E. *Film Propaganda and American Politics: An Analysis and Filmography.* New York: Garland, 1994.

Condon-Rall, Ellen, and Albert E. Cowdrey. *Medical Service in the War against Japan (United States Army in World War II, the Technical Services).* Washington, DC: Center for Military History, 1998.

Cooke, Blanche. *Eleanor Roosevelt.* Vol. 2: *The Defining Years, 1933–1938.* New York: Penguin, 2000.

———. *Eleanor Roosevelt.* Vol. 3: *The War Years and After, 1939–1962.* New York: Penguin Books, 2016.

Cooper, Rachel. *Classifying Madness: A Philosophical Examination of the Diagnostic and Statistical Manual of Mental Disorders.* New York, 2005.

Copp, Terry, and Bill McAndrew. *Battle Exhaustion: Soldiers and Psychiatrists in the Canadian Army, 1939–1945.* Montreal: McGill-Queens University Press, 1990.

Cowdrey, Albert E. *Fighting for Life: American Military Medicine in World War II.* New York: Free Press, 1994.

Cripps, Thomas. *Making Movies Black.* New York: Oxford University Press, 1993.

Dalfiume, Richard M. *Fighting on Two Fronts: Desegregation of US Armed Forces, 1939–1953.* Columbia: University of Missouri Press, 1969.

Decker, Hannah. *The Making of DSM-III.* New York: Oxford University Press, 2013.

D'Emilio, John. *Lost Prophet: The Life and Times of Bayard Rustin.* Chicago: University of Chicago Press, 2004.

———. *Sexual Politics, Sexual Communities.* Chicago: University of Chicago Press, 1998.

DeSalvo, Louise. *Chasing Ghosts: A Memoir of a Father Gone to War.* New York: Fordham University Press, 2016.
D'Este, Carlo. *Patton: A Genius for War.* New York: Harper, 1995.
Deutsch, Albert. *The History of the Group for Advancement of Psychiatry.* Washington, DC: GAP, 1959.
———. *The Mentally Ill in America: A History of their Care and Treatment from Colonial Times.* New York: Columbia University Press, 1946.
Doubler, Michael D. *Closing with the Enemy: How GIs Fought the War in Europe, 1944–1945.* Lawrence: University Press of Kansas, 1994.
Dowbiggin, Ian. *The Quest for Mental Health: A Tale of Science, Medicine, Scandal, Sorrow, and Mass Society.* New York: Cambridge University Press, 2011.
Dower, John W. *War without Mercy: Race and Power in the Pacific War.* New York: Pantheon, 1986.
Eiler, Keith. *Mobilizing America: Robert P. Patterson and the War Effort.* Ithaca, NY: Cornell University Press, 1997.
Eisan, Leslie. *Pathways of Peace: A History of the Civilian Public Service Program Administered by the Brethren Service Committee.* Elgin, IL, 1948.
Eisenhower, David. *Eisenhower at War: 1943–1945.* New York: Random House, 1986.
Eskridge, William. *Dishonorable Passions: Sodomy Laws in America, 1861–2003.* New York: Penguin, 2008.
Estes, Steve. *Ask and Tell: Gay and Lesbian Veterans Speak Out.* Chapel Hill: University of North Carolina Press, 2007.
Evans, F. Barton. *Harry Stack Sullivan: Interpersonal Theory and Psychotherapy.* New York: Routledge, 1996.
Evans, Richard. *The Coming of the Third Reich.* New York, 2003.
———. *The Third Reich in Power.* New York, 2005.
Faderman, Lillian. *Odd Girls and Twilight Lovers: A History of Lesbian Life in Twentieth-Century America.* New York: Columbia University Press, 2011.
Feldstein, Ruth. *Motherhood in Black and White: Race and Sex in American Liberalism, 1930–1965.* Ithaca, NY: Cornell University Press, 2000.
Finkel, David. *Thank You for Your Service.* New York: Farrar, Straus and Giroux, 2013.
———. *The Good Soldiers.* New York: Farrar, Straus and Giroux, 2009.
Fish, Hamilton. *FDR, the Other Side of the Coin: How We Were Tricked into World War II.* New York, 1976.
Flynn, George Q. *The Draft: 1940–1973.* Lawrence: University Press of Kansas, 1993.
———. *Lewis B. Hershey, Mr. Selective Service.* Chapel Hill: University of North Carolina Press, 1985.
Franks, Lucinda. *My Father's Secret War: A Memoir.* New York: Miramax, 2007.

Friedman, Lawrence, and Anke M. Schreiber. *The Lives of Erich Fromm: Love's Prophet.* New York: Columbia University Press, 2013.
———. *Menninger: The Family and the Clinic.* Lawrence: University Press of Kansas, 1990.
Fussell, Paul. *Wartime: Understanding and Behavior in the Second World War.* New York: Oxford University Press, 1990.
Gabbard, Krin, and Glen O. Gabbard. *Psychiatry and the Cinema.* Chicago: University of Chicago Press, 1987.
Gabriel, Richard. *The Painful Field.* New York: Greenwood, 1988.
Ginzberg, Eli. *The Ineffective Soldier: Lessons for Management and the Nation.* 3 vols. New York: Columbia University Press, 1959.
———. *The Negro Potential.* New York: Columbia University Press, 1956.
———. *Psychiatry and Military Manpower Policy.* New York: Columbia University, 1953.
Glass, Charles. *The Deserters: A Hidden History of World War II.* London: Penguin, 2013.
Goldensohn, Leonard. *The Nuremberg Interviews: An American Psychiatrist's Conversations with Defendants and Witnesses.* New York: Viking, 2004.
Goltermann, Svenja. *The War in Their Minds: German Soldiers and Their Violent Pasts in West Germany.* Trans. Philip Schmitz. Ann Arbor: University of Michigan Press, 2017.
Gould, Stephen Jay. *The Mismeasure of Man.* New York, 1996.
Graebner, William. *The Age of Doubt: American Thought and Culture in the 1940s.* Boston: Twayne, 1991.
Grinker, Roy Richard. *Nobody's Normal: How Culture Created the Stigma of Mental Illness.* New York: Norton, 2021.
Grob, Gerald. *From Asylum to Community Mental Health Policy in Modern America.* Princeton, NJ: Princeton University Press, 1991.
Hale, Nathan. *Freud and the Americans: The Beginnings of Psychoanalysis in the United States, 1876–1917.* New York: Oxford University Press, 1971.
———. *The Rise and Crisis of Psychoanalysis in America, 1917 to 1985.* New York: Oxford University Press, 1995.
Hampf, M. Michaela. *Release a Man for Combat: The Women's Army Corps during World War II.* Cologne, 2010.
Hartmann, Susan M. *The Home Front and Beyond: American Women in the 1940s.* New York, 1983.
Hechler, Ken. *The Bridge at Remagen.* New York: Ballantine, 1957.
Heller, Joseph. *Catch-22.* New York: Simon and Schuster, 1961.
Herman, Ellen. *The Romance of American Psychology.* Berkeley: University of California Press, 1995.
Herzog, Dagmar. *Cold War Freud.* Cambridge: Cambridge University Press, 2017.
Hillenbrand, Laura. *Unbroken: A World War II Story of Survival, Resilience, and Redemption.* New York, 2010.

Hodgson, Godfrey, Colonel. *The Life and Wars of Henry Stimson, 1867–1950*. New York, 1990.

Hough, Frank O. *Pearl Harbor to Guadalcanal: History of the U.S. Marine Corps Operations in World War II*, Washington, DC, 1958.

Huie, William Patrick. *The Execution of Private Slovik*. New York, 1954.

Huston, John. *An Open Book*. New York: Knopf, 1980.

Jaffe, Eric. *A Curious Madness: An American Combat Psychiatrist*. New York: Simon and Schuster, 2014.

Johnson, Paul. *Eisenhower: A Life*. New York: Penguin, 2015.

Jones, Edgar. *Shell Shock to PTSD: Military Psychiatry from 1900 to Gulf War*. Psychology Press, 2006.

Jordan, Jonathan. *Brothers, Rivals, Victors: Eisenhower, Patton, Bradley, and the Partnership That Drove the Allied Conquest in Europe*. New York: Penguin, 2011.

Junger, Sebastian. *Tribe: On Homecoming and Belonging*. New York: Hachette, 2016.

Kaplan, Alice. *The Interpreter*. New York: Free Press, 2005.

Kershaw, Alex. *The First Wave: The D-Day Warriors Who Led the Way to Victory in World War II*. New York: Penguin, 2019.

———. *The Liberator: One World War II Soldier's 500-Day Odyssey from the Beaches of Sicily to the Gates of Dachau*. New York: Crown, 2012.

———. *The Longest Winter: The Battle of the Bulge and the Epic Story of World War II's Most Decorated Platoon*. New York: Da Capo, 2006.

Kieran, David. *Signature Wounds: The Untold Story of the Military's Mental Health Crisis*. New York: New York University Press, 2019.

Kindsvatter, Peter S. *American Soldiers: Ground Combat in the World Wars, Korea, and Vietnam*. Lawrence: University Press of Kansas, 2003.

Krehbiel, Nicholas A. *Hershey and the Conscientious Objector during World War II*. Columbia: University of Missouri Press, 2012.

Lamb, S. D. *Pathologist of the Mind: Adolf Meyer and the Origins of American Psychiatry*. Baltimore, MD: Johns Hopkins University Press, 2014.

Lee, Ulysses. *US Army in World War II Special Studies: The Employment of Negro Troops*. Washington, DC, 1966.

Lerner, Paul. *Hysterical Men: War, Psychiatry, and the Politics of Trauma in Germany, 1890–1938*. Ithaca, NY: Cornell University Press, 2003.

Levinson, Leila. *Gated Grief: The Daughter of a GI Concentration Camp Liberator Discovers a Legacy of Trauma*. Madison: University of Wisconsin Press, 2011.

Lewes, Kenneth. *The Psychoanalytic Theory of Male Homosexuality*. New York: Simon and Schuster, 1988.

Lifton, Robert Jay. *Nazi Doctors*. New York: Basic Books, 2000.

Linderman, Gerald. *The World within War*. New York, 2013.

MacLean, French L., Colonel. *The Fifth Field: The Story of the Ninety-Six American Soldiers Sentenced to Death and Executed in Europe and North Africa in World War II*. Pennsylvania, 2013.

MacLeod, A. D. *Shell Shock Doctors: Neuropsychiatry in the Trenches, 1914–1918.* Cambridge: Cambridge Scholars Publication, 2019.

McBride, Joseph. *Frank Capra: The Catastrophe of Success.* Tuscaloosa: University of Mississippi Press, 2011.

McGuire, Philip, ed. *Taps for a Jim Crow Army: Letters from Black Soldiers in World War II.* Lexington: University of Kentucky Press, 1983.

McManus, John. *The Deadly Brotherhood: The American Combat Soldier in World War II.* San Francisco: Presidio, 2003.

Malcolm X. *The Autobiography of Malcolm X.* New York: Grove, 1964.

Manchester, William. *Goodbye Darkness.* New York, 1979.

Marable, Manning. *Malcolm X: A Life of Reinvention.* New York: Viking, 2011.

Marsh, Alec. *Ezra Pound.* London: Reaktion, 2011.

Mendes, Gabriel. *Under the Strain of Color.* Ithaca, NY: Cornell University Press, 2015.

Menninger, Roy, et al. *American Psychiatry after World War II.* Washington, DC: American Psychiatric Association, 2000.

Meyer, Leisa. *Creating GI Jane: Women Serving in World War II.* New York: Columbia University Press, 1996.

Miller, Donald. *Masters of the Air.* New York: Simon and Schuster, 2016.

Monahan, Evelyn. *A Few Good Women: America's Military Women from World War I to the Wars in Iraq and Afghanistan.* New York: Knopf, 2009.

Moore, Deborah Dash. *GI Jews: How World War II Changed a Generation.* Cambridge, MA: Harvard University Press, 2004.

Morehouse, Maggi. *Fighting in the Jim Crow Army.* Maryland, 2000.

Morrison, Elting. *Turmoil and Tradition: A Study of the Life and Times of Henry Stimson.* History Book Club, 2003.

Motley, Mary Penick. *The Invisible Soldier: Experience of the Black Soldier in World War II.* Michigan, 1975.

Mullahy, Patrick. *The Beginnings of Modern American Psychiatry: Ideas of Harry Stack Sullivan.* New York, 1973.

Murdoch, Stephen. *IQ: A Smart History of a Failed Idea.* New York: Wiley, 2007.

Nalty, Bernard. *Strength for the Fight: A History of Black Americans in the Military.* New York: Free Press, 1986.

Napoli, Donald, *Architects of Adjustment: The History of the Psychological Profession in the United States.* New York: Kennikat, 1981.

Norman, Elizabeth M. *We Band of Angels.* New York: Simon and Schuster, 1999.

Norman, Michael, and Elizabeth Norman. *Tears in the Darkness.* New York, 2009.

O'Neill, William. *A Democracy at War: America's Fight at Home and Abroad in World War II.* Cambridge, MA: Harvard University Press, 1998.

Ossad, Steven L. *Omar Nelson Bradley.* Missouri: University of Missouri Press, 2017.

O'Sullivan, John, ed. *The Draft and Its Enemies.* Chicago, 1974.

Perry, Helen Swick. *Psychiatrist of America: The Life of Harry Stack Sullivan.* Cambridge, MA: Harvard University Press, 1980.
Perry, Mark. *Partners in Command: George Marshall and Dwight Eisenhower in War and Peace.* New York: Penguin, 2008.
Piehler, G. Kurt. *A Religious History of the American GI in World War II.* Lincoln: University of Nebraska Press, December 2021.
Piehler, G. Kurt, and Sidney Pash. *The United States and the Second World War: New Perspectives on Diplomacy, War, and the Home Front.* New York: Fordham University Press, 2013.
Plant, Rebecca Jo. *Mom: The Transformation of Motherhood in Modern America.* Chicago: University of Chicago Press, 2015.
Pogue, Forrest. *George C. Marshall.* Vol. 2: *Ordeal and Hope, 1939–1942.* New York: Viking, 1973.
———. *George C. Marshall.* Vol. 3: *Organizer of Victory, 1943–1945.* New York: Viking, 1973.
Poitier, Sidney. *The Measure of a Man.* New York: Harper Collins, 2000.
———. *This Life.* New York: Knopf, 1980.
Polenberg, Richard. *America at War: Home Front, 1941–1945.* New Jersey, 1968.
———. *War and Society.* Philadelphia, 1972.
Porter, Bruce D. *War and the Rise of the State: The Military Foundations of Modern Politics.* New York: Free Press, 1994.
Puckett, Kent. *War Pictures: Cinema, Violence, and Style in Britain, 1939–1945.* New York: Fordham University Press, 2017.
Rawley, Hazel. *Richard Wright: The Life and Times.* New York: Holt, 2001.
Richardson, Theresa. *The Century of the Child: The Mental Hygiene Movement and Social Policy.* New York: SUNY Press, 1989.
Roll, David L. *The Hopkins Touch: Harry Hopkins and the Forging of the Alliance to Defeat Hitler.* New York: Oxford University Press, 2013.
Ross, Davis. *Preparing for Ulysses.* New York, 1969.
Rothman, David. *The Discovery of the Asylum.* New York: Little, Brown, 1971.
Rowland, Lewis P. *The Legacy of Tracy J. Putnam and H. Houston Merritt.* New York: Oxford University Press, 2009.
Ryan, Joseph W. *Samuel Stouffer and the GI Survey: Sociologists and Soldiers during the Second World War.* Knoxville: University of Tennessee Press, 2013.
Salmon, Thomas, and Norman Fenton. *Neuropsychiatry in the American Expeditionary Force.* Vol. 10 of *The Medical Department in the United States Army in The World War.* Washington, DC: US Government Printing Office, 1929.
Scull, Andrew. *Psychiatry and Its Discontents.* Berkeley: University of California Press, 2019.
Shephard, Ben. *A War of Nerves.* Cambridge, MA: Harvard University Press, 1999.

Shorter, Edward. *A History of Psychiatry: From the Era of the Asylum to the Age of Prozac.* New York: Wiley, 1997.

———. *How Everyone Became Depressed: The Rise and Fall of the Nervous Breakdown.* New York: Oxford University Press, 2013.

Smith, Jean Edward. *FDR.* New York: Random House, 2008.

Smith, Lee Carraway. *A River Swift and Deadly: The 36th "Texas" Infantry Division at the Rapido River.* Fort Worth, TX: Eaken, 1989.

Starr, Paul. *Remedy and Reaction: The Peculiar American Struggle over Health Care Reform.* New Haven, CT: Yale University Press, 2011.

———. *The Social Transformation of American Medicine.* New York: Basic Books, 1982.

Stevenson, George S. *Mental Health Planning for Social Action.* New York, 1956.

Symonds, Craig L. *Neptune: The Allied Invasion of Europe and the D-Day Landings.* New York: Oxford University Press, 2014.

Taylor, Steven. *Acts of Conscience: World War II, Mental Institutions, and Religious Objectors.* Syracuse, NY: Syracuse University Press, 2009.

Terkel, Studs. *"The Good War": An Oral History of World War II.* New York: Ballantine, 1984.

Tobin, James. *The Man He Became: How FDR Defied Polio to Win the Presidency.* New York: Simon and Schuster, 2013.

Treadwell, Mattie E. *US Army in World War II Special Studies: The Women's Army Corps.* Washington, DC, 1954.

Tsika, Noah. *Traumatic Imprints: Cinema, Military Psychiatry, and the Aftermath of War.* Berkeley: University of California Press, 2018.

Tuttle, William. *Daddy's Gone to War: The Second World War in the Lives of American Children.* New York: Oxford University Press, 1993.

US Army Medical Department. *Neuropsychiatry in World War II.* Vols. 1–2. Washington, DC, 1966–1975.

Van Ellis, Mark D. *To Hear Only Thunder Again: America's World War II Vets Come Home.* New York: Lexington, 2001.

Vento, Carol Schultz. *The Hidden Legacy of World War II.* Mechanicsburg, PA: Sunbury, 2011.

Wake, Naoko. *Private Practices: Harry Stack Sullivan, the Science of Homosexuality, and American Liberalism.* New Brunswick, NJ: Rutgers University Press, 2011.

Wallace, Edwin R., and John Gach, ed. *History of Psychiatry and Medical Psychology,* 2008.

Ward, Thomas J. *Black Physicians in the Jim Crow South.* Fayetteville: University of Arkansas Press, 2003.

Weigley, Russell F. *Eisenhower's Lieutenants: The Campaigns of France and Germany, 1944–1945.* Bloomington: Indiana University Press, 1981.

Wells, Mark. *Courage and Air Warfare: The Allied Aircrew Experience in the Second World War.* London: Frank Cass, 1995.

Wersten, Irving. *Guadalcanal*. New York: Thomas Y. Crowell, 1963.
Wilhelm, J. J. *Ezra Pound: The Tragic Years, 1925–1972*. State College: Penn State University Press, 1994.
Wiltse, Charles M. *US Army in World War II the Technical Services the Medical Department: Medical Services in the Mediterranean and Minor Theaters.* Washington, DC, 1965.
Wright, Richard. *Richard Wright: Writing America at Home and from Abroad.* Ed. Virginia Whatley Smith. Jackson: University Press of Mississippi, 1998.
Wright, Stuart. *An Emotional Gauntlet: From Life in Peacetime America to the War in European Skies.* Madison: University of Wisconsin Press, 2004.
Wylie, Philip. *Sons and Daughters of Mom.* New York, 1971.
Yellin, Emily. *Our Mother's War: American Women at Home and at the Front.* New York: Free Press, 2004.
Zimmerman, John L. *The Guadalcanal Campaign.* Washington, DC, 1949.

Other Sources

DOCUMENTARIES

Dong, Arthur, and Allan Bérubé. *Coming Out under Fire.* 1994.

DOCTORAL DISSERTATIONS

Bresnahan, Josephine Callisen. *Danger in Paradise: The Battle against Combat Fatigue in the Pacific War.* Cambridge, MA: Harvard University Press, 1999.

UNPUBLISHED PAPERS

Johnson, Paul M. "Every Man Has His Breaking Point: The Attitudes of American Infantrymen towards Combat Fatigue in World War II." Final paper, University of Wisconsin, Eau Claire, 2006.
Lilly, Robert J., and J. Michael Thomson. "Death Penalty Cases in World War II Military Courts: Lessons Learned from North Africa and Italy." Paper presented at the 41st Annual Meeting of the Academy of Criminal Justice Sciences, Las Vegas, NV, March 10–13, 2004.
Suzuki, Akihito. "Psychiatry in the Land of Suicide: Medicalization of Self-Killing in Early Twentieth-Century Japan." Paper presented at the Institute on History of Psychiatry, New York Hospital–Cornell Medical Center, New York City, January 2013.

Index

Aberdeen Proving Grounds training camp, 82, 150, 165, 186, 187, 257, 346
abortion, 219
Abraham, Karl (doctor), 18, 255, 269
abreaction, 191
absence without leave (AWOL), 154, 253. *See also* Mauldin, Bill
Ackerly, S. Spafford (doctor), 55, 59, 255, 282, 304n78. *See also* homosexuality
Adaptability Rating for Military Aeronautics (ARMA), 134, 253
adviser system, 263, 378n59. *See also* Kraines, Samuel (doctor)
Afghanistan, 9, 178, 233, 245, 292
Aita, John (doctor), 48, 312n10
alcoholism, concerned about: Roosevelts, 27, 301nn58,59; Ruggles, Arthur (doctor), 89; Salmon, Thomas (doctor), 17; U.S. Senate, 222; military service, rejection for: 3, 40; psychopath, diagnosed as: 53; Medical Survey Program (MSP), used to detect: 126, 347n20; prisoners of war (POWs), having history of: 237; stress reaction, manifestation of: 227; veterans' pensions, effort to get for: 401n34
Alexander, Franz (doctor), 90, 214, 255, 260, 265
Allen, A. Leonard (U.S. representative), 111, 341, 343n69
American Civil Liberties Union (ACLU), 130, 253
American Legion, 29, 117, 118, 222, 360n45

American Medical Association (AMA), 50
American Museum of Natural History, 19
American Psychiatric Association, 4, 30, 35, 46, 59, 80, 124, 147, 155, 212, 241, 250
American Psychoanalytic Association, 25, 214, 219, 263, 380n69
American Student Union, 20
American Sociological Association, 133. *See also* Stouffer, Samuel
amytal (sodium amytal), 34, 84, 86, 194, 236
antisemitism, 22, 23, 266, 298
anxiety reaction, 202
Appel, John (doctor), 255; allegiance to Marshall instead of Hippocrates, opinion on, 7; Army Mental Hygiene Branch, director of, 148; combat days, limits of, 157, 177; job classifications being correct and mental health, 162 (*see also* Spiegel, Herbert); Lancaster juvenile guidance clinic, director of, 17; military intolerance to psychiatry, recalled 202; Neuropsychiatric Screening Adjunct (NSA), developer of with Stouffer, 133 (*see also* personality tests); officer selection and screening, 179, 374n16; predisposition, questions about, 123; "Prevention of Manpower Loss from Psychiatric Disorders," memorandum, 156, 364nn21–23; preventive psychiatry after World War II, involvement with, 225; replacements at front,

442 | Index

Appel, John (doctor) *(continued)*
sending in groups, 185; Stouffer, Samuel (sociologist), working with on surveys of soldiers, 7; tour of duty, limited, recommended, 177; "Why We Fight" films, working with Stouffer and Frank Capra, 181, 271

Armed Forces Qualification Test (AFQT), 243

Army Adjutant General, psychologists assigned to, 290n11

Army Adjutant General Memorandum No. 600-30-43, toughening screening, 98

Army Air Forces, Eighth Air Force, 158, 193, 372n5

Army Circular Letter No. 19, 38, 39, 45, 51, 52, 277

Army General Classification Test (AGCT), 17, 112, 294

Army Inspector General, investigations of psychoneurotics in Zone of Interior, Pacific Ocean Areas, European Theater of Operations and Mediterranean Theater of Operations, 197, 200–5

Army Medical Bulletin No. 58, 38, 52, 123

Army Morale Branch, 37, 71, 72, 183, 266. *See also* Information and Education Division; Osborn, Frederick

Army Neuropsychiatric Consultants Division, 89, 124, 147, 152, 155, 156, 167

Army Research Branch, 133, 136, 255, 270, 353. *See also* Information and Education Division; Stouffer, Samuel

Army School of Neuropsychiatry, Lawson General Hospital, Atlanta, Georgia, 91

Army Special Committee investigating mental cases at induction stations, 121–22, 256, 267, 271

Army Special Committee investigating mental cases in training camps, 122

Army Special Committee investigating mental cases in the WAC, 174

Army Surgeon General, Kirk, Norman (doctor), chief of, 262

Arnold, Harold (Hap), Commanding Gen., Army Air Forces, 170

Arnold, William, Chief of Army Chaplains, 107

Assistant Army Chief of Staff for Personnel (G-1), 151, 152, 177, 202, 203, 261

Atomic Energy Commission (AE), 395n80

Auschwitz, 215

Austin, Warren, (senator), 103, 107

Bailey, Pearce, 18, 222, 255

Bataan, 80, 239

Battle Noise Test, 131, 133, 134

Battle of the Bulge, 139, 161, 199, 239, 340n45

Baukhage, Hilmar Robert (H. R.) (journalist), 144, 357n24

Beers, Clifford, 17, 255, 256

Berezin, Dr. Martin (doctor), 79, 140, 214, 256. *See also* Guadalcanal

Berlien, Ivan C. (doctor), 174, 256

The Best Years of Our Lives (film), 229, 238

Biehler, William A., 198, 382n91. *See also* Utah Beach

Birnbaum, Dr. Karl, 25, 256, 299n52

blackout by Army of news: on Malaria, 138; on psychoneuroses, 149

Blacks, discharges, psychiatric: bias against officers, complaints of, 116, 117. *See also* Section VIII discharges

Blacks, psychological testing at local boards, complaints of bias: AGCT, related to, 112; Conference of Negro Educators from, 112; insufficient number of Black psychologists, 117

Blacks, rejections from military service: aptitude, 103, 115; biased, 5, 68, 101, 115, 117; illiteracy, 103; impact of rejections on employment, 118; mental deficiency, 103; NAACP, complaints from, 111; NMA, complaints from, 111; rejections by Navy, complaints of, 111,

112; rejections, psychiatric, in Arkansas, 116; rejections, psychiatric, VD related to, 115; rejections of prominent figures: Malcolm X (activist), 114; Wright, Richard (author), 113, 114
Blacks, riots, 114
Blacks, segregation, 3, 112, 113; Army, 109; Black hospitals, 109; "Double V Campaign," 110; housing, Camp Claiborne, La, 109; Kubie, Lawrence (doctor), views on, 169; Kaufman, M. Ralph (doctor), views on, 170–71; low morale because of, 110; Menninger, William (doctor), views on, 169; Navy, 109; recreation, 109
Blacks, under representation in military compared to percentage, complaints of, 110, 111
Blain, Daniel (doctor), 224, 256. See also Veterans Affairs
Blitsten, Dorothy, 24. See also Sullivan, Harry Stack (doctor)
Blitzsten, Lloyd, 24
blue discharges, 53, 58, 68, 63, 117, 216, 249, 336n23, 390n34. See also Section VIII discharges
Bly, Nelly, 223. See also Manhattan State Hospital
Bora Bora Airfield, 159
Boston Psychoanalytic Society, 25
Bougainville, 116, 154, 158, 160–62,
Boyce, Westray Battle, 200, 384n1. See also Women's Army Corps
Braceland, Francis (doctor), 111, 127, 212, 236, 256, 395n80
Bradley, Omar (general), 138, 145, 149, 211, 258, 357n21
Brav, Rabbi Stanley, 233
Brigham, Carl (psychologist), 256, 294n7. See also Yerkes, Robert (psychologist)
Brill, Norman, 119, 256, 344n86
Brown versus Topeka, 212, 243
Buck, Pearl, 221, 222
Bullard, Dexter Means (doctor), 32, 60. See also schizoid personality
Bundy, Harvey, 148, 359n40. See also Appel, John (doctor)

Bureau of the Budget, 29, 127, 303n72, 351n99. See also Smith, Harold (director)
Burling, Temple (doctor), 104, 257
Burlingame, Charles, 257

cages, 82, 235
Calderone, Thomas, 77, 239
Camp Callan Anti-Aircraft Replacement Training Center, Calif., 180. See also Schreiber, Julius (doctor)
Camp Claiborne, La., 109
Campbell, C. MacFie (doctor), 35, 257, 333n85, 312n56
Capra, Frank. See Appel, John (doctor)
Caribbean, neuropsychiatric cases in military, 83. See also Osborn, Frederick
Cassino, Italy, xii, 157, 158
"Catch 22," 159. See also Army Air Forces
Cathcart, John (doctor), 35, 257, 305n3. See also Menninger, William
Catholic criticism of psychiatry, 107, 108, 196, 215, 226, 339n37
certificate of disability for discharge (C. D. D.), 58, 217
Challman, Samuel A. (doctor, colonel), 153
child guidance clinics, 17, 137, 229, 294n8
Chisholm, G. Brock (doctor), 147, 257, 227. See also Menninger, William
Chiwy, Augusta, 340n45
Churchill, Winston, 138
Civil War, 140, 244, 386n3
Civilian Conservation Corps (CCC), 125, 318n75
Clark, Mark (general), 145, 178. See also Rapido, Italy
clergy, 7, 184, 195–96, 218, 251
Cohen, R. Robert (doctor), 186, 257, 346n9. See also Aberdeen Proving Grounds training camp; "Mack & Mike" pamphlet
Cohen, Seymour. See also Army Air Forces
Colman, William (general), 109, 110, 340n47

combat exhaustion, 6, 141, 142, 149, 150, 154, 155, 189, 192, 193, 205
"combat fatigue," 138, 141, 149, 155, 189, 216, 362n4, 378n53
combat, fear of, 80, 185, 188, 189. See also Dollard, John (psychoanalyst)
Community Mental Health Act (1963), 252
concentration camps, 43, 164
Conference of Negro Educators, 112
conscientious objector (CO), 33, 104
constitutionalism, 19. See also Draper, George (doctor)
conversion reaction, 203, 384n111
Cooke, Elliot (general), 200, 335n11, 380n71
Cooley, Martin (doctor), 257, 304n78
Cornell Selectee Index, 131, 132, 134–36, 154, 266, 272, 273
Cortez, Stanley (cinematographer), 188
Costello, John M. (U.S. representative), 106
Craighill, Margaret (doctor). See Women's Army Corps (WAC)
Creel Committee, 37
Crighton, Kyle (journalist), 199, 382n97
Crowther, Bosley (journalist), 220

Daniels, Jonathan, 384nn110,111
Daniels, Josephus, 316n59, 384n110
The Dark Mirror (movie), 220, 391n47
de Jarnette, Joseph S. (doctor), 56, 57, 258
de River, Paul (doctor), 56, 61, 258, 358n48
Deutsch, Albert (journalist), 219, 220, 294n8, 333n85
Deutsch, Harry (doctor), 67, 258
Diagnostic Statistical Manual No. 1 (1952) (DSM-I), 203, 313, 396n83
displaced person (DP), 226
division psychiatrist, 6, 92, 151, 360n49
Dollard, John (psychoanalyst), 185, 258, 378n55
"Double V Campaign," 110
Douglas, Michael, 237
draft evasion, 49, 102, 103

Draper, George (doctor), 19, 258, 262. See also constitutionalism; Roosevelt, Franklin Delano
Dravo, E., 315n53. See also psychopath
DSM II, 313
DSM III, 313, 317n64
Dunn, William, 57. See also heredity of mental illness; psychopath
Dyas, Timothy, 240, 401n37
Dykstra, Clarence, 22

Eanes, Richard, 65, 67, 103, 105, 115, 123,
Ebaugh, Franklin (doctor), 89, 258, 354n2
Eighth Air Force, 158, 193, 372n5
eighteen- and nineteen-year-old draft, 98–100
"eighty-eight" ("88" or "88" mm gun), 145, 188, 195, 198, 368n58
Eighty-Second Airborne, 232
Eisenhower, Dwight D. (general), 5, 356n14; Abilene, Kansas, from, 148; British air force psychiatry, endorse, 151, 152; Carentan, Battle of, 199; Columbia University, president, 241; Conservation for Human Resources, Columbia University, 242; Kenner, Albert (doctor), consulted with, 199; manpower shortages, concerned about, 177, 197, 198, 262, 371n2; Marshall, George C. (general), 147, 364n25; McC. Snyder, Howard, (IG and personal physician), 233, 269; Patton, George, reaction to, 138, 142, 143, 145, 147, 248; Pershing, John (general), aide to, World War I, 356n114; psychiatric evacuations, interest in limiting, 138, 155, 198; psychiatric profession, views on, 140, 241, 245, 402n40; stamp collector, 148; WAC's, appreciation of, 172, 370n91, 381n89
electric shock, films covering, 235, 295n13, 398n16
electroconvulsive therapy (ECT; also called electric shock), 34
émigré analysts, 25, 26, 214, 215

enemy weapons, 188
enuresis (bed wetting), 38, 103, 154
epilepsy, 16, 43, 98, 103, 124, 175, 235, 258
Erikson, Erik (psychoanalyst), 324, 259
eugenics, 19
"everyone has his breaking point," 138, 167–68, 209, 229, 231

Farrell, Malcolm (doctor), 89, 103, 148, 150, 153, 212, 218, 259
fathers to exempt from draft, bill in Congress, 103. See also Wheeler, Burton K. (senator)
Federal Bureau of Investigation (FBI), 56, 113, 114, 131, 180, 221, 315n49, 342n63, 351n55, 352n56. See also Malcolm X; Wright, Richard
Federal Employment Practices Commission (FEPC), 226
Fenichel, Otto (doctor), 214, 394
Fish, Hamilton (U.S. rep., New York), 143, 357n17
Fitchberg Sentinel, 224, 394n67
flashback, 1, 219, 229, 237, 238, 239, 241. See also Post-Traumatic Stress Disorder (PTSD)
Fort Hood, Texas, Tank Destroyer Replacement Training Center, 165
Fort Huachuca, Arizona, 109
Frank, Lawrence (social scientist), 259, 333n86
Fremont-Smith, Frank (doctor), 35, 136, 259
Freud, Anna (psychoanalyst), 226, 259
Freud, Sigmund (doctor), 18, 26, 36, 84, 162, 255, 260, 267, 269, 273
Fromm, Erich (psychoanalyst), 22, 214, 259, 298n38, 324n129
Fromm-Reichman, Frieda (doctor), 214, 229, 259, 298n38. See also Sullivan, Harry Stack (doctor)

Garrett, Henry (psychologist), 179, 259
Gavin, Jim (general), 232
Geneva Convention, 199
Gibson, Truman K. (general), 169. See also Blacks

GI Bill, 63, 215
Ginzberg, Eli (economist), 130, 233, 242, 243, 287, 402n41
Glass, Albert (doctor), 193
Glueck, Bernard (doctor), 36, 260, 306n9
Gold, Michael, 238
Goring, Hermann, 226
Governor's Island, New York, 112, 347n19
Graham, Billy (chaplain), 238
Graham, Clarence (psychologist), 135
Grant, David (general), Army Air Forces, 361n52
Great Lakes Naval Training Station, Chicago, Ill., 57
Gregg, Alan (doctor), 124, 347n19
Grinker, Roy (doctor): Don Ce-Sar Hotel, Florida, 85; "everyone has his breaking point," conception of, 167; Freud, Sigmund, trained with, 260; Group for the Advancement of Psychiatry (GAP), founder of, 212; hatred of enemy, inspiring, reservations about, 376n35; Kenton, Colman (British military doctor), worked with, 84; narcosynthesis, 85, 380n73; North Africa, work in hospitals, 150; psychotherapy, evaluation of, 380n73; rest camps, evaluation of, 178; Twelfth Army Air Force, psychiatrist at, 178
Grotjahn, Martin (doctor), 260
gross stress reaction, 227
group cohesion, 7, 184–85, 377n44
Group for the Advancement of Psychiatry (GAP), 211
group psychotherapy, 181, 209, 225, 230, 267, 377n45, 396n84, 397n5. See also Paster, Samuel (doctor)
Grumman Aircraft, 105
Guadalcanal, 87, 397n5; Berezin, Martin (doctor), 79, 81, 256; Carlson, Evans F., leadership training, 179; combat, 161; killing, soldiers' recollections of, 233; malaria, 81; neuropsychiatric casualties, extent of, 77, 80, 124, 328n44, 367n50;

Guadalcanal *(continued)*
  Patch, Alexander (general), 140; predisposition, questioned, 184; Rosner, Albert (doctor), 79, 80, 325n1, 326n13; Smith, E. Rogers (naval commander), 80, 326n14; Tregaskis, Richard, 79, 325; veterans of, 363n12
Guam, 77, 161

Hadley, Ernest (doctor), 260. *See also* Sullivan, Harry Stack (doctor)
Hall, Roscoe (doctor), 56, 97
Halloran, Roy (doctor): candidate of Overholser, Winfred (doctor), 90; Chief, Army Neuropsychiatric Consultants Branch, appointed to, 4, 90, 261; death, coronary occlusion, 261; division psychiatrist, views on, 151; Medical Survey Program (MSP), views on, 127; screening, concerns about, 363n15; Special Committee investigations mental rejections at induction, member of, 121; WAC psychiatry, criticism of, 174
Hammond, John, 341, 387n10
Hanson, Frederick (doctor): G-1, appointed to, 261; hatred of Germans indoctrination, skeptical about, 7; Inspector General, investigation of psychoneurotics in Mediterranean and European Theaters of Operation, participation in, 204; Mediterranean Theater, psychiatric consultant, 148, 149, 376n35; mental health in war, concept of, 192; North Africa, in, 4, 87; tour of duty, views on, 177; training films, worked on, 189; treatment at the front, 149, 190
Harrison, Malcolm, (Malcolm H, Native American), 65–68
Hartmann, Heinz (doctor), 26, 261, 300n52, 388n19
Hatfield, Malcolm (Michigan judge), 28, 102, 303n70, 335n8
Hawley, Paul (doctor), 211
heredity of mental illness, 48, 57, 313n29. *See also* eugenics

Hershey, Lewis (general): Army-Navy War Readiness Committee Selective Service bill, drafting of, 20; Army Selective Service induction examinations, interest in combining, 69, 70; bill to exempt fathers from draft, 103, 106; Blacks, call up by Selective Service, criticism of, 110, 342n56; democratic nature of draft, extol, 21; eighteen- and nineteen-year-old draft, in favor, 98; FBI, contacts with, 56, 131; fear in combat, paper on, 20, 297n28; Malcolm H, receipt of appeal, 66, 67; MSP, interest in, 124; National Neuropsychiatric Institute (NNI) hearings, testify at, 220; prehabilitation (rehabilitation) of 4Fs, interest in, 68; psychiatric rejections viewed as biased, excessive, stigmatic, 48, 49, 65, 103, 343n68; Sullivan, Harry Stack, differences with, 72, 73; Waggoner, Raymond (doctor), approved as successor to Sullivan, Harry Stack, 49, 90, 125
Hess, Rudolph, 226
Hines, Frank, director, Veterans Affairs, 27, 29, 123, 151, 211
hippocratic oath, conflict between obligations military and medical role, 99, 182, 249
Hitchcock, Alfred, 220
Hitler, Adolf, 206
Hobby, Oveta Culp (colonel, WAC director), 172
Home of the Brave (film), 220, 391
homicides, 83, 235, 237
homosexuality, doctors' opinions: Mira y Lopez, Emilio, non-combat assignments in Spanish Republic, 35; psychoanalytic interpretations between World Wars, 58; Sullivan, Harry Stack, 58–60, Sullivan's own homosexuality, 317nn66,67; Madigan, Patrick, 61, 329n54; on administrative discharges: Kaufman, M. Ralph 61, 62; Overholser, Winfred, 62; McIntire, Ross T., 62, 63; on rejections: Putnam, Tracy, 60–61

homosexuality, enforcement: administrative discharges, including Section VIII (blue), 58, 216, 217, 249; criminal prosecution, 9; JAG, views on, 62; locked wards, 235; navy court-martial, 318n78; sodomy, 3
homosexuality, examinations: Army Circular No. 22, Examinations in Nervous and Mental Disease, World War I, 58; *DSM* II (1973), disorder removed, 250; Medical Circular No. 1 REVISED, Army Circular Letter No. 19, "homosexual proclivities," included, 3, 39, 53, 58, 61
homosexuality, experiences of men: outside military: Civilian Conservation Corps, 318; service men in World War II: Allenby, Ted, 63; Winn, Dr. Ted, 63; Jordan, Paul and Bill Taylor, 319n85; as told by others: *Coming Out under Fire*, documentary, 63; Fry, Clements, survey of former student who served in World War II, 64; Greer, Lionel, oral recollections of an examination, 61
homosexuality, numbers rejected/discharged for homosexuality, 63, 64
homosexuality, Roosevelt, Franklin Delano, interest in: 1919 navy investigation of Newport, Rhode Island, YMCA while Roosevelt, Assistant Secretary of Navy, 316n59; de River, J. Paul (doctor) correspondence with President Roosevelt's personal secretary, Stephen P. Early on psychiatric rejections, 61
homosexuality, treatment for (glandular), 62
homosexuality, women in military: numbers unknown, 175, 320n92; screening or lack of, 173
Hopkins, Harry, as analyzed by Williams, Frankwood (doctor), 26, 273
Horney, Karen (doctor), 22, 214, 261
Hunt, William, psychologist, 132
Huie, William Bradford, 229. See also Slovik, Eddie

Huston, John, 230. See also *Let There Be Light*
hydrotherapy, 235
hypnosis, 12, 7, 86, 87, 191, 194, 195, 230, 231, 270. *See also* Spiegel, Herbert (doctor)
hysteria, 44, 84, 194, 230, 262

illiterates, psychiatric examination of for service, 97, 103, 118
immigrants, 16, 25, 36, 260, 268. *See also* Salmon, Thomas (doctor)
individualism in America, 18, 44, 71, 149, 163, 182
industrial psychiatry, 213, 251, 395n74
Information and Education Division: name of division, reason for it, 37; news media, current events, news maps, *Stars and Stripes*, 162; Osborn, Frederick, director of, 30, 266; political orientation lectures, 376n39 (*see also* Schreiber, Julius [doctor]; Stouffer, Samuel [sociologist]); religion, 165; surveys by Army Research Branch of attitudes toward war, 7, 180, 362n1
insulin therapy, 152, 235
intelligence quotient (IQ), 16
International Conference on Mental Health, 1948, 73, 227, 271
International Psychoanalytical Association, 25
"intestinal fortitude," 156
Iowa Psychopathic Hospital, 129
Iraq, 9, 178, 133, 245
isolation, mental effects of, 6, 159, 161, 176, 196
isolationism, 14, 20, 56, 143, 247, 359. *See also* de Jarnette, Joseph (doctor); de River, Paul (doctor)
Italian campaign, 139, 157, 163
Iwo Jima, 140

Jaffe, Daniel (doctor), 226, 261
Japanese, battles fought: Guadalcanal, 79–80, 179; Guam, 77; Okinawa, 190; Pearl Harbor, 77; Philippines, 77–80, 325n5; Solomon Islands, 365n34

448 | Index

Japanese, military psychiatry, use of by, 44, 80: predisposition, extent believe in, 44
Japanese, Patton's views on, 141
Japanese, prisoner of war (POW) camps, 79, 237, 238–40, 400n26
Japanese, psychological warfare by Americans: character study of, 226; hatred against, inspiring of, 80, 164, 180
Japanese, warfare of: Army Criminal Code 1908, 80; cave fighting, 140; suicide, 45, 310n42. *See also* Stouffer, Samuel
Japanese American internment camps, 131
Jews (Jewish), 43, 180, 226, 233, 238, 262, 267, 269
job assignments, psychological impact, 183. *See also* Appel, John (doctor); Spiegel, Herbert(doctor)
Joint Army-Navy Selective Service Committee (JANSSS), 20. *See also* Hershey, Lewis (general); Osborn, Frederick
Jones, Ernest (doctor), 18, 25, 261, 299n51. *See also* Kubie, Lawrence (doctor); Freud, Sigmund (doctor)
Jung, Carl (doctor), 28, 262, 310n36

Kardiner, Abram (doctor), 12, 36, 262,
Kaufman, M. Ralph (doctor): analysts, assist in emigrating to U.S., 8, 25; discharge for psychopathy, 53; homosexuality in Army, employment of administrative discharge, 53, 61, 62; hypnosis, 12, 192; narcoanalysis, use of, 190; segregation, opposition to, 168, 170 (*see also* Maxwell, Earl [general], 93rd Div.); training films, development of, 189; treatment in Okinawa on battlefront, 190, 191
Keehn, Robert, 237
Kennedy, Foster (doctor), 26, 54, 99, 220, 262, 345n2. *See also* Kolb, Lawrence (doctor); Roosevelt, Franklin Delano

Kenner, Albert, 199, 202, 262; supported by Patton for Surgeon General, 202. *See also* Eisenhower, Dwight D. (general)
Kenton, Colman (doctor), 84. *See also* Grinker, Roy (doctor)
Kerouac, Jack, 3, 83
killer, reconversion to peacetime man, 233, 234. *See also* Brav, Rabbi Stanley
killing, moral conflict over, 33, 165, 195, 232, 368n58. *See also* Paster, Samuel (doctor)
King, Ernest, Chief, Naval Operations, 106
Kirk, Norman, Commander of Army Surgeon General, Office of: division psychiatrists, views on placement of, 151; Magee, James (doctor and Surgeon General), successor to, 264; physicians appointed by President to investigate hospitalization of American fliers in England, part of, 361n52; predisposition, views on, 155; presidential commission to review requirements for admission to army, navy and marine corps, appointed to, 122; profile, 262; psychiatrists' defense of military role, support for, 202; Roosevelt, Eleanor, copy of letter received regarding William Menninger's appointment, 147, 259; Women's Army Corps (WAC) social history program, arranged for, 175
Kolb, Lawrence (doctor), 36, 38, 94, 123, 220, 263, 330, 392
Korean War, 9, 242–44, 260, 261
Kraines, Samuel (doctor), 188, 263. *See also* adviser system
Kubie, Lawrence (doctor): analysts, assisted emigrating, 8, 25, 261, 262; industrial psychiatry, views on, 395n73; National Neuropsychiatric Institute hearings on, witness at, 220; NYC Committee on Mental Hygiene, Memorandum on the Selection Process, principal author,

92–94, 397n7; profile, 263; propaganda, views on, 72; psychiatric screening, criticism of, 88; psychoanalyst, contributions as, 214; rehabilitation of veterans, correspondence with Roosevelt, Eleanor, 211, 386n7, 398n11; segregation, opposition to, 168–70, 369n84; training in military psychiatry, program proposed, 90. *See also* Oscoda Airfield; Ruggles, Arthur (doctor)

labor battalions, 34, 37, 55, 69, 150, 170
lacking moral fiber (LMF), 149, 365n29
Lady in the Dark (film), 220
Lafargue clinic, Harlem, New York City, 212, 272, 387n11. *See also* Wright, Richard
La Guardia, Fiorello, 27. *See also* Office of Civilian Defense; Roosevelt, Eleanor
Lahey, Frank (doctor), 263, 346n11
Landis, Carney (psychologist), 132. *See also* Shipley Inventory
Lasswell, Harold, 22
Langer, Walter, 226, 264
Lawson General Hospital, Atlanta, Georgia, 57, 91, 267, 329n52
Lazarsfeld, Paul F., 24
leadership, psychiatric casualties, relationship to, 20, 72, 82, 98, 159. *See also* Stouffer, Samuel
leadership training, 178–80,
Let There Be Light (film), 229–31
Lewis, Aubrey (doctor), 35, 264
Lewis, Gordon, 187, 381n88
Lewis, Nolan D. C. (doctor), 55, 315n45
Leyte, Philippines, 140, 171
Liebman, Rabbi Joshua Loth, 215
Lifton, Robert F. (doctor), 241, 401n38
line officers, role of, 2, 51, 146, 151, 155, 156, 169, 199, 200. *See also* Spiegel, Herbert (doctor)
Link, Henry, 103, 335n11
Little, George (doctor), 170, 171. *See also* segregation
Lovett, Robert (doctor), 28. *See also* Roosevelt, Franklin Delano

Luce, Claire Boothe (U.S. representative), 177
Luce, Henry (journalist), 221, 222, 372n1
Luzon, Philippines, 77, 80

MacArthur, Douglas (general), 78, 79, 402n42
MacIntyre, Marvin, 94
MacLeish, Archibald, 20
"Mack & Mike" pamphlet, 186, 187, 257, 378. *See also* Cohen, R. Robert (doctor)
Madigan, Patrick (doctor): Army Circular Letter No. 9, designer of, 39; homosexuals in the military, concerned about, 61; profile, 39, 264; psychiatric screening to promote teamwork, 38, 308n21; replaced as head of Army Neuropsychiatric Branch by Dr. Roy Halloran, 4, 89; request from Dr. Edward Strecker to expand Selective Service psychiatric examination's function, 88; Selective Service Psychiatric Advisory Committee, member of, 30, 304n78; William Alanson White Psychiatric Foundation (WAWPF), member of, 22
Magee, James C. Army Surgeon General, 89, 151, 329n50
malaria, 78, 79, 81, 139, 146, 239, 362n8. *See also* Guadalcanal
Malcolm X, 114, 342n60, 342n65
malingering, 22, 54–55, 102, 103, 105, 122, 205, 210, 236, 248
Manhattan State Hospital, Ward's Island, New York City, 223. *See also* Bly, Nelly; Deutsch, Albert (journalist)
Manhoff, Bert, 165, 232, 240, 364n23
manpower shortages, 13, 171, 197, 199
Marlowe, David, 367n57. *See also* group cohesion
Marshall, George C., Army Chief of Staff: American individualism, critical of, 182; dual role satisfying President and military, 198;

Marshall, George C *(continued)*
government's prior coddling of youth, concerned about, 228; ineffective leadership, concerned about, 82; limited service assignments, extent supports, 150; limited tour of duty recommended by Appel, endorsed in memo to generals, 158, 364n25; memorandum on psychoneuroses skeptical of psychiatric expertise and reality of psychoneuroses, 138, 146–47; military equipment, paucity, concerned about, 82; morale of soldiers, concerned about, 322n120, 323nn126,127, 363n20, 338n35; O'Hara, John F. Bishop, correspondence with, 108; Osborn, Frederick, appointment of, 30; Patton, George, attitudes toward, 5; psychiatric rehabilitation before induction, opposition to, 69; segregation, opinion on, 169

Marshall, S. L. A., *Men Against Fire*, 367n57

Mason General Hospital, Long Island, 57, 91, 217, 230, 267. See also *Let There Be Light* (film)

Mauldin, Bill, 164, 366n43, 373n8

Maxwell, Earl (general), 93rd Div., 170. See also segregation

McCormick, Robert Rutherford (publisher), 172. See also Patton, George (general)

McIntire, Ross T., Navy Surgeon General, 28, 155; homosexuality and discharges for, views on, 62; inquiry ordered by President regarding treatment American airmen in England, involved in, 152, 361n52; Perkins, Frances, correspondence with, 94, 95; Presidential commission participated in reviewing requirements for admission to army, marines, navy, 122; profile, 264; Railey Report, 72; speech praising psychiatric screening before College Physicians and Surgeons, 29. See also Roosevelt, Franklin Delano

McKenzie, Charles E. (U.S. representative) 111

McNair, Lesley (general): Japanese, inspiring hatred for during training, 80, 326n19; Railey Report, 72, 323n127; segregation, 340n42, 369n87

McNutt, Paul, 110, 123, 124. See also War Manpower Commission (WMC)

Medical Circular No. 1, 24, 28, 30–34, 45, 49, 50, 52, 56, 59

Medical Circular No. 1 REVISED, 60

Medical Survey Program (MSP), Medical Circular No. 4, 123–25, 175, 270, 273, 348n25. See also Waggoner, Raymond (doctor)

medics, 139, 161, 305n91. See also Battle of the Bulge; isolation, mental effects of

Mella, Hugo (doctor), 264

Menninger, Karl (doctor), 38, 121, 148, 212, 214, 215, 265

Menninger, William: Alexander, Franz (doctor), analyzed by, 214, 255; "arbiter of life and death," referring to military psychiatrist, 191; combat exhaustion, transient, views on, 236; division psychiatrists sent to front, 151, 360n49; Kansas Selective Service examination, 38; malingering, medical opinion on, 55; MSP, support for, 124; Neuropsychiatric Consultants Div., appointed chief, 301n60; OSRD investigation of psychoneuroses, participated in, 373n10; piano player, 178; political orientation, 7, 162; profile, 147, 148, 257, 265; psychiatric rehabilitation of soldiers, 360n46, 391n44; psychiatric training after the war, 214; psychoanalysis, involved in, 90, 210, 214; replacements, sending into combat by self or in group, 185; rest and recuperation (R&R), 178; returning to combat too soon, concerned about, 192; segregation views, during and after war, 226, 291n21, 369n75; stamp collector,

148; veterans, employment of, study of, 118, 119, 344n86; WAC psychiatry, views on, 256, 348n21. See also Berlien, Ivan C. (doctor); Marshall, George C.; Menninger, Karl (doctor)
mental defectives, 155
Meyer, Adolf: case history, 18; etiology of mental illness, social and biological, 17; Kubie, Lawrence, differences with, 96; National Mental Health Act, support, 22; Selective Training and Service Act, Section 8a, critic of, 120; Sullivan, Harry Stack (doctor), relationship to, 96, 296n20; training of: Wertham, Fredric, 212; Wolff, Harold, 132
Mira y Lopez, Emilio (doctor), 35, 266, 306
Mittelman, Bela (doctor), 132, 266, 353n63
Momism, 228–29
Monahan, John F., Army chaplain for Roman Catholic priests, 196
Mondale, Walter, 230. See also *Let There Be Light* (film)
morphine, 235, 301n58
Mott, F. W. (doctor), 266, 295. See also predisposition; "shell-shock"
Murray, John (doctor): American Psychoanalytical Emergency Committee on Relief & Immigration, 25; Army Air Force psychiatric consultant, appointed, 266; Freud, Sigmund, trained by, 108; GAP founder, 212; rest camps, Air Force, views on, 373n7; segregation, response to Kubie's criticism of, 170
Myrdal, Gunnar, 215

narcoanalysis, 190, 196, 209
National Academy of Sciences (NAS), National Research Council (NRC), Committee on Neuropsychiatry, 34, 49, 120
National Association for the Advancement of Colored People (NAACP), 109, 111, 116, 168, 171, 216, 383n109

National Committee for Mental Hygiene (NCMH), 17, 25, 82, 98, 124, 147, 174, 255. See also Beers, Clifford; Salmon, Thomas (doctor)
National Defense Research Committee (NDRC), 179, 374n16
National Institute of Mental Health (NIMH), 225, 394n70
National Medical Association (NMA), 111
National Mental Health Act (NMHA), 27, 209, 220–22
National Mental Health Foundation, 222
National Neuropsychiatric Institute Act (NNIA) bill, hearings on S.1160, 224, 373n10, 392n50
National Neuropsychiatric Institute Act (NNIA) bill, hearings on HR 2550, 221, 224, 392n50
National Research Council (NRC) Committee on Neuropsychiatry, subcommittee on war neuroses, 49; on psychiatry, 89, 136; on neurology, 313n28, 324n129
National Service Act, bill on, 249, 338nn32,35
National Vietnam Veterans Longitudinal Study, 241
National Vietnam Veterans Readjustment Study, 241
Native Americans (American Indians), 3, 5, 65–68, 401n37. See also Harrison, Malcolm
Navy, Bureau of Medicine and Surgery 118; Braceland, Francis, Chief, Psychiatry Branch, 111, 127, 212; Kerouac, Jack (author), 3, 83; Kolb, Lawrence (doctor), 36, 38, 94; psychiatric examinations, 38; rotation system, 157; Sutton, Dallas (doctor), 38, 136; switch to no discharge without definite sign mental illness, 155; toughness of men compared to Army, perception of, 98; training camps, Great Lakes, Chicago, 57; written personality tests, 134, 137. See also McIntire, Ross T.
The Negro Soldier (film), 109

neuropsychiatric casualties, 11, 12, 50, 102, 167, 230, 328n44, 367n50

Neuropsychiatric Institute, proposal before Congress, 1939, 127

Neuropsychiatric Screening Adjunct (NSA), 133

New Georgia campaign, 139, 160

New York Psychoanalytic Association (NYPA), 25, 263

Niederland, William (doctor), 401n38

"No disease, temperamentally unqualified for service," 149

nomenclature, psychiatric, 4, 149, 150, 203, 227, 251. *See also* Bradley, Omar (general); Overholser, Winfred (doctor)

Normandy, 105, 138, 139, 178, 198, 199

Nuremberg war crimes trials, 226, 264

Oberwager, Jerry (puppeteer), 187

occupational therapy, 235, 303n71, 398n14

Office of Civilian Defense (OCD), 27, 101. *See also* La Guardia, Fiorello (mayor); Roosevelt, Eleanor

Office of Scientific Research and Development (OSRD), 35, 135, 162, 295n11, 373n10

Office of Strategic Services (OSS), 226, 394n79

Office of War Information (OWI), 37, 110, 114, 180, 324n129. *See also* Appel, John (doctor), Osborn, Frederick

officer training in American Army, 179, 183, 323n127

Okinawa, 7, 12, 140, 189–92, 230, 267. *See also* Kaufman, M. Ralph (doctor)

"Old Sergeant Syndrome," 269. *See also* Sobel, Raymond (doctor)

Orr, Douglass (doctor), 48

Osborn, Frederick: Appel, John (doctor) working with, 148; Black morale, efforts to improve, 110; Caribbean, military psychiatric conditions, concerned about, 83; eugenics, views on, 19; JANSSC, head of, 30; morale, efforts to improve, working with Roosevelt, Eleanor, 364n27; political orientation efforts by I&E, 156, 162, 269, 307n16; profile, 266; reducing number of psychiatric 4Fs through proposals to combine Army Selective Service examinations, establish labor battalions, and rehabilitate (medically treat) 4Fs, opposed to all three, 69, 70; Selective Service Psychiatric Advisory Committee, head, 30; surveys of attitudes of soldiers toward war, 7. *See also* Stouffer, Samuel (sociologist)

Osborn, Henry Fielding, 19. *See also* American Museum of Natural History

Oscoda Airfield, 169, 170. *See also* Blacks; Kubie, Lawrence (doctor); segregation

Overholser, Winfred (doctor): examinations of prisoners in Massachusetts, 2; Freudian psychoanalysts, differences with, 289; homosexuality in military, discharge and court-martial, views on, 62; lobbying for Roosevelt's approval of Medical Circular No. 1, 14, 26; McIntire, Ross (doctor), correspondence with, 88, 94; MSP, 124; nomenclature for psychiatric conditions, views on, 150; Perkins, Frances (Secretary of Labor), correspondence with, 94; Pound, Ezra, role in his trial and institutionalization at St. Elizabeth's Hospital, 227; psychoneuroses, severity minimizes, 236; reducing number of psychiatric 4Fs through proposals to combine Army Selective Service examinations, establish labor battalions, and rehabilitate (medically treat) 4Fs, opposed to all three, 69, 70; Roosevelt, Mrs. Eleanor, correspondence with about mental hospitals, 27; Section 8a of Selective Service and Training Act, opposed to, 120, 345n2; Special Committee Appointed by War Department to Investigate Rejections of Mental Cases, role in,

311n7; St. Elizabeth's Hospital, superintendent, 2, 14, 26; veterans, problems getting jobs, concerned about, 216, 218, 399n18; WAC psychiatry, criticism of, 174; World War I, doctor in 26

pacifism, 2, 20, 21, 23, 163, 305n91, 367n50
Paris, 27, 178
Parran, Thomas (doctor), 220, 224, 314n43, 393n59
Parsons, Frederick (doctor), 88, 130, 267, 345n6. *See also* Roosevelt, Franklin Delano
Paster, Samuel (doctor), 181, 267, 375n28. *See also* group psychotherapy
Patch, Alexander (general), 140, 256. *See also* Guadalcanal
Patterson, Robert, Assistant Secretary of War, 110, 322n120, 323n127
Patton, George (general), slapping of neuropsychiatric patients in Army hospitals, 4, 138, 140; diary of Patton with his reaction to Eisenhower's actions, 143; Eisenhower, Dwight D. (general), 142; Fish, Hamilton (U.S. representative), defense of Patton to Congress, 143; Marshall, George C. (general), 145; Pearson, Drew (journalists), report, 143; press about the slapping incident, 140, 142–43; profile, 141; psychoanalysis (recent) of Patton, 144–45; psychoneurosis, concern of Patton about faking, 140; public letters to Mrs. Roosevelt and to General Marshall, 141, 143; Roosevelt, Franklin Delano, 5, 144; Senate investigates, 144, 145; Stimson, Henry P. (Secretary of War), 144
Payne Whitney Psychiatric Clinic, NYC, 211, 268. *See also* Rennie, Thomas (doctor)
Pearl Harbor, 27, 46, 77, 80, 117, 122, 163, 237, 337n29
pentothal, 84, 193
Pepper, Claude (Senator), 220

Perkins, Frances, Secretary of Labor, 24, 26, 94. *See also* Roosevelt, Eleanor; Roosevelt, Franklin Delano; McIntire, Ross T.
Pershing, John (general), 18, 20, 22, 356n14
phenobarbital, 79, 194. *See also* Spiegel, Herbert (doctor)
Philbin, Philip J. (U.S. representative), 222
pioneer corps of British Army, 34, 169, 322n117. *See also* labor battalions
Plesset, Marvin, 154
Poitier, Sidney, 217
political orientation (propaganda), 7, 44, 156, 164, 180, 182, 184, 295n11. *See also* Information and Education Division; Kubie, Lawrence (doctor); Menninger, William
Porter, William (doctor), 55, 91, 120, 161, 267, 313n28. *See also* Army School of Neuropsychiatry, Lawson General Hospital, Atlanta, Georgia
Possessed (film), 220, 391n47
Post-Traumatic Stress Disorder (PTSD), 232; alcoholism, 238; characteristics of, 237; *Diagnostic Statistical Manual III*, included as diagnosis in, 10; German prisoners of war, suffering from, 240; German veterans, recognizing disability, 235; Lifton, Robert (doctor), Vietnam, 241; Manhoff, Burt, recollections of, 240; media, portrayal of, 400n31; National Viet Nam Veterans Longitudinal Study (2013), 241; National Viet Nam Veterans Readjustment Study (1983), 241; Native Americans, experience with, 401n37; Niederland, William (doctor), study of Holocaust survivors, 402n39; Schultz, Arthur ("Dutch"), victim of, 400n31; Steele, Ben, Japanese prisoner of war, suffering, 79; Zamperini, Louis, Japanese prisoner of war, suffering, 238
Pound, Ezra (poet), 227, 267. *See also* Overholser, Winfred (doctor)
Pratt, George (doctor), 228. *See also* Momism

454 | Index

predisposition, 5, 137; British experience in World War I, 295n13; definition, 17; favoring instead an environmental etiology, 34, 168, 305n1; fiscal incentive in military to espouse, 153; Japanese belief in, 44; questioning predisposition, 153–55, 157, 167, 203, 210

predisposition, theories related to: childhood socialization (related to William Alanson White), 18; constitutionalism, 19; eugenics, 19; "habit theory," (White and Adolf Meyer), 18; interpersonal relations (Harry Stack Sullivan), 19; Momism (Edward Strecker), 251; "shell-shock," 17, 18, 266

Pride of the Marines (film), 220, 229. See also Schmid, Al

psychiatric clinics, 52, 105, 124, 211, 216, 221

psychiatric label, stigma, 48, 49, 101, 106, 201, 383n105. See also Hershey, Lewis (general); Sullivan, Harry Stack (doctor)

"Psychiatric Toll of Warfare," *Fortune*, 167

psychiatrists, shortage of, 44, 196, 311n2

psychoanalysis in movies, 220

psychoanalysts, 1, 4, 8, 22, 88, 90, 108, 148, 192, 210, 213, 214, 248

psychologists: Army General Classification Test (AGCT), bias of, 112; Army General Classification Test (AGCT), use of, 17, 330n62; bias in psychological examinations, 115; Black psychologists, paucity of, 112, 117; character studies, 226; character studies by Leighton, Alexander (psychologist), 395n79; intelligence quotient test (IQ), limited role, World War II, 16; leadership selection, 178; mental hygiene units in training camps, involvement in, 82; Shipley Inventory, design of, 131, 135

psychologists and psychiatrists, extent of collaboration or lack thereof: Adjutant General, not Surgeon General, training psychologists, 97; illiterates, selected for service by psychiatrists, aptitude tests given by psychologists, 97; in general, 4, 92–94, 247, 290n11, 332n78; Inspector General investigation recommending employing psychologists in lieu of psychiatrists, 200

psychoneurotics: limited assignments for, 147; treatment in Pacific Zone, 82, 146

psychopath, 52. See also Kaufman, M. Ralph (doctor); Overholser, Winfred (doctor)

Public Health Service, U.S., psychiatrists in, 36, 68, 116, 220, 261, 263, 268, 314n43

Putnam, Tracy (doctor), 60, 72, 88, 267

Quen, Jacques (doctor), 281, 373

Rado, Sandor (doctor), 214, 300n52

"Raiders on Guadalcanal" (Col. Evans F. Carlson), 374n15

Railey Report, 71–72, 323nn122, 127

"railway spine," 295n12

Rapido, Italy, 145. See also Clark, Mark (general)

Rees, John R. (doctor), 147, 267. See also Tavistock Clinic

rehabilitation of 4Fs for military service (prehabilitation), 69, 70, 151, 321n110, 322n114

rehabilitation of military for further service, 151, 197, 203, 205. See also Roosevelt, Franklin Delano

rehabilitation of veterans, 392n51. See also Kubie, Lawrence (doctor)

religion, 159, 164–65, 181, 215, 389n24

Renfrow, Lewis (doctor), 124. See also Medical Survey Program

Rennie, Thomas (doctor), 118, 211, 212, 216, 268. See also Group for the Advancement of Psychiatry; Payne Whitney Psychiatric Clinic

"Repairing War-Cracked Minds," *Colliers*, 199

replacements, 107, 139, 152, 161, 162, 171, 178, 185, 193, 198, 242, 243, 365n34
rest and recuperation (R&R), 9, 177, 249
rest camps, 178, 373n7
Reynolds, Robert (senator), 105
Riker's Island, New York City, 132
Roosevelt, Eleanor: alcoholism/addiction in family, 58, 59; Black morale, 110; Blacks, concerns for conditions in segregated hospitals, including Tuskegee, 109; Byberry mental hospital, Philadelphia, concerns about conditions, 223; morale, promotion of, 363n20; "My Day," Oct. 6 and Oct. 7, 1942, 96; NNPI, interest in after World War II, 220, 222; NNPI, interest in before World War II, 27; NYC Selective Service Memorandum, authored by Kubie, opposed to, 97; tour of duty (limited), promoted, 158, 225, 364; WAC, defended respectability, 172, 370n91, 371n103. *See also* Marshall, George C.; Osborn, Frederick
Roosevelt, Eleanor, correspondence: letter from Brav, Stanley (Rabbi) concerning veterans' readjustment to civilian life, 233; letter from NCMH recommending Menninger as head Neuropsychiatric Consultants Division, 147; letters from the public about, 143; with Kubie, Lawrence (doctor), on Heinz Hartmann, 26; with Kubie on her family's health, 126; with La Guardia, Fiorello, about getting passport for British child psychiatrist Viola Bernard, 302n6; and to McIntire, Ross T., regarding the need for more psychiatrists, 95; with Overholser, Winfred (doctor), on conditions in mental hospitals, 27; with Perkins, Frances, Secretary of Labor, on excessive psychiatric casualties, 94; with Stimson regarding giving Frederick Hanson (doctor) an Army appointment,

152; with Stimson, Henry, Secretary of War, proposing vocational reassignments for soldiers, 100; with Stimson, regarding excessive numbers of veterans being committed to mental hospitals, 151; with Strecker, Edward (doctor) on her family's health, 26
Roosevelt, Franklin Delano: American fliers, England, concerned with level medical treatment, 151, 152, 361n52; Army and Selective Service examinations, favored combining, 69, 70; death, 206; election eve speech 1940 promising not to get into war, 21; McIntire, Ross T, relationship with, 264; one-minute psychiatric examination proposed, 70; Osborn, Frederick, appointed head of Selective Service Psychiatric Advisory Committee, 266; Perkins, Frances, speaking to, about role for psychiatrist in war, 21; rehabilitation of men rejected from service, in favor of, 321n110; rehabilitation of soldiers, advocacy, 138; rejections of Blacks on psychiatric grounds from service, responded to, 111; rotation in Army, 9, 157, 372n3; Selective Service Medical Circular No. 1, approved, 33, 247; stamp collector, 148; Warm Springs, Ga. polio program, directed, 302n64
Rowntree, Leonard (doctor), 97, 98, 125, 335n13
Ruggles, Arthur (doctor), 88, 147, 170, 268, 329n49
Rush, Benjamin (doctor), 223, 268
Rusk, Howard, 85, 268
Russia (Soviet Union), etiology of mental illness, 43, 163
Russian psychiatric treatment and evacuation in World War II, 44
Russian view of Patton, 141
Russians' motivation to fight, 7, 162, 182. *See also* Zilboorg, Gregory (doctor)

456 | Index

Salmon, Thomas (doctor): Ellis Island, medical examinations, administered, 16, 293n5; eugenics, 19; hysteria, etiology of, 18; National Committee for Mental Hygiene, director of, 17; profile, 265, 268; World War I, chief American Expeditionary Forces psychiatry, 17

Sargant, William, 34, 305n1

Schilder, Paul (psychoanalyst), 214

schizoid personality, 51

schizophrenia, 19, 27, 47, 54, 67, 214, 229, 259, 296

Schmid, Al, 229. See also *Pride of Marines* (film)

Schreiber, Julius (doctor), 180, 269, 346n9. *See also* Information and Education Division

Schwab, Sidney (doctor), 269, 331n73

Section VIII discharges (including blue), 45, 52, 53, 58, 61, 63, 64, 97, 117, 135, 174, 216

segregation: Delaware public schools, 212; GAP resolution endorsing, *To Secure these Rights: Report of the President's Committee on Civil Rights*, 226; Hammond, John, 341; housing, 109; Kaufman, M. Ralph, views on, 168, 170–71; Kubie, Lawrence, views on, 168–70; Menninger, William (doctor), 168, 169; Negro press, response to, 369n78; Ruggles, Arthur (doctor), 170; Selective Training and Service Act (Selective Service Act) (September 1940), Section 8a, psychiatric records open to registrants, response to, 52, 120, 121, 123, 313n28; Selfridge Air Base, 109; theaters, 109

Senna, Albert, 240

Servicemen's Dependency Act of 1942, 219

sexual psychopath, 64, 116, 315n55. *See also* Kaufman, Dr. M. Ralph

Shades of Gray (film), 229, 231, 251. See also *Let There Be Light* (film)

Shafer, Paul, (U.S. representative), 110

The Shame of the States (book and film), 219. *See also* Deutsch, Albert (journalist)

Sheen, Fulton J. Bishop, 215

"shell-shock," 28, 34, 143, 282

Shipley Inventory, 131, 132, 134–36, 261, 263, 269, 273

Shipley, Walter (psychologist), 132, 269

Sicilian campaign, 105, 157, 159, 160

Sillman, Leonard, (doctor), 183

Simmel, Ernst (doctor), 53, 266, 269

Slater, Eliot (doctor), 34, 305

Slovik, Eddie, 205, 229. *See also* Huie, William Bradford

Snake Pit (film), 220, 223

Snyder, Howard McC., 198, 233, 269, 360n49. *See also* Boyce, Westray Battle; Eisenhower, Dwight D. (general); Women's Army Corps

Sobel, Raymond (doctor)183, 269. *See also* "Old Sergeant Syndrome"

sodium amytal, 34, 84, 194, 236. *See also* narcoanalysis

sodomy, 58, 63, 316n58, 318n80

Solomon Islands, 139, 154, 158, 365n34

Special Committee Appointed by War Department to Investigate Rejections at Induction, 256, 271, 279

Spellbound (film), 220

Spiegel, Herbert (doctor), 270: adviser system used by psychiatrists to aid commanders, 156; battalion surgeon, Tunisia, 7, 86; "cogs in the machine of war," 154; homosexuals, 64; hypnotism, 86; job assignments, correct ones, and mental health, 162; love not hate inspirational on the battlefield, 183, 184; narcosynthesis, evaluation of, 85; pentothal, amytal drawbacks, 86; phenobarbital, evaluation of, 194; predisposition, evaluation of, 154

Spiegel, John, 84–85, 190, 214, 260, 270, 327n33. *See also* Grinker, Roy (doctor)

Spock, Benjamin (doctor), 229

Spruit, Charles (doctor), 21

Index | 457

Stars and Stripes, 162, 180, 222. See also Information and Education Division; Osborn, Frederick
Steckel, Harry (doctor), 26, 35, 94, 270, 345n2
Stevens, Rutherford (doctor), 113. See also segregation
Stevenson, George (doctor), 17, 98, 124, 147, 174, 219. See also Medical Survey Program; National Neuropsychiatric Institute Act
Stimson, Henry, Secretary of War: Hanson, Frederick, correspondence with Mrs. Roosevelt about getting Army appointment for, 152; Kenner, Albert, his candidate for Army Surgeon General, 202; Medical Survey Program, in favor of, 124; rehabilitation of psychiatric 4Fs, combining Army/Selective Service exams, both opposed, 69, 70; Roosevelt, Franklin Delano, correspondence with, 1945, 205–6; segregation, views on, 168, 169; veterans, correspondence with Mrs. Roosevelt about too many in asylums, 151
Stouffer, Samuel (sociologist), 7, 72, 133, 148, 180, 255, 271, 291n19. See also Appel, John (doctor); Information and Education Division; Osborn, Frederick
Strecker, Edward (doctor): Appel, John (doctor), training of, 148; Brav, Stanley (Rabbi), 234; British medical facilities for airmen, ordered by Roosevelt to study, 151, 152; malingering, opinion on whether mental disability, 55; Medical Survey Program, 124, 127, 130; "Momism," 228, 257; psychiatric screening, for tougher, 88; rehabilitation of soldiers before discharge, correspondence with Roosevelt on, 151; segregation, response to criticism of by Kubie, 170; special committee of War Department investigating rejections of mental cases at induction centers, appointed to, 121; stutterer, 3, 84, 195; suicide among American soldiers in World War II, 83, 144, 178, 235; suicide among veterans Iraq and Afghanistan, 292n29, 372n4; suicide among veterans World War II, 221, 222, 235, 237, 240; suicide, German soldiers World War II, 43; suicide of Adolf Hitler, 206; suicide, Japanese soldiers World War II, 45, 190; suicide, reason given by Overholser to get rid open records allowed in Section 8a, 121; WAC psychiatry at induction boards, criticized, 174; World War I, psychiatrist in, 18; World War II, psychiatric consultant to both Army and Navy, 18
Sullivan, Harry Stack (doctor): Army/Selective Services/Hershey, differences in objectives of screening and personality differences, 47, 48, 72, 73; Benedict, Ruth (anthropologist), 22; Blitsten, Dorothy, 24; Bullard, Dexter (doctor), 32, 60; *Bulletin from William Alanson White Psychiatric Foundation to the Chairman and the Physician-Member of Each Local Selective Board,* 29; conflicts between Sullivan and other psychiatrists over psychiatric rejections Native Americans, Malcolm H. case, 68; death, 271; differences between Sullivan and other psychiatrists over a family history leading to rejection from service, 48; difficulties encountered with screenings, unanticipated, 46 establishing Selective Service seminars for examiners, 7; Fromm-Reichmann, Frieda (on schizophrenia), 214, 259; Fromm, Erich, 22; homosexuality, conflict between Sullivan's persona as gay and military obligations, stigma from rejection from service recognized, 58–60; Horney, Karen, 261; International Conference on

Sullivan, Harry Stack (doctor) *(continued)*
Mental Health, attended, 227; Lasswell, Harold, (influenced on playing a political role), 23; Madigan, Patrick (doctor, from William Alanson White Psychiatric Foundation [WAWPF]), 22; Medical Circular No. 1, focus on interpersonal relations, 14; Medical Circular No. 1, reasons for adoption, 2, 15, 22; *Memorandum on the Utilization of Psychiatrists in the Promotion of National Security*, 22; Meyer, Adolf (doctor), influenced theories, 96, 271, 296n20; Osborn, Frederick, 19; Overholser, Winfred (doctor), on getting psychiatric screening approved, 29; Pershing, Lewis (general), medical officer under, 22; predisposition, views on, 18, 19; resignation from Selective Service, reasons for, 72–74; Roosevelt, Franklin, approved screening, 2; Sutton, Dallas, (doctor, WAWPF member), 22; treatment of homosexual patients at Enoch Pratt, 58–60; Veterans Bureau, liaison between and St. Elizabeth's Hospital, 22; White, William Alanson (influenced on theories), 18. *See also* Hershey, Lewis; Madigan, Patrick (doctor); Osborn, Frederick; Overholser, Winfred (doctor); Roosevelt, Franklin Delano

Tavistock Clinic, 147
Thompson, Lloyd, 189, 204, 271, 373n6
Tunisia, 84, 86, 87, 141, 154, 161, 179, 325n1
unemployment: amount after war, 215; Preventive Psychiatry Committee (Appel), role in trying to reduce, 225; psychiatric rejections from service, history, 3; psychiatric veterans' experience of, 216, 234; psychological impact, studies of, 23, 24, 218; stigma from psychiatric rejection, 118

United Nations, 227
University of Michigan, Psychiatric Clinic, 17, 46, 271, 295n11. *See also* Waggoner, Raymond (doctor)
Utah Beach, 198, 382n92. *See also* Biehler, William A.

Valenti, Jack, 230
venereal disease (VD), 69, 108, 115, 172, 173, 343n68, 390n34
Veterans Affairs (Veterans Administration), 14, 27, 29, 30, 36, 122, 154, 211, 233, 234
Veterans Vocational Rehabilitation Act (1943), 382n98
Vietnam, 241, 244, 245

Waggoner, Raymond (doctor), 17, 46, 90, 125, 271. *See also* Hershey, Lewis (general)
Warburg, Bettina (doctor), 125, 272
War Department Technical Bulletin, Medical 203, 227
War Manpower Commission (WMC), 123, 124. *See also* McNutt, Paul
Wechsler, David (psychologist), 132
Wechsler Intelligence Test, 13
Weed, Lewis (doctor), 89, 175, 272, 347n18
Wells, Federic Lyman (psychologist), 92, 272. *See also* Ruggles, Arthur (doctor)
Wells, James, 161
Wheeler, Burton K. (senator), 103, 123. *See also* fathers to exempt from draft
White, Walter, 116, 171. *See also* National Association for the Advancement of Colored People
White, William Alanson (doctor), 17, 26, 267, 272. *See* National Committee for Mental Hygiene; Sullivan, Harry Stack (doctor)
Whitehorn, John (doctor), 273, 295n11, 345n2, 373n10
"Why We Fight" series of films, 37, 162, 181. *See also* Appel, John (doctor); Capra, Frank; Stouffer, Samuel (sociologist)

Index | 459

William Alanson White Psychiatric Foundation (WAWPF), 2, 13, 29, 227
Williams, Frankwood, 26, 272
Wittson, Cecil (doctor), 261, 273
Wolff, Harold G. (doctor), 132, 273
Women's Army Auxiliary Corps (WAAC), 172, 173, "Sex Hygiene Course for Officers and Officer Candidates," 173
Women's Army Corps (WAC), 8, 65, 171, 172, 370n88. *See also* Hobby, Oveta Culp
Woman's Home Companion (Oct. 1944), 167
Woodward, Luther, MSW, 125, 127, 273
World Health Organization (WHO), 227, 257
WPA, 3, 14, 24, 33, 123, 125
Wright, Richard, 113, 130, 212, 387n10

Yank Magazine, 162, 180, 183, 380n69. *See also* Information and Education Division
Yerkes, Robert (psychologist), 16

Zilboorg, Gregory (doctor), 162, 221, 273, 333n85, 393n59
Zubin, Joseph (psychologist), 160

Rebecca Schwartz Greene is Visiting Scholar at Seton Hall University in South Orange, New Jersey. She is a historian who specializes in American social history, history of medicine, and modern American history.

World War II: The Global, Human, and Ethical Dimension
G. Kurt Piehler, *series editor*

Lawrence Cane, David E. Cane, Judy Barrett Litoff, and David C. Smith, eds., *Fighting Fascism in Europe: The World War II Letters of an American Veteran of the Spanish Civil War*

Angelo M. Spinelli and Lewis H. Carlson, *Life behind Barbed Wire: The Secret World War II Photographs of Prisoner of War Angelo M. Spinelli*

Don Whitehead and John B. Romeiser, *"Beachhead Don": Reporting the War from the European Theater, 1942–1945*

Scott H. Bennett, ed., *Army GI, Pacifist CO: The World War II Letters of Frank and Albert Dietrich*

Alexander Jefferson with Lewis H. Carlson, *Red Tail Captured, Red Tail Free: Memoirs of a Tuskegee Airman and POW*

Jonathan G. Utley, *Going to War with Japan, 1937–1941*

Grant K. Goodman, *America's Japan: The First Year, 1945–1946*

Patricia Kollander with John O'Sullivan, *"I Must Be a Part of This War": One Man's Fight against Hitler and Nazism*

Judy Barrett Litoff, *An American Heroine in the French Resistance: The Diary and Memoir of Virginia d'Albert-Lake*

Thomas R. Christofferson and Michael S. Christofferson, *France during World War II: From Defeat to Liberation*

Don Whitehead, *Combat Reporter: Don Whitehead's World War II Diary and Memoirs*, edited by John B. Romeiser

James M. Gavin, *The General and His Daughter: The Wartime Letters of General James M. Gavin to His Daughter Barbara*, edited by Barbara Gavin Fauntleroy et al.

Carol Adele Kelly, ed., *Voices of My Comrades: America's Reserve Officers Remember World War II*, Foreword by Senators Ted Stevens and Daniel K. Inouye

John J. Toffey IV, *Jack Toffey's War: A Son's Memoir*

Lt. General James V. Edmundson, *Letters to Lee: From Pearl Harbor to the War's Final Mission*, edited by Dr. Celia Edmundson

John K. Stutterheim, *The Diary of Prisoner 17326: A Boy's Life in a Japanese Labor Camp*, Foreword by Mark Parillo

G. Kurt Piehler and Sidney Pash, eds., *The United States and the Second World War: New Perspectives on Diplomacy, War, and the Home Front*

Susan E. Wiant, *Between the Bylines: A Father's Legacy*, Foreword by Walter Cronkite

Deborah S. Cornelius, *Hungary in World War II: Caught in the Cauldron*

Gilya Gerda Schmidt, *Süssen Is Now Free of Jews: World War II, The Holocaust, and Rural Judaism*

Emanuel Rota, *A Pact with Vichy: Angelo Tasca from Italian Socialism to French Collaboration*

Panteleymon Anastasakis, *The Church of Greece under Axis Occupation*

Louise DeSalvo, *Chasing Ghosts: A Memoir of a Father, Gone to War*

Alexander Jefferson with Lewis H. Carlson, *Red Tail Captured, Red Tail Free: Memoirs of a Tuskegee Airman and POW, Revised Edition*

Kent Puckett, *War Pictures: Cinema, Violence, and Style in Britain, 1939–1945*

Marisa Escolar, *Allied Encounters: The Gendered Redemption of World War II Italy*

Courtney A. Short, *The Most Vital Question: Race and Identity in the U.S. Occupation of Okinawa, 1945–1946*

James Cassidy, *NBC Goes to War: The Diary of Radio Correspondent James Cassidy from London to the Bulge,* edited by Michael S. Sweeney

Rebecca Schwartz Greene, *Breaking Point: The Ironic Evolution of Psychiatry in World War II*

Franco Baldasso, *Against Redemption: Democracy, Memory, and Literature in Post-Fascist Italy*

www.ingramcontent.com/pod-product-compliance
Lightning Source LLC
Chambersburg PA
CBHW020348080526
44584CB00014B/933